STAR STATS
WHO'S WHOSE IN HOLLYWOOD

KENNETH S. MARX

PRICE/STERN/SLOAN

Publishers, Inc., Los Angeles

1979

Researched by
GERALDINE GONZALES ECKERT

Data Base Services Designed
and Implemented by
PAMELA R. PFAU

Cover Illustration by Jeani Brunnick

Copyright © 1979 by Kenneth S. Marx
Published by Price/Stern/Sloan Publishers, Inc.
410 North La Cienega Boulevard/Los Angeles, California 90048
Printed in the United States of America. All rights reserved.

ISBN: 0-8431-0498-8

DEDICATION

To star-crossed lovers

ACKNOWLEDGEMENTS

The researching of this work was accomplished for the most part in the comfort of the Margaret Herrick Library of the Academy of Motion Pictures Arts and Sciences in Beverly Hills, California. Though the staff most likely dreaded to see the research team sign the register on the many days they invaded the archives, they were unfailingly kind, considerate and encouraging. More than candy and balloons can indicate, the publishers are indebted to Mildred Simpson, the librarian, and her staff: Cheryl Behnke, Debra Bergman, Carol Cullen, Dennis Croy, Stacy Endres, Sylvia Fischer, Samuel Gill, Alice Mitchell, Mary Olivares, Terry Roach, Bonnie Rothbart, David Sanders and Jon Sandler.

When that library was closed we traveled to the West Los Angeles Regional Branch of the City Library system and were there assisted, equally kindly, by Irma King, Frances Moriwaki and Fontayne Holmes.

Among the many private sources of information we are pleased to acknowledge are: Bud Abbott, Jr., Jan Clayton, Gale and Ken Delpit, Alan J. Factor, Jack Haimer, Irene Hayman, George Kirvay, June Levant Ephron, Samuel Marx, Irene and Jimmy McHugh, Cele and Irv Rudman, March J. Schwartz, Robyn and John Scrimgeour, Anne Shirley, Harvey J. Shotz, Salvatore Tomasello, Wayne Tourrell and Denis B. Wright.

TABLE OF CONTENTS

INTRODUCTION

The celebrities of the Hollywood film business are the focus of this work. They were and still are the people willing to expose themselves to the public through their films, publicity, and news stories. The more recognizable their names became, the more valued they were in the industry.

Once a person embarked on the journey to stardom, it was almost impossible to change directions. It was a one-way trip from which no one would ever be able to return to his or her original home. Time and events precluded any rejuvenation, though cosmetics and surgery could be a mask a sympathetic camera operator could shoot but not penetrate.

In the bedroom communities of the film business there were merry-go-rounds for both the young and older. Though the elders appeared to have other activities, the play seemed to be the same. Identifying the players was a problem as things kept spinning around. But that was an effect that was desired.

In recent times many film celebrities have been writing their memoirs. Their stories are worthy of print, as everyone's life should be. But librarians seem concerned about classifying these books. Non-fiction is often inappropriate and the new term, "Faction," not yet widely accepted.

Memories, like memoirs, are selective and also subject to editing. Large blocks of data may be omitted from recollections and the passing of time often does, obliterate traces of reality. So often has the magic of these glamorous lives been discounted, it would seem the happiness we heard about, or imagined, was really not happening. Those are the stories to be read between the lines of this compilation of facts.

A final note: The information contained in this work was derived from many sources and is as accurate as humanly possible. If any errors are noted, the author and publisher offer their sincerest apologies as well as their promise that corrections will be made in any future printing.

KSM

February, 1979
Los Angeles, California

THE STARS

```
---------------------------------------------------------------------------------
ABBOTT, BUD           BORN:  WILLIAM ALEXANDER ABBOTT
                             OCT 02,'95 AT ASBURY PARK, NJ  DIED IN '74
   FATHER: HARRY ABBOTT, CIRCUS PERFORMER
   MOTHER: RAE FISHER, CIRCUS BAREBACK RIDER
   SISTER: OLIVE VICTORIA ABBOTT
   SISTER: FLORENCE 'BABE' ABBOTT
   BROTHER: HARRY ABBOTT, JR.
   *** MARRIED:  '16 JENNIE MAE 'BETTY' PRATT, BURLESQUE DANCER
   ADOPTED SON: WILLIAM HARRY 'BUD' ABBOTT, ACTOR, FILM TECHNICIAN
   ADOPTED DAUGHTER: RAE VICTORIA ABBOTT
   FRIEND: ERROL FLYNN
   FRIEND: TOM MIX
   PARTNER: LOU COSTELLO
   RESIDENCE: OJAI, CA
   RESIDENCE: ENCINO, CA
   POSSESSION: COLLECTION OF FIREARMS INCLUDING HITLER'S SHOTGUN
   TALENT: ACTOR
   CREDIT:  '40 ONE NIGHT IN THE TROPICS, DEBUT
   CREDIT:  '41 BUCK PRIVATES
   CREDIT:  '48 THE NOOSE HANGS HIGH
   CREDIT:  '52 JACK AND THE BEANSTALK
   CREDIT:  '56 DANCE WITH ME HENRY, LAST FILM
---------------------------------------------------------------------------------
ADAMS, EDIE           BORN:  EDITH ADAMS ENKE
                             APR 16,'29 AT KINGSTON, PA
   FATHER: SHELDON A. ENKE
   MOTHER: ADA ADAMS
   BROTHER: --
   *** MARRIED:  '54 ERNIE KOVACS, ACTOR  (DIED '62)
   STEP-DAUGHTER: BETTY KOVACS
   STEP-DAUGHTER: KIP KOVACS
   DAUGHTER:  '60 MIA KOVACS
   *** MARRIED:  '64 MARTY MILLS, MUSIC PUBLISHER
   SON:  '68 JOSHUA MILLS
   *** MARRIED:  '72 PETE CANDOLI
   STEP-DAUGHTER: CAROLYN CANDOLI
   TALENT: ACTRESS-SINGER
   CREDIT:  '60 THE APARTMENT
   CREDIT:  '62 LOVER COME BACK
   CREDIT:  '63 LOVE WITH THE PROPER STRANGER
   CREDIT:  '64 THE BEST MAN
   CREDIT:  '67 THE HONEY POT
---------------------------------------------------------------------------------
ADAMS, NICK           BORN:  NICHOLAS ALOYSIUS ADAMSCHOCK
                             JUL 10,'31 AT NANTICOKE, PA  DIED IN '68
   FATHER: PETER ADAMSCHOCK, COAL MINER
   MOTHER: CATHERINE
   BROTHER: ANDREW D. ADAMS, DOCTOR
   *** MARRIED:  '59 CAROL NUGENT, ACTRESS  (DIVORCED '66)
   DAUGHTER:  '60 ALLYSON LEE ADAMS
   SON:  '61 JEB STUART ADAMS
   FRIEND: ERVIN RODER, ATTORNEY
   FRIEND: JAMES DEAN, ACTOR
   ENEMY: PAUL RAPP, FILM EXECUTIVE
   RESIDENCE: BEVERLY HILLS, CA
   TALENT: ACTOR
   CREDIT:  '52 SOMEBODY LOVES ME, DEBUT
```

```
CREDIT:  '53 OUR MISS BROOKS
CREDIT:  '54 STRANGE LADY IN TOWN
CREDIT:  '56 PICNIC
AA-NOM  SUP.ACT:  '63 TWILIGHT OF HONOR
CREDIT:  '65 YOUNG DILLINGER
CREDIT:  '67 FEVER HEAT
```

```
AGAR, JOHN          BORN:  JOHN G. AGAR, 2ND
                           JAN 31,'21 AT CHICAGO, IL
   FATHER: JOHN G. AGAR
   *** MARRIED:  '46 SHIRLEY TEMPLE  (DIVORCED '49)
   DAUGHTER:  '47 LINDA SUSAN AGAR
   *** MARRIED:  '51 LORETTA BARNETT COMBS
   SON:  '52 MARTIN DAVID AGAR
   ADOPTED SON: JOHN GEORGE AGAR, 3RD
   TALENT: ACTOR
   CREDIT:  '48 FORT APACHE
   CREDIT:  '53 THE GOLDEN MISTRESS
   CREDIT:  '63 OF LOVE AND DESIRE
   CREDIT:  '67 THE CURSE OF THE SWAMP CREATURE
   CREDIT:  '71 BIG JAKE
```

```
AHERNE, BRIAN       BORN:  WILLIAM BRIAN DE LACY AHERNE
                           MAY 02,'02 AT KING'S NORTON, WORCESTERSHIRE, ENGLAND
   FATHER: WILLIAM DE LACY AHERNE, ARCHITECT
   MOTHER: LOUISE 'LULU' THOMAS, ACTRESS
   SISTER: ELANA AHERNE
   BROTHER: PATRICK AHERNE
   *** MARRIED:  '39 JOAN FONTAINE  (DIVORCED '44)
   MOTHER-IN-LAW: LILLIAN AUGUSTA RUSE, ACTRESS
   SISTER-IN-LAW: OLIVIA DE HAVILLAND, ACTRESS
   *** MARRIED:  '46 ELEANOR DE LIAGRE LABROT
   RESIDENCE: CHATEAU DE L'AILE, VEVEY, SWITZERLAND
   RESIDENCE: NYC
   POSSESSION: BEACH HOUSE IN SANTA MONICA BOUGHT FROM BARBARA HUTTON
   POSSESSION: GRAPE RANCH AT THERMAL, CALIF.
   MEMOIRS:  '69 A PROPER JOB
   TALENT: ACTOR
   COMMENT: FOUNDER OF AIRCRAFT OWNERS' & PILOTS' ASSOCIATION
   CREDIT:  '33 SONG OF SONGS, DEBUT
   AA-NOM  SUP.ACT:  '39 JUAREZ
   CREDIT:  '48 SMART WOMAN
   CREDIT:  '59 THE BEST OF EVERYTHING
   CREDIT:  '68 ROSIE!
```

```
AIMEE, ANOUK        BORN:  FRANCOISE SORYA DREYFUS
                           APR 27,'32 AT PARIS, FRANCE
   FATHER: --, ACTOR
   *** MARRIED: NICOS PAPATAKIS
   *** MARRIED:  '66 PIERRE BAROUH, SINGER
   *** MARRIED:  '70 ALBERT FINNEY, ACTOR
   ROMANCE: RYAN O'NEAL
   TALENT: ACTRESS
   CREDIT:  '59 LA DOLCE VITA
   CREDIT:  '61 LOLA
   CREDIT:  '62 SODOM AND GOMMORAH
   AA-NOM  ACTRESS:  '66 A MAN AND A WOMAN
   CREDIT:  '69 THE APPOINTMENT
```

ALBERGHETTI, ANNA MARIA
                              MAY 15,'36 AT PESARO, ITALY
    FATHER: DANIELE ALBERGHETTI, MUSICIAN
    MOTHER: VITTORIA, MUSICIAN
    SISTER: CARLA ALBERGHETTI
    BROTHER: PAOLO ALBERGHETTI
    *** MARRIED: '64 CLAUDIO GUZMAN, DIRECTOR
    DAUGHTER: '65 PILAR GUZMAN
    SON: '66 ALEXANDER GUZMAN
    DAUGHTER: DANIELLE ALBERGHETTI, CELLIST
    ROMANCE: LOUIS 'BUDDY' BREGMAN, MUSICAL DIRECTOR
    RESIDENCE: HOLLYWOOD, CA
    TALENT: SINGER-ACTRESS
    CREDIT: '51 HERE COMES THE GROOM
    CREDIT: '53 THE STARS ARE SINGING
    CREDIT: '55 THE LAST COMMAND
    CREDIT: '57 TEN THOUSAND BEDROOMS
    CREDIT: '60 CINDERFELLA

ALBERT, EDDIE   BORN: EDDIE ALBERT HEIMBERGER
                         APR 22,'08 AT ROCK ISLAND, IL
    FATHER: FRANK HEIMBERGER
    MOTHER: JULIA JONES
    *** MARRIED: '45 MARIA MARGARITA BOLADO, ACTRESS - MARGO
    SON: '51 EDWARD ALBERT
    ADOPTED DAUGHTER: MARISA ALBERT
    RESIDENCE: LOS ANGELES, CA
    POSSESSION: '54 COLLECTOR OF 1ST EDITION BOOKS
    TALENT: ACTOR
    CREDIT: '38 BROTHER RAT
    CREDIT: '46 THE PERFECT MARRIAGE
    AA-NOM SUP.ACT: '53 ROMAN HOLIDAY
    CREDIT: '56 TEAHOUSE OF THE AUGUST MOON
    AA-NOM SUP.ACT: '72 THE HEARTBREAK KID

ALBRIGHT, LOLA   BORN: LOLA JEAN ALBRIGHT
                         JUL 20,'24 AT AKRON,OH
    FATHER: JOHN PAUL ALBRIGHT
    MOTHER: MARION
    *** MARRIED: --, TEENAGE MARRIAGE
    *** MARRIED: '52 JACK CARSON, ACTOR (DIVORCED '58)
    *** MARRIED: '61 WILLIAM C. CHADNEY, RESTAURATEUR, PIANIST (DIVORCED '67)
    RESIDENCE: ENCINO, CA
    POSSESSION: '66 BERLIN FILM FESTIVAL BEST ACTRESS AWARD-'LORD LOVE A DUCK'
    TALENT: ACTRESS
    CREDIT: '49 CHAMPION
    CREDIT: '50 THE GOOD HUMOR MAN
    CREDIT: '56 THE TENDER TRAP
    CREDIT: '65 THE LOVE CAGE
    CREDIT: '68 THE IMPOSSIBLE YEARS

ALDA, ALAN
                         JAN 28,'36 AT NYC
    FATHER: ROBERT ALDA, ACTOR
    MOTHER: JOAN BROWNE
    STEP-MOTHER: FLORA MARINO, ACTRESS
    STEP-BROTHER: ANTHONY ALDA, ACTOR

```
    AUNT: ANN D'ABRUZZO
    UNCLE: VINCENT D'ABRUZZO
    *** MARRIED: '57 ARLENE WEISS, CLARINETIST
    DAUGHTER:  '58 EVE ALDA
    DAUGHTER:  '59 ELIZABETH ALDA
    DAUGHTER:  '60 BEATRICE ALDA
    RESIDENCE: LEONIA NJ
    TALENT: ACTOR
    CREDIT:  '63 GONE ARE THE DAYS
    CREDIT:  '68 THE EXTRAORDINARY SEAMAN
    CREDIT:  '70 THE MOONSHINE WAR
    CREDIT:  '71 THE MEPHISTO WALTZ
    CREDIT:  '72 TO KILL A CLOWN
```

ALDA, ROBERT   BORN: ALPHONSO ROBERTO D'ABRUZZO
                                  FEB 26, '14 AT NYC
```
    SISTER: ANN D'ABRUZZO
    BROTHER: VINCENT D'ABRUZZO
    *** MARRIED: '32 JOAN BROWNE
    SON:  '36 ALAN ALDA, ACTOR
    DAUGHTER-IN-LAW: ARLENE WEISS  (MARRIED '57)
    *** MARRIED: '56 FLORA MARINO, ACTRESS
    SON:  '57 ANTHONY ALDA, ACTOR
    GRANDDAUGHTER: EVE ALDA
    GRANDDAUGHTER: ELIZABETH ALDA
    GRANDDAUGHTER: BEATRICE ALDA
    POSSESSION: DELICATESSEN IN ROME
    TALENT: ACTOR
    CREDIT:  '45 RHAPSODY IN BLUE
    CREDIT:  '51 TWO GALS AND A GUY
    CREDIT:  '55 BEAUTIFUL BUT DANGEROUS
    CREDIT:  '59 IMITATION OF LIFE
    CREDIT:  '68 THE GIRL WHO KNEW TOO MUCH
```

ALEXANDER, JANE   BORN: JANE QUIGLEY
                                     OCT 28, '39 AT BOSTON,MS
```
    FATHER: THOMAS BARTLETT QUIGLEY, ORTHOPEDIC SURGEON
    MOTHER: RUTH PEARSON
    SISTER: PAMELA QUIGLEY
    BROTHER: THOMAS QUIGLEY, JR.
    *** MARRIED:  '62 ROBERT ALEXANDER  (DIVORCED '69)
    SON:  '63 JASON ALEXANDER
    *** MARRIED:  '75 EDWIN SHERIN
    POSSESSION: FARM IN PUTNAM COUNTY, NY
    TALENT: ACTRESS
    AA-NOM  ACTRESS:  '70 THE GREAT WHITE HOPE
    CREDIT:  '71 A GUNFIGHT
    CREDIT:  '71 WELCOME HOME JOHNNY BRISTOL
    CREDIT:  '72 THE NEW CENTURIONS
    AA-NOM  SUP.ACT:  '76 ALL THE PRESIDENT'S MEN
```

ALLEN, FRED   BORN: JOHN FLORENCE SULLIVAN
                                 MAY 31,'94 AT CAMBRIDGE, MS DIED IN '56
```
    FATHER: --  (DIED '09)
    MOTHER: --  (DIED '98)
    BROTHER: ROBERT ALLEN
    AUNT: ELIZABETH HERLIHY
    NIECE: BARBARA BOND
```

```
NIECE: MARY BOND
NIECE: FRANCES HERSHKOWITZ
*** MARRIED:  '28 PORTLAND HOFFA
FRIEND: JACK BENNY
RESIDENCE: ALLEN'S ALLEY, 57TH STREET,NYC
MEMOIRS:  '54 TREADMILL TO OBLIVION
MEMOIRS: MUCH ADO ABOUT ME
TALENT: ACTOR, JOURNALIST, DIRECTOR
COMMENT: KNOWN AS FREDDIE JAMES, WORLDS WORST JUGGLER - VAUDEVILLE ACT
CREDIT:  '35 THANKS A MILLION
CREDIT:  '41 LOVE THY NEIGHBOR
CREDIT:  '45 IT'S IN THE BAG
CREDIT:  '52 WE'RE NOT MARRIED
CREDIT:  '53 O. HENRY'S FULL HOUSE
```

```
ALLEN, GRACIE          BORN:  GRACE ETHEL CECILE ROSALIE ALLEN
                              JUL 26,'06 AT SAN FRANCISCO,CA  DIED IN '64
   FATHER: EDWARD ALLEN
   *** MARRIED:  '27 GEORGE BURNS, ACTOR
   ADOPTED DAUGHTER: SANDRA JEAN BURNS
   ADOPTED SON: ROLAND JON BURNS
   TALENT: ACTRESS
   CREDIT:  '33 COLLEGE HUMOR
   CREDIT:  '34 WE'RE NOT DRESSING
   CREDIT:  '38 A DAMSEL IN DISTRESS
   CREDIT:  '39 GRACIE ALLEN MURDER CASE
   CREDIT:  '44 TWO GIRLS AND A SAILOR
```

```
ALLEN, STEVE           BORN:  STEPHEN VALENTINE ALLEN
                              DEC 26,'21 AT NYC
   FATHER: CARROLL ALLEN, VAUDEVILLE ENTERTAINER
   MOTHER: ISABELLE DONOHU, AKA BELLE MONTROSE
   *** MARRIED:  '43 DOROTHY GOODMAN  (DIVORCED '52)
   SON:  '44 STEVE ALLEN, JR.
   SON:  '45 BRIAN ALLEN
   SON:  '46 DAVID ALLEN
   *** MARRIED:  '54 JAYNE MEADOWS
   BROTHER-IN-LAW: FRANCIS COTTER, JR., EXECUTIVE-CONTINENTAL AIRLINES
   SISTER-IN-LAW: AUDREY MEADOWS, ACTRESS
   SON:  '57 WILLIAM CHRISTOPHER ALLEN
   MEMOIRS:  '60 MARK IT AND STRIKE IT
   TALENT: PERFORMER,AUTHOR,MUSICIAN
   CREDIT:  '49 DOWN MEMORY LANE
   CREDIT:  '55 THE BENNY GOODMAN STORY
   CREDIT:  '59 THE BIG CIRCUS
   CREDIT:  '66 WARNING SHOT
   CREDIT:  '70 THE COMIC
```

```
ALLEN, WOODY           BORN:  ALLEN STEWART KONIGSBERG
                              DEC 01,'35 AT BROOKLYN,NY
   FATHER: MARTIN KONIGSBERG
   MOTHER: NETTIE CHERRY
   SISTER: LETTI KONIGSBERG
   *** MARRIED:  '54 HARLENE ROSEN, TEACHER  (DIVORCED)
   *** MARRIED:  '66 LOUISE LASSER, ACTRESS  (DIVORCED)
   ROMANCE: DIANE KEATON, ACTRESS
   RESIDENCE: NYC
   BIOGRAPHY:  '75 ON BEING FUNNY, BY ERIC LAX
```

```
TALENT: ACTOR, DIRECTOR, WRITER
CREDIT:  '66 WHAT'S NEW PUSSYCAT?
CREDIT:  '69 TAKE THE MONEY AND RUN
CREDIT:  '72 EVERYTHING YOU ALWAYS WANTED  TO KNOW ABOUT SEX
CREDIT:  '76 THE FRONT
AA-NOM  ACTOR:  '77 ANNIE HALL WON ACADEMY AWARD AS DIRECTOR
```

```
ALLYSON, JUNE          BORN:  ELLA GEISMAN
                              OCT 07,'17 AT BRONX,NY
   FATHER: ROBERT GEISMAN
   MOTHER: CLARA
   BROTHER: HENRY GEISMAN
   *** MARRIED:  '45 DICK POWELL, ACTOR  (DIED '63)
   STEP-DAUGHTER: ELLEN POWELL
   STEP-SON: NORMAN SCOTT BARNES
   ADOPTED DAUGHTER: PAMELA POWELL
   SON:  '50 RICHARD KEITH POWELL, JR.
   *** MARRIED:  '63 ALFRED GLENN MAXWELL  (DIVORCED '65)
   *** MARRIED:  '66 ALFRED GLENN MAXWELL, BARBER  (DIVORCED '70)
   *** MARRIED:  '76 DR. DAVID ASHROW
   POSSESSION:  '52 MINIATURE CHINA PIG COLLECTION
   TALENT: ACTRESS
   CREDIT:  '43 BEST FOOT FORWARD
   CREDIT:  '46 TILL THE CLOUDS ROLL BY
   CREDIT:  '48 THE BRIDE GOES WILD
   CREDIT:  '54 THE GLENN MILLER STORY
   CREDIT:  '56 THE OPPOSITE SEX
```

```
AMECHE, DON            BORN:  DOMINIC FELIX AMECHE
                              MAY 31,'08 AT KENOSHA,WI
   FATHER: FELIX AMECHE
   MOTHER: BARBARA HERTLE
   SISTER: KATHERINE AMECHE
   BROTHER: JIM AMECHE, RADIO ANNOUNCER
   *** MARRIED:  '32 HONORE PRENDERGAST
   SON:  '40 DOMINIC 'DON' AMECHE, JR.
   SON:  '41 THOMAS AMECHE
   SON:  '42 LONNIE AMECHE
   DAUGHTER: CONSTANCE AMECHE
   DAUGHTER: BONNIE AMECHE
   TALENT: ACTOR
   CREDIT:  '36 SINS OF MAN
   CREDIT:  '40 THE STORY OF ALEXANDER GRAHAM BELL
   CREDIT:  '41 MOON OVER MIAMI
   CREDIT:  '44 WING AND A PRAYER
   CREDIT:  '48 SLEEP, MY LOVE
   CREDIT:  '66 PICTURE MOMMY DEAD
```

```
AMES, LEON             BORN:  LEON WYCOFF
                              JAN 20,'03 AT PORTLAND,IN
   FATHER: CHARLES ELMER WYCOFF
   MOTHER: CORA ALICE DE MASSE
   *** MARRIED:  '38 CHRISTINE GOSSETT
   DAUGHTER:  '41 SHELLEY AMES
   SON:  '44 LEON AMES, JR.
   DAUGHTER-IN-LAW: MELANIE CONSTANCE MORRIS  (MARRIED '70)
   FRIEND: LLOYD NOLAN, ACTOR
   RESIDENCE: STUDIO CITY, CA
```

```
TALENT: ACTOR
COMMENT: PRESIDENT OF SCREEN ACTORS GUILD - 1957
CREDIT:  '32 MURDERS IN THE RUE MORGUE, DEBUT
CREDIT:  '41 NO GREATER SIN
CREDIT:  '49 LITTLE WOMEN
CREDIT:  '57 PEYTON PLACE
CREDIT:  '63 SON OF FLUBBER
```

AMSTERDAM, MOREY
                              DEC 14,'14 AT CHICAGO,IL

```
    FATHER: MAX AMSTERDAM
    MOTHER: JENNY FINDER
    *** MARRIED:  '41 CATHERINE AMAYIA PATRICK
    DAUGHTER: CATHY AMSTERDAM
    SON: GEOFFREY AMSTERDAM
    MEMOIRS: KEEP LAUGHING
    TALENT: ACTOR, WRITER
    CREDIT:  '60 MURDER, INC.
    CREDIT:  '63 BEACH PARTY
    CREDIT:  '64 MUSCLE BEACH PARTY
    CREDIT:  '68 THE HORSE IN THE GREY FLANNEL  SUIT
```

ANDERSON, "BRONCO BILLY"   BORN: MAX ARONSON
                              MAR 21,'82 AT LITTLE ROCK,AR   DIED IN '71

```
    PARTNER: EVELYN SELBIE, ACTRESS-'THE BRONCO BILLY GIRL'
    PARTNER: RUTH STONEHOUSE, ACTRESS-PARTNER ESSANAY STUDIO
    RESIDENCE: LOS ANGELES, CA
    TALENT: ACTOR, PRODUCER
    COMMENT: CO-FOUNDER ESSANAY FILM CO.
    CREDIT:  '03 THE GREAT TRAIN ROBBERY, DEBUT
    AA-SPECIAL AWARD:  '57 HONORARY AWARD AS A MOTION PICTURE PIONEER
    CREDIT: BRONCHO BILLY, SERIES
    CREDIT: SNAKE VILLE COMEDY, SERIES
    CREDIT: ALKALI IKE, SERIES
```

ANDERSON, EDDIE "ROCHESTER"
                              SEP 18,'05 AT OAKLAND, CA   DIED IN '77

```
    FATHER: BIG ED ANDERSON, CIRCUS PERFORMER
    MOTHER: ELLA MAE, CIRCUS PERFORMER
    SISTER: MARY ANDERSON
    BROTHER: CORNELIUS ANDERSON
    BROTHER: DAVID ANDERSON
    *** MARRIED: MAMIE
    ADOPTED SON: WILLIAM ANDERSON
    *** MARRIED:  '56 EVANGELA  (DIVORCED)
    DAUGHTER:  '56 EVANGELA ANDERSON
    DAUGHTER:  '57 STEPHANIE ANDERSON
    SON: EDMOND ANDERSON
    FRIEND: JACK BENNY
    TALENT: ACTOR
    CREDIT:  '30 WHAT PRICE HOLLYWOOD
    CREDIT:  '36 GREEN PASTURES
    CREDIT:  '39 GONE WITH THE WIND
    CREDIT:  '43 CABIN IN THE SKY
    CREDIT:  '63 IT'S A MAD MAD MAD MAD WORLD
```

ANDERSON, BIBI
                          NOV 11,'35 AT STOCKHOLM, SWEDEN
FATHER: JOSEF ANDERSSON
MOTHER: KARIN
SISTER: GERD ANDERSSON, BALLERINA
*** MARRIED: '60 KJELL GREDE, WRITER, DIRECTOR (DIVORCED '73)
DAUGHTER: '71 JENNY MATILDA GREDE
ROMANCE: MILOS FORMAN, DIRECTOR
RESIDENCE: LIDINGO, STOCKHOLM, SWEDEN
TALENT: ACTRESS
CREDIT: '53 SMILES OF A SUMMER NIGHT
CREDIT: '57 WILD STRAWBERRIES
CREDIT: '65 DUEL AT DIABLO, AMERICAN DEBUT
CREDIT: '71 THE TOUCH
CREDIT: '77 I NEVER PROMISED YOU A ROSE GARDEN

ANDRESS, URSULA
                          MAR 19,'36 AT BERNE, SWITZERLAND
FATHER: ROLF ANDRESS, DIPLOMAT
MOTHER: ANNA
SISTER: KATHI ANDRESS
SISTER: ERICA ANDRESS
SISTER: GISELA ANDRESS
SISTER: CHARLOTTE ANDRESS
BROTHER: HEINZ ANDRESS
*** MARRIED: '57 JOHN DEREK, DIRECTOR, ACTOR (DIVORCED '66)
STEP-DAUGHTER: SEAN CATHERINE DEREK
STEP-SON: RUSSELL ANDRE DEREK
ROMANCE: COUNT FRANCESCO DI BORGOLO
ROMANCE: MARLON BRANDO
ROMANCE: JAMES DEAN
FRIEND: DANIEL GELIN, ACTOR
POSSESSION: '55 CONTRACT AT PARAMOUNT STUDIOS
TALENT: ACTRESS
CREDIT: '54 THE LOVES OF CASANOVA
CREDIT: '62 DR. NO
CREDIT: '65 SHE
CREDIT: '67 CASINO ROYALE
CREDIT: '72 FIVE AGAINST CAPRICORN

ANDREWS, DANA   BORN: CARVER DANIEL ANDREWS
                         JAN 01,'09 AT COLLINS, MS
FATHER: CHARLES FORREST ANDREWS, MINISTER
MOTHER: ANNIS SPEED
BROTHER: STEVE FOREST, ACTOR
*** MARRIED: '32 JANET MURRAY (DIED '35)
SON: '34 DAVID ANDREWS, PIANIST COMPOSER (DIED '64)
*** MARRIED: '39 MARY TODD
SON: '44 STEPHEN ANDREWS
DAUGHTER: '48 KATHRYN ANDREWS
DAUGHTER: '49 SUSAN ANDREWS
RESIDENCE: TOLUCA LAKE, CA
POSSESSION: 50 FT YAWL RIG SAILBOAT
TALENT: ACTOR
CREDIT: '40 THE WESTERNER
CREDIT: '46 THE BEST YEARS OF OUR LIVES

```
CREDIT:  '55 STRANGE LADY IN TOWN
CREDIT:  '62 MADISON AVENUE
CREDIT:  '67 HOT RODS TO HELL
```

ANDREWS, JULIE   BORN: JULIA ELIZABETH WELLS ANDREWS
                                    OCT 01,'34 AT WALTON-ON-THAMES, SURREY, ENG.
```
FATHER: EDWARD C. WELLS, TEACHER
MOTHER: BARBARA MORRIS, PIANIST
STEP-FATHER: TED ANDREWS, MUSIC HALL SINGER  (DIED '66)
BROTHER: JOHN WELLS
STEP-BROTHER: DONALD ANDREWS
STEP-BROTHER: CHRIS ANDREWS
*** MARRIED:  '59 TONY WALTON, SET DESIGNER  (DIVORCED '68)
DAUGHTER:  '62 EMMA KATE WALTON
*** MARRIED:  '69 BLAKE EDWARDS, DIRECTOR
RESIDENCE: SURREY, ENGLAND
POSSESSION:  '56 BENNY GOODMAN RECORDS
BIOGRAPHY:  '75 JULIE, BY MARCHAK & HUNTER
TALENT: ACTRESS,SINGER
AA-WIN  ACTRESS:  '64 MARY POPPINS
AA-NOM  ACTRESS:  '65 THE SOUND OF MUSIC
CREDIT:  '67 THOROUGHLY MODERN MILLIE
CREDIT:  '68 STAR!
CREDIT:  '70 DARLING LILI
```

ANDREWS, LAVERNE
                          JUL 06,'15 AT MINNEAPOLIS, MN DIED IN '67
```
FATHER: PETER ANDREWS  (DIED '49)
MOTHER: OLLIE  (DIED '48)
SISTER: MAXENE ANDREWS
SISTER: PATRICIA ANDREWS
BROTHER-IN-LAW: LOU LEVEY
BROTHER-IN-LAW: MARTIN MELCHER
BROTHER-IN-LAW: WALTER WECHSLER
NIECE: ALEDA LEVEY
NEPHEW: PETER LEVEY
*** MARRIED:  '48 LOUIS A. RUGGIERO, AKA LOU ROGERS  (DIED '67)
RESIDENCE: LOS ANGELES, CA
POSSESSION:  '46 THE EIGHT-TO-THE-BAR RANCH INC
TALENT: ACTRESS, SINGER
COMMENT: THE SISTERS' ACT SPLIT UP FOR 2 YEARS IN 1954
CREDIT:  '40 ARGENTINE NIGHTS
CREDIT:  '42 GIVE OUT, SISTERS
CREDIT:  '43 ALWAYS A BRIDESMAID
CREDIT:  '48 MELODY TIME
```

ANDREWS, MAXENE
                          JAN 03,'18 AT MINNEAPOLIS, MN
```
FATHER: PETER ANDREWS  (DIED '49)
MOTHER: OLLIE  (DIED '48)
SISTER: LAVERNE ANDREWS
SISTER: PATRICIA ANDREWS
BROTHER-IN-LAW: LOUIS A. RUGGIERO
BROTHER-IN-LAW: MARTIN MELCHER
BROTHER-IN-LAW: WALTER WECHSLER
*** MARRIED:  '41 LOU LEVEY  (DIVORCED '50)
DAUGHTER:  '42 ALEDA LEVEY
SON:  '43 PETER LEVEY
```

RESIDENCE: LOS ANGELES, CA
POSSESSION: '46 THE EIGHT-TO-THE-BAR RANCH INC
TALENT: ACTRESS, SINGER
COMMENT: THE SISTERS' ACT SPLIT UP FOR 2 YEARS IN 1954
COMMENT: SEE CREDITS LISTED ABOVE
COMMENT: TEACHER OF SPEECH AND DRAMA AT TAHOE PARADISE COLLEGE IN 1969

ANDREWS, PATRICIA
                              FEB 16,'20 AT MINNEAPOLIS, MN
   FATHER: PETER ANDREWS (DIED '49)
   MOTHER: OLLIE (DIED '48)
   SISTER: LAVERNE ANDREWS
   SISTER: MAXENE ANDREWS
   BROTHER-IN-LAW: LOUIS A. RUGGIERO
   BROTHER-IN-LAW: LOU LEVEY
   NIECE: ALEDA LEVEY
   NEPHEW: PETER LEVEY
   *** MARRIED: '40 MARTIN MELCHER, AGENT, PRODUCER (DIVORCED '50)
   *** MARRIED: '50 WALTER WECHSLER, PIANIST
   RESIDENCE: ENCINO, CA
   POSSESSION: '46 THE EIGHT-TO-THE-BAR RANCH INC
   TALENT: ACTRESS, SINGER
   COMMENT: THE SISTERS' ACT SPLIT UP FOR 2 YEARS IN 1954
   COMMENT: SEE CREDITS LISTED ABOVE

ANGELI, PIER   BORN: ANNA MARIA PIERANGELI
                              JUN 19,'32 AT CAGLIARI, SARDINIA DIED IN '71
   FATHER: LUIGI PIERANGELI, ARCHITECT
   MOTHER: INRICA
   SISTER: MARISA PAVAN, TWIN
   SISTER: PATRICIA PIERANGELI
   BROTHER-IN-LAW: JEAN-PIERRE AUMONT, ACTOR
   NEPHEW: JEAN-CLAUDE AUMONT, ACTOR
   NEPHEW: PATRICK AUMONT
   *** MARRIED: '54 VIC DAMONE, SINGER (DIVORCED)
   SON: '55 PERRY ROCCO LUIGI DAMONE
   *** MARRIED: '62 ARMANDO TRAVAJOLI
   SON: '63 HOWARD ANDREA TRAVAJOLI, NICKNAME-POPPINO
   ROMANCE: JAMES DEAN, ACTOR
   FRIEND: DEBBIE REYNOLDS
   FRIEND: PERRY COMO
   RESIDENCE: BEVERLY HILLS, CA
   TALENT: ACTRESS
   CREDIT: '52 THE DEVIL MAKES THREE
   CREDIT: '59 THE ANGRY SILENCE
   CREDIT: '62 SODOM AND GOMORRAH
   CREDIT: '65 EVERY BASTARD A KING
   CREDIT: '70 ONE FOOT IN HELL

ANN-MARGRET   BORN: ANN-MARGRET OLSSON
                              APR 28,'41 AT VALSOBYN, JAMTLAND, SWEDEN
   FATHER: GUSTAV OLSSON
   MOTHER: ANNA ARONSON
   *** MARRIED: '67 ROGER SMITH
   FATHER-IN-LAW: DALLAS SMITH
   STEP-SON: JORDAN SMITH
   STEP-DAUGHTER: TRACEY SMITH
   STEP-SON: DALLAS THOMAS SMITH

```
RESIDENCE: BEVERLY HILLS, CA
POSSESSION: AUTOMOBILE & MOTORCYCLE COLLECTION AND A BULLDOZER
POSSESSION: 14 KARAT GOLD GOLF CART AND A 6 WHEELED AMPHIBIAN
TALENT: SINGER, ACTRESS
CREDIT:  '61 POCKETFUL OF MIRACLES
CREDIT:  '62 BYE BYE BIRDIE
CREDIT:  '64 KITTEN WITH A WHIP
AA-NOM  SUP.ACT:  '71 CARNAL KNOWLEDGE
AA-NOM  ACTRESS:  '75 TOMMY
CREDIT:  '78 THE CHEAP DETECTIVE
--------------------------------------------------------------------------------
ARBUCKLE, FATTY        BORN:  ROSCOE CONKLIN ARBUCKLE
                              MAY 24,'87 AT SMITH CENTER, AK   DIED IN '33
FATHER: WILLIAM GOODRICH ARBUCKLE
MOTHER: MARY GORDON
NEPHEW: AL 'FUZZY' ST. JOHN, ACTOR (AKA FUZZY Q. JONES)
*** MARRIED:  '08 MINTA DURFEE
*** MARRIED:  '98 DORIS DEANE, ACTRESS  (DIVORCED)
*** MARRIED:  '99 ADDIE MCPHAIL, ACTRESS
ROMANCE: MARY MILES MINTER
ROMANCE: VIRGINIA RAPPE, ACTRESS  (DIED '21)
FRIEND: LAURA ANSON, ACTRESS
FRIEND: JOSEPH M. SCHENCK, STUDIO EXECUTIVE
TALENT: ACTOR, DIRECTOR
COMMENT: AFTER SCANDAL ABOUT RAPPE,USED NAME-WILLIAM GOODRICH; BUT WAS
         ALSO KNOWN AS WILL B. GOODE
CREDIT: THE GANGSTERS, DEBUT IN 1913
CREDIT: FATTY AND MABEL (NORMAND), SERIES
CREDIT: FICKLE FATTY'S FALL
CREDIT: BREWSTER'S MILLIONS
CREDIT: LIFE OF THE PARTY
CREDIT: HOLLYWOOD
--------------------------------------------------------------------------------
ARDEN, EVE        BORN:  EUNICE QUEDENS
                         APR 30,'12 AT MILL VALLEY,CA
FATHER: CHARLES PETER QUEDENS
MOTHER: LUCILLE FRANK
*** MARRIED:  '39 EDWARD G. BERGEN  (DIVORCED '48)
DAUGHTER:  '40 ELIZABETH BERGEN
ADOPTED DAUGHTER: CONSTANCE BERGEN
*** MARRIED:  '51 BROOKS WEST, ACTOR
ADOPTED SON: DUNCAN PARIS WEST
SON:  '54 DOUGLAS BROOKS WEST
RESIDENCE: WESTHAVEN RANCH, HIDDEN VALLEY CA
POSSESSION:  '53 COLLECTION OF ANTIQUES
TALENT: ACTRESS
CREDIT:  '37 OH, DOCTOR
AA-NOM  SUP.ACT:  '45 MILDRED PIERCE
CREDIT:  '53 THE LADY WANTS MINK
CREDIT:  '56 OUR MISS BROOKS
CREDIT:  '65 SGT. DEADHEAD
CREDIT:  '78 GREASE
```

ARKIN, ALAN

MAR 26,'34 AT NYC

FATHER: DAVID I. ARKIN
MOTHER: BEATRICE WORTIS
SISTER: --
BROTHER: --
*** MARRIED: '55 --, A BENNINGTON COLLEGE GIRL (DIVORCED)
SON: '56 ADAM ARKIN
SON: '60 MATTHEW ARKIN
*** MARRIED: '64 BARBARA DANA
SON: '65 ANTHONY ARKIN
RESIDENCE: NYC
TALENT: ACTOR
AA-NOM ACTOR: '66 THE RUSSIANS ARE COMING- THE RUSSIANS ARE COMING
CREDIT: '67 WAIT UNTIL DARK
AA-NOM ACTOR: '68 THE HEART IS A LONELY HUNTER
CREDIT: '69 POPI
CREDIT: '72 LAST OF THE RED HOT LOVERS

ARLISS, GEORGE

BORN: AUGUSTUS GEORGE ANDREWS
APR 10,1868 AT LONDON, ENGLAND DIED IN '46

FATHER: WILLIAM ARLISS-ANDREWS
SISTER: DAISY ARLISS
BROTHER: CHARLES ARLISS
BROTHER: FRED ARLISS
*** MARRIED: '99 FLORENCE MONTGOMERY, ACTRESS
SON: LESLIE ANDREWS, DIRECTOR - LESLIE ARLISS
RESIDENCE: ST. MARGARET'S-AT-CLIFFE, KENT ENGLAND
MEMOIRS: UP THE YEARS FROM BLOOMSBURY
MEMOIRS: MY TEN YEARS IN THE STUDIOS
TALENT: ACTOR
AA-NOM ACTOR: '29 THE GREEN GODDESS
AA-WIN ACTOR: '29 DISRAELI
CREDIT: '31 THE MILLIONAIRE
CREDIT: '33 THE ADOPTED FATHER
CREDIT: '34 THE HOUSE OF ROTHSCHILD
CREDIT: '35 THE IRON DUKE

ARMENDARIZ, PEDRO

MAY 09,'12 AT MEXICO CITY, DISTRICT FEDERAL DIED IN '63

FATHER: PEDRO ARMENDARIZ, SR. (DIED '20)
MOTHER: DELLA HASTINGS (DIED '19)
BROTHER: FRANCISCO ARMENDARIZ
*** MARRIED: '39 CARMEN PARDO
SON: '40 PEDRO ARMENDARIZ, JR., ACTOR
DAUGHTER: '45 CARMEN ARMENDARIZ
FRIEND: EMILIO FERNANDES, DIRECTOR
RESIDENCE: LOS ANGELES, CA
POSSESSION: '45 CONTRACT AT GOLDWYN STUDIO
TALENT: ACTOR
CREDIT: '43 MARIA CANDELARIA, ONE OF 40 MEXICAN FILMS
CREDIT: '47 THE FUGITIVE
CREDIT: '55 THE LITTLEST OUTLAW
CREDIT: '63 FROM RUSSIA WITH LOVE
CREDIT: LIFE OF SIMON BOLIVAR

```
-------------------------------------------------------------------------------------------------
ARMSTRONG, LOUIS          BORN:  DANIEL LOUIS ARMSTRONG
                               JUL 04,'00 AT NEW ORLEANS, LA  DIED IN '71
     FATHER: WILLIE ARMSTRONG, TURPENTINE WORKER
     MOTHER: MARY ANN, DOMESTIC
     SISTER: BEATRICE ARMSTRONG
     *** MARRIED: '17 DAISY PARKER  (DIVORCED)
     *** MARRIED: '24 LILLIAN HARDIN, JAZZ PIANIST  (DIVORCED '32)
     *** MARRIED: '42 LUCILLE WILSON, CHORUS GIRL
     FRIEND: JOE ' KING' OLIVER, JAZZ PERFORMER
     RESIDENCE: NYC
     BIOGRAPHY:  '75 AMBASSADOR SATCHMO, BY JEAN G. CORNELL
     TALENT: MUSICIAN, ACTOR
     COMMENT: NICKNAME 'SATCHELMOUTH' BECAME 'SATCHMO' IN 1930'S
     COMMENT: WON 'DOWN BEAT' MAGAZINE'S HALL OF FAME AWARD IN 1952
     CREDIT:  '36 PENNIES FROM HEAVEN
     CREDIT:  '47 NEW ORLEANS
     CREDIT:  '54 THE GLENN MILLER STORY
     CREDIT:  '66 A MAN CALLED ADAM
     CREDIT:  '69 HELLO, DOLLY!
-------------------------------------------------------------------------------------------------
ARNAZ, DESI          BORN:  DESIDERIO ALBERTO ARNAZ, III
                            MAR 02,'17 AT SANTIAGO, CUBA
     FATHER: DESIDERIO ALBERTO ARNAZ, II, MAYOR OF SANTIAGO, CUBA
     MOTHER: LOLITA DE ACHA
     *** MARRIED:  '40 LUCILLE BALL, ACTRESS  (DIVORCED '60)
     DAUGHTER:  '51 LUCIE ARNAZ, ACTRESS
     SON:   '53 DESI ARNAZ, JR., ACTOR
     POSSESSION: DESILU STUDIO & PRODUCTION CO.
     MEMOIRS:'A BOOK'
     TALENT: ACTOR-SINGER
     COMMENT: ARNAZ FAMILY FLED CUBAN REVOLUTION IN 1933
     CREDIT:  '36 SANG WITH XAVIER CUGAT'S BAND
     CREDIT:  '41 FATHER TAKES A WIFE
     CREDIT:  '46 BATAAN CUBAN PETE
     CREDIT:  '54 THE LONG, LONG TRAILER
     CREDIT:  '56 FOREVER DARLING
-------------------------------------------------------------------------------------------------
ARNESS, JAMES          BORN:  JAMES AURNESS
                             MAY 16,'23 AT MINNEAPOLIS, MN
     FATHER: ROLF C. AURNESS, MANAGER OF SON'S RANCH
     MOTHER: RUTH DUESLER
     BROTHER: PETER AURNESS, ACTOR - PETER GRAVES
     *** MARRIED: VIRGINIA CHAPMAN  (DIVORCED '60)
     SON:  '47 CRAIG ARNESS
     DAUGHTER:  '51 JENNY LEE ARNESS, ACTRESS  (SUICIDE '75)
     SON:  '52 ROLF ARNESS
     RESIDENCE: PACIFIC PALISADES, CA
     POSSESSION: 4 HOUSES, 2 AIRPLANES
     TALENT: ACTOR
     CREDIT: THE FARMER'S DAUGHTER, DEBUT
     CREDIT:  '52 THE THING
     CREDIT:  '54 THEM
     CREDIT:  '56 THE FIRST TRAVELLING SALESLADY
     CREDIT: GUNSMOKE, TV SERIES
```

ARNOLD, EDWARD   BORN: GUNTHER SCHNEIDER
                                  FEB 18,'90 AT NYC   DIED IN '56
   BROTHER: CHARLES SCHNEIDER
   *** MARRIED: '17 HARRIET MARSHALL (DIVORCED '27)
   DAUGHTER: '18 ELIZABETH ORLANDO ARNOLD
   DAUGHTER: '19 DOROTHY JANE ARNOLD
   SON: '20 WILLIAM EDWARD ARNOLD, JR., ACTOR
   *** MARRIED: '29 OLIVE EMERSON, SOPRANO (DIVORCED '48)
   *** MARRIED: '51 CLEO MCCLAIN
   RESIDENCE: LOS ANGELES, CA
   MEMOIRS: '40 LORENZO GOES TO HOLLYWOOD
   TALENT: ACTOR
   CREDIT: '16 WHEN THE MAN SPEAKS
   CREDIT: '32 RASPUTIN AND THE EMPRESS
   CREDIT: '37 EASY LIVING
   CREDIT: '48 COMMAND DECISION
   CREDIT: '56 THE AMBASSADOR'S DAUGHTER

ARTHUR, BEATRICE   BORN: BERNICE FRANKEL
                                    MAY 13,'24 AT NYC
   FATHER: PHILIP FRANKEL
   MOTHER: REBECCA
   SISTER: --
   SISTER: --
   *** MARRIED: '50 GENE SAKS, ACTOR, DIRECTOR
   ADOPTED SON: MATTHEW SAKS
   ADOPTED SON: DANIEL SAKS
   RESIDENCE: NYC
   TALENT: ACTRESS
   CREDIT: '67 THAT KIND OF WOMAN
   CREDIT: '70 LOVERS AND OTHER STRANGERS
   CREDIT: '73 MAME, WON TONY AWARD FOR STAGE ROLE
   CREDIT: '74 MAUDE, TV SERIES

ARTHUR, JEAN   BORN: GLADYS GEORGIANNE GREENE
                                OCT 17,'05 AT NYC
   FATHER: HERBERT SIDNEY GREENE
   MOTHER: JOHANNA AUGUSTA NIELSEN
   *** MARRIED: '28 JULIAN ANKER (ANNULLED '28)
   *** MARRIED: '32 FRANK J. ROSS, PRODUCER (DIVORCED '49)
   ROMANCE: GEORGE K. ARTHUR, ACTOR
   RESIDENCE: CARMEL-BY-THE-SEA, CA
   TALENT: ACTRESS
   COMMENT: VASSAR COLLEGE-DRAMA DEPARTMENT CHAIRMAN
   CREDIT: '23 CAMEO KIRBY, DEBUT
   CREDIT: '27 THE POOR NUT
   CREDIT: '37 EASY LIVING
   CREDIT: '40 TOO MANY HUSBANDS
   AA-NOM ACTRESS: '43 THE MORE THE MERRIER
   CREDIT: '52 SHANE

ASHLEY, ELIZABETH
                                AUG 30,'39 AT OCALA, FL
   *** MARRIED: RICHARD MATHEWS
   *** MARRIED: '62 JAMES FARENTINO, ACTOR
   *** MARRIED: '63 GEORGE PEPPARD, ACTOR (DIVORCED)
   STEP-DAUGHTER: JULIE LOUISE PEPPARD

```
STEP-SON: BRADFORD DAVIES PEPPARD
SON:  '68 CHRISTOPHER PEPPARD
*** MARRIED:  '75 JAMES MCCARTHY, ACTOR
ROMANCE: THOMAS MCGUANE
MEMOIRS:  '78 ACTRESS - POSTCARDS FROM THE ROAD
TALENT: ACTRESS
CREDIT:  '64 THE CARPETBAGGERS
CREDIT:  '65 SHIP OF FOOLS
CREDIT:  '65 THE THIRD DAY
CREDIT:  '71 MARRIAGE OF A YOUNG STOCKBROKE
-------------------------------------------------------------------------------------------
ASNER, EDWARD
                         NOV 15,'25 AT KANSAS CITY, KA
    FATHER: MORRIS DAVID ASHER
    MOTHER: LIZZIE SELIGER
    *** MARRIED:  '59 NANCY LOU SYKES
    DAUGHTER:  '63 LIZA ASNER, TWIN
    SON:  '63 MATTHEW ASNER, TWIN
    DAUGHTER:  '65 KATHRYN ASNER
    TALENT: ACTOR
    CREDIT:  '65 THE SATAN BUG
    CREDIT:  '66 EL DORADO
    CREDIT:  '67 GUNN
    CREDIT:  '70 THE MARY TYLER MOORE SHOW, TV SERIES
    CREDIT:  '71 THE SKIN GAME
-------------------------------------------------------------------------------------------
ASTAIRE, FRED           BORN:   FREDERIC AUSTERLITZ
                         MAY 10,'99 AT OMAHA,NE
    FATHER: FREDERIC AUSTERLITZ, SALESMAN
    MOTHER: ANN GEILUS
    SISTER: ADELE ASTAIRE, DANCER
    BROTHER-IN-LAW: SIR CHARLES CAVENDISH
    BROTHER-IN-LAW: KINGMAN DOUGLASS
    *** MARRIED:  '33 PHYLLIS BAKER POTTER  (DIED '54)
    SON:  '41 FRED ASTAIRE, JR.
    DAUGHTER:  '42 AVA ASTAIRE
    STEP-SON: PETER POTTER
    PARTNER: CLAIRE LUCE
    PARTNER: GINGER ROGERS
    PARTNER: CYD CHARISSE
    PARTNER: BARRIE CHASE
    RESIDENCE: BEVERLY HILLS, CA
    POSSESSION: RACE HORSE 'TRIPLICATE'
    POSSESSION: FRED ASTAIRE DANCE STUDIOS
    MEMOIRS:  '59 STEPS IN TIME
    TALENT: DANCER-ACTOR
    CREDIT:  '34 THE GAY DIVORCEE
    CREDIT:  '48 EASTER PARADE
    AA-SPECIAL AWARD:  '49 HONORING HIS ARTISTRY
    CREDIT:  '55 DADDY LONG LEGS
    CREDIT:  '57 SILK STOCKINGS
    CREDIT:  '62 THE PLEASURE OF HIS COMPANY
    AA-NOM  SUP.ACT:  '74 THE TOWERING INFERNO
```

ASTIN, JOHN
                    MAR 30,'30 AT BALTIMORE, MD
    GRANDMOTHER: EDITH A. MACKENZIE, ACTRESS-AKA 'MOTHER MACK' (DIED '65)
    FATHER: ALLEN VARLEY ASTIN
    MOTHER: MARGARET LINNIE MACKENZIE
    *** MARRIED: '60 SUZANNE HAHN, ACTRESS
    SON: '60 DAVID ASTIN
    SON: '61 ALLEN ASTIN
    SON: '65 THOMAS ASTIN
    *** MARRIED: '68 PATRICIA OWENS
    SON: '71 SEAN ASTIN, MOTHER - PATTY DUKE
    *** MARRIED: '72 PATTY DUKE, ACTRESS
    SON: '73 MACKENZIE ASTIN
    POSSESSION: '73 BANJO FILMS LTD.
    TALENT: ACTOR
    CREDIT: '61 WEST SIDE STORY
    CREDIT: '62 THAT TOUCH OF MINK
    CREDIT: '68 CANDY
    CREDIT: '72 EVIL ROY SLADE
    CREDIT: '73 THE BROTHERS O'TOOLE

ASTOR, MARY   BORN: LUCILLE VASCONCELLOS LANGHANKE
                    MAY 03,'06 AT QUINCY,IL
    FATHER: OTTO L. W. LANGHANKE
    MOTHER: HELEN VASCONCELLOS
    *** MARRIED: '28 KENNETH HAWKS, DIRECTOR (DIED '30)
    *** MARRIED: '31 DR. FRANKLIN THORPE (DIVORCED '36)
    DAUGHTER: '32 MARYLYN HAUOLI THORPE
    *** MARRIED: '36 MANUEL DEL COMPOS (DIVORCED '41)
    SON: '37 ANTHONY DEL COMPOS
    *** MARRIED: '45 THOMAS WHEELOCK (DIVORCED '55)
    BROTHER-IN-LAW: HOWARD HAWKS, DIRECTOR
    ROMANCE: JOHN BARRYMORE
    ROMANCE: GEORGE S. KAUFMAN, PLAYWRIGHT
    FRIEND: FERRIS HALL, ACTOR
    RESIDENCE: MOTION PICTURE AND TV COUNTRY HOME
    MEMOIRS: '59 MY STORY
    TALENT: ACTRESS
    CREDIT: '21 THE BEGGAR MAID, DEBUT
    CREDIT: '26 DON JUAN
    CREDIT: '33 EASY TO LOVE
    AA-WIN SUP.ACT.: '41 THE GREAT LIE
    CREDIT: '49 ANY NUMBER CAN PLAY
    CREDIT: '56 A KISS BEFORE DYING
    CREDIT: '64 HUSH, HUSH SWEET CHARLOTTE

AUER, MISCHA   BORN: MISCHA OUNSKOWSKI
                    NOV 17,'05 AT ST. PETERSBURG, RUSSIA   DIED IN '67
    GRANDFATHER: LEOPOLD AUER, VIOLIN TEACHER
    FATHER: --, ARMY OFFICER (DIED '16)
    MOTHER: --, NURSE (DIED '17)
    *** MARRIED: '31 NORMA TILLMAN (DIVORCED '41)
    SON: '34 ANTHONY AUER
    ADOPTED DAUGHTER: ZOE AUER
    *** MARRIED: '41 JOYCE HUNTER, SINGER
    *** MARRIED: '50 SUSANNE KALISH (DIVORCED '57)
    *** MARRIED: '65 ELISE SOULS

```
          RESIDENCE: GLOVERSVILLE, NY
          TALENT: ACTOR
          CREDIT:   '30 JUST IMAGINE
          AA-NOM  SUP.ACT:  '36 MY MAN GODFREY
          CREDIT:   '37 MARRY THE GIRL
          CREDIT:   '42 DON'T GET PERSONAL
          CREDIT:   '50 ARRIVEDERCI, BABY!
          CREDIT:   '66 DROP DEAD DARLING
------------------------------------------------------------------------------------------------
AUMONT, JEAN-PIERRE          BORN:  JEAN-PIERRE SALOMONS
                                    JAN 05,'09 AT PARIS, FRANCE
          BROTHER: FRANCOIS AUMONT
          *** MARRIED:  '43 MARIA VIDAL SILAS Y GARCIA, ACTRESS - MARIA MONTEZ  (DIED '51)
          DAUGHTER:  '46 MARIA CHRISTINE AUMONT
          SON-IN-LAW: CHRISTIAN MARQUAND, ACTOR, DIRECTOR
          *** MARRIED:  '56 MARISA PAVAN, ACTRESS  (DIVORCED '65)
          SISTER-IN-LAW: PIER ANGELI, ACTRESS  (DIED '71)
          SISTER-IN-LAW: PATRICIA PIERANGELI
          SON:  '57 JEAN-CLAUDE AUMONT
          SON:  '58 PATRICK AUMONT
          *** MARRIED:  '69 MARISA PAVAN, RE-MARRIED
          MEMOIRS:  '77 SUN AND SHADOW
          TALENT: ACTOR
          CREDIT:   '32 JEAN DE LA LUNE
          CREDIT:   '42 THE CROSS OF LORRAINE
          CREDIT:   '53 LILI
          CREDIT:   '69 CASTLE KEEP
          CREDIT:   '73 LA NUIT AMERICAINE
------------------------------------------------------------------------------------------------
AUTRY, GENE          BORN:  ORVON GENE AUTRY
                            SEP 29,'07 AT TIOGA, TX
          GRANDFATHER: WILLIAM T. AUTRY
          FATHER: DELBERT AUTRY
          MOTHER: ELNORA OZMONT
          SISTER: VELDA AUTRY
          SISTER: WILMA AUTRY
          BROTHER: DUDLEY (DOUG) AUTRY
          *** MARRIED:  '32 INA MAE SPIVEY
          FRIEND: WILL ROGERS
          FRIEND: ROY ROGERS
          FRIEND: RICHARD M. NIXON
          PARTNER: CHAMPION, HIS HORSE
          RESIDENCE: PALM SPRINGS, CA
          RESIDENCE: MELODY RANCH, SAN FERNANDO, CA
          POSSESSION:  '47 3 AIRPLANES & 1 HELICOPTER
          POSSESSION: PLATINUM RECORD FOR RUDOLPH THE RED-NOSED REINDEER
          POSSESSION: GENE AUTRY FILM PRODUCTION CO.
          POSSESSION: GENE AUTRY HOTELS
          MEMOIRS:  '78 BACK IN THE SADDLE AGAIN
          TALENT: ACTOR,SINGER
          CREDIT:   '34 IN OLD SANTA FE, DEBUT
          CREDIT:   '39 IN OLD MONTERREY
          CREDIT:   '46 RANGE WARS
          CREDIT:   '49 GUNS AND SADDLES
          CREDIT:   '53 GOLDTOWN GHOST RIDERS
```

AVALON, FRANKIE   BORN: FRANCIS THOMAS AVALLONE
                          SEP 18,'40 AT PHILADELPHIA,PA
   FATHER: NICOLAS AVALLONE
   MOTHER: MARY
   *** MARRIED: '63 KAY DEIBEL
   SON: '63 FRANK AVALON, JR.
   SON: '64 ANTHONY AVALON
   DAUGHTER: '65 DINA MARY AVALON
   DAUGHTER: '66 LAURA AVALON
   SON: '69 JOSEPH AVALON
   TALENT: ACTOR, ENTERTAINER
   CREDIT: '60 GUNS OF THE TIMBERLINE
   CREDIT: '65 BEACH BLANKET BINGO
   CREDIT: '66 HOW TO STUFF A WILD BIKINI
   CREDIT: '78 GREASE

AYRES, LEW   BORN: LEWIS FREDRICK AYRES, III
                      DEC 28,'08 AT MINNEAPOLIS, MN
   *** MARRIED: '31 LOLA LANE (DIVORCED '33)
   *** MARRIED: '33 GINGER ROGERS, ACTRESS (DIVORCED '43)
   *** MARRIED: '64 DIANA HALL, AIRLINE STEWARDESS
   SON: '68 JUSTIN BRET AYRES
   RESIDENCE: BRENTWOOD, CA
   TALENT: ACTOR, DIRECTOR
   CREDIT: '29 THE SOPHOMORE, DEBUT
   CREDIT: '31 ALL QUIET ON THE WESTERN FRONT
   CREDIT: '38 DR. KILDARE, MGM SERIES
   AA-NOM ACTOR: '48 JOHNNY BELINDA
   CREDIT: '62 ADVISE AND CONSENT
   CREDIT: '64 THE CARPETBAGGERS

AZNAVOUR, CHARLES   BORN: VARENAGH AZNAORIAN
                      MAY 22,'24 AT PARIS, FRANCE
   FATHER: MISHA AZNAOURIAN, CHEF
   *** MARRIED: '67 ULLA THORSSELL
   DAUGHTER: '69 PATRICIA AZNAVOUR
   SON: '71 PATRICK AZNAVOUR
   FRIEND: EDITH PIAF, CHANTEUSE
   RESIDENCE: GALLIUS, SEINE-ET-OISE, FRANCE
   TALENT: SINGER, ACTOR
   COMMENT: FAMILY FLED TURKISH REVOLUTION
   CREDIT: '60 SHOOT THE PIANIST
   CREDIT: '68 CANDY
   CREDIT: '69 THE ADVENTURERS
   CREDIT: '69 THE GAMES

```
---------------------------------------------------------------------------------------------
BACALL, LAUREN          BORN:   BETTE JOAN PERSKE
                                SEP 16,'24 AT NYC

    FATHER: WILLIAM PERSKE
    MOTHER: NATALIE WEINSTEIN BACAL
    *** MARRIED:  '45 HUMPHREY BOGART  (DIED '57)
    SON:  '48 STEPHEN BOGART
    DAUGHTER-IN-LAW: DALE GEMELLI  (MARRIED '69)
    DAUGHTER:  '52 LESLIE HOWARD BOGART
    *** MARRIED:  '61 JASON ROBARDS, JR., ACTOR  (DIVORCED '69)
    STEP-DAUGHTER: SARA LOUISE ROBARDS
    STEP-SON: JASON ROBARDS, III
    STEP-SON: DAVID ROBARDS
    SON: '62 SAM ROBARDS
    CREDIT:  '45 TO HAVE AND HAVE NOT, DEBUT
    CREDIT:  '57 DESIGNING WOMAN
    CREDIT:  '64 SEX AND THE SINGLE GIRL
    CREDIT:  '74 MURDER ON THE ORIENT EXPRESS
---------------------------------------------------------------------------------------------
BACKUS, JIM
                        FEB 25,'13 AT CLEVELAND, OH
    FATHER: RUSSELL GOULD BACKUS
    MOTHER: DAISY GILMORE TAYLOR
    *** MARRIED:  '43 HENRIETTE KAYE
    RESIDENCE: BEL AIR, LOS ANGELES, CA
    MEMOIRS:  '58 ROCKS ON THE ROOF
    TALENT: ACTOR,AUTHOR
    CREDIT:  '49 THE GREAT LOVER
    CREDIT:  '55 REBEL WITHOUT A CAUSE
    CREDIT:  '57 A MAN OF A THOUSAND FACES
    CREDIT:  '62 BOYS' NIGHT OUT
    CREDIT:  '68 WHERE WERE YOU WHEN THE LIGHTS  WENT OUT?
---------------------------------------------------------------------------------------------
BAER, JR., MAX
                        1937 AT OAKLAND, CA
    FATHER: MAX BAER, HEAVYWEIGHT BOXER, ACTOR  (DIED '59)
    MOTHER: DOROTHY DUNBAR, ACTRESS
    UNCLE: JACOB HENRY 'BUDDY' BAER, ACTOR, BOXER
    *** MARRIED: JOANNA HILL, ACTRESS
    RESIDENCE: LOS ANGELES, CA
    POSSESSION: CONTRACT AT WARNER BROS.
    TALENT: ACTOR, PRODUCER
    CREDIT: THE LONG RIDE HOME
    CREDIT: THE MCCULLOCHS
    CREDIT: THE BEVERLY HILLBILLIES, TV SERIES
    CREDIT: ODE TO BILLIE JOE
    CREDIT: MACON COUNTY LINE
---------------------------------------------------------------------------------------------
BAILEY, PEARL           BORN:   PEARL MAE BAILEY
                                MAR 29,'18 AT NEWPORT NEWS, VA
    FATHER: JOSEPH JAMES BAILEY
    MOTHER: ELLA MAE
    SISTER: VIRGINIA BAILEY
    SISTER: EURA BAILEY
    BROTHER: BILL BAILEY, DANCER
    BROTHER: HENRY BAILEY
    *** MARRIED:  '48 JOHN RANDOLPH PINKETT  (DIVORCED '52)
```

```
*** MARRIED:  '52 LOUIS BELLSON
ADOPTED SON: TONY BELLSON
ADOPTED DAUGHTER: DEE DEE JEAN BELLSON
RESIDENCE: APPLE VALLEY, CA
POSSESSION:  '68 TONY AWARD FOR HELLO, DOLLY
MEMOIRS:  '68 THE RAW PEARL
TALENT: ENTERTAINER
CREDIT:  '47 VARIETY GIRL, DEBUT
CREDIT:  '54 CARMEN JONES
CREDIT:  '55 THAT CERTAIN FEELING
CREDIT:  '60 PORGY AND BESS
```

BAINTER, FAY
```
                          DEC 07,'91 AT LOS ANGELES, CA   DIED IN '68
FATHER: CHARLES FRANCIS BAINTER
MOTHER: MARY OKELL
*** MARRIED:  '22 REGINALD S. H. VENABLE  (DIED '64)
SON:  '23 REGINALD S. H. VENABLE, JR.
RESIDENCE: SANTA MONICA, CA
CREDIT:  '34 THIS SIDE OF HEAVEN, DEBUT
AA-NOM  ACTRESS:  '38 WHITE BANNERS
AA-WIN  SUP.ACT.:  '38 JEZEBEL
CREDIT:  '51 CLOSE TO MY HEART
AA-NOM  SUP.ACT  '61 THE CHILDREN'S HOUR
```

BAKER, CARROLL
```
                          MAY 28,'31 AT JOHNSTOWN, PA
FATHER: WILLIAM BAKER
MOTHER: VIRGINIA
SISTER: VIRGINIA BAKER
*** MARRIED:  '55 JACK GARFEIN
SON:  '58 HERSHEL GARFEIN
DAUGHTER:  '59 BLANCHE GARFEIN
TALENT: ACTRESS
AA-NOM  ACTRESS:  '56 BABY DOLL
CREDIT:  '56 GIANT
CREDIT:  '58 THE BIG COUNTRY
CREDIT:  '62 THE CARPETBAGGERS
CREDIT:  '65 HARLOW
CREDIT:  '71 CAPTAIN APACHE
```

BALL, LUCILLE   BORN: LUCILLE DESIREE BALL
```
                          AUG 06,'10 AT CELORON, NY
FATHER: HENRY BALL, ELECTRICIAN
MOTHER: DESIREE HUNT, MODEL, CONCERT PIANIST
BROTHER: FRED BALL
*** MARRIED:  '40 DESI ARNAZ  (DIVORCED '60)
DAUGHTER:  '51 LUCIE ARNAZ
SON:  '53 DESI ARNAZ, JR.
*** MARRIED:  '61 GARY MORTON
RESIDENCE: BEVERLY HILLS, CA
POSSESSION: DESILU PRODUCTIONS COMPANY-BOUGHT OUT ARNAZ IN 1962
BIOGRAPHY:  '73 LUCY: THE BITTERSWEET LIFE
TALENT: ACTRESS
CREDIT:  '34 BROADWAY BILL
CREDIT:  '54 THE LONG, LONG TRAILER
CREDIT:  '60 THE FACTS OF LIFE
CREDIT:  '68 YOURS, MINE AND OURS
```

```
CREDIT:  '73 MAME
---------------------------------------------------------------------------------------------
BALSAM, MARTIN          BORN:  MARTIN HENRY BALSAM
                               NOV 04,'19 AT NYC
    FATHER: ALBERT BALSAM
    MOTHER: LILLIAN WEINSTEIN
    *** MARRIED:  '52 PEARL L. SOMNER  (DIVORCED '54)
    *** MARRIED:  '57 JOYCE VAN PATTEN  (DIVORCED '62)
    BROTHER-IN-LAW: DICK VAN PATTEN, ACTOR
    DAUGHTER:  '58 TALIA BALSAM
    *** MARRIED:  '63 IRENE MILLER
    SON:  '64 ADAM BALSAM
    DAUGHTER:  '68 ZOE BALSAM
    RESIDENCE: NYC
    TALENT: ACTOR
    CREDIT:  '54 ON THE WATERFRONT
    CREDIT:  '58 MARJORIE MORNINGSTAR
    CREDIT:  '60 PSYCHO
    AA-WIN  SUP.ACT.:  '65 A THOUSAND CLOWNS
    CREDIT:  '67 HOMBRE
---------------------------------------------------------------------------------------------
BANCROFT, ANNE          BORN:  ANNA MARIA LUISA ITALIANO
                               SEP 17,'31 AT NYC
    FATHER: MICHAEL ITALIANO, ACTOR - GEORGE BANCROFT
    MOTHER: MILDRED DINAPOLI
    SISTER: JOANNE ITALIANO
    SISTER: PHYLLIS ITALIANO
    *** MARRIED:  '54 MARTY MAY, ACTOR  (DIVORCED '57)
    *** MARRIED:  '64 MEL BROOKS, ACTOR, DIRECTOR
    STEP-DAUGHTER: STEFANIE BROOKS
    STEP-SON: NICHOLAS BROOKS
    STEP-SON: EDWARD BROOKS
    SON:  '72 MAXIMILIAN BROOKS
    RESIDENCE: NYC
    TALENT: ACTRESS
    CREDIT:  '52 DON'T BOTHER TO KNOCK, DEBUT
    CREDIT:  '57 THE RESTLESS BREED
    AA-WIN  ACTRESS:  '62 THE MIRACLE WORKER
    AA-NOM  ACTRESS:  '64 THE PUMPKIN EATER
    AA-NOM  ACTRESS:  '67 THE GRADUATE
    AA-NOM  ACTRESS:  '77 THE TURNING POINT
---------------------------------------------------------------------------------------------
BANKHEAD, TALLULAH          BORN:  TALLULAH BROCKMAN BANKHEAD
                                   JAN 31,'02 AT HUNTSVILLE,AL  DIED IN '68
    GRANDFATHER: JOHN H. BANKHEAD, SENATOR FROM ALABAMA
    FATHER: WILLIAM BROCKMAN BANKHEAD, CONGRESSMAN
    MOTHER: ADELINE EUGENIA SLEDGE  (DIED '02)
    SISTER: EUGENIA BANKHEAD
    *** MARRIED:  '37 JOHN EMERY, ACTOR  (DIVORCED '41)
    ADOPTED DAUGHTER: BARBARA NICHOLAI EMERY
    FRIEND: ESTELLE WINWOOD, ACTRESS
    FRIEND: TONIO SELWART, ACTOR
    RESIDENCE: BEDFORD VILLAGE, NY
    POSSESSION: AUGUSTUS JOHN'S'PORTRAIT OF THE ACTRESS AS A YOUNG WOMAN'
    MEMOIRS: TALLULAH
    TALENT: ACTRESS
    CREDIT:  '18 THIRTY A WEEK, DEBUT
    CREDIT:  '28 HIS HOUSE IN ORDER
```

```
CREDIT:  '44 LIFEBOAT
CREDIT:  '53 MAIN STREET TO BROADWAY
CREDIT:  '45 A ROYAL SCANDAL
CREDIT:  '53 MAIN STREET TO BROADWAY
CREDIT:  '64 FANATIC
```

BANKS, MONTAGUE "MONTY"   BORN: MARIO BIANCHI
                              JUL 17,'97 AT CASENE, ITALY   DIED IN '50
```
*** MARRIED: GLADYS FRAZIN  (DIVORCED)
*** MARRIED: '40 GRACIE FIELDS, ACTRESS
RESIDENCE: CAPRI, ITALY
POSSESSION: '36 CONTRACT AT 20TH CENTURY FOX
TALENT: ACTOR, DIRECTOR
CREDIT:  '27 A PERFECT GENTLEMAN
CREDIT:  '29 WEEKEND WIVES
CREDIT:  '31 ALMOST A HONEYMOON  FRONT
CREDIT:  '35 NO LIMIT
CREDIT:  '45 A BELL FOR ADANO
```

BANKY, VILMA   BORN: VILMA LONCIT
                    JAN 09,'03 AT BUDAPEST, HUNGARY
```
FATHER: VILMOS LONCIT, AKA JOHN BAULSEY
MOTHER: ULBERT KATALIN
*** MARRIED:  '27 ROD LA ROCQUE, ACTOR  (DIED '69)
ROMANCE: RONALD COLMAN
FRIEND: LOUIS B. MAYER
FRIEND: SAMUEL GOLDWYN, DISCOVERED HER IN BUDAPEST
RESIDENCE: BEVERLY HILLS, CA
POSSESSION: RANCH IN SAN FERNANDO VALLEY
TALENT: ACTRESS
COMMENT: GOLF CHAMPION AT THE WILSHIRE COUNTRY CLUB IN LOS ANGELES
CREDIT:  '25 DARK ANGEL
CREDIT:  '26 SON OF THE SHEIK
CREDIT:  '28 TWO LOVERS
CREDIT:  '30 A LADY TO LOVE
CREDIT:  '33 THE REBEL
```

BARA, THEDA   BORN: THEODOSIA GOODMAN
                   APR 07,'90 AT CHILLICOTHE, OH DIED IN '55
```
GRANDFATHER: BARRANGER, FROM WHOM STAGENAME DEVELOPED
FATHER: BERNARD GOODMAN, TAILOR
MOTHER: PAULINE DE COPPET
SISTER: LORI GOODMAN
BROTHER: MARQUE GOODMAN
*** MARRIED: '21 CHARLES BRABIN, DIRECTOR
RESIDENCE: LOS ANGELES, CA
TALENT: ACTRESS
COMMENT: 1ST STAGE NAME THEODOSIA DE COPPETT
COMMENT: THEDA BARA IS AN ANAGRAM OF 'ARAB DEATH'
CREDIT:  '15 THE TWO ORPHANS, DEBUT
CREDIT:  '16 ROMEO AND JULIET
CREDIT:  '17 CAMILLE
CREDIT:  '18 SALOME
CREDIT:  '19 THE SIREN'S SONG
```

BARDOT, BRIGITTE   BORN: CAMILLE JAVAL BARDOT
                              SEP 28,'34 AT PARIS, FRANCE
 FATHER: LOUIS BARDOT, INDUSTRIAL ENGINEER
 MOTHER: ANN-MARIE
 SISTER: MIJANOU BARDOT
 *** MARRIED: '52 ROGER VADIM PLEMIANIKOFF, JOURNALIST, DIRECTOR (DIVORCED '57)
 *** MARRIED: '59 JACQUES CHARRIER (DIVORCED '63)
 SON: '60 NICOLAS JACQUES CHARRIER
 *** MARRIED: '66 GUNTHER SACHS VON OPEL (DIVORCED '69)
 STEP-SON: ROLF SACHS
 ROMANCE: BOB ZAGURI, PROMOTER
 FRIEND: GHISLAIN DUSSART, ARTIST
 RESIDENCE: LA MADRAGUE, ST. TROPEZ, FRANCE
 BIOGRAPHY: '75 BRIGITTE BARDOT - A CLOSE-UP, BY FRANCOISE SAGAN
 TALENT: ACTRESS
 CREDIT: '53 ACT OF LOVE
 CREDIT: '56 HELEN OF TROY
 CREDIT: '57 AND GOD CREATED WOMAN
 CREDIT: '65 VIVA MARIA!
 CREDIT: '68 SHALAKO

BARKER, LEX   BORN: ALEXANDER CRICHELOW BARKER
                         MAY 08,'19 AT RYE, NY DIED IN '73
 *** MARRIED: '42 CONSTANCE THURLOW (DIVORCED '51)
 DAUGHTER: '43 LYNNE ALEXANDER BARKER
 SON: '44 ALEXANDER BARKER
 *** MARRIED: '51 ARLENE DAHL (DIVORCED '52)
 *** MARRIED: '53 LANA TURNER, ACTRESS (DIVORCED '57)
 STEP-DAUGHTER: CHERYL CRANE
 *** MARRIED: '59 IRENE LABHART (DIED '62)
 SON: '60 CHRISTOPHER BARKER
 *** MARRIED: '65 MARIA CERVERA
 TALENT: ACTOR
 CREDIT: '45 DOLL FACE
 CREDIT: '50 TARZAN AND THE SLAVE GIRL
 CREDIT: '57 THE DEERSLAYER
 CREDIT: '64 CODE 7, VICTIM 5
 CREDIT: '68 DEVIL MAY CARE

BARNES, BINNIE   BORN: GITELLE ENOYCE BARNES
                            MAR 25,'06 AT LONDON, ENGLAND
 *** MARRIED: '32 SAMUEL JOSEPH (DIVORCED '36)
 *** MARRIED: '40 MICHAEL J. FRANKOVICH, PRODUCER
 SON: '42 MICHAEL FRANKOVICH, JR.
 DAUGHTER: '44 MICHELLE FRANKOVICH
 SON: '46 PETER FRANKOVICH
 CREDIT: '31 NIGHT IN MONTMARTRE
 CREDIT: '39 DAYTIME WIFE
 CREDIT: '45 GETTING GERTIE'S GARTER
 CREDIT: '55 SHADOW OF THE EAGLE
 CREDIT: '68 WHERE ANGELS GO...TROUBLE FOLLOWS

BARRIE, WENDY   BORN: MARGARET WENDY JENKINS
                                 APR 18,'13 AT HONG KONG DIED IN '78
  GRANDFATHER: GEN. SIR CHARLES WARREN, HEAD OF SCOTLAND YARD
  FATHER: FRANK C. JENKINS, BARRISTER (DIED '35)
  MOTHER: NELL MACDONAGH
  GODFATHER: SIR JAMES MATTHEW BARRIE, AUTHOR OF PETER PAN
  SISTER: BARBARA PATRICIA JENKINS (DIED '38)
  UNCLE: SIR JAMES BARRIE, SURGEON
  *** MARRIED: '45 DAVID L. MEYERS, TEXTILE MANUFACTURER (DIVORCED '50)
  ROMANCE: CHARLES 'BUGSY' SIEGEL
  ROMANCE: WOOLWORTH DONAHUE
  ROMANCE: MARCO 'SCHMOOPEE' CAZES, WAITER
  FRIEND: ZEPPO MARX, HER AGENT
  ENEMY: MELODY CAZES, SINGER-MICKEY LANE
  RESIDENCE: NYC
  POSSESSION: '33 PARAMOUNT CONTRACT
  POSSESSION: '38 RKO CONTRACT
  TALENT: ACTRESS
  CREDIT: '32 COLLISION, DEBUT
  CREDIT: '37 DEAD END
  CREDIT: '41 REPENT AT LEISURE
  CREDIT: '43 FOREVER AND A DAY
  CREDIT: '54 IT SHOULD HAPPEN TO YOU

BARRY, GENE   BORN: EUGENE KLASS
                                 JUN 14,'21 AT NYC
  FATHER: MARTIN KLASS (DIED '69)
  MOTHER: EVA CONN
  *** MARRIED: JULIE CARSON
  *** MARRIED: '44 BETTY CLAIRE KALB
  SON: '46 MICHAEL BARRY, PRODUCER
  DAUGHTER-IN-LAW: FRANCINE GREENSTEIN (MARRIED '66)
  SON: '53 FREDERIC JAMES BARRY, ACTOR
  ADOPTED DAUGHTER: LIZA BARRY
  RESIDENCE: BEVERLY HILLS, CA
  POSSESSION: BARBETY PRODUCTION CO.
  TALENT: ACTOR
  CREDIT: '52 THE ATOMIC CITY
  CREDIT: '54 RED GARTERS
  CREDIT: '54 NAKED ALIBI
  CREDIT: '69 SUBTERFUGE
  CREDIT: '73 THE SECOND COMING OF SUZANNE

BARRYMORE, ETHEL   BORN: ETHEL MAE BARRYMORE
                                 AUG 15,'79 AT PHILADELPHIA, PA DIED IN '59
  GRANDMOTHER: LOUISA LANE, ACTRESS
  FATHER: MAURICE BARRYMORE, AUTHOR
  MOTHER: GEORGIANA DREW, ACTRESS
  BROTHER: LIONEL BARRYMORE
  BROTHER: JOHN BARRYMORE
  SISTER-IN-LAW: DORIS RANKIN
  SISTER-IN-LAW: KATHERINE CORRI HARRIS
  SISTER-IN-LAW: BLANCHE OELRICHS THOMAS, KNOWN AS POET MICHAEL STRANGE
  SISTER-IN-LAW: IRENE FRIZZEL, ACTRESS - IRENE FENWICK
  SISTER-IN-LAW: DOLORES COSTELLO, ACTRESS
  SISTER-IN-LAW: ELAINE JACOBS, ACTRESS - ELAINE BARRIE
  NIECE: DIANA BARRYMORE, ACTRESS

```
NIECE: DOLORES ETHEL MAE BARRYMORE
NIECE: ETHEL BARRYMORE, SECOND
NEPHEW: JOHN BARRYMORE, JR.
UNCLE: JOHN DREW, ACTOR
UNCLE: SIDNEY DREW, ACTOR
*** MARRIED:  '05 RUSSELL GRISWOLD COLT, N.Y. SOCIALITE  (DIVORCED '23)
SON:  '10 SAMUEL PEABODY COLT
SON:  '11 JOHN DREW COLT
DAUGHTER:  '12 ETHEL BARRYMORE COLT, ACTRESS, SINGER  (DIED '77)
SON-IN-LAW: JOHN ROMEO MIGLIETTA, OIL COMPANY EXEC.  (MARRIED '44)
GRANDSON: JOHN MIGLIETTA, ACTOR
FRIEND: TALLULAH BANKHEAD
MEMOIRS:  '68 MEMORIES
TALENT: ACTRESS
AA-WIN  SUP.ACT.:  '44 NONE BUT THE LONELY HEART
AA-NOM  SUP.ACT:  '46 THE SPIRAL STAIRCASE
AA-NOM  SUP.ACT:  '47 THE PARADINE CASE
AA-NOM  SUP.ACT:  '49 PINKY
```

BARRYMORE, JOHN   BORN: JOHN SIDNEY BLYTHE BARRYMORE
                                    FEB 15,'82 AT PHILADELPHIA,PA DIED IN '42
```
GRANDMOTHER: LOUISA LANE, ACTRESS
FATHER: MAURICE BARRYMORE, AUTHOR
MOTHER: GEORGIANA DREW, ACTRESS
SISTER: ETHEL BARRYMORE
BROTHER-IN-LAW: RUSSELL GRISWOLD COLT
BROTHER: LIONEL BARRYMORE
SISTER-IN-LAW: DORIS RANKIN
SISTER-IN-LAW: IRENE FRIZZEL, ACTRESS- IRENE FENWICK
NIECE: ETHEL BARRYMORE, SECOND
NIECE: ETHEL BARRYMORE COLT, ACTRESS, SINGER
NEPHEW: SAMUEL PEABODY COLT
NEPHEW: JOHN DREW COLT
UNCLE: JOHN DREW, ACTOR
UNCLE: SIDNEY DREW, ACTOR
*** MARRIED:  '10 KATHERINE CORRI HARRIS  (DIVORCED '17)
*** MARRIED:  '20 BLANCHE OELRICHS THOMAS, POET - MICHAEL STRANGE  (DIVORCED '28)
DAUGHTER:  '21 DIANA BARRYMORE, ACTRESS  (SUICIDE '60)
SON-IN-LAW: BRAMWELL FLETCHER
SON-IN-LAW: JOHN ROBERT HOWARD
SON-IN-LAW: ROBERT WILCOX
*** MARRIED:  '28 DOLORES COSTELLO  (DIVORCED '35)
FATHER-IN-LAW: MAURICE COSTELLO, ACTOR
MOTHER-IN-LAW: RUTH REEVES, ACTRESS
SISTER-IN-LAW: HELENE COSTELLO, ACTRESS
DAUGHTER:  '32 DOLORES ETHEL MAE BARRYMORE
SON:  '32 JOHN BARRYMORE, JR.
*** MARRIED:  '36 ELAINE JACOBS, ACTRESS - ELAINE BARRIE  (DIVORCED '40)
ROMANCE: EVELYN NESBIT
ROMANCE: MARY ASTOR
FRIEND: POLA NEGRI
POSSESSION: SCHOONER 'MARINER'
MEMOIRS:  '26 CONFESSIONS OF AN ACTOR
BIOGRAPHY:  '77 DAMNED IN PARADISE, BY JOHN KOBLER
BIOGRAPHY: TOO MUCH TOO SOON, BY DIANA BARRYMORE
TALENT: ACTOR
CREDIT:  '13 AN AMERICAN CITIZEN
CREDIT:  '20 DR. JEKYLL AND MR. HYDE
```

CREDIT: '32 GRAND HOTEL
CREDIT: '38 TRUE CONFESSIONS
CREDIT: '42 PLAYMATES

BARRYMORE, JR., JOHN   BORN: JOHN BLYTH BARRYMORE, JR.
                                          JUN 04,'32 AT BEVERLY HILLS, CA
GRANDFATHER: MAURICE COSTELLO, ACTOR
GRANDMOTHER: GEORGIANA DREW
FATHER: JOHN BARRYMORE
MOTHER: DOLORES COSTELLO
SISTER: DOLORES ETHEL MAE BARRYMORE
STEP-SISTER: DIANA BARRYMORE, ACTRESS   (SUICIDE '60)
BROTHER-IN-LAW: LEW BEDELL
AUNT: HELENE COSTELLO, ACTRESS
COUSIN: ETHEL BARRYMORE COLT, ACTRESS, SINGER
COUSIN: SAMUEL PEABODY COLT
COUSIN: JOHN DREW COLT
COUSIN: JOHN MIGLIETTA, ACTOR
COUSIN: ETHEL BARRYMORE, SECOND
UNCLE: LIONEL BARRYMORE, ACTOR
*** MARRIED: '52 CARA WILLIAMS, ACTRESS   (DIVORCED '56)
SON: '53 JOHN BLYTH BARRYMORE
*** MARRIED: '60 GABRIELLA 'GABY' PALAZZOLI, ACTRESS   (DIVORCED)
DAUGHTER: '62 DOROTHY BLYTH BARRYMORE
ROMANCE: GEORGIA MOLL, ACTRESS
ROMANCE: EVA BARTOK, ACTRESS
FRIEND: DAVID CARRADINE, ACTOR
TALENT: ACTOR
CREDIT: '50 THE SUNDOWNERS
CREDIT: '56 WHILE THE CITY SLEEPS
CREDIT: '60 THE COSSACKS
CREDIT: '63 WAR OF THE ZOMBIES

BARRYMORE, LIONEL   BORN: LIONEL BLYTHE BARRYMORE
                                       APR 28,1878 AT PHILADELPHIA, PA   DIED IN '54
GRANDMOTHER: LOUISA LANE, ACTRESS
FATHER: MAURICE BARRYMORE, AUTHOR
MOTHER: GEORGIANA DREW, ACTRESS
SISTER: ETHEL BARRYMORE
BROTHER-IN-LAW: RUSSELL GRISWOLD COLT
BROTHER: JOHN BARRYMORE
SISTER-IN-LAW: KATHERINE CORRI HARRIS
SISTER-IN-LAW: BLANCHE OELRICHS THOMAS, KNOWN AS POET MICHAEL STRANGE
SISTER-IN-LAW: DOLORES COSTELLO, ACTRESS
SISTER-IN-LAW: ELAINE JACOBS, ACTRESS - ELAINE BARRIE
NIECE: ETHEL BARRYMORE COLT, ACTRESS, SINGER
NIECE: DIANA BARRYMORE, ACTRESS
NIECE: DOLORES ETHEL MAE BARRYMORE
NEPHEW: SAMUEL PEABODY COLT
NEPHEW: JOHN DREW COLT
NEPHEW: JOHN BARRYMORE, JR.
UNCLE: JOHN DREW, ACTOR
UNCLE: SIDNEY DREW, ACTOR
*** MARRIED: '04 DORIS RANKIN (DIVORCED '23)
DAUGHTER: '08 ETHEL BARRYMORE, SECOND
*** MARRIED: '23 IRENE FRIZZEL, ACTRESS - IRENE FENWICK (DIED '36)
MEMOIRS: WE BARRYMORES
TALENT: ACTOR

```
CREDIT:   '13 THE TENDER-HEARTED BOY
AA-NOM  DIRECTOR:  '28 MADAME X
AA-WIN  ACTOR:  '30 A FREE SOUL
CREDIT:   '36 CAMILLE
CREDIT:   '37 CAPTAINS COURAGEOUS
CREDIT:   '38 DR. KILDARE,   MGM SERIES
CREDIT:   '46 DUEL IN THE SUN
```

BARTHELMESS, RICHARD   BORN: RICHARD SAMLAR BARTHELMESS
                                     MAY 09,'95 AT NYC   DIED IN '63
```
FATHER: ALFRED BARTHELMESS  (DIED '98)
MOTHER: CAROLINA HARRIS, ACTRESS
*** MARRIED:  '20 MARY HAY CALDWELL, AKA MARY HALY - SHOWGIRL  (DIVORCED '26)
FATHER-IN-LAW: F. M. CALDWELL, U.S. ARMY GENERAL OFFICER
DAUGHTER:  '22 MARY HAY BARTHELMESS, ACTRESS  (MARRIED '46)
SON-IN-LAW: RICHARD ROBER, ACTOR
*** MARRIED:  '28 JESSICA SARGEANT
ADOPTED SON: STEWART BARTHELMESS, HIS STEP-SON
ROMANCE: CONSTANCE TALMADGE
ROMANCE: KATHERINE YOUNG WILSON, ACTRESS
FRIEND: NAZIMOVA, ACTRESS
RESIDENCE: SOUTHAMPTON, NY & NYC
POSSESSION:  '20 INSPIRATION PICTURES CO.
POSSESSION: COLLECTION OF MAPS AND PRINTS
TALENT: ACTOR
CREDIT:   '16 WAR BRIDES, DEBUT
AA-NOM  ACTOR:  '27 THE NOOSE THE PATENT LEATHER KID
CREDIT:   '28 WHEEL OF CHANCE
CREDIT:   '30 THE DAWN PATROL
CREDIT:   '42 THE SPOILERS, LAST FILM
```

BARTHOLOMEW, FREDDIE   BORN: FREDERIC LLEWELLYN BARTHOLOMEW
                                     MAR 28,'24 AT LONDON, ENGLAND
```
MOTHER: LILLIE MAE LLEWELLYN
*** MARRIED:  '46 MAELY DANIELE  (DIVORCED '53)
DAUGHTER:  '47 CELIA BARTHOLOMEW
*** MARRIED:  '53 AILEEN PAUL
SON:  '54 FREDERICK ROBERT BARTHOLOMEW
DAUGHTER:  '55 KATHLEEN MILLICENT BARTHOLOMEW
RESIDENCE: NEW JERSEY
TALENT: ACTOR
COMMENT: VICE-PRESIDENT BENTON & BOWLES ADVERTISING AGENCY IN NYC
CREDIT:   '35 THE PERSONAL HISTORY, DEBUT
CREDIT:   '36 LITTLE LORD FAUNTLEROY
CREDIT:   '37 CAPTAINS COURAGEOUS
CREDIT:   '40 TOM BROWN'S SCHOOLDAYS
CREDIT:   '42 A YANK AT ETON
```

BASEHART, RICHARD
                                     AUG 31,'14 AT ZANESVILLE, OH
```
FATHER: HARRY T. BASEHART
MOTHER: MAE WETHERALD
*** MARRIED:  '40 STEPHANIE KLEIN
*** MARRIED:  '51 VALENTINA CORTESA, ACTRESS
SON:  '51 JOHN BASEHART
DAUGHTER:  '52 JENNA BASEHART
DAUGHTER:  '53 GAYLA BASEHART
*** MARRIED:  '70 DIANA LOTERY
```

```
TALENT: ACTOR
CREDIT: '45 CRY WOLF, DEBUT
CREDIT: '49 THE BLACK BOOK
CREDIT: '56 MOBY DICK
CREDIT: '60 PORTRAIT IN BLACK
CREDIT: '63 KINGS OF THE SUN
```

BATES, ALAN　　　　　BORN:　ALAN ARTHUR BATES
```
                          MAR 17,'34 AT ALLESTREE, ENGLAND
    FATHER: HAROLD ARTHUR BATES, INSURANCE BROKER
    MOTHER: FLORENCE MARY WHEATCROFT
    BROTHER: --
    BROTHER: --
    *** MARRIED:  '70 VALERIE WARD
    SON:  '70 --, TWIN
    SON:  '70 --, TWIN
    FRIEND: JEREMY BRETT, ACTOR
    RESIDENCE: HAMPSTEAD, LONDON, ENGLAND
    TALENT: ACTOR
    CREDIT: '59 THE ENTERTAINER
    CREDIT: '67 FAR FROM THE MADDING CROWD
    AA-NOM  ACTOR:  '68 THE FIXER
    CREDIT: '69 WOMEN IN LOVE
    CREDIT: '73 IMPOSSIBLE OBJECT
```

BAXTER, ANNE
```
                    MAY 07,'23 AT MICHIGAN CITY, IN
    GRANDFATHER: FRANK LLOYD WRIGHT, ARCHITECT
    FATHER: KENNETH STUART BAXTER, DISTILLERY EXECUTIVE
    MOTHER: CATHERINE WRIGHT
    *** MARRIED:  '46 JOHN HODIAK  (DIVORCED '53)
    DAUGHTER:  '51 KATRINA BAXTER HODIAK
    *** MARRIED:  '60 RANDOLPH GALT, RANCHER  (DIED '75)
    DAUGHTER:  '63 MELISSA GALT
    DAUGHTER:  '64 MAGINEL GALT
    POSSESSION: GIRO STATION, NEAR WORCESTER, AUSTRALIA
    MEMOIRS:  '76 INTERMISSION
    TALENT: ACTRESS
    CREDIT:  '42 THE MAGNIFICENT AMBERSONS
    AA-WIN  SUP.ACT.:  '46 THE RAZOR'S EDGE
    AA-NOM  ACTRESS:  '50 ALL ABOUT EVE
    CREDIT:  '56 THE TEN COMMANDMENTS
    CREDIT:  '62 WALK ON THE WILD SIDE
    CREDIT:  '71 FOOL'S PARADE
```

BAXTER, WARNER
```
                    MAR 29,'91 AT COLUMBUS, OH  DIED IN '51
    FATHER: EDWIN F. BAXTER (DIED '92)
    MOTHER: JANE BARRETT
    *** MARRIED:  '11 VIOLA CALDWELL
    *** MARRIED:  '17 WINIFRED BRYSON, ACTRESS
    PARTNER: DOROTHY SHOEMAKER, DANCING PARTNER
    RESIDENCE: BEVERLY HILLS, CA
    TALENT: ACTOR
    AA-WIN  ACTOR:  '28 IN OLD ARIZONA
    CREDIT: '36 THE ROAD TO GLORY
    CREDIT: '37 SLAVE SHIP
    CREDIT: '43 CRIME DOCTOR, COLUMBIA SERIES
```

CREDIT: '44 LADY IN THE DARK

BEATTY, WARREN
                        MAR 30,'38 AT RICHMOND, VA
FATHER: IRA O. BEATTY
MOTHER: KATHLYN MACLEAN, DANCER
SISTER: SHIRLEY MACLAINE, ACTRESS
BROTHER-IN-LAW: STEVE PARKER
NIECE: STEPHANIE SACHIKO PARKER
ROMANCE: MICHELLE PHILLIPS, SINGER-MAMAS AND THE PAPAS
ROMANCE: JULIE CHRISTIE, ACTRESS
ROMANCE: KATE JACKSON, ACTRESS
ROMANCE: DIANE KEATON, ACTRESS
RESIDENCE: LOS ANGELES, CA
BIOGRAPHY: '76 WARREN BEATTY, BY JIM BURKE
TALENT: ACTOR
CREDIT: '61 SPLENDOR IN THE GRASS
CREDIT: '61 THE ROMAN SPRING OF MRS. STONE
AA-NOM ACTOR: '67 BONNIE AND CLYDE
CREDIT: '68 THE ONLY GAME IN TOWN
CREDIT: '74 SHAMPOO
CREDIT: '78 HEAVEN CAN WAIT

BEAVERS, LOUISE
                        MAR 08,'98 AT CINCINNATI, OH DIED IN '62
*** MARRIED: LEROY MOORE
TALENT: ACTRESS
CREDIT: '29 COQUETTE
CREDIT: '32 WHAT PRICE HOLLYWOOD?
CREDIT: '35 IMITATION OF LIFE
CREDIT: '46 DELIGHTFULLY DANGEROUS
CREDIT: '61 THE FACTS OF LIFE

BEERY, WALLACE
                        APR 01,'85 AT KANSAS CITY, MR DIED IN '49
FATHER: NOAH BEERY, POLICE OFFICER
MOTHER: MARGARET
BROTHER: WILLIAM BEERY
BROTHER: NOAH BEERY
NEPHEW: NOAH BEERY, JR., ACTOR
*** MARRIED: '16 GLORIA SWANSON (DIVORCED '18)
*** MARRIED: '24 RITA GILMAN, ACTRESS (DIVORCED '39)
ADOPTED DAUGHTER: CAROL ANN BEERY
ROMANCE: MAE MURRAY
ROMANCE: COBINA WRIGHT, SR.
ROMANCE: GLORIA WHITNEY
RESIDENCE: BEVERLY HILLS, CA
POSSESSION: '40 CONTRACT AT M-G-M STUDIOS
TALENT: ACTOR
COMMENT: WORKED AS ELEPHANT TRAINER AT RINGLING BROTHERS CIRCUS
CREDIT: '16 SWEEDIE, SERIES
AA-NOM ACTOR: '29 THE BIG HOUSE
CREDIT: '30 MIN AND BILL
AA-WIN ACTOR: '31 THE CHAMP
CREDIT: '34 TREASURE ISLAND
CREDIT: '41 BARNACLE BILL

BEGLEY, ED   BORN: EDWARD JAMES BEGLEY
                                 MAR 21,'01 AT HARTFORD, CN   DIED IN '70
     FATHER: MICHAEL JOSEPH BEGLEY
     MOTHER: HANNAH CLIFFORD
     SISTER: HELENE BEGLEY
     BROTHER: MARTIN BEGLEY
     *** MARRIED: '22 AMANDA HUFF (DIED '57)
     SON: '23 THOMAS ALLENE BEGLEY
     SON: '24 ED BEGLEY, JR.
     *** MARRIED: '61 DOROTHY BATES (DIVORCED '63)
     *** MARRIED: '63 HELEN JORDAN
     DAUGHTER: '64 MAUREEN K. BEGLEY
     RESIDENCE: VAN NUYS, CA
     POSSESSION: '56 TONY AWARD-INHERIT THE WIND
     TALENT: ACTOR
     CREDIT: '47 BOOMERANG
     CREDIT: '50 BACKFIRE
     CREDIT: '57 TWELVE ANGRY MEN
     AA-WIN SUP.ACT.: '62 SWEET BIRD OF YOUTH
     CREDIT: '68 WILD IN THE STREETS

BEL GEDDES, BARBARA   BORN: BARBARA GEDDES
                                      OCT 31,'22 AT NYC
     FATHER: NORMAN GEDDES, DESIGNER
     MOTHER: HELEN BELLE SNEIDER
     SISTER: JOAN GEDDES
     *** MARRIED: '44 CARL L. SCHREUER (DIVORCED '51)
     DAUGHTER: '45 SUSAN SCHREUER
     DAUGHTER: '46 BETSY LEWIS SCHREUER
     *** MARRIED: '51 WINDSOR LEWIS
     TALENT: ACTRESS
     CREDIT: '47 THE GANGSTER
     AA-NOM SUP.ACT: '48 I REMEMBER MAMA
     CREDIT: '58 VERTIGO
     CREDIT: '61 BY LOVE POSSESSED
     CREDIT: '71 SUMMERTREE

BELAFONTE, HARRY   BORN: HAROLD GEORGE BELAFONTE, JR.
                                    MAR 01,'27 AT NYC
     FATHER: HAROLD GEORGE BELAFONTE
     MOTHER: MELVINE LOVE
     *** MARRIED: '48 MARGUERITE BYRD
     DAUGHTER: '49 ADRIENNE BELAFONTE
     DAUGHTER: '50 SHARI BELAFONTE
     *** MARRIED: '57 JULIE ROBINSON
     DAUGHTER: GINA BELAFONTE
     SON: DAVID BELAFONTE
     TALENT: ACTOR,SINGER
     CREDIT: '54 CARMEN JONES
     CREDIT: '57 ISLAND IN THE SUN
     CREDIT: '62 ODDS AGAINST TOMORROW
     CREDIT: '70 THE ANGEL LEVINE
     CREDIT: '72 UPTOWN SATURDAY NIGHT

```
------------------------------------------------------------------------------------------
BELLAMY, RALPH
                          JUN 17,'04 AT CHICAGO,IL
      FATHER: CHARLES REXFORD BELLAMY
      MOTHER: LILLA LOUISE SMITH
      *** MARRIED: '22 ALICE DELDRIDGE  (DIVORCED '30)
      *** MARRIED: '31 CATHERINE WILLARD, ACTRESS  (DIVORCED '45)
      DAUGHTER: '32 LYNN BELLAMY
      SON:  '33 WILLARD BELLAMY
      *** MARRIED: '45 ETHEL SMITH, MUSICIAN-ACTRESS  (DIVORCED '47)
      *** MARRIED: '49 ALICE MURPHY
      TALENT: ACTOR
      CREDIT: '31 THE SECRET SIX
      AA-NOM SUP.ACT: '37 THE AWFUL TRUTH
      CREDIT: '45 LADY ON A TRAIN
      CREDIT: '55 THE COURT-MARTIAL OF BILLY MITCHELL
      CREDIT: '68 ROSEMARY'S BABY
------------------------------------------------------------------------------------------
BELMONDO, JEAN-PAUL          BORN:  JEAN-PAUL 'BEBEL' BELMONDO
                                    APR 09,'33 AT NEUILLY-SUR-SEINE, FRANCE
      FATHER: JEAN-PAUL BELMONDO, SR., SCULPTOR
      *** MARRIED: '52 ELODIE, BALLERINA
      DAUGHTER: '60 FLORENCE BELMONDO
      ROMANCE: BRIGITTE BARDOT
      ROMANCE: URSULA ANDRESS
      ROMANCE: CHRISTINA ONASSIS
      FRIEND: ANNIE GIRARDOT, PARTNER IN THEATRE GROUP
      FRIEND: GUY BEDOS, PARTNER IN THEATRE GROUP
      RESIDENCE: PARIS, FRANCES
      TALENT: ACTOR, BOXER
      CREDIT: '59 TWO WOMEN
      CREDIT: '63 THAT MAN FROM RIO
      CREDIT: '66 IS PARIS BURNING?
      CREDIT: '72 BORSALINO
      CREDIT: '75 STAVISKY
------------------------------------------------------------------------------------------
BENCHLEY, ROBERT          BORN:  ROBERT CHARLES BENCHLEY
                                 SEP 15,'89 AT WORCESTER, MS   DIED IN '45
      FATHER: CHARLES HENRY BENCHLEY
      MOTHER: JANE
      *** MARRIED: '14 GERTRUDE DARLING
      SON:  '15 NATHANIEL GODDARD BENCHLEY  (MARRIED)
      DAUGHTER-IN-LAW: MARJORIE BRADFORD
      SON:  '16 ROBERT J. BENCHLEY, JR.
      GRANDSON:  '40 PETER BRADFORD BENCHLEY, NOVELIST
      GRANDSON:  '42 NATHANIEL ROBERT BENCHLEY
      PARTNER: DOROTHY PARKER, WRITER & CO-PRESIDENT OF UTICA
      RESIDENCE: SCARSDALE, NY
      POSSESSION: UTICA DROP FORGE & TOOL CO.,NY CABLE ADDRESS-PARKBENCH
      MEMOIRS: '36 MY TEN YEARS IN A QUANDARY
      BIOGRAPHY: '55 A BIOGRAPHY, BY NATHANIEL BENCHLEY
      TALENT: WRITER, CRITIC, ACTOR
      CREDIT: '33 DANCING LADY
      AA-SPECIAL AWARD: '35 HOW TO SLEEP-SHORT SUBJECT
      CREDIT: '40 FOREIGN CORRESPONDENT
      CREDIT: '41 YOU'LL NEVER GET RICH
      CREDIT: '42 I MARRIED A WITCH
      CREDIT: '45 KISS AND TELL
```

BENDIX, WILLIAM
                              JAN 14,'06 AT NYC   DIED IN '64
    FATHER: OSCAR 'MAX' BENDIX, VIOLINIST & CONDUCTOR
    *** MARRIED: '28 TERESA STEFANOTTI
    ADOPTED DAUGHTER: STEPHANIE BENDIX
    DAUGHTER: LORRAINE BENDIX
    TALENT: ACTOR
    COMMENT: BAT BOY FOR NY GIANTS BASEBALL TEAM
    AA-NOM SUP.ACT: '42 WAKE ISLAND
    CREDIT: '44 LIFEBOAT
    CREDIT: '44 LIFE OF RILEY
    CREDIT: '51 DETECTIVE STORY
    CREDIT: '62 BOYS' NIGHT OUT
    CREDIT: '63 FOR LOVE OR MONEY

BENJAMIN, RICHARD
                              MAY 22,'39 AT NYC
    *** MARRIED: '60 PAULA PRENTISS, ACTRESS
    SON: '74 ROSS THOMAS BENJAMIN
    RESIDENCE: BEVERLY HILLS, CA
    TALENT: ACTOR
    CREDIT: '53 THUNDER OVER THE PLAINS
    CREDIT: '69 GOODBYE COLUMBUS
    CREDIT: '70 DIARY OF A MAD HOUSEWIFE
    CREDIT: '72 PORTNOY'S COMPLAINT
    CREDIT: '75 THE SUNSHINE BOYS

BENNETT, CONSTANCE   BORN: CONSTANCE CAMPBELL BENNETT
                              OCT 22,'05 AT NYC   DIED IN '65
    FATHER: RICHARD BENNETT, ACTOR
    MOTHER: ADRIENNE MORRISON
    STEP-FATHER: TULLY MARSHALL, ACTOR
    STEP-MOTHER: AIMEE RAISCH HASTINGS, ACTRESS
    SISTER: JOAN BENNETT, ACTRESS
    SISTER: BARBARA BENNETT, ACTRESS (DIED '58)
    BROTHER-IN-LAW: JOHN MARTIN FOX
    BROTHER-IN-LAW: MORTON DOWNEY, SINGER
    BROTHER-IN-LAW: ADDISON 'JACK' RANDALL, ACTOR
    BROTHER-IN-LAW: GENE MARKEY, WRITER
    BROTHER-IN-LAW: WALTER WANGER, PRODUCER
    *** MARRIED: '21 CHESTER HIRST MOORHEAD (ANNULLED '23)
    *** MARRIED: '25 PHILIP MORGAN HAYWARD PLANT (DIVORCED '30)
    ADOPTED SON: PETER BENNETT PLANT
    *** MARRIED: '31 MARQUIS HENRI DE LA FALAISE, DE LA COUDRAY (DIVORCED '40)
    *** MARRIED: '41 GILBERT ROLAND, ACTOR (DIVORCED '45)
    BROTHER-IN-LAW: CHICO ALONSO, DIRECTOR
    DAUGHTER: '42 LORINDA ALONZO ROLAND
    DAUGHTER: '43 GYL CHRISTINA ROLAND
    *** MARRIED: '46 THERON 'JOHN' COULTER, US AIR FORCE GENERAL OFFICER
    ROMANCE: JOEL MCCREA
    RESIDENCE: HOLMBY HILLS, CA
    BIOGRAPHY: '76 CONSTANCE BENNETT, BY M. H. MCBRIDE
    TALENT: ACTRESS
    CREDIT: '32 WHAT PRICE HOLLYWOOD?
    CREDIT: '37 TOPPER, SERIES OF FILMS
    CREDIT: '47 THE UNSUSPECTED
    CREDIT: '54 IT SHOULD HAPPEN TO YOU

CREDIT: '65 MADAME X

BENNETT, JOAN
                        FEB 27,'10 AT PALISADES, NJ
    FATHER: RICHARD BENNETT, ACTOR
    MOTHER: ADRIENNE MORRISON
    STEP-FATHER: TULLY MARSHALL, ACTOR
    STEP-MOTHER: AIMEE RAISCH HASTINGS, ACTRESS
    SISTER: CONSTANCE BENNETT, ACTRESS
    SISTER: BARBARA BENNETT, ACTRESS (DIED '58)
    BROTHER-IN-LAW: PHILIP MORGAN HAYWARD PLANT
    BROTHER-IN-LAW: MORTON DOWNEY, SINGER
    BROTHER-IN-LAW: ADDISON 'JACK' RANDALL, ACTOR
    BROTHER-IN-LAW: LAURENT SUPRENANT, WRITER
    BROTHER-IN-LAW: MARQUIS HENRI DE LA FALAISE DE LA COUDRAY
    BROTHER-IN-LAW: GILBERT ROLAND
    BROTHER-IN-LAW: THERON 'JOHN' COULTER
    *** MARRIED: '26 JOHN MARTIN FOX (DIVORCED '28)
    DAUGHTER: '29 DIANA BENNETT FOX
    DAUGHTER: '30 ADRIENNE FOX
    *** MARRIED: '32 GENE MARKEY, WRITER (DIVORCED '37)
    DAUGHTER: '33 MELINDA MARKEY
    *** MARRIED: '38 WALTER WANGER, PRODUCER (DIVORCED '62)
    SON: '40 JUSTIN WANGER
    DAUGHTER: '43 STEPHANIE WANGER
    DAUGHTER: '48 SHELLEY WANGER
    ROMANCE: ERROL FLYNN
    ROMANCE: JOHN CONSIDINE
    ROMANCE: JOHN EMERY, ACTOR
    FRIEND: JENNINGS LANG
    RESIDENCE: LOS ANGELES, CA
    RESIDENCE: SCARSDALE, NY
    MEMOIRS: '70 THE BENNETT PLAYBILL
    TALENT: ACTRESS
    COMMENT: VICE PRES & TREA OF DIANA PROD
    CREDIT: '29 BULLDOG DRUMMOND, DEBUT
    CREDIT: '39 THE MAN IN THE IRON MASK
    CREDIT: '45 SCARLET STREET
    CREDIT: '50 FATHER OF THE BRIDE
    CREDIT: '56 THERE'S ALWAYS TOMORROW

BENNETT, RICHARD
                        MAY 21,1873 AT DEACON'S MILLS, IN DIED IN '44
    FATHER: GEORGE W. BENNETT
    MOTHER: ELIZA L. HOFFMAN
    *** MARRIED: '01 GRENA, ACTRESS (DIVORCED '02)
    *** MARRIED: '03 ADRIENNE MORRISON
    DAUGHTER: '05 CONSTANCE BENNETT, ACTRESS
    SON-IN-LAW: CHESTER HIRST MOORHEAD
    SON-IN-LAW: PHILIP MORGAN HAYWARD PLANT
    SON-IN-LAW: MARQUIS HENRI DE LA FALAISE, DE LA COUDRAY
    SON-IN-LAW: GILBERT ROLAND, ACTOR
    DAUGHTER: '10 JOAN BENNETT, ACTRESS
    SON-IN-LAW: JOHN MARTIN FOX
    DAUGHTER: '11 BARBARA BENNETT, ACTRESS
    SON-IN-LAW: GENE MARKEY, WRITER
    SON-IN-LAW: WALTER WANGER, PRODUCER
    *** MARRIED: '27 AIMEE RAISCH HASTINGS, ACTRESS (DIVORCED '37)

```
TALENT: ACTOR
CREDIT:  '23 THE ETERNAL CITY
CREDIT:  '28 HOME TOWERS
CREDIT:  '32 IF I HAD A MILLION
CREDIT:  '42 THE MAGNIFICENT AMBERSONS
CREDIT: .'43 JOURNEY INTO FEAR
```

BENNETT, TONY   BORN: ANTHONY DOMINICK BENEDETTO
                                   JAN 04,'26 AT ASTORIA, NY
```
FATHER: JOHN BENEDETTO, TAILOR  (DIED '34)
MOTHER: ANNA SURACI, SEAMSTRESS
*** MARRIED:  '52 PATRICIA BUCH, AKA PATRICIA BEECH  (DIVORCED '57)
SON:  '54 D'ANDREA BENNETT
SON:  '55 DAEGAL BENNETT
*** MARRIED:  '72 SANDRA GRANT
DAUGHTER:  '74 JOANNA BENNETT
DAUGHTER:  '75 ANTONIA BENNETT
RESIDENCE: ENGLEWOOD, NEW JERSEY
POSSESSION:  '53 RAGS TO RICHES-GOLD RECORD
POSSESSION:  '54 STRANGER IN PARADISE-GOLD RECORD
POSSESSION:  '62 I LEFT MY HEART IN SAN FRANCISCO - GOLD RECORD
TALENT: SINGER, ACTOR
COMMENT: FIRST STAGE NAME-JOE BARI
CREDIT: THE OSCAR
```

BENNY, JACK   BORN: BENJAMIN KUBELSKY
                                 MAR 14,'94 AT WAUKEGAN, IL DIED IN '74
```
FATHER: MEYER KUBELSKY, TAVERN KEEPER
MOTHER: EMMA SACHS
*** MARRIED:  '28 SADYE MARKS, ACTRESS- MARY LIVINGSTONE
ADOPTED DAUGHTER: JOAN NAOMI BENNY
RESIDENCE: BEVERLY HILLS, CA
POSSESSION: STRADIVARIUS VIOLIN
TALENT: ACTOR,COMEDIAN
CREDIT:  '37 ARTISTS AND MODELS
CREDIT:  '39 MAN ABOUT TOWN
CREDIT:  '40 BUCK BENNY RIDES AGAIN
CREDIT:  '41 CHARLEY'S AUNT
CREDIT:  '67 A GUIDE FOR THE MARRIED MAN
```

BERGEN, CANDICE
                         MAY 09,'46 AT LOS ANGELES, CA
```
GRANDFATHER: JOHN BERGREN
FATHER: EDGAR BERGEN, ACTOR, VENTRILOQUIST  (DIED '78)
MOTHER: FRANCES WESTERMANN, ACTRESS - FRANCES WESTON
BROTHER: KRIS EDGAR BERGEN
ROMANCE: TERRY MELCHER
ROMANCE: BERT SCHNEIDER
RESIDENCE: NYC
TALENT: ACTRESS, PHOTO-JOURNALIST
CREDIT:  '65 THE GROUP, DEBUT
CREDIT:  '66 THE SAND PEBBLES
CREDIT:  '68 THE MAGUS
CREDIT:  '70 GETTING STRAIGHT
CREDIT:  '71 CARNAL KNOWLEDGE
```

```
-------------------------------------------------------------------------------
BERGEN, EDGAR          BORN:   EDGAR JOHN BERGREN
                               MAR 16,'03 AT CHICAGO,IL   DIED IN '78
    FATHER: JOHN BERGREN
    MOTHER: NELL SWANSON  (DIED '45)
    *** MARRIED:  '45 FRANCES WESTERMANN, ACTRESS FRANCES WESTON
    DAUGHTER:  '46 CANDICE BERGEN, ACTRESS
    SON:  '61 KRIS EDGAR BERGEN
    PARTNER: CHARLIE MCCARTHY
    PARTNER: MORTIMER SNERD
    PARTNER: EFFIE
    RESIDENCE: LIDO ISLAND, NEWPORT HARBOR,
    POSSESSION:  '37 HONORARY MASTER OF ARTS DEGREE FROM NORTHWESTERN UNIVERSITY
    TALENT: ACTOR, VENTRILOQUIST
    AA-SPECIAL AWARD:  '37 FOR HIS CREATION 'CHARLIE MC- CARTHY' - A WOODEN STATUETTE
    CREDIT:  '39 YOU CAN'T CHEAT AN HONEST MAN
    CREDIT:  '42 HERE WE GO AGAIN
    CREDIT:  '48 I REMEMBER MAMA
    CREDIT:  '64 THE HANGED MAN
    CREDIT:  '67 DON'T MAKE WAVES
-------------------------------------------------------------------------------
BERGEN, POLLY          BORN:   NELLIE PAULINA BURGIN
                               JUL 14,'30 AT KNOXVILLE,TN
    FATHER: WILLIAM BURGIN, CONSTRUCTION ENGINEER
    MOTHER: LUCY LAWHORN
    SISTER: BARBARA BURGIN
    *** MARRIED:  '50 JEROME COURTLAND  (DIVORCED '55)
    *** MARRIED:  '56 FREDDIE FIELDS, AGENT
    BROTHER-IN-LAW: SHEP FIELDS, MUSICIAN
    DAUGHTER: KATHY FIELDS
    DAUGHTER: PAMELA FIELDS
    SON: PETER FIELDS
    POSSESSION:  '58 EMMY AWARD
    TALENT: SINGER, ACTRESS
    CREDIT:  '50 AT WAR WITH THE ARMY
    CREDIT:  '62 CAPE FEAR
    CREDIT:  '63 MOVE OVER DARLING
    CREDIT:  '64 KISSES FOR MY PRESIDENT
    CREDIT:  '67 A GUIDE FOR THE MARRIED MAN
-------------------------------------------------------------------------------
BERGER, SENTA
                               MAY 13,'41 AT VIENNA, AUSTRIA
    FATHER: JOSEF BERGER, COMPOSER
    MOTHER: THERESA
    *** MARRIED:  '64 DR. MICHAEL VERHOEVEN
    RESIDENCE: LOS ANGELES & MUNICH, GERMANY
    TALENT: ACTRESS
    CREDIT:  '61 THE SECRET WAYS
    CREDIT:  '63 CAST A GIANT SHADOW
    CREDIT:  '65 THE GLORY GUYS
    CREDIT:  '67 THE AMBUSHERS
    CREDIT:  '70 PERCY
```

BERGMAN, INGRID
                              AUG 29,'15 AT STOCKHOLM, SWEDEN
    FATHER: JUSTUS BERGMAN
    MOTHER: FRIEDEL ADLER
    *** MARRIED: '37 DR. PETER LINDSTROM (DIVORCED '50)
    DAUGHTER: '38 PIA LINDSTROM, TV REPORTER
    SON-IN-LAW: JOSEPH DALY (MARRIED '71)
    *** MARRIED: '50 ROBERTO ROSSELLINI, DIRECTOR (ANNULLED '57)
    SON: '50 ROBERTO ROSSELLINI, JR.
    DAUGHTER: '52 ISABELLA ROSSELLINI, TWIN TV REPORTER
    DAUGHTER: '52 INGRID ISOTTA ROSSELLINI, TWIN
    *** MARRIED: '58 LARS SCHMIDT, PRODUCER
    RESIDENCE: DANNHOLMEN, SWEDEN
    RESIDENCE: CHOISEL, FRANCE
    POSSESSION: PLANTATION ON BARBADOS ISLAND
    BIOGRAPHY: '59 AN INTIMATE PORTRAIT, BY JOSEPH HENRY STEELE
    TALENT: ACTRESS
    CREDIT: '43 CASABLANCA
    AA-NOM ACTRESS: '43 FOR WHOM THE BELL TOLLS
    AA-WIN ACTRESS: '44 GASLIGHT
    AA-NOM ACTRESS: '45 THE BELLS OF ST. MARY'S
    AA-NOM ACTRESS: '48 JOAN OF ARC
    AA-WIN ACTRESS: '56 ANASTASIA
    AA-WIN SUP.ACT.: '74 MURDER ON THE ORIENT EXPRESS

BERKELEY, BUSBY   BORN: WILLIAM BERKELEY ENOS
                              NOV 29,'95 AT LOS ANGELES, CA DIED IN '76
    FATHER: WILLIAM ENOS, SR., DIRECTOR OF REPERTORY COMPANY
    MOTHER: GERTRUDE BERKELEY, ACTRESS
    BROTHER: GEORGE ENOS
    *** MARRIED: '29 ESTHER MUIR (DIVORCED)
    *** MARRIED: '34 MERNA KENNEDY (DIVORCED)
    *** MARRIED: '42 CLAIR JAMES
    *** MARRIED: '43 MYRA STEFFIN, LASTED 3 WEEKS (ANNULLED '43)
    *** MARRIED: '45 MARTE PEMBERTON (DIVORCED '53)
    *** MARRIED: '58 ETTA DUNN
    FRIEND: AMY BUSBY, ACTRESS IN FATHER'S COMPANY
    FRIEND: MACK SENNETT
    FRIEND: RUBY KEELER
    TALENT: DANCE DIRECTOR, DIRECTOR
    COMMENT: SERVED AS GEN. PERSHING'S ENTERTAINMENT OFFICER - 1918
    CREDIT: '32 BIRD OF PARADISE, CHOREOGRAPHED
    CREDIT: '38 MEN ARE SUCH FOOLS, DIRECTED
    CREDIT: '42 FOR ME AND MY GAL, DIRECTED
    CREDIT: '49 TAKE ME OUT TO THE BALLGAME, DIRECTED
    CREDIT: '51 CALL ME MISTER, CHOREOGRAPHED

BERLE, MILTON   BORN: MENDEL BERLINGER
                              JUL 12,'08 AT NYC
    FATHER: MOSES BERLINGER
    MOTHER: SARAH GLANTZ, ACTRESS - SANDRA BERLE
    SISTER: ROSALIND BERLINGER
    *** MARRIED: BERYL WALLACE, ACTRESS (DIVORCED)
    *** MARRIED: '41 JOYCE MATHEWS (DIVORCED '47)
    *** MARRIED: '49 JOYCE MATHEWS, RE-MARRIAGE
    *** MARRIED: '53 RUTH COSGROVE
    ADOPTED DAUGHTER: VICTORIA BERLE

```
           SON: WILLIAM BERLE
           MEMOIRS:  '74 AN AUTOBIOGRAPHY
           TALENT: ACTOR
           CREDIT:  '37 NEW FACES OF 1937
           CREDIT:  '41 TALL DARK AND HANDSOME
           CREDIT:  '49 ALWAYS LEAVE THEM LAUGHING
           CREDIT:  '60 LET'S MAKE LOVE
           CREDIT:  '68 FOR SINGLES ONLY
```

BERMAN, SHELLEY
```
                           FEB 03,'26 AT CHICAGO,IL
           FATHER: NATHAN BERMAN
           MOTHER: IRENE MARKS
           *** MARRIED:  '47 SARAH HERMAN
           DAUGHTER: RACHEL BERMAN
           SON: JOSHUA BERMAN
           TALENT: ACTOR
           CREDIT:  '64 THE BEST MAN
           CREDIT:  '69 DIVORCE AMERICAN STYLE
           CREDIT:  '70 EVERY HOME SHOULD HAVE ONE
```

BERNARDI, HERSHEL
```
                           OCT 20,'23 AT NYC
           FATHER: BERNARD BERNARDI, ACTOR
           MOTHER: HELEN, ACTRESS
           *** MARRIED:  '56 CYNTHIA GRIFFITH, ARTIST  (DIVORCED)
           SON:  '57 ADAM BERNARDI
           DAUGHTER:  '61 BERYL BERNARDI
           DAUGHTER:  '63 ROBIN BERNARDI
           TALENT: ACTOR
           CREDIT:  '37 GREEN FIELDS
           CREDIT:  '46 MISS SUSIE SLAGLE'S
           CREDIT:  '58 STAKEOUT ON DOPE STREET
           CREDIT:  '63 IRMA LA DOUCE
           CREDIT:  '67 THE HONEY POT
```

BERNHARDT, SARAH   BORN: ROSINE BERNARD
```
                           OCT 22,1844 AT PARIS, FRANCE   DIED IN '23
           FATHER: EDOUARD BERNARD, LAWYER
           MOTHER: JULIE
           SISTER: JEANNE BERNARD
           SISTER: REGINE BERNARD
           *** MARRIED:  '82 JACQUES DAMALA  (DIED '89)
           SON: MAURICE DAMALA
           ROMANCE: PIERRE BERTON
           ROMANCE: JUAN LOPEZ, BULLFIGHTER
           RESIDENCE: PARIS, FRANCE
           POSSESSION:  '98 THEATRE SARAH BERNHARDT
           POSSESSION:  '14 GRAND CROSS OF LEGION OF HONOR
           MEMOIRS:  '07 MEMORIES OF MY LIFE
           BIOGRAPHY:  '77 SARAH BERNHARDT AND HER WORLD, BY JOANNA RICHARDSON
           TALENT: ACTRESS
           CREDIT:  '00 HAMLET, PLAYED TITLE ROLE
           CREDIT:  '11 CAMILLE
           CREDIT:  '12 QUEEN ELIZABETH
           CREDIT:  '17 MOTHERS OF FRANCE
```

BICKFORD, CHARLES
JAN 01,'91 AT CAMBRIDGE, MS   DIED IN '67
```
     GRANDFATHER: THOMAS WOODS, SAILOR
     FATHER: LORETUS BICKFORD
     MOTHER: MARY ELLEN WOODS
     SISTER: RUTH BICKFORD
     SISTER: ESTHER BICKFORD
     SISTER: DOROTHY BICKFORD
     BROTHER: THOMAS BICKFORD
     BROTHER: JONATHAN BICKFORD
     BROTHER: WILLIAM BICKFORD
     *** MARRIED:  '19 BEATRICE LORING
     DAUGHTER: '20 DORIS BICKFORD
     SON:  '21 REX BICKFORD
     RESIDENCE: LOS ANGELES, CA
     MEMOIRS:  '65 BULLS, BALLS, BICYCLES & ACTORS
     TALENT: ACTOR
     CREDIT:  '29 DYNAMITE, DEBUT IN 1929
     CREDIT:  '40 OF MICE AND MEN
     AA-NOM  SUP.ACT:  '43 THE SONG OF BERNADETTE
     AA-NOM  SUP.ACT:  '47 THE FARMER'S DAUGHTER
     AA-NOM  SUP.ACT:  '48 JOHNNY BELINDA
     CREDIT:  '54 A STAR IS BORN
     CREDIT:  '66 A BIG HAND FOR THE LITTLE LADY
```

BIKEL, THEODORE
MAY 02,'24 AT VIENNA, AUSTRIA
```
     FATHER: JOSEF BIKEL
     MOTHER: MIRIAM RIEGLER
     *** MARRIED:  '55 OFRA ICHILOV
     *** MARRIED:  '67 RITA WEINBERG, PRODUCER
     SON:  '69 ROBERT SIMON BIKEL
     SON:  '71 DAVID MARTIN BIKEL
     RESIDENCE: NYC
     POSSESSION: 2 EXPRESSO COFFEE HOUSES IN LOS ANGELES
     TALENT: ACTOR, FOLK-SINGER
     CREDIT:  '51 THE AFRICAN QUEEN
     CREDIT:  '57 THE PRIDE AND THE PASSION
     AA-NOM  SUP.ACT:  '58 THE DEFIANT ONES
     CREDIT:  '64 MY FAIR LADY
     CREDIT:  '68 MY SIDE OF THE MOUNTAIN
     CREDIT:  '71 THE LITTLE ARK
```

BISSET, JACQUELINE
BORN: JACQUELINE FRAZER BISSET
SEP 13,'44 AT WEYBRIDGE, ENGLAND
```
     FATHER: FRAZER BISSET, PHYSICIAN
     MOTHER: ARLETTE ALEXANDER, BARRISTER
     BROTHER: --
     ROMANCE: MICHAEL SARRAZIN, ACTOR
     ROMANCE: VICTOR DRAI
     RESIDENCE: LOS ANGELES, CA
     TALENT: ACTRESS
     CREDIT:  '67 TWO FOR THE ROAD
     CREDIT:  '68 THE DETECTIVE
     CREDIT:  '70 AIRPORT
     CREDIT:  '73 THE THIEF WHO CAME TO DINNER
     CREDIT:  '77 THE DEEP
```

```
-----------------------------------------------------------------------------------------------
BIXBY, BILL
                            JAN 22,'34 AT SAN FRANCISCO, CA
      FATHER: WILFRED BIXBY
      MOTHER: JANE
      *** MARRIED: BRENDA BENET
      SON:  '74 CHRISTOPHER SEAN BIXBY
      RESIDENCE: BRENTWOOD, CA
      POSSESSION:  '72 FARM IN OREGON
      TALENT: ACTOR
      CREDIT:  '62 LONELY ARE THE BRAVE
      CREDIT:  '63 IRMA LA DOUCE
      CREDIT:  '64 UNDER THE YUM YUM TREE
      CREDIT:  '67 SPINOUT
      CREDIT:  '68 SPEEDWAY
-----------------------------------------------------------------------------------------------
BLACK, KAREN           BORN:  KAREN BLANCHE ZIEGLER
                            JUL 01,'42 AT PARK RIDGE, IL
      FATHER: NORMAN A. ZIEGLER, ENGINEER
      MOTHER: ELSIE REIF, WRITER
      SISTER: GAIL ZIEGLER, DANCER-AKA GAIL BROWN
      BROTHER: PETER ZIEGLER
      *** MARRIED:  '60 CHARLES BLACK  (DIVORCED)
      *** MARRIED:  '73 SKIP BURTON, ACTOR  (DIVORCED '74)
      *** MARRIED:  '75 KIT CARSON, WRITER
      SON:  '75 HUNTER CARSON
      RESIDENCE: LOS ANGELES, CA
      POSSESSION: COLLECTION OF ANTIQUES
      TALENT: ACTRESS
      CREDIT:  '66 YOU'RE A BIG BOY NOW, DEBUT
      CREDIT:  '69 EASY RIDER
      AA-NOM  SUP.ACT:  '70 FIVE EASY PIECES
      CREDIT:  '72 PORTNOY'S COMPLAINT
      CREDIT:  '73 RHINOCEROS
      CREDIT:  '78 CAPRICORN ONE
-----------------------------------------------------------------------------------------------
BLACKMER, SIDNEY
                            JUL 13,'98 AT SALISBURY, NC  DIED IN '73
      FATHER: WALTER STEELE BLACKMER
      MOTHER: CLARA DE ROULHAC ALDERMAN
      *** MARRIED:  '28 LENORE ULRIC  (DIVORCED '39)
      *** MARRIED:  '42 SUSANNE KAAREN
      POSSESSION: HINSDALE, ILLINOIS, SUMMER THEATRE
      TALENT: ACTOR
      COMMENT: COME BACK, LITTLE SHEBA (PLAY) WON ANTOINETTE PERRY AWARD
      CREDIT:  '29 A MOST IMMORAL LADY
      CREDIT:  '36 EARLY TO BED
      CREDIT:  '46 DUEL IN THE SUN
      CREDIT:  '56 HIGH SOCIETY
      CREDIT:  '65 HOW TO MURDER YOUR WIFE
-----------------------------------------------------------------------------------------------
BLAINE, VIVIAN         BORN:  VIVIAN S. STAPLETON
                            NOV 21,'21 AT NEWARK, NJ
      FATHER: LIONEL P. STAPLETON
      *** MARRIED:  '45 MANUEL G. FRANK  (DIVORCED '56)
      *** MARRIED:  '59 MILTON R. RACKMIL, FILM BUSINESS EXECUTIVE  (DIVORCED '61)
      POSSESSION: CONTRACT AT 20TH CENTURY-FOX IN 1942
      TALENT: ACTRESS
```

```
CREDIT:  '42 JITTERBUGS
CREDIT:  '45 STATE FAIR
CREDIT:  '52 SKIRTS AHOY
CREDIT:  '55 GUYS AND DOLLS
CREDIT:  '57 PUBLIC PIGEON NUMBER ONE
```

BLAIR, JANET   BORN: MARTHA JANE LAFFERTY
                               APR 23,'21 AT ALTOONA, PA
```
FATHER: FRED LAFFERTY
MOTHER: FLORENCE
SISTER: LOUISE LAFFERTY
BROTHER: FRED LAFFERTY, JR.
*** MARRIED:  '43 LOUIS BUSCH, PIANIST  (DIVORCED '50)
*** MARRIED:  '52 NICK MAYO  (DIVORCED '72)
DAUGHTER:  '59 AMANDA MAYO
SON:  '61 ANDREW MAYO
TALENT: ACTRESS
CREDIT:  '41 THREE GIRLS ABOUT TOWN
CREDIT:  '42 MY SISTER EILEEN
CREDIT:  '48 I LOVE TROUBLE
CREDIT:  '62 NIGHT OF THE EAGLE
CREDIT:  '68 THE ONE AND ONLY GENUINE ORIGINAL FAMILY BAND
```

BLAKE, ROBERT   BORN: MICHAEL J. VIJENCIO GUBITOSI
                               SEP 18,'33 AT NUTLEY, NJ
```
FATHER: JAMES GUBITOSI
MOTHER: ELIZABETH
SISTER: LOVANNY GUBITOSI, ACTRESS
BROTHER: JAMES GUBITOSI, JR., ACTOR
*** MARRIED:  '64 SONDRA KERRY, ACTRESS  (SEPARATED '77)
SON:  '65 NOAH LUTHER BLAKE
DAUGHTER:  '66 DELINAH RAYAH 'DELL' BLAKE
FRIEND: SALLY KELLERMAN, ACTRESS
RESIDENCE: HOLLYWOOD HILLS, CA
POSSESSION:  '42 CONTRACT AT M-G-M STUDIOS
TALENT: ACTOR
CREDIT:  '43 ANDY HARDY'S DOUBLE LIFE
CREDIT:  '59 BATTLE FLAME
CREDIT:  '67 IN COLD BLOOD
CREDIT:  '69 TELL THEM WILLIE BOY IS HERE
CREDIT:  '73 ELECTRA GLIDE IN BLUE
```

BLANC, MEL   BORN: MELVIN JEROME BLANC
                             MAY 30,'07 AT SAN FRANCISCO, CA
```
FATHER: FREDERICK BLANC, HABERDASHER
MOTHER: EVA KATZ
BROTHER: HENRY CHARLES BLANC, RADIO ANNOUNCER-HENRY CHARLES
COUSIN: JACK HAIMER, HORTICULTURIST
*** MARRIED:  '33 ESTELLE ROSENBAUM
SON:  '38 NOEL BLANC
RESIDENCE: PACIFIC PALISADES, CA
POSSESSION:  '60 BLANC COMMUNICATIONS CORP.
POSSESSION: HONORARY MAYOR-BIG BEAR LAKE CALIFORNIA
TALENT: MUSICIAN, VOICE, SPECIAL EFFECT RECORDING ACTOR
CREDIT:  '31 CONDUCTOR ORPHEUM THEATRE ORCHESTRA, PORTLAND, OREGON
CREDIT:  '37 WARNER BROS, CARTOONS
CREDIT:  '40 JACK BENNY RADIO SHOW
CREDIT:  '60 THE FLINTSTONES, SERIES
```

BLONDELL, JOAN
                        AUG 30,'09 AT NYC
    FATHER: EDDIE BLONDELL, ACTOR-THE KATZENJAMMER KID
    MOTHER: KATHRYN CAIN, ACTRESS
    SISTER: GLORIA BLONDELL, ACTRESS
    BROTHER: EDWARD BLONDELL, FILM TECHNICIAN
    *** MARRIED: '33 GEORGE BARNES, CAMERAMAN (DIVORCED '36)
    SON: '34 NORMAN SCOTT BARNES
    *** MARRIED: '36 DICK POWELL, ACTOR (DIVORCED '44)
    DAUGHTER: '38 ELLEN POWELL
    *** MARRIED: '46 MICHAEL TODD, PRODUCER (DIVORCED '50)
    STEP-SON: MICHAEL TODD, JR.
    POSSESSION: '30 CONTRACT AT WARNER BROS.
    MEMOIRS: CENTER DOOR FANCY
    TALENT: ACTRESS
    COMMENT: DEBUT ON STAGE AGE 3 IN FAMILY VAUDEVILLE ACT
    CREDIT: '30 SINNER'S HOLIDAY, DEBUT
    CREDIT: '37 STAND IN
    CREDIT: '45 A TREE GROWS IN BROOKLYN
    AA-NOM SUP.ACT: '51 THE BLUE VEIL
    CREDIT: '65 THE CINCINNATI KID
    CREDIT: '78 GREASE

BLOOM, CLAIRE
                     FEB 15,'31 AT LONDON, ENGLAND
    FATHER: EDWARD MAX BLUM
    MOTHER: ELIZABETH GREW
    *** MARRIED: '59 ROD STEIGER, ACTOR (DIVORCED '69)
    DAUGHTER: '60 ANNA JUSTINE STEIGER
    *** MARRIED: '69 HILLIARD ELKINS, PRODUCER
    TALENT: ACTRESS
    CREDIT: '48 THE BLIND GODDESS
    CREDIT: '51 LIMELIGHT
    CREDIT: '62 THE CHAPMAN REPORT
    CREDIT: '68 THREE INTO TWO WON'T GO
    CREDIT: '71 A DOLL'S HOUSE

BLYTH, ANN   BORN: ANN MARIE BLYTH
                        AUG 16,'28 AT MT. KISCO, NY
    SISTER: DOROTHY BLYTH
    AUNT: CISSY, SURROGATE MOTHER
    UNCLE: PAT, SURROGATE FATHER
    *** MARRIED: '53 DR. JAMES MCNULTY
    BROTHER-IN-LAW: DENNIS DAY, ACTOR
    SON: '54 TIMOTHY PATRICK MCNULTY
    DAUGHTER: '55 MAUREEN ANN MCNULTY
    DAUGHTER: '57 KATHLEEN MARY MCNULTY
    SON: '60 TERENCE GRADY MCNULTY
    DAUGHTER: '63 EILEEN ALANA MCNULTY
    RESIDENCE: TOLUCA LAKE, CA
    TALENT: ACTRESS
    AA-NOM SUP.ACT: '45 MILDRED PIERCE
    CREDIT: '49 TOP O' THE MORNING
    CREDIT: '51 THE GREAT CARUSO
    CREDIT: '55 KISMET
    CREDIT: '57 THE HELEN MORGAN STORY

BOARDMAN, ELEANOR
                              AUG 19,'99 AT PHILADELPHIA, PA
    FATHER: GEORGE BOARDMAN
    MOTHER: MIRIAM STOCKMAN
    *** MARRIED: '26 KING LOUIS WALLIS VIDOR, DIRECTOR (DIVORCED '33)
    DAUGHTER: '27 ANTONIA VIDOR
    DAUGHTER: '30 BELINDA VIDOR
    *** MARRIED: '40 HENRI D'ABBADIE D'ARRAST, DIRECTOR (DIED '68)
    RESIDENCE: SANTA BARBARA, CA
    TALENT: ACTRESS MADE LAST FILM-1932
    COMMENT: WINNING A BEAUTY CONTEST IN PHILADELPHIA LED TO M-G-M PACT
    CREDIT: '23 SOULS FOR SALE
    CREDIT: '24 SINNERS IN SILK
    CREDIT: '25 THE CIRCLE
    CREDIT: '28 THE CROWD
    CREDIT: '31 THE SQUAW MAN

BOGARDE, DIRK   BORN: DEREK NIVEN VAN DEN BOGAERDE
                                 MAR 28,'21 AT LONDON, ENGLAND
    FATHER: ULRICH JULES VAN DEN BOGAERDE, ART EDITOR OF LONDON TIMES
    MOTHER: MARGARET NIVEN, ACTRESS
    SISTER: ELIZABETH BOGAERDE
    ROMANCE: JEAN SIMMONS, ACTRESS
    RESIDENCE: SURREY, ENGLAND 16TH CENTURY MANOR HOUSE
    POSSESSION: SCHOLARSHIP ROYAL COLLEGE ART
    MEMOIRS: '77 A POSTILLION STRUCK BY LIGHTNING
    TALENT: ACTOR, ARTIST, POET
    CREDIT: '48 ESTHER WATERS
    CREDIT: '51 BLACKMAILED
    CREDIT: '56 ILL MET BY MOONLIGHT
    CREDIT: '65 DARLING
    CREDIT: '66 MODETY BLAISE
    CREDIT: '69 JUSTINE

BOGART, HUMPHREY   BORN: HUMPHREY DEFOREST BOGART
                                    JAN 23,'99 AT NYC DIED IN '57
    FATHER: BELMONT DEFOREST BOGART, DOCTOR
    MOTHER: MAUDE HUMPHREY, ARTIST, ILLUSTRATOR
    SISTER: FRANCES BOGART
    SISTER: CATHERINE ELIZABETH BOGART
    BROTHER-IN-LAW: STUART ROSE, STORY EDITOR
    SISTER-IN-LAW: GRACE MENKEN, STAGE ACTRESS
    *** MARRIED: '26 HELEN MENKEN, ACTRESS (DIVORCED '27)
    *** MARRIED: '28 MARY PHILLIPS, ACTRESS (DIVORCED '37)
    *** MARRIED: '38 MAYO METHOT (DIVORCED '45)
    *** MARRIED: '45 LAUREN BACALL, ACTRESS
    SON: '48 STEPHEN BOGART
    DAUGHTER: '52 LESLIE HOWARD BOGART
    FRIEND: LESLIE HOWARD
    FRIEND: JOHN HUSTON
    POSSESSION: YACHT 'SANTANA'
    BIOGRAPHY: '76 BOGART & BACALL, A LOVE STORY, BY JOSEPH HYAMS
    TALENT: ACTOR
    CREDIT: '30 A DEVIL WITH WOMEN
    CREDIT: '41 THE MALTESE FALCON
    AA-NOM ACTOR: '43 CASABLANCA
    AA-WIN ACTOR: '51 THE AFRICAN QUEEN

AA-NOM ACTOR: '54 THE CAINE MUTINY

BOLGER, RAY   BORN: RAYMOND WALLACE BOLGER
                              JAN 10,'06 AT DORCHESTER,MS
    FATHER: JAMES EDWARD BOLGER
    MOTHER: ANN WALLACE
    *** MARRIED: '29 GWENDOLYN RICKARD
    TALENT: DANCER-ACTOR
    CREDIT: '37 ROSALIE
    CREDIT: '39 THE WIZARD OF OZ
    CREDIT: '49 LOOK FOR THE SILVER LINING
    CREDIT: '60 BABES IN TOYLAND
    CREDIT: '66 THE DAYDREAMER

BOND, WARD
                        APR 09,'03 AT BENDELMAN, NB DIED IN '60
    FATHER: JOHN W. BOND
    MOTHER: MABEL
    SISTER: BERNICE BOND
    *** MARRIED: '36 DORIS SELLERS CHILDS (DIVORCED '44)
    *** MARRIED: '54 MARY LOUISE MAY, AGENT
    FRIEND: JOHN WAYNE, ACTOR
    FRIEND: HENRY FONDA
    RESIDENCE: BEVERLY HILLS, CA
    POSSESSION: 20 GAUGE SHOTGUN BEQUEATHED TO JOHN WAYNE
    POSSESSION: 2 RANCHES IN KERN COUNTY, CA
    TALENT: ACTOR
    CREDIT: '29 SALUTE, DEBUT IN 1929
    CREDIT: '39 DRUMS ALONG THE MOHAWK
    CREDIT: '47 THE FUGITIVE
    CREDIT: '55 MR. ROBERTS
    CREDIT: '59 ALIAS JESSE JAMES

BONO, SONNY   BORN: SALVATORE BONO
                              FEB 16,'40 AT DETROIT, MH
    FATHER: SANTO BONO
    MOTHER: JEAN
    *** MARRIED: '54 DONNA
    DAUGHTER: '54 JEAN BONO
    SON: '56 SANTINO BONO
    DAUGHTER: '58 CHRISTINE BONO
    *** MARRIED: '64 CHER, ACTRESS, SINGER (DIVORCED)
    DAUGHTER: '69 CHASTITY BONO
    TALENT: SINGER, ACTOR-DIRECTOR,WRITER
    CREDIT: '74 CHASTITY
    CREDIT: GOOD TIMES

BOONE, PAT   BORN: CHARLES EUGENE BOONE
                              JUN 01,'34 AT JACKSONVILLE, FL
    FATHER: ARCHIE BOONE, BUILDING CONTRACTOR
    MOTHER: MARGARET PRICHARD, NURSE
    SISTER: MARGUERITE BOONE
    SISTER: JUDY BOONE
    BROTHER: NICK BOONE, SINGER - NICK TODD
    *** MARRIED: '53 SHIRLEY FOLEY
    DAUGHTER: CHERYL LYNN BOONE
    DAUGHTER: LINDA LEE BOONE
    DAUGHTER: DEBORAH ANN BOONE

DAUGHTER: LAURA GENE BOONE
RESIDENCE: TEANECK, NJ
RESIDENCE: BEVERLY HILLS, CA
POSSESSION: '59 RADIO STATIONS WKDA AND KNOK, NASHVILLE & FORT WORTH
POSSESSION: COOGA MOOGA INC.
MEMOIRS: '77 THE HONEYMOON IS OVER
TALENT: SINGER, AUTHOR, ACTOR
CREDIT: '56 BERNADINE, DEBUT
CREDIT: '57 APRIL LOVE
CREDIT: '58 MARDI GRAS
CREDIT: '64 GOODBYE CHARLIE
CREDIT: '67 THE PERILS OF PAULINE
CREDIT: '70 THE CROSS AND THE SWITCHBLADE

BOONE, RICHARD   BORN: RICHARD ALLEN BOONE
                                   JUN 18,'17 AT LOS ANGELES, CA
FATHER: KIRK BOONE, LAWYER
MOTHER: CECILE BECKERMAN
*** MARRIED: JANE HOPPER, PAINTER (DIVORCED)
*** MARRIED: '49 MIMI KELLY, SINGER (DIVORCED '51)
*** MARRIED: '51 CLAIR MCALOON
SON: '53 PETER BOONE
TALENT: ACTOR
COMMENT: FAMILY RELATED TO EXPLORER DANIEL BOONE
CREDIT: '49 THE HALLS OF MONTEZUMA, DEBUT
CREDIT: '53 VICKI
CREDIT: '55 MAN WITHOUT A STAR
CREDIT: '60 THE ALAMO
CREDIT: '65 THE WAR LORD
CREDIT: '71 BIG JAKE

BOOTH, SHIRLEY   BORN: THELMA BOOTH FORD
                                   AUG 30,'07 AT NYC
FATHER: ALBERT FORD
MOTHER: VIRGINIA WRIGHT
*** MARRIED: '29 EDWARD F. GARDNER, RADIO COMEDIAN (DIVORCED '41)
*** MARRIED: '43 WILLIAM H. BAKER (DIED '51)
RESIDENCE: NYC
POSSESSION: '53 CANNES FILM FESTIVAL BEST ACTRESS AWARD
TALENT: ACTRESS
AA-WIN ACTRESS: '52 COME BACK, LITTLE SHEBA
CREDIT: '54 ABOUT MRS. LESLIE
CREDIT: '58 HOT SPELL
CREDIT: '58 THE MATCHMAKER

BORGNINE, ERNEST   BORN: ERMES EFFRON BORGNINE
                                     JAN 24,'17 AT HAMDEN, CN
GRANDFATHER: COUNT PAOLO BOSELLI, ADVISOR-KING VICTOR EMMANUEL
FATHER: CHARLES B. BORGNINE
MOTHER: ANNA BOSELLI
*** MARRIED: '49 RHODA KEMINS (DIVORCED '58)
DAUGHTER: '53 NANCY BORGNINE
*** MARRIED: '59 KATY JURADO, ACTRESS (DIVORCED '61)
STEP-DAUGHTER: SANDRAMARIA CRISTINA VELAZQUEZ
STEP-SON: VICTOR HUGO VELAZQUEZ
*** MARRIED: '64 ETHEL MERMAN (DIVORCED '64)
STEP-DAUGHTER: ETHEL LEVITT
STEP-SON: ROBERT LEVITT, JR.

```
*** MARRIED:  '65 DONNA GRANOUCCI RANCOURT  (DIVORCED)
SON:  '66 CHRISTOPHER BORGNINE
DAUGHTER:  '67 SHARON BORGNINE
*** MARRIED:  '72 TOVE TRAESNER·
TALENT: ACTOR
CREDIT:  '51 THE MOB
AA-WIN  ACTOR:  '55 MARTY
CREDIT:  '67 THE DIRTY DOZEN
CREDIT:  '68 ICE STATION ZEBRA
CREDIT:  '71 WILLARD
CREDIT:  '78 CONVOY
```

BOTTOMS, TIMOTHY
                         AUG 30,'51 AT SANTA BARBARA, CA
```
FATHER: JAMES 'BUD' BOTTOMS
MOTHER: BETTY
BROTHER: JOSEPH BOTTOMS, ACTOR
BROTHER: SAM BOTTOMS, ACTOR
BROTHER: BEN BOTTOMS
*** MARRIED:  '75 ALICIA CORY, SINGER, COMPOSER
SON:  '77 BARTHOLOMEW BOTTOMS
RESIDENCE: SANTA BARBARA, CA
TALENT: ACTOR
CREDIT:  '71 JOHNNY GOT HIS GUN
CREDIT:  '71 THE LAST PICTURE SHOW
CREDIT:  '72 THE PAPER CHASE
CREDIT:  '76 A SMALL TOWN IN TEXAS
CREDIT:  '78 HURRICANE
```

BOW, CLARA   BORN: CLARA GORDON BOW
                         AUG 08,'05 AT BROOKLYN, NY DIED IN '65
```
FATHER: ROBERT BOW
MOTHER: SARAH GORDON
*** MARRIED: REX BELL, ACTOR
COMMENT: BELL WAS LT. GOV. NEVADA 54-62
ROMANCE: GILBERT ROLAND
ROMANCE: GARY COOPER
BIOGRAPHY:  '76 THE IT GIRL, BY MORELLA & EPSTEIN
TALENT: ACTRESS
CREDIT:  '22 BEYOND THE RAINBOW
CREDIT:  '25 THE PLASTIC AGE
CREDIT:  '27 THE SHADOW OF THE LAW
CREDIT:  '30 LOVE AMONG THE MILLIONAIRES
CREDIT:  '33 HOOPLA
```

BOYD, STEPHEN   BORN: WILLIAM MILLAR
                         JUL 04,'28 AT GLEN GORMLEY, BELFAST, IRELAND DIED IN '77
```
FATHER: JAMES ALEXANDER MILLAR, TRUCK DRIVER
MOTHER: MARTHA BOYD
*** MARRIED:  '58 MARIELLA DI SARZANA  (DIVORCED '59)
RESIDENCE: ENCINO, CA
COMMENT: AMERICAN CITIZENSHIP IN DEC 63
TALENT: ACTOR
CREDIT:  '56 THE MAN WHO NEVER WAS
CREDIT:  '58 BEN-HUR
CREDIT:  '59 THE BEST OF EVERYTHING
CREDIT:  '61 THE BIG GAMBLE
CREDIT:  '68 THE SHALAKO
```

CREDIT: '71 KILL

BOYD, WILLIAM
                        JUN 05,'95 AT CAMBRIDGE, OH DIED IN '72
FATHER: CHARLES W. BOYD
MOTHER: LIDA ALBERTA WILKINS
*** MARRIED: '21 RUTH MILLER, ACTRESS
*** MARRIED: '25 ELINOR FAIR (DIVORCED '29)
*** MARRIED: '30 DOROTHY SEBASTIAN, ACTRESS (DIVORCED '36)
*** MARRIED: '37 GRACE BRADLEY, ACTRESS
PARTNER: GABBY HAYES
RESIDENCE: PALM DESERT, CA
POSSESSION: '50 'BOYD'S NEST' CALIFORNIA RANCH
TALENT: ACTOR & EQUESTRIAN
CREDIT: '19 WHY CHANGE YOUR WIFE?, DEBUT
CREDIT: '28 LADY OF THE PAVEMENT
CREDIT: '35 HOPALONG CASSIDY, SERIES

BOYER, CHARLES
                        AUG 28,'99 AT FIGEAC, FRANCE DIED IN '78
FATHER: MAURICE BOYER
MOTHER: AUGUSTINE LOUISE DURAND
*** MARRIED: '34 PAT PATERSON, SHE DIED TWO DAYS BEFORE HIM
SON: '44 MICHAEL BOYER, DIALOGUE DIRECTOR (SUICIDE '65)
RESIDENCE: PARADISE VALLEY, PHEONIX, AR.
POSSESSION: '42 AMERICAN CITIZENSHIP IN FEB 42
POSSESSION: '51 PARTNER IN FOUR STAR PROD CO. WITH LUPINO, NIVEN & POWELL
TALENT: ACTOR
AA-NOM ACTOR: '37 CONQUEST
AA-NOM ACTOR: '38 ALGIERS
AA-SPECIAL AWARD: '42 HONORING HIS ESTABLISHING THE FRENCH RESEARCH FOUNDATION
AA-NOM ACTOR: '44 GASLIGHT
AA-NOM ACTOR: '61 FANNY
CREDIT: '76 STAVISKY

BRANDO, MARLON   BORN: MARLON "BUD" BRANDO, JR.
                        APR 30,'24 AT OMAHA, NB
FATHER: MARLON BRANDO, SR.
MOTHER: DOROTHY PENNEBAKER MYERS
SISTER: FRANCES BRANDO, ARTIST
SISTER: JOCELYN BRANDO, ACTRESS
*** MARRIED: '57 ANNA KASHFI (DIVORCED '60)
SON: '58 CHRISTIAN DEVI BRANDO
*** MARRIED: '60 MOVITA CASTANEDA, ACTRESS
SON: '60 MIKO BRANDO
DAUGHTER: '61 REBECCA BRANDO
SON: '61 TEHOTO
*** MARRIED: '62 TARITA
DAUGHTER: '70 CHEYENNE 'TARITA' BRANDO
ROMANCE: JOSANNE MARIANNA BERENGER
ROMANCE: RITA MORENO
ROMANCE: FRANCE NUYEN
FRIEND: WALLY COX, ACTOR
RESIDENCE: TETIAROA, FRENCH POLYNESIA
TALENT: ACTOR
AA-NOM ACTOR: '51 A STREETCAR NAMED DESIRE
AA-NOM ACTOR: '52 VIVA ZAPATA!
AA-NOM ACTOR: '53 JULIUS CAESAR

```
AA-WIN  ACTOR:    '54 ON THE WATERFRONT
AA-NOM  ACTOR:    '57 SAYONARA
AA-WIN  ACTOR:    '72 THE GODFATHER
AA-NOM  ACTOR:    '73 LAST TANGO IN PARIS
```

BRAZZI, ROSSANO
<pre>
                              SEP 18,'15 AT BOLOGNA, ITALY
    FATHER: ADELMO BRAZZI
    MOTHER: MARIA GHEDINI
    SISTER: FRANCA BRAZZI
    BROTHER: OSCAR BRAZZI
    *** MARRIED: '40 LYDIA BERTOLINI
    TALENT: ACTOR
    CREDIT: '49 LITTLE WOMEN
    CREDIT: '54 THREE COINS IN THE FOUNTAIN
    CREDIT: '58 SOUTH PACIFIC
    CREDIT: '69 THE ITALIAN JOB
    CREDIT: '72 THE GREAT WALTZ
</pre>

BRENNAN, WALTER   BORN: WALTER ANDREW BRENNAN
<pre>
                          JUL 25,'94 AT SWAMPSCOTT, MS   DIED IN '74
    FATHER: WILLIAM JOHN BRENNAN
    MOTHER: MARGARET ELIZABETH FLANAGAN
    *** MARRIED: '20 RUTH WELLS
    DAUGHTER: RUTH BRENNAN
    SON: WALTER BRENNAN, JR.
    SON: ARTHUR WELLS BRENNAN
    RESIDENCE: NORTH HOLLYWOOD, CA
    POSSESSION: '41 COLLECTION OF OLD PANTS
    TALENT: ACTOR
    AA-WIN SUP.ACT.: '36 COME AND GET IT
    AA-WIN SUP.ACT.: '38 KENTUCKY
    AA-WIN SUP.ACT.: '40 THE WESTERNER
    AA-NOM SUP.ACT: '41 SERGEANT YORK
    CREDIT: '54 BAD DAY AT BLACK ROCK
    CREDIT: '66 THE OSCAR
</pre>

BRICE, FANNY   BORN: FANNY BORACH
<pre>
                          OCT 29,'91 AT BROOKLYN, NY DIED IN '51
    FATHER: CHARLES BORACH, SALOON OWNER
    MOTHER: ROSE STERN
    BROTHER: LEW BORACH
    *** MARRIED: '18 NICKY ARNSTEIN, GAMBLER (DIVORCED '27)
    DAUGHTER: '19 FRANCES ARNSTEIN
    SON: '20 WILLIAM JULES ARNSTEIN
    *** MARRIED: '30 BILLY ROSE, PRODUCER (DIVORCED '39)
    FATHER-IN-LAW: DAVID ROSENBERG
    MOTHER-IN-LAW: FANNY WERNICK
    TALENT: ACTRESS
    CREDIT: '28 MY MAN, DEBUT IN 1928
    CREDIT: '30 BE YOURSELF
    CREDIT: '36 THE GREAT ZIEGFELD
    CREDIT: '38 EVERYBODY SINGS
    CREDIT: '45 ZIEGFELD FOLLIES
</pre>

BRIDGES, JEFF
DEC 04,'49 AT LOS ANGELES, CA
    FATHER: LLOYD BRIDGES, ACTOR
    MOTHER: DOROTHY SIMPSON
    SISTER: LUCINDA BRIDGES
    BROTHER: BEAU BRIDGES, ACTOR
    ROMANCE: IDA RANDOM
    ROMANCE: CYBILL SHEPHERD, ACTRESS
    ROMANCE: CANDY CLARK
    ROMANCE: VALERIE PERRINE, ACTRESS
    ROMANCE: SUSAN GESTON
    TALENT: ACTOR
    CREDIT: '70 HALLS OF ANGER
    AA-NOM SUP.ACT: '71 THE LAST PICTURE SHOW
    CREDIT: '71 FAT CITY
    CREDIT: '72 BAD COMPANY
    AA-NOM SUP.ACT: '74 THUNDERBOLT AND LIGHTFOOT
    CREDIT: '78 HURRICANE

BRIDGES, LLOYD
JAN 15,'13 AT SAN LEANDRO, CA
    MOTHER: HARRIET BROWN
    *** MARRIED: '38 DOROTHY SIMPSON
    SON: '41 BEAU BRIDGES, ACTOR
    SON: '49 JEFF BRIDGES, ACTOR
    DAUGHTER: '53 LUCINDA BRIDGES
    TALENT: ACTOR
    CREDIT: '48 FORCES OF EVIL
    CREDIT: '67 THE INCIDENT
    CREDIT: '69 GAILY GAILY
    CREDIT: '72 CHILDS PLAY

BROLIN, JAMES   BORN: JAMES BRUDERLIN
JUN 18,'40 AT LOS ANGELES, CA
    FATHER: HENRY BRUDERLIN, ENGINEER
    MOTHER: HELEN SUE
    *** MARRIED: '66 JANE CAMERON AGEE
    SON: '68 JOSH BROLIN
    SON: '72 JESS BROLIN
    FRIEND: JIM MITCHUM, ACTOR
    FRIEND: CLINT EASTWOOD, ACTOR
    RESIDENCE: PASO ROBLES, CA
    TALENT: ACTOR
    CREDIT: '65 VON RYAN'S EXPRESS
    CREDIT: '72 SKYJACKED
    CREDIT: '73 MARCUS WELBY, MD, TV SERIES
    CREDIT: '75 GABLE & LOMBARD

BRONSON, CHARLES   BORN: CHARLES BUCHINSKY
NOV 03,'21 AT SCOOPTOWN, PA
    BROTHER: JOHN BUCHINSKY
    *** MARRIED: '49 HARRIET TENDLER
    DAUGHTER: '55 SUZANNE BRONSON
    SON: '61 ANTHONY BRONSON
    *** MARRIED: '68 JILL IRELAND
    STEP-SON: PAUL MCCALLUM
    STEP-SON: JASON MCCALLUM

```
STEP-SON: VALENTINE MCCALLUM
DAUGHTER:  '71 ZULEIKA BRONSON
RESIDENCE: BEL AIR, LOS ANGELES, CA
POSSESSION: FARM AT WEST WINDSOR, VERMONT
BIOGRAPHY:  '75 CHARLES BRONSON SUPERSTAR, BY STEVE WHITNEY
TALENT: ACTOR
CREDIT:  '51 YOU'RE IN THE NAVY NOW
CREDIT:  '60 THE MAGNIFICENT SEVEN
CREDIT:  '67 THE DIRTY DOZEN
CREDIT:  '70 YOU CAN'T WIN THEM ALL
CREDIT:  '72 THE VALACHI PAPERS
```

BROOKS, MEL   BORN: MELVIN KAMINSKY
                               JUN 28,'26 AT BROOKLYN, NY
```
MOTHER: KITTY BROOKMAN
BROTHER: --
BROTHER: --
BROTHER: --
*** MARRIED:  '50 FLORENCE BAUM
DAUGHTER:  '51 STEFANIE BROOKS
SON:  '52 NICHOLAS BROOKS
SON:  '53 EDWARD BROOKS
*** MARRIED:  '64 ANNE BANCROFT, ACTRESS
FATHER-IN-LAW: MICHAEL ITALIANO, ACTOR
MOTHER-IN-LAW: MILDRED DINAPOLI
SISTER-IN-LAW: JOANNE ITALIANO
SISTER-IN-LAW: PHYLLIS ITALIANO
SON:  '72 MAXIMILIAN BROOKS
RESIDENCE: BEVERLY HILLS, CA & NYC
TALENT: WRITER, DIRECTOR, ACTOR
CREDIT:  '54 NEW FACES
CREDIT:  '68 THE PRODUCERS
CREDIT:  '70 THE TWELVE CHAIRS
CREDIT:  '76 SILENT MOVIE
```

BROWN, JOE E.   BORN: JOSEPH EVANS BROWN
                               JUL 28,'91 AT HOLGATE, OH DIED IN '73
```
FATHER: MATHIAS BROWN
MOTHER: ANNA EVANS
*** MARRIED:  '15 KATHRYN MCGRAW
ADOPTED SON: MICHAEL J. FRANKOVICH, PRODUCER
DAUGHTER-IN-LAW: BINNIE BARNES, ACTRESS
ADOPTED DAUGHTER: MARY ELIZABETH ANN BROWN
ADOPTED DAUGHTER: KATHRYN FRANCES BROWN
SON: DONALD BROWN, DIED IN COMBAT WW2
SON: JOE LEROY BROWN
PARTNER: W.C. FIELDS
RESIDENCE: LOS ANGELES,CA
POSSESSION: '45  JACK DEMPSEY'S BOXING GLOVES AND BABE RUTH'S BASEBALL BAT
POSSESSION: PERFUME BOTTLE COLLECTION
MEMOIRS: '59  LAUGHTER IS A WONDERFUL THING
TALENT: ACTOR-BASEBALL PLAYER
COMMENT: FIRST STAR TO APPEAR IN SANTA CLAUS LANE PARADE IN 1931
CREDIT:  '28 CROOKS CAN'T WIN
CREDIT:  '32 YOU SAID A MOUTHFUL
CREDIT:  '40 SO YOU WON'T TALK
CREDIT:  '51 SHOW BOAT
CREDIT:  '59 SOME LIKE IT HOT
```

BRUCE, NIGEL BORN: WILLIAM NIGEL BRUCE
                              FEB 04,'95 AT ENSENADA, BAJA CALIF., MEXICO DIED IN '53
FATHER: SIR WILLIAM WALLER BRUCE
MOTHER: ANGELICA MARY SELBY
BROTHER: SIR MICHAEL WALLER SELBY BRUCE, BARONET OF STENHOUSE
*** MARRIED: '21 VIOLET SHELTON, ACTRESS - VIOLET CAMPBELL
DAUGHTER: PAULINE BRUCE
DAUGHTER: JENNIFER BRUCE
FRIEND: GLADYS COOPER
RESIDENCE: LOS ANGELES, CA
TALENT: ACTOR
CREDIT: '29 RED ACES
CREDIT: '39 SHERLOCK HOLMES SERIES, PLAYED DR. WATSON
CREDIT: '41 FREE AND EASY
CREDIT: '43 LASSIE, COME HOME
CREDIT: '52 B'WANA DEVIL

BRUCE, VIRGINIA BORN: HELEN VIRGINIA BRIGGS
                              SEP 29,'10 AT MINNEAPOLIS, MN
FATHER: EARL F. BRIGGS
MOTHER: MARGARET MORRIS
BROTHER: STANLEY BRIGGS
*** MARRIED: '32 JOHN GILBERT (DIVORCED '34)
MOTHER-IN-LAW: SARAH IDA APPERLEY, ACTRESS- ADA ADAIR
DAUGHTER: '33 SUSAN ANN GILBERT
*** MARRIED: '37 J. WALTER RUBIN, DIRECTOR (DIED '42)
SON: '41 CHRISTOPHER RUBIN
*** MARRIED: '46 ALI IPAR, SOLDIER (DIVORCED '51)
*** MARRIED: '52 ALI IPAR, FILM PRODUCER, REMARRIED
ROMANCE: DAVID NIVEN
RESIDENCE: PACIFIC PALISADES, CA
TALENT: ACTRESS
CREDIT: '29 WOMAN TRAP
CREDIT: '34 JANE EYRE
CREDIT: '45 LOVE HONOR AND GOODBY
CREDIT: '52 THE RELUCTANT BRIDE
CREDIT: '60 STRANGERS WHEN WE MET

BRYNNER, YUL BORN: YOUL BRYNER
                              JUL 11,'15 AT CAPE ELIZAVETY, SAKHALIN, USSR
FATHER: BORIS BRYNER, MINING ENGINEER
MOTHER: MARIA BLAGOVIDOVA, GYPSY
SISTER: VERA BRYNNER
*** MARRIED: '44 VIRGINIA GILMORE, ACTRESS (DIVORCED '60)
SON: '45 YUL 'ROCKY' BRYNNER, II
*** MARRIED: '60 DORIS KLEINER (DIVORCED)
DAUGHTER: '62 VICTORIA BRYNNER
*** MARRIED: '71 JACQUELINE DE CROISSET
ADOPTED DAUGHTER: MIA BRYNNER
ADOPTED DAUGHTER: MELODY BRYNNER
RESIDENCE: NORMANDY, FRANCE
MEMOIRS: BRING FORTH THE CHILDREN
TALENT: ACTOR, PHOTOGRAPHER
CREDIT: '49 PORT OF NEW YORK
AA-WIN ACTOR: '56 THE KING AND I
CREDIT: '60 THE MAGNIFICENT SEVEN
CREDIT: '64 INVITATION TO A GUNFIGHT

CREDIT: '74 WESTWORLD

BUCHHOLZ, HORST   BORN: HORST WERNER BUCHHOLTZ
                                    DEC 04,'33 AT BERLIN, GERMANY
     FATHER: --, SHOE-MAKER
     MOTHER: MARIA
     SISTER: HEIDI BUCHHOLTZ
     *** MARRIED: '58 MYRIAM BRU, ACTRESS
     SON: '62 CHRISTOPHER BUCHHOLZ
     DAUGHTER: '63 BEATRICE BUCHHOLZ
     RESIDENCE: PARIS, FRANCE
     RESIDENCE: SWITZERLAND
     TALENT: ACTOR
     COMMENT: AKA HENRY BROOKHOLT
     CREDIT: '59 TIGER BAY
     CREDIT: '60 THE MAGNIFICENT SEVEN
     CREDIT: '61 ONE, TWO, THREE
     CREDIT: '64 MARCO POLO
     CREDIT: '72 THE GREAT WALTZ

BUJOLD, GENEVIEVE
                             JUL 01,'42 AT MONTREAL, CANADA
     FATHER: FERMIN BUJOLD
     MOTHER: LAURETTE
     *** MARRIED: '65 PAUL ALMOND, DIRECTOR (DIVORCED '73)
     SON: '68 MATTHEW JAMES ALMOND
     RESIDENCE: MONTREAL, CANADA
     TALENT: ACTRESS
     CREDIT: '56 FRENCH CAN CAN
     CREDIT: '67 KING OF HEARTS
     CREDIT: '67 ISABEL
     AA-NOM ACTRESS: '69 ANNE OF THE THOUSAND DAYS
     CREDIT: '70 ACE OF HEARTS

BURKE, BILLIE   BORN: MARY WILLIAM ETHELBERT BURKE
                                    AUG 07,'84 AT WASHINGTON, DC   DIED IN '70
     FATHER: WILLIAM BURKE, CLOWN-BARNUM & BAILEY
     MOTHER: BLANCHE
     *** MARRIED: '14 FLORENZ ZIEGFELD, STAGE PRODUCER (DIED '32)
     DAUGHTER: '16 PATRICIA ZIEGFELD
     TALENT: ACTRESS
     CREDIT: '16 GLORIA'S ROMANCE, SERIES
     CREDIT: '33 DINNER AT EIGHT
     AA-NOM SUP.ACT: '38 MERRILY WE LIVE
     CREDIT: '55 THREE HUSBANDS
     CREDIT: '60 PEPE

BURNETT, CAROL   BORN: CAROL CREIGHTON BURNETT
                                    APR 26,'35 AT SAN ANTONIO, TX
     FATHER: JODY BURNETT
     MOTHER: LOUISE CREIGHTON
     SISTER: CHRISTINE BURNETT
     *** MARRIED: '63 JOE HAMILTON
     DAUGHTER: '63 CARRIE LOUISE HAMILTON
     DAUGHTER: '67 JODY ANN HAMILTON
     DAUGHTER: '68 ERIN KATE HAMILTON
     BIOGRAPHY: '75 THE CAROL BURNETT STORY, BY GEORGE CARPOZI
     TALENT: ACTRESS

CREDIT: '63 WHO'S BEEN SLEEPING IN MY BED
CREDIT: '72 PETE'N TILLIE
CREDIT: THE FRONT PAGE

BURNETTE, SMILEY   BORN: LESTER ALVIN BURNETT
                              MAR 18,'11 AT SUMMUM, IL   DIED IN '67
FATHER: REV. GEORGE BURNETTE
*** MARRIED: DALLAS MACDONNELL, JOURNALIST
ADOPTED DAUGHTER: LINDA BURNETTE
ADOPTED SON: STEPHEN BURNETTE
DAUGHTER: CAROLYN BURNETTE
SON: BRIAN BURNETTE
PARTNER: GENE AUTRY, ACTOR, SINGER
RESIDENCE: SAN FERNANDO VALLEY, CA. AND SPRINGFIELD, MR.
TALENT: ACTOR, SONGWRITER
COMMENT: HONORARY MAYOR OF STUDIO CITY, CA
CREDIT: '35 MYSTERY MOUNTAIN, SERIAL
CREDIT: '37 MEET THE BOYFRIEND, SERIAL
CREDIT: '38 THE SMILEY BURNETTE SONG BOOK
CREDIT: '40 ROY ROGERS SERIES OF PICTURES
CREDIT: '50 GENE AUTRY SERIES OF PICTURES

BURNS, GEORGE   BORN: NATHAN BIRNBAUM
                           JAN 20,'96 AT NYC
SISTER: MAMIE BIRNBAUM
SISTER: GOLDIE BIRNBAUM
BROTHER: WILLIAM BIRNBAUM
BROTHER: SAMUEL BIRNBAUM
*** MARRIED: HANNAH SIEGEL, HIS VAUDEVILLE PARTNER
*** MARRIED: '26 GRACIE ALLEN, ACTRESS (DIED '64)
ADOPTED DAUGHTER: SANDRA JEAN BURNS
ADOPTED SON: ROLAND JON BURNS
RESIDENCE: BEVERLY HILLS, CA
POSSESSION: '77 HONORARY DIPLOMA FROM P.S. 22 (HE DROPPED OUT IN 4TH GRADE)
TALENT: ROLLER SKATER,DANCER, COMEDIAN
CREDIT: '32 THE BIG BROADCAST, DEBUT
CREDIT: '34 WE'RE NOT DRESSING
AA-WIN SUP.ACT.: '75 THE SUNSHINE BOYS
CREDIT: '78 'OH, GOD!'

BURR, RAYMOND   BORN: RAYMOND WILLIAM STACEY BURR
                           MAY 21,'17 AT NEW WESTMINSTER, B.C., CANADA
FATHER: WILLIAM JOHNSTON BURR, SR., HARDWARE DEALER
MOTHER: MINERVA SMITH, CONCERT PIANIST
SISTER: MINERVA SMITH BURR
BROTHER: WILLIAM JOHNSTON BURR
*** MARRIED: '39 ANNETTE SUTHERLAND, DIED IN WARTIME PLANE CRASH (DIED '43)
SON: '40 MICHAEL EVAN BURR
*** MARRIED: '46 ISABELLA WARD (DIVORCED)
*** MARRIED: '50 LAURA ANDRINA MORGAN (DIED '55)
RESIDENCE: MALIBU, CA
POSSESSION: ISLAND IN FIJI GROUP
POSSESSION: SWARTHE-BURR ART GALLERY
TALENT: ACTOR
CREDIT: '46 SAN QUENTIN
CREDIT: '51 M
CREDIT: '57 CRIME OF PASSION
CREDIT: '68 P.J.

```
-----------------------------------------------------------------------------------------
BURSTYN, ELLEN          BORN:  EDNA RAE GILLOOLY
                               DEC 07,'32 AT DETROIT, MN
     FATHER: --, PLUMBER
     BROTHER: JACK GILLOOLY
     STEP-BROTHER: STEPHEN SCHWARTZ
     *** MARRIED:  '50 WILLIAM ALEXANDER, POET, SALESMAN  (DIVORCED)
     *** MARRIED:  '57 PAUL ROBERTS, DIRECTOR  (DIVORCED)
     *** MARRIED:  '61 NEIL BURSTYN  (DIVORCED '70)
     SON:  '62 JEFFERSON BURSTYN
     FRIEND: BILL SMITH, ACTOR, ARTIST
     RESIDENCE: ROCKLAND COUNTY, NY
     TALENT: ACTRESS
     COMMENT: AKA - EDNA RAE, KERRI FLYNN, ERICA DEAN AND ELLEN MCRAE
     AA-NOM  SUP.ACT:  '71 THE LAST PICTURE SHOW
     AA-NOM  ACTRESS:  '73 THE EXORCIST
     AA-WIN  ACTRESS:  '74 ALICE DOESN'T LIVE HERE ANYMORE
-----------------------------------------------------------------------------------------
BURTON, RICHARD         BORN:  RICHARD WALTER JENKINS
                               NOV 10,'25 AT PONTRHYDYFEN, WALES, U.K.
     FATHER: THOMAS JENKINS, COAL MINER
     MOTHER: EDITH
     *** MARRIED:  '49 SYBIL WILLIAMS  (DIVORCED '63)
     DAUGHTER:  '50 JESSICA BURTON
     DAUGHTER:  '51 KATE BURTON
     *** MARRIED:  '64 ELIZABETH TAYLOR  (DIVORCED '74)
     STEP-SON: MICHAEL HOWARD WILDING, JR.
     STEP-DAUGHTER: ELIZABETH FRANCES TODD
     STEP-SON: CHRISTOPHER EDWARD WILDING
     STEP-DAUGHTER: MARIA-PETRA FISHER
     *** MARRIED:  '75 ELIZABETH TAYLOR, ACTRESS  (DIVORCED '76)
     *** MARRIED:  '76 SUZY HUNT
     FRIEND: PHILIP BURTON, TEACHER AT OXFORD UNIVERSITY
     POSSESSION: COMMANDER OF THE BRIT. EMPIRE
     TALENT: ACTOR
     AA-NOM  SUP.ACT:  '52 MY COUSIN RACHEL
     AA-NOM  ACTOR:  '53 THE ROBE
     AA-NOM  ACTOR:  '64 BECKET
     AA-NOM  ACTOR:  '65 THE SPY WHO CAME IN FROM THE- COLD
     AA-NOM  ACTOR:  '66 WHO'S AFRAID OF VIRGINIA WOOLF
     AA-NOM  ACTOR:  '69 ANNE OF THE THOUSAND DAYS
     AA-NOM  ACTOR:  '77 EQUUS
-----------------------------------------------------------------------------------------
BUSHMAN, FRANCIS X.       BORN:  FRANCIS XAVIER BUSHMAN
                                 JAN 10,'83 AT BALTIMORE, MD   DIED IN '66
     FATHER: JOHN BUSHMAN
     MOTHER: MARY
     *** MARRIED:  '09 JOSEPHINE FLADUME
     DAUGHTER:  '10 JOSEPHINE BUSHMAN
     SON:  '11 RALPH BUSHMAN
     *** MARRIED:  '18 BEVERLY BAYNE, ACTRESS  (DIVORCED '24)
     DAUGHTER:  '20 VIRGINIA BUSHMAN, ACTRESS  (MARRIED)
     SON:  '20 RICHARD STANBURY BUSHMAN  (DIED '60)
     SON-IN-LAW: JACK CONWAY, DIRECTOR
     DAUGHTER:  '21 LEONORE BUSHMAN, ACTRESS
     SON:  '22 BRUCE BUSHMAN, ARTIST
     RESIDENCE: PACIFIC PALISADES, CA
     TALENT: ACTOR
```

```
CREDIT:   '11 LAST YEAR, DEBUT
CREDIT:   '17 BLOOD WILL TELL
CREDIT:   '26 BEN-HUR
CREDIT:   '45 DICK TRACY, SERIES
CREDIT:   '66 GHOST IN THE INVISIBLE BIKINI
```

BUTTONS, RED   BORN: AARON CHWATT
                                 FEB 05,'19 AT NYC
```
FATHER: MICHAEL CHWATT
MOTHER: SOPHIE BAKER
SISTER: IDA CHWATT
BROTHER: JOSEF CHWATT
*** MARRIED:  '47 ROXANNE, BURLESQUE PERFORMER  (DIVORCED '51)
*** MARRIED:  '51 HELAYNE MCNORTON  (DIVORCED '63)
*** MARRIED:  '64 ALICIA PRATT
DAUGHTER:  '66 AMY BUTTONS
TALENT: ACTOR
CREDIT:   '44 WINGED VICTORY
AA-WIN  SUP.ACT.:  '57 SAYONARA
CREDIT:   '63 A TICKLISH AFFAIR
CREDIT:   '69 THEY SHOOT HORSES, DON'T THEY?
CREDIT:   '72 THE POSEIDON ADVENTURE
```

BUZZI, RUTH
                          JUL 24,'36 AT WESTERLY, RI
```
FATHER: --, STONE CARVER
BROTHER: HAROLD BUZZI
BROTHER: ED BUZZI
*** MARRIED:  '65 BILL KEKO, WRITER
FRIEND: GLADYS ORMPHBY
FRIEND: AGNES GOOCH
RESIDENCE: HOLLYWOOD, CA
POSSESSION: PARK BENCH IN WESTERLY, RI
POSSESSION: PARTNER-BUZZI MEMORIALS, WEQUETQUOCK, CN
TALENT: ACTRESS
CREDIT:   '61 AUNTIE MAME
CREDIT:   '68 LAUGH-IN TV SHOW, 3 EMMY NOMINATIONS
CREDIT:   '69 IN NAME ONLY, TV MOVIE
CREDIT:   '75 THE LOST SAUCER
CREDIT:   '77 FREAKY FRIDAY, FILM DEBUT
```

BYINGTON, SPRING
                          OCT 17,'93 AT COLORADO SPRINGS, CO   DIED IN '71
```
FATHER: EDWIN LEE BYINGTON  (DIED '98)
MOTHER: HELEN CLEGHORN, DOCTOR
*** MARRIED: ROY CAREY CHANDLER  (DIVORCED)
DAUGHTER: PHYLLIS CHANDLER
DAUGHTER: LOIS CHANDLER
FRIEND: FRANCES RAFFERTY
RESIDENCE: HOLLYWOOD HILLS, CA
POSSESSION: COFFEE PLANTATION IN BRAZIL
TALENT: ACTRESS
CREDIT:   '33 LITTLE WOMEN
CREDIT:   '35 AH, WILDERNESS
AA-NOM  SUP.ACT:  '38 YOU CAN'T TAKE IT WITH YOU
CREDIT:   '43 HEAVEN CAN WAIT
CREDIT:   '52 BECAUSE YOU'RE MINE
CREDIT:   '60 PLEASE DON'T EAT THE DAISIES
```

CAAN, JAMES
                        MAR 26,'39 AT NYC
    FATHER: ARTHUR CAAN, BUTCHER
    MOTHER: SOPHIE FALKENSTEIN
    SISTER: BARBARA CAAN
    BROTHER: RONALD CAAN
    *** MARRIED: '61 DEE JAY MATTIS, DANCER (DIVORCED '66)
    DAUGHTER: '64 TARA ALISA CAAN
    *** MARRIED: '76 SHEILA RYAN, MODEL (SEPARATED '78)
    SON: '76 SCOTT ANDREW CAAN
    ROMANCE: CONNIE KRESKI, MODEL
    RESIDENCE: BEVERLY HILLS, CA
    TALENT: ACTOR-RODEO RIDER
    CREDIT: '64 LADY IN A CAGE
    CREDIT: '67 GAMES
    CREDIT: '70 RABBIT RUN
    CREDIT: '71 BRIAN'S SONG
    AA-NOM SUP.ACT: '72 THE GODFATHER
    CREDIT: '73 SCARECROW
    CREDIT: '78 ANOTHER MAN, ANOTHER CHANCE

CABOT, BRUCE   BORN: JACQUES ETIENNE DE BUJAC JR.
                        1904 AT CARLSBAD, NM   DIED IN '72
    SISTER: ADELE DE BUJAC
    *** MARRIED: GRACE MARY MATHER SMITH, ACTRESS (DIVORCED)
    DAUGHTER: '29 JENNIFER DE BUJAC
    *** MARRIED: '33 ADRIENNE AMES, ACTRESS (DIVORCED '37)
    SISTER-IN-LAW: LINDA MARCH
    STEP-DAUGHTER: DOROTHY J. AMES
    *** MARRIED: '50 FRANCESCA JUANA SOFIA ARNAUDT, ACTRESS (DIVORCED '51)
    DAUGHTER: '50 ALPHONSINE CABOT
    SON: '53 BRUCE MICHAEL CABOT
    ROMANCE: LAILA STOCKING
    ROMANCE: LADY SYLVIA HAWKES ASHLEY
    ROMANCE: LORI CAMPBELL
    FRIEND: JOHN WAYNE, ACTOR
    POSSESSION: BROWN-CABOT CO. LIQUOR IMPORTERS
    MEMOIRS: WHICH WAY DID THEY GO?
    TALENT: ACTOR
    CREDIT: '33 KING KONG
    CREDIT: '50 LAST OF THE MOHICANS
    CREDIT: '59 JOHN PAUL JONES
    CREDIT: '65 CAT BALLOU
    CREDIT: '71 DIAMONDS ARE FOREVER

CAESAR, SID
                        SEP 08,'22 AT YONKERS, NY
    FATHER: MAX CAESAR, RESTAURATEUR
    MOTHER: IDA RAPHAEL
    *** MARRIED: '43 FLORENCE LEVY
    DAUGHTER: '44 MICHELE ANDREA CAESAR
    PARTNER: IMOGENE COCA, ACTRESS
    POSSESSION: '51 COLLECTION OF FIREARMS
    TALENT: ACTOR
    CREDIT: '45 TARS AND SPARS
    CREDIT: '47 THE GUILT OF JANET AMES
    CREDIT: '67 A GUIDE FOR MARRIED MEN

```
CREDIT:  '67 THE BUSY BODY
CREDIT:  '78 GREASE
```

CAGNEY, JAMES   BORN: JAMES FRANCIS CAGNEY, JR.
                               JUL 17,'99 AT NYC
```
FATHER: JAMES FRANCIS CAGNEY, SALOON OWNER
MOTHER: CAROLYN NELSON
SISTER: GRACE CAGNEY (DIED '05)
SISTER: JEANNE CAGNEY, ACTRESS
BROTHER-IN-LAW: JACK MORRISON
BROTHER: EDDIE CAGNEY
BROTHER: BILL CAGNEY
BROTHER: ROBERT CAGNEY (DIED '17)
BROTHER: HARRY CAGNEY (DIED '64)
*** MARRIED:  '20 FRANCIS WILLARD VERNON, NICKNAMED BILLIE
ADOPTED DAUGHTER: CATHLEEN CAGNEY, NICKNAMED CASEY
ADOPTED SON: JIMMY CAGNEY
FRIEND: JOAN BLONDELL
RESIDENCE: MARTHA'S VINEYARD, MS
POSSESSION: SWIFT OF IPSWICH-TOPSAIL SCHOONER
POSSESSION: FARM IN DUCHESS COUNTY, NY
MEMOIRS:  '76 CAGNEY BY CAGNEY
TALENT: ACTOR, POET, SAILOR
CREDIT:  '31 PUBLIC ENEMY
AA-NOM  ACTOR:  '38 ANGELS WITH DIRTY FACES
AA-WIN  ACTOR:  '42 YANKEE DOODLE DANDY
AA-NOM  ACTOR:  '55 LOVE ME OR LEAVE ME
CREDIT:  '60 THE GALLANT HOURS
```

CAINE, MICHAEL   BORN: MAURICE JOSEPH MICKLEWHITE
                                MAR 14,'33 AT LONDON, ENGLAND
```
FATHER: MAURICE MICKLEWHITE
MOTHER: ELLEN FRANCES MARIE
BROTHER: STANLEY MICKELWHITE, ACTOR-STANLEY HUNTER
*** MARRIED:  '55 PATRICIA HAINES, ACTRESS
DAUGHTER:  '56 DOMINIQUE CAINE
*** MARRIED:  '73 SHAKIRA BAKSH, ACTRESS-BEAUTY QUEEN
TALENT: ACTOR
CREDIT:  '56 HOW TO MARRY A RICH UNCLE
CREDIT:  '63 ZULU
AA-NOM  ACTOR:  '66 ALFIE
CREDIT:  '67 BILLION DOLLAR BRAIN
AA-NOM  ACTOR:  '72 SLEUTH
CREDIT:  '78 THE SWARM
```

CALHERN, LOUIS   BORN: CARL HENRY VOGT
                                FEB 19,'95 AT BROOKLYN, NY DIED IN '56
```
FATHER: EUGENE ADOLPH VOGT
MOTHER: HUBERTINA FRIESE
SISTER: EMMY VOGT
*** MARRIED: ILKA CHASE, ACTRESS
*** MARRIED: JULIA HOYT, ACTRESS
*** MARRIED: NATALIE SCHAFER, ACTRESS
*** MARRIED:  '46 MARIANNE STEWART, ACTRESS
TALENT: ACTOR
CREDIT:  '31 STOLEN HEAVEN
CREDIT:  '33 20,000 YEARS IN SING SING
CREDIT:  '44 THE BRIDGE OF SAN LUIS REY
```

AA-NOM ACTOR: '50 THE MAGNIFICENT YANKEE
CREDIT: '54 EXECUTIVE SUITE

CALHOUN, RORY   BORN: FRANCIS TIMOTHY DURGIN
                                 AUG 08,'22 AT LOS ANGELES, CA
*** MARRIED: '48 LITA BARON, ACTRESS (DIVORCED '70)
DAUGHTER: '57 CINDY FRANCES CALHOUN
DAUGHTER: '58 TAMI ELIZABETH CALHOUN
DAUGHTER: '59 LORRIE MARIE CALHOUN
*** MARRIED: '71 SUSAN LANGLEY
DAUGHTER: '71 RORYE CALHOUN
PARTNER: VICTOR ORSATTI, AGENT
TALENT: ACTOR
CREDIT: '44 SOMETHING FOR THE BOYS
CREDIT: '52 WITH A SONG IN MY HEART
CREDIT: '55 THE SPOILERS
CREDIT: '61 MARCO POLO
CREDIT: '68 DAYTON'S DEVILS

CALVET, CORINNE   BORN: CORINNE DIBOS
                                 APR 30,'25 AT PARIS, FRANCE
FATHER: PIERRE DIBOS
MOTHER: JULIETTE MUNIER
*** MARRIED: '48 JOHN BROMFIELD, ACTOR (DIVORCED '54)
*** MARRIED: '55 JOHN FORREST FONTAINE, ACTOR - JEFF STONE
SON: '56 ROBIN JOHN STONE
ADOPTED SON: MICHAEL CALVET
*** MARRIED: '66 AL GANNOWAY, PRODUCER (DIVORCED '68)
STEP-SON: GARY GANNOWAY
*** MARRIED: '68 ROBERT WIRT, PHOTOGRAPHER
ROMANCE: DONALD P. SCOTT
FRIEND: DENISE DARCEL, ACTRESS
POSSESSION: '66 RANCH IN VENTURA COUNTY, CALIF
POSSESSION: CONTRACT AT PARAMOUNT PICTURES AS CORINNE CALVAY
TALENT: ACTRESS
CREDIT: '49 ROPE OF SAND
CREDIT: '52 WHAT PRICE GLORY
CREDIT: '54 THE FAR COUNTRY
CREDIT: '60 BLUEBEARD'S TEN HONEYMOONS
CREDIT: '65 APACHE UPRISING

CAMBRIDGE, GODFREY   BORN: GODFREY MACARTHUR CAMBRIDGE
                                 FEB 26,'33 AT NYC   DIED IN '76
FATHER: ALEXANDER CAMBRIDGE, BOOKKEEPER
MOTHER: SARAH, STENOGRAPHER
SISTER: --, BIOLOGIST
*** MARRIED: '62 BARBARA ANN TEER, ACTRESS (DIVORCED '65)
RESIDENCE: NYC
TALENT: ACTOR
CREDIT: '59 THE LAST ANGRY MAN
CREDIT: '63 GONE ARE THE DAYS
CREDIT: '67 THE BUSY BODY
CREDIT: '69 WATERMELON MAN
CREDIT: '70 COTTON COMES TO HARLEM

CANNON, DYAN   BORN: SAMILLE DIANE 'FROSTY' FRIESEN
                             JAN 04,'37 AT TACOMA, WA
   FATHER: BENJAMIN W. FRIESEN
   MOTHER: CLARA
   BROTHER: DAVID FRIESEN
   *** MARRIED: '65 CARY GRANT, ACTOR (DIVORCED '68)
   DAUGHTER: '66 JENNIFER GRANT
   RESIDENCE: MALIBU, CA
   TALENT: ACTRESS
   CREDIT: '59 THE RISE AND FALL OF LEGS DIAMOND
   AA-NOM SUP.ACT: '69 BOB & CAROL & TED & ALICE
   CREDIT: '72 SUCH GOOD FRIENDS
   CREDIT: '73 THE LAST OF SHEILA
   CREDIT: '78 REVENGE OF THE PINK PANTHER

CANOVA, JUDY   BORN: JULIET CANOVA
                             NOV 20,'16 AT JACKSONVILLE, FL
   FATHER: JOE CANOVA
   MOTHER: HENRIETTA PERRY
   SISTER: DIANE 'ANNE' CANOVA
   BROTHER: LEO 'PETE' CANOVA
   *** MARRIED: '36 WILLIAM BURNS (DIVORCED '39)
   *** MARRIED: '41 JAMES RIPLEY (ANNULLED '41)
   *** MARRIED: '43 CHESTER B. ENGLAND (DIVORCED '49)
   DAUGHTER: '44 JULIETA ENGLAND
   *** MARRIED: '50 PHILIP RIVERO
   DAUGHTER: '53 DIANA CANOVA RIVERO
   ROMANCE: EDGAR BERGEN, ACTOR
   ROMANCE: ROBERT THOMPSON, DOCTOR (DIED '49)
   RESIDENCE: SAN FERNANDO VALLEY, CA
   TALENT: ACTRESS, SINGER
   CREDIT: '35 IN CALIENTE
   CREDIT: '41 NAVY BLUES
   CREDIT: '45 HIT THE HAY
   CREDIT: '54 UNTAMED HEIRESS
   CREDIT: '60 THE ADVENTURES OF HUCKLEBERRY FINN
   CREDIT: '70 HOW DO I LOVE THEE?

CANTINFLAS   BORN: MARIO MORENO
                          AUG 12,'11 AT MEXICO CITY, MEXICO
   FATHER: JOSE MORENO, POST OFFICE EMPLOYEE
   MOTHER: MARIA GAIZAR
   *** MARRIED: '37 VALENTINA ZUBAREFF, DANCER
   TALENT: ACTOR, BULLFIGHTER
   CREDIT: '41 NEITHER BLOOD OR SAND
   CREDIT: '44 ROMEO AND JULIET
   CREDIT: '56 AROUND THE WORLD IN EIGHTY DAYS
   CREDIT: '59 PEPE

CANTOR, EDDIE   BORN: EDWARD ISIDORE ITZKOWITZ
                             JAN 31,'92 AT NYC   DIED IN '64
   GRANDMOTHER: ESTHER
   FATHER: MICHAEL ITZKOWITZ
   MOTHER: MINNIE (DIED '93)
   *** MARRIED: '14 IDA TOBIAS (DIED '62)
   DAUGHTER: MARJORIE CANTOR
   DAUGHTER: NATALIE CANTOR

```
DAUGHTER: EDNA CANTOR
DAUGHTER: MARILYN CANTOR
DAUGHTER: JANET CANTOR
RESIDENCE: LONG ISLAND, NY
POSSESSION: '31 FILM CONTRACT WITH GOLDWYN
MEMOIRS:  '57 TAKE MY LIFE
MEMOIRS:  '59 THE WAY I SEE IT
MEMOIRS:  '62 AS I REMEMBER THEM
TALENT: ACTOR
CREDIT:  '26 KID BOOTS, DEBUT
CREDIT:  '30 WHOOPEE
CREDIT:  '37 KID MILLIONS
CREDIT:  '40 THANK YOUR LUCKY STARS
CREDIT:  '48 IF YOU KNEW SUSIE
AA-SPECIAL AWARD:  '56 HONORARY AWARD FOR HIS SERVICE TO THE FILM INDUSTRY
```

CARDINALE, CLAUDIA
                              APR 15,'39 AT TUNIS, TUNISIA
```
*** MARRIED:  '67 FRANCO CRISTALDI, PRODUCER  (DIVORCED)
SON: '67 PATRICK FRANK CRISTALDI
TALENT: ACTRESS
CREDIT:  '60 ROCCO AND HIS BROTHERS
CREDIT:  '63 EIGHT AND A HALF
CREDIT:  '64 THE PINK PANTHER
CREDIT:  '67 DON'T MAKE WAVES
CREDIT:  '73 DAYS OF FURY
```

CAREY, HARRY
             BORN: HARRY DEWITT CAREY, II
                    JAN 16,1878 AT NYC DIED IN '47
```
*** MARRIED:  '13 OLIVE GOLDEN
DAUGHTER: ELLEN CAREY
SON: HARRY CAREY, JR., ACTOR
RESIDENCE: LOS ANGELES, CA
TALENT: ACTOR, PLAYWRIGHT
CREDIT:  '17 THE SOUL HERDER
CREDIT:  '19 THE OUTCASTS OF POKER FLAT
CREDIT:  '31 TRADER HORN
AA-NOM  SUP.ACT:  '39 MR. SMITH GOES TO WASHINGTON
CREDIT:  '48 RED RIVER
```

CAREY, MACDONALD
                              MAR 15,'13 AT SIOUX CITY, IO
```
*** MARRIED:  '41 BETTY HECKSHER  (DIVORCED '69)
SON:  '42 MACDONALD CAREY, JR.
SON:  '43 PAUL GORDON CAREY
DAUGHTER:  '44 ANNA THERESE CAREY
DAUGHTER:  '45 LYNN CAREY
DAUGHTER:  '46 LISA CAREY
SON:  '47 STEVEN CAREY
*** MARRIED:  '70 NORMA DAUPHIN
TALENT: ACTOR
CREDIT:  '42 DR. BROADWAY
CREDIT:  '47 DREAM GIRL
CREDIT:  '52 MY WIFE'S BEST FRIEND
CREDIT:  '62 THE DAMNED
CREDIT:  '65 BROKEN SABRE
```

CARLISLE, KITTY   BORN: CATHERINE HOLZMAN
                             SEP 03,'14 AT NEW ORLEANS, LA
MOTHER: HORTENSE
*** MARRIED: '46 MOSS HART, WRITER '(DIED '61)
SON: '48 CHRISTOPHER HART
DAUGHTER: '50 CATHERINE HART
RESIDENCE: NYC AND IN BUCKS, COUNTY, PA
TALENT: ACTRESS
COMMENT: CHAIRPERSON NY STATE COUNCIL ON ARTS - 1976
CREDIT: '34 MURDER AT THE VANITIES
CREDIT: '34 HERE IS MY HEART
CREDIT: '34 SHE LOVES ME NOT
CREDIT: '35 A NIGHT AT THE OPERA
CREDIT: '43 HOLLYWOOD CANTEEN

CARMICHAEL, HOAGY   BORN: HOAGLAND HOWARD CARMICHAEL
                               NOV 22,'99 AT BLOOMINGTON, IN
FATHER: HOWARD CLYDE CARMICHAEL
MOTHER: --, PIANIST
*** MARRIED: '20 LIDA MARY ROBISON
SON: '21 HOAGY BIX CARMICHAEL
SON: '22 RANDY BOB CARMICHAEL
*** MARRIED: '36 RUTH MEINARDI (DIVORCED '55)
*** MARRIED: '77 WANDA MCKAY
FRIEND: BIX BEIDERBECKE, MUSICIAN
RESIDENCE: LOS ANGELES, CA
MEMOIRS: THE STARDUST ROAD
TALENT: ACTOR, COMPOSER
CREDIT: '46 THE BEST YEARS OF OUR LIVES
CREDIT: '51 IN THE COOL, COOL, COOL OF THE EVENING - WROTE TITLE SONG
CREDIT: '52 BELLES ON THEIR TOES
CREDIT: '62 HATARI! - WROTE SONG

CARNEY, ART   BORN: ARTHUR WILLIAM MATTHEW CARNEY
                         NOV 04,'18 AT MT. VERNON, NY
FATHER: EDWARD CARNEY
MOTHER: HELEN FARRELL
BROTHER: JOHN CARNEY, PRODUCER
BROTHER: FREDERIC CARNEY, DIRECTOR
*** MARRIED: '40 JEAN MYERS
DAUGHTER: '41 EILEEN CARNEY
SON: '42 BRIAN CARNEY
SON: '52 PAUL CARNEY
*** MARRIED: '99 BARBARA ISAACS
RESIDENCE: YONKERS, NY
TALENT: PERFORMER, ACTOR
CREDIT: '41 POT O'GOLD
CREDIT: '64 THE YELLOW ROLLS ROYCE
CREDIT: '67 A GUIDE FOR THE MARRIED MAN
AA-WIN ACTOR: '74 HARRY AND TONTO

CARON, LESLIE   BORN: LESLIE CLAIRE MARGARET CARON
                           JUL 01,'31 AT PARIS, FRANCE
FATHER: CLAUDE CARON, CHEMIST
MOTHER: MARGARET PETIT
BROTHER: AIMERY CARON
*** MARRIED: '51 GEORGE HORMEL, MEAT PACKER (DIVORCED '54)

```
*** MARRIED:  '56 PETER HALL, PRODUCER-DIRECTOR  (DIVORCED '66)
SON:  '57 CHRISTOPHER JOHN HALL
DAUGHTER:  '58 JENNIFER CARON HALL
*** MARRIED:  '69 MICHAEL LAUGHTON, PRODUCER
ROMANCE: WARREN BEATTY
TALENT: DANCER, ACTRESS
CREDIT:  '51 AN AMERICAN IN PARIS
AA-NOM  ACTRESS:  '53 LILI
CREDIT:  '58 GIGI
CREDIT:  '61 FANNY
AA-NOM  ACTRESS:  '63 THE L-SHAPED ROOM
CREDIT:  '66 IS PARIS BURNING?
```

```
CARRADINE, JOHN          BORN:  RICHMOND REED CARRADINE
                                FEB 05,'06 AT NYC
    GRANDFATHER: --, FOUNDER - HOLY ROLLERS
    FATHER: WILLIAM REED CARRADINE, JOURNALIST
    MOTHER: GENEVIEVE WINIFRED RICHMOND, DOCTOR
    *** MARRIED:  '35 ARDANELLE COSNER  (DIVORCED '44)
    SON:  '40 DAVID CARRADINE, ACTOR
    DAUGHTER-IN-LAW: LINDA GILBERT  (MARRIED '77)
    SON:  '41 BRUCE JOHN CARRADINE
    *** MARRIED:  '45 SONIA SOREL  (DIVORCED '55)
    SON:  '46 JOHN ARTHUR CARRADINE, JR.
    SON:  '47 CHRISTOPHER JOHN CARRADINE
    SON:  '49 KEITH IAN CARRADINE, SONGWRITER
    SON:  '53 ROBERT REED CARRADINE
    *** MARRIED:  '56 DORIS RICH  (DIED '71)
    *** MARRIED:  '75 EMILY CISNEROS
    GRANDSON:  '72 SEAGULL CARRADINE, SON OF DAVID & BARBARA HERSHEY
    TALENT: ACTOR
    COMMENT: EARLY STAGE NAME - JOHN PETER RICHMOND
    CREDIT:  '32 THE SIGN OF THE CROSS
    CREDIT:  '38 FOUR MEN AND A PRAYER
    CREDIT:  '45 FALLEN ANGEL
    CREDIT:  '56 THE TEN COMMANDMENTS
    CREDIT:  '69 THE GOOD GUYS AND THE BAD GUYS
```

```
CARRILLO, LEO
                         AUG 06,'80 AT LOS ANGELES, CA  DIED IN '61
    FATHER: JUAN J. CARRILLO
    MOTHER: FRANCISCA ROLDAN
    *** MARRIED:  '40 EDITH SHAKESPEARE HAESELBARTH  (DIED '53)
    ADOPTED DAUGHTER: MARIE ANTOINETTE CARRILLO
    RESIDENCE: SANTA MONICA CANYON, CA
    TALENT: ACTOR-POLITICIAN-EQUESTRIAN
    COMMENT: GREAT GRDFATHER-CARLOS ANTONIO CARRILLO, GOV. OF CALIF., 1837
    CREDIT:  '27 VIVA VILLA!
    CREDIT:  '42 SIN TOWN
    CREDIT:  '48 THE GAY AMIGO
    CREDIT:  '50 PANCHO VILLA RETURNS
```

```
CARROLL, DIAHANN         BORN:  CAROL DIAHANN JOHNSON
                                JUL 17,'35 AT NYC
    FATHER: JOHN JOHNSON
    MOTHER: MABEL FAULK
    *** MARRIED: MONTE KAY  (DIVORCED)
    DAUGHTER:  '60 SUZANNE KAY
```

```
*** MARRIED:  '73 FREDERICK GLUSMAN  (DIVORCED '74)
*** MARRIED:  '75 ROBERT DE LEON, EDITOR
ROMANCE: DAVID FROST
TALENT: SINGER, ACTRESS
CREDIT:  '54 CARMEN JONES
CREDIT:  '59 PORGY AND BESS
CREDIT:  '67 HURRY SUNDOWN
AA-NOM  ACTRESS:  '74 CLAUDINE
```

CARSON, JACK   BORN: JOHN ELMER CARSON
                      OCT 27,'10 AT CARMEN, MANITOBA, CANADA   DIED IN '63
```
FATHER: E. L. CARSON
*** MARRIED: BETTY LYNN (DIVORCED)
*** MARRIED:  '40 KAY ST. GERMAINE  (DIVORCED '50)
SON:  '41 JOHN CARSON
DAUGHTER:  '42 GERMAINE CARSON
*** MARRIED:  '52 LOLA ALBRIGHT  (DIVORCED '58)
*** MARRIED:  '61 SANDRA TUCKER
TALENT: ACTOR
CREDIT:  '37 YOU ONLY LIVE ONCE
CREDIT:  '39 THE HONEYMOON'S OVER
CREDIT:  '47 LOVE AND LEARN
CREDIT:  '55 AIN'T MISBEHAVIN'
CREDIT:  '61 KING OF THE ROARING TWENTIES
```

CARUSO, ENRICO
                  FEB. 25, 1873 AT NAPLES, ITALY   DIED IN '21
```
FATHER: MARCELLIUS CARUSO
MOTHER: ANNA BALDINI
*** MARRIED:  '18 DOROTHY BENJAMIN
RESIDENCE: FLORENCE, ITALY
TALENT: OPERA SINGER, ACTOR
CREDIT:  '18 MY COUSIN
CREDIT: THE SPLENDID ROMANCE
```

CASSIDY, JACK   BORN: JOHN EDWARD JOSEPH CASSIDY
                      MAR 05,'25 AT RICHMOND HILL, LONG ISLAND, NY   DIED IN '76
```
*** MARRIED:  '48 EVELYN WARD
SON:  '49 DAVID CASSIDY, SINGER
DAUGHTER-IN-LAW: KAY LENZ
*** MARRIED:  '56 SHIRLEY JONES, ACTRESS, SINGER  (DIVORCED '75)
SON:  '59 SHAUN CASSIDY, ACTOR
SON:  '62 PATRICK CASSIDY
SON:  '66 RYAN JOHN CASSIDY
FRIEND: MILTON BERLE
RESIDENCE: WEST HOLLYWOOD, CA
POSSESSION:  '74 MOLLY - A GOLDEN RETRIEVER AND LITTER MATE OF LIBERTY 'FORD'
POSSESSION:  '75 RICHMOND HILL PRODUCTION CO.
POSSESSION: HOUSE AT PALM SPRINGS, CA
TALENT: ACTOR-SINGER
CREDIT:  '62 LOOK IN ANY WINDOW
CREDIT:  '64 FBI CODE 98
CREDIT:  '67 GUIDE FOR THE MARRIED MAN
```

```
-------------------------------------------------------------------------------
CASTELLANO, RICHARD
                            SEP 04,'33 AT NYC
    BROTHER-IN-LAW: JOSEPH LARAIA
    *** MARRIED: '53 MARGARET TIERNAN
    FATHER-IN-LAW: MICHAEL LARAIA
    MOTHER-IN-LAW: ROSE MORENO
    DAUGHTER: MARGARET CASTELLANO
    POSSESSION: '72 STRANGWAYS PRODUCTIONS CO.
    TALENT: ACTOR, PRODUCER
    AA-NOM SUP.ACT: '70 LOVERS AND OTHER STRANGERS
    CREDIT: '73 THE GODFATHER
-------------------------------------------------------------------------------
CASTLE, IRENE          BORN:  IRENE FOOTE
                            1893 AT NEW ROCHELLE, NY  DIED IN '69
    *** MARRIED: '10 VERNON BLYTHE CASTLE, ACTOR, DANCING PARTNER  (DIED '18)
    *** MARRIED: '20 ROBERT E. TREMAN
    MEMOIRS: '58 CASTLES IN THE AIR
    TALENT: DANCER, ACTRESS
    CREDIT: '15 THE WHIRL OF LIFE
    CREDIT: '21 THE BROADWAY BRIDE
    CREDIT: '23 BROADWAY AFTER DARK
-------------------------------------------------------------------------------
CAULFIELD, JOAN          BORN:  JOAN BEATRICE CAULFIELD
                            JUN 01,'22 AT WEST ORANGE, NJ
    FATHER: HENRY R. CAULFIELD
    SISTER: BETTY CAULFIELD
    SISTER: MARY CAULFIELD
    *** MARRIED: '50 FRANK ROSS  (DIVORCED '59)
    SON: '59 CAULFIELD ROSS
    *** MARRIED: '60 ROBERT PETERSON, DENTIST  (DIVORCED '66)
    SON: '62 JOHN PETERSON
    RESIDENCE: BEVERLY HILLS, CA
    TALENT: ACTRESS
    CREDIT: '46 MISS SUSIE SLAGLE'S
    CREDIT: '50 DEAR WIFE
    CREDIT: '51 THE LADY SAYS NO
    CREDIT: '55 THE RAINS OF RANCHIPUR
    CREDIT: '68 BUCKSKIN
-------------------------------------------------------------------------------
CAWTHORN, JOSEPH
                      MARCH 29, 1867 AT NYC  DIED IN '49
    FATHER: ALFRED CAWTHORN
    MOTHER: SARAH E. WILLETT
    *** MARRIED: '01 QUEENIE VASSAR, ACTRESS
    RESIDENCE: BEVERLY HILLS, CA
    TALENT: ACTOR
    CREDIT: '28 HOLD 'EM YALE
    CREDIT: '29 DANCE HALL
    CREDIT: '35 GO INTO YOUR DANCE
    CREDIT: '36 BRIDES ARE LIKE THAT
    CREDIT: '42 THE POSTMAN DIDN'T RING
```

CHAMBERLAIN, RICHARD BORN: GEORGE RICHARD CHAMBERLAIN
MAR 31,'35 AT BEVERLY HILLS, CA
FATHER: CHARLES CHAMBERLAIN, MANUFACTURER
MOTHER: ELSA, SINGER
BROTHER: WILLIAM CHAMBERLAIN
TALENT: ACTOR
CREDIT: '62 A THUNDER OF DRUMS, DEBUT
CREDIT: '68 PETULIA
CREDIT: '70 THE MUSIC LOVERS
CREDIT: '72 LADY CAROLINE LAMB
CREDIT: '74 THE THREE MUSKETEERS

CHAMPION, GOWER
JUN 22,'20 AT GENEVA, IL
FATHER: JOHN W. CHAMPION, ADVERTISING EXECUTIVE
MOTHER: BEATRICE CARLISLE
BROTHER: ROBERT CHAMPION (MARRIED '58)
SISTER-IN-LAW: LINDA CRISTAL, ACTRESS (MARRIED '58)
*** MARRIED: '47 MARGE CHAMPION (DIVORCED '72)
FATHER-IN-LAW: ERNEST BELCHER, HIS DANCE TEACHER
SON: '60 GREGG ERNEST CHAMPION
SON: '62 BLAKE CHAMPION
PARTNER: JEAN TYLER, DANCER
POSSESSION: '52 CONTRACT AT M-G-M
TALENT: DANCER, ACTOR, & DIRECTOR
CREDIT: '46 TILL THE CLOUDS ROLL BY
CREDIT: '50 MR. MUSIC
CREDIT: '51 SHOW BOAT
CREDIT: '52 EVERYTHING I HAVE IS YOURS
CREDIT: '55 JUPITER'S DARLING

CHAMPION, MARGE BORN: MARJORIE CELESTE BELCHER
SEP 02,'23 AT LOS ANGELES, CA
FATHER: ERNEST BELCHER, BALLET TEACHER (DIED '73)
MOTHER: GLADYS BASQUETTE
STEP-SISTER: LINA BASQUETTE
*** MARRIED: ART BABBITT (DIVORCED)
*** MARRIED: '47 GOWER CHAMPION, DANCER, ACTOR, DIRECTOR (DIVORCED '72)
SON: '60 GREGG ERNEST CHAMPION
SON: '62 BLAKE CHAMPION
TALENT: ACTRESS, DANCER
CREDIT: '52 LOVELY TO LOOK AT
CREDIT: '67 THE SWIMMER
CREDIT: '68 THE PARTY
CREDIT: '70 THE COCKEYED COWBOYS OF CALICO COUNTY

CHANDLER, JEFF BORN: IRA GROSSEL
DEC 15,'18 AT BROOKLYN, NY DIED IN '61
*** MARRIED: '46 MARJORIE HOSHELLE (DIVORCED '54)
SON: '47 JAMIE CHANDLER
SON: '48 DANA CHANDLER
POSSESSION: '49 CONTRACT AT UNIVERSAL STUDIOS
TALENT: ACTOR
CREDIT: '49 JOHNNY O'CLOCK
AA-NOM SUP.ACT: '50 BROKEN ARROW
CREDIT: '54 SIGN OF THE PAGAN
CREDIT: '57 RAW WIND IN EDEN

CREDIT: '61 MERRILL'S MARAUDERS

CHANEY, LON
                         APR 01,'83 AT COLORADO SPRINGS, CO   DIED IN '30
  *** MARRIED: '05 CLEVA CREIGHTON (DIVORCED '14)
  SON: '06 LON CHANEY, JR., ACTOR
  *** MARRIED: '15 FRANCES CLEVELAND BUSH
  BIOGRAPHY: '57 MAN OF A THOUSAND FACES
  TALENT: ACTOR, WRITER, DIRECTOR
  COMMENT: PANTOMIMIST BECAUSE PARENTS WERE DEAF AND MUTE
  CREDIT: '13 THE EMBEZZLER
  CREDIT: '19 THE MIRACLE MAN
  CREDIT: '23 THE HUNCHBACK OF NOTRE DAME
  CREDIT: '25 THE PHANTOM OF THE OPERA
  CREDIT: '30 THE UNHOLY THREE, HIS ONLY TALKIE

CHANEY, JR., LON   BORN: CREIGHTON CHANEY
                            FEB 10,'06 AT OKLAHOMA CITY, OK   DIED IN '73
  FATHER: LON CHANEY, ACTOR, WRITER, DIRECTOR
  MOTHER: CLEVA CREIGHTON
  STEP-MOTHER: FRANCES CLEVELAND BUSH
  *** MARRIED: '37 PATSY BECK
  SON: LON CHANEY, 3RD
  SON: RONALD CHANEY
  TALENT: ACTOR
  CREDIT: '32 BIRD OF PARADISE
  CREDIT: '39 OF MICE AND MEN
  CREDIT: '42 THE GHOST OF FRANKENSTEIN
  CREDIT: '45 FRANKENSTEIN MEETS THE WOLFMAN
  CREDIT: '52 HIGH NOON
  CREDIT: '64 WITCHCRAFT

CHAPLIN, CHARLES   BORN: CHARLES SPENCER CHAPLIN, JR.
                            APR 16,'89 AT WALWORTH, LONDON, ENGLAND   DIED IN '77
  FATHER: CHARLES SPENCER CHAPLIN, ENTERTAINER (DIED '95)
  MOTHER: HANNAH HILL, SINGER- AKA LILY HARLEY
  STEP-BROTHER: WHEELER DRYDEN
  STEP-BROTHER: SYDNEY CHAPLIN (DIED '65)
  *** MARRIED: '18 MILDRED HARRIS, ACTRESS (DIVORCED '20)
  SON: '19 --, DIED THREE DAYS OLD (DIED '19)
  *** MARRIED: '24 LILLITA LOUISE MCMURRAY, ACTRESS - LITA GREY (DIVORCED '27)
  SON: '25 CHARLES SPENCER CHAPLIN, 3RD (DIED '68)
  SON: '26 SYDNEY EARLE CHAPLIN
  *** MARRIED: '36 PAULETTE GODDARD, ACTRESS (DIVORCED '42)
  *** MARRIED: '43 OONA O'NEILL
  FATHER-IN-LAW: EUGENE O'NEILL, PLAYWRIGHT
  DAUGHTER: '44 GERALDINE CHAPLIN, ACTRESS
  SON: '45 MICHAEL CHAPLIN
  DAUGHTER: '46 JOSEPHINE CHAPLIN
  SON-IN-LAW: NIKOLAS SISTOUARIS (MARRIED '69)
  DAUGHTER: '47 VICTORIA CHAPLIN
  SON-IN-LAW: JEAN-PIERRE THIERREE, CIRCUS PERFORMER (MARRIED '74)
  DAUGHTER: '48 JANE CHAPLIN
  DAUGHTER: '49 ANNETTE CHAPLIN
  SON: '50 EUGENE CHAPLIN
  SON: '51 CHRISTOPHER CHAPLIN
  ROMANCE: JOAN BARRY, FILED PATERNITY CASE SUIT
  ROMANCE: POLA NEGRI, ACTRESS

GRANDSON: '74 SHANE CHAPLIN
PARTNER: EDNA PURVIANCE, ACTRESS & HIS LEADING LADY
RESIDENCE: VEVEY, SWITZERLAND
POSSESSION: YACHT 'PANACEA'
MEMOIRS: MY AUTOBIOGRAPHY
TALENT: ACTOR,WRITER,COMPOSER,DIRECTOR,PRODUCER
CREDIT: '14 MAKING A LIVING
AA-NOM ACTOR: '27 THE CIRCUS
AA-SPECIAL AWARD: '27 THE CIRCUS **FOR** 'VERSATILITY AND GENIUS'
AA-NOM DIRECTOR: '27 THE CIRCUS
CREDIT: '36 MODERN TIMES
AA-NOM ACTOR: '40 THE GREAT DICTATOR
CREDIT: '52 LIMELIGHT
CREDIT: '67 A CONTESS FROM HONG KONG
AA-SPECIAL AWARD: '71 HONORING HIS 'INCALCULABLE EFFECT' ON MOVIE MAKING

CHAPLIN, GERALDINE
                         JUL 31,'44 AT SANTA MONICA, CA
GRANDFATHER: EUGENE O'NEILL, PLAYWRIGHT
FATHER: CHARLES CHAPLIN, ACTOR,WRITER,COMPOSER,DIRECTOR
MOTHER: OONA O'NEILL
SISTER: JOSEPHINE CHAPLIN
SISTER: VICTORIA CHAPLIN
SISTER: JANE CHAPLIN
SISTER: ANNETTE CHAPLIN
BROTHER: MICHAEL CHAPLIN
BROTHER: EUGENE CHAPLIN
BROTHER: CHRISTOPHER CHAPLIN
STEP-BROTHER: CHARLES SPENCER CHAPLIN, III
STEP-BROTHER: SYDNEY EARLE CHAPLIN
SON: '74 SHANE CHAPLIN, FATHER-CARLOS SAURA, DIRECTOR
ROMANCE: CARLOS SAURA, DIRECTOR
TALENT: ACTRESS
CREDIT: '65 DOCTOR ZHIVAGO
CREDIT: '70 THE HAWAIIANS
CREDIT: '73 THE THREE MUSKETEERS

CHARISSE, CYD   BORN: TULA ELLICE FINKLEA
                         MAR 08,'22 AT AMARILLO, TX
FATHER: ERNEST FINKLEA, JEWELER
MOTHER: LELA NORWOOD
*** MARRIED: '39 NICO CHARISSE, BALLET TEACHER (DIVORCED '47)
SON: '40 NICKY CHARISSE
BROTHER-IN-LAW: PIERRE CHARISSE, DANCER, DEL MAR HOTEL
BROTHER-IN-LAW: ANDRE CHARISSE, DANCER
BROTHER-IN-LAW: NOEL CHARISSE, DANCER
SISTER-IN-LAW: KATHRYN CHARISSE, CHOREOGRAPHER
SISTER-IN-LAW: NANETTE CHARISSE, BALLERINA
SISTER-IN-LAW: RITA CHARISSE, CHOREOGRAPHER
SISTER-IN-LAW: MARIE CHARISSE, DANCER
SISTER-IN-LAW: LUCILLE CHARISSE, DANCER
*** MARRIED: '48 TONY MARTIN, SINGER
SON: '50 TONY MARTIN, JR.
MEMOIRS: '76 THE TWO OF US
TALENT: DANCER, ACTRESS
CREDIT: '45 THE HARVEY GIRLS
CREDIT: '54 BRIGADOON
CREDIT: '57 SILK STOCKINGS
CREDIT: '66 THE SILENCERS

```
--------------------------------------------------------------------------------
CHASE, ILKA          BORN:   EDNA WOOLMAN CHASE
                            APR 08,'05 AT NYC   DIED IN '78
   FATHER: FRANK D. CHASE
   MOTHER: EDNA ALLAWAY
   *** MARRIED:  '26 LOUIS CALHERN, ACTOR  (DIVORCED)
   *** MARRIED:  '35 WILLIAM B. MURRAY  (DIVORCED)
   *** MARRIED:  '45 NORTON S. BROWN, PHYSICIAN
   ENEMY: MARION DAVIES
   RESIDENCE: NYC
   TALENT: ACTRESS, WRITER
   CREDIT: PARIS BOUND, DEBUT IN 1929
   CREDIT: THE BIG PARTY
   CREDIT: JOHNNY DARK
   CREDIT: THE BIG KNIFE
   CREDIT: OCEAN'S 11
--------------------------------------------------------------------------------
CHATTERTON, RUTH
                         DEC 24,'93 AT NYC   DIED IN '61
   FATHER: WALTER CHATTERTON
   MOTHER: LILIAN REED
   *** MARRIED:  '24 RALPH FORBES, ACTOR  (DIVORCED '32)
   MOTHER-IN-LAW: MARY TAYLOR FORBES, ACTRESS
   SISTER-IN-LAW: BRENDA FORBES, ACTRESS
   *** MARRIED:  '32 GEORGE BRENT, ACTOR  (DIVORCED '34)
   *** MARRIED:  '42 BARRY THOMSON, ACTOR  (DIED '60)
   TALENT: ACTRESS
   AA-NOM  ACTRESS:  '28 MADAME X
   CREDIT:  '28 SONS OF THE FATHERS, DEBUT
   AA-NOM  ACTRESS:  '29 SARAH AND SON
   CREDIT:  '36 LADY OF SECRETS
   CREDIT:  '38 A ROYAL DIVORCE
--------------------------------------------------------------------------------
CHEKHOV, MICHAEL
                     AUG 29,'91 AT ST. PETERSBURG, RUSSIA   DIED IN '55
   UNCLE: ANTON CHEKHOV, AUTHOR
   *** MARRIED: OLGA KNIPPER, ACTRESS  (DIVORCED)
   *** MARRIED: XENIA J. CHEKOV
   RESIDENCE: BEVERLY HILLS, CA
   TALENT: ACTOR, DIRECTOR
   CREDIT:  '44 SONG OF RUSSIA
   AA-NOM  SUP.ACT:  '45 SPELLBOUND
   CREDIT:  '46 SPECTRE OF THE ROSE
   CREDIT:  '52 HOLIDAY FOR SINNERS
   CREDIT:  '54 RHAPSODY
--------------------------------------------------------------------------------
CHER        BORN:   CHERILYN LA PIERE
                         MAY 20,'46 AT EL CENTRO, CA
   FATHER: GILBERT LA PIERE, BANKER
   MOTHER: JACKIE JEAN CROUCH, SINGER - GEORGIA HOLT
   SISTER: GEORGANNE LA PIERE, ACTRESS
   *** MARRIED:  '64 SONNY BONO, ACTOR, SINGER, DIRECTOR  (DIVORCED '75)
   STEP-DAUGHTER: CHRISTINE BONO
   STEP-DAUGHTER: JEAN BONO
   STEP-SON: SANTINO BONO
   DAUGHTER:  '69 CHASTITY BONO
   *** MARRIED:  '75 GREGG ALLMAN, ROCK SINGER
   SON:  '76 ELIJAH BLUE ALLMAN
```

```
        RESIDENCE: LOS ANGELES, CA
        POSSESSION: COLLECTION OF ANTIQUES & AUTOS
        BIOGRAPHY:  '75 CHER, BY VICKI PELLEGRINO
        TALENT: ACTRESS, SINGER
        CREDIT: GOOD TIMES
        CREDIT: CHASTITY
        CREDIT: I GOT YOU BABE, 1ST HIT RECORD
```

CHEVALIER, MAURICE   BORN: M.EDOUARD SAINT-LEON CHEVALIER
```
                                    SEP 12,'88 AT MENILMONTANT, PARIS, FRANCE   DIED IN '72
        FATHER: VICTOR CHARLES CHEVALIER, HOUSE PAINTER
        MOTHER: JOSEPHINE VANDEN-BOOSCHE
        BROTHER: PAUL CHEVALIER
        BROTHER: CHARLES CHEVALIER
        *** MARRIED:  '26 YVONNE VALLEE  (ANNULLED '35)
        ROMANCE: NITA RYAN, COMPANION DURING WW2
        PARTNER: MISTINGUETT, DANCER, ACTRESS
        RESIDENCE: LA LOUQUE, SEINE ET OISE, FR.
        POSSESSION:  '38 LEGION OF HONOR OF FRANCE
        MEMOIRS:  '60 WITH LOVE
        MEMOIRS:  '70 THE WHITE HAIRED BOY
        MEMOIRS:  '72 I REMEMBER IT WELL
        TALENT: ACTOR, ENTERTAINER
        AA-NOM  ACTOR:  '29 THE LOVE PARADE THE BIG POND
        CREDIT:  '34 THE MERRY WIDOW
        CREDIT:  '57 GIGI
        AA-SPECIAL AWARD:  '58 HONORING MORE THAN HALF A CENTURY OF ENTERTAINMENT
        CREDIT:  '61 FANNY
```

CHRISTIAN, LINDA   BORN: BLANCA ROSA WELTER
```
                                    NOV 13,'24 AT TAMPICO, TAMAULIPAS, MEXICO
        FATHER: GERALD WELTER
        COUSIN: KATY JURADO, ACTRESS
        *** MARRIED:  '49 TYRONE POWER  (DIVORCED '55)
        DAUGHTER:  '49 ROMINA POWER, ACTRESS
        SON-IN-LAW: AL BANO, SINGER
        DAUGHTER:  '53 TARYN POWER, ACTRESS
        *** MARRIED:  '62 EDMUND PURDOM  (DIVORCED '63)
        ROMANCE: HUGH O'BRIAN
        ROMANCE: ERROL FLYNN
        ROMANCE: TURHAN BEY
        ROMANCE: MARQUIS ALFONSO DE PORTAGO
        ROMANCE: FRANCISCO 'BABY' PIGNATARI
        RESIDENCE: MARBELLA, SPAIN
        TALENT: ACTRESS
        CREDIT:  '46 HOLIDAY IN MEXICO
        CREDIT:  '48 TARZAN AND THE MERMAIDS
        CREDIT:  '52 THE HAPPY TIME
        CREDIT:  '63 THE VIP'S
        CREDIT:  '66 HOW TO SEDUCE A PLAYBOY
```

CHRISTIE, JULIE
```
                            APR 14,'40 AT CHUKUR, ASSAM, INDIA
        ROMANCE: DON BESSANT
        ROMANCE: WARREN BEATTY
        RESIDENCE: MADRID, SPAIN
        TALENT: ACTRESS
        COMMENT: MEMBER OF ROYAL SHAKESPEARE CO
```

```
CREDIT:  '62 FAST LADY
AA-WIN  ACTRESS:  '65 DARLING
CREDIT:  '68 PETULIA
AA-NOM  ACTRESS:  '71 MCCABE & MRS. MILLER
CREDIT:  '74 SHAMPOO
CREDIT:  '77 DEMON SEED
```

CLAIRE, INA   BORN: INA FAGAN
                                 OCT 15,'92 AT WASHINGTON, DC
```
FATHER: JOSEPH FAGAN
MOTHER: CORA B. LIEURANCE CLAIRE
*** MARRIED:  '19 JAMES WHITTAKER, JOURNALIST  (DIVORCED '25)
*** MARRIED:  '29 JOHN GILBERT, ACTOR  (DIVORCED '31)
FATHER-IN-LAW: JOHN PRINGLE, ACTOR
MOTHER-IN-LAW: SARAH IDA APPERLEY, ACTRESS-ADA ADAIR
*** MARRIED:  '39 WILLIAM R. WALLACE, LAWYER
ROMANCE: GENE MARKEY, WRITER
FRIEND: MARION DAVIES
RESIDENCE: SAN FRANCISCO, CA
POSSESSION:  '36 GOLD MEDAL OF ACADEMY OF ARTS & LETTERS FOR GOOD DICTION
POSSESSION:  '54 RANCH IN SONOMA, CA
TALENT: ACTRESS
CREDIT:  '15 THE PUPPET CLOWN
CREDIT:  '20 POLLY WITH A PAST
CREDIT:  '29 THE AWFUL TRUTH
CREDIT:  '31 REBOUND
CREDIT:  '43 CLAUDIA
```

CLARK, DANE   BORN: BERNARD ZANVILLE
                                 MAR 18,'13 AT NYC
```
*** MARRIED:  '41 MARGO YODER  (DIED '70)
*** MARRIED:  '72 GERALDINE FRANK, STOCKBROKER
TALENT: ACTOR
CREDIT:  '43 TENNESSEE JOHNSON
CREDIT:  '49 MOONRISE
CREDIT:  '50 WITHOUT HONOUR
CREDIT:  '57 THE OUTLAW'S SON
CREDIT:  '70 THE MCMASTERS
```

CLARK, DICK   BORN: RICHARD WAGSTAFF CLARK
                                 NOV 30,'29 AT MT. VERNON, NY
```
FATHER: RICHARD AUGUSTUS CLARK
MOTHER: JULIA
BROTHER: BRADLEY CLARK
*** MARRIED:  '52 BARBARA MALLERY, SCHOOLTEACHER  (DIVORCED '61)
SON:  '57 RICHARD AUGUSTUS CLARK, III
*** MARRIED:  '62 LORETTA MARTIN  (DIVORCED)
SON:  '63 DWAYNE CLARK
DAUGHTER:  '65 CYNTHIA CLARK
ROMANCE: KARI WIGTON
POSSESSION:  '65 DICK CLARK PRODUCTION CO.
MEMOIRS:  '63 TO GOOF OR NOT TO GOOF
TALENT: ACTOR, PRODUCER
CREDIT:  '60 BECAUSE THEY'RE YOUNG
CREDIT:  '61 THE YOUNG DOCTORS
CREDIT:  '68 WILD IN THE STREETS
CREDIT:  '69 THE PHYNX
```

```
----------------------------------------------------------------------------------------------
CLARK, FRED            BORN:   FREDERIC LEONARD CLARK
                               MAR 09,'14 AT LINCOLN, CA   DIED IN '68
   *** MARRIED:  '52 BENAY VENUTA, ACTRESS  (DIVORCED '63)
   *** MARRIED:  '66 GLORIA GLASER
   TALENT: ACTOR
   CREDIT:  '47 RIDE THE PINK HORSE
   CREDIT:  '50 SUNSET BOULEVARD
   CREDIT:  '56 THE SOLID GOLD CADILLAC
   CREDIT:  '68 SKIDOO
----------------------------------------------------------------------------------------------
CLARK, PETULA          BORN:   PETULA SALLY OLWEN CLARK
                               NOV 15,'34 AT EPSOM, SURREY, ENGLAND
   FATHER: LESLIE CLARK, HER MANAGER
   SISTER: --
   *** MARRIED:  '61 CLAUDE WOLFF
   DAUGHTER:  '62 BARBARA MICHELE WOLFF
   DAUGHTER:  '63 CATHERINE NATALIE WOLFF
   SON:  '72 PATRICK PHILIPPE WOLFF
   RESIDENCE: GENEVA, SWITZERLAND
   POSSESSION: VILLA AT VALLAURIS, FRANCE
   TALENT: ACTRESS, VOCALIST
   CREDIT:  '44 MEDAL FOR THE GENERAL
   CREDIT:  '48 EASY MONEY
   CREDIT:  '52 THE CARD
   CREDIT:  '69 GOODBYE MR. CHIPS
   CREDIT:  '70 FINIAN'S RAINBOW
----------------------------------------------------------------------------------------------
CLAYTON, JAN           BORN:   JANE BYRAL CLAYTON
                               AUG 26,'17 AT TULAROSA, NM
   FATHER: G. VERNER CLAYTON
   MOTHER: VERA CARTER
   BROTHER-IN-LAW: ALAN JAY LERNER, LYRICIST
   *** MARRIED:  '39 RUSSELL HAYDEN  (DIVORCED '46)
   DAUGHTER:  '40 SANDRA JANE HAYDEN  (DIED '56)
   *** MARRIED:  '46 ROBERT WARREN LERNER  (DIVORCED '58)
   DAUGHTER:  '48 ROBIN LERNER
   SON:  '49 JOSEPH LERNER
   DAUGHTER:  '50 KAREN 'KIMMY' LERNER  (MARRIED '74)
   SON-IN-LAW: JOSE LUIS PEREZ
   *** MARRIED:  '65 GEORGE GREELEY, MUSICIAN  (DIVORCED '68)
   GRANDSON:  '75 LUIS ROBERTO PEREZ
   RESIDENCE: LOS ANGELES, CA
   POSSESSION: HER OWN COVER ON LIFE MAGAZINE
   TALENT: ACTRESS
   COMMENT: MEMBER NATIONAL BOARD OF USO
   COMMENT: MEMBER OF BOARD OF ALCOHOLISM COUNCIL OF LOS ANGELES
   COMMENT: SPOKESPERSON FOR SCHICK CENTER SMOKING & WEIGHT CONTROL
   CREDIT:  '39 HOPALONG CASSIDY, SERIES
   CREDIT:  '44 CAROUSEL, STAGE PRODUCTION
   CREDIT:  '45 THIS MAN'S NAVY
   CREDIT:  '48 THE SNAKEPIT
   CREDIT:  '60 LASSIE, TV SERIES
```

```
---------------------------------------------------------------------------------
CLIFT, MONTGOMERY         BORN:   EDWARD MONTGOMERY CLIFT
                                  OCT 17,'20 AT OMAHA,NB   DIED IN '66
     FATHER: WILLIAM BROOKS CLIFT, SALESMAN
     MOTHER: ETHEL FOGG ANDERSON
     SISTER: ROBERTA 'ETHEL' CLIFT, TWIN
     BROTHER: WILLIAM BROOKS CLIFT, JR.
     ROMANCE: LIBBY HOLMAN
     FRIEND: MIRA ROSTOVA, ACTING COACH
     FRIEND: ELIZABETH TAYLOR, ACTRESS
     RESIDENCE: NYC
     BIOGRAPHY:  '77 MONTY, BY ROBERT LAGUARDIA
     BIOGRAPHY:  '78 MONTGOMERY CLIFT, BY PATRICIA BOSWORTH
     TALENT: ACTOR
     AA-NOM  ACTOR:  '48 THE SEARCH
     CREDIT:  '48 RED RIVER
     AA-NOM  ACTOR:  '51 A PLACE IN THE SUN
     AA-NOM  ACTOR:  '53 FROM HERE TO ETERNITY
     AA-NOM  SUP.ACT:  '61 JUDGMENT AT NUREMBERG
     CREDIT:  '62 FREUD
     CREDIT:  '66 THE DEFECTOR
---------------------------------------------------------------------------------
CLOONEY, ROSEMARY
                          MAY 23,'28 AT MAYSVILLE, KT
     FATHER: ANDREW CLOONEY, HOUSE PAINTER
     MOTHER: FRANCES GUILFOYLE
     SISTER: GAIL CLOONEY
     SISTER: ELIZABETH CLOONEY, SINGER
     BROTHER: NICHOLAS CLOONEY
     *** MARRIED:  '53 JOSE FERRER, ACTOR
     SON:  '54 MIGUEL FERRER
     SON:  '55 RAPHAEL FERRER
     DAUGHTER:  '56 MARIA FERRER
     DAUGHTER:  '57 GABRIEL FERRER
     DAUGHTER:  '58 MONSITA FERRER
     RESIDENCE: BEVERLY HILLS, CA
     MEMOIRS:  '77 THIS IS FOR REMEMBRANCE
     TALENT: ACTRESS
     CREDIT:  '53 THE STARS ARE SINGING
     CREDIT:  '54 RED GARTERS
     CREDIT:  '54 WHITE CHRISTMAS
     CREDIT:  '54 DEEP IN MY HEART
---------------------------------------------------------------------------------
COBB, LEE J.             BORN:   LEO JACOB COBB
                                  DEC 08,'11 AT NYC  DIED IN '76
     FATHER: BENJAMIN JACOB COBB
     MOTHER: KATE NEILECHT
     *** MARRIED:  '40 HELEN BEVERLY, HEIRESS  (DIVORCED '52)
     SON:  '43 VINCENT COBB
     DAUGHTER:  '44 JULIE COBB
     *** MARRIED:  '57 MARY HIRSCH
     SON:  '60 ANTHONY COBB
     SON:  '61 GERALD COBB
     TALENT: ACTOR
     CREDIT:  '39 GOLDEN BOY
     CREDIT:  '44 WINGED VICTORY
     AA-NOM  SUP.ACT:  '54 ON THE WATERFRONT
     AA-NOM  SUP.ACT:  '58 THE BROTHERS KARAMAZOV
```

CREDIT: '62 THE FOUR HORSEMEN OF THE APOCALYPSE

COBURN, CHARLES

BORN: CHARLES DOUVILLE COBURN
JUN 19,'77 AT SAVANNAH, GE   DIED IN '61
FATHER: MOSES DOUVILLE COBURN
MOTHER: EMMA LOUISE SPRIGMAN
*** MARRIED: '06 IVAH WILLS, ACTRESS (DIED '37)
*** MARRIED: '59 WINIFRED NATZKA
RESIDENCE: BEVERLY HILLS, CA
TALENT: ACTOR
CREDIT: '33 BOSS TWEED
AA-NOM SUP.ACT: '41 THE DEVIL AND MISS JONES
AA-WIN SUP.ACT.: '43 THE MORE THE MERRIER
AA-NOM SUP.ACT: '46 THE GREEN YEARS
CREDIT: '53 GENTLEMEN PREFER BLONDES

COBURN, JAMES

AUG 31,'28 AT LAUREL, NB
FATHER: JAMES COBURN, SR.
*** MARRIED: '58 BEVERLY KELLY
DAUGHTER: LISA COBURN
SON: JAMES COBURN, IV
RESIDENCE: BEVERLY HILLS, CA
POSSESSION: PANPIPER PRODUCTIONS CO.
POSSESSION: PERCUSSION INSTRUMENT COLLECTION
TALENT: ACTOR
CREDIT: '60 THE MAGNIFICENT SEVEN
CREDIT: '65 OUR MAN FLINT
CREDIT: '67 WATERHOLE THREE
CREDIT: '71 A FISTFUL OF DYNAMITE
CREDIT: '73 THE LAST OF SHEILA

COCA, IMOGENE

BORN: IMOGENE FERNANDEZ Y COCA
NOV 18,'20 AT PHILADELPHIA, PA
FATHER: JOSE FERNANDEZ Y COCA, ORCHESTRA LEADER - JOE COCA
MOTHER: SADIE BRADY, VAUDEVILLIAN
*** MARRIED: '35 BOB BURTON
*** MARRIED: '60 KING DONOVAN, ACTOR
PARTNER: SID CAESAR
RESIDENCE: NYC
TALENT: ACTRESS
CREDIT: '37 THE BASHFUL BALLERINA
CREDIT: '64 THE SOUND OF LAUGHTER
CREDIT: '65 PROMISE HER ANYTHING
CREDIT: '78 ON THE 20TH CENTURY, PLAY ON BROADWAY

COCHRAN, STEVE

BORN: ROBERT ALEXANDER COCHRAN
MAY 25,'17 AT EUREKA, CA   DIED IN '65
*** MARRIED: '40 FLORENCE LOCKWOOD (DIVORCED '46)
DAUGHTER: '41 XANDRA COCHRAN
*** MARRIED: '46 FAYE MCKENZIE, SINGER (DIVORCED '48)
*** MARRIED: '61 JONNA JENSEN (DIVORCED)
TALENT: ACTOR
CREDIT: '45 BOSTON BLACKIE, SERIES
CREDIT: '47 COPACABANA
CREDIT: '58 I, MOBSTER
CREDIT: '65 MOZAMBIQUE

```
------------------------------------------------------------------------------------------
COLBERT, CLAUDETTE          BORN:  LILY CLAUDETTE CHAUCHOIN
                                   SEP 13,'05 AT PARIS, FRANCE
     FATHER: GEORGE CHAUCHOIN
     MOTHER: JEANNE LOEW
     BROTHER: CHARLES CHAUCHOIN
     *** MARRIED:  '28 NORMAN FOSTER, DIRECTOR  (DIVORCED '35)
     *** MARRIED:  '35 DR. JOEL PRESSMAN  (DIED '68)
     FRIEND: FRANK SINATRA
     FRIEND: LILLIAN HELLMAN
     FRIEND: DEBORAH KERR
     FRIEND: SLIM KEITH
     RESIDENCE: BELLERIVE, ST. PETER, VIRGIN ISLANDS
     TALENT: ACTRESS
     CREDIT:  '27 FOR THE LOVE OF MIKE
     AA-WIN  ACTRESS:  '34 IT HAPPENED ONE NIGHT
     AA-NOM  ACTRESS:  '35 PRIVATE WORLDS
     CREDIT:  '38 IMITATION OF LIFE
     AA-NOM  ACTRESS:  '44 SINCE YOU WENT AWAY
     CREDIT:  '61 PARRISH
------------------------------------------------------------------------------------------
COLE, NAT "KING"            BORN:  NATHANIEL ADAMS COLES
                                   MAR 17,'19 AT MONTGOMERY, AL   DIED IN '65
     FATHER: EDWARD COLES, MINISTER
     MOTHER: PERLINA ADAMS
     *** MARRIED:  '37 NADINE ROBINSON, DANCER  (DIVORCED '46)
     *** MARRIED:  '48 MARIE ELLINGTON
     DAUGHTER:  '49 STEPHANIE NATALIE MARIA COLE, SINGER
     ADOPTED DAUGHTER: CAROL COLE, HIS WIFE'S NIECE
     TALENT: ACTOR, SINGER, COMPOSER
     CREDIT:  '49 MAKE BELIEVE BALLROOM
     CREDIT:  '53 THE BLUE GARDENIA
     CREDIT:  '58 ST. LOUIS BLUES
     CREDIT:  '65 CAT BALLOU
------------------------------------------------------------------------------------------
COLLINS, JOAN
                            MAY 23,'33 AT LONDON, ENGLAND
     FATHER: WILLIAM COLLINS
     MOTHER: ELSA
     SISTER: JACQUELINE COLLINS
     BROTHER: WILLIAM COLLINS, JR.
     *** MARRIED:  '52 MAXWELL REED  (DIVORCED '57)
     *** MARRIED:  '63 ANTHONY NEWLEY, ACTOR, SINGER
     DAUGHTER:  '63 TARA NEWLEY
     SON:  '65 ANTHONY NEWLEY, JR.
     *** MARRIED:  '72 RON KASS, PRODUCER
     DAUGHTER:  '72 KATHARINE KASS
     ROMANCE: WARREN BEATTY
     MEMOIRS: PAST IMPERFECT
     TALENT: ACTRESS
     CREDIT:  '52 I BELIEVE IN YOU, DEBUT
     CREDIT:  '56 THE OPPOSITE SEX
     CREDIT:  '66 WARNING SHOT
     CREDIT:  '71 QUEST FOR LOVE
     CREDIT:  '73 TALES THAT WITNESS MADNESS
     CREDIT:  '78 THE STUD
```

```
----------------------------------------------------------------------------------------------------
COLMAN, RONALD          BORN:  RONALD CHARLES COLMAN
                               FEB 09,'91 AT RICHMOND, SURREY, ENGLAND  DIED IN '58
    FATHER: CHARLES COLMAN, SILK IMPORTER
    MOTHER: MARJORY READ FRASER
    *** MARRIED:  '19 THELMA RAYE, ACTRESS - VICTORIA MAUD  (DIVORCED '34)
    *** MARRIED:  '38 BENITA HUME, ACTRESS
    DAUGHTER:  '39 JULIET COLMAN
    ROMANCE: VILMA BANKY
    FRIEND: DAVID NIVEN
    FRIEND: WILLIAM POWELL
    ENEMY: SAMUEL GOLDWYN
    RESIDENCE: BEVERLY HILLS, CA
    RESIDENCE: SAN YSIDRO RANCH IN SANTA BARBARA COUNTY
    BIOGRAPHY:  '75 A VERY PRIVATE PERSON, BY JULIET COLMAN
    TALENT: ACTOR
    COMMENT: OWNED 85' KETCH 'DRAGON
    CREDIT:  '19 THE TOILERS
    CREDIT:  '25 STELLA DALLAS
    AA-NOM  ACTOR:  '29 BULLDOG DRUMMOND CONDEMNED
    CREDIT:  '35 A TALE OF TWO CITIES
    AA-NOM  ACTOR:  '42 RANDOM HARVEST
    AA-WIN  ACTOR:  '47 A DOUBLE LIFE
----------------------------------------------------------------------------------------------------
COMO, PERRY             BORN:  PIETRO 'PIERINO' COMO
                               MAY 18,'12 AT CANONSBURG, PA
    FATHER: PIETRO COMO
    MOTHER: LUCILLE TRAVAGLINI
    *** MARRIED:  '33 ROSELLE BELINE
    SON:  '40 RONALD COMO
    DAUGHTER-IN-LAW: MELANIE ELAINE ADAMS  (MARRIED '60)
    SON:  '46 DAVID COMO
    DAUGHTER:  '47 TERRI COMO
    GRANDDAUGHTER:  '61 MELANIE ROSELLE COMO
    FRIEND: VIC DAMONE
    RESIDENCE: JUPITER, FA
    RESIDENCE: SANDS POINT, LONG ISLAND, NY
    POSSESSION:  '76 15TH GOLD RECORD FOR 'AND I LOVE YOU SO'
    TALENT: SINGER
    CREDIT:  '44 SOMETHING FOR THE BOYS
    CREDIT:  '45 DOLL FACE
    CREDIT:  '46 IF I'M LUCKY
    CREDIT:  '48 WORDS AND MUSIC
----------------------------------------------------------------------------------------------------
CONNERY, SEAN           BORN:  THOMAS CONNERY
                               AUG 25,'30 AT EDINBURGH, SCOTLAND
    FATHER: JOSEPH CONNERY, TRUCK DRIVER
    MOTHER: EUPHAMIA
    *** MARRIED:  '62 DIANE CILENTO, ACTRESS  (DIVORCED '74)
    SON:  '63 JASON CONNERY
    DAUGHTER:  '64 GIOVANNA CONNERY
    *** MARRIED:  '74 MICHELINE ROQUEBRUNE
    *** MARRIED:  '75 MICHELINE ROQUEBRUNE, RE-MARRIED
    RESIDENCE: MARBELLA, SPAIN
    POSSESSION: TANTALLON FILM PRODUCTION CO.
    TALENT: ACTOR
    CREDIT:  '53 SOUTH PACIFIC, STAGE DEBUT
    CREDIT:  '57 HELL DRIVERS
```

```
CREDIT:   '62 JAMES BOND, SERIES
CREDIT:   '71 THE ANDERSON TAPES
CREDIT:   '76 ZARDOZ
```

CONNORS, CHUCK   BORN: KEVIN JOSEPH CONNORS
                                  APR 10,'21 AT BROOKLYN, NY
```
*** MARRIED:  '42 BETTY JANE RIDDLE  (DIVORCED '61)
SON:  '43 MICHAEL CONNORS
SON:  '44 JEFFREY CONNORS
SON:  '45 STEVEN CONNORS
SON:  '46 KEVIN CONNORS
*** MARRIED:  '63 KAMALA DEVI
RESIDENCE: PALM SPRINGS, CA
TALENT: BASEBALL PLAYER, ACTOR
CREDIT:   '52 PAT AND MIKE
CREDIT:   '54 NAKED ALIBI
CREDIT:   '62 GERONIMO
CREDIT:   '69 CAPTAIN NEMO AND THE UNDERWATER CITY
CREDIT:   '72 SOYLENT GREEN
```

CONTE, RICHARD   BORN: NICHOLAS CONTE
                                  MAR 24,'14 AT JERSEY CITY, NJ   DIED IN '75
```
FATHER: PASQUALE CONTE, BARBER
MOTHER: JULIA FINA
*** MARRIED:  '72 SHIRLEY COLLEEN KREIGER
SON: MARK CONTE
POSSESSION: CONTRACT AT 20TH CENTURY FOX
TALENT: ACTOR
CREDIT:   '43 GUADALCANAL DIARY
CREDIT:   '48 CALL NORTHSIDE 777
CREDIT:   '60 OCEAN'S 11
CREDIT:   '65 SYNANON
```

COOGAN, JACKIE   BORN: JOHN LESLIE COOGAN
                                  OCT 26,'14 AT LOS ANGELES, CA
```
FATHER: JOHN HENRY COOGAN
MOTHER: LILLIAN RITA DOLLIVER
*** MARRIED:  '36 BETTY GRABLE, ACTRESS  (DIVORCED '39)
*** MARRIED:  '40 FLOWER PARRY  (DIVORCED '43)
SON:  '42 JOHN ANTHONY COOGAN
*** MARRIED:  '46 ANN MCCORMACK  (DIVORCED '50)
DAUGHTER:  '48 JOANN DOLLIVER COOGAN
*** MARRIED:  '50 DOROTHEA ODETTA HANSON
*** MARRIED:  '53 DODIE LAMPHERE
DAUGHTER:  '54 LESLIE DIANE COOGAN
SON:  '67 CHRISTOPHER FENTON COOGAN
RESIDENCE: PALM SPRINGS, CA
TALENT: ACTOR
CREDIT:   '20 THE KID, DEBUT
CREDIT:   '21 OLIVER TWIST
CREDIT:   '31 HUCKLEBERRY FINN
CREDIT:   '52 OUTLAW WOMEN
CREDIT:   '69 MARLOWE
```

```
-----------------------------------------------------------------------------------------
COOPER, GARY          BORN:  FRANK JAMES COOPER
                             MAY 07,'01 AT HELENA, MT  DIED IN '61
    FATHER: CHARLES HENRY COOPER, STATE SUPREME CT. JUSTICE
    MOTHER: ALICE BRAZIER
    BROTHER: ARTHUR COOPER
    *** MARRIED:  '33 VERONICA BALFE, ACTRESS-SANDRA SHAW
    SPOUSE'S AUNT: DOLORES DEL RIO, ACTRESS
    DAUGHTER:  '37 MARIA VERONICA COOPER
    ROMANCE: LUPE VELEZ
    ROMANCE: CONTESSA DOROTHY DI FRASSO
    ROMANCE: CLARA BOW
    ROMANCE: EVELYN BRENT
    ROMANCE: PATRICIA NEAL
    ROMANCE: KAY WILLIAMS SPRECKELS
    FRIEND: ERNEST HEMINGWAY
    FRIEND: JACK BENNY
    FRIEND: JAMES STEWART
    RESIDENCE: HOLMBY HILLS, CA
    POSSESSION:  '27 CONTRACT AT PARAMOUNT PICTURES
    BIOGRAPHY:  '70 THE COOPER STORY, BY GEORGE CARPOZI, JR.
    TALENT: ACTOR, COWBOY
    AA-NOM  ACTOR:  '36 MR. DEEDS GOES TO TOWN
    AA-WIN  ACTOR:  '41 SERGEANT YORK
    AA-NOM  ACTOR:  '42 THE PRIDE OF THE YANKEES
    AA-NOM  ACTOR:  '43 FOR WHOM THE BELL TOLLS
    AA-WIN  ACTOR:  '52 HIGH NOON
    AA-SPECIAL AWARD:  '60 HONORARY AWARD FOR HIS MANY MEMORABLE SCREEN PERFORMANCES
-----------------------------------------------------------------------------------------
COOPER, GLADYS          BORN:  GLADYS CONSTANCE COOPER
                               DEC 18,'88 AT LEWISHAM, LONDON, ENGLAND  DIED IN '71
    FATHER: CHARLES F. COOPER, JOURNALIST
    MOTHER: MABEL BARNETT
    *** MARRIED:  '08 HERBERT J. BUCKMASTER  (DIVORCED '22)
    DAUGHTER:  '10 JOAN BUCKMASTER
    SON-IN-LAW: ROBERT MORLEY, ACTOR  (MARRIED '40)
    SON:  '15 JOHN BUCKMASTER, ACTOR
    *** MARRIED:  '28 SIR NEVILLE PEARSON  (DIVORCED '36)
    DAUGHTER:  '29 SALLY PEARSON
    SON-IN-LAW: ROBERT HARDY
    *** MARRIED:  '37 PHILIP MERIVALE, ACTOR  (DIED '46)
    STEP-SON: JOHN MERIVALE
    FRIEND: NIGEL BRUCE
    FRIEND: LAURENCE OLIVIER
    RESIDENCE: PACIFIC PALISADES, CA
    MEMOIRS: GLADYS
    TALENT: ACTRESS
    COMMENT: DAME COMMANDER, ORDER OF THE BRITISH EMPIRE
    CREDIT:  '17 MASKS AND FACES
    CREDIT:  '35 THE IRON DUKE
    AA-NOM  SUP.ACT:  '42 NOW, VOYAGER
    AA-NOM  SUP.ACT:  '43 THE SONG OF BERNADETTE
    CREDIT:  '58 SEPARATE TABLES
    AA-NOM  SUP.ACT:  '64 MY FAIR LADY
    CREDIT:  '69 A NICE GIRL LIKE ME
```

```
--------------------------------------------------------------------------------
COOPER, JACKIE          BORN:   JOHN COOPER, JR.
                                SEP 15,'22 AT LOS ANGELES, CA
    FATHER: JOHN COOPER
    MOTHER: MABEL LEONARD
    UNCLE: NORMAN TAUROG, DIRECTOR
    *** MARRIED:  '44 JUNE HORNE  (DIVORCED '49)
    SON:  '46 JOHN ANTHONY COOPER
    *** MARRIED:  '50 HILDY PARKS  (DIVORCED '50)
    *** MARRIED:  '54 BARBARA KRAUSE
    SON:  '56 RUSSELL COOPER
    DAUGHTER:  '57 JULIE COOPER
    DAUGHTER:  '58 CHRISTINA COOPER
    RESIDENCE: BEVERLY HILLS, CA
    TALENT: CHILD ACTOR,PRODUCER,DIRECTOR
    AA-NOM  ACTOR:  '30 SKIPPY
    CREDIT:  '34 TREASURE ISLAND
    CREDIT:  '41 HER FIRST BEAU
    CREDIT:  '61 EVERYTHING'S DUCKY
    CREDIT:  '71 THE LOVE MACHINE
--------------------------------------------------------------------------------
CORD, ALEX              BORN:   ALEXANDER VIESPI
                                AUG 03,'31 AT FLORAL PARK, NY
    *** MARRIED:  '68 JOANNA PETTET, ACTRESS
    SON:  '68 DAMION CORD
    TALENT: ACTOR
    CREDIT:  '65 SYNANON
    CREDIT:  '66 STAGECOACH
    CREDIT:  '70 THE BROTHERHOOD
    CREDIT:  '73 CHOSEN SURVIVORS
--------------------------------------------------------------------------------
COREY, WENDELL
                                MAR 20,'14 AT DRACUT, MS   DIED IN '68
    FATHER: MILTON ROTHWELL COREY, MINISTER
    MOTHER: JULIA REID MACKENNEY
    *** MARRIED:  '39 ALICE NEVIN WILEY
    SON:  '46 JONATHAN WENDELL COREY
    SON:  '47 RONALD COREY
    DAUGHTER: LUCY ROBIN COREY
    DAUGHTER: JENNIFER JULIA COREY
    DAUGHTER: BONNIE ALICE ELSIE COREY
    TALENT: ACTOR
    CREDIT:  '47 DESERT FURY, DEBUT IN 1947
    CREDIT:  '48 SORRY, WRONG NUMBER
    CREDIT:  '55 THE BIG KNIFE
    CREDIT:  '59 ALIAS JESSE JAMES
    CREDIT:  '69 YOUNG BILLY YOUNG
--------------------------------------------------------------------------------
CORRELL, CHARLES        BORN:   CHARLES JAMES CORRELL
                                FEB 03,'80 AT PEORIA, IL   DIED IN '72
    FATHER: JOSEPH BOLAND CORRELL
    MOTHER: ANNA FISS
    *** MARRIED:  '27 ALYCE MCLAUGHLIN
    DAUGHTER:  '40 DOROTHY ALYCE CORRELL
    DAUGHTER:  '42 BARBARA JOAN CORRELL
    SON:  '44 CHARLES JAMES CORRELL, JR.
    SON:  '46 JOHN JOSEPH CORRELL
    SON:  '48 RICHARD THOMAS CORRELL
```

FRIEND: JIM JORDAN
FRIEND: HARRY R. 'TIM' MOORE, KINGFISH
RESIDENCE: HOLMBY HILLS, CALIF.
MEMOIRS: '31 HERE THEY ARE
TALENT: ACTOR
CREDIT: '28 THE AMOS AND ANDY SHOW (RADIO), RAN 25 YEARS
CREDIT: '31 CHECK AND DOUBLE CHECK
CREDIT: '61 CALVIN AND THE COLONEL

CORTEZ, RICARDO   BORN: JACOB KRANZ
                             SEP 19,'99 AT VIENNA, AUSTRIA
MOTHER: SARAH
SISTER: HELEN KRANZ
BROTHER: STANLEY KRANZ, CAMERAMAN - STANLEY CORTEZ
*** MARRIED: ALMA RUBENS, ACTRESS (DIED '31)
*** MARRIED: CHRISTINE CONNIFF LEE
*** MARRIED: '50 MARGARETTE BELL
DAUGHTER: '51 HELEN CORTEZ
TALENT: ACTOR, DIRECTOR
CREDIT: '23 SIXTY CENTS AN HOUR
CREDIT: '32 THIRTEEN WOMEN
CREDIT: '39 FREE, BLONDE AND 21
CREDIT: '40 MAKE YOUR OWN BED
CREDIT: '41 BLACKMAIL

COSBY, BILL
                             JUL 12,'37 AT PHILADELPHIA, PA
FATHER: WILLIAM COSBY
MOTHER: ANNA COSBY
*** MARRIED: '64 CAMILLE HANKS
DAUGHTER: '65 ERIKE RANEE COSBY
DAUGHTER: '66 ERINN CHARLENE COSBY
SON: '70 ENNIS WILLIAM COSBY
DAUGHTER: '73 ENSA COSBY
DAUGHTER: '76 EVIN HARRAH COSBY
RESIDENCE: BEVERLY HILLS, CA
TALENT: ACTOR, COMEDIAN
CREDIT: HICKEY AND BOGGS
CREDIT: LET'S DO IT AGAIN
CREDIT: UPTOWN SATURDAY NIGHT

COSTELLO, DOLORES
                             SEP 17,'06 AT PITTSBURGH, PA
FATHER: MAURICE COSTELLO, ACTOR
MOTHER: RUTH REEVES, ACTRESS
SISTER: HELENE COSTELLO, ACTRESS
BROTHER-IN-LAW: LOVELL SHERMAN, ACTOR
*** MARRIED: '28 JOHN BARRYMORE, ACTOR (DIVORCED '35)
BROTHER-IN-LAW: LIONEL BARRYMORE, ACTOR
FATHER-IN-LAW: MAURICE BARRYMORE, AUTHOR
MOTHER-IN-LAW: GEORGIANA DREW
SISTER-IN-LAW: ETHEL BARRYMORE, ACTRESS
STEP-DAUGHTER: DIANA BARRYMORE, ACTRESS
SON: '32 JOHN BARRYMORE, JR.
DAUGHTER: '34 DOLORES ETHEL MAE BARRYMORE
*** MARRIED: '39 DR. JOHN VRUWINK (DIVORCED '51)
RESIDENCE: DEL MAR, CA
TALENT: ACTRESS

```
CREDIT:   '25 THE SEA BEAST
CREDIT:   '29 NOAH'S ARK
CREDIT:   '31 EXPENSIVE WOMAN
CREDIT:   '42 THE MAGNIFICENT AMBERSONS
```

COSTELLO, LOU   BORN: LOUIS FRANCIS CRISTILLO
```
                              MAR 06,'08 AT PATERSON, NJ   DIED IN '59
   FATHER: SEBASTIAN CRISTILLO
   MOTHER: HELEN REGE
   SISTER: MARIE THERESA CRISTILLO
   BROTHER: ANTHONY SEBASTIAN CRISTILLO
   *** MARRIED:  '34 ANNE BATTLER
   SON:  '42 LOU COSTELLO, JR., DROWNED IN BACKYARD POOL  (DIED '43)
   DAUGHTER: PATRICIA COSTELLO
   DAUGHTER: CAROLE LOU COSTELLO
   DAUGHTER: CHRISTINE COSTELLO
   PARTNER: BUD ABBOTT
   RESIDENCE: SAN FERNANDO VALLEY, CA
   POSSESSION: RACE HORSES
   POSSESSION: RANCH IN CHATSWORTH, CA
   TALENT: ACTOR
   COMMENT: WAS SUED IN 1958 BY ABBOTT FOR MONIES CLAIMED DUE
   CREDIT:  '40 ONE NIGHT IN THE TROPICS
   CREDIT:  '41 BUCK PRIVATES
   CREDIT:  '42 RIO RITA
   CREDIT:  '47 BUCK PRIVATES COME HOME
   CREDIT:  '59 THE 30' BRIDE OF CANDY ROCK, APPEARED WITHOUT ABBOTT
```

COTTEN, JOSEPH   BORN: JOSEPH CHESIRE COTTON
```
                              MAY 13,'05 AT PETERSBURG, VA
   FATHER: JOSEPH COTTON, SR., POST OFFICE SUPERINTENDENT
   MOTHER: SALLY WILLSON
   *** MARRIED:  '31 LENORE KIP  (DIED '60)
   STEP-DAUGHTER: JUDITH KIP COTTEN
   SON-IN-LAW: JAMES D. YOUNG
   *** MARRIED:  '60 PATRICIA MEDINA, ACTRESS
   RESIDENCE: LOS ANGELES, CA
   POSSESSION:  '50 CONTRACT AT 20TH CENTURY FOX
   POSSESSION:  '56 FORDYCE PRODUCTIONS
   POSSESSION: COLLECTION OF COMMEDIA DELL' ARTE ART
   TALENT: ACTOR
   CREDIT:  '42 THE MAGNIFICENT AMBERSONS
   CREDIT:  '53 NIAGARA
   CREDIT:  '55 THE BOTTOM OF THE BOTTLE
   CREDIT:  '69 TORA! TORA! TORA!
   CREDIT:  '72 BARON BLOOD
```

COURTENAY, TOM   BORN: THOMAS DANIEL COURTENAY
```
                              MAR 25,'37 AT HULL, YORKSHIRE, ENGLAND
   FATHER: THOMAS HENRY COURTENAY
   MOTHER: ANNIE ELIZA QUEST
   SISTER: --
   *** MARRIED:  '73 CHERYL KENNEDY, ACTRESS
   RESIDENCE: LONDON, ENGLAND
   TALENT: ACTOR
   CREDIT:  '60 MEMBER OF OLD VIC COMPANY
   CREDIT:  '62 LONELINESS OF THE LONG DISTANCE RUNNER
   AA-NOM  SUP.ACT:  '65 DOCTOR ZHIVAGO
```

CREDIT: '65 KING RAT
CREDIT: '68 A DANDY IN ASPIC

COWARD, NOEL
BORN: NOEL PIERCE COWARD
                          DEC 16,'99 AT TEDDINGTON, ENGLAND   DIED IN '73
FATHER: ARTHUR SABIN COWARD
MOTHER: VIOLET VEITCH
FRIEND: JEFFREY HOLMSDALE, COMPANION
RESIDENCE: JAMAICA, WEST INDIES
MEMOIRS: PRESENT INDICATIVE
MEMOIRS: FUTURE INDEFINITE
TALENT: PLAYRIGHT,ACTOR,PRODUCER, ENTERTAINER
CREDIT: '18 HEARTS OF THE WORLD
CREDIT: '25 PRIVATE LIVES
CREDIT: '33 DESIGN FOR LIVING
AA-SPECIAL AWARD: '42 SPECIAL CERTIFICATE HONORING 'IN WHICH WE SERVE'-WAR FILM
CREDIT: '45 BLITHE SPIRIT
CREDIT: '60 OUR MAN IN HAVANA

CRABBE, BUSTER
BORN: CLARENCE LINDEN 'LARRY' CRABBE
                          FEB 07,'07 AT OAKLAND, CA
*** MARRIED: '33 ADAH HELD
DAUGHTER: CAREN CRABBE
DAUGHTER: SUSAN CRABBE
SON: CULLEN 'CUFFY' CRABBE
FRIEND: EDWARD SMALL, PRODUCER
RESIDENCE: SCOTTSDALE, ARIZONA
POSSESSION: OLYMPIC GAMES GOLD MEDAL FOR SWIMMING - 1932
TALENT: ACTOR
COMMENT: EDUCATED AND SPENT EARLY YEARS IN HAWAII
COMMENT: PUBLICITY MAN FOR CASCADE POOL
CREDIT: '33 KING OF THE JUNGLE, DEBUT
CREDIT: '39 BUCK ROGERS
CREDIT: '59 GUNFIGHTERS OF ABILENE
CREDIT: '65 ARIZONA RAIDERS
CREDIT: '75 BOOK ON PHYSICAL FITNESS - 'ENERGISTICS'

CRAIN, JEANNE
                          MAY 25,'25 AT BARSTOW, CA
FATHER: GEORGE A. CRAIN
MOTHER: LORETTA CARR
SISTER: RITA CRAIN
*** MARRIED: '45 PAUL BRINKMAN
SON: '47 PAUL FREDERICK BRINKMAN
SON: '48 MICHAEL ANTHONY BRINKMAN
SON: '50 CHRISTOPHER BRINKMAN
DAUGHTER: '52 JEANINE BRINKMAN
DAUGHTER: '57 LISABETTE BRINKMAN
DAUGHTER: '60 MARIA BRINKMAN
SON: '65 TIMOTHY BRINKMAN
RESIDENCE: BEVERLY HILLS, CA
POSSESSION: '51 COLLECTION OF MOVIE MAGAZINES
TALENT: ACTRESS
COMMENT: MODEL - MISS LONG BEACH, CALIF IN 1941
CREDIT: '43 THE GANG'S ALL HERE
AA-NOM ACTRESS: '49 PINKY
CREDIT: '54 DUEL IN THE JUNGLE
CREDIT: '67 HOT RODS TO HELL

```
        CREDIT:   '72 SKYJACKED
------------------------------------------------------------------------------
CRAWFORD, BRODERICK        BORN:   WILLIAM B. PENDERGAST
                                   DEC 09,'11 AT PHILADELPHIA, PA
        GRANDFATHER: WILLIAM E. BRODERICK, SINGER
        FATHER: LESTER PENDERGAST, ACTOR - LESTER CRAWFORD  (DIED '62)
        MOTHER: HELEN BRODERICK, ACTRESS  (DIED '56)
        *** MARRIED:  '40 KAY GRIFFITH, SINGER  (DIVORCED '61)
        ADOPTED SON: KIM CRAWFORD
        SON:  '48 CHRISTOPHER CRAWFORD
        SON:  '51 KELLY CRAWFORD
        *** MARRIED:  '62 JOAN TABOR, ACTRESS  (DIVORCED '67)
        STEP-DAUGHTER: LAUREN GOLD
        *** MARRIED:  '73 MARY ALICE MITCHELL
        RESIDENCE: TUCSON, ARIZONA
        POSSESSION: CONTRACT AT GOLDWYN STUDIO
        TALENT: ACTOR
        CREDIT:  '37 WOMAN CHASES MAN
        CREDIT:  '48 THE TIME OF YOUR LIFE
        AA-WIN  ACTOR:  '49 ALL THE KING'S MEN
        CREDIT:  '54 NIGHT PEOPLE
------------------------------------------------------------------------------
CRAWFORD, JOAN        BORN:   LUCILLE LESUEUR
                              MAR 23,'04 AT SAN ANTONIO, TX  DIED IN '77
        FATHER: THOMAS LESUEUR
        MOTHER: ANNA JOHNSON
        STEP-FATHER: HENRY CASSIN, THEATRE OWNER
        BROTHER: HAL LESUEUR
        *** MARRIED:  '29 DOUGLAS FAIRBANKS, JR.  (DIVORCED '33)
        MOTHER-IN-LAW: ELIZABETH SULLY
        MOTHER-IN-LAW: MARY PICKFORD, ACTRESS
        *** MARRIED:  '35 FRANCHOT TONE  (DIVORCED '39)
        *** MARRIED:  '42 PHILLIP TERRY  (DIVORCED '45)
        ADOPTED SON: CHRISTOPHER TERRY
        *** MARRIED:  '55 ALFRED N. STEELE, CHAIRMAN-PEPSI COLA CO.   (DIED '59)
        ADOPTED DAUGHTER: CHRISTINA CRAWFORD
        ADOPTED DAUGHTER: CATHARINE CRAWFORD, TWIN
        ADOPTED DAUGHTER: CYNTHIA CRAWFORD, TWIN
        ROMANCE: CLARK GABLE
        ROMANCE: MICHAEL CUDAHY
        FRIEND: WILLIAN HAINES, ACTOR
        FRIEND: JERRY ASHER
        RESIDENCE: BRENTWOOD, CA
        RESIDENCE: NYC
        POSSESSION: COLLECTION OF DOLLS
        MEMOIRS:  '62 A PORTRAIT OF JOAN
        MEMOIRS:  '72 MY WAY OF LIFE
        BIOGRAPHY:  '78 MOMMIE DEAREST, BY CHRISTINA CRAWFORD
        TALENT: ACTRESS, EXECUTIVE
        CREDIT:  '26 TRAMP, TRAMP, TRAMP
        CREDIT:  '32 GRAND HOTEL
        AA-WIN  ACTRESS:  '45 MILDRED PIERCE
        AA-NOM  ACTRESS:  '47 POSSESSED
        AA-NOM  ACTRESS:  '52 SUDDEN FEAR
        CREDIT:  '62 WHAT EVER HAPPENED TO BABY JANE?
```

CRENNA, RICHARD
                              NOV 30,'27 AT LOS ANGELES, CA
FATHER: DOMENICK CRENNA
MOTHER: EDITH POLETTE
*** MARRIED: '50 PENNI SMITH
DAUGHTER: '52 SEANA CRENNA
SON: '59 RICHARD CRENNA, JR.
DAUGHTER: '65 MARIA CRENNA
POSSESSION: PENDICK ENTERPRISES
TALENT: ACTOR
CREDIT: '52 IT GROWS ON TREES
CREDIT: '56 OVER EXPOSED
CREDIT: '67 WAIT UNTIL DARK
CREDIT: '71 DOCTORS' WIVES
CREDIT: '73 THE MAN CALLED NOON

CRISTAL, LINDA.   BORN: MARTA VICTORIA MOYA BURGES
                          FEB 24,'36 AT BUENOS AIRES, ARGENTINA
BROTHER: MIGUEL BURGES
*** MARRIED: '53 --, TEENAGE MARRIAGE (ANNULLED '53)
*** MARRIED: '58 ROBERT CHAMPION (DIVORCED '59)
BROTHER-IN-LAW: GOWER CHAMPION
*** MARRIED: '60 YALE WEXLER
SON: '62 GREGORY SIMON WEXLER
*** MARRIED: '72 CHARLES COLLINS
POSSESSION: '56 CONTRACT AT UNIVERSAL STUDIOS
POSSESSION: '70 COLLECTION OF AMERICAN INDIAN JEWELRY
TALENT: ACTRESS
CREDIT: '56 COMANCHE
CREDIT: '58 THE PERFECT FURLOUGH
CREDIT: '59 CRY TOUGH
CREDIT: '60 THE ALAMO
CREDIT: '68 PANIC IN THE CITY

CRONYN, HUME   BORN: HUME BLAKE, JR.
                        JUL 18,'11 AT LONDON, ONTARIO CANADA
FATHER: HUME BLAKE
MOTHER: FRANCES AMELIA LABATT
*** MARRIED: '42 JESSICA TANDY, ACTRESS
STEP-DAUGHTER: SUSAN HAWKINS
SON: '43 CHRISTOPHER CRONYN
DAUGHTER: '45 TANDY CRONYN
RESIDENCE: NYC
POSSESSION: '32 MEMBER CANADIAN OLYMPIC BOXING TEAM
POSSESSION: '54 ISLAND IN THE BAHAMAS
TALENT: ACTOR, WRITER, DIRECTOR
AA-NOM SUP.ACT: '44 THE SEVENTH CROSS
CREDIT: '47 THE BEGINNING OR THE END
CREDIT: '51 PEOPLE WILL TALK
CREDIT: '56 CROWDED PARADISE
CREDIT: '60 SUNRISE AT CAMPOBELLO
CREDIT: '69 GAILY GAILY

```
-------------------------------------------------------------------------------------------------------
CROSBY, BING          BORN:  HARRY LILLIS CROSBY
                             MAY 02,'04 AT TACOMA, WA.  DIED IN '77
    GRANDFATHER: DENNIS HARRIGAN
    FATHER: HARRY LOWE CROSBY
    MOTHER: CATHERINE H. HARRIGAN
    SISTER: CATHERINE CROSBY
    SISTER: MARY ROSE CROSBY
    BROTHER: BOB CROSBY, PERFORMER
    BROTHER: EVERETT CROSBY
    BROTHER: LAWRENCE CROSBY
    BROTHER: THEODORE CROSBY
    SISTER-IN-LAW: FLORENCE GEORGE, SINGER
    NEPHEW: CHRISTOPHER CROSBY
    *** MARRIED:  '30 WILMA W. WYATT, ACTRESS - DIXIE LEE  (DIED '52)
    SON:  '33 GARY EVAN CROSBY
    SON:  '34 PHILIP LANG CROSBY
    SON:  '35 DENNIS MICHAEL CROSBY
    SON:  '37 HOWARD LINDSAY CROSBY
    *** MARRIED:  '57 KATHRYN GRANT, AKA-OLIVE GRANDSTAFF
    DAUGHTER:  '59 MARY FRANCES CROSBY
    SON:  '60 HARRY LILLIS CROSBY, III
    SON:  '61 NATHANIEL PATRICK CROSBY
    RESIDENCE: HOLMBY HILLS, CA
    POSSESSION:  '53 RANCH IN ARGENTINA
    POSSESSION:  '54 CATTLE RANCH IN NEVADA
    MEMOIRS:  '53 CALL ME LUCKY
    TALENT: SINGER,ACTOR
    CREDIT:  '30 THE KING OF JAZZ, DEBUT
    CREDIT:  '33 GOING HOLLYWOOD
    AA-WIN  ACTOR:  '44 GOING MY WAY
    AA-NOM  ACTOR:  '45 THE BELLS OF ST. MARY'S
    AA-NOM  ACTOR:  '54 THE COUNTRY GIRL
    CREDIT:  '62 THE ROAD TO HONG KONG
-------------------------------------------------------------------------------------------------------
CUGAT, XAVIER         BORN:  FRANCISCO DE ASIS JAVIER CUGAT MINGALL DE BRU Y DEULOFEO
                             JAN 01,'00 AT BARCELONA, SPAIN
    FATHER: JUAN CUGAT DE BRU
    MOTHER: MINGALL DEULOFEO
    SISTER: REGINA CUGAT
    BROTHER: FRANCIS CUGAT, ART DIRECTOR
    BROTHER: ALBERT CUGAT
    BROTHER: HENRY CUGAT
    NIECE: MARIA MARGARITA BOLADO, ACTRESS - MARGO
    *** MARRIED:  '29 CARMEN CASTILLO, SINGER
    *** MARRIED:  '47 LORRAINE ALLEN
    *** MARRIED:  '50 ABBE LANE
    *** MARRIED:  '66 CHARO
    POSSESSION: CASA CUGAT RESTAURANT IN LOS ANGELES
    MEMOIRS:  '48 RUMBA IS MY LIFE
    TALENT: MUSICIAN, CARICATURIST, ACTOR
    CREDIT:  '42 YOU WERE NEVER LOVELIER
    CREDIT:  '44 TWO GIRLS AND A SAILOR
    CREDIT:  '48 A DATE WITH JUDY
    CREDIT:  '49 NEPTUNE'S DAUGHTER
    CREDIT:  '55 CHICAGO SYNDICATE
```

CULP, ROBERT

AUG 16,'30 AT BERKELEY, CA
```
*** MARRIED: NANCY WILNER  (DIVORCED '67)
SON:  '61 JOSHUA CULP
SON:  '62 JASON CULP
SON:  '63 JOSEPH CULP
DAUGHTER:  '64 RACHEL CULP
*** MARRIED:  '67 FRANCE NUYEN, ACTRESS  (DIVORCED '69)
*** MARRIED:  '71 SHEILA SULLIVAN
TALENT: ACTOR,WRITER, DIRECTOR
CREDIT:  '62 PT 109, DEBUT
CREDIT:  '64 SUNDAY IN NEW YORK
CREDIT:  '69 BOB & CAROL & TED & ALICE
CREDIT:  '71 HANNIE CAULDER
CREDIT:  '72 HICKEY AND BOGGS
```

CUMMINGS, ROBERT   BORN: ROBERT ORVILLE CUMMINGS

JUN 09,'10 AT JOPLIN, MR
```
FATHER: CHARLES CUMMINGS, DOCTOR
MOTHER: RUTH A. KRAFT, MINISTER
*** MARRIED: EDMA EMMA MYERS
*** MARRIED:  '33 VIVIENNE AUDREY JANIS  (DIVORCED '43)
*** MARRIED:  '45 MARY ELLIOTT  (DIVORCED '69)
DAUGHTER:  '46 LAUREL CUMMINGS
DAUGHTER:  '48 SHARON PATRICIA CUMMINGS
DAUGHTER:  '51 MARY MELINDA CUMMINGS
DAUGHTER:  '55 MICHELLE HELENE CUMMINGS
SON:  '55 ROBERT RICHARD CUMMINGS
SON:  '57 ANTHONY CUMMINGS
SON:  '59 CHARLES CLARENCE CUMMINGS
*** MARRIED:  '71 REGINA YOUNG
RESIDENCE: BEVERLY HILLS, CA
POSSESSION:  '35 CONTRACT AT PARAMOUNT STUDIOS
TALENT: ACTOR, DIRECTOR
COMMENT: EARLY STAGE NAME-BRICE HUTCHENS
CREDIT:  '36 HOLLYWOOD BOULEVARD
CREDIT:  '41 THE DEVIL AND MISS JONES
CREDIT:  '48 SLEEP, MY LOVE
CREDIT:  '54 DIAL M FOR MURDER
CREDIT:  '66 STAGECOACH
```

CURTIS, TONY   BORN: BERNARD SCHWARTZ

JUN 01,'25 AT NYC
```
FATHER: MONO SCHWARTZ, ACTOR
BROTHER: ROBERT SCHWARTZ
*** MARRIED:  '51 JANET LEIGH  (DIVORCED '63)
DAUGHTER:  '56 KELLY LEE CURTIS
DAUGHTER:  '58 JAMIE LEIGH CURTIS
*** MARRIED:  '64 CHRISTINE KAUFMANN, ACTRESS  (DIVORCED '67)
DAUGHTER:  '64 ALEXANDRA CURTIS
DAUGHTER:  '66 ALLEGRA CURTIS
*** MARRIED:  '68 LESLIE ALLEN
SON:  '70 NICHOLAS CURTIS
SON:  '73 BENJAMIN CURTIS
RESIDENCE: BEVERLY HILLS, CA
POSSESSION:  '50 CONTRACT AT UNIVERSAL PICTURES
TALENT: ACTOR, AUTHOR
```

CREDIT: '48 CRISS CROSS
CREDIT: '53 HOUDINI
CREDIT: '56 TRAPEZE
AA-NOM ACTOR: '58 THE DEFIANT ONES
CREDIT: '60 SPARTACUS
CREDIT: '65 THE GREAT RACE
CREDIT: '68 THE BOSTON STRANGLER
CREDIT: '77 KID ANDREW CODY AND JULIE SPARROW - NOVEL

DAHL, ARLENE   BORN: ARLENE CAROL DAHL
                                  AUG 11,'24 AT MINNEAPOLIS, MN
    FATHER: RUDOLPH DAHL
    MOTHER: IDELLE SWAN
    *** MARRIED: '51 LEX BARKER (DIVORCED '52)
    STEP-DAUGHTER: LYNNE ALEXANDER BARKER
    STEP-SON: ALEXANDER BARKER
    *** MARRIED: '54 FERNANDO LAMAS (DIVORCED '60)
    SON: '58 LORENZO FERNANDO LAMAS
    *** MARRIED: '60 CHRISTIAN HOLMES, III (DIVORCED '64)
    DAUGHTER: '61 CAROL HOLMES
    *** MARRIED: '65 ALEXIS LICHINE (DIVORCED '67)
    *** MARRIED: '69 ROUSEVELLE W. SCHAUM
    SON: '70 ROUSEVELLE SCHAUM
    TALENT: ACTRESS, DESIGNER, AUTHOR OF 12 BEAUTY BOOKS
    CREDIT: '47 MY WILD IRISH ROSE, DEBUT
    CREDIT: '55 IT'S A WOMAN'S WORLD
    CREDIT: '59 JOURNEY TO THE CENTER OF THE EARTH
    CREDIT: '64 KISSES FOR MY PRESIDENT
    CREDIT: '70 THE LAND RAIDERS

DAILEY, DAN   BORN: DAN DAILEY, JR.
                                 DEC 14,'17 AT NYC   DIED IN '78
    *** MARRIED: ESTHER RODIER (DIVORCED '41)
    *** MARRIED: '42 ELIZABETH HOFERT (DIVORCED '51)
    SON: '47 DAN DAILEY, 3RD (SUICIDE '75)
    *** MARRIED: '54 GWEN CARTER (DIVORCED '61)
    STEP-DAUGHTER: DONNA O'CONNOR
    *** MARRIED: '68 NORA WARNER
    POSSESSION: '40 CONTRACT AT M-G-M
    TALENT: ACTOR
    CREDIT: '40 THE MORTAL STORM
    CREDIT: '47 MOTHER WORE TIGHTS
    AA-NOM ACTOR: '48 WHEN MY BABY SMILES AT ME
    CREDIT: '54 THERE'S NO BUSINESS LIKE SHOW BUSINESS

DALY, JAMES   BORN: JAMES FIRMAN DALY
                                 OCT 23,'18 AT WISCONSIN RAPIDS, WI DIED IN '78
    FATHER: PERCIFER DALY, FUEL MERCHANT
    MOTHER: DOROTHY HOGAN MULLEN, CIA EMPLOYEE
    SISTER: MARY ELLEN DALY, CAPTAIN-US AIR FORCE
    SISTER: CYNTHIA ANN DALY, SPEECH PATHOLOGIST
    BROTHER: DAVID DALY, FBI AGENT
    *** MARRIED: '42 HOPE NEWELL
    DAUGHTER: '43 PEGEEN DALY
    DAUGHTER: '44 TYNE DALY, ACTRESS
    SON-IN-LAW: GEORGE STANFORD BROWN, ACTOR (MARRIED)
    DAUGHTER: '45 GLYNN DALY
    SON: '46 TIMOTHY DALY
    RESIDENCE: SUFFERN, NY
    TALENT: ACTOR
    CREDIT: '57 THE YOUNG STRANGER
    CREDIT: '60 I AIM AT THE STARS
    CREDIT: '68 PLANET OF THE APES
    CREDIT: '72 WILD IN THE SKY
    CREDIT: THE COURT MARTIAL OF BILLY MITCHELL

```
-------------------------------------------------------------------------------
DAMITA, LILI          BORN:  LILLIANE CARRE DAMITA
                             JUL 20,'07 AT PARIS, FRANCE
     FATHER: PIERRE DAMITA  (DIED '15)
     MOTHER: ISABELLE
     *** MARRIED:  '36 ERROL FLYNN, ACTOR  (DIVORCED '42)
     FATHER-IN-LAW: THEODORE THOMSON FLYNN
     MOTHER-IN-LAW: MARELLE YOUNG
     SON:  '41 SEAN LESLIE FLYNN, ACTOR, PHOTOGRAPHER
     *** MARRIED:  '62 ALLEN LOOMIS
     ROMANCE: PRINCE LOUIS VON HOHENZOLLERN
     ROMANCE: SIDNEY A. SMITH, FINANCIER
     RESIDENCE: MIAMI BEACH,FL
     TALENT: ACTRESS
     CREDIT:  '28 THE RESCUE
     CREDIT:  '29 THE BRIDGE OF SAN LUIS REY
     CREDIT:  '30 THE COCK-EYED WORLD
     CREDIT:  '32 THIS IS THE NIGHT
     CREDIT:  '33 GOLDIE GETS ALONG
     CREDIT:  '35 THE FRISCO KID
-------------------------------------------------------------------------------
DAMONE, VIC           BORN:  VITO FARINOLA
                             JUN 12,'28 AT BROOKLYN, NY
     FATHER: ROCCO FARINOLA
     MOTHER: MAMIE DAMONE, PIANO AND VOICE TEACHER
     SISTER: PEARL FARINOLA
     SISTER: TERESA FARINOLA
     SISTER: ELAINE FARINOLA
     SISTER: SANDRA FARINOLA
     COUSIN: DORETTA MORROW, ACTRESS, SINGER
     *** MARRIED:  '54 PIER ANGELI  (DIVORCED '59)
     SISTER-IN-LAW: MARISA PAVAN, ACTRESS
     SON:  '55 PERRY ROCCO LUIGI DAMONE
     *** MARRIED:  '63 JUDITH RAWLINGS, ACTRESS-SUICIDE 1974  (DIVORCED)
     DAUGHTER:  '65 VICTORIA CATHERINE DAMONE
     DAUGHTER:  '66 ANDREA DAMONE
     DAUGHTER:  '68 DANIELLA DAMONE
     *** MARRIED:  '74 BECKY ANN JONES
     TALENT: SINGER,ACTOR
     CREDIT:  '51 RICH, YOUNG AND PRETTY
     CREDIT:  '51 THE STRIP
     CREDIT:  '55 DEEP IN MY HEART
     CREDIT:  '55  KISMET
     CREDIT:  '60 HELL TO ETERNITY
-------------------------------------------------------------------------------
DANIELS, BEBE         BORN:  VIRGINIA DANIELS
                             JAN 14,'01 AT DALLAS,TX  DIED IN '71
     FATHER: MELVILLE DANIELS, ACTOR
     MOTHER: PHYLLIS GRIFFIN
     *** MARRIED:  '30 BEN LYON, ACTOR
     DAUGHTER: BARBARA LYON
     ROMANCE: JACK PICKFORD
     ROMANCE: HAROLD LLOYD
     FRIEND: JACK DEMPSEY
     FRIEND: BILL TILDEN
     FRIEND: ROD LA ROCQUE
     RESIDENCE: LONDON, ENGLAND
     TALENT: ACTRESS,SINGER
```

```
CREDIT:   '08 A COMMON ENEMY, DEBUT IN 1908
CREDIT:   '16 LONESOME LUKE, SERIES
CREDIT:   '26 MRS. BREWSTER'S MILLIONS
CREDIT:   '40 HI, GANG!
CREDIT:   '55 THE LYONS IN PARIS
```

DARBY, KIM   BORN: DEBORAH ELIAS ZERBY
                               JUL 08,'48 AT NORTH HOLLYWOOD, CA
```
   GRANDFATHER: CLYDE ZERBY
   MOTHER: WEIERE, DANCER
   *** MARRIED:  '67 JAMES STACY, ACTOR  (DIVORCED '69)
   DAUGHTER:  '68 HEATHER STACY
   *** MARRIED:  '70 JAMES WESTMORELAND  (DIVORCED)
   ROMANCE: JOHN CARSON, ACTOR
   ROMANCE: ANDREW STEVENS, ACTOR, MUSICIAN
   RESIDENCE: STUDIO CITY, CA
   TALENT: ACTRESS
   CREDIT:   '65 BUS RILEY'S BACK IN TOWN
   CREDIT:   '69 TRUE GRIT
   CREDIT:   '71 THE GRISSOM GANG
   CREDIT:   '77 THE ONE AND ONLY
```

DARIN, BOBBY   BORN: ROBERT WALDEN CASSOTTO
                                 MAY 14,'36 AT NYC   DIED IN '73
```
   FATHER: SAVERIO CASSOTTO  (DIED '36)
   MOTHER: VIVIAN FERNE WALDEN
   SISTER: VANINA CASSOTTO
   *** MARRIED:  '60 SANDRA DEE  (DIVORCED '67)
   SON:  '61 DODD MITCHELL CASSOTTO DARIN
   *** MARRIED:  '73 AUDREY YEAGER
   TALENT: ACTOR-SINGER
   CREDIT:   '60 COME SEPTEMBER
   AA-NOM  SUP.ACT:  '63 CAPTAIN NEWMAN, M.D.
   CREDIT:   '65 THE FUNNY FEELING
   CREDIT:   '67 STRANGER IN THE HOUSE
   CREDIT:   '69 THE HAPPY ENDING
```

DARNELL, LINDA   BORN: MONETTA ELOYSE DARNELL
                                   OCT 16,'21 AT DALLAS, TX   DIED IN '65
```
   FATHER: CALVIN ROY DARNELL, POST OFFICE CLERK  (DIED '77)
   MOTHER: MARGARET PEARL BROWN
   SISTER: UNDEEN DARNELL
   SISTER: MONTE MALOYA DARNELL
   *** MARRIED:  '43 J. PEVERELL MARLEY, CAMERAMAN  (DIVORCED '51)
   ADOPTED DAUGHTER: CHARLOTTE MILDRED MARLEY
   *** MARRIED:  '54 PHILIP LIEBMAN  (DIVORCED '55)
   *** MARRIED:  '57 MERLE ROBERTSON  (DIVORCED '63)
   TALENT: ACTRESS
   CREDIT:   '39 HOTEL FOR WOMEN
   CREDIT:   '41 BLOOD AND SAND
   CREDIT:   '47 FOREVER AMBER
   CREDIT:   '53 SECOND CHANCE
   CREDIT:   '65 BLACK SPURS
```

```
--------------------------------------------------------------------------------
DARREN, JAMES          BORN:  JAMES WILLIAM ERCOLANI
                              JUN 08,'36 AT PHILADELPIA, PA
   FATHER: WILLIAM ERCOLANI
   MOTHER: VIRGINIA DI JOSIE
   BROTHER: JOHN DARREN
   *** MARRIED:  '54 GLORIA TERLITZKY, MODEL  (DIVORCED '59)
   SON:  '56 JAMES DARREN, JR.
   *** MARRIED:  '60 EVY NORLUND LARSEN, MODEL
   SON:  '63 CHRISTIAN DARREN
   SON:  '64 ANTHONY DARREN
   POSSESSION:  '63 CONTRACT AT UNIVERSAL PICTURES
   TALENT: ACTOR
   CREDIT:  '56 RUMBLE ON THE DOCKS
   CREDIT:  '59 GIDGET
   CREDIT:  '61 THE GUNS OF NAVARONE
   CREDIT:  '63 DIAMONDHEAD
   CREDIT:  '64 FOR THOSE WHO THINK YOUNG
--------------------------------------------------------------------------------
DASSIN, JULES
                              DEC 18,'11 AT MIDDLETOWN,CN
   FATHER: SAMUEL DASSIN
   MOTHER: BERTHE VOGEL
   *** MARRIED:  '33 BEATRICE LAUNER  (DIVORCED '62)
   DAUGHTER:  '34 RICHELLE DASSIN
   DAUGHTER:  '35 JULIE DASSIN
   SON:  '36 JOSEPH DASSIN
   *** MARRIED:  '66 MELINA MERCOURI, ACTRESS
   TALENT: ACTOR,WRITER,DIRECTOR
   CREDIT:  '44 THE CANTERVILLE GHOST
   CREDIT:  '54 RIFIFI
   AA-NOM  DIRECTOR:  '60 NEVER ON SUNDAY
   CREDIT:  '66 10:30 P.M. SUMMER EVENING
   CREDIT:  '70 PROMISE AT DAWN
   CREDIT:  '78 A DREAM OF PASSION
--------------------------------------------------------------------------------
DAVIES, MARION         BORN:  MARION CECILIA DOURAS
                              JAN 03,'97 AT BROOKLYN,NY  DIED IN '61
   FATHER: BERNARD J. DOURAS
   MOTHER: ROSE REILLY
   SISTER: ETHEL DOURAS
   SISTER: IRENE DOURAS
   SISTER: ROSE MARIE DOURAS
   BROTHER: CHARLES DOURAS
   NEPHEW: CHARLES LEDERER, WRITER
   NEPHEW: ARTHUR LAKE, ACTOR
   *** MARRIED:  '51 HORACE M. BROWN, STUNTMAN, MERCHANT MARINE CAPT
   ROMANCE: ANGIER BIDDLE DUKE
   ROMANCE: PAUL BLOCK
   ROMANCE: GENE BUCK
   ROMANCE: WM. RANDOLPH HEARST
   FRIEND: IRVING THALBERG
   FRIEND: CONSTANCE TALMADGE
   FRIEND: GEORGE BERNARD SHAW
   FRIEND: JOHN F. KENNEDY
   RESIDENCE: BEVERLY HILLS, CA
   RESIDENCE: PALM SPRINGS, CA
   RESIDENCE: SANTA MONICA, CA
```

```
MEMOIRS: THE TIMES WE HAD-LIFE WITH WM. RANDOLPH HEARST
TALENT: ACTRESS, PHILANTHROPIST,AUTHOR
CREDIT:  '17 RUNAWAY, ROMANY, DEBUT
CREDIT:  '23 LITTLE OLD NEW YORK
CREDIT:  '28 HER CARDBOARD LOVER
CREDIT:  '32 POLLY OF THE CIRCUS
CREDIT:  '37 EVER SINCE EVE, LAST FILM
```

DAVIS, BETTE   BORN: RUTH ELIZABETH DAVIS
```
                          APR 05,'08 AT LOWELL,MS
FATHER: HARLOW MORRELL DAVIS, LAWYER
MOTHER: RUTH FAVOR
SISTER: BARBARA DAVIS
*** MARRIED:  '32 HARMON O. NELSON, JR.  (DIVORCED '38)
*** MARRIED:  '40 ARTHUR FARNSWORTH  (DIED '43)
*** MARRIED:  '45 WILLIAM GRANT SHERRY  (DIVORCED '49)
DAUGHTER:  '46 BARBARA DAVIS SHERRY
*** MARRIED:  '50 GARY MERRILL, ACTOR  (DIVORCED '60)
ADOPTED SON: MICHAEL MERRILL
ADOPTED DAUGHTER: MARGOT MERRILL
FRIEND: JACK WARNER
RESIDENCE: WESTPORT, CN
MEMOIRS: THE LONELY LIFE
TALENT: ACTRESS
COMMENT: PRESIDENT OF ACADEMY OF MOTION PICTURE ARTS & SCIENCES - '42
AA-WIN  ACTRESS:  '35 DANGEROUS
AA-WIN  ACTRESS:  '38 JEZEBEL
AA-NOM  ACTRESS:  '39 DARK VICTORY
AA-NOM  ACTRESS:  '40 THE LETTER
AA-NOM  ACTRESS:  '41 THE LITTLE FOXES
AA-NOM  ACTRESS:  '42 NOW, VOYAGER
AA-NOM  ACTRESS:  '44 MR. SKEFFINGTON
AA-NOM  ACTRESS:  '50 ALL ABOUT EVE
AA-NOM  ACTRESS:  '52 THE STAR
AA-NOM  ACTRESS:  '62 WHAT EVER HAPPENED TO BABY JANE?
```

DAVIS, JR., SAMMY
```
                          DEC 08,'25 AT NYC
FATHER: SAMMY DAVIS, SR.
MOTHER: ELVIRA SANCHEZ
SISTER: RAMONA DAVIS
UNCLE: WILL MASTIN, SINGER, DANCER
*** MARRIED:  '58 LORAY WHITE (DIVORCED '59)
*** MARRIED:  '60 MAY BRITT, ACTRESS  (DIVORCED)
DAUGHTER:  '61 TRACEY DAVIS
SON:  '62 MARK DAVIS
SON:  '63 JEFF DAVIS
*** MARRIED:  '70 ALTOVISE GORE
RESIDENCE: BEVERLY HILLS, CA
MEMOIRS:  '66 YES I CAN
TALENT: ENTERTAINER
CREDIT:  '56 THE BENNY GOODMAN STORY
CREDIT:  '59 PORGY AND BESS
CREDIT:  '60 OCEAN'S ELEVEN
CREDIT:  '64 ROBIN AND THE SEVEN HOODS
CREDIT:  '68 SWEET CHARITY
```

```
----------------------------------------------------------------------------------------
DAY, DENNIS            BORN:   EUGENE DENNIS MCNULTY
                               MAY 21,'17 AT NYC
     FATHER: PATRICK MCNULTY
     MOTHER: MARY ELIZABETH
     BROTHER: DR. JAMES MCNULTY
     SISTER-IN-LAW: ANN BLYTH, ACTRESS  (MARRIED '53)
     *** MARRIED:  '48 MARGARET ELLEN ALMQUIST
     SON:  '49 PATRICK JAMES MCNULTY
     SON:  '50 EUGENE DENNIS MCNULTY
     SON:  '51 MICHAEL JOSEPH MCNULTY
     DAUGHTER:  '52 MARGARET MARY MCNULTY
     DAUGHTER:  '54 EILEEN MARIA MCNULTY
     SON:  '56 PAUL THOMAS MCNULTY
     SON:  '58 THOMAS FRANCIS MCNULTY
     DAUGHTER:  '61 MARY KATE MCNULTY
     SON:  '63 DANIEL GERARD MCNULTY
     DAUGHTER:  '66 THERESE MARIE MCNULTY
     TALENT: ACTOR, SINGER
     CREDIT:  '40 BUCK BENNY RIDES AGAIN
     CREDIT:  '44 MUSIC IN MANHATTAN
     CREDIT:  '50 I'LL GET BY
     CREDIT:  '51 GOLDEN GIRL
     CREDIT:  '53 THE GIRL NEXT DOOR
----------------------------------------------------------------------------------------
DAY, DORIS             BORN:   DORIS KAPPELHOFF
                               APR 03,'24 AT CINCINNATI, OH
     FATHER: FREDERICK WILHELM KAPPELHOFF
     MOTHER: ALMA SOPHIA
     BROTHER: PAUL KAPPELHOFF
     *** MARRIED:  '41 AL JORDAN  (DIVORCED '43)
     SON:  '42 TERRY JORDAN, AKA-TERRY MELCHER
     *** MARRIED:  '46 GEORGE WEIDLER  (DIVORCED '49)
     *** MARRIED:  '51 MARTIN MELCHER, AGENT, PRODUCER  (DIED '68)
     *** MARRIED:  '76 BARRY COMDEN
     RESIDENCE: SAN FERNANDO VALLEY, CA
     POSSESSION:  '48 CONTRACT AT WARNER BROTHERS
     BIOGRAPHY:  '76 HER OWN STORY, BY A. E. HOTCHNER
     TALENT: ACTRESS, SINGER
     CREDIT:  '48 ROMANCE ON THE HIGH SEAS
     CREDIT:  '53 CALAMITY JANE
     AA-NOM  ACTRESS:  '59 PILLOW TALK
     CREDIT:  '62 THAT TOUCH OF MINK
     CREDIT:  '68 WITH SIX YOU GET EGGROLL
----------------------------------------------------------------------------------------
DAY, LARAINE           BORN:   LARAINE JOHNSON
                               OCT 13,'19 AT ROOSEVELT, UT
     FATHER: CLARENCE IRWIN JOHNSON
     MOTHER: ADA
     SISTER: NILA JOHNSON
     SISTER: THERMA JOHNSON
     BROTHER: NARVILLE JOHNSON
     BROTHER: ETHRIDGE JOHNSON
     BROTHER: DE ARMAN JOHNSON
     BROTHER: LAMAR JOHNSON, TWIN
     *** MARRIED:  '42 JAMES RAY HENDRICKS, SINGER  (DIVORCED '47)
     ADOPTED DAUGHTER: ANGELA HENDRICKS
     ADOPTED DAUGHTER: MICHELE HENDRICKS
```

```
ADOPTED SON: CHRISTOPHER HENDRICKS
*** MARRIED:  '47 LEO DUROCHER, BASEBALL PLAYER, COACH  (DIVORCED '60)
*** MARRIED:  '60 MICHAEL GRILKHAS
DAUGHTER:  '62 DANA GRILKHAS
DAUGHTER:  '65 GIGI GRILKHAS
FRIEND: ELIAS DAY, ACTING TEACHER
RESIDENCE: 'THE SYCAMORES'  SANTA MONICA, CA
MEMOIRS: A DAY WITH THE GIANTS
TALENT: ACTRESS, AUTHOR
COMMENT: MEMBER OF THE AROHANUI MAORI PA IN NEW ZEALAND
CREDIT:  '31 SCANDAL SHEET
CREDIT:  '38 BORDER G-MEN, DEBUT
CREDIT:  '41 THE TRIAL OF MARY DUGAN
CREDIT:  '46 THE LOCKET
CREDIT:  '49 I MARRIED A COMMUNIST
CREDIT:  '59 THE THIRD VOICE
```

DE CAMP, ROSEMARY
```
                         NOV 14,'13 AT PRESCOTT, AR
*** MARRIED:  '41 JOHN SHIDLER, JUDGE
DAUGHTER:  '46 MARGARET SHIDLER
DAUGHTER:  '47 MARTHA SHIDLER
DAUGHTER:  '52 VALERIE SHIDLER
DAUGHTER:  '54 NITA SHIDLER
TALENT: ACTRESS
CREDIT:  '41 CHEERS FOR MISS BISHOP
CREDIT:  '45 RHAPSODY IN BLUE
CREDIT:  '51 ON MOONLIGHT BAY
CREDIT:  '55 MANY RIVERS TO CROSS
CREDIT:  '60 THIRTEEN GHOSTS
```

DE CARLO, YVONNE   BORN: PEGGY YVONNE MIDDLETON
```
                         SEP 01,'22 AT VANCOUVER, BRITISH COLUMBIA, CANADA
*** MARRIED:  '55 ROBERT MORGAN, STUNTMAN
SON:  '56 BRUCE MORGAN
SON:  '57 MICHAEL MORGAN
POSSESSION:  '42 CONTRACT AT PARAMOUNT PICTURES
TALENT: ACTRESS
CREDIT:  '42 THIS GUN FOR HIRE
CREDIT:  '45 SALOME
CREDIT:  '57 BAND OF ANGELS
CREDIT:  '63 MCLINTOCK
```

DE HAVEN, GLORIA   BORN: GLORIA MILDRED DE HAVEN
```
                         JUL 23,'24 AT LOS ANGELES, CA
FATHER: CARTER DE HAVEN
MOTHER: FLORA PARKER, ACTRESS
SISTER: MARJORIE DE HAVEN
BROTHER: CARTER DE HAVEN, JR.
*** MARRIED:  '45 JOHN PAYNE, ACTOR  (DIVORCED '50)
DAUGHTER:  '45 KATHLEEN PAYNE
STEP-DAUGHTER: JULIE ANNE PAYNE
SON:  '47 THOMAS PAYNE
*** MARRIED:  '53 MARTIN KIMMEL, LAND DEVELOPER  (DIVORCED '55)
*** MARRIED:  '57 RICHARD FINCHER, AUTO DEALER  (DIVORCED '63)
SON:  '58 HARRY FINCHER
DAUGHTER:  '62 FAITH FINCHER
*** MARRIED:  '64 RICHARD FINCHER, FLORIDA SENATOR  (DIVORCED '68)
```

TALENT: ACTRESS
CREDIT: '40 SUSAN AND GOD
CREDIT: '44 TWO GIRLS AND A SAILOR
CREDIT: '51 TWO TICKETS TO BROADWAY
CREDIT: '55 SO THIS IS PARIS
CREDIT: '55 THE GIRL RUSH

DE HAVILLAND, OLIVIA
                         JUL 01, '16 AT TOKYO, JAPAN
FATHER: WALTER AUGUSTUS DE HAVILLAND, ATTORNEY
MOTHER: LILLIAN AUGUSTA RUSE, ACTRESS
STEP-FATHER: GEORGE M. FONTAINE
SISTER: JOAN FONTAINE, ACTRESS
BROTHER-IN-LAW: BRIAN AHERNE, ACTOR (MARRIED '39)
BROTHER-IN-LAW: WILLIAM DOZIER, PRODUCER (MARRIED '46)
BROTHER-IN-LAW: COLLIER YOUNG, PRODUCER
BROTHER-IN-LAW: ALFRED WRIGHT, JR., JOURNALIST
NIECE: DEBORAH LESLIE DOZIER
NIECE: MARTITA VALENTINA CALDERON
*** MARRIED: '46 MARCUS AURELIUS GOODRICH (DIVORCED '52)
SON: '49 BENJAMIN BRIGGS GOODRICH
*** MARRIED: '55 PIERRE PAUL GALANTE
DAUGHTER: '56 GISELE GALANTE
RESIDENCE: PARIS, FRANCE
POSSESSION: '35 CONTRACT AT WARNER BROTHERS - LATER CONTESTED IN COURT
MEMOIRS: '62 EVERY FRENCHMAN HAS ONE
BIOGRAPHY: '76 OLIVIA DE HAVILLAND, BY JUDITH KASS
TALENT: ACTRESS
CREDIT: '35 A MIDSUMMER NIGHT'S DREAM
AA-NOM SUP.ACT: '39 GONE WITH THE WIND
AA-NOM ACTRESS: '41 HOLD BACK THE DAWN
AA-WIN ACTRESS: '46 TO EACH HIS OWN
AA-NOM ACTRESS: '48 THE SNAKE PIT
AA-WIN ACTRESS: '49 THE HEIRESS
CREDIT: '69 THE ADVENTURERS
CREDIT: '78 THE SWARM

DE LAURENTIIS, DINO
                         AUG 08,'19 AT TORRE ANNUNZIATA, ITALY
FATHER: ROSARIO AURELIO DE LAURENTIIS
MOTHER: GIUSEPPINA SALVATORE
BROTHER: ALFREDO DE LAURENTIIS
*** MARRIED: '49 SYLVANA MANGANO, ACTRESS
DAUGHTER: '50 VERONICA DE LAURENTIIS
DAUGHTER: '52 RAFAELLA DE LAURENTIIS
DAUGHTER: '54 FRANCESCA DE LAURENTIIS
SON: FEDERICO DE LAURENTIIS
FRIEND: JOHN HUSTON
PARTNER: CARLO PONTI, PRODUCER
RESIDENCE: LOS ANGELES, CA
POSSESSION: '65 FILM STUDIO IN 'MEZZOGIORNO' SOLD TO GOVERNMENT IN '71
TALENT: ACTOR, PRODUCER
CREDIT: '54 LA STRADA, WON ACADEMY AWARD-FOREIGN FILM
CREDIT: '66 THE BIBLE
CREDIT: '70 WATERLOO
CREDIT: '76 KING KONG

DE MILLE, C. B.   BORN: CECIL BLOUNT DE MILLE
                                AUG 12,'81 AT ASHFIELD,MS DIED IN '59
    FATHER: HENRY CHURCHILL DE MILLE, ACTOR, WRITER
    MOTHER: MATILDA BEATRICE SAMUEL, ACTRESS
    BROTHER: WILLIAM DE MILLE, WRITER
    *** MARRIED: '02 CONSTANCE ADAMS, ACTRESS
    DAUGHTER: '03 CECILIA HOYT DE MILLE
    ADOPTED DAUGHTER: KATHERINE DE MILLE, ACTRESS (MARRIED '37)
    SON-IN-LAW: ANTHONY QUINN, ACTOR, DIRECTOR
    ADOPTED SON: JOHN DE MILLE
    ADOPTED SON: RICHARD DE MILLE
    GRANDSON: '38 CHRISTOPHER QUINN, DROWNED (DIED '41)
    GRANDDAUGHTER: '41 CHRISTINA QUINN
    GRANDDAUGHTER: '42 KATHLEEN QUINN, ACTRESS
    GRANDSON: '45 DUNCAN QUINN
    GRANDDAUGHTER: '52 VALENTINA QUINN
    FRIEND: JESSE LASKY
    FRIEND: SAMUEL GOLDWYN
    FRIEND: ARTHUR FRIEND
    RESIDENCE: ON DEMILLE DRIVE, LOS ANGELES
    POSSESSION: '52 IRVING THALBERG MEMORIAL AWARD
    POSSESSION: DE MILLE CORPORATION FOR POLITICAL LIBERTY
    MEMOIRS: '59 AUTOBIOGRAPHY OF C. B. DEMILLE
    TALENT: ACTOR, DIRECTOR, PRODUCER
    COMMENT: REPUBLICAN PARTY NOMINEE FOR SENATE IN 1937-BUT DIDN'T RUN
    CREDIT: '15 THE GIRL OF THE GOLDEN WEST
    CREDIT: '27 THE KING OF KINGS
    CREDIT: '39 UNION PACIFIC
    CREDIT: '40 LAND OF LIBERTY
    AA-SPECIAL AWARD: '49 HONORING HIS 37 YEARS OF BRILLIANT SHOWMANSHIP
    CREDIT: '49 SAMSON AND DELILAH
    AA-NOM DIRECTOR: '52 THE GREATEST SHOW ON EARTH
    CREDIT: '56 THE TEN COMMANDMENTS

DE NIRO, ROBERT   BORN: ROBERT DE NIRO, JR.
                                  AUG 17,'43 AT NYC
    FATHER: ROBERT DE NIRO, SR., ARTIST
    MOTHER: --, ARTIST
    *** MARRIED: '76 DIAHNNE ABBOTT, ACTRESS
    STEP-DAUGHTER: DRINA
    POSSESSION: 'NEGRESS IN A BATHTUB' HIS FATHER'S FIRST PAINTING
    TALENT: ACTOR
    AA-WIN SUP.ACT.: '74 THE GODFATHER PART II
    AA-NOM ACTOR: '76 TAXI DRIVER
    CREDIT: '77 NEW YORK, NEW YORK

DEAN, JAMES   BORN: JAMES BYRON DEAN
                                FEB 08,'31 AT MARION, IN DIED IN '55
    FATHER: WINTON DEAN, DENTAL TECHNICIAN
    MOTHER: MILDRED WILSON (DIED '40)
    STEP-MOTHER: ETHEL CASE
    ROMANCE: PIER ANGELI, ACTRESS
    FRIEND: URSULA ANDRESS
    FRIEND: LESLIE CARON
    FRIEND: KATY JURADO
    TALENT: ACTOR
    CREDIT: '51 FIXED BAYONETS

```
       CREDIT:   '53 TROUBLE ALONG THE WAY
       AA-NOM  ACTOR:  '55 EAST OF EDEN
       CREDIT:   '55 REBEL WITHOUT A CAUSE
       AA-NOM  ACTOR:  '56 GIANT
------------------------------------------------------------------------------------------------
DEE, SANDRA          BORN:  ALEXANDRA CYMBOLIAK
                            APR 23,'42 AT BAYONNE, NJ
    MOTHER: MARY
    STEP-FATHER: EUGENE DOUVAN  (DIED '56)
    *** MARRIED:  '60 BOBBY DARIN  (DIVORCED '67)
    SON:  '61 DODD MITCHELL CASSOTTO DARIN
    POSSESSION:  '57 CONTRACT AT UNIVERSAL PICTURES
    TALENT: ACTRESS
    CREDIT:  '57 UNTIL THEY SAIL, DEBUT
    CREDIT:  '59 A SUMMER PLACE
    CREDIT:  '63 TAMMY AND THE DOCTOR
    CREDIT:  '64 TAKE HER SHE'S MINE
------------------------------------------------------------------------------------------------
DEL RIO, DOLORES         BORN:  LOLITA DOLORES MARTINEZ
                                AUG 03,'05 AT DURANGO, MEXICO
    FATHER: JESUS MARTINEZ ASUNSOLO, RANCHER
    MOTHER: ANTONIA LOPEZ NEGRETTE
    COUSIN: RAMON NOVARRO, ACTOR
    *** MARRIED:  '21 JAIME DEL RIO, ATTORNEY  (DIED '28)
    *** MARRIED:  '31 CEDRIC GIBBONS, DESIGNER (OF ACADEMY OSCAR)  (DIVORCED '41)
    FATHER-IN-LAW: AUSTIN PATRICK GIBBONS, ARCHITECT
    *** MARRIED:  '59 LEWIS RILEY
    ROMANCE: EDWIN CAREWE, DIRECTOR
    ROMANCE: ORSON WELLES, ACTOR,DIRECTOR,WRITER
    RESIDENCE: SANTA MONICA, CA
    RESIDENCE: COYOACAN, MEXICO CITY, MEXICO
    POSSESSION: DIEGO RIVERA PORTRAIT OF THE ACTRESS
    TALENT: ACTRESS
    CREDIT:  '25 JOANNA
    CREDIT:  '32 THE GIRL OF THE RIO
    CREDIT:  '47 THE FUGITIVE
    CREDIT:  '60 FLAMING STAR
------------------------------------------------------------------------------------------------
DENEUVE, CATHERINE        BORN:  CATHERINE DORLEAC
                                 OCT 22,'43 AT PARIS, FRANCE
    FATHER: MAURICE DORLEAC, ACTOR
    SISTER: FRANCOISE DORLEAC, ACTRESS  (DIED '68)
    SON:  '63 CHRISTIAN DENEUVE, FATHER - ROGER VADIM
    *** MARRIED:  '65 DAVID BAILEY, PHOTGRAPHER  (DIVORCED '70)
    DAUGHTER:  '72 CHIARA-CHARLOTTE DENEUVE, FATHER -MARCELLO MASTROIANNI
    ROMANCE: MARCELLO MASTROIANNI, ACTOR
    ROMANCE: ROGER VADIM, DIRECTOR
    RESIDENCE: PARIS, FRANCE
    TALENT: ACTRESS, MODEL
    CREDIT:  '62 VICE AND VIRTUE
    CREDIT:  '64 THE UMBRELLAS OF CHERBOURG
    CREDIT:  '67 BELLE DE JOUR
    CREDIT:  '68 MAYERLING
    CREDIT:  '69 THE APRIL FOOLS
    CREDIT:  '75 MODEL FOR CHANEL PERFUMES
```

```
-------------------------------------------------------------------------------------------------
DENNIS, SANDY          BORN:  SANDRA DALE DENNIS
                              APR 27,'37 AT HASTINGS, NB
     FATHER: JACK DENNIS
     BROTHER: FRANK DENNIS
     *** MARRIED:  '65 GERRY MULLIGAN, MUSICIAN
     RESIDENCE: NYC
     RESIDENCE: CONNECTICUT FARMHOUSE
     TALENT: ACTRESS
     CREDIT:  '61 SPLENDOUR IN THE GRASS
     AA-WIN  SUP.ACT.:  '66 WHO'S AFRAID OF VIRGINIA WOOLF?
     CREDIT:  '67 UP THE DOWN STAIRCASE
     CREDIT:  '68 SWEET NOVEMBER
     CREDIT:  '69 A TOUCH OF LOVE
-------------------------------------------------------------------------------------------------
DENNY, REGINALD         BORN:  REGINALD LEIGH DUGMORE DENNY
                              NOV 20,'91 AT RICHMOND, SURREY, ENGLAND   DIED IN '67
     FATHER: W. H. DENNY
     MOTHER: GEORGINA PIKE
     *** MARRIED:  '13 IRENE HAISMAN  (DIVORCED '27)
     DAUGHTER:  '14 BARBARA DENNY
     *** MARRIED:  '28 ISOBEL STIEFEL
     SON:  '29 REGINALD DENNY, JR.
     DAUGHTER:  '30 JOAN DENNY
     CREDIT:  '15 THE LEATHER PUSHERS
     CREDIT:  '21 DISRAELI
     CREDIT:  '30 MADAM SATAN
     CREDIT:  '40 REBECCA
     CREDIT:  '50 IROQUOIS TRAIL
     CREDIT:  '66 BATMAN
-------------------------------------------------------------------------------------------------
DEREK, JOHN          BORN:  DERECK HARRIS
                            AUG 12,'26 AT LOS ANGELES,CA
     FATHER: LAWSON HARRIS, PRODUCER, DIRECTOR, WRITER
     MOTHER: DELORES JOHNSON, ACTRESS
     *** MARRIED:  '50 PATRICIA BEHRS  (DIVORCED '55)
     SON:  '50 RUSSELL ANDRE DEREK
     DAUGHTER:  '53 SEAN CATHERINE DEREK
     *** MARRIED:  '57 URSULA ANDRESS  (DIVORCED '66)
     *** MARRIED:  '69 LINDA EVANS, ACTRESS  (DIVORCED '74)
     ROMANCE: CATHLEEN COLLINS
     RESIDENCE: MALIBU, CALIF.
     POSSESSION:  '39 CONTRACT AT 20TH CENTURY FOX
     POSSESSION:  '46 CONTRACT AT COLUMBIA PICTURES
     TALENT: ACTOR, DIRECTOR
     CREDIT:  '49 KNOCK ON ANY DOOR
     CREDIT:  '57 OMAR KHAYYAM
     CREDIT:  '60 EXODUS
-------------------------------------------------------------------------------------------------
DEVINE, ANDY
                            OCT 07,'05 AT FLAGSTAFF,AR   DIED IN '77
     GRANDFATHER: JAMES WARD, ADMIRAL, USN
     FATHER: --, HOTEL OWNER
     *** MARRIED:  '33 DOROTHY IRENE HOUSE
     SON:  '34 TIMOTHY DEVINE
     SON: DENNIS DEVINE
     SON: TOD DEVINE
     RESIDENCE: ORANGE, CA
```

```
         TALENT: ACTOR
         CREDIT:  '28 WE AMERICANS
         CREDIT:  '39 STAGECOACH
         CREDIT:  '51 THE RED BADGE OF COURAGE
         CREDIT:  '60 THE ADVENTURES OF HUCKLEBERRY  FINN
         CREDIT:  '68 THE BALLAD OF JOSIE
-------------------------------------------------------------------------------------
DEWHURST, COLLEEN
                         JUN 03,'26 AT MONTREAL, CANADA
    FATHER: --, PROFESSIONAL ATHLETE
    MOTHER: --, CHRISTIAN SCIENCE PRACTITIONER
    *** MARRIED:  '47 JAMES VICKERY  (ANNULLED '59)
    *** MARRIED:  '60 GEORGE C. SCOTT, ACTOR  (DIVORCED '65)
    SON:  '61 ALEXANDER SCOTT
    SON:  '62 CAMPBELL SCOTT
    *** MARRIED:  '67 GEORGE C. SCOTT, RE-MARRIED  (DIVORCED '72)
    RESIDENCE: FARM IN WESTCHESTER COUNTY, NY
    TALENT: ACTRESS
    CREDIT:  '59 THE NUN'S STORY
    CREDIT:  '60 MAN ON A STRING
    CREDIT:  '66 A FINE MADNESS
    CREDIT:  '68 THE LAST RUN
    CREDIT:  '70 MCQ.
-------------------------------------------------------------------------------------
DICKINSON, ANGIE         BORN:  ANGELINE BROWN
                                SEP 30,'31 AT KULM, ND
    FATHER: --, JOURNALIST
    SISTER: MARYLOU BROWN
    SISTER: JANET BROWN
    *** MARRIED:  '52 GENE DICKINSON
    *** MARRIED:  '65 BURT BACHARACH, COMPOSER, PERFORMER  (SEPARATED '76)
    FATHER-IN-LAW: BERT BACHARACH, JOURNALIST
    DAUGHTER:  '66 LEA 'NIKKI' BACHARACH
    FRIEND: IRA GERSHWIN
    RESIDENCE: BEVERLY HILLS, CA
    POSSESSION:  '63 INSURANCE POLICY ON HER LEGS
    TALENT: ACTRESS
    CREDIT:  '55 LUCKY ME
    CREDIT:  '60 OCEAN'S 11
    CREDIT:  '71 PRETTY MAIDS ALL IN A ROW
-------------------------------------------------------------------------------------
DIETRICH, MARLENE        BORN:  MARIA MAGDA DIETRICH VON LOSCH
                                DEC 27,'01 AT SCHOENBERG, BERLIN, GERMANY
    FATHER: LOUIS ERICH OTTO DIETRICH
    MOTHER: WILHELMINA ELIZABETH FELSING
    SISTER: ELIZABETH DETRICH
    *** MARRIED:  '24 RUDOLPH SIEBER
    DAUGHTER:  '25 MARIA SIEBER, ACTRESS
    ROMANCE: JOHN GILBERT, ACTOR
    ROMANCE: NOEL COWARD, PLAYWRITE
    ROMANCE: CECIL BEATON
    ROMANCE: DOUGLAS FAIRBANKS, JR., ACTOR
    ROMANCE: ERICH MARIA REMARQUE
    ROMANCE: JOSEF VON STERNBERG
    FRIEND: GERDA HUBER
    POSSESSION: FRENCH LEGION OF HONOR AWARD
    MEMOIRS:  '62 MARLENE DIETRICH'S ABC
    TALENT: SINGER, ACTRESS
```

```
CREDIT:  '23 TRAGEDIES OF LOVE
AA-NOM ACTRESS:  '30 MOROCCO
CREDIT:  '30 THE BLUE ANGEL
CREDIT:  '39 DESTRY RIDES AGAIN
CREDIT:  '44 KISMET
CREDIT:  '57 WITNESS FOR THE PROSECUTION
```

DILLER, PHYLLIS   BORN: PHYLLIS DRIVER
                             JUL 17,'17 AT LIMA, OH
```
    FATHER: PERRY MARCUS DRIVER
    MOTHER: FRANCES ADA ROMSHE
*** MARRIED:  '39 SHERWOOD ANDERSON DILLER  (DIVORCED '65)
*** MARRIED:  '65 WARD DONOVAN, ACTOR      (DIVORCED)
*** MARRIED:  '67 WARD DONOVAN, RE-MARRIED  (DIVORCED '75)
    DAUGHTER: SALLY DILLER
    DAUGHTER: SUZANNE DILLER
    DAUGHTER: STEPHANIE DILLER
    SON: PETER DILLER, III
    SON: PERRY DILLER
    POSSESSION: DILLER BROADCASTING CORP.
    POSSESSION: LINCOLN CROSSING THE DELAWARE ETCHING
    MEMOIRS: HOUSEKEEPING HINTS
    TALENT: ACTRESS
    CREDIT:  '66 BOY DID I GET A WRONG NUMBER
    CREDIT:  '67 EIGHT ON THE LAM
    CREDIT:  '68 DID YOU HEAR THE ONE ABOUT THE TRAVELING SALESLADY?
    CREDIT:  '69 THE ADDING MACHINE
```

DILLMAN, BRADFORD
                             APR 14,'30 AT SAN FRANCISCO, CA
```
    FATHER: DEAN DILLMAN
    MOTHER: JOSEPHINE MOORE
*** MARRIED:  '56 FRIEDA HARDING, ACTRESS  (DIVORCED '62)
    SISTER-IN-LAW: JANET MEDICI
    DAUGHTER:  '58 JEFFREY DILLMAN
    DAUGHTER:  '59 PAMELA DILLMAN
*** MARRIED:  '63 SUZY PARKER, ACTRESS-MODEL
    BROTHER-IN-LAW: IDDO BEN-GURION, WRITER
    SISTER-IN-LAW: DORIAN LEIGH PARKER
    STEP-DAUGHTER: GEORGINA BELLE LA SALLE
    DAUGHTER:  '65 DINAH DILLMAN
    SON:  '69 CHRISTOPHER PARKER DILLMAN
    CREDIT:  '58 A CERTAIN SMILE
    CREDIT:  '58 IN LOVE AND WAR
    CREDIT:  '59 COMPULSION
    CREDIT:  '61 SANCTUARY
    CREDIT:  '62 A RAGE TO LIVE
    CREDIT:  '78 THE SWARM
```

DISNEY, WALT   BORN: WALTER ELIAS DISNEY
                             DEC 05,'01 AT CHICAGO, IL   DIED IN '66
```
    FATHER: ELIAS DISNEY, FARMER
    MOTHER: FLORA CALL
    BROTHER: ROY O. DISNEY  (DIED '71)
*** MARRIED:  '25 LILLIAN MARIE BONDS
    DAUGHTER:  '26 DIANE MARIE DISNEY
    DAUGHTER:  '27 SHARON MAE DISNEY
*** MARRIED:  '53 KATHERINE CALPASS
```

```
         PARTNER: UB IWERKS, ARTIST
         POSSESSION:  '41 IRVING THALBERG MEMORIAL AWARD
         BIOGRAPHY:  '56 THE DISNEY STORY, BY DIANE DISNEY MILLER
         TALENT: CARTOONIST, PRODUCER
         AA-SPECIAL AWARD:  '31 HONORING HIS CREATION OF MICKEY MOUSE
         AA-SPECIAL AWARD:  '38 FOR 'SNOW WHITE AND THE SEVEN DWARFS'
         AA-SPECIAL AWARD:  '41 FOR USE OF SOUND IN 'FANTASIA'
         CREDIT:  '53 THE LIVING DESERT
         CREDIT:  '65 MARY POPPINS
-------------------------------------------------------------------------------
DONAHUE, TROY        BORN:  MERLE JOHNSON, JR.
                            JAN 27,'36 AT NYC
         FATHER: MERLE JOHNSON
         *** MARRIED:  '64 SUZANNE PLESHETTE, ACTRESS  (DIVORCED '64)
         FATHER-IN-LAW: EUGENE PLESHETTE, FILM EXHIBITOR
         MOTHER-IN-LAW: GERALDINE, DANCER
         *** MARRIED:  '66 VALERIE ALLEN  (DIVORCED '68)
         *** MARRIED:  '69 ALMA SHARPE
         ROMANCE: PAT RUSSELL
         RESIDENCE: SANTA MONICA, CA
         POSSESSION:  '59 CONTRACT AT WARNER BROTHERS
         TALENT: ACTOR
         CREDIT:  '58 A SUMMER PLACE
         CREDIT:  '59 IMITATION OF LIFE
         CREDIT:  '61 PALM SPRINGS WEEKEND
         CREDIT:  '67 ROCKET TO THE MOON
         CREDIT:  '74 THE GODFATHER PART II
-------------------------------------------------------------------------------
DONAT, ROBERT
                     MAR 18,'05 AT MANCHESTER, ENGLAND  DIED IN '58
         FATHER: ERNST EMILE DONAT
         MOTHER: ROSE ALICE GREEN
         *** MARRIED: ELLA ANNESLERY VOYSEY
         *** MARRIED: RENEE ASHERSON
         RESIDENCE: LONDON, ENGLAND
         BIOGRAPHY:  '68 ROBERT DONAT, BY J. C. TREWIN
         TALENT: ACTOR, DIRECTOR
         CREDIT:  '32 MEN OF TOMORROW, DEBUT IN 1932
         CREDIT:  '35 THE 39 STEPS
         AA-NOM  ACTOR:  '38 THE CITADEL
         AA-WIN  ACTOR:  '39 GOODBYE, MR. CHIPS
         CREDIT:  '59 INN OF THE SIXTH HAPPINESS
-------------------------------------------------------------------------------
DONLEVY, BRIAN       BORN:  WALDO BRUCE DONLEVY
                            FEB 09,'03 AT PORTADOWN, IRELAND  DIED IN '72
         *** MARRIED:  '36 MARJORIE LANE  (DIVORCED '47)
         DAUGHTER:  '37 JUDITH DONLEVY
         *** MARRIED:  '66 LILLIAN ARCH
         RESIDENCE: LOS ANGELES, CA
         TALENT: ACTOR
         CREDIT:  '28 MOTHER'S BOY
         AA-NOM  SUP.ACT:  '39 BEAU GESTE
         CREDIT:  '44 AN AMERICAN ROMANCE
         CREDIT:  '56 A CRY IN THE NIGHT
         CREDIT:  '65 HOW TO STUFF A BIKINI
```

PAGE 100

```
------------------------------------------------------------------------------------------
DORS, DIANA          BORN:  DIANA FLUCK
                            OCT 23,'31 AT SWINDON, WILTSHIRE, ENGLAND
   *** MARRIED: RICHARD 'DICKIE' DAWSON
   SON:  '60 MARK DAWSON
   SON:  '62 GARY DAWSON
   *** MARRIED:  '68 ALAN LAKE
   SON:  '69 JASON LAKE
   POSSESSION:  '46 CONTRACT A J. ARTHUR RANK CO.
   TALENT: ACTRESS
   CREDIT:  '45 THE SHOP AT SLY CORNER, DEBUT
   CREDIT:  '50 LADY GODIVA RIDES AGAIN
   CREDIT:  '69 BABY LOVE
   CREDIT:  '71 DEEP END
------------------------------------------------------------------------------------------
DOUGLAS, KIRK         BORN:  ISSUR DANIELOVITCH DEMSKY
                            DEC 09,'16 AT AMSTERDAM, NY
   FATHER: HARRY DANIELOVITCH DEMSKY
   MOTHER: BRYNA SANGLEL
   *** MARRIED:  '43 DIANA DILL  (DIVORCED '50)
   SON:  '45 MICHAEL DOUGLAS
   SON:  '47 JOEL DOUGLAS
   DAUGHTER-IN-LAW: SUSAN JORGENSON
   SON:  '53 PETER DOUGLAS, MOTHER - ANNE BUYDENS
   *** MARRIED:  '54 ANNE BUYDENS
   SON:  '55 VINCENT DOUGLAS
   SON:  '58 ERIC DOUGLAS
   SON:  '60 ANTHONY DOUGLAS
   ROMANCE: EVELYN KEYES
   RESIDENCE: BEVERLY HILLS, CA
   POSSESSION:  '55 BRYNA PRODUCTION COMPANY
   TALENT: ACTOR
   CREDIT:  '46 THE STRANGE LOVE OF MARTHA IVERS
   AA-NOM  ACTOR:  '49 CHAMPION
   AA-NOM  ACTOR:  '52 THE BAD AND THE BEAUTIFUL
   AA-NOM  ACTOR:  '56 LUST FOR LIFE
   CREDIT:  '60 SPARTACUS
   CREDIT:  '70 THERE WAS A CROOKED MAN
------------------------------------------------------------------------------------------
DOUGLAS, MELVYN        BORN:  MELVYN EDOUARD HESSELBERG
                            APR 05,'01 AT MACON, GE
   FATHER: EDOUARD G. HESSELBERG, PIANIST
   MOTHER: LENA SHACKLEFORD
   BROTHER: GEORGE HESSELBERG
   BROTHER: LAMAR HESSELBERG
   SON:  '20 GREGORY DOUGLAS
   SON:  '21 MELVYN DOUGLAS, JR.
   *** MARRIED:  '31 HELEN GAHAGAN, ACTRESS, CONGRESSWOMAN
   SON:  '33 PIERRE GAHAGAN 'PETER' DOUGLAS
   DAUGHTER:  '35 MARY HELEN DOUGLAS
   RESIDENCE: NYC
   RESIDENCE: FAIRLEE, VT
   TALENT: ACTOR
   CREDIT:  '31 TONIGHT OR NEVER
   CREDIT:  '39 NINOTCHKA
   CREDIT:  '46 THE SEA OF GRASS
   AA-WIN  SUP.ACT.:  '63 HUD
   AA-NOM  ACTOR:  '70 I NEVER SANG FOR MY FATHER
```

DOUGLAS, MICHAEL
SEP 25,'45 AT NEW BRUNSWICK, NJ

FATHER: KIRK DOUGLAS
MOTHER: DIANA DILL
STEP-MOTHER: ANNE BUYDENS
BROTHER: JOEL DOUGLAS
STEP-BROTHER: PETER DOUGLAS
STEP-BROTHER: VINCENT DOUGLAS
STEP-BROTHER: ERIC DOUGLAS
STEP-BROTHER: ANTHONY DOUGLAS
*** MARRIED: '77 DIANDRA MURRELL LUKER
ROMANCE: BRENDA VACCARO
TALENT: ACTOR
CREDIT: HAIL HERO
CREDIT: SUMMERTREE
CREDIT: NAPOLEON AND SAMANTHA

DOUGLAS, PAUL
NOV 04,'07 AT PHILADELPHIA, PA DIED IN '59

*** MARRIED: ELIZABETH FARNSWORTH (DIVORCED)
*** MARRIED: SUSSIE WELLES (DIVORCED)
*** MARRIED: GERALDINE HIGGINS (DIVORCED)
*** MARRIED: '40 VIRGINIA FIELD, ACTRESS (DIVORCED '46)
DAUGHTER: '41 MARGARET DOUGLAS
*** MARRIED: '50 JAN STERLING, ACTRESS
TALENT: ACTOR
CREDIT: '49 A LETTER TO THREE WIVES
CREDIT: '52 WE'RE NOT MARRIED
CREDIT: '57 THIS COULD BE THE NIGHT
CREDIT: '59 THE MATING GAME

DOVE, BILLIE
BORN: LILLIAN BOHNY
MAY 14,'03 AT NYC

*** MARRIED: '23 IRVING WILLAT, DIRECTOR (DIVORCED '29)
*** MARRIED: '33 ROBERT KENASTON (DIVORCED '71)
ADOPTED DAUGHTER: GAIL KENASTON
SON: ROBERT ALAN KENASTON
ROMANCE: HOWARD HUGHES
RESIDENCE: LOS ANGELES, CA
TALENT: MODEL, ACTRESS
CREDIT: '22 BEYOND THE RAINBOW
CREDIT: '27 SENSATION SEEKERS
CREDIT: '29 HER PRIVATE LIFE
CREDIT: '30 PAINTED ANGEL
CREDIT: '62 DIAMONDHEAD

DRESSER, LOUISE
BORN: LOUISE KERLIN
OCT 05,'82 AT EVANSVILLE, IN DIED IN '65

FATHER: WILLIAM KERLIN, RAILROAD CONDUCTOR
*** MARRIED: JOHN NORWORTH, ACTOR (DIVORCED)
*** MARRIED: '23 JACK GARDNER (DIED '50)
POSSESSION: '53 RANCH IN ENCINO, CA
TALENT: ACTRESS
CREDIT: '22 ENTER MADAME
CREDIT: '26 BROKEN HEARTS OF HOLLYWOOD
AA-NOM ACTRESS: '27 A SHIP COMES IN
CREDIT: '37 MAID OF SALEM

DRESSLER, MARIE   BORN: LEILA MARIE VON KOERBER
                          NOV 09, 1869 AT COBURG, ONTARIO CANADA   DIED IN '34
    FATHER: ALEXANDER RUDOLPH VON KOERBER
    MOTHER: ANNE HENDERSON
    SISTER: BONITA VON KOERBER
    ROMANCE: GEORGE HOPPERT
    ROMANCE: JAMES DALTON
    FRIEND: LILLIAN RUSSELL, ACTRESS
    FRIEND: FRANCES MARION, WRITER
    FRIEND: LOUIS B. MAYER
    RESIDENCE: SANTA BARBARA, CA
    MEMOIRS: MY OWN STORY
    MEMOIRS: STORY OF AN UGLY DUCKLING
    TALENT: SINGER, ACTRESS
    CREDIT: '15 TILLIE'S PUNCTURED ROMANCE
    AA-WIN ACTRESS: '30 MIN AND BILL
    AA-NOM ACTRESS: '31 EMMA
    CREDIT: '33 TUGBOAT ANNIE

DREYFUSS, RICHARD
                          OCT 29,'45 AT BROOKLYN, NY
    FATHER: RICHARD DREYFUSS, SR., LAWYER, RESTAURATEUR
    MOTHER: GERRY
    SISTER: CATHERINE DREYFUSS
    BROTHER: LOREN DREYFUSS
    ROMANCE: LUCINDA
    RESIDENCE: LOS ANGELES, CA
    TALENT: ACTOR
    COMMENT: NAMED MAN OF THE YEAR - 1978 HARVARD UNIVERSITY THEATRE
    CREDIT: '68 THE GRADUATE
    CREDIT: '69 VALLEY OF THE DOLLS
    CREDIT: '73 AMERICAN GRAFFITI
    CREDIT: '75 JAWS
    AA-WIN ACTOR: '77 THE GOODBYE GIRL

DRU, JOANNE   BORN: JOANNE LETITIA LAYCOCK
                          JAN 31,'23 AT LOGAN, WV
    *** MARRIED: '41 DICK HAYMES, SINGER (DIVORCED '49)
    BROTHER-IN-LAW: ROBERT STANTON, ACTOR
    SON: '42 RICHARD HAYMES
    DAUGHTER: '44 HELEN HAYMES
    DAUGHTER: '48 BARBARA HAYMES
    *** MARRIED: '49 JOHN IRELAND, ACTOR (DIVORCED '56)
    STEP-SON: JOHN ANTHONY IRELAND, PRODUCER
    STEP-SON: PETER IRELAND
    *** MARRIED: '63 GEORGE PIEROSE
    TALENT: ACTRESS
    COMMENT: 1ST STAGE NAME-JOAN MARSHALL
    CREDIT: '46 ABIE'S IRISH ROSE
    CREDIT: '53 THUNDER BAY
    CREDIT: '56 HELL ON FRISCO BAY
    CREDIT: '65 SYLVIA

```
--------------------------------------------------------------------------------
DUFF, HOWARD
                         NOV 14,'17 AT BREMMERTON, WA
     FATHER: CARLTON DUFF, WHOLESALE GROCER
     BROTHER: DOUGLAS DUFF
     *** MARRIED:  '52 IDA LUPINO, ACTRESS  (DIVORCED '54)
     FATHER-IN-LAW: STANLEY LUPINO, ACTOR
     MOTHER-IN-LAW: CONSTANCE O'SHAY
     SISTER-IN-LAW: RITA LUPINO, ACTRESS
     DAUGHTER:  '52 BRIDGET MARELIA DUFF
     RESIDENCE: BRENTWOOD, CA
     TALENT: ACTOR
     CREDIT:  '47 BRUTE FORCE
     CREDIT:  '50 SHAKEDOWN
     CREDIT:  '56 WHILE THE CITY SLEEPS
     CREDIT:  '62 BOY'S NIGHT OUT
     CREDIT:  '63 SARDANAPOLUS THE GREAT
--------------------------------------------------------------------------------
DUKE, PATTY          BORN:  ANNA MARIE DUKE
                         DEC 14,'46 AT NYC
     FATHER: JOHN DUKE, CAB DRIVER
     MOTHER: FRANCES MCMAHON
     SISTER: CAROL DUKE
     BROTHER: RAYMOND DUKE
     *** MARRIED:  '65 HENRY FALK, JR., DIRECTOR  (DIVORCED '69)
     *** MARRIED:  '70 MICHAEL TELL, MUSIC PRODUCER, PROMOTER  (DIVORCED '70)
     SON:  '71 SEAN DUKE, FATHER - JOHN ASTIN
     *** MARRIED:  '72 JOHN ASTIN
     STEP-SON: DAVID ASTIN
     STEP-SON: ALLEN ASTIN
     STEP-SON: THOMAS ASTIN
     SON: '73 MACKENZIE ASTIN
     POSSESSION:  '73 BANJO FILM PRODUCTION CO., LTD
     TALENT: ACTRESS
     CREDIT:  '58 THE GODDESS
     AA-WIN  SUP.ACT.:  '62 THE MIRACLE WORKER
     CREDIT:  '67 VALLEY OF THE DOLLS
     CREDIT:  '69 ME NATALIE
     CREDIT:  '71 IF TOMORROW COMES
     CREDIT:  '77 CAPTAINS AND KINGS
     CREDIT:  '78 THE SWARM, CREDIT AS PATTY DUKE ASTIN
--------------------------------------------------------------------------------
DUNAWAY, FAYE        BORN:  DOROTHY FAYE DUNAWAY
                         JAN 14,'41 AT BASCOM, FL
     FATHER: JOHN DUNAWAY, US ARMY SERGEANT
     MOTHER: GRACE DUNAWAY HARTSHORN
     BROTHER: --
     *** MARRIED:  '74 PETER WOLFE, ROCK MUSICIAN
     ENEMY: ROMAN POLANSKI
     RESIDENCE: BOSTON, MS
     RESIDENCE: NYC
     POSSESSION:  '64 FULBRIGHT SCHOLARSHIP FOR THEA TRE STUDIES
     POSSESSION:  '66 CONTRACT WITH DIRECTOR OTTO PREMINGER-LATER CONTESTED
     TALENT: ACTRESS
     CREDIT:  '60 MEMBER LINCOLN CENTER REPERTORY COMPANY
     AA-NOM  ACTRESS:  '67 BONNIE AND CLYDE
     CREDIT:  '70 PUZZLE OF A DOWNFALL CHILD
     AA-NOM  ACTRESS:  '74 CHINATOWN
```

AA-WIN ACTRESS: '76 NETWORK
  CREDIT: '78 EYES OF LAURA MARS

DUNCAN, SANDY   BORN: SANDRA KAY DUNCAN
                                  FEB 20,'46 AT HENDERSON,TX
  FATHER: MANCIL DUNCAN
  MOTHER: SYLVIA
  SISTER: ROBIN DUNCAN
  *** MARRIED: '69 BRUCE ZAHARIADES, ACTOR, MUSICIAN - BRUCE SCOTT (DIVORCED '72)
  *** MARRIED: '73 THOMAS C. CATCATERRA, DOCTOR (HER SURGEON IN 1971)
  RESIDENCE: LOS ANGELES, CA
  POSSESSION: '72 GOLDEN KEWPIE DOLL' KINDNESS AWARD OF ROSE O'NEILL CLUB
  BIOGRAPHY: '73 THE SANDY DUNCAN STORY, BY ROCHELLE REED
  TALENT: ACTRESS,SINGER
  CREDIT: '68 THE $1,000,000 DUCK
  CREDIT: '70 STAR SPANGLED GIRL
  CREDIT: '78 THE CAT FROM OUTER SPACE

DUNNE, IRENE   BORN: IRENE MARIE DUNN
                                  DEC 20,'04 AT LOUISVILLE,KT
  FATHER: JOSEPH JOHN DUNN, STEAMSHIP INSPECTOR
  MOTHER: ADELAIDE ANTOINETTE HENRY
  BROTHER: CHARLES DUNN
  *** MARRIED: '28 FRANCIS GRIFFIN, DENTIST (DIED '65)
  ADOPTED DAUGHTER: MARY FRANCES GRIFFIN
  RESIDENCE: LOS ANGELES, CA
  TALENT: ACTRESS
  COMMENT: ACTIVE SUPPORTER OF UNITED NATIONS ORGANIZATION
  AA-NOM ACTRESS: '30 CIMARRON
  AA-NOM ACTRESS: '36 THEODORA GOES WILD
  AA-NOM ACTRESS: '37 THE AWFUL TRUTH
  AA-NOM ACTRESS: '39 LOVE AFFAIR
  AA-NOM ACTRESS: '48 I REMEMBER MAMA
  CREDIT: '52 IT GROWS ON TREES, LAST FILM

DUNNOCK, MILDRED   BORN: MILDRED DOROTHY DUNNOCK
                                   JAN 25,'06 AT BALTIMORE, MD
  *** MARRIED: '33 KEITH URMY
  DAUGHTER: '34 LINDA URMY
  DAUGHTER: '35 MARY URMY
  TALENT: ACTRESS
  CREDIT: '45 THE CORN IS GREEN
  AA-NOM SUP.ACT: '51 DEATH OF A SALESMAN
  AA-NOM SUP.ACT: '56 BABY DOLL
  CREDIT: '62 SWEET BIRD OF YOUTH
  CREDIT: '69 WHATEVER HAPPENED TO AUNT ALICE?

DURANTE, JIMMY   BORN: JAMES FRANCIS DURANTE
                                   FEB 10,'93 AT NYC
  FATHER: BARTHOLOMEW DURANTE, CIRCUS BARKER
  MOTHER: ROSEA MILLINO
  SISTER: LILIAN DURANTE
  BROTHER-IN-LAW: ROMANO GENARO
  BROTHER: MICHAEL DURANTE (DIED '20)
  BROTHER: ALBERT DURANTE
  *** MARRIED: '16 JEANNE OLSEN (DIED '43)
  *** MARRIED: '60 MARY ALICE LITTLE
  DAUGHTER: '61 CE CE ALICIA DURANTE

```
FRIEND: LOU CLAYTON, COINED-SCHNOZZOLA
FRIEND: EDDIE JACKSON
FRIEND: LOUIS B. MAYER
RESIDENCE: BEVERLY HILLS, CA
TALENT: ACTOR, ENTERTAINER
CREDIT:   '30 ROADHOUSE NIGHTS
CREDIT:   '41 YOU'RE IN THE ARMY NOW
CREDIT:   '50 THE MILKMAN
CREDIT:   '60 PEPE
CREDIT:   '63 IT'S A MAD MAD MAD MAD WORLD
```

DURBIN, DEANNA

```
                        BORN:  EDNA MAE DURBIN
                               DEC 04,'21 AT WINNIPEG, MANITOBA, CANADA
FATHER: JAMES DURBIN, CONTRACTOR
MOTHER: ADA READ
SISTER: EDITH DURBIN
*** MARRIED:  '41 VAUGHN PAUL, STUDIO EXECUTIVE  (DIVORCED '43)
*** MARRIED:  '45 FELIX JACKSON, PRODUCER  (DIVORCED '49)
DAUGHTER:  '46 JESSICA JACKSON
SON-IN-LAW: JAY DAVIS  (MARRIED '73)
*** MARRIED:  '50 CHARLES HENRI DAVID, DIRECTOR
SON:  '51 PETER DAVID
RESIDENCE: NEAUPHLE-LE-CHATEAU, FRANCE
POSSESSION:  '36 CONTRACT AT UNIVERSAL STUDIOS
TALENT: ACTRESS,SINGER
CREDIT:  '36 THREE SMART GIRLS
AA-SPECIAL AWARD:  '38 AN HONORARY MINIATURE AWARD
CREDIT:  '39 THREE SMART GIRLS GROW UP
CREDIT:  '44 CHRISTMAS HOLIDAY
```

DURYEA, DAN

```
                        BORN:  DANIEL DURYEA
                               JAN 23,'07 AT WHITE PLAINS, NY  DIED IN '68
FATHER: RICHARD HEWLETT DURYEA
MOTHER: MABEL HOFFMAN
*** MARRIED:  '31 HELEN BRYAN  (DIED '67)
SON: PETER DURYEA, ACTOR
SON: RICHARD DURYEA, 'BEACHBOYS' ROCK GROUP MGR.
RESIDENCE: LOS ANGELES, CA
POSSESSION: LODGE AT LAKE ARROWHEAD, CA
TALENT: ACTOR
CREDIT:  '41 THE LITTLE FOXES
CREDIT:  '45 SCARLET STREET
CREDIT:  '50 WINCHESTER '73
CREDIT:  '57 BATTLE HYMN
CREDIT:  '68 FIVE GOLDEN DRAGONS
```

EASTWOOD, CLINT BORN: CLINTON EASTWOOD, JR.
MAY 31,'30 AT SAN FRANCISCO, CA
FATHER: CLINTON EASTWOOD
MOTHER: RUTH
SISTER: JEANNE EASTWOOD
*** MARRIED: '53 MAGGIE JOHNSON
SON: '68 KYLE CLINTON EASTWOOD
DAUGHTER: '72 ALISON EASTWOOD
RESIDENCE: CARMEL-BY-THE-SEA, CA
POSSESSION: '55 CONTRACT AT UNIVERSAL STUDIOS
POSSESSION: '69 MALPASO PRODUCTION CO.
POSSESSION: '77 THE HOG'S BREATH INN, CARMEL
TALENT: ACTOR-DIRECTOR
CREDIT: '55 FRANCIS IN THE NAVY
CREDIT: '64 FOR A FISTFUL OF DOLLARS
CREDIT: '71 DIRTY HARRY
CREDIT: '75 THE OUTLAW JOSIE WALES
CREDIT: '78 THE GAUNTLET

EBSEN, BUDDY BORN: CHRISTIAN RUDOLF EBSEN
APR 02,'08 AT BELLEVILLE,IL
FATHER: CHRISTIAN EBSEN, DANCE TEACHER
SISTER: VILMA EBSEN, DANCING PARTNER ON STAGE
SISTER: HELGA EBSEN
SISTER: NORMA EBSEN
*** MARRIED: '33 RUTH CAMBRIDGE
DAUGHTER: '36 ELIZABETH 'LIBBY' EBSEN
DAUGHTER: '43 ALIX EBSEN
*** MARRIED: '45 NANCY WOLCOTT
DAUGHTER: '47 SUSANNAH EBSEN
DAUGHTER: '49 CATHERINE EBSEN
DAUGHTER: '51 BONNIE EBSEN
DAUGHTER: '58 KIRSTEN EBSEN
SON: '59 DUSTIN EBSEN
RESIDENCE: BALBOA ISLAND, CA
RESIDENCE: RANCH IN AGOURA, CA
POSSESSION: CATAMARAN SAILBOAT MANUFACTURING COMPANY
POSSESSION: EBSEN SCHOOL OF DANCING
TALENT: DANCER-ACTOR
CREDIT: '36 BROADWAY MELODY OF 1936
CREDIT: '42 SING YOUR WORRIES AWAY
CREDIT: '55 DAVY CROCKETT
CREDIT: '62 BREAKFAST AT TIFFANY'S
CREDIT: '72 POLYNESIAN CONCEPT, BOOK ON THE '68 HONOLULU RACE

EDDY, NELSON
JUN 29,'01 AT PROVIDENCE,RI   DIED IN '67
GRANDMOTHER: CAROLINE KENDRICK, SINGER
FATHER: WILLIAM DARIUS EDDY, SINGER
MOTHER: ISABEL KENDRICK, SINGER
*** MARRIED: '39 ANNE DENITZ, AKA ANNE FRANKLIN
RESIDENCE: BRENTWOOD, CA
POSSESSION: T'ANG CHINA HORSE COLLECTION
TALENT: SINGER, JOURNALIST,ACTOR
COMMENT: FAMILY ANCESTOR-PRESIDENT MARTIN VAN BUREN
CREDIT: '33 BROADWAY TO HOLLYWOOD
CREDIT: '35 NAUGHTY MARIETTA

```
CREDIT:   '40 BITTER SWEET
CREDIT:   '47 NORTHWEST OUTPOST
```

EDEN, BARBARA   BORN: BARBARA MOORHEAD
                                   AUG 23,'34 AT TUCSON, AR
```
FATHER: HUBERT MOORHEAD
MOTHER: MARY ALICE FRANKLIN
STEP-FATHER: HARRISON C. HUFFMAN
*** MARRIED:   '58 MICHAEL ANSARA, ACTOR   (DIVORCED '73)
SON:   '65 MATTHEW MICHAEL ANSARA
TALENT: ACTRESS
CREDIT:   '56 BACK FROM ETERNITY
CREDIT:   '60 TWELVE HOURS TO KILL
CREDIT:   '64 THE BRASS BOTTLE
CREDIT:   '78 HARPER VALLEY P.T.A.
```

EDWARDS, CLIFF   BORN: CLIFTON A. EDWARDS
                                   JUN 14,'95 AT HANNIBAL, MR   DIED IN '71
```
FATHER: EDWARD EDWARDS
*** MARRIED:   '19 GERTRUDE RYRHOLM   (DIVORCED '23)
SON:   '20 GEORGE CLIFTON EDWARDS
*** MARRIED:   '23 IRENE WILEY, SINGER   (DIVORCED '31)
*** MARRIED:   '32 LUCILLE KELLY, ACTRESS - NANCY DOVER
FRIEND: JEAN HARLOW
FRIEND: ADDIE GREEN, HOUSEKEEPER
RESIDENCE: BEVERLY HILLS, CA
POSSESSION:   '28 CONTRACT AT M-G-M STUDIOS
COMMENT: KNOWN AS 'UKELELE IKE'
CREDIT:   '29 HOLLYWOOD REVUE OF 1929
CREDIT:   '35 RED SALUTE
CREDIT:   '39 BAD GUY
CREDIT:   '40 PINOCCHIO
CREDIT:   '45 SHE COULDN'T SAY NO
CREDIT:   '53 THE AVENGING RIDER
```

EGGAR, SAMANTHA   BORN: VICTORIA LOUISE SAMANTHA EGGAR
                                     MAR 05,'39 AT LONDON,ENGLAND
```
FATHER: RALPH A. J. EGGAR, ROYAL ARMY GENERAL OFFICER
UNCLE: JACK EGGAR, STAGE PRODUCER
*** MARRIED:   '64 TOM STERN, ACTOR, PRODUCER   (DIVORCED '71)
SON:   '65 NICOLAS STERN
DAUGHTER:   '67 JENNA LOUISE STERN
ROMANCE: ALBERT FINNEY, ACTOR
ROMANCE: EDWARD RUSCHA, ARTIST
FRIEND: MICHAEL 'DANDY KIM' WATERFIELD, JOCKEY, JEWELRY THIEF
RESIDENCE: LOS ANGELES, CA
POSSESSION:   '69 SAMANTHA FILM PRODUCTION CO.
TALENT: ACTRESS
CREDIT:   '62 THE WILD AND THE WILLING
AA-NOM  ACTRESS:   '65 THE COLLECTOR
CREDIT:   '67 DOCTOR DOLITTLE
CREDIT:   '70 THE LADY IN THE CAR
CREDIT:   '72 THE LIGHT ON THE EDGE OF THE WORLD
```

EKBERG, ANITA
SEP 29,'31 AT MALMO,SWEDEN
FATHER: GUSTAV EKBERG
MOTHER: ALVAH
*** MARRIED: '56 ANTHONY STEELE, ACTOR (DIVORCED '62)
*** MARRIED: '63 RIK VAN NUTTER, ACTOR
ROMANCE: ROD TAYLOR, ACTOR
TALENT: ACTRESS-MODEL
COMMENT: MISS SWEDEN OF 1950
CREDIT: '55 BLOOD ALLEY
CREDIT: '59 LA DOLCE VITA
CREDIT: '63 FOUR FOR TEXAS
CREDIT: '66 THE ALPHABET MURDERS
CREDIT: '67 THE GLASS SPHINX
CREDIT: '78 THE MUD

EKLAND, BRITT
OCT 06,'42 AT STOCKHOLM,SWEDEN
*** MARRIED: '64 PETER SELLERS, ACTOR, DIRECTOR (DIVORCED '69)
FATHER-IN-LAW: WILLIAM SELLERS, PIANIST
MOTHER-IN-LAW: AGNES MARKS
STEP-DAUGHTER: SARAH JANE PETERS SELLERS
STEP-SON: MICHAEL PETER ANTHONY SELLERS
DAUGHTER: '65 VICTORIA SELLERS
ROMANCE: LOU ADLER
SON: '73 NICOLAI EKLAND, FATHER- LOU ADLER
ROMANCE: ROD STUART
TALENT: ACTRESS
CREDIT: '66 AFTER THE FOX
CREDIT: '68 THE DOUBLE MAN
CREDIT: '71 GET A GARTER
CREDIT: '71 A TIME FOR LOVING
CREDIT: '72 ENDLESS NIGHT

EMERSON, FAYE
BORN: FAYE MARGARET EMERSON
JUL 08,'17 AT ELIZABETH,LA
FATHER: LAWRENCE L. EMERSON
*** MARRIED: '41 WILLIAM CRAWFORD (DIVORCED '42)
SON: '42 'SCOOP' CRAWFORD
*** MARRIED: '44 ELLIOTT ROOSEVELT (DIVORCED '50)
*** MARRIED: '50 SKITCH HENDERSON (DIVORCED '57)
RESIDENCE: PALMA DE MALLORCA, SPAIN
RESIDENCE: NEW YORK CITY
TALENT: ACTRESS
CREDIT: '44 BETWEEN TWO WORLDS
CREDIT: '45 DANGER SIGNAL
CREDIT: '50 GUILTY BYSTANDER
CREDIT: '57 A FACE IN THE CROWD

EVANS, DALE
BORN: FRANCES OCTAVIA SMITH
OCT 31,'12 AT UVALDE,TX
FATHER: WALTER HILLMAN SMITH, COTTON FARMER
MOTHER: BETTIE SUE WOOD
BROTHER: WALTER HILLMAN SMITH, JR.
*** MARRIED: '28 THOMAS FOX (DIED '29)
SON: '29 THOMAS FOX, JR.
*** MARRIED: '30 ROBERT DALE BUTTS (DIVORCED '45)

```
*** MARRIED:   '47 ROY ROGERS, ACTOR
STEP-DAUGHTER: CHERYL DARLENE ROGERS
STEP-SON: ROY ROGERS, JR.
STEP-DAUGHTER: LINDA LOU ROGERS
STEP-SON: SCOTT WARD ROGERS
STEP-DAUGHTER: MARION ROGERS
 DAUGHTER:  '49 ROBIN ROGERS
SON:  '49 JOHN ROGERS
DAUGHTER:  '50 MARY LITTLE DOE ROGERS
DAUGHTER:  '51 MARION ROGERS
DAUGHTER:  '52 DEBORAH ROGERS
RESIDENCE: DOUBLE R RANCH, CHATSWORTH,CA
MEMOIRS: TRIALS, TEARS & TRIUMPH
TALENT: SINGER,ACTRESS,AUTHOR,COMPOSER
CREDIT:   '42 ORCHESTRA WIVES
CREDIT:   '43 SWING YOUR PARTNER
CREDIT:   '44 THE YELLOW ROSE OF TEXAS
CREDIT:   '50 TWILIGHT IN THE SIERRAS
CREDIT:   '51 PALS OF THE GOLDEN WEST
----------------------------------------------------------------------------
EVANS, ROBERT          BORN:   ROBERT J. EVANS
                               JUN 29,'30 AT NYC
   FATHER: ARCHIBALD EVANS
   MOTHER: FLORENCE KRASNE
   SISTER: ALICE EVANS
   BROTHER: CHARLES EVANS
   *** MARRIED:   '61 SHARON HUGUENY, ACTRESS  (DIVORCED '62)
   *** MARRIED:   '64 CAMILLA SPARV, ACTRESS  (DIVORCED)
   MOTHER-IN-LAW: COUNTESS ANTONIA VON GREVNER
   *** MARRIED:   '69 ALI MACGRAW, ACTRESS, MODEL  (DIVORCED)
   SON:  '71 JOSHUA EVANS
   *** MARRIED:   '77 PHYLLIS GEORGE, JOURNALIST
   ROMANCE: BARBARA CARRERA, MODEL-CHIQUITA BANANA GIRL
   PARTNER: JOSEPH PICONE, EVAN-PICONE CLOTHING CO.
   TALENT: ACTOR,PRODUCER
   CREDIT:   '52 LYDIA BAILEY
   CREDIT:   '56 MAN OF A THOUSAND FACES
   CREDIT:   '58 THE FIEND WHO WALKED THE WEST SIDE
   CREDIT:   '59 THE BEST OF EVERTHING
----------------------------------------------------------------------------
EVERETT, CHAD          BORN:   RAYMON LEE CRAMTON
                               JUN 11,'36 AT SOUTH BEND, IN
   FATHER: HARRY CLYDE CRAMTON
   MOTHER: VIRDEEN RUTH HOPPER
   *** MARRIED: SHELBY GRANT
   *** MARRIED:   '66 BRENDA LEE THOMPSON
   DAUGHTER:  '69 KATHERINE KERRIE EVERETT
   DAUGHTER:  '71 SHANNON KIMBERLY EVERETT
   TALENT: ACTOR
   COMMENT: THE LAST LONG TERM CONTRACT PLAYER AT M-G-M STUDIOS
   CREDIT:   '62 THE CHAPMAN REPORT
   CREDIT:   '65 GET YOURSELF A COLLEGE GIRL
   CREDIT:   '66 THE SINGING NUN
   CREDIT:   '67 THE LAST CHALLENGE
```

EWELL, TOM   BORN: YEWELL TOMPKINS
                             APR 29,'09 AT OWENSBORO,KT
     FATHER: SAMUEL WILLIAM TOMPKINS
     MOTHER: MARTINE YEWELL
     *** MARRIED: '46 JUDITH ANN ABBOTT (DIVORCED '47)
     FATHER-IN-LAW: GEORGE ABBOTT, PRODUCER
     *** MARRIED: '48 MARJORIE GWYNNE SANBORN
     SON: '49 TAYLOR ALLEN EWELL
     RESIDENCE: NEW HOPE, PA
     RESIDENCE: NYC
     POSSESSION: RACING FORMS COLLECTION
     TALENT: ACTOR
     CREDIT: '40 THEY KNEW WHAT THEY WANTED
     CREDIT: '49 ADAM'S RIB
     CREDIT: '55 THE SEVEN YEAR ITCH
     CREDIT: '62 STATE FAIR

```
--------------------------------------------------------------------------------
FABARES, SHELLEY          BORN:   MICHELE MARIE FABARES
                                  JAN 19,'42 AT SANTA MONICA, CA
    FATHER: JAMES FABARES
    MOTHER: ELSA
    SISTER: NANETTE 'SMOKEY' FABARES
    AUNT: NANETTE FABRAY, ACTRESS
    *** MARRIED:  '64 LOU ADLER
    TALENT: ACTRESS
    CREDIT:  '56 NEVER SAY GOODBYE
    CREDIT:  '58 SUMMER LOVE
    CREDIT:  '65 GIRL HAPPY
    CREDIT:  '66 HOLD ON
    CREDIT:  '67 CLAMBAKE
--------------------------------------------------------------------------------
FABRAY, NANETTE           BORN:   NANETTE FABARES
                                  OCT 27,'20 AT SAN DIEGO, CA
    FATHER: RAOUL FABARES, RAILROAD ENGINEER
    MOTHER: LILLIAN MCGOVERN
    NIECE: SHELLEY FABARES, ACTRESS
    NIECE: NANETTE 'SMOKEY' FABARES
    *** MARRIED:  '47 DAVID TEBET  (DIVORCED '51)
    *** MARRIED:  '57 RANALD MACDOUGALL, WRITER  (DIED '73)
    SON: JAMIE MACDOUGALL
    POSSESSION:  '55 COLLECTION OF ROCKS
    TALENT: ACTRESS
    COMMENT: VAUDEVILLE DEBUT AT AGE FOUR- KNOWN AS BABY NANETTE
    CREDIT:  '39 ELIZABETH AND ESSEX
    CREDIT:  '53 BAND WAGON
    CREDIT:  '69 THE HAPPY ENDING
    CREDIT:  '78 HARPER VALLEY P.T.A.
    CREDIT: OUR GANG, SERIES
--------------------------------------------------------------------------------
FAIRBANKS, DOUGLAS        BORN:   DOUGLAS ELTON ULMAN
                                  MAY 23,'83 AT DENVER,CO   DIED IN '39
    FATHER: HEZEKIAH CHARLES DOUGLAS ULMAN, LAWYER
    MOTHER: ELLA ADELAIDE MARSH FAIRBANKS
    BROTHER: ROBERT ULMAN
    STEP-BROTHER: JOHN FAIRBANKS
    *** MARRIED:  '07 ELIZABETH SULLY  (DIVORCED '12)
    FATHER-IN-LAW: DANIEL J. SULLY, FINANCIER
    SON:  '09 DOUGLAS FAIRBANKS, JR.
    *** MARRIED:  '20 MARY PICKFORD, ACTRESS  (DIVORCED '35)
    *** MARRIED:  '35 LADY SYLVIA HAWKES ASHLEY, ACTRESS
    ROMANCE: AMY SEMPLE MACPHERSON
    RESIDENCE: PICKFAIR, BEVERLY HILLS
    POSSESSION:  '17 ARTCRAFT FILM CO.
    BIOGRAPHY:  '53 THE FOURTH MUSKETEER, BY ELTON THOMAS
    BIOGRAPHY:  '77 DOUG AND MARY, BY GARY CAREY
    BIOGRAPHY:  '77 MARY AND DOUG, BY BOOTON HERNDON
    TALENT: ACTOR, WRITER
    COMMENT: WROTE SCRIPTS UNDER PSEUDONYM ELTON THOMAS
    CREDIT:  '15 THE LAMB, DEBUT IN 1915
    CREDIT:  '19 KNICKERBOCKER BUCKEROO
    CREDIT:  '21 THE THREE MUSKETEERS
    CREDIT:  '27 SHOW PEOPLE
    CREDIT:  '34 PRIVATE LIFE OF DON JUAN
    AA-SPECIAL AWARD:  '39 COMMEMORATIVE AWARD TO THE 1ST PRESIDENT OF THE ACADEMY
```

FAIRBANKS, JR., DOUGLAS   BORN: DOUGLAS ELTON ULMAN, JR.
                                             DEC 09,'09 AT NYC
    GRANDFATHER: DANIEL J. SULLY
    FATHER: DOUGLAS FAIRBANKS
    MOTHER: ELIZABETH SULLY
    STEP-FATHER: JACK WHITING, ACTOR, SINGER
    STEP-MOTHER: MARY PICKFORD, ACTRESS
    STEP-MOTHER: LADY SYLVIA HAWKES ASHLEY, ACTRESS
    *** MARRIED: '29 JOAN CRAWFORD, ACTRESS (DIVORCED '33)
    *** MARRIED: '39 MARY LEE EPLING
    DAUGHTER: '40 MELISSA FAIRBANKS
    DAUGHTER: '42 DAPHNE FAIRBANKS
    DAUGHTER: '47 VICTORIA FAIRBANKS
    ROMANCE: GERTRUDE LAWRENCE
    ROMANCE: MARLENE DIETRICH
    RESIDENCE: PALM BEACH, FL
    POSSESSION: '51 THE DOUGFAIR CORPORATION
    BIOGRAPHY: '55 KNIGHT ERRANT, BY BRIAN CONNELL
    TALENT: ACTOR-PRODUCER
    CREDIT: '23 STEPHEN STEPS OUT
    CREDIT: '28 THE CORSICAN BROTHERS
    CREDIT: '30 THE DAWN PATROL
    CREDIT: '37 THE PRISONER OF ZENDA
    CREDIT: '48 THE EXILE

FALK, PETER   BORN: PETER MICHAEL FALK
                                  SEP 16,'27 AT NYC
    FATHER: MICHAEL FALK
    MOTHER: MADELINE HAUSER
    *** MARRIED: '60 ALYCE MAYO
    DAUGHTER: '61 KATHERINE FALK
    DAUGHTER: '62 JACQUELINE FALK
    *** MARRIED: '77 SHERRA LYNN DANESE, ACTRESS
    FRIEND: JOHN CASSAVETES
    FRIEND: TELLY SAVALAS, BILLIARDS PARTNER
    RESIDENCE: BEVERLY HILLS, CA
    TALENT: ACTOR
    CREDIT: '58 WIND ACROSS THE EVERGLADES
    AA-NOM SUP.ACT: '60 MURDER, INC.
    AA-NOM SUP.ACT: '61 POCKETFUL OF MIRACLES
    CREDIT: '65 THE GREAT RACE
    CREDIT: '69 CASTLE KEEP
    CREDIT: '78 THE CHEAP DETECTIVE

FARENTINO, JAMES
                         FEB 24,'38 AT BROOKLYN,NY
    FATHER: ANTHONY FARENTINO
    MOTHER: HELEN ENRICO
    *** MARRIED: '66 MICHELLE LEE DUSICK
    SON: '69 DAVID MICHAEL FARENTINO
    TALENT: ACTOR
    CREDIT: '64 PSYCHOMANIA
    CREDIT: '65 THE WAR LORD
    CREDIT: '68 ROSIE
    CREDIT: '69 ME NATALIE
    CREDIT: '70 THE STORY OF A WOMAN

FARNUM, DUSTIN
                    MAY 27, 1874 AT HAMPTON BEACH, MAINE   DIED IN '29
     GRANDFATHER: STOVER LA GROS
     FATHER: GREENLEAF D. FARNUM
     MOTHER: CLARA
     BROTHER: MARSHALL FARNUM
     BROTHER: WILLIAM FARNUM, ACTOR
     SISTER-IN-LAW: MABEL EATON
     SISTER-IN-LAW: OLIVE ANN WHITE
     NIECE: ADELE FARNUM
     *** MARRIED: AGNES MUIR JOHNSTONE, ACTRESS - PEARL FARNUM (DIVORCED '08)
     *** MARRIED: MARY ELIZABETH CONWELL
     DAUGHTER: '02 ESTELLE FARNUM
     *** MARRIED: '10 ELIZABETH CARROL, ACTRESS (DIVORCED '24)
     *** MARRIED: '24 WINIFRED KINGSTON, ACTRESS
     ROMANCE: GLORIA GOULD
     TALENT: ACTOR
     CREDIT: '13 THE SQUAW MAN
     CREDIT: '17 THE SCARLET PIMPERNEL
     CREDIT: '23 THE VIRGINIAN
     CREDIT: '26 THE FLAMING FRONTIER

FARNUM, WILLIAM
                    JUL 04,'76 AT BOSTON, MS   DIED IN '53
     FATHER: GREENLEAF D. FARNUM
     MOTHER: CLARA
     BROTHER: MARSHALL FARNUM
     BROTHER: DUSTIN FARNUM
     SISTER-IN-LAW: MARY ELIZABETH CONWELL
     SISTER-IN-LAW: ELIZABETH CARROL, ACTRESS
     SISTER-IN-LAW: WINIFRED KINGSTON
     SISTER-IN-LAW: AGNES MUIR JOHNSTON, ACTRESS
     NIECE: ESTELLE FARNUM
     *** MARRIED: '01 MABEL EATON
     *** MARRIED: '06 OLIVE ANN WHITE (DIVORCED '32)
     ADOPTED DAUGHTER: ADELE FARNUM
     *** MARRIED: '32 ISABELLE LIND, WRITER - ISABELLE LYNDS MAJOR
     STEP-DAUGHTER: ISABELLE MAJOR, TWIN
     STEP-DAUGHTER: ELIZABETH MAJOR, TWIN
     ADOPTED SON: WILLIAM FARNUM, JR., HIS STEPSON - THOMAS MAJOR
     RESIDENCE: SAG HARBOR, NY
     RESIDENCE: ROBINSON HOUSE, BUCKSPORT, ME.
     RESIDENCE: HOLLYWOOOD HILLS, CA
     TALENT: ACTOR
     CREDIT: '14 THE SPOILERS, DEBUT
     CREDIT: '24 THE MAN WHO FIGHTS ALONE
     CREDIT: '35 SILVER STREAK
     CREDIT: '38 IF I WERE KING
     CREDIT: '45 CAPTAIN KIDD
     CREDIT: '52 LONE STAR

FARRELL, CHARLES
                    AUG 09,'01 AT ONSET BAY,MS
     FATHER: DAVIS FARRELL, FILM EXHIBITOR
     *** MARRIED: '31 VIRGINIA VALLI, ACTRESS
     *** MARRIED: '60 BOBBIE MCMANUS
     FRIEND: JANET GAYNOR

```
FRIEND: RALPH BELLAMY
RESIDENCE: PALM SPRINGS, CA
TALENT: ACTOR-TENNIS PLAYER
COMMENT: OWNER OF PALM SPRINGS RACQUET CLUB FOR MANY YEARS
CREDIT:  '23 THE TEN COMMANDMENTS
CREDIT:  '27 SEVENTH HEAVEN
CREDIT:  '30 HIGH SOCIETY
CREDIT:  '33 MAKER OF MEN
CREDIT:  '42 THE DEADLY GAME
```

FARROW, MIA   BORN: MIA VILLIERS FARROW
                               FEB 09,'46 AT LOS ANGELES, CA
```
FATHER: JOHN VILLIERS FARROW, DIRECTOR  (DIED '63)
MOTHER: MAUREEN O'SULLIVAN, ACTRESS
SISTER: PRUDENCE FARROW
SISTER: TERESA FARROW
SISTER: STEPHANIE FARROW
BROTHER: JOHN FARROW, JR.
BROTHER: MICHAEL FARROW  (DIED '58)
BROTHER: PATRICK FARROW
*** MARRIED:  '66 FRANK SINATRA, SINGER, ACTOR  (DIVORCED '68)
STEP-DAUGHTER: NANCY SINATRA
STEP-SON: FRANK SINATRA, JR.
STEP-DAUGHTER: CHRISTINE SINATRA
*** MARRIED:  '70 ANDRE PREVIN, CONDUCTOR
ADOPTED DAUGHTER: GIGI PREVIN
SON:  '74 KYM LARK PREVIN
SON: MATTHEW PHINEAS PREVIN, TWIN
SON: SASCHA VILLIERS PREVIN, TWIN
RESIDENCE: LONDON, ENGLAND
TALENT: ACTRESS
CREDIT:  '64 GUNS AT BATASI
CREDIT:  '68 ROSEMARY'S BABY
CREDIT:  '69 JOHN AND MARY
CREDIT:  '71 BLIND TERROR
CREDIT:  '73 THE GREAT GATSBY
```

FAWCETT-MAJORS, FARRAH   BORN: MARY FARRAH LENI FAWCETT
                                        FEB 02,'47 AT CORPUS CHRISTI, TX
```
FATHER: JAMES WILLIAM FAWCETT, REFINERY PIPEFITTER
MOTHER: PAULINE ALICE EVANS
SISTER: THERESA DIANNE FAWCETT
*** MARRIED:  '73 LEE MAJORS, ACTOR
ROMANCE: BURT REYNOLDS, ACTOR
FRIEND: VINCE VAN PATTEN, TENNIS PARTNER
RESIDENCE: LOS ANGELES, CA
BIOGRAPHY:  '77 AN UNAUTHORIZED BIOGRAPHY, BY PATRICIA BURSTEIN
TALENT: MODEL-ACTRESS
CREDIT:  '76 CHARLIES' ANGELS, TV SERIES
CREDIT:  '78 SOMEBODY KILLED HER HUSBAND
CREDIT: LOVE IS A FUNNY THING
```

FAYE, ALICE   BORN: ANN JEANNE 'ALICE' LEPPERT
                               MAY 05,'12 AT NYC
```
BROTHER: WILLIAM LEPPERT, TALENT AGENT
*** MARRIED: '37 TONY MARTIN  (DIVORCED '40)
*** MARRIED:  '41 PHIL HARRIS
STEP-SON: PHIL HARRIS, JR.
```

```
DAUGHTER:   '42 ALICE HARRIS
DAUGHTER:   '44 PHYLLIS HARRIS
RESIDENCE: PALM SPRINGS, CA
TALENT: ACTRESS
CREDIT:   '34 GEORGE WHITE'S SCANDALS
CREDIT:   '38 ALEXANDER'S RAGTIME BAND
CREDIT:   '41 WEEKEND IN HAVANA
CREDIT:   '45 FALLEN ANGEL
CREDIT:   '62 STATE FAIR
```

FAZENDA, LOUISE
                          JUN 17,'89 AT LAFAYETTE, IN   DIED IN '62
```
FATHER: JOSEPH A. FAZENDA  (DIED '33)
MOTHER: NELDA
AUNT: MAY FAZENDA, AKA MAY RICK
UNCLE: ANTHONY FAZENDA
UNCLE: ULYSSES FAZENDA
*** MARRIED:   '17 NOEL M. SMITH, DIRECTOR   (DIVORCED '26)
*** MARRIED:   '27 HAL B. WALLIS, PRODUCER
SISTER-IN-LAW: MINNA WALLIS, TALENT AGENT
SON:   '33 HAL BRENT WALLIS, PSYCHOLOGIST
TALENT: ACTRESS
CREDIT:   '13 THE CHEESE SPECIAL
CREDIT:   '20 DOWN ON THE FARM
CREDIT:   '25 BROADWAY BUTTERFLY
CREDIT:   '31 GUN SMOKE
CREDIT:   '39 THE OLD MAID
```

FERRER, JOSE   BORN: JOSE VICENTE FERRER Y CINTRON
                              JAN 08,'09 AT SANTURCE, PUERTO RICO
```
FATHER: RAFAEL FERRER
MOTHER: MARIA PROVIDENCIA CINTRON
*** MARRIED:   '38 UTA HAGEN, ACTRESS  (DIVORCED '48)
DAUGHTER:   '40 LETICIA THYRA FERRER
*** MARRIED:   '48 PHYLLIS HILL  (DIVORCED '53)
*** MARRIED:   '53 ROSEMARY CLOONEY, SINGER
SON:   '54 MIGUEL FERRER
SON:   '55 RAPHAEL FERRER
DAUGHTER:   '56 MARIA FERRER
DAUGHTER:   '57 GABRIEL FERRER
DAUGHTER:   '58 MONSITA FERRER
TALENT: ACTOR-DIRECTOR
CREDIT:   '44 LAURA
AA-NOM  SUP.ACT:   '48 JOAN OF ARC
AA-WIN  ACTOR:   '50 CYRANO DE BERGERAC
AA-NOM  ACTOR:   '52 MOULIN ROUGE
CREDIT:   '54 THE CAINE MUTINY
CREDIT:   '65 SHIP OF FOOLS
CREDIT:   '78 THE SWARM
```

FERRER, MEL   BORN: MELCHIOR GASTON FERRER
                              AUG 25,'17 AT ELBERON,NJ
```
FATHER: DR. JOSE FERRER
MOTHER: IRENE O'DONOHUE
*** MARRIED:   '40 BARBARA C. TRIPPS
DAUGHTER:   '40 MELA FERRER
DAUGHTER:   '41 PEPA FERRER
SON: '41 CHRIS FERRER
```

```
*** MARRIED: '42 FRANCES PILCHARD (DIVORCED '53)
SON: '44 MARK FERRER
*** MARRIED: '54 AUDREY HEPBURN, ACTRESS (DIVORCED '68)
SON: '60 SEAN FERRER
*** MARRIED: '71 ELIZABETH SOUKOTINE
TALENT: DANCER,ACTOR,DIRECTOR
COMMENT: FOUNDER OF LA JOLLA, CALIF. PLAYHOUSE
CREDIT: '51 THE BRAVE BULLS
CREDIT: '57 THE SUN ALSO RISES
CREDIT: '56 WAR AND PEACE
CREDIT: '61 BLOOD AND ROSES
CREDIT: '64 THE FALL OF THE ROMAN EMPIRE
CREDIT: '71 A TIME FOR LOVING
```

FETCHIT, STEPIN   BORN: LINCOLN THEODORE PERRY
                             MAY 30,'02 AT KEY WEST,FL
```
*** MARRIED: '51 BERNICE SLIMS
FRIEND: WILL ROGERS
FRIEND: MOHAMMED ALI
RESIDENCE: CHICAGO, IL
TALENT: ACTOR
CREDIT: '29 IN OLD KENTUCKY
CREDIT: '35 STEAMBOAT 'ROUND THE BEND
CREDIT: '37 ON THE AVENUE
CREDIT: '52 BEND OF THE RIVER
CREDIT: '53 THE SUN SHINES BRIGHTER
```

FIELD, SALLY
                             NOV 06,'46 AT PASADENA,CA
```
MOTHER: MARGARET 'MAGGIE' FIELD, ACTRESS
STEP-FATHER: JOCK MAHONEY
SISTER: PRINCESS FIELD
*** MARRIED: '68 STEVE CRAIG
SON: '69 PETER CRAIG
SON: '72 ELI CRAIG
TALENT: ACTRESS
CREDIT: '67 THE WAY WEST
CREDIT: '72 HOME FOR THE HOLIDAYS
CREDIT: '78 THE END
```

FIELDS, W. C.   BORN: WILLIAM CLAUDE DUKENFIELD
                           FEB 10,'79 AT PHILADELPHIA,PA   DIED IN '46
```
FATHER: JAMES C. DUKENFIELD, FOOD WHOLESALER, TAVERN OWNER
MOTHER: KATE FELTON
SISTER: ELSIE MAE DUKENFIELD
SISTER: ADELE DUKENFIELD
BROTHER: LEROY DUKENFIELD
BROTHER: WALTER DUKENFIELD
*** MARRIED: '00 HARRIET V. HUGHES
SON: '04 WILLIAM CLAUDE FIELDS, JR.
GRANDSON: '44 WILLIAM CLAUDE FIELDS, III
GRANDSON: '45 EVERETT FIELDS
GRANDSON: '49 RONALD J. FIELDS
FRIEND: CAROL DEMPSTER
MEMOIRS: '39 FIELDS FOR PRESIDENT
MEMOIRS: '73 W. C. FIELDS BY HIMSELF RONALD J. FIELDS, EDITOR
TALENT: ACTOR
COMMENT: PEN NAME - OTIS CRIBLECOLIS
```

```
CREDIT:   '15 POOL SHARKS, DEBUT IN 1915
CREDIT:   '25 SALLY OF THE SAWDUST
CREDIT:   '33 ALICE IN WONDERLAND
CREDIT:   '40 THE BANK DICK
CREDIT:   '45 SENSATIONS OF 1945
```

FINCH, PETER   BORN: WILLIAM PETER INGLE-FINCH
                                  SEP 28,'16 AT LONDON, ENGLAND   DIED IN '77
```
FATHER: GEORGE INGLE-FINCH, PHYSICIST AND LEGAL FATHER
MOTHER: ALICIA GLADYS FISHER
STEP-FATHER: CAMPBELL, NATURAL FATHER
*** MARRIED:  '43 TAMARA TCHINAROVA  (DIVORCED '59)
DAUGHTER:  '44 ANITA FINCH
*** MARRIED:  '59 YOLANDE TURNER  (DIVORCED '66)
DAUGHTER:  '60 SAMANTHA FINCH
SON:  '61 CHARLES FINCH
DAUGHTER:  '70 DIANA FINCH, MOTHER - ELETHA BARRETT
*** MARRIED:  '73 ELETHA BARRETT
ROMANCE: SHIRLEY BASSEY, SINGER
RESIDENCE: JAMAICA
TALENT: ACTOR
CREDIT:  '50 THE WOODEN HORSE
CREDIT:  '61 NO LOVE FOR JOHNNIE
CREDIT:  '67 FAR FROM THE MADDING CROWD
AA-NOM  ACTOR:  '71 SUNDAY BLOODY SUNDAY
AA-WIN  ACTOR:  '76 NETWORK
```

FINNEY, ALBERT   BORN: ALBERT FINNEY, JR.
                                   MAY 09,'36 AT SALFORD, LANCASTER, ENGLAND
```
FATHER: ALBERT FINNEY, SR., BOOKIE
MOTHER: ALICE HOBSON
SISTER: --
SISTER: --
*** MARRIED:  '57 JANE WENHAM  (DIVORCED '61)
SON:  '58 SIMON FINNEY
*** MARRIED:  '70 ANOUK AIMEE, ACTRESS
TALENT: ACTOR
CREDIT:  '60 SATURDAY NIGHT AND SUNDAY MORNING
AA-NOM  ACTOR:  '63 TOM JONES
CREDIT:  '67 CHARLIE BUBBLES
CREDIT:  '70 SCROOGE
AA-NOM  ACTOR:  '74 MURDER ON THE ORIENT EXPRESS
```

FISHER, EDDIE   BORN: EDWIN JACK FISHER
                                   AUG 10,'28 AT PHILADELPHIA, PA
```
FATHER: JOSEPH FISHER
MOTHER: KATE MINICKER
*** MARRIED:  '55 DEBBIE REYNOLDS, ACTRESS  (DIVORCED '59)
DAUGHTER:  '56 CARRIE FISHER, ACTRESS
SON:  '58 TODD FISHER
*** MARRIED:  '59 ELIZABETH TAYLOR, ACTRESS  (DIVORCED '64)
STEP-SON: MICHAEL HOWARD WILDING, JR.
STEP-SON: CHRISTOPHER EDWARD WILDING
STEP-DAUGHTER: ELIZABETH FRANCES TODD
ADOPTED DAUGHTER: MARIA-PETRA FISHER
*** MARRIED:  '66 CONCERTA ANN INGOLIE, ACTRESS - CONNIE STEVENS
DAUGHTER:  '68 JOELY FISHER
DAUGHTER:  '70 TRICIA LEIGH FISHER
```

```
    *** MARRIED:  '75 TERRY RICHARD
    TALENT: ACTOR-SINGER
    CREDIT:  '56 BUNDLE OF JOY
    CREDIT:  '60 BUTTERFIELD 8
```

FITZGERALD, BARRY   BORN: WILLIAM JOSEPH SHIELDS
```
                          MAR 10,'88 AT DUBLIN, IRELAND  DIED IN '61
    FATHER: ADOLPHUS SHIELDS, COLUMNIST, DUBLIN TELEGRAPH
    MOTHER: FANNY
    SISTER: UNA SHIELDS
    BROTHER: ARTHUR SHIELDS, ACTOR  (DIED '70)
    FRIEND: GUS TALLOWN, COMPANION
    RESIDENCE: DUBLIN, IRELAND
    TALENT: ACTOR
    CREDIT:  '30 JUNO AND THE PAYCOCK
    CREDIT:  '38 DAWN PATROL
    AA-NOM  ACTOR: '44 GOING MY WAY
    AA-WIN  SUP.ACT.:  '44 GOING MY WAY
    CREDIT:  '56 THE CATERED AFFAIR
    CREDIT:  '59 BROTH OF A BOY
```

FITZGERALD, GERALDINE
```
                          NOV 24,'14 AT DUBLIN, IRELAND  DIED IN '77
    FATHER: EDWARD FITZGERALD, LAWYER
    MOTHER: EDITH
    *** MARRIED:  '36 EDWARD LINDSAY-HOGG, SONGWRITER  (DIVORCED '46)
    SON:  '40 MICHAEL LINDSAY-HOGG, TV DIRECTOR
    *** MARRIED:  '46 STUART SHEFTEL
    DAUGHTER:  '47 SUSAN SHEFTEL
    RESIDENCE: NYC
    TALENT: ACTRESS
    CREDIT:  '35 TURN OF THE TIDE
    AA-NOM  SUP.ACT: '39 WUTHERING HEIGHTS
    CREDIT:  '44 WILSON
    CREDIT:  '58 TEN NORTH FREDERICK
    CREDIT:  '65 THE PAWNBROKER
    CREDIT:  '73 THE LAST AMERICAN HERO
```

FLEMING, RHONDA   BORN: MARILYN LOUIS
```
                        AUG 10,'23 AT LOS ANGELES,CA
    FATHER: HAROLD LOUIS
    MOTHER: EFFIE GRAHAM
    *** MARRIED:  '40 TOM LANE  (DIVORCED '42)
    SON:  '41 KENT LANE
    *** MARRIED:  '52 DR. LEWIS MORRILL  (DIVORCED '54)
    *** MARRIED:  '60 LANG JEFFRIES  (DIVORCED '62)
    *** MARRIED:  '65 HALL BARTLETT
    RESIDENCE: BEVERLY HILLS, CA
    TALENT: ACTRESS-SINGER
    CREDIT:  '44 SINCE YOU WENT AWAY
    CREDIT:  '51 CRY DANGER
    CREDIT:  '54 YANKEE PASHA
    CREDIT:  '58 HOME BEFORE DARK
    CREDIT:  '66 RUN FOR YOUR WIFE
```

```
----------------------------------------------------------------------------------------
FLYNN, ERROL          BORN:   ERROL LESLIE FLYNN
                              JUN 20,'09 AT HOBART, TASMANIA, AUSTRALIA   DIED IN '59
     FATHER: THEODORE THOMSON FLYNN, PROFESSOR
     MOTHER: MARELLE YOUNG
     *** MARRIED:  '36 LILI DAMITA, ACTRESS  (DIVORCED '42)
     SON:  '41 SEAN LESLIE FLYNN, PHOTOGRAPHER
     *** MARRIED:  '43 NORA EDDINGTON  (DIVORCED '49)
     DAUGHTER:  '45 DEIDRE FLYNN
     DAUGHTER:  '47 RORY FLYNN
     *** MARRIED:  '50 PATRICE WYMORE, ACTRESS
     DAUGHTER:  '53 ARLETTA FLYNN
     ROMANCE: OLIVIA DE HAVILLAND, ACTRESS
     ROMANCE: DENISE DUVIVIER
     ROMANCE: JOAN BENNETT, ACTRESS
     ROMANCE: BEVERLY AADLAND, SINGER-DANCER
     FRIEND: DAVID NIVEN
     FRIEND: DIEGO RIVERA, PAINTER
     FRIEND: JOHN BARRYMORE, ACTOR
     RESIDENCE: LOS ANGELES,CA
     RESIDENCE: JAMAICA
     POSSESSION: YACHT 'ZACA'
     POSSESSION: RHODESIAN RIDGEBACK SHOW DOGS
     MEMOIRS:  '34 BEAM ENDS
     MEMOIRS:  '59 MY WICKED, WICKED WAYS
     TALENT: ACTOR-SAILOR
     CREDIT:  '33 IN THE WAKE OF THE BOUNTY
     CREDIT:  '35 CAPTAIN BLOOD
     CREDIT:  '40 THE SEA HAWK
     CREDIT:  '51 ADVENTURES OF CAPTAIN FABIAN
     CREDIT:  '59 CUBAN REBEL GIRLS
----------------------------------------------------------------------------------------
FOCH, NINA            BORN:   NINA CONSUELO MAUD FOCH
                              APR 20,'24 AT LEYDEN,NETHERLANDS
     FATHER: DIRK FOCH, ORCHESTRA CONDUCTOR
     MOTHER: CONSUELO FLOWERTON, ACTRESS
     *** MARRIED:  '54 JAMES LIPTON, ACTOR  (DIVORCED '58)
     *** MARRIED:  '59 DENNIS R. BRITE, WRITER  (DIVORCED '63)
     SON:  '62 SCHUYLER DIRK BRITE
     *** MARRIED:  '67 MICHAEL DEWELL
     TALENT: ACTRESS
     CREDIT:  '43 THE RETURN OF THE VAMPIRE, DEBUT
     CREDIT:  '51 AN AMERICAN IN PARIS
     AA-NOM  SUP.ACT:  '54 EXECUTIVE SUITE
     CREDIT:  '60 CASH MCCALL
     CREDIT:  '71 SUCH GOOD FRIENDS
----------------------------------------------------------------------------------------
FONDA, HENRY          BORN:   HENRY JAYNES FONDA
                              MAY 16,'05 AT GRAND ISLAND,NB
     FATHER: WM. BRACE FONDA
     MOTHER: HERBERTA JAYNES
     SISTER: HARRIET FONDA
     SISTER: JAYNE FONDA
     *** MARRIED:  '31 MARGARET SULLAVAN  (DIVORCED '33)
     *** MARRIED:  '36 FRANCES SEYMOUR, AKA FRANCES BROKAW  (SUICIDE '50)
     STEP-DAUGHTER: FRANCES DE VILLERS BROKAW
     DAUGHTER:  '37 JANE FONDA
     SON-IN-LAW: ROGER VADIM
```

```
SON-IN-LAW: THOMAS HAYDEN
SON:   '39 PETER FONDA
DAUGHTER-IN-LAW: SUSAN BREWER
*** MARRIED:  '50 SUSAN BLANCHARD  (DIVORCED '56)
ADOPTED DAUGHTER: AMY FONDA
*** MARRIED:  '57 ALFREDA FRANCHETTI  (DIVORCED '62)
*** MARRIED:  '65 SHIRLEE MAE ADAMS
GRANDDAUGHTER:  '68 VANESSA VADIM
GRANDSON:   '73 TROY HAYDEN
GRANDDAUGHTER: BRIDGET FONDA
GRANDSON: JUSTIN FONDA
FRIEND: MARLON BRANDO, SR.
FRIEND: JAMES STEWART
FRIEND: LELAND HAYWARD
RESIDENCE: NYC
BIOGRAPHY:  '70 THE FONDAS, BY JOHN SPRINGER
TALENT: ACTOR
CREDIT:   '35 THE FARMER TAKES A WIFE
AA-NOM  ACTOR:  '40 THE GRAPES OF WRATH
CREDIT:   '46 THE FUGITIVE
CREDIT:   '55 MISTER ROBERTS
CREDIT:   '66 BATTLE OF THE BULGE
CREDIT:   '78 THE SWARM
```

FONDA, JANE   BORN: JAYNE SEYMOUR FONDA
                                DEC 21,'37 AT NYC

```
FATHER: HENRY FONDA
MOTHER: FRANCES SEYMOUR
STEP-MOTHER: SUSAN BLANCHARD
STEP-MOTHER: ALFREDA FRANCHETTI
STEP-MOTHER: SHIRLEE MAE ADAMS
STEP-SISTER: FRANCES DE VILLERS BROKAW
STEP-SISTER: AMY FONDA
BROTHER: PETER FONDA
SISTER-IN-LAW: SUSAN BREWER
NIECE: BRIDGET FONDA
NEPHEW: JUSTIN FONDA
*** MARRIED:  '65 ROGER VADIM  (DIVORCED)
STEP-DAUGHTER: NATALIE STROYBERG VADIM
DAUGHTER:  '68 VANESSA VADIM
*** MARRIED:  '73 THOMAS HAYDEN
SON:  '73 TROY HAYDEN
FRIEND: BROOKE HAYWARD
RESIDENCE: SANTA MONICA, CA
TALENT: ACTRESS
CREDIT:   '61 TALL STORY
CREDIT:   '67 HURRY SUNDOWN
AA-NOM  ACTRESS:  '69 THEY SHOOT HORSES, DON'T THEY?
AA-WIN  ACTRESS:  '71 KLUTE
AA-NOM  ACTRESS:  '77 JULIA
CREDIT:  '78 COMING HOME
```

FONDA, PETER   BORN: PETER HENRY FONDA
                                 FEB 23,'39 AT NYC

```
FATHER: HENRY FONDA
MOTHER: FRANCES SEYMOUR
STEP-MOTHER: SUSAN BLANCHARD
STEP-MOTHER: ALFREDA FRANCHETTI
```

```
STEP-MOTHER: SHIRLEE MAE ADAMS
STEP-SISTER: FRANCES DE VILLERS BROKAW
STEP-SISTER: AMY FONDA
SISTER: JANE FONDA
BROTHER-IN-LAW: ROGER VADIM, DIRECTOR
BROTHER-IN-LAW: THOMAS HAYDEN
NIECE: VANESSA VADIM
NEPHEW: TROY HAYDEN
*** MARRIED: SUSAN BREWER  (DIVORCED '74)
DAUGHTER: BRIDGET FONDA
SON: JUSTIN FONDA
FRIEND: WILLIAM 'BILL' HAYWARD
FRIEND: DENNIS HOPPER, ACTOR
TALENT: ACTOR-DIRECTOR
CREDIT:  '63 TAMMY AND THE DOCTOR
CREDIT:  '66 WILD ANGELS
CREDIT:  '69 EASY RIDER
CREDIT:  '71 THE HIRED HAND
CREDIT:  '73 TWO PEOPLE
```

```
FONTAINE, JOAN          BORN:  JOAN DE BEAUVOIR DE HAVILLAND
                               OCT 22,'17 AT TOKYO,JAPAN
     FATHER: WALTER AUGUSTUS DE HAVILLAND
     MOTHER: LILLIAN AUGUSTA RUSE, ACTRESS
     STEP-FATHER: GEORGE M. FONTAINE
     SISTER: OLIVIA DE HAVILLAND
     *** MARRIED:  '39 BRIAN AHERNE, ACTOR  (DIVORCED '44)
     MOTHER-IN-LAW: LOUISE 'LULU' THOMAS
     *** MARRIED:  '46 WILLIAM DOZIER, PRODUCER  (DIVORCED '51)
     DAUGHTER:  '47 DEBORAH LESLIE DOZIER
     *** MARRIED:  '52 COLLIER YOUNG  (DIVORCED '61)
     *** MARRIED:  '64 ALFRED WRIGHT, JR., JOURNALIST
     ADOPTED DAUGHTER: MARTITA VALENTINA CALDERON
     ROMANCE: CONRAD NAGEL
     RESIDENCE: BEVERLY HILLS, CA
     MEMOIRS:  '78 NO BED OF ROSES
     TALENT: ACTRESS
     CREDIT:  '37 QUALITY STREET
     AA-NOM  ACTRESS:  '40 REBECCA
     AA-WIN  ACTRESS:  '41 SUSPICION
     AA-NOM  ACTRESS:  '43 THE CONSTANT NYMPH
     CREDIT:  '44 JANE EYRE
     CREDIT:  '52 THE DECAMERON NIGHTS
     CREDIT:  '62 TENDER IS THE NIGHT
```

```
FORD, FRANCIS           BORN:  FRANCIS O'FEENEY
                               AUG 15,'82 AT PORTLAND, ME  DIED IN '53
     SISTER: JOSEPHINE O'FEENEY
     SISTER: MAMIE O'FEENEY
     BROTHER: EDWARD O'FEENEY
     BROTHER: PATRICK O'FEENEY
     BROTHER: SEAN ALOYSIUS O'FEENEY, DIRECTOR AKA JOHN FORD  (DIED '73)
     NIECE: BARBARA FORD
     *** MARRIED:  '35 MARY ARMSTRONG
     SON: PHILIP FORD
     SON: ROBERT FORD
     SON: FRANCIS FORD, JR.
     PARTNER: GRACE CUNARD, ACTRESS
```

```
        RESIDENCE: LOS ANGELES, CA
        TALENT: ACTOR, DIRECTOR
        CREDIT:  '14 THE PURPLE MASK, SERIES
        CREDIT:  '15 PEG O' THE RING, SERIES
        CREDIT:  '35 THE INFORMER
        CREDIT:  '46 MY DARLING CLEMENTINE
        CREDIT:  '53 THE MARSHAL'S DAUGHTER
-------------------------------------------------------------------------------
FORD, GLENN          BORN:  GWYLLYN SAMUEL NEWTON FORD
                            MAY 01,'16 AT QUEBEC, CANADA
    FATHER: NEWTON FORD, RAILROAD EXEC. & MILL OWNER
    MOTHER: HANNAH
    UNCLE: SIR JOHN MACDONALD, PRIME MINISTER OF CANADA
    *** MARRIED:  '43 ELEANOR POWELL  (DIVORCED '60)
    SON:  '45 PETER FORD
    *** MARRIED:  '66 KATHRYN HAYS
    *** MARRIED:  '77 CYNTHIA HAYWARD, ACTRESS
    FRIEND: ROBERT GOULET
    FRIEND: FRANK SINATRA
    FRIEND: JOHN WAYNE
    RESIDENCE: BEVERLY HILLS, CA
    RESIDENCE: RETREAT IN MAUI, HAWAII
    MEMOIRS:  '70 RFD BEVERLY HILLS
    TALENT: ACTOR, HORTICULTURIST
    COMMENT: DESCENDENT MARTIN VAN BUREN 8TH PRESIDENT OF USA
    CREDIT:  '40 THE LADY IN QUESTION
    CREDIT:  '46 GILDA
    CREDIT:  '55 THE BLACKBOARD JUNGLE
    CREDIT:  '61 POCKETFUL OF MIRACLES
    CREDIT:  '67 THE LAST CHALLENGE
    CREDIT:  '78 EVENING IN BYZANTIUM, TV FEATURE FILM
-------------------------------------------------------------------------------
FORSYTHE, JOHN       BORN:  JOHN LINCOLN FREUND
                            JAN 29,'18 AT PENNS GROVE, NJ
    FATHER: SAMUEL JEREMIAH FREUND
    MOTHER: BLANCHE MATERSON BLOHM
    *** MARRIED: JULIE WARREN
    DAUGHTER:  '54 DALL FORSYTHE
    DAUGHTER:  '55 BROOKE FORSYTHE
    SON:  '56 PAGE FORSYTHE
    *** MARRIED: '69 PARKER MCCORMICK
    RESIDENCE: PELHAM MANOR, NY
    TALENT: ACTOR
    CREDIT:  '43 DESTINATION TOKYO
    CREDIT:  '56 THE AMBASSADOR'S DAUGHTER
    CREDIT:  '66 MADAME X
    CREDIT:  '67 IN COLD BLOOD
    CREDIT:  '69 TOPAZ
-------------------------------------------------------------------------------
FOX, WILLIAM         BORN:  WILLIAM FRIED
                            JAN 01,'79 AT TULCHVA, HUNGARY  DIED IN '52
    BROTHER: AARON FOX, FILM EXEC.
    *** MARRIED:  '00 EVE LEE
    DAUGHTER: VIRGINIA FOX
    SON-IN-LAW: DARRYL F. ZANUCK, PRODUCER, WRITER
    GRANDSON:  '34 RICHARD DARRYL ZANUCK, PRODUCER
    POSSESSION:  '15 FOX FILM CORPORATION SOLD IN 1930
    BIOGRAPHY:  '33 WILLIAM FOX, BY UPTON SINCLAIR
```

TALENT: EXECUTIVE

FOXX, REDD   BORN: JOHN ELROY SANFORD
                            DEC 09,'22 AT ST. LOUIS,MO
    FATHER: FRED SANFORD, ELECTRICIAN
    BROTHER: FRED SANFORD, JR.
    *** MARRIED: EVELYN KILLIBREW (DIVORCED '51)
    *** MARRIED: '55 BETTY JEAN HARRIS (DIVORCED '76)
    ADOPTED DAUGHTER: DEBRACA FOXX
    PARTNER: SLAPPY WHITE
    TALENT: ACTOR
    COMMENT: TWO SISTERS DIED BEORE 1922
    CREDIT: '75 SANFORD & SON, TV SERIES
    CREDIT: COTTON COMES TO HARLEM

FOY, JR., EDDIE   BORN: EDWARD F. FOY, JR.
                                 FEB 04,'05 AT NEW ROCHELLE, NY
    FATHER: EDWARD FITZGERALD FOY, SR., VAUDEVILLIAN (DIED '28)
    MOTHER: MADELINE MORONDO, ACTRESS, DANCER
    SISTER: MARY FOY
    SISTER: MADELEINE FOY
    BROTHER-IN-LAW: LYLE LATELL, MARRIED MARY FOY
    BROTHER: BRYAN FOY, PRODUCER
    BROTHER: CHARLES FOY, RESTAURATEUR
    BROTHER: RICHARD FOY, FILM EXHIBITOR
    BROTHER: IRVING FOY
    *** MARRIED: ANNA MARIE KENNEY (DIED '52)
    SON: '35 EDDIE FOY, 3RD
    TALENT: ACTOR
    CREDIT: '28 FOYS FOR JOYS
    CREDIT: '40 FUGITIVE FROM JUSTICE
    CREDIT: '54 LUCKY ME
    CREDIT: '57 THE PAJAMA GAME
    CREDIT: '67 THIRTY IS A DANGEROUS AGE

FRANCIOSA, ANTHONY   BORN: ANTHONY GEORGE PAPALEO
                                    OCT 25,'28 AT NYC
    FATHER: ANTHONY PAPALEO
    MOTHER: JEAN FRANCIOSA
    *** MARRIED: '52 BEATRICE BAKALYAR (DIVORCED '57)
    *** MARRIED: '57 SHELLEY WINTERS, ACTRESS (DIVORCED '60)
    *** MARRIED: '62 JUDY BALABAN KANTOR
    STEP-DAUGHTER: VICTORIA KANTOR
    STEP-DAUGHTER: AMY KANTOR
    DAUGHTER: '64 NINA FRANCIOSA
    RESIDENCE: NYC
    TALENT: ACTOR
    CREDIT: '56 A FACE IN THE CROWD, DEBUT
    AA-NOM ACTOR: '57 A HATFUL OF RAIN
    CREDIT: '58 THE LONG HOT SUMMER
    CREDIT: '65 THE PLEASURE SEEKERS
    CREDIT: '72 ACROSS 110TH STREET

FRANCIS THE MULE
                    JAN 01,'50 AT UNIVERSAL-INTERNATIONAL STUDIO   DIED IN '56
    FRIEND: ZASU PITTS, ACTRESS
    PARTNER: ALLAN LANE, HIS VOICE
    PARTNER: DONALD O'CONNOR, HIS FIRST SCREEN MASTER
    PARTNER: MICKEY ROONEY, HIS SECOND SCREEN MASTER
    TALENT: ACTOR
    CREDIT: FRANCIS THE TALKING MULE, SERIES OF FILMS

FRANCIS, ANNE
                    SEP 16,'30 AT OSSINING,NY
    FATHER: PHILIP FRANCIS
    MOTHER: EDITH ABBERTSON
    *** MARRIED: '52 BAMLET L. PRICE, JR. (DIVORCED '55)
    *** MARRIED: '60 DR. ROBT. ABELOFF (DIVORCED '64)
    DAUGHTER: '63 ELIZABETH JANE ABELOFF
    ADOPTED DAUGHTER: MARGARET WEST FRANCIS
    POSSESSION: '46 CONTRACT AT M-G-M
    TALENT: MODEL-ACTRESS
    CREDIT: '47 SUMMER HOLIDAY, DEBUT
    CREDIT: '55 THE BLACKBOARD JUNGLE
    CREDIT: '68 FUNNY GIRL
    CREDIT: '70 MORE DEAD THAN ALIVE
    CREDIT: '72 HAUNTS OF THE VERY RICH

FRANCISCUS, JAMES   BORN: JAMES GROVER FRANCISCUS
                    JAN 31,'34 AT CLAYTON,MR
    FATHER: JOHN ALLEN FRANCISCUS
    MOTHER: LORAINE GROVER
    *** MARRIED: '60 KATHLEEN KENT WELLMAN, BALLERINA
    FATHER-IN-LAW: WILLIAM WELLMAN, DIRECTOR
    DAUGHTER: '63 JAMIE FRANCISCUS
    DAUGHTER: '65 JOLIE FRANCISCUS
    DAUGHTER: '73 KELLIE FRANCISCUS
    DAUGHTER: '75 KORIE FRANCISCUS
    ROMANCE: DANNI CRAYNE
    RESIDENCE: LOS ANGELES, CA
    TALENT: ACTOR
    CREDIT: '56 FOUR BOYS AND A GUN
    CREDIT: '60 I PASSED FOR WHITE
    CREDIT: '64 YOUNGBLOOD HAWKE
    CREDIT: '69 MAROONED
    CREDIT: '71 CAT O'NINE TAILS

FRAWLEY, WILLIAM
                    FEB 26,'87 AT BURLINGTON, IO DIED IN '66
    SISTER: MARY FRAWLEY
    BROTHER: PAUL FRAWLEY, VAUDEVILLE PARTNER
    BROTHER: JAY FRAWLEY
    *** MARRIED: '14 LOUISE, VAUDEVILLE PARTNER (DIVORCED '27)
    RESIDENCE: LOS ANGELES, CA
    TALENT: ACTOR
    CREDIT: '29 TURKEY FOR TWO
    CREDIT: '36 STRIKE ME PINK
    CREDIT: '41 THE BRIDE CAME C.O.D.
    CREDIT: '50 KISS TOMORROW GOODBYE
    CREDIT: '62 SAFE AT HOME!

FURNESS, BETTY   BORN: ELIZABETH MARY FURNESS
                                   JAN 03,'16 AT DOUGLASTON, LONG ISLAND, NY
     FATHER: GEORGE CHOATE FURNESS, MARKET RESEARCHER
     MOTHER: FLORENCE STURTEVANT, ARTIST
     STEP-MOTHER: MARGARET ROGERS, SOCIAL WORKER
     *** MARRIED: '37 JOHN GREEN, MUSIC COMPOSER, CONDUCTOR (DIVORCED '42)
     BROTHER-IN-LAW: RICHARD GREEN, ASST. DIRECTOR (DIED)
     DAUGHTER: '39 BARBARA BABETTE 'BABBIE' GREEN, MUSIC COMPOSER, LYRICIST (MARRIED '61)
     SON-IN-LAW: DENTON MCCOY SNYDER, THEATRE ARTS PROFESSOR (DIVORCED '73)
     *** MARRIED: '44 HUGH 'BUD' ERNST, PRODUCER (DIVORCED)
     *** MARRIED: '45 HUGH 'BUD' ERNST, REMARRIED (DIED '50)
     *** MARRIED: '67 LESLIE GRANT MIDGLEY, JOURNALIST, PRODUCER
     STEP-DAUGHTER: ANDRE MIDGLEY, DESIGNER
     STEP-SON: PETER JEDEDIAH 'JEDDY' MIDGLEY
     GRANDSON: '66 CHRISTOPHER JOHN SNYDER
     GRANDDAUGHTER: '68 ELIZABETH ANNE SNYDER
     FRIEND: ANNE SHIRLEY, ACTRESS
     FRIEND: JUDY CRICHTON, PRODUCER
     RESIDENCE: NYC
     POSSESSION: '32 CONTRACT AT M-G-M STUDIOS
     POSSESSION: NEEDLEPOINT WORK-SOME OF HER OWN HAS BEEN EXHIBITED
     TALENT: MODEL, ACTRESS, SPOKESPERSON
     COMMENT: SPOKESPERSON FOR WESTINGHOUSE CORPORATION
     CREDIT: '66 SPECIAL ASST-CONSUMER AFFAIRS, GOVT OFFICE-APPOINTED BY LBJ
     CREDIT: SWING TIME
     CREDIT: THE MAGNIFICENT OBSESSION

GABLE, CLARK   BORN: WILLIAM CLARK 'BILLY' GABLE
                             FEB 01,'01 AT CADIZ,OH DIED IN '60
     FATHER: WILLIAM H. GABLE, OIL FIELD WORKER,FARMER
     MOTHER: ADELINE HERSHELMAN
     STEP-MOTHER: JENNIE DUNLAP
     *** MARRIED: '24 JOSEPHINE DILLON (DIVORCED '30)
     *** MARRIED: '31 RHEA LUCAS LANGHAM (DIVORCED '39)
     *** MARRIED: '39 CAROLE LOMBARD, ACTRESS (DIED '42)
     *** MARRIED: '49 LADY SYLVIA HAWKES ASHLEY, ACTRESS (DIVORCED '52)
     *** MARRIED: '55 KAY WILLIAMS SPRECKELS, SUGAR HEIRESS
     STEP-DAUGHTER: JOAN SPRECKELS
     SON: '60 JOHN CLARK GABLE
     ROMANCE: FRANCES DOETLER
     ROMANCE: JANE COWL
     ROMANCE: PAULINE FREDERICK
     ROMANCE: ALICE BRADY
     ROMANCE: JOAN CRAWFORD
     ROMANCE: LORETTA YOUNG, DURING CALL OF THE WILD
     ROMANCE: MILLICENT ROGERS
     ROMANCE: VIRGINIA GREY
     FRIEND: MINNA WALLIS, AGENT
     FRIEND: JEAN HARLOW
     FRIEND: LIONEL BARRYMORE
     BIOGRAPHY: '63 THE KING, BY CHARLES SAMUELS
     TALENT: ACTOR
     CREDIT: '24 FORBIDDEN PARADISE, DEBUT IN 1924
     AA-WIN ACTOR: '34 IT HAPPENED ONE NIGHT
     AA-NOM ACTOR: '35 MUTINY ON THE BOUNTY
     AA-NOM ACTOR: '39 GONE WITH THE WIND
     CREDIT: '53 MOGAMBO
     CREDIT: '61 THE MISFITS

GABOR, EVA
                        FEB 11,'21 AT BUDAPEST, HUNGARY
     FATHER: VILMOS GABOR
     MOTHER: JOLIE
     SISTER: ZSA ZSA GABOR
     SISTER: MAGDA GABOR
     BROTHER-IN-LAW: BURHAN BELGE
     BROTHER-IN-LAW: HAL B. HAYES
     BROTHER-IN-LAW: CONRAD NICHOLSON HILTON, SR.
     BROTHER-IN-LAW: GEORGE SANDERS
     BROTHER-IN-LAW: HERBERT L. HUTNER
     BROTHER-IN-LAW: JOSHUA COSDEN, JR.
     BROTHER-IN-LAW: JACK RYAN
     BROTHER-IN-LAW: MICHAEL O'HARA
     BROTHER-IN-LAW: HELTAI TIBOR
     BROTHER-IN-LAW: ARTHUR GALLUCI
     NIECE: FRANCESCA HILTON
     *** MARRIED: '39 ERIC DRIMMER, PHYSICIAN (DIVORCED '42)
     *** MARRIED: '43 CHARLES ISAACS, REALTOR (DIVORCED '49)
     *** MARRIED: '56 DR. JOHN WILLIAMS
     *** MARRIED: '59 RICHARD BROWN, STOCKBROKER
     *** MARRIED: '73 FRANK G. JAMESON
     RESIDENCE: BEVERLY HILLS, CA
     MEMOIRS: '54 ORCHIDS AND SALAMI
     TALENT: ACTRESS

```
CREDIT:   '41 PACIFIC BLACKOUT
CREDIT:   '54 TARZAN AND THE SLAVE GIRL
CREDIT:   '56 THE TRUTH ABOUT WOMEN
CREDIT:   '58 GIGI
CREDIT:   '63 A NEW KIND OF LOVE
```

GABOR, ZSA ZSA   BORN: SARI GABOR
                                FEB 06,'19 AT HUNGARY
```
     FATHER: VILMOS GABOR
     MOTHER: JOLIE
     SISTER: EVA GABOR
     SISTER: MAGDA GABOR
     BROTHER-IN-LAW: ERIC DRIMMER
     BROTHER-IN-LAW: CHARLES ISAACS
     BROTHER-IN-LAW: DR. JOHN WILLIAMS
     BROTHER-IN-LAW: RICHARD BROWN
     BROTHER-IN-LAW: FRANK G. JAMESON
     BROTHER-IN-LAW: GEORGE SANDERS
     BROTHER-IN-LAW: HELTAI TIBOR
     BROTHER-IN-LAW: ARTHUR GALLUCI
     BROTHER-IN-LAW: HAL B. HAYES
 *** MARRIED: BURHAN BELGE
 *** MARRIED: CONRAD NICHOLSON HILTON, SR.
 *** MARRIED: GEORGE SANDERS
 *** MARRIED: HERBERT L. HUTNER
 *** MARRIED: JOSHUA COSDEN, JR.
 *** MARRIED: JACK RYAN
 *** MARRIED: MICHAEL O'HARA
     DAUGHTER: FRANCESCA HILTON
     ROMANCE: PORFIRIO RUBIROSA, DIPLOMAT
     MEMOIRS:  '61 MY STORY
     MEMOIRS:  '70 HOW TO CATCH A MAN,HOW TO KEEP A MAN,HOW TO GET RID OF A MAN
     TALENT: ACTRESS
     COMMENT: MISS HUNGARY OF 1936
     CREDIT:   '52 LOVELY TO LOOK AT
     CREDIT:   '59 QUEEN OF OUTER SPACE
     CREDIT:   '66 ARRIVEDERCI BABY
     CREDIT:   '72 UP FRONT
```

GARBO, GRETA   BORN: GRETA LOVISA GUSTAFSSON
                               SEP 18,'05 AT STOCKHOLM, SWEDEN
```
     FATHER: KARL ALFRED GUSTAFSSON  (DIED '20)
     MOTHER: ANNA LOVISA KARLSSON
     SISTER: ALVA GUSTAFSSON, ACTRESS  (DIED '26)
     BROTHER: SVEN GUSTAFSSON
     ROMANCE: JOHN GILBERT, ACTOR
     ROMANCE: GEORGE SCHLEE, FINANCIER
     ROMANCE: GAYLORD HAUSER, DIETICIAN
     ROMANCE: LEOPOLD STOKOWSKI, CONDUCTOR
     FRIEND: CECILE DE ROTHSCHILD
     FRIEND: MAURITZ STILLER, DIRECTOR
     FRIEND: CECIL BEATON, DESIGNER
     FRIEND: ARISTOTLE ONASSIS, SHIP OWNER
     FRIEND: SALKA VIERTEL
     FRIEND: CLARENCE BROWN, DIRECTOR
     RESIDENCE: NYC
     BIOGRAPHY:  '55 GARBO, BY JOHN BAINBRIDGE
     TALENT: ACTRESS
```

COMMENT: GAYELORD HAUSER DEDICATED HIS WILD RICE HAMBURGER TO HER
COMMENT: AKA - HARRIET BROWN
CREDIT: '24 THE STORY OF GOSTA BERLING
CREDIT: '27 LOVE
AA-NOM ACTRESS: '29 ANNA CHRISTIE
AA-NOM ACTRESS: '30 ROMANCE
AA-NOM ACTRESS: '37 CAMILLE
AA-NOM ACTRESS: '39 NINOTCHKA
CREDIT: '41 TWO-FACED WOMAN
AA-SPECIAL AWARD: '54 HONORARY AWARD FOR HER 'UNFORGETTABLE SCREEN PERFORMANCES'

GARDNER, AVA   BORN: AVA LAVINIA GARDNER
                          DEC 24,'22 AT SMITHFIELD, NC
FATHER: JONAS B. GARDNER, FARMER
MOTHER: MARY ELIZABETH
SISTER: BEATRICE GARDNER
SISTER: INEZ GARDNER
*** MARRIED: '42 MICKEY ROONEY, ACTOR (DIVORCED '43)
FATHER-IN-LAW: JOE YULE, VAUDEVILLIAN
*** MARRIED: '45 ARTIE SHAW, BANDLEADER
STEP-SON: STEVEN KERN SHAW
*** MARRIED: '51 FRANK SINATRA, ACTOR (DIVORCED '54)
STEP-DAUGHTER: NANCY SINATRA, SINGER
STEP-SON: FRANK SINATRA, JR.
STEP-DAUGHTER: CHRISTINE SINATRA
ROMANCE: HOWARD HUGHES
ROMANCE: JOHNNY STOMPANATO
ROMANCE: MARIO CABRE, MATADOR
RESIDENCE: MADRID, SPAIN
POSSESSION: '41 CONTRACT AT M-G-M UNTIL 1958
BIOGRAPHY: '74 AVA, BY CHARLES HIGHAM
TALENT: ACTRESS
CREDIT: '43 YOUNG IDEAS
CREDIT: '50 MY FORBIDDEN PAST
AA-NOM ACTRESS: '53 MOGAMBO
CREDIT: '59 THE NAKED MAJA
CREDIT: '69 MAYERLING

GARFIELD, JOHN   BORN: JULIUS GARFINKLE
                          MAR 04,'13 AT NYC DIED IN '52
FATHER: DAVID GARFINKLE
MOTHER: HANNAH (DIED '70)
BROTHER: MAX GARFINKLE
*** MARRIED: '33 ROBERTA MANN
SON: '43 JOHN GARFIELD, JR., ACTOR
DAUGHTER: '46 JULIE GARFIELD
POSSESSION: '38 CONTRACT AT WARNER BROTHERS
POSSESSION: '47 ENTERPRISE PRODUCTIONS
BIOGRAPHY: '75 BODY AND SOUL, BY LARRY SWINDELL
TALENT: ACTOR
COMMENT: SEMI-FINALIST, GOLDEN GLOVES BOXING CONTEST
CREDIT: '33 FOOTLIGHT PARADE
AA-NOM SUP.ACT: '38 FOUR DAUGHTERS
CREDIT: '42 TORTILLA FLAT
AA-NOM ACTOR: '47 BODY AND SOUL
CREDIT: '52 HE RAN ALL THE WAY

```
-----------------------------------------------------------------------------------------
GARLAND, JUDY          BORN:   FRANCES ETHEL GUMM
                              JUN 10,'22 AT GRAND RAPIDS, MN  DIED IN '69
      FATHER: FRANK AVENT GUMM, SINGER
      MOTHER: ETHEL MARION MILNE, PIANIST
      SISTER: DOROTHY VIRGINIA GUMM
      SISTER: MARY JANE SUZANNE GUMM
      *** MARRIED:  '41 DAVID ROSE, MUSICIAN  (DIVORCED '44)
      *** MARRIED:  '45 VINCENTE MINNELLI, DIRECTOR  (DIVORCED '51)
      MOTHER-IN-LAW: MINA GENNELL, ACTRESS, SINGER, DANCER
      DAUGHTER:  '46 LIZA MINNELLI, ACTRESS
      *** MARRIED:  '52 SID LUFT  (DIVORCED '65)
      DAUGHTER:  '52 LORNA LUFT
      SON:  '55 JOEY LUFT
      *** MARRIED:  '66 MARK HERRIN, ACTOR  (DIVORCED '67)
      *** MARRIED:  '69 MICKEY DEANS, CLUB MANAGER
      ROMANCE: GLENN FORD
      ROMANCE: ARTIE SHAW, BANDLEADER, ACTOR
      TALENT: SINGER, ACTRESS
      POSSESSION:  '37 CONTRACT AT M-G-M UNTIL 1950
      BIOGRAPHY:  '74 I REMEMBER IT WELL, BY VINCENTE MINNELLI
      COMMENT: APPEARED WITH SISTERS ON STAGE AS THE 'GUMM SISTERS'
      CREDIT:  '36 PIGSKIN PARADE
      AA-SPECIAL AWARD:  '39 AN HONORARY MINIATURE AWARD
      CREDIT:  '39 THE WIZARD OF OZ
      CREDIT:  '48 EASTER PARADE
      AA-NOM ACTRESS:  '54 A STAR IS BORN
      AA-NOM  SUP.ACT:  '61 JUDGMENT AT NUREMBERG
      CREDIT:  '63 I COULD GO ON SINGING
-----------------------------------------------------------------------------------------
GARNER, JAMES          BORN:   JAMES SCOTT BAUMGARNER
                              APR 07,'28 AT NORMAN, OK
      FATHER: WELDON BAUMGARNER, UPHOLSTERER
      MOTHER: MILDRED  (DIED '33)
      BROTHER: JACK BAUMGARNER
      BROTHER: CHARLES BAUMGARNER
      *** MARRIED:  '56 LOIS CLARKE
      STEP-DAUGHTER: KIMBERLY CLARKE GARNER
      DAUGHTER:  '58 GRETA GARNER
      PARTNER: CLINT EASTWOOD, IN REAL ESTATE IN CARMEL, CAL.
      RESIDENCE: BRENTWOOD, CA
      POSSESSION: OIL LANDS IN TEXAS & COLORADO
      TALENT: ACTOR
      CREDIT:  '56 TOWARD THE UNKNOWN
      CREDIT:  '59 CASH MCCALL
      CREDIT:  '64 THE AMERICANIZATION OF EMILY
      CREDIT:  '68 HOW SWEET IT IS
-----------------------------------------------------------------------------------------
GARSON, GREER
                              SEP 29,'08 AT CO. DOWN, N. IRELAND
      FATHER: GEORGE GARSON
      MOTHER: NINA GREER
      *** MARRIED:  '32 EDWIN A. SNELSON  (DIVORCED '37)
      *** MARRIED:  '43 RICHARD NEY  (DIVORCED '47)
      *** MARRIED:  '49 ELIJAH 'BUDDY' FOGELSON
      FRIEND: LOUIS B. MAYER
      RESIDENCE: DALLAS, TEXAS
      RESIDENCE: PECOS, NEW MEXICO
```

```
TALENT: ACTRESS
COMMENT: GRADUATED CUM LAUDE, GRENOBLE UNIVERSITY
AA-NOM  ACTRESS:   '39 GOODBYE, MR. CHIPS
AA-NOM  ACTRESS:   '41 BLOSSOMS IN THE DUST
AA-WIN  ACTRESS:   '42 MRS. MINIVER
AA-NOM  ACTRESS:   '43 MADAME CURIE
AA-NOM  ACTRESS:   '44 MRS. PARKINGTON
AA-NOM  ACTRESS:   '45 THE VALLEY OF DECISION
AA-NOM  ACTRESS:   '60 SUNRISE AT CAMPOBELLO
```

```
GAYNOR, JANET        BORN:  LAURA GAINOR
                            NOV 06,'06 AT PHILADELPHIA, PA
   FATHER: FRANK GAINOR
   MOTHER: LAURA BUHL
   SISTER: HILARY GAINOR
   *** MARRIED:  '29 LYDELL PECK, ATTORNEY  (DIVORCED '34)
   *** MARRIED:  '39 GILBERT ADRIAN, DESIGNER  (DIED '59)
   SON:  '40 ROBIN ADRIAN
   *** MARRIED:  '65 PAUL GREGORY, PRODUCER
   ROMANCE: LEW AYRES
   ROMANCE: CHARLES FARRELL
   ROMANCE: TYRONE POWER
   RESIDENCE: PALM SPRINGS, CA
   TALENT: ACTRESS, ARTIST
   COMMENT: THE 1ST ACADEMY AWARD FOR BEST ACTRESS IN 1927
   CREDIT:  '26 THE JOHNSTOWN FLOOD
   AA-WIN  ACTRESS:  '27 SEVENTH HEAVEN, STREET ANGEL, AND SUNRISE (3 MOVIES)
   CREDIT:  '29 LUCKY STAR
   CREDIT:  '30 HAPPY DAYS
   AA-NOM  ACTRESS:  '37 A STAR IS BORN
   CREDIT:  '57 BERNARDINE
```

```
GAYNOR, MITZI        BORN:  FRANCESCA MITZI GERBER
                            SEP 04,'31 AT CHICAGO,IL
   FATHER: HENRY GERBER, MUSICAL DIRECTOR
   MOTHER: PAULINE FISHER, DANCER
   *** MARRIED:  '54 JACK BEAN, ACTOR
   ROMANCE: HOWARD HUGHES
   RESIDENCE: BEVERLY HILLS, CA
   TALENT: ACTRESS-DANCER
   CREDIT:  '50 MY BLUE HEAVEN
   CREDIT:  '54 THERE'S NO BUSINESS LIKE SHOW  BUSINESS
   CREDIT:  '56 ANYTHING GOES
   CREDIT:  '58 SOUTH PACIFIC
   CREDIT:  '63 FOR LOVE OR MONEY
```

```
GIBSON, HOOT         BORN:  EDWARD GIBSON
                            AUG 06,'92 AT TEKAMAH, NB  DIED IN '62
   *** MARRIED: HELEN JOHNSON, ACTRESS  (DIVORCED)
   *** MARRIED:  '30 SALLY EILERS, ACTRESS  (DIVORCED '33)
   *** MARRIED:  '42 DOROTHY DUNSTAN, SINGER
   DAUGHTER: LOIS GIBSON
   TALENT: ACTOR
   CREDIT:  '15 THE HAZARDS OF HELEN
   CREDIT:  '22 THE GALLOPING KID
   CREDIT:  '29 SMILING GUNS
   CREDIT:  '30 CONCENTRATIN' KID
   CREDIT:  '32 GAY BUCKAROO
```

```
         CREDIT:  '61 OCEAN'S ELEVEN
---------------------------------------------------------------------------------------------------
GIELGUD, JOHN          BORN:  ARTHUR JOHN GIELGUD
                              APR 14,'04 AT LONDON, ENGLAND
     GRANDMOTHER: MME. ASZBERGER, ACTRESS
     FATHER: FRANK GIELGUD
     MOTHER: KATE TERRY-LEWIS, ACTRESS
     BROTHER: VAL GIELGUD, WRITER
     BROTHER: LEWIS GIELGUD
     SISTER-IN-LAW: BARBARA DILLON
     SISTER-IN-LAW: RITA VALE WEILL
     SISTER-IN-LAW: MONICA GREEY
     RESIDENCE: WESTMINSTER, LONDON
     POSSESSION: KNIGHTED IN 1953
     MEMOIRS:  '73 DISTINGUISHED COMPANY
     MEMOIRS:  '76 EARLY STAGES
     TALENT: ACTOR
     CREDIT:  '32 THE GOOD COMPANIONS
     CREDIT:  '55 RICHARD III
     AA-NOM  SUP.ACT:  '64 BECKET
---------------------------------------------------------------------------------------------------
GILBERT, JOHN          BORN:  JOHN PRINGLE, JR.
                              JUL 10,'97 AT LOGAN, UT   DIED IN '36
     FATHER: JOHN PRINGLE, ACTOR  (DIED '29)
     MOTHER: SARAH IDA APPERLEY, ACTRESS - ADA ADAIR
     STEP-FATHER: WALTER B. GILBERT
     *** MARRIED:  '17 OLIVE BURWELL  (DIVORCED '18)
     *** MARRIED:  '22 LEATRICE JOY, ACTRESS  (DIVORCED '25)
     DAUGHTER:  '23 LEATRICE JOY GILBERT
     *** MARRIED:  '29 INA CLAIRE, ACTRESS  (DIVORCED '31)
     *** MARRIED:  '32 VIRGINIA BRUCE  (DIVORCED '34)
     DAUGHTER:  '33 SUSAN ANN GILBERT
     ROMANCE: NORMA SHEARER
     ROMANCE: GRETA GARBO
     FRIEND: PAUL BERN
     FRIEND: MARLENE DIETRICH
     FRIEND: IRVING THALBERG
     RESIDENCE: BEVERLY HILLS, CA
     POSSESSION: YACHT 'TEMPTRESS'
     TALENT: WRITER, DIRECTOR, ACTOR
     CREDIT:  '15 THE MOTHER INSTINCT
     CREDIT:  '23 CALIFORNIA ROMANCE
     CREDIT:  '24 HE WHO GETS SLAPPED
     CREDIT:  '29 HIS GLORIOUS NIGHT
     CREDIT:  '34 THE CAPTAIN HATES THE SEA, LAST PICTURE
---------------------------------------------------------------------------------------------------
GINGOLD, HERMIONE        BORN:  HERMIONE FERDINANDA GINGOLD
                                DEC 09,'97 AT LONDON, ENGLAND
     FATHER: JAMES GINGOLD
     MOTHER: KATE WALTER
     SISTER: MARGARET GINGOLD
     AUNT: BARONESS HELENE GINGOLD, OF THE AUSTRIAN COURT
     UNCLE: BARON NICOLA DI SAN GREGORIO, OF THE ITALIAN COURT
     *** MARRIED: MICHAEL JOSEF
     SON:  '21 STEPHEN JOSEF
     SON:  '22 LESLIE JOSEF
     *** MARRIED:  '30 ERIC MASCHWITZ, WRITER, DRAMATIST  (DIVORCED)
     MEMOIRS: THE WORLD IS SQUARE
```

```
TALENT: ACTRESS-SINGER
CREDIT:  '36 SOMEONE AT THE DOOR
CREDIT:  '52 PICKWICK PAPERS
CREDIT:  '58 BELL, BOOK AND CANDLE
CREDIT:  '71 BANYON
```

GISH, DOROTHY   BORN: DOROTHY ELIZABETH GISH
                                  MAR 11,'98 AT MASSILLON, OH   DIED IN '68
```
FATHER: JAMES LEIGH GISH
MOTHER: MARY ROBINSON MCCONELL, ACTRESS - MAY BERNARD
SISTER: LILLIAN GISH, ACTRESS
*** MARRIED: JAMES RENNIE, ACTOR
RESIDENCE: RAPALLO, ITALY
BIOGRAPHY:  '73 DOROTHY & LILLIAN GISH, BY LILLIAN GISH
TALENT: ACTRESS
CREDIT:  '03 EAST LYNNE, STAGE DEBUT
CREDIT:  '12 THE NEW YORK HAT
CREDIT:  '22 ORPHANS OF THE STORM
CREDIT:  '44 OUR HEARTS WERE YOUNG AND GAY
CREDIT:  '64 THE CHALK GARDEN
```

GISH, LILLIAN   BORN: LILLIAN DIANA GISH
                                  OCT 14,'96 AT SPRINGFIELD,OH
```
FATHER: JAMES LEIGH GISH
MOTHER: MARY ROBINSON MCCONNELL, ACTRESS - MAY BERNARD
SISTER: DOROTHY GISH, ACTRESS
BROTHER-IN-LAW: JAMES RENNIE, ACTOR
ROMANCE: D.W. GRIFFITH, PRODUCER
ROMANCE: GEORGE JEAN NATHAN, WRITER
MEMOIRS:  '73 DOROTHY & LILLIAN GISH
MEMOIRS: THE MOVIES, MR. GRIFFITH  AND ME
TALENT: ACTRESS
CREDIT:  '12 TWO DAUGHTERS OF EVE
CREDIT:  '22 ORPHANS OF THE STORM
CREDIT:  '30 ONE ROMANTIC NIGHT
AA-NOM  SUP.ACT:  '46 DUEL IN THE SUN
CREDIT:  '55 THE NIGHT OF THE HUNTER
CREDIT:  '67 THE COMEDIANS
AA-SPECIAL AWARD:  '70 HONORARY AWARD FOR SUPERLATIVE ARTISTRY IN MOTION PICTURES
```

GLEASON, JACKIE   BORN: HERBERT JOHN GLEASON
                                  FEB 26,'16 AT BROOKLYN, NY
```
FATHER: HERBERT GLEASON
MOTHER: MAE KELLY
BROTHER: --  (DIED '19)
*** MARRIED: '36 GENEVIEVE HALFORD  (DIVORCED '71)
DAUGHTER:  '40 GERALDINE GLEASON
DAUGHTER:  '42 LINDA GLEASON
*** MARRIED:  '71 BEVERLY MCKITTRICK  (DIVORCED '74)
*** MARRIED:  '75 MARILYN TAYLOR
TALENT: ACTOR-ENTERTAINER
CREDIT:  '41 NAVY BLUES
CREDIT:  '50 LIFE OF RILEY
AA-NOM  SUP.ACT:  '61 THE HUSTLER
CREDIT:  '62 GIGOT
CREDIT:  '63 REQUIEM FOR A HEAVYWEIGHT
CREDIT:  '69 HOW DO I LOVE THEE?
```

GLEASON, JAMES "JIMMY"
                                    MAY 23,'86 AT NYC DIED IN '59
    FATHER: WILLIAM GLEASON, ACTOR, PRODUCER
    MOTHER: MINA CROLINS, ACTRESS
    *** MARRIED: '05 LUCILLE WEBSTER, ACTRESS (DIED '47)
    SON: '08 RUSSELL GLEASON, ACTOR (SUICIDE '45)
    DAUGHTER-IN-LAW: CYNTHIA LINDSAY, WRITER
    GRANDSON: '40 MICHAEL GLEASON LINDSAY, WRITER
    TALENT: ACTOR
    CREDIT: '22 POLLY OF THE FOLLIES
    CREDIT: '29 THE SHANNONS OF BRAODWAY
    CREDIT: '35 MURDER ON A HONEYMOON
    AA-NOM SUP.ACT: '41 HERE COMES MR. JORDAN
    CREDIT: '58 THE LAST HURRAH

GODDARD, PAULETTE   BORN: PAULINE MARION GODDARD LEVEE
                                     JUN 03,'11 AT GREAT NECK, NY
    FATHER: JOSEPH RUSSELL LEVEE
    MOTHER: ALTA GODDARD
    *** MARRIED: '27 EDWARD JAMES (DIVORCED '32)
    *** MARRIED: '36 CHARLES CHAPLIN, ACTOR (DIVORCED '42)
    MOTHER-IN-LAW: HANNAH HILL, SINGER-AKA LILY HARLEY
    STEP-SON: CHARLES SPENCER CHAPLIN, III (DIED '68)
    STEP-SON: SYDNEY EARLE CHAPLIN
    *** MARRIED: '44 BURGESS MEREDITH, ACTOR (DIVORCED '48)
    *** MARRIED: '58 ERICH MARIA REMARQUE, WRITER
    RESIDENCE: PARIS, FRANCE
    RESIDENCE: NYC
    TALENT: ACTRESS
    CREDIT: '36 MODERN TIMES
    CREDIT: '39 THE CAT AND CANARY
    AA-NOM SUP.ACT: '43 SO PROUDLY WE HAIL
    CREDIT: '48 AN IDEAL HUSBAND
    CREDIT: '52 BABES IN BAGDAD

GOLDWYN, SAMUEL   BORN: SAMUEL GOLDFISH
                                   AUG 27,'82 AT WARSAW, POLAND DIED IN '74
    FATHER: ABRAHAM GOLDFISH
    MOTHER: HANNAH
    *** MARRIED: '10 BLANCHE LASKY (DIVORCED)
    BROTHER-IN-LAW: JESSE LASKY, PRODUCER
    *** MARRIED: '25 FRANCES HOWARD, ACTRESS
    SON: '26 SAMUEL GOLDWYN, JR., PRODUCER
    FRIEND: CECIL B. DE MILLE, PRODUCER
    FRIEND: EDGAR SELWYN, PRODUCER
    FRIEND: LOUIS B. MAYER, PRODUCER
    FRIEND: DOUGLAS FAIRBANKS, ACTOR
    FRIEND: MARY PICKFORD, ACTRESS
    RESIDENCE: BEVERLY HILLS, CA
    POSSESSION: '46 IRVING THALBERG MEMORIAL AWARD
    MEMOIRS: BEHIND THE SCREEN
    TALENT: PRODUCER
    COMMENT: GOLDFISH AND SELWYN FORMED GOLDWYN CO.
    COMMENT: THEN GOLDFISH CHANGED HIS NAME TO GOLDWYN
    CREDIT: '19 JUBILO
    CREDIT: '26 STELLA DALLAS
    CREDIT: '38 THE GOLDWYN FOLLIES

CREDIT: '46 THE BEST YEARS OF OUR LIVES
CREDIT: '55 GUYS AND DOLLS

GORCEY, LEO   BORN: LEO BERNARD GORCEY
                                JUN 03,'17 AT NYC   DIED IN '69
   FATHER: BERNARD GORCEY, ACTOR
   MOTHER: JOSEPHINE
   SISTER: AUDREY GORCEY
   BROTHER: DAVID GORCEY, ACTOR
   BROTHER: FRED GORCEY
   *** MARRIED: '39 KATHERINE MARVIS (DIVORCED '45)
   *** MARRIED: '45 EVALENE BANKSTON (DIVORCED '49)
   *** MARRIED: '49 AMELITA WARD (DIVORCED '56)
   DAUGHTER: '50 JAN GORCEY
   SON: '51 LEO GORCEY, JR.
   DAUGHTER: '52 BRANDY JOSEPHINE GORCEY
   *** MARRIED: '56 BRANDY
   *** MARRIED: '68 MARY GANNON
   RESIDENCE: LOS MOLINOS, CA
   POSSESSION: '56 RANCH AT CALABASAS, CA
   MEMOIRS: '67 AN ORIGINAL DEAD END KID ...
   TALENT: ACTOR-FARMER
   CREDIT: '37 DEAD END, SERIES
   CREDIT: '42 JUNIOR G-MEN OF THE AIR, SERIES
   CREDIT: '56 DIG THAT URANIUM
   CREDIT: '69 THE PHYNX

GORDON, RUTH   BORN: RUTH GORDON JONES
                                OCT 30,'96 AT WOLLASTON, MS
   FATHER: CLINTON JONES
   MOTHER: ANNIE TAPLEY ZIEGLER
   *** MARRIED: '18 GREGORY KELLY, ACTOR (DIED '27)
   SON: '20 JONES HARRIS KELLY
   *** MARRIED: '42 GARSON KANIN, PROD-DIR.-AUTHOR
   RESIDENCE: BEVERLY HILLS, CA
   RESIDENCE: NYC
   RESIDENCE: MARTHA'S VINEYARD, MASS.
   MEMOIRS: '72 MYSELF AMONG OTHERS
   MEMOIRS: '76 MY SIDE
   TALENT: ACTRESS
   CREDIT: '40 ABE LINCOLN IN ILLINOIS
   CREDIT: '43 EDGE OF DARKNESS
   CREDIT: '52 THE MARRYING KIND
   AA-NOM SUP.ACT: '65 INSIDE DAISY CLOVER
   AA-WIN SUP.ACT.: '68 ROSEMARY'S BABY
   CREDIT: '72 HAROLD AND MAUDE

GOSDEN, FREEMAN   BORN: FREEMAN FISHER GOSDEN
                                   MAY 05,'89 AT RICHMOND, VA
   FATHER: WALTER WAY GOSDEN
   *** MARRIED: '27 LETA MARIE SCHREIBER (DIED)
   SON: '28 FREEMAN GOSDEN, JR. (MARRIED)
   DAUGHTER-IN-LAW: ELIZABETH FITE
   DAUGHTER: '29 VIRGINIA MARIA GOSDEN (MARRIED '53)
   SON-IN-LAW: RICHARD EMERY JACKSON
   *** MARRIED: '44 JANE STONEHAM
   FATHER-IN-LAW: CHARLES STONEHAM, OWNED NY GIANTS BASEBALL TEAM
   DAUGHTER: '53 LINDA GOSDEN

PARTNER: CHARLES CORRELL, 'ANDY'
RESIDENCE: BEVERLY HILLS, CA
TALENT: ACTOR
CREDIT: '19 AMOS OF AMOS AND ANDY RADIO, SHOW FOR 25 YEARS
CREDIT: '30 CHECK AND DOUBLE CHECK

GOULD, ELLIOT

BORN: ELLIOTT GOLDSTEIN
AUG 29,'38 AT BROOKLYN, NY
FATHER: BERNARD GOLDSTEIN
MOTHER: LUCILLE RAVER
*** MARRIED: '63 BARBRA STREISAND, SINGER, ACTRESS (DIVORCED '71)
SON: '66 JOSHUA GOULD
DAUGHTER: '71 MOLLY BOGART
*** MARRIED: '73 JENNIFER BOGART (DIVORCED '75)
SON: '73 SAMUEL GOULD
ROMANCE: JENNIFER O'NEILL, ACTRESS
TALENT: ACTOR
CREDIT: '66 THE CONFESSION
AA-NOM SUP.ACT: '69 BOB & CAROL & TED & ALICE
CREDIT: '70 M.A.S.H.
CREDIT: '70 THE TOUCH
CREDIT: '72 THE LONG GOODBYE
CREDIT: '78 CAPRICORN ONE

GOULET, ROBERT

NOV 26,'33 AT LAWRENCE, MS
FATHER: JOSEPH GOULET (DIED '47)
MOTHER: JEANETTE GAUTHIER
*** MARRIED: '55 LOUISE LONGMORE (DIVORCED '63)
DAUGHTER: '56 NICOLETTE GOULET
*** MARRIED: '63 CAROL LAWRENCE
BROTHER-IN-LAW: JOSEPH LARAIA
FATHER-IN-LAW: MICHAEL LARAIA
MOTHER-IN-LAW: ROSE MORENO
SON: '64 CHRISTOPHER GOULET
SON: '66 MICHAEL GOULET
RESIDENCE: LOS ANGELES, CA
POSSESSION: '71 MERLIN RECORDS
POSSESSION: '72 FROG COLLECTION
POSSESSION: '77 ROGO RECORDS
POSSESSION: '77 CHESNICK PUBLISHING
TALENT: ACTOR-SINGER
CREDIT: '63 HONEYMOON HOTEL
CREDIT: '64 I'D RATHER BE RICH
CREDIT: '70 UNDERGROUND

GRABLE, BETTY

BORN: ELIZABETH RUTH GRABLE
DEC 18,'16 AT ST. LOUIS, MR DIED IN '73
FATHER: CONN GRABLE
MOTHER: LILLIAN HOFFMAN
SISTER: MARJORIE GRABLE
*** MARRIED: '37 JACKIE COOGAN, ACTOR (DIVORCED '40)
*** MARRIED: '43 HARRY JAMES, BAND LEADER (DIVORCED '65)
DAUGHTER: VICTORIA JAMES
DAUGHTER: ELIZABETH JAMES
DAUGHTER: JESSICA JAMES
ROMANCE: ARTIE SHAW, BAND LEADER
ROMANCE: GEORGE RAFT, ACTOR

TALENT: ACTRESS
CREDIT: '29 LET'S GO PLACES
CREDIT: '36 FOLLOW THE FLEET
CREDIT: '40 DOWN ARGENTINE WAY
CREDIT: '49 THE BEAUTIFUL BLONDE FROM BASHFUL BEND
CREDIT: '55 THREE FOR THE SHOW

GRAHAME, GLORIA   BORN: GLORIA GRAHAME HALLWARD
                                    NOV 28,'25 AT LOS ANGELES, CA
    FATHER: MICHAEL HALLWARD, DESIGNER
    MOTHER: JEAN GRAHAME, ACTRESS
    *** MARRIED: '45 STANLEY CLEMENTS, ACTOR (DIVORCED '47)
    *** MARRIED: '47 NICHOLAS RAY, DIRECTOR (DIVORCED '52)
    STEP-SON: ANTHONY RAY
    SON: '48 TIMOTHY NICHOLAS RAY
    *** MARRIED: '54 CY HOWARD, PRODUCER (DIVORCED '57)
    DAUGHTER: '56 MARIANNE PAULETTE HOWARD
    *** MARRIED: '62 ANTHONY RAY, HER STEPSON
    FATHER-IN-LAW: NICHOLAS RAY, HER EX-HUSBAND
    POSSESSION: '47 CONTRACT AT RKO STUDIOS
    TALENT: ACTRESS
    CREDIT: '44 BLONDE FEVER, DEBUT
    AA-NOM SUP.ACT: '47 CROSSFIRE
    AA-WIN SUP.ACT.: '52 THE BAD AND THE BEAUTIFUL
    CREDIT: '59 ODDS AGAINST TOMORROW
    CREDIT: '72 BLOOD AND LACE

GRANGER, STEWART   BORN: JAMES LABLANCHE STEWART
                                     MAY 06,'13 AT LONDON, ENGLAND
    FATHER: MAJOR JAMES STEWART, MILITARY OFFICER
    MOTHER: FREDERICA LABLANCHE
    *** MARRIED: '46 ELSPETH MARCH, ACTRESS
    FATHER-IN-LAW: HARRY MALCOLM MACKENZIE, ARMY OFFICER
    SON: '47 JAIME GRANGER
    DAUGHTER-IN-LAW: MARTA JACKSON (MARRIED '68)
    SON: '48 LINDSAY GRANGER
    *** MARRIED: '50 JEAN SIMMONS, ACTRESS (DIVORCED)
    DAUGHTER: '56 TRACY GRANGER
    *** MARRIED: '64 CAROLINE LECERF, MISS BELGIUM 1962-MODEL
    DAUGHTER: '68 SAMANTHA GRANGER
    FRIEND: MICHAEL WILDING
    FRIEND: DAVID NIVEN
    RESIDENCE: COSTA DEL SOL, SPAIN 300 ACRE ESTATE
    POSSESSION: OWNS CHAROLAIS CATTLE RANCH ARIZONA
    TALENT: ACTOR
    CREDIT: '39 SO THIS IS LONDON
    CREDIT: '44 LOVE STORY
    CREDIT: '50 KING SOLOMON'S MINES
    CREDIT: '56 BHOWANI JUNCTION
    CREDIT: '67 THE LAST SAFARI

GRANT, CARY   BORN: ALEXANDER ARCHIBALD LEACH
                                JAN 18,'04 AT BRISTOL, ENGLAND
    FATHER: ELIAS LEACH
    MOTHER: ELSIE KINGDOM
    *** MARRIED: '33 VIRGINIA CHERRILL, ACTRESS (DIVORCED '34)
    *** MARRIED: '42 BARBARA HUTTON, WOOLWORTH'S HEIRESS (DIVORCED '45)
    *** MARRIED: '49 BETSY DRAKE, ACTRESS (DIVORCED '62)

*** MARRIED: '65 DYAN CANNON, ACTRESS (DIVORCED '68)
DAUGHTER: '66 JENNIFER GRANT
ROMANCE: SOPHIA LOREN
ROMANCE: YUGOSLAVIAN BASKETBALL PLAYER, KNOWN AS LUBA
ROMANCE: PHYLLIS BROOKS
ROMANCE: MAUREEN DONALDSON, PHOTOGRAPHER
RESIDENCE: BEVERLY HILLS, CA
POSSESSION: IMPRESSIONIST ART COLLECTION
BIOGRAPHY: '71 THE FILMS OF CARY GRANT, BY DONALD DESCHNER
TALENT: ACTOR
COMMENT: DIRECTOR OF FABERGE PERFUME CO
CREDIT: '32 THIS IS THE NIGHT, DEBUT
AA-NOM ACTOR: '41 PENNY SERENADE
AA-NOM ACTOR: '44 NONE BUT THE LONELY HEART
CREDIT: '55 TO CATCH A THIEF
CREDIT: '63 CHARADE
AA-SPECIAL AWARD: '69 HONORARY AWARD FOR 'UNIQUE MASTERY OF THE ART OF ACTING'

GRANVILLE, BONITA
                              FEB 02,'23 AT NYC
FATHER: BERNARD GRANVILLE, ACTOR
MOTHER: ROSINA TIMPONI, ACTRESS
*** MARRIED: '47 JACK WRATHER, PRODUCER
SON: '48 JACK WRATHER, JR.
DAUGHTER: '49 LINDA WRATHER
DAUGHTER: '50 MOLLY WRATHER
SON: '52 CHRISTOPHER WRATHER
ROMANCE: JACKIE COOPER, ACTOR
ROMANCE: TIM HOLT, ACTOR
RESIDENCE: LOS ANGELES, SAN FRANCISCO, PALM SPRINGS AND NEWPORT, CA
POSSESSION: YACHT 'LONE RANGER'
TALENT: ACTRESS
COMMENT: JOINED PARENT'S VAUDEVILLE ACT AT AGE THREE
CREDIT: '32 WESTWARD PASSAGE
AA-NOM SUP.ACT: '36 THESE THREE
CREDIT: '45 THE BEAUTIFUL CHEAT
CREDIT: '48 STRIKE IT RICH
CREDIT: '56 THE LONE RANGER

GRAYSON, KATHRYN   BORN: ZELMA KATHRYN HEDRICK
                              FEB 09,'22 AT WINSTON-SALEM, NC
FATHER: CHARLES E. HEDRICK, REALTOR
MOTHER: LILLIAN GRAY
SISTER: FRANCES RAEBURN HEDRICK
BROTHER: BUDDY HEDRICK
BROTHER: HAL HEDRICK
*** MARRIED: '41 JOHN SHELTON, ACTOR (DIVORCED '46)
*** MARRIED: '47 JOHN JOHNSTON, ACTOR (DIVORCED '51)
DAUGHTER: '48 PATRICIA KATHRYN JOHNSTON
ROMANCE: ROBERT EVANS
ROMANCE: HANK HENDLER, BUTCHER
TALENT: ACTRESS-SINGER
CREDIT: '41 ANDY HARDY'S PRIVATE SECRETARY
CREDIT: '50 GROUNDS FOR MARRIAGE
CREDIT: '52 LOVELY TO LOOK AT
CREDIT: '56 THE VAGABOND KING

GREENE, LORNE
FEB 12,'15 AT OTTAWA, ONTARIO, CANADA
FATHER: DANIEL GREENE
MOTHER: DORA
*** MARRIED: '40 RITA HANDS (DIVORCED '60)
DAUGHTER: '41 BELINDA SUSAN GREENE, TWIN
SON: '41 CHARLES GREENE, TWIN
*** MARRIED: '61 NANCY ANN DEAL
DAUGHTER: '68 GILLIAN DONNA GREENE
RESIDENCE: BEVERLY HILLS, CA
POSSESSION: '65 CANADA'S 1965 MAN OF THE YEAR
TALENT: ACTOR
CREDIT: '54 THE SILVER CHALICE
CREDIT: '55 TIGHT SPOT
CREDIT: '57 PEYTON PLACE
CREDIT: '58 THE TRAP
CREDIT: '71 THE HARNESS

GREENSTREET, SYDNEY
BORN: SYDNEY HUGHES GREENSTREET
DEC 27,'79 AT SANDWICH, KENT, ENGLAND DIED IN '54
FATHER: JOHN GREENSTREET
MOTHER: ANN BAKER
*** MARRIED: '18 DOROTHY OGDEN
SON: JOHN OGDEN GREENSTREET, SALESMAN
FRIEND: WOODROW WILSON
TALENT: ACTOR
AA-NOM SUP.ACT: '41 THE MALTESE FALCON DEBUT
CREDIT: '44 ONE MAN'S SECRET
CREDIT: '47 THE HUCKSTERS
CREDIT: '50 MALAYA

GREY, JOEL
BORN: JOEL KATZ
APR 11,'32 AT CLEVELAND,OH
FATHER: MICKIE KATZ, ENTERTAINER
MOTHER: GRACE
BROTHER: RONALD KATZ
*** MARRIED: '58 JO WILDER
DAUGHTER: '61 JENNIFER GREY
SON: '63 JAMES GREY
RESIDENCE: NYC
RESIDENCE: MALIBU, CA
TALENT: ACTOR
CREDIT: '52 ABOUT FACE
CREDIT: '61 COME SEPTEMBER
AA-WIN SUP.ACT.: '72 CABARET
CREDIT: BUFFALO BILL AND THE INDIANS
CREDIT: MAN ON A SWING

GRIFFITH, CORINNE
NOV 24,'96 AT TEXARKANA,TX
*** MARRIED: '20 WEBSTER CAMPBELL (DIVORCED '23)
*** MARRIED: '24 WALTER MOROSCO (DIVORCED '34)
*** MARRIED: '36 GEORGE P. MARSHALL (DIVORCED '58)
*** MARRIED: '66 DANNY SCHOLL (DIVORCED '66)
RESIDENCE: BEVERLY HILLS, CA
POSSESSION: GLOUCESTER SCHOONER - WANDERLUST
MEMOIRS: '55 EGGS I HAVE KNOWN AUTOBIOGRAPHY & COOKBOOK

```
TALENT: ACTRESS
CREDIT:  '22 THE YELLOW GIRL
CREDIT:  '24 LOVE'S WILDERNESS
CREDIT:  '25 THE MARRIAGE WHIRL
CREDIT:  '25 INFATUATION
CREDIT:  '28 THE GARDEN OF EDEN
```

```
GRIFFITH, D. W.          BORN:  DAVID WARK GRIFFITH
                         JAN 22,'75 AT LA GRANGE, KT   DIED IN '48
*** MARRIED: LINDA ARVIDSON, ACTRESS, WRITER  (DIVORCED)
*** MARRIED: EVELYN MARJORIE BALDWIN, ACTRESS  (DIVORCED)
FRIEND: BILLY BITZER, CAMERAMAN
BIOGRAPHY: THE MOVIES, MR. GRIFFITH  AND ME, BY LILLIAN GISH
TALENT: ACTOR, WRITER, DIRECTOR
COMMENT: CO-FOUNDER OF UNITED ARTISTS
CREDIT:  '07 RESCUED FROM AN EAGLE'S NEST
CREDIT:  '15 THE BIRTH OF A NATION
CREDIT:  '16 INTOLERANCE
CREDIT:  '22 WHEN KNIGHTHOOD WAS IN FLOWER
CREDIT:  '31 ORPHANS OF THE STORM
AA-SPECIAL AWARD:  '35 SPECIAL AWARD FOR INITIATIVE AND LASTING CONTRIBUTIONS
```

```
GUARDINO, HARRY
                         DEC 23,'25 AT NYC
FATHER: JOSEPH GUARDINO, BANDLEADER
MOTHER: MARGARET
BROTHER: LOUIS GUARDINO, WRITER
*** MARRIED:  '58 ANN  (DIVORCED '69)
DAUGHTER:  '59 MICHELLE GUARDINO
SON:  '62 MICHAEL GUARDINO
*** MARRIED:  '73 JENNIFER REVSON, COSMETICS HEIRESS  (DIVORCED '74)
BROTHER-IN-LAW: PETER REVSON  (DIED '74)
FATHER-IN-LAW: MARTIN REVSON
SISTER-IN-LAW: JULIE REVSON, AKA JULIE COX
RESIDENCE: LOS ANGELES, CA
TALENT: ACTOR
CREDIT:  '58 HOUSEBOAT
CREDIT:  '61 KING OF KINGS
CREDIT:  '62 HELL IS FOR HEROES
CREDIT:  '69 LOVERS AND OTHER STRANGERS
CREDIT:  '71 DIRTY HARRY
```

```
GUINNESS, ALEC
                         APR 02,'14 AT LONDON,ENGLAND
*** MARRIED:  '37 NERULA SALAMAN
SON:  '38 MATTHEW GUINNESS
RESIDENCE: KETTLEBROOK MEADOWS, HAMPSHIRE, ENGLAND
POSSESSION:  '55 KNIGHTHOOD
BIOGRAPHY:  '55 GUINNESS, BY KENNETH TYNAN
TALENT: ACTOR
COMMENT: MEMBER OLD VIC THEATRE COMPANY 1937
CREDIT:  '46 GREAT EXPECTATIONS
AA-NOM  ACTOR:  '52 THE LAVENDER HILL MOB
AA-WIN  ACTOR:  '57 THE BRIDGE ON THE RIVER KWAI
CREDIT:  '67 THE COMEDIANS
CREDIT:  '70 CROMWELL
AA-NOM  SUP.ACT:  '77 STAR WARS
```

GWENN, EDMUND   BORN: EDMUND KELLAWAY, JR.
                               SEP 26, 1875 AT GLAMORGAN, WALES   DIED IN '59
   FATHER: EDMUND KELLAWAY, CIVIL SERVANT
   SISTER: ELSIE KELLAWAY
   *** MARRIED: '01 MINNIE TERRY (DIVORCED '18)
   RESIDENCE: BEVERLY HILLS, CA
   TALENT: ACTOR
   CREDIT: '16 THE REAL THING AT LAST
   CREDIT: '20 THE SKIN GAME
   CREDIT: '36 THE WALKING DEAD
   AA-WIN SUP.ACT.: '47 MIRACLE ON 34TH STREET
   AA-NOM SUP.ACT: '50 MISTER 880
   CREDIT: '55 THE TROUBLE WITH HARRY

```
------------------------------------------------------------------------------------------
HACKETT, BUDDY          BORN:  LEONARD HACKER
                               1924 AT BROOKLYN, NY
     FATHER: PHILIP HACKER, INVENTOR
     MOTHER: ANNA
     SISTER: MILDRED HACKER
     *** MARRIED: SHERRY DUBOIS, DANCE TEACHER
     DAUGHTER: SANY ZADE HACKETT
     DAUGHTER: IVY JULIE HACKETT
     DAUGHTER: LISA JEAN HACKETT
     TALENT: ACTOR
     CREDIT:  '58 GOD'S LITTLE ACRE
     CREDIT:  '62 THE MUSIC MAN
     CREDIT:  '66 MUSCLE BEACH PARTY
------------------------------------------------------------------------------------------
HACKETT, RAYMOND
                               JUL 15,'02 AT NYC  DIED IN '58
     MOTHER: FLORENCE, ACTRESS
     BROTHER: ALBERT HACKETT, ACTOR, WRITER
     SISTER-IN-LAW: FRANCES GOODRICH, WRITER
     *** MARRIED: BLANCHE SWEET, ACTRESS
     RESIDENCE: NYC
     TALENT: ACTOR
     CREDIT:  '18 CRUISE OF THE MAKE-BELIEVE
     CREDIT:  '28 THE LOVES OF SUNYA
     CREDIT:  '29 OUR BLUSHING BRIDES
     CREDIT:  '30 THE SEA WOLF
     CREDIT:  '31 THE CAT CREEPS
     CREDIT:  '31 SEED
------------------------------------------------------------------------------------------
HACKMAN, GENE           BORN:  EUGENE ALDEN HACKMAN
                               JAN 30,'31 AT SAN BERNARDINO, CA
     FATHER: EUGENE EZRA HACKMAN, PRINTER
     MOTHER: LYDIA
     *** MARRIED:  '56 KAY MALTESE
     DAUGHTER: ELIZABETH HACKMAN
     DAUGHTER: LESLIE HACKMAN
     SON: CHRISTOPHER HACKMAN
     TALENT: ACTOR
     CREDIT:  '64 LILITH
     AA-NOM  SUP.ACT:  '67 BONNIE AND CLYDE
     AA-NOM  SUP.ACT:  '70 I NEVER SANG FOR MY FATHER
     AA-WIN  ACTOR:  '71 THE FRENCH CONNECTION
     CREDIT:  '73 SCARECROW
     CREDIT:  '73 THE CONVERSATION
     CREDIT:  '78 SUPERMAN
------------------------------------------------------------------------------------------
HALE, ALAN          BORN:  RUFUS ALAN MCKANAN
                           FEB 10,'92 AT WASHINGTON, D.C.  DIED IN '50
     *** MARRIED:  '14 GRETCHEN HARTMAN, ACTRESS
     SON:  '15 ALAN HALE, JR., ACTOR
     DAUGHTER-IN-LAW: NAOMI INGRIM
     DAUGHTER:  '16 JEANNE HALE
     DAUGHTER:  '17 KAREN HALE
     *** MARRIED:  '43 BETTY REED DOER
     TALENT: ACTOR
     CREDIT:  '11 THE COWBOY AND THE LADY, DEBUT IN 1911
     CREDIT:  '22 A DOLL'S HOUSE
```

```
       CREDIT:   '34 OF HUMAN BONDAGE
       CREDIT:   '40 COLT .45
       CREDIT:   '50 ROGUES OF SHERWOOD FOREST
```

HALEY, JACK   BORN: JONATHAN HALEY
                                 AUG 10,'02 AT BOSTON,MS
```
       FATHER: JOHN HALEY
       MOTHER: ELLEN CURLY
       *** MARRIED: FLORENCE MCFADDEN, ACTRESS
       DAUGHTER:  '28 GLORIA HALEY, ACTRESS
       SON-IN-LAW: LOUIS A. PORCHIA, AKA - PHILIP CASEY - ACTOR   (MARRIED '47)
       SON-IN-LAW: LOUIS 'BUDDY' BREGMAN, MUSICAL DIRECTOR  (MARRIED '50)
       SON-IN-LAW: MILAN RADOVICH, REAL ESTATE MAN  (MARRIED '58)
       SON-IN-LAW: DR. WILLIAM PARNASSUS  (MARRIED '74)
       SON:  '35 JOHN JOSEPH 'JACK' HALEY, JR., PRODUCER
       DAUGHTER-IN-LAW: LIZA MINNELLI, ACTRESS  (MARRIED '74)
       GRANDSON:  '52 BARRY BREGMAN
       GRANDDAUGHTER:  '59 ADRIENNE RADOVICH
       FRIEND: FRED ALLEN
       FRIEND: JACK BENNY
       FRIEND: GEORGE BURNS
       RESIDENCE: BEVERLY HILLS, CA.
       POSSESSION: COLLECTION OF JOKE BOOKS
       TALENT: ACTOR-SINGER
       CREDIT:  '30 FOLLOW THRU
       CREDIT:  '36 POOR LITTLE RICH GIRL
       CREDIT:  '38 ALEXANDER'S RAGTIME BAND
       CREDIT:  '39 THE WIZARD OF OZ
       CREDIT:  '45 PEOPLE ARE FUNNY
```

HALL, JON   BORN: CHARLES HALL LOCHER
                               FEB 23,'13 AT FRESNO, CA
```
       COUSIN: JAMES NORMAN HALL, AUTHOR
       *** MARRIED:  '38 FRANCES LANGFORD, ACTRESS  (DIVORCED '55)
       *** MARRIED:  '59 RACQUEL AMES  (DIVORCED)
       *** MARRIED:  '60 RACQUEL AMES, RE-MARRIED
       PARTNER: MARIA MONTEZ, ACTRESS
       TALENT: ACTOR
       CREDIT:  '36 THE CLUTCHING HAND, SERIES
       CREDIT:  '37 THE HURRICANE
       CREDIT:  '43 WHITE SAVAGE
       CREDIT:  '51 CHINA CORSAIR
       CREDIT:  '59 FORBIDDEN ISLAND
```

HAMILTON, GEORGE   BORN: GEORGE STEVENS HAMILTON
                                      AUG 12,'39 AT MEMPHIS, TN
```
       FATHER: GEORGE WILLIAM HAMILTON, MUSICIAN
       MOTHER: ANNE STEVENS SPALDING
       BROTHER: WILLIAM HAMILTON
       BROTHER: DAVID HUBBARD HAMILTON
       SISTER-IN-LAW: HELLE BIRTE MELCHIOR  (MARRIED '67)
       *** MARRIED:  '72 ALANA COLLINS  (DIVORCED '76)
       SON:  '74 ASHLEY STEVEN HAMILTON
       ROMANCE: WENDY VANDERBILT
       ROMANCE: LYNDA B. JOHNSON
       RESIDENCE: BEVERLY HILLS, CA
       TALENT: ACTOR
       CREDIT:  '58 CRIME AND PUNISHMENT USA, DEBUT
```

```
CREDIT:  '61 ANGEL BABY
CREDIT:  '63 ACT ONE
CREDIT:  '72 EVIL KNIEVEL
CREDIT:  '73 THE MAN WHO LOVED CAT DANCING
CREDIT:  '78 LOVE AT FIRST BITE
```

HARDING, ANN

```
                    BORN:  DOROTHY WALTON GATLEY
                           AUG 17,'04 AT FORT SAM HOUSTON, TX
FATHER: GEORGE G. GATLEY, US ARMY GENERAL OFFICER
MOTHER: ELIZABETH CRABBE
SISTER: EDITH GATLEY
*** MARRIED:  '26 HARRY BANNISTER  (DIVORCED '32)
DAUGHTER:  '29 JANE BANNISTER
*** MARRIED:  '37 WERNER JANSSEN, MUSIC CONDUCTOR  (DIVORCED '63)
TALENT: ACTRESS
CREDIT:  '29 PARIS BOUND
AA-NOM ACTRESS:  '30 HOLIDAY
CREDIT:  '45 THOSE ENDEARING YOUNG CHARMS
CREDIT:  '50 TWO WEEKS WITH LOVE
CREDIT:  '56 STRANGE INTRUDER
```

HARDWICKE, CEDRIC

```
                      BORN:  CEDRIC WEBSTER HARDWICKE
                             FEB 19,'93 AT LYE, STOURBRIDGE, ENGLAND  DIED IN '64
FATHER: EDWIN WEBSTER HARDWICKE, PHYSICIAN
MOTHER: JESSIE MASTERSON
*** MARRIED:  '28 HELENA PICKARD, ACTRESS  (DIVORCED '48)
SON:  '29 EDWARD HARDWICKE, ACTOR
*** MARRIED:  '50 MARY SCOTT  (DIVORCED '61)
POSSESSION:  '34 KNIGHTHOOD
MEMOIRS:  '32 LET'S PRETEND
MEMOIRS:  '61 A VICTORIAN ORBIT
TALENT: ACTOR
CREDIT:  '31 DREYFUS, DEBUT IN 1931
CREDIT:  '39 STANLEY AND LIVINGSTONE
CREDIT:  '43 FOREVER AND A DAY
CREDIT:  '55 HELEN OF TROY
CREDIT:  '64 THE PUMPKIN EATER
```

HARDY, OLIVER

```
                    BORN:  OLIVER NORVELL HARDY
                           JAN 18,'92 AT ATLANTA, GE  DIED IN '57
*** MARRIED:  '21 MYRTLE REEVES  (DIVORCED '37)
*** MARRIED:  '40 LUCILLE JONES
PARTNER: STAN LAUREL
BIOGRAPHY:  '61 MR. LAUREL AND MR. HARDY, BY JOHN MCCABE
TALENT: ACTOR, SINGER
CREDIT:  '13 OUTWITTING DAD, DEBUT
CREDIT:  '20 FLY COP, SERIES
CREDIT:  '32 SCRAM
CREDIT:  '39 ELEPHANTS NEVER FORGET
CREDIT:  '49 THE FIGHTING KENTUCKIAN
```

HARLOW, JEAN

```
                    BORN:  HARLEAN CARPENTIER
                           MAR 03,'11 AT KANSAS CITY,MR  DIED IN '37
FATHER: MONTCLAIR CARPENTIER, DENTIST
MOTHER: JEAN  HARLOW
STEP-FATHER: MARINO BELLO
*** MARRIED:  '27 CHARLES F. MCGREW  (ANNULLED '30)
*** MARRIED:  '32 PAUL BERN, PRODUCER  (SUICIDE '32)
```

```
*** MARRIED:  '33 HAL ROSSON, CAMERAMAN  (DIVORCED '34)
ROMANCE: HOWARD HUGHES
ROMANCE: JESSE LASKY, JR.
ROMANCE: WILLIAM POWELL
FRIEND: ARTHUR LANDAU, AGENT
FRIEND: JEANETTE MACDONALD
FRIEND: NELSON EDDY
BIOGRAPHY:  '65 HARLOW, BY IRVING SHULMAN
TALENT: ACTRESS
CREDIT:  '29 THE SATURDAY NIGHT KID
CREDIT:  '30 HELL'S ANGELS
CREDIT:  '32 RED HEADED WOMAN
CREDIT:  '34 THE GIRL FROM MISSOURI
CREDIT:  '37 SARATOGA
```

```
HARPER, VALERIE          BORN:  VALERIE CATHRYN HARPER
                                AUG 22,'40 AT SUFFERN,NY
FATHER: HOWARD HARPER
MOTHER: IVA, NURSE
STEP-MOTHER: ANGELA POSILLICO
SISTER: LEAH HARPER, FOLKSINGER
BROTHER: DON HARPER, LUMBERJACK
*** MARRIED:  '64 DICK SCHAAL, ACTOR-WRITER  (DIVORCED '78)
RESIDENCE: WEST LOS ANGELES, CA
BIOGRAPHY:  '75 THE UNFORGETTABLE SNOWFLAKE, BY LINDA JACOBS
TALENT: ACTRESS
CREDIT:  '73 RHODA, TV SERIES
CREDIT:  '77 STING RAY
CREDIT:  FREEBIE AND THE BEAN
```

```
HARRIS, JULIE           BORN:  JULIA ANN HARRIS
                               DEC 02,'25 AT GROSSE POINTE PARK,MH
FATHER: WILLIAM PICKETT HARRIS
MOTHER: ELSIE SMITH
*** MARRIED:  '46 JAY I. JULIEN  (DIVORCED '54)
*** MARRIED:  '54 MANNING GURIAN
SON:  '55 PETER GURIAN
*** MARRIED:  '77 WALTER CARROLL
TALENT: ACTRESS
AA-NOM ACTRESS:  '52 THE MEMBER OF THE WEDDING
CREDIT:  '55 EAST OF EDEN
CREDIT:  '58 THE TRUTH ABOUT WOMEN
CREDIT:  '67 REFLECTIONS IN A GOLDEN EYE
CREDIT:  '70 THE PEOPLE NEXT DOOR
```

```
HARRIS, PHIL
                        JUN 24,'06 AT LINTON, IN
*** MARRIED: MARCIA RALSTON
SON:  '36 PHIL HARRIS, JR.
*** MARRIED:  '41 ALICE FAYE, ACTRESS
BROTHER-IN-LAW: WILLIAM LEPPERT, TALENT AGENT
DAUGHTER:  '42 ALICE HARRIS
DAUGHTER:  '44 PHYLLIS HARRIS
RESIDENCE: ENCINO, CA
POSSESSION:  '76 TEQUILA IMPORTING CO.
POSSESSION: GUN COLLECTION
POSSESSION: COWBOY BOOT COLLECTION
TALENT: ACTOR-BANDLEADER
```

```
      CREDIT:  '33 MELODY CRUISE
      CREDIT:  '51 HERE COMES THE GROOM
      CREDIT:  '54 THE HIGH AND THE MIGHTY
      CREDIT:  '63 THE WHEELER DEALERS
      CREDIT:  '67 THE COOL ONES
--------------------------------------------------------------------------------------------------
HARRIS, RICHARD          BORN:   RICHARD ST. JOHN HARRIS
                                 OCT 01,'33 AT LIMERICK,IRELAND
      FATHER: IVAN HARRIS
      MOTHER: MILDRED
      BROTHER: DERMOT HARRIS
      *** MARRIED:  '57 JOAN ELIZABETH REESE-WILLIAMS  (DIVORCED '69)
      FATHER-IN-LAW: LORD OGMORE
      SON:   '58 DAMIAN HARRIS
      SON:   '61 JARED HARRIS
      SON:   '64 JAMIE HARRIS
      *** MARRIED:  '74 ANN TURKEL, ACTRESS
      ROMANCE: CHRIS RUDAS
      ENEMY: OLIVER REED, ACTOR
      RESIDENCE: KENSINGTON, LONDON, ENGLAND
      POSSESSION: VICTORIAN BIRDCAGE FOR HIS CANARY
      MEMOIRS:  '74 I, IN THE MEMBERSHIP OF MY DAYS - POETRY
      BIOGRAPHY:  '77 LOVE, HONOR AND DISMAY, BY JOAN ELIZABETH REESE-WILLIAMS
      TALENT: ACTOR-DIRECTOR
      CREDIT:  '59 SHAKE HANDS WITH THE DEVIL
      AA-NOM  ACTOR:  '63 THIS SPORTING LIFE
      CREDIT:  '66 HAWAII
      CREDIT:  '70 A MAN CALLED HORSE
      CREDIT:  '71 BLOOMFIELD
--------------------------------------------------------------------------------------------------
HARRISON, GEORGE
                          FEB 25,'43 AT LIVERPOOL, ENGLAND
      FATHER: HAROLD HARRISON
      MOTHER: LOUISE
      SISTER: LOUISE HARRISON
      BROTHER: PETER HARRISON
      BROTHER: HARRY HARRISON
      *** MARRIED:  '66 PATTI BOYD, ACTRESS
      *** MARRIED:  '78 OLIVIA ARIAS, SECRETARY
      SON:   '78 DHANI ARIAS
      PARTNER: JOHN LENNON, IN THE BEATLES & THE APPLE CO.
      PARTNER: PAUL MCCARTNEY, IN THE BEATLES & THE APPLE CO.
      PARTNER: RINGO STARR, IN THE BEATLES & THE APPLE CO.
      RESIDENCE: WEYBRIDGE, ENGLAND
      TALENT: GUITARIST, COMPOSER, ACTOR
      CREDIT:  '65 A HARD DAY'S NIGHT, WITH BEATLES
      CREDIT:  '65 HELP!, WITH BEATLES
--------------------------------------------------------------------------------------------------
HARRISON, REX          BORN:   REGINALD CAREY HARRISON
                                MAR 05,'08 AT HUYTON,LANCASHIRE,ENGLAND
      FATHER: WILLIAM REGINALD HARRISON
      MOTHER: EDITH CAREY
      *** MARRIED:  '34 MARJORIE THOMAS  (DIVORCED '42)
      SON:   '35 NOEL HARRISON
      DAUGHTER-IN-LAW: MARGARET BENSON  (MARRIED '72)
      *** MARRIED:  '43 LILLI PALMER  (DIVORCED '57)
      SON:   '44 CAREY HARRISON
      *** MARRIED:  '57 KAY KENDALL  (DIED '59)
```

FATHER-IN-LAW: TERRY KENDALL, DANCER
MOTHER-IN-LAW: PAT, DANCER
SISTER-IN-LAW: KIM KENDALL
*** MARRIED: '62 RACHEL ROBERTS (DIVORCED '71)
*** MARRIED: '71 JOAN ELIZABETH REESE-WILLIAMS
FATHER-IN-LAW: LORD OGMORE
MEMOIRS: '75 REX: AN AUTOBIOGRAPHY
BIOGRAPHY: '75 CHANGE LOBSTERS AND DANCE, BY LILLI PALMER
BIOGRAPHY: '77 LOVE, HONOR AND DISMAY, BY JOAN ELIZABETH REESE-WILLIAMS
TALENT: ACTOR
CREDIT: '30 SCHOOL FOR SCANDAL
CREDIT: '48 UNFAITHFULLY YOURS
CREDIT: '55 THE CONSTANT HUSBAND
AA-NOM ACTOR: '63 CLEOPATRA
AA-WIN ACTOR: '64 MY FAIR LADY

HART, WILLIAM S.   BORN: WILLIAM SURREY HART
                              DEC 06,'62 AT DAKOTA TERRITORY DIED IN '46
SISTER: MARY HART
*** MARRIED: '22 WINIFRED WESTOVER, ACTRESS
*** MARRIED: '25 DOROTHY DAVENPORT, ACTRESS
BROTHER-IN-LAW: ARTHUR RANKIN, ACTOR
FATHER-IN-LAW: HARRY DAVENPORT, ACTOR, DIRECTOR (DIED '49)
MOTHER-IN-LAW: PHYLLIS RANKIN, ACTRESS
SISTER-IN-LAW: ANN DAVENPORT, ACTRESS
STEP-SON: WILLIAM WALLACE REID, JR.
SISTER-IN-LAW: KATE DAVENPORT, ACTRESS
ROMANCE: JANE NOVAK
ROMANCE: ANNA Q. NILSSON
PARTNER: THOMAS H. INCE, PRODUCER
MEMOIRS: '28 MY LIFE EAST AND WEST
TALENT: ACTOR
COMMENT: WROTE 'PINTO BEN' STORY IN VER SE PUBLISHED 1919
COMMENT: LIVED 15 YEARS IN DAKOTA TERR.
CREDIT: '13 THE FUGITIVE
CREDIT: '15 BETWEEN MEN
CREDIT: '17 THE GUNFIGHTER
CREDIT: '25 TUMBLEWEEDS
CREDIT: '43 ONE FOOT IN HEAVEN

HARVEY, LAURENCE   BORN: LAURUSKA MISCHA SKIKNE
                              OCT 01,'28 AT YONISHKIS, LITHUANIA DIED IN '73
FATHER: BER SKIKNE ZOTNICKAITA
MOTHER: ELLA
*** MARRIED: '57 MARGARET LEIGHTON, ACTRESS (DIVORCED '61)
*** MARRIED: '68 JOAN PERRY, ACTRESS
*** MARRIED: '72 PAULINE STONE
DAUGHTER: '73 DOMINO HARVEY
TALENT: ACTOR
CREDIT: '48 HOUSE OF DARKNESS
CREDIT: '54 THE GOOD DIE YOUNG
AA-NOM ACTOR: '59 ROOM AT THE TOP
CREDIT: '63 THE CEREMONY
CREDIT: '65 DARLING

```
--------------------------------------------------------------------------------
HAVER, JUNE          BORN:   JUNE STOVENOUR
                             JUN 10,'26 AT ROCK ISLAND, IL
     FATHER: STOVENOUR, MUSICIAN
     STEP-FATHER: BERT HAVER
     *** MARRIED:  '47 JIMMY ZITO, MUSICIAN  (DIVORCED '48)
     *** MARRIED:  '54 FRED MACMURRAY, ACTOR
     FATHER-IN-LAW: FREDERICK MACMURRAY, VIOLINIST
     MOTHER-IN-LAW: MALETA MARTIN
     STEP-DAUGHTER: SUSAN MACMURRAY
     STEP-SON: ROBERT MACMURRAY
     ADOPTED DAUGHTER: LAURIE MACMURRAY, TWIN
     ADOPTED DAUGHTER: KATHARINE MACMURRAY, TWIN
     ROMANCE: DAVID ROSE, MUSICIAN
     RESIDENCE: WILLIAMSBURG, VA.
     TALENT: MUSICIAN-ACTRESS
     CREDIT:  '44 HOME IN INDIANA, DEBUT
     CREDIT:  '45 THE DOLLY SISTERS
     CREDIT:  '49 LOOK FOR THE SILVER LINING
     CREDIT:  '51 LOVE NEST
     CREDIT:  '53 THE GIRL NEXT DOOR
--------------------------------------------------------------------------------
HAVOC, JUNE          BORN:   JUNE HOVICK
                             NOV 08,'16 AT VANCOUVER,BRITISH COLUMBIA,CAN
     FATHER: JOHN OLAV HOVICK
     MOTHER: ROSE
     SISTER: GYPSY ROSE LEE, ACTRESS
     BROTHER-IN-LAW: ALEXANDER KIRKLAND
     BROTHER-IN-LAW: ARNOLD R. MIZZY
     NEPHEW: ERIK KIRKLAND PREMINGER
     *** MARRIED:  '29 BOBBY, DANCER  (DIVORCED)
     DAUGHTER:  '30 APRIL
     *** MARRIED:  '39 DONALD GIBBS, ADVERTISING EXECUTIVE  (DIVORCED)
     *** MARRIED:  '48 WILLIAM SPIER, PRODUCER  (DIED '73)
     RESIDENCE: WESTON, CN
     MEMOIRS: EARLY HAVOC
     TALENT: ACTRESS
     CREDIT:  '42 FOUR JACKS AND A JILL
     CREDIT:  '45 BREWSTER'S MILLIONS
     CREDIT:  '50 ONCE A THIEF
     CREDIT:  '51 A LADY POSSESSED
     CREDIT:  '57 THREE FOR JAMIE DAWN
--------------------------------------------------------------------------------
HAWN, GOLDIE         BORN:   GOLDIE JEAN HAWN
                             NOV 21,'45 AT WASHINGTON,D.C.
     FATHER: EDWARD RUTLEDGE HAWN, MUSICIAN
     MOTHER: LAURA STEINHOFF, JEWELRY WHOLESALER
     SISTER: PATRICIA HAWN
     *** MARRIED:  '69 GUS TRIKONIS
     *** MARRIED:  '76 BILL HUDSON, SINGER
     SON:  '76 OLIVER HUDSON
     TALENT: ACTRESS
     AA-WIN  SUP.ACT.:  '69 CACTUS FLOWER
     CREDIT:  '70 THER'S A GIRL IN MY SOUP
     CREDIT:  '72 BUTTERFLIES ARE FREE
     CREDIT:  '73 THE SUGARLAND EXPRESS
     CREDIT:  '74 SHAMPOO
     CREDIT:  '78 FOUL PLAY
```

HAYAKAWA, SESSUE   BORN: KINTARO HAYAKAWA
                                      JAN 10,'90 AT NAAURA, HONSHU, JAPAN DIED IN '73
  FATHER: YOICHORO HAYAKAWA, GOVERNOR OF CHIBA PREFECTURE
  MOTHER: KANE
  *** MARRIED: '14 TSURA AOKI (DIED '61)
  SON: YUKIO HAYAKAWA
  SON: YOSHIKO HAYAKAWA
  SON: FUJIKO HAYAKAWA
  MEMOIRS: '61 ZEN SHOWED ME THE WAY
  TALENT: ACTOR
  CREDIT: '14 THE TYPHOON
  CREDIT: '15 THE CHEAT
  CREDIT: '49 TOKYO JOE
  AA-NOM SUP.ACT: '57 THE BRIDGE ON THE RIVER KWAI
  CREDIT: '59 THE GEISHA BOY
  CREDIT: '61 HELL TO ETERNITY

HAYDEN, RUSSELL   BORN: HAYDEN MICHAEL LUCID
                                     JUN 10,'12 AT CHICO,CA
  *** MARRIED: '39 JAN CLAYTON, ACTRESS (DIVORCED '46)
  FATHER-IN-LAW: G. VERNER CLAYTON
  MOTHER-IN-LAW: VERA CARTER
  DAUGHTER: '40 SANDRA JANE HAYDEN (DIED '56)
  *** MARRIED: '46 LILLIAN PORTER
  RESIDENCE: PALM SPRINGS, CA
  TALENT: ACTOR-PRODUCER-DIRECTOR
  CREDIT: '37 HILLS OF OLD WYOMING, DEBUT
  CREDIT: '42 LUCKY LEGS
  CREDIT: '47 SEVEN WERE SAVED
  CREDIT: '49 SILVER CITY
  CREDIT: '51 VALLEY OF FIRE

HAYDEN, STERLING   BORN: JOHN HAMILTON
                                      MAR 26,'16 AT MONTCLAIR, NJ
  *** MARRIED: '37 MADELEINE CARROLL, ACTRESS (DIVORCED '46)
  *** MARRIED: '47 BETTY ANN DE NOON (DIVORCED '54)
  SON: '48 CHRISTIAN HAYDEN
  DAUGHTER: '50 DANA HAYDEN
  DAUGHTER: '52 GRETCHEN HAYDEN
  *** MARRIED: '60 CATHERINE MCCONNELL
  SON: '61 MATTHEW HAYDEN
  POSSESSION: SAILBOAT 'WANDERER'
  MEMOIRS: THE WANDERER
  TALENT: SAILOR-ACTOR
  CREDIT: '41 VIRGINIA, DEBUT
  CREDIT: '50 THE ASPHALT JUNGLE
  CREDIT: '54 JOHNNY GUITAR
  CREDIT: '63 DR. STRANGELOVE
  CREDIT: '70 LOVING

HAYES, GABBY   BORN: GEORGE F. HAYES
                                  MAY 07,'85 AT WELLSVILLE, NY DIED IN '69
  SISTER: HATTIE HAYES
  BROTHER: CLARK B. HAYES
  *** MARRIED: '14 DOROTHY EARLE, ACTRESS (DIED '45)
  PARTNER: WILLIAM BOYD
  RESIDENCE: LOS ANGELES, CA

```
        TALENT: ACTOR
        CREDIT:  '29 BIG NEWS
        CREDIT:  '36 HOPALONG CASSIDY, SERIES
        CREDIT:  '40 WAGONS WESTWARD
        CREDIT:  '46 UNDER NEVADA SKIES
        CREDIT:  '50 THE CARIBOU TRAIL
--------------------------------------------------------------------------------
HAYES, HELEN          BORN:   HELEN HAYES BROWN
                              OCT 10,'00 AT WASHINGTON, D.C.
        FATHER: FRANCIS VAN ARNUUM BROWN
        MOTHER: CATHERINE ESTELL HAYES
        *** MARRIED:  '28 CHARLES MACARTHUR, WRITER
        BROTHER-IN-LAW: JOHN MACARTHUR
        DAUGHTER:  '30 MARY MACARTHUR  (DIED '49)
        ADOPTED SON: JAMES MACARTHUR, ACTOR
        DAUGHTER-IN-LAW: JOYCE BULIFANT
        *** MARRIED:  '43 HAL NEIDES
        FRIEND: IRVING THALBERG
        RESIDENCE: NYACK, NY
        MEMOIRS:  '69 ON REFLECTION
        TALENT: ACTRESS
        CREDIT:  '17 THE WEAVERS OF LIFE
        AA-WIN  ACTRESS:  '31 THE SIN OF MADELON CLAUDET
        CREDIT:  '34 WHAT EVERY WOMAN KNOWS
        CREDIT:  '56 ANASTASIA
        AA-WIN  SUP.ACT.:  '70 AIRPORT
--------------------------------------------------------------------------------
HAYES, PETER LIND        BORN:   JOSEPH CONRAD LIND, JR.
                                 JUN 25,'15 AT SAN FRANCISCO, CA
        FATHER: JOSEPH CONRAD LIND
        MOTHER: GRACE DOLORES HAYES, VAUDEVILLE ENTERTAINER
        *** MARRIED:  '40 MARY HEALY, ACTRESS
        DAUGHTER: CATHY LIND HAYES
        SON: PETER MICHAEL HAYES
        TALENT: ACTOR
        CREDIT:  '38 OUTSIDE OF PARADISE
        CREDIT:  '39 THESE GLAMOUR GIRLS
        CREDIT:  '41 ZIS BOOM BAH!
        CREDIT:  '41 PLAYMATES
        CREDIT:  '68 SUDDEN DEATH
--------------------------------------------------------------------------------
HAYMES, DICK
                         SEP 13,'18 AT BUENOS AIRES, ARGENTINA
        MOTHER: MARGUERITE
        BROTHER: ROBERT STANTON, ACTOR
        *** MARRIED:  '38 EDITH HARPER  (ANNULLED '38)
        *** MARRIED:  '41 JOANNE DRU, ACTRESS  (DIVORCED '49)
        SON:  '42 RICHARD HAYMES
        DAUGHTER:  '44 HELEN HAYMES
        DAUGHTER:  '48 BARBARA HAYMES
        *** MARRIED:  '50 NORA EDDINGTON  (DIVORCED)
        STEP-DAUGHTER: DEIDRE FLYNN
        STEP-DAUGHTER: RORY FLYNN
        *** MARRIED:  '53 RITA HAYWORTH  (DIVORCED '55)
        FATHER-IN-LAW: EDUARDO CANSINO, DANCER
        MOTHER-IN-LAW: VOLGA HAWORTH, DANCER
        STEP-DAUGHTER: REBECCA WELLES
        STEP-DAUGHTER: JASMIN KHAN
```

```
*** MARRIED:  '56 FRAN MAKRIS  (DIVORCED)
*** MARRIED:  '57 FRAN JEFFRIES  (DIVORCED)
*** MARRIED:  '58 WENDY SMITH
ENEMY: RICHARD QUINE, BECAUSE OF FRAN JEFFRIES
RESIDENCE: DUBLIN, IRELAND
TALENT: ACTOR-SINGER
CREDIT:  '44 IRISH EYES ARE SMILING, DEBUT
CREDIT:  '45 STATE FAIR
CREDIT:  '46 DO YOU LOVE ME?
CREDIT:  '48 ONE TOUCH OF VENUS
CREDIT:  '53 ALL ASHORE
```

HAYWARD, SUSAN   BORN: EDYTHE MARRENER
                              JUN 30,'19 AT BROOKLYN,NY DIED IN '75

```
GRANDMOTHER: KATE HARRIGAN, ACTRESS
FATHER: WALTER MARRENER
MOTHER: ELLEN PEARSON
SISTER: FLORENCE MARRENER, MODEL, SHOWGIRL
BROTHER: WALTER MARRENER, JR.
*** MARRIED:  '44 JESS BARKER, ACTOR  (DIVORCED '54)
SON:  '45 TIMOTHY BARKER, TWIN  (DIED '72)
SON:  '45 GREGORY BARKER, TWIN
*** MARRIED:  '57 FLOYD EATON CHALKLEY, ATTORNEY, RANCHER  (DIED '66)
STEP-SON: JOSEPH CHALKLEY  (DIED '64)
ROMANCE: JOHN CARROLL
RESIDENCE: CARROLTON, GA
POSSESSION: YACHT 'OH, SUSANNAH'
BIOGRAPHY:  '73 THE DIVINE BITCH, BY DOUG MCCLELLAND
TALENT: ACTRESS
AA-NOM  ACTRESS:  '47 SMASH UP - STORY OF A WOMAN
AA-NOM  ACTRESS:  '49 MY FOOLISH HEART
AA-NOM  ACTRESS:  '52 WITH A SONG IN MY HEART
AA-NOM  ACTRESS:  '55 I'LL CRY TOMORROW
AA-WIN  ACTRESS:  '58 I WANT TO LIVE!
```

HAYWORTH, RITA   BORN: MARGARITA CARMEN CANSINO
                              OCT 17,'18 AT NYC

```
FATHER: EDUARDO CANSINO, DANCER
MOTHER: VOLGA HAWORTH, DANCER
BROTHER: EDUARDO CANSINO, JR., ACTOR
BROTHER: VERNON CANSINO
AUNT: LELA HAWORTH, AKA LELA OWENS  (DIED '77)
COUSIN: GINGER ROGERS, DANCER, ACTRESS
*** MARRIED:  '36 EDWARD C. JUDSON  (DIVORCED '42)
*** MARRIED:  '43 ORSON WELLES, ACTOR-PRODUCER-WRITER  (DIVORCED '47)
FATHER-IN-LAW: RICHARD HEAD WELLES, INVENTOR
MOTHER-IN-LAW: BEATRICE IVES, PIANIST, POLITICAL SUFFRAGETTE
DAUGHTER:  '44 REBECCA WELLES
*** MARRIED:  '49 PRINCE ALY KHAN  (DIVORCED '51)
DAUGHTER:  '50 JASMIN KHAN, MODEL
*** MARRIED:  '53 DICK HAYMES, SINGER  (DIVORCED '55)
STEP-DAUGHTER: HELEN HAYMES
STEP-SON: RICHARD HAYMES
STEP-DAUGHTER: BARBARA HAYMES
*** MARRIED:  '58 JAMES HILL, PRODUCER  (DIVORCED '61)
RESIDENCE: BEVERLY HILLS, CA
POSSESSION:  '39 CONTRACT AT COLUMBIA STUDIOS
BIOGRAPHY:  '76 RITA, BY JOHN KOBAL
```

```
TALENT: ACTRESS
COMMENT: THE CANSINO DANCE ACT BILLED - 'FANTASIA ESPANOLA'
CREDIT:  '35 DANTE'S INFERNO
CREDIT:  '38 THERE'S ALWAYS A WOMAN
CREDIT:  '41 YOU'LL NEVER GET RICH
CREDIT:  '46 GILDA
CREDIT:  '48 THE LADY FROM SHANGHAI
CREDIT:  '54 MISS SADIE THOMPSON
CREDIT:  '72 THE WRATH OF GOD
```

HEATHERTON, JOEY   BORN: DAVENIE JOHANNA HEATHERTON
                                  SEP 14,'44 AT ROCKVILLE CENTRE, NY
```
FATHER: RAY HEATHERTON, ACTOR
MOTHER: DAVENIE
BROTHER: RICHARD HEATHERTON
*** MARRIED:  '69 LANCE RENTZELL, FOOTBALL PLAYER  (DIVORCED '72)
ENEMY: PAUL ANKA, SUED FOR BREACH OF CONTRACT
TALENT: ACTRESS
CREDIT:  '64 TWILIGHT OF HONOUR
CREDIT:  '64 WHERE LOVE HAS GONE
CREDIT:  '64 MY BLOOD RUNS COLD
CREDIT:  '72 BLUEBEARD
```

HEFLIN, VAN   BORN: EMMETT EVAN HEFLIN, JR.
                             DEC 13,'10 AT WALTERS, OK DIED IN '71
```
FATHER: EMMETT HEFLIN, DENTIST
MOTHER: FANNY SHIPPEY
SISTER: FRANCES HEFLIN, ACTRESS
BROTHER: MARTIN HEFLIN
*** MARRIED:  '42 FRANCES NEAL, ACTRESS  (DIVORCED '67)
DAUGHTER:  '43 VANA HEFLIN
DAUGHTER:  '46 CATHLEEN HEFLIN
SON:  '54 TRACY NEAL HEFLIN
TALENT: ACTOR
CREDIT:  '36 A WOMAN REBELS
CREDIT:  '40 SANTE FE TRAIL
AA-WIN  SUP.ACT.:  '42 JOHNNY EAGER
CREDIT:  '53 SHANE
CREDIT:  '56 PATTERNS
CREDIT:  '69 AIRPORT
```

HENIE, SONJA
                          APR 08,'12 AT OSLO,NORWAY DIED IN '69
```
FATHER: WILHELM HENIE
MOTHER: SELMA LOCHMAN-NIELSEN
BROTHER: LEIF HENIE
*** MARRIED:  '40 DAN TOPPING  (DIVORCED '46)
*** MARRIED:  '49 WINTHROP GARDNER, JR.  (DIVORCED '55)
*** MARRIED:  '56 NILS ONSTAD
ROMANCE: RICHARD GREENE
ROMANCE: CARL CARLSON
FRIEND: TYRONE POWER
PARTNER: MICHAEL KIRBY
RESIDENCE: OSLO, NORWAY
RESIDENCE: LOS ANGELES, CA
POSSESSION:  '18 FIRST PAIR OF ICE SKATES- A CHRISTMAS GIFT
MEMOIRS:  '40 WINGS ON MY FEET
TALENT: ICE SKATER-ACTRESS
```

```
     CREDIT:   '36 ONE IN A MILLION
     CREDIT:   '37 THIN ICE
     CREDIT:   '42 ICELAND
     CREDIT:   '45 IT'S A PLEASURE
     CREDIT:   '58 HELLO, LONDON
```

HEPBURN, AUDREY   BORN: AUDREY HEPBURN-RUSTON
```
                             MAY 04,'29 AT BRUSSELS, BELGIUM
     GRANDFATHER: BARON ARNOUD VAN HEEMSTRA, GOVERNOR OF DUTCH GUIANA
     FATHER: JOSEPH ANTHONY HEPBURN-RUSTON
     MOTHER: BARONESS ELLA VAN HEEMSTRA
     *** MARRIED:  '54 MEL FERRER, ACTOR-DIRECTOR   (DIVORCED '68)
     STEP-DAUGHTER: MELA FERRER
     STEP-SON: CHRIS FERRER
     STEP-DAUGHTER: PEPA FERRER
     STEP-SON: MARK FERRER
     SON:  '60 SEAN FERRER
     *** MARRIED:  '69 ANDREA DOTTI, DOCTOR
     SON:  '70 LUCA DOTTI
     TALENT: ACTRESS
     AA-WIN  ACTRESS:  '53 ROMAN HOLIDAY
     AA-NOM  ACTRESS:  '54 SABRINA
     AA-NOM  ACTRESS:  '59 THE NUN'S STORY
     AA-NOM  ACTRESS:  '61 BREAKFAST AT TIFFANY'S
     CREDIT:  '62 THE CHILDREN'S HOUR
     AA-NOM  ACTRESS:  '67 WAIT UNTIL DARK
```

HEPBURN, KATHARINE   BORN: KATHARINE HOUGHTON HEPBURN
```
                              NOV 08,'07 AT HARTFORD,CN
     FATHER: DR. THOMAS NORVAL HEPBURN
     MOTHER: KATHERINE MARTHA HOUGHTON
     SISTER: MARION HEPBURN
     SISTER: MARGARET HEPBURN
     BROTHER: THOMAS HEPBURN, JR.
     BROTHER: RICHARD HEPBURN
     BROTHER: ROBERT HEPBURN
     *** MARRIED:  '28 LUDLOW OGDEN SMITH, AKA OGDEN LUDLOW  (DIVORCED '34)
     ROMANCE: LELAND HAYWARD, AGENT
     ROMANCE: SPENCER TRACY, ACTOR
     ROMANCE: ROBERT MCKNIGHT, SCULPTOR
     ROMANCE: HOWARD HUGHES
     FRIEND: LAURA HARDING
     FRIEND: GEORGE CUKOR, DIRECTOR
     RESIDENCE: NYC
     POSSESSION:  '77 M. CAREY THOMAS AWARD OF BRYN MAWR COLLEGE (HER ALMA MATER)
     BIOGRAPHY:  '71 THE FILMS OF KATHARINE HEPBURN, BY HOMER DICKENS
     TALENT: ACTRESS
     AA-WIN  ACTRESS:  '32 MORNING GLORY
     AA-NOM  ACTRESS:  '35 ALICE ADAMS
     AA-NOM  ACTRESS:  '40 THE PHILADELPHIA STORY
     AA-NOM  ACTRESS:  '42 WOMAN OF THE YEAR
     AA-NOM  ACTRESS:  '51 THE AFRICAN QUEEN
     AA-NOM  ACTRESS:  '55 SUMMERTIME
     AA-NOM  ACTRESS:  '56 THE RAINMAKER
     AA-NOM  ACTRESS:  '59 SUDDENLY  LAST SUMMER
     AA-NOM  ACTRESS:  '62 LONG DAY'S JOURNEY INTO NIGHT
     AA-WIN  ACTRESS:  '67 GUESS WHO'S COMING TO DINNER
     AA-WIN  ACTRESS:  '68 THE LION IN WINTER
```

HERSHOLT, JEAN
                         JUL 12,'86 AT COPENHAGEN, DENMARK   DIED IN '56
     FATHER: HENRY HERSHOLT, ACTOR
     MOTHER: CLAIRE, ACTRESS
     *** MARRIED: '14 VIA ANDERSEN
     SON: '14 ALLAN HERSHOLT, ACTOR, PUBLICIST
     TALENT: ACTOR
     CREDIT: '15 DON QUIXOTE
     CREDIT: '32 GRAND HOTEL
     AA-SPECIAL AWARD: '49 HONORING HIS WORK ON BEHALF OF THE MOTION PICTURE RELIEF FUND
     CREDIT: '49 DANCING IN THE DARK
     CREDIT: '55 RUN FOR COVER
     CREDIT: 'DR. CHRISTIAN, SERIES

HESTON, CHARLTON   BORN: CHARLTON CARTER
                                    OCT 04,'23 AT EVANSTON, IL
     FATHER: RUSSELL WHITFORD CARTER
     MOTHER: LILLA CHARLTON
     STEP-FATHER: CHESTER HESTON
     SISTER: LILLA CARTER
     BROTHER: ALAN CARTER
     *** MARRIED: '44 LYDIA CLARKE, ACTRESS
     SON: '55 FRASER CLARKE HESTON, ACTING DEBUT AT 3 MONTHS
     DAUGHTER: HOLLY ANN HESTON
     POSSESSION: FARM AT ST. HELEN, MICHIGAN
     MEMOIRS: '78 THE ACTOR'S LIFE
     BIOGRAPHY: '76 CHARLTON HESTON, BY MICHAEL DRUXMAN
     TALENT: ACTOR-DIRECTOR
     CREDIT: '50 DARK CITY
     CREDIT: '56 THE TEN COMMANDMENTS
     AA-WIN ACTOR: '59 BEN-HUR
     CREDIT: '65 THE WAR LORD
     CREDIT: '67 PLANET OF THE APES
     CREDIT: '73 SOYLENT GREEN

HILLIARD, HARRIET   BORN: PEGGY LOU SNYDER
                                    JUL 18,'14 AT DES MOINES, IO
     FATHER: ROY SNYDER, ACTOR- AKA ROY HILLIARD
     MOTHER: HAZEL HILLIARD
     *** MARRIED: OZZIE NELSON, ACTOR
     SON: '36 DAVID NELSON
     DAUGHTER-IN-LAW: JUNE BLAIR, ACTRESS (MARRIED '64)
     SON: '40 RICK NELSON, ACTOR, SINGER
     DAUGHTER-IN-LAW: KRISTIN HARMON (MARRIED '63)
     GRANDDAUGHTER: '63 TRACY KRISTIN NELSON
     GRANDSON: '67 ERIC NELSON, JR., TWIN
     GRANDSON: '67 MATTHEW NELSON, TWIN
     GRANDSON: '69 GUNNAR NELSON
     RESIDENCE: LOS ANGELES, CA
     TALENT: ACTRESS
     CREDIT: '36 FOLLOW THE FLEET
     CREDIT: '38 COCOANUT GROVE
     CREDIT: '43 HI, BUDDY!
     CREDIT: '44 SWINGTIME JOHNNY
     CREDIT: '52 HERE COME THE NELSONS

HITCHCOCK, ALFRED   BORN: ALFRED JOSEPH HITCHCOCK
                                       AUG 13,'99 AT LONDON, ENGLAND

```
      MOTHER: EMMA WHELAN
      *** MARRIED:  '26 ALMA REVILLE, WRITER
      DAUGHTER: PATRICIA HITCHCOCK
      RESIDENCE: LOS ANGELES, CA
      RESIDENCE: RANCH  NEAR SAN FRANCISCO, CA
      POSSESSION: '67 IRVING THALBERG MEMORIAL AWARD
      BIOGRAPHY:  '67 HITCHCOCK, BY FRANCOIS TRUFFAUT
      TALENT: DIRECTOR-ACTOR
      CREDIT:  '25 THE PLEASURE GARDEN
      AA-NOM  DIRECTOR:  '40 REBECCA
      AA-NOM  DIRECTOR:  '44 LIFEBOAT
      AA-NOM  DIRECTOR:  '45 SPELLBOUND
      AA-NOM  DIRECTOR:  '54 REAR WINDOW
      CREDIT:  '59 NORTH BY NORTHWEST
      AA-NOM  DIRECTOR:  '60 PSYCHO
```

HODIAK, JOHN
                              APR 16,'14 AT PITTSBURGH,PA   DIED IN '55
```
      FATHER: HODIAK
      *** MARRIED:  '46 ANNE BAXTER, ACTRESS  (DIVORCED '53)
      FATHER-IN-LAW: KENNETH STUART BAXTER
      MOTHER-IN-LAW: CATHERINE WRIGHT
      DAUGHTER:  '51 KATRINA BAXTER HODIAK
      TALENT: ACTOR
      CREDIT:  '43 A STRANGER IN TOWN
      CREDIT:  '48 HOMECOMING
      CREDIT:  '52 THE SELLOUT
      CREDIT:  '55 ON THE THRESHOLD OF SPACE
```

HOFFMAN, DUSTIN
                              AUG 08,'37 AT LOS ANGELES, CA
```
      FATHER: HARRY HOFFMAN, FURNITURE DESIGNER
      BROTHER: RONALD HOFFMAN, ECONOMICS TEACHER
      *** MARRIED:  '69 ANNE BYRNE, DANCER, ACTRESS - ANNE HOFFMAN
      DAUGHTER:  '70 JENNIFER CELIA HOFFMAN
      RESIDENCE: NYC
      TALENT: ACTOR
      AA-NOM  ACTOR:  '67 THE GRADUATE
      AA-NOM  ACTOR:  '69 MIDNIGHT COWBOY
      CREDIT:  '70 LITTLE BIG MAN
      CREDIT:  '71 STRAW DOGS
      AA-NOM  ACTOR:  '74 LENNY
      CREDIT:  '76 ALL THE PRESIDENT'S MEN
```

HOLBROOK, HAL   BORN: HAROLD ROWE HOLBROOK, JR.
                                 FEB 17,'25 AT CLEVELAND,OH
```
      FATHER: HAROLD ROWE HOLBROOK
      MOTHER: AILEEN DAVENPORT, SHOWGIRL-ZIEGFELD FOLLIES
      SISTER: --
      SISTER: --
      BROTHER: --  (DIED)
      UNCLE: GEORGE H. ROWE, ACTOR, DIRECTOR
      *** MARRIED:  '45 RUBY ELAINE JOHNSTON, ACTRESS  (DIVORCED '64)
      DAUGHTER:  '52 VICTORIA HOLBROOK
```

```
        SON:  '55 DAVID HOLBROOK
        *** MARRIED:  '67 CAROL ROSSEN, ACTRESS
        FATHER-IN-LAW: ROBERT ROSSEN, DIRECTOR
        DAUGHTER:  '70 EVE HOLBROOK
        RESIDENCE: PACIFIC PALISADES, CA
        POSSESSION: KETCH 'DOUBLOON'
        TALENT: ACTOR
        CREDIT:  '66 THE GROUP
        CREDIT:  '68 WILD IN THE STREETS
        CREDIT:  '70 THE PEOPLE NEXT DOOR
        CREDIT:  '76 ALL THE PRESIDENT'S MEN
-----------------------------------------------------------------------------
HOLDEN, WILLIAM         BORN:  WILLIAM FRANKLIN BEEDLE, JR.
                               APR 17,'18 AT O'FALLON, IL
        FATHER: WILLIAM FRANKLIN BEEDLE, CHEMIST
        MOTHER: MARY BELL
        BROTHER: ROBERT HOLDEN  (DIED '44)
        BROTHER: RICHARD HOLDEN
        *** MARRIED:  '41 BRENDA MARSHALL, ACTRESS  (DIVORCED)
        SON:  '43 PETER WESTFIELD HOLDEN
        SON:  '46 SCOTT PORTER HOLDEN
        DAUGHTER: VIRGINIA HOLDEN
        ROMANCE: STEPHANIE POWERS
        FRIEND: HARVEY BERNHARD
        RESIDENCE: SANTA MONICA
        TALENT: ACTOR-CONSERVATIONIST
        CREDIT:  '39 GOLDEN BOY
        CREDIT:  '48 RACHEL AND THE STRANGER
        AA-NOM  ACTOR:  '50 SUNSET BOULEVARD
        AA-WIN  ACTOR:  '53 STALAG 17
        CREDIT:  '55 LOVE IS A MANY-SPLENDORED THING
        AA-NOM  ACTOR:  '76 NETWORK
-----------------------------------------------------------------------------
HOLLIDAY, JUDY          BORN:  JUDITH TUVIM
                               JUN 21,'23 AT NYC  DIED IN '65
        FATHER: ABRAHAM TUVIM
        MOTHER: HELEN GOLLUMB
        *** MARRIED:  '48 DAVID OPPENHEIM, MUSICIAN  (DIVORCED '58)
        SON:  '49 JONATHAN OPPENHEIM
        PARTNER: ADOLPH GREEN
        PARTNER: BETTY COMDEN
        TALENT: ACTRESS
        CREDIT:  '44 GREENWICH VILLAGE
        AA-WIN  ACTRESS:  '50 BORN YESTERDAY
        CREDIT:  '53 IT SHOULD HAPPEN TO YOU
        CREDIT:  '56 THE SOLID GOLD CADILLAC
        CREDIT:  '60 BELLS ARE RINGING
-----------------------------------------------------------------------------
HOLLOWAY, STANLEY       BORN:  STANLEY AUGUSTUS HOLLOWAY
                               OCT 01,'90 AT LONDON,ENGLAND
        FATHER: --, LAW CLERK
        *** MARRIED:  '39 VIOLET MARION LANE
        SON:  '53 JULIAN HOLLOWAY
        DAUGHTER-IN-LAW: TESSA DAHL
        RESIDENCE: THE NIGHTINGALES, PENN, BUCKINGHAMSHIRE, ENGLAND
        POSSESSION:  '60 ORDER OF THE BRITISH EMPIRE- SERVICES TO THE THEATRE
        MEMOIRS:  '69 WIV' A LITTLE BIT OF LUCK
        TALENT: ACTOR-SINGER
```

```
CREDIT:  '21 ROTTERS
CREDIT:  '34 LOVE AT SECOND SIGHT
CREDIT:  '45 BRIEF ENCOUNTER
AA-NOM  SUP.ACT:  '64 MY FAIR LADY
CREDIT:  '71 FLIGHT OF THE DOVES
```

HOLM, CELESTE
                         APR 29,'19 AT NYC
```
FATHER: THEODORE HOLM
MOTHER: JEAN PARKE
*** MARRIED:  '38 RALPH NELSON  (DIVORCED)
SON:  '39 THEODORE NELSON
*** MARRIED:  '40 FRANCIS DAVIS
*** MARRIED:  '46 A. SCHUYLER DUNNING  (DIVORCED '52)
SON:  '46 DANIEL DUNNING
TALENT: ACTRESS
CREDIT:  '46 THREE LITTLE GIRLS IN BLUE
AA-WIN  SUP.ACT.:  '47 GENTLEMAN'S AGREEMENT
AA-NOM  SUP.ACT:  '49 COME TO THE STABLE
AA-NOM  SUP.ACT:  '50 ALL ABOUT EVE
CREDIT: .'56 HIGH SOCIETY
```

HOLM, ELEANOR
                         DEC 06,'14 AT BROOKLYN,NY
```
*** MARRIED:  '33 ARTHUR JARRETT, SINGER  (DIVORCED '38)
*** MARRIED:  '39 BILLY ROSE, PRODUCER  (DIVORCED '54)
FATHER-IN-LAW: DAVID ROSENBERG
MOTHER-IN-LAW: FANNY WERNICK
*** MARRIED:  '74 TOMMY WHALEN
RESIDENCE: MIAMI BEACH, FL
TALENT: SWIMMER-ACTRESS
COMMENT: 'WAR OF THE ROSES' DIVORCE CASE PUBLICIZED IN 1954
COMMENT: OLYMPIC GAMES COMPETITOR FOR SWIMMING
CREDIT: TARZAN'S REVENGE
```

HOPE, BOB   BORN: LESLIE TOWNES HOPE
                         MAY 29,'03 AT ELTHAM, LONDON, ENGLAND
```
MOTHER: AGNES TOWNES
BROTHER: FREDERICK HOPE
BROTHER: JACK HOPE, HIS PERSONAL MANAGER  (DIED '62)
BROTHER: JAMES HOPE, DIRECTOR OF HOPE ENTERPRISES
BROTHER: SIDNEY HOPE  (DIED '46)
BROTHER: IVOR HOPE, PRESIDENT-HOPE METAL PRODUCTS  (DIED '69)
BROTHER: GEORGE HOPE, PRODUCTION CO. CO-ORDINATOR  (DIED '69)
*** MARRIED:  '33 DOLORES READE
ADOPTED DAUGHTER: LINDA ROBERTA THERESA HOPE
ADOPTED DAUGHTER: HONORA AVIS MARY HOPE
ADOPTED SON: ANTHONY READE HOPE
ADOPTED SON: WILLIAM KELLY FRANCIS HOPE
SON-IN-LAW: SAMUEL MCCULLAGH, JR.  (MARRIED '69)
SON-IN-LAW: NATHANIEL GREENBLATT  (MARRIED '69)
FRIEND: FERNANDO D. MIRON, (HIS MASSEUR FOR 35 YEARS)  (DIED '78)
RESIDENCE: BEVERLY HILLS, CA
MEMOIRS:  '44 I NEVER LEFT HOME
MEMOIRS: THE ROAD TO HOLLYWOOD
TALENT: ACTOR
CREDIT:  '38 THE BIG BROADCAST OF 1938
AA-SPECIAL AWARD:  '40 HONORING HIS UNSELFISH SERVICE TO THE MOTION PICTURE INDUSTRY
```

AA-SPECIAL AWARD: '44 HONORARY LIFE MEMBERSHIP IN ACADEMY OF MOTION PICTURES
AA-SPECIAL AWARD: '52 HONORARY AWARD OF A STATUETTE
AA-SPECIAL AWARD: '65 HONORARY GOLD MEDAL AWARD FOR UNIQUE AND DISTINGUISHED WORK
CREDIT: '69 HOW TO COMMIT MARRIAGE

HOPPER, DENNIS
                    MAY 17,'36 AT DODGE CITY,KA
*** MARRIED: '61 BROOKE HAYWARD (DIVORCED '67)
BROTHER-IN-LAW: WILLIAM 'BILL' HAYWARD, PRODUCER
FATHER-IN-LAW: LELAND HAYWARD, AGENT, PRODUCER
DAUGHTER: '62 MARIN HOPPER
*** MARRIED: '70 MICHELLE PHILLIPS, SINGER (DIVORCED)
*** MARRIED: '73 DARLENE HALPIN
FRIEND: PETER FONDA
TALENT: ACTOR-PRODUCER WRITER
CREDIT: '55 REBEL WITHOUT A CAUSE
CREDIT: '60 KEY WITNESS
CREDIT: '67 COOL HAND LUKE
CREDIT: '69 EASY RIDER
CREDIT: '71 THE LAST MOVIE

HOPPER, HEDDA   BORN: ELDA FURRY
                          MAY 02,'85 AT HOLLIDAYSBURG,PA   DIED IN '66
FATHER: DAVID FURRY, BUTCHER
MOTHER: MARGARETT MILLER
SISTER: MARGARET FURRY
SISTER: DORA FURRY
BROTHER: SHERMAN FURRY
BROTHER: CAMMON FURRY
BROTHER: FRANK FURRY
BROTHER: EDGAR FURRY
*** MARRIED: '13 WILLIAM DEWOLF HOPPER, STAGE ACTOR (DIVORCED '22)
STEP-SON: JOHN HOPPER, II
SON: '15 WILLIAM DEWOLF HOPPER, JR., ACTOR (DIED '70)
DAUGHTER-IN-LAW: JANE GILBERT (MARRIED '40)
GRANDDAUGHTER: '41 JOAN HOPPER
FRIEND: FRANCES MARION, WRITER
FRIEND: CHARLOTTE GREENWOOD
FRIEND: ALICE BRADY, ACTRESS
RESIDENCE: BEVERLY HILLS, CA
MEMOIRS: '52 FROM UNDER MY HAT
MEMOIRS: '63 'THE WHOLE TRUTH & NOTHING BUT
TALENT: ACTRESS-JOURNALIST
COMMENT: GOSSIP COLUMN STARTED IN 1936
CREDIT: '16 BATTLE OF HEARTS, DEBUT IN 1916
CREDIT: '26 PLEASURES OF THE RICH
CREDIT: '36 DRACULA'S DAUGHTER
CREDIT: '46 BREAKFAST IN HOLLYWOOD
CREDIT: '66 THE OSCAR

HORNE, LENA   BORN: LENA CALHOUN HORNE
                         JUN 30,'17 AT BROOKLYN, NY
FATHER: EDWIN F. HORNE
MOTHER: EDNA CALHOUN, ACTRESS
*** MARRIED: '37 LEWIS JONES (DIVORCED '44)
DAUGHTER: '38 GAIL JONES
SON-IN-LAW: SIDNEY LUMET, DIRECTOR (MARRIED '63)
SON: '39 TERRY JONES

```
*** MARRIED:   '48 LENNIE HAYTON, MUSICIAN  (DIED '71)
SON:  '49 LEONARD HAYTON
RESIDENCE: LOS ANGELES, CA
MEMOIRS: IN PERSON-LENA HORNE
TALENT: SINGER-ACTRESS
CREDIT:  '42 PANAMA HATTIE
CREDIT:  '46 CABIN IN THE SKY
CREDIT:  '48 WORDS AND MUSIC
CREDIT:  '56 MEET ME IN LAS VEGAS
CREDIT:  '69 DEATH OF A GUNFIGHTER
-------------------------------------------------------------------------------
HOWARD, LESLIE           BORN:   LESLIE HOWARD STAINER
                              APR 03,'93 AT LONDON, ENGLAND  DIED IN '43
FATHER: FRANK STAINER, STOCKBROKER
MOTHER: LILIAN HOWARD
SISTER: IRENE STAINER
SISTER: DORICE STAINER
BROTHER: JAMES STAINER
BROTHER: ARTHUR STAINER
*** MARRIED:   '16 RUTH EVELYN MARTIN
SON:  '18 RONALD HOWARD, ACTOR
DAUGHTER:  '24 LESLIE RUTH HOWARD
BIOGRAPHY:  '59 A QUITE REMARKABLE FATHER, BY LESLIE RUTH HOWARD
TALENT: ACTOR
CREDIT:  '19 THE LACKEY AND THE LADY
CREDIT:  '30 OUTWARD BOUND
AA-NOM  ACTOR:  '32 BERKELEY SQUARE
CREDIT:  '36 ROMEO AND JULIET
AA-NOM  ACTOR:  '38 PYGMALION
CREDIT:  '39 GONE WITH THE WIND
CREDIT:  '39 INTERMEZZO
CREDIT:  '43 SPITFIRE
-------------------------------------------------------------------------------
HOWARD, RON
                    MAR 01,'54 AT DUNCAN,OK
FATHER: RANCE HOWARD, ACTOR
MOTHER: JEAN, ACTRESS
BROTHER: CLINT HOWARD, ACTOR
*** MARRIED:   '75 CHERYL ALLEY
TALENT: ACTOR
CREDIT:  '62 THE MUSIC MAN
CREDIT:  '69 SMOKE
CREDIT:  '71 THE WILD COUNTRY
CREDIT:  '73 AMERICAN GRAFFITI
-------------------------------------------------------------------------------
HOWARD, TREVOR          BORN:   TREVOR WALLACE HOWARD
                             SEP 29,'16 AT CLIFTONVILLE, KENT, ENGLAND
FATHER: ARTHUR JOHN HOWARD, LLOYD'S OF LONDON UNDERWRITER
MOTHER: MABEL GREY WALLACE
*** MARRIED:   '44 HELEN MARY CHERRY
POSSESSION: JAZZ RECORD COLLECTION
TALENT: ACTOR
CREDIT:  '43 THE WAY AHEAD
CREDIT:  '53 THE GIFT HORSE
AA-NOM  ACTOR:  '60 SONS AND LOVERS
CREDIT:  '65 VON RYAN'S EXPRESS
CREDIT:  '71 KIDNAPPED
```

```
-----------------------------------------------------------------------------------------
HUDSON, ROCK          BORN:   ROY SHERER FITZGERALD
                              NOV 17,'25 AT WINNETKA, IL
      FATHER: ROY SHERER, HUDSON AUTOMOBILE MECHANIC
      MOTHER: KATHERINE M. OLSEN
      STEP-FATHER: WALLACE FITZGERALD
      *** MARRIED:  '55 PHYLLIS GATES, HENRY WILSON'S SECRETARY  (DIVORCED '58)
      PARTNER: HENRY WILSON, THE SEVEN PICTURES CO.
      RESIDENCE: NEWPORT HARBOR, CA
      POSSESSION: SAILBOAT 'KHARIOZAZ'
      TALENT: ACTOR
      CREDIT:  '49 FIGHTER SQUADRON
      AA-NOM ACTOR:  '56 GIANT
      CREDIT:  '61 LOVER COME BACK
      CREDIT:  '64 STRANGE BEDFELLOWS
      CREDIT:  '71 PRETTY MAIDS ALL IN A ROW
-----------------------------------------------------------------------------------------
HUGHES, HOWARD        BORN:   HOWARD ROBARDS HUGHES
                              DEC 24,'05 AT HOUSTON, TX  DIED IN '76
      FATHER: HOWARD ROBARD HUGHES
      MOTHER: ALENE GANO
      *** MARRIED:  '57 JEAN PETERS, ACTRESS  (DIVORCED '71)
      ROMANCE: TERRY MOORE, ACTRESS
      ROMANCE: KATHARINE HEPBURN, ACTRESS
      ROMANCE: BILLIE DOVE, ACTRESS
      ROMANCE: JUNE LANG, ACTRESS
      ROMANCE: GINGER ROGERS, ACTRESS
      ROMANCE: FAITH DOMERGUE, ACTRESS
      ROMANCE: AVA GARDNER, ACTRESS
      ROMANCE: JEAN HARLOW, ACTRESS
      RESIDENCE: BEVERLY HILLS, CA UNTIL 1948 - THEN PERIPATETICALLY
      POSSESSION:  '48 33% OF RKO STUDIOS
      POSSESSION:  '50 THE SPRUCE GOOSE WOOD SEAPLANE
      BIOGRAPHY:  '68 THE BASHFUL BILLIONAIRE, BY ALBERT B. GERBER
      TALENT: EXECUTIVE-PILOT
      CREDIT:  '30 HELL'S ANGELS
      CREDIT:  '31 THE FRONT PAGE
      CREDIT:  '40 THE OUTLAW, MADE IN '40-RELEASED '46
-----------------------------------------------------------------------------------------
HUME, BENITA
                      OCT 14,'06 AT EGERTON, LANCASHIRE, ENGLAND  DIED IN '67
      SISTER: PAMELA MILBURNE
      *** MARRIED: ERIC SIEPMAN  (DIVORCED '33)
      *** MARRIED:  '38 RONALD COLMAN, ACTOR  (DIED '58)
      DAUGHTER:  '39 JULIET COLMAN
      *** MARRIED:  '58 GEORGE SANDERS, ACTOR
      ROMANCE: JACK DUNFEE
      RESIDENCE: BEVERLY HILLS, CALIF.
      POSSESSION:  '33 CONTRACT AT RKO
      POSSESSION: SAN YSIDRO RESORT IN SANTA BARBARA, CA.
      TALENT: ACTRESS
      CREDIT:  '28 SOUTH SEA BUBBLE
      CREDIT:  '30 THE LADY OF THE LAKE
      CREDIT:  '34 THE PRIVATE LIFE OF DON JUAN
      CREDIT:  '38 PECK'S BAD BOY WITH THE CIRCUS
      CREDIT:  '40 THE CONSTANT NYMPH
```

HUNTER, JEFFREY   BORN: HENRY HERMAN MCKINNIES, JR.
                          NOV 25,'25 AT NEW ORLEANS, LA   DIED IN '69
    FATHER: HENRY MCKINNIES
    *** MARRIED: '50 BARBARA RUSH, ACTRESS (DIVORCED '54)
    SON: '52 CHRISTOPHER HUNTER
    *** MARRIED: '57 DUSTY BARTLETT (DIVORCED '67)
    SON: '59 TODD HUNTER
    TALENT: ACTOR
    CREDIT: '51 CALL ME MISTER
    CREDIT: '56 A KISS BEFORE DYING
    CREDIT: '61 KING OF KINGS
    CREDIT: '61 MAN TRAP
    CREDIT: '62 THE LONGEST DAY
    CREDIT: '68 FIND A PLACE TO DIE

HUNTER, TAB   BORN: ARTHUR GELIEN
                      JUL 11,'31 AT NYC
    MOTHER: GERTRUDE
    BROTHER: WALTER GELIEN (DIED)
    ROMANCE: MARY ANN MOBLEY, ACTRESS
    ROMANCE: JOAN PERRY, ACTRESS
    FRIEND: CHARLES WILLIAMS
    RESIDENCE: MIDDLEBURG, VIRGINIA
    TALENT: ACTOR
    CREDIT: '48 THE LAWLESS, DEBUT
    CREDIT: '54 TRACK OF THE CAT
    CREDIT: '58 DAMN YANKEES
    CREDIT: '66 BIRDS DO IT
    CREDIT: '73 THE TENDER TRAP

HUSSEY, RUTH   BORN: RUTH CAROL HUSSEY O'ROURKE
                       OCT 30,'15 AT PROVIDENCE, RI
    FATHER: GEORGE HUSSEY
    MOTHER: JULIA CORBETT
    STEP-FATHER: O'ROURKE
    *** MARRIED: '42 C. ROBERT LONGENECKER
    SON: '44 GEORGE R. LONGENECKER
    SON: '47 JOHN W. LONGENECKER
    DAUGHTER: '53 MARY E. LONGENECKER
    RESIDENCE: CARLSBAD-BY-THE-SEA, CALIF.
    TALENT: ACTRESS
    CREDIT: '37 MADAM X
    AA-NOM SUP.ACT: '40 THE PHILADELPHIA STORY
    CREDIT: '44 THE UNINVITED
    CREDIT: '53 THE LADY WANTS MINK
    CREDIT: '60 THE FACTS OF LIFE

HUSTON, JOHN
                      AUG 05,'06 AT NEVADA,MR
    FATHER: WALTER HUSTON, ACTOR
    MOTHER: RHEA GORE
    STEP-MOTHER: BAYONNE WHIPPLE
    STEP-MOTHER: NAN SUNDERLAND
    *** MARRIED: '37 E. LESLEY (DIVORCED)
    *** MARRIED: '46 EVELYN KEYES, ACTRESS (DIVORCED)
    ADOPTED SON: PAUL ALBERRAN 'PABLO' HUSTON
    *** MARRIED: '49 ENRICA SOMA (DIVORCED)

```
    SON:  '50 WALTER ANTHONY HUSTON
    DAUGHTER:  '51 ANGELICA HUSTON
    *** MARRIED:  '72 CE CE SHANE
    FRIEND: GLADYS HILL
    FRIEND: PAUL KOHNER, AGENT
    RESIDENCE: NYC
    BIOGRAPHY:  '65 KING REBEL, BY W. F. NOLAN
    TALENT: ACTOR-DIRECTOR-WRITER
    AA-WIN  DIRECTOR:  '48 TREASURE OF SIERRA MADRE
    AA-NOM  DIRECTOR:  '50 THE ASPHALT JUNGLE
    AA-NOM  DIRECTOR:  '51 THE AFRICAN QUEEN
    AA-NOM  DIRECTOR:  '52 MOULIN ROUGE
    AA-NOM  SUP.ACT:  '63 THE CARDINAL
    CREDIT:  '66 THE BIBLE
    CREDIT:  '71 MAN IN THE WILDERNESS
---------------------------------------------------------------------------------
HUSTON, WALTER          BORN:  WALTER HOUGHSTON
                            APR 06,'84 AT TORONTO, ONTARIO,CANADA   DIED IN '50
    FATHER: ROBERT HOUGHSTON, CONTRACTOR
    MOTHER: ELIZABETH MCGIBBON
    *** MARRIED:  '05 RHEA GORE  (DIVORCED '13)
    SON:  '06 JOHN HUSTON, ACTOR-DIRECTOR
    DAUGHTER-IN-LAW: E. LESLEY
    DAUGHTER-IN-LAW: EVELYN KEYES, ACTRESS
    DAUGHTER-IN-LAW: ENRICA SOMA
    *** MARRIED:  '14 BAYONNE WHIPPLE, VAUDEVILLE PARTNER
    *** MARRIED:  '31 NAN SUNDERLAND
    RESIDENCE: RUNNING SPRINGS, CA
    POSSESSION:  '49 CATTLE RANCH, PORTERVILLE, CA
    TALENT: ACTOR
    CREDIT:  '30 THE VIRGINIAN
    AA-NOM  ACTOR:  '36 DODSWORTH
    AA-NOM  ACTOR:  '41 ALL THAT MONEY CAN BUY
    AA-NOM  SUP.ACT:  '42 YANKEE DOODLE DANDY
    AA-WIN  SUP.ACT.:  '48 TREASURE OF SIERRA MADRE
    CREDIT:  '50 THE FURIES
---------------------------------------------------------------------------------
HUTTON, BETTY           BORN:  ELIZABETH JUNE THORNBURG
                            FEB 26,'21 AT BATTLE CREEK,MH
    FATHER: PERCY THORNBURG, RAILROAD BRAKEMAN
    MOTHER: MABEL LUM
    SISTER: MARION THORNBURG
    *** MARRIED:  '45 TED BRISKIN  (DIVORCED '51)
    DAUGHTER:  '46 LINDSAY BRISKIN
    DAUGHTER:  '48 CANDICE BRISKIN
    *** MARRIED:  '52 CHARLES O'CURRAN, DANCE DIRECTOR  (DIVORCED '54)
    *** MARRIED:  '55 ALAN LIVINGSTON  (DIVORCED '58)
    *** MARRIED:  '61 PETE CANDOLI  (DIVORCED '68)
    DAUGHTER:  '62 CAROLYN CANDOLI
    TALENT: ACTRESS-SINGER
    COMMENT: ONCE WORKED AS DOMESTIC HELP AT ST. ANTHONY'S RECTORY, R.I.
    CREDIT:  '42 THE FLEET'S IN
    CREDIT:  '48 DREAM GIRL
    CREDIT:  '50 ANNIE GET YOUR GUN
    CREDIT:  '52 THE GREATEST SHOW ON EARTH
    CREDIT:  '57 SPRING REUNION
```

HYDE WHITE, WILFRED
                          MAY 12,'03 AT BOURTON, GLOUCESTER, ENGLAND
    FATHER: WILLIAM EDWARD WHITE, CANON OF GLOUCESTER
    MOTHER: ETHEL ADELAIDE DROUGHT
    *** MARRIED: '27 BLANCHE HOPE AITKEN, AKA-BLANCHE GLYNNE (DIVORCED '48)
    SON: '28 MICHAEL HYDE WHITE
    *** MARRIED: '57 ETHEL KORENMANN, AKA-ETHEL DREW
    SON: '59 ALEXANDER 'PUNCH' HYDE WHITE
    DAUGHTER: '61 JULIET HYDE WHITE
    RESIDENCE: LONDON, ENGLAND
    TALENT: ACTOR
    CREDIT: '34 REMBRANDT, DEBUT
    CREDIT: '58 UP THE CREEK
    CREDIT: '59 BAD GIRL
    CREDIT: '64 MY FAIR LADY
    CREDIT: '69 GAILY, GAILY

HYER, MARTHA
                          AUG 10,'24 AT FORT WORTH,TX
    FATHER: JULIEN C. HYER, JUDGE
    MOTHER: AGNES BARNHART
    SISTER: AGNES ANN HYER
    SISTER: JEANNE HYER
    *** MARRIED: '51 C. RAY STAHL (DIVORCED '54)
    *** MARRIED: '66 HAL B. WALLIS, PRODUCER
    STEP-SON: HAL BRENT WALLIS, JR., PSYCHOLOGIST
    POSSESSION: '45 CONTRACT AT RKO STUDIOS
    TALENT: ACTRESS
    CREDIT: '46 THE LOCKET
    CREDIT: '53 SO BIG
    AA-NOM SUP.ACT: '58 SOME CAME RUNNING
    CREDIT: '63 WIVES AND LOVERS
    CREDIT: '67 THE HAPPENING
    CREDIT: '70 ONCE YOU KISS A STRANGER

IRELAND, JILL   APR 24,'36 AT LONDON, ENGLAND
    FATHER: JOHN ALFRED IRELAND
    MOTHER: DOROTHY CONNOLL EBORN
    *** MARRIED: '57 DAVID MCCALLUM, ACTOR (DIVORCED)
    SON: '58 PAUL MCCALLUM
    SON: '59 JASON MCCALLUM
    SON: '60 VALENTINE MCCALLUM
    *** MARRIED: '68 CHARLES BRONSON, ACTOR
    STEP-DAUGHTER: SUZANNE BRONSON
    STEP-SON: ANTHONY BRONSON
    DAUGHTER: '71 ZULEIKA BRONSON
    RESIDENCE: BEL AIR, LOS ANGELES, CA.
    TALENT: ACTRESS
    CREDIT: '55 OH ROSALINDA
    CREDIT: '59 CARRY ON NURSE
    CREDIT: '62 TWICE AROUND THE DAFFODILS
    CREDIT: '68 VILLA RIDES
    CREDIT: '73 WILD HORSES

IRELAND, JOHN   BORN: JOHN BENJAMIN IRELAND
                           JAN 30,'14 AT VANCOUVER, B.C. CANADA
    FATHER: JOHN IRELAND, SR.
    MOTHER: KATHERINE FERGUSON
    STEP-SISTER: KATHERINE NOONAN
    STEP-BROTHER: TOMMY NOONAN, ACTOR, WRITER (DIED '68)
    STEP-BROTHER: MICHAEL NOONAN
    *** MARRIED: '40 ELAINE SHELDON (DIVORCED '48)
    SON: '42 JOHN ANTHONY IRELAND, PRODUCER
    SON: '45 PETER IRELAND, ACTOR
    *** MARRIED: '49 JOANNE DRU, ACTRESS (DIVORCED '56)
    STEP-DAUGHTER: HELEN HAYMES
    STEP-SON: RICHARD HAYMES
    STEP-DAUGHTER: BARBARA HAYMES
    *** MARRIED: '62 DAPHNE MYRICK
    RESIDENCE: SANTA BARBARA, CALIF.
    POSSESSION: '75 IRELAND'S RESTAURANT IN SANTA BARBARA, CA
    TALENT: ACTOR
    CREDIT: '45 A WALK IN THE SUN
    AA-NOM SUP.ACT: '49 ALL THE KING'S MEN
    CREDIT: '57 GUNFIGHT AT THE OK CORRAL
    CREDIT: '63 THE CEREMONY
    CREDIT: '73 THE HOUSE OF THE SEVEN CORPSES

ITURBI, JOSE   NOV 28,'95 AT VALENCIA, SPAIN
    FATHER: RICARDO ITURBI
    MOTHER: TERESA BAGUENO, SINGER
    SISTER: AMPARA ITURBI, PIANIST (DIED '69)
    *** MARRIED: MARIA GINER (DIED '29)
    DAUGHTER: MARIA ITURBI (DIED '44)
    RESIDENCE: BEVERLY HILLS, CA
    RESIDENCE: VALENCIA, SPAIN
    TALENT: PIANIST, CONDUCTOR, COMPOSER, PILOT, ACTOR
    CREDIT: '43 THOUSANDS CHEER
    CREDIT: '44 MUSIC FOR MILLIONS
    CREDIT: '45 ANCHORS AWEIGH

```
    CREDIT:  '46 HOLIDAY IN MEXICO
    CREDIT:  '49 THAT MIDNIGHT KISS
------------------------------------------------------------------------------------------------------
IVES, BURL         BORN:  ICLE IVANHOE IVES
                          JUN 14,'09 AT HUNT,IL
    FATHER: FRANK IVES
    MOTHER: CORDELLA WHITE
    UNCLE: SAMUEL ICLE IVANHOE
    *** MARRIED:  '45 HELEN EHRLICH
    *** MARRIED:  '71 DOROTHY KOSTER
    SON:   '72 ALEXANDER IVES
    POSSESSION: HONORARY DOCTORATE OF LAWS FAIRLEIGH DICKINSON UNIVERSITY
    MEMOIRS:  '62 THE WAYFARING STRANGER'S NOTEBOOK
    TALENT: SINGER-ACTOR
    CREDIT:  '46 SMOKY, DEBUT
    CREDIT:  '57 CAT ON A HOT TIN ROOF
    AA-WIN  SUP.ACT.:  '58 THE BIG COUNTRY
    CREDIT:  '59 OUR MAN IN HAVANA
    CREDIT:  '70 THE ONLY WAY OUT IS DEAD
```

JACKSON, GLENDA   MAY 09,'37 AT BIRKENHEAD, CHESIRE, ENGLAND
    FATHER: HARRY JACKSON, BRICKLAYER
    MOTHER: JOAN
    SISTER: --
    SISTER: --
    SISTER: --
    *** MARRIED: ROY HODGES
    SON: '69 DANIEL HODGES
    RESIDENCE: BLACKHEATH, LONDON, ENGLAND
    TALENT: ACTRESS
    AA-WIN ACTRESS: '70 WOMEN IN LOVE
    AA-NOM ACTRESS: '71 SUNDAY BLOODY SUNDAY
    CREDIT: '71 MARY QUEEN OF SCOTS
    AA-WIN ACTRESS: '73 A TOUCH OF CLASS
    AA-NOM ACTRESS: '75 HEDDA

JAFFE, SAM   MAR 08,'91 AT NYC
    FATHER: BERNARD JAFFEE
    MOTHER: ADA STEINBERG, VAUDEVILLE PERFORMER
    *** MARRIED: '26 LILLIAN TAIZ (DIED '41)
    *** MARRIED: '56 BETTYE LOUISE ACKERMAN
    TALENT: ACTOR
    CREDIT: '34 THE SCARLET EMPRESS
    CREDIT: '39 GUNGA DIN
    AA-NOM SUP.ACT: '50 THE ASPHALT JUNGLE
    CREDIT: '59 BEN-HUR
    CREDIT: '69 THE KREMLIN LETTERS
    CREDIT: '71 BEDKNOBS AND BROOMSTICKS

JAGGER, DEAN   BORN: DEAN JEFFRIES JAGGER
                              NOV 07,'05 AT COLUMBUS GROVE, OH
    FATHER: ALBERT JAGGER
    MOTHER: LILY MAYBERRY
    *** MARRIED: '35 ANTOINETTE LOWRENCE (DIVORCED '45)
    *** MARRIED: '47 GLORIA JOAN LING (DIVORCED '67)
    DAUGHTER: '48 DIANE MARION JAGGER
    TALENT: ACTOR
    CREDIT: '29 WOMEN FROM HELL
    CREDIT: '40 BRIGHAM YOUNG
    AA-WIN SUP.ACT.: '49 TWELVE O'CLOCK HIGH
    CREDIT: '54 EXECUTIVE SUITE
    CREDIT: '71 VANISHING POINT

JANSSEN, DAVID   BORN: DAVID HAROLD MYER
                              MAR 27,'30 AT NAPONEE,NB
    FATHER: HAROLD MYER
    MOTHER: BERNICE GRAF, SHOWGIRL
    STEP-FATHER: EUGENE JANSSEN
    STEP-SISTER: TERI JANSSEN
    STEP-SISTER: JILL JANSSEN
    *** MARRIED: ELLIE GRAHAM
    *** MARRIED: DANNI CRAYNE, EX-MRS. BUDDY GRECO
    RESIDENCE: BEVERLY HILLS, CA
    TALENT: ACTOR
    CREDIT: '52 YANKEE BUCCANEER

```
     CREDIT:  '60 HELL TO ETERNITY
     CREDIT:  '63 MY SIX LOVES
     CREDIT:  '69 WHERE IT'S AT
     CREDIT:  '70 MACHO CALLAHAN
```

JESSEL, GEORGE   BORN: GEORGE ALBERT JESSEL
                                   APR 15,'98 AT NYC
```
     FATHER: JOSEPH AARON JESSEL, PLAYWRIGHT
     MOTHER: CHARLOTTE SCHWARTZ
     *** MARRIED:  '19 FLORENCE COURTNEY  (DIVORCED '32)
     *** MARRIED:  '34 NORMA TALMADGE, ACTRESS  (DIVORCED '39)
     SISTER-IN-LAW: CONSTANCE TALMADGE, ACTRESS
     SISTER-IN-LAW: NATALIE TALMADGE, ACTRESS
     *** MARRIED:  '40 LORRAINE GOURLEY, ACTRESS-LOIS ANDREWS  (DIVORCED '43)
     DAUGHTER: '41 JERILYN JESSEL
     RESIDENCE: LOS ANGELES, CA
     POSSESSION:  '43 COLLECTION OF RELIGIOUS ARTIFACTS
     MEMOIRS:  '43 SO HELP ME
     TALENT: ACTOR
     CREDIT:  '19 THE OTHER MAN'S WIFE
     CREDIT:  '29 LUCKY BOY
     CREDIT:  '43 STAGE DOOR CANTEEN
     CREDIT:  '53 THE I DON'T CARE GIRL
     CREDIT:  '57 THE BUSY BODY
```

JOHNS, GLYNIS
                           OCT 05,'23 AT DURBAN, SOUTH AFRICA
```
     FATHER: MERVYN JOHNS, ACTOR
     MOTHER: ALYS MAUDE STEEL-PAYNE, PIANIST
     STEP-MOTHER: DIANA CHURCHILL
     *** MARRIED:  '40 ANTHONY FORWOOD, ACTOR  (DIVORCED)
     SON:  '41 GARETH FORWOOD, ACTOR
     *** MARRIED:  '50 DAVID RAMSEY FOSTER  (DIVORCED)
     *** MARRIED:  '60 CECIL HENDERSON  (DIVORCED)
     *** MARRIED:  '64 ELLIOT ARNOLD, WRITER
     TALENT: ACTRESS
     CREDIT:  '36 SOUTH RIDING, DEBUT
     CREDIT:  '47 MIRANDA
     CREDIT:  '56 THE COURT JESTER
     AA-NOM  SUP.ACT:  '60 THE SUNDOWNERS
     CREDIT:  '69 LOCK UP YOUR DAUGHTERS
     CREDIT:  '73 VAULT OF HORRORS
```

JOHNSON, VAN   BORN: CHARLES VAN JOHNSON
                                 AUG 25,'16 AT NEWPORT, RI
```
     FATHER: CHARLES JOHNSON, REALTOR
     MOTHER: LORETTA
     *** MARRIED:  '47 EVE ABBOTT, ACTRESS  (DIVORCED '68)
     STEP-SON: EDMUND WYNN
     STEP-SON: TRACY WYNN
     DAUGHTER: '48 SCHUYLER JOHNSON
     FRIEND: KEENAN WYNN
     FRIEND: SPENCER TRACY
     RESIDENCE: BEVERLY HILLS,CA
     RESIDENCE: NYC
     POSSESSION: RED SOCKS
     TALENT: ACTOR
     CREDIT:  '40 TOO MANY GIRLS, DEBUT
```

```
     CREDIT:   '48 THE BRIDE GOES WILD
     CREDIT:   '54 THE CAINE MUTINY
     CREDIT:   '63 WIVES AND LOVES
     CREDIT:   '67 DIVORCE AMERICAN STYLE
     CREDIT:   '69 BATTLE SQUADRON
-------------------------------------------------------------------------------------
JOLSON, AL          BORN:   ASA YOELSON
                            MAR 26,'88 AT ST. PETERSBURG, RUSSIA   DIED IN '50
   *** MARRIED:  '06 HENRIETTA KELLER  (DIVORCED '19)
   *** MARRIED:  '22 ALMA OSBORNE CARLTON, ACTRESS - ETHEL DELMAR  (DIVORCED '26)
   *** MARRIED:  '28 RUBY KEELER, DANCER-ACTRESS  (DIVORCED '40)
   ADOPTED SON: AL 'PETER' JOLSON, JR.
   *** MARRIED:  '45 ERLE CHENAULT GALBRAITH
   DAUGHTER:  '46 ASA JOLSON
   RESIDENCE: ENCINO, CA
   TALENT: JAZZ SINGER
   CREDIT:   '27 THE JAZZ SINGER
   CREDIT:   '29 SONNY BOY
   CREDIT:   '36 THE SINGING KID
   CREDIT:   '39 SWANEE RIVER
   CREDIT:   '45 BURLESQUE
-------------------------------------------------------------------------------------
JONES, ALLAN
                            OCT 14,'07 AT SCRANTON, PA
   FATHER: DANIEL JONES, COAL MINER
   MOTHER: ELIZABETH
   *** MARRIED:  '36 IRENE HERVEY (DIVORCED '57)
   SON:  '37 JACK JONES, SINGER  (MARRIED '67)
   DAUGHTER-IN-LAW: JILL SAINT JOHN, ACTRESS
   *** MARRIED:  '57 MARY FLORSHEIM, SHOE MANUFACTURING HEIRESS  (DIVORCED '64)
   RESIDENCE: NYC
   POSSESSION:  '40 BEVERLY HILLS RIDING ACADEMY
   POSSESSION: CONTRACT AT MGM
   TALENT: SINGER-ACTOR
   CREDIT:   '35 RECKLESS
   CREDIT:   '37 THE FIREFLY
   CREDIT:   '42 THERE'S MAGIC IN MUSIC
   CREDIT:   '45 HONEYMOON AHEAD
   CREDIT:   '67 STAGE TO THUNDER ROCK
-------------------------------------------------------------------------------------
JONES, BUCK         BORN:   CHARLES FREDERICK GEBHART
                            DEC 04,'89 AT VINCENNES, IN   DIED IN '42
   *** MARRIED:  '15 ODELLE OSBORNE, EQUESTRIENNE
   DAUGHTER: MAXINE JONES
   SON-IN-LAW: NOAH BEERY, JR., ACTOR  (MARRIED '40)
   TALENT: ACTOR, DIRECTOR
   CREDIT:   '17 BLOOD WILL TELL
   CREDIT:   '24 WESTERN LUCK
   CREDIT:   '30 THE LONE RIDER
   CREDIT:   '36 THE BOSS OF GUN CREEK
   CREDIT:   '42 DOWN ON THE GREAT DIVIDE
-------------------------------------------------------------------------------------
JONES, JAMES  EARL
                            JAN 17,'31 AT ARKABUTLA, MP
   GRANDFATHER: JOHN CONNOLLY
   FATHER: ROBERT EARL JONES, ACTOR
   MOTHER: RUTH WILLIAMS
   *** MARRIED:  '67 JULIENNE MARIE, ACTRESS
```

```
     TALENT: ACTOR
     AA-NOM ACTOR: '70 THE GREAT WHITE HOPE
     CREDIT: DR. STRANGELOVE
     CREDIT: THE COMEDIANS
     CREDIT: CLAUDINE
     CREDIT: THE END OF THE ROAD
```

JONES, JENNIFER   BORN: PHYLLIS ISLEY
                                    MAR 02,'19 AT TULSA,OK
```
     FATHER: PHILIP R. ISLEY, THEATRE OWNER
     MOTHER: FLORA MAE SUBER
     *** MARRIED: '39 ROBERT WALKER (DIVORCED '45)
     SON: '40 ROBERT WALKER, JR., ACTOR
     SON: '41 MICHAEL WALKER
     *** MARRIED: '49 DAVID O. SELZNICK, PRODUCER  (DIED '65)
     DAUGHTER: '54 MARY JENNIFER SELZNICK  (SUICIDE '76)
     *** MARRIED: '71 NORTON SIMON, BUSINESS EXEC.
     RESIDENCE: MALIBU, CA
     TALENT: ACTRESS
     AA-WIN ACTRESS:  '43 THE SONG OF BERNADETTE
     AA-NOM SUP.ACT:  '44 SINCE YOU WENT AWAY
     AA-NOM ACTRESS:  '45 LOVE LETTERS
     AA-NOM ACTRESS:  '46 DUEL IN THE SUN
     AA-NOM ACTRESS:  '55 LOVE IS A MANY-SPLENDORED THING
```

JONES, SHIRLEY   BORN: SHIRLEY MAE JONES
                                   MAR 31,'34 AT SMITHTOWN, PA
```
     FATHER: PAUL JONES, BREWER
     MOTHER: MARJORIE WILLIAMS
     *** MARRIED: '56 JACK CASSIDY (DIVORCED '75)
     STEP-SON: DAVID CASSIDY, SINGER
     DAUGHTER-IN-LAW: KAY LENZ
     SON: '59 SHAUN CASSIDY, ACTOR
     SON: '62 PATRICK CASSIDY
     SON: '66 RYAN JOHN CASSIDY
     *** MARRIED: '77 MARTY INGELS, PRODUCER
     POSSESSION: '52 MISS PITTSBURGH OF 1952
     TALENT: ACTRESS-SINGER
     CREDIT: '55 OKLAHOMA!
     AA-WIN SUP.ACT.: '60 ELMER GANTRY
     CREDIT: '62 THE MUSIC MAN
     CREDIT: '65 FLUFFY
     CREDIT: '70 THE HAPPY ENDING
```

JOURDAN, LOUIS   BORN: LOUIS GENDRE
                                   JUN 19,'21 AT MARSEILLES, FRANCE
```
     FATHER: HENRI GENDRE
     MOTHER: YVONNE JOURDAN
     *** MARRIED: '46 BERTHE FREDERIQUE
     SON: '51 LOUIS HENRY JOURDAN
     RESIDENCE: NYC
     TALENT: ACTOR
     CREDIT: '39 LE CORSAIRE, DEBUT
     CREDIT: '52 THE HAPPY TIME
     CREDIT: '54 THREE COINS IN THE FOUNTAIN
     CREDIT: '58 GIGI
     CREDIT: '62 THE VIP'S
```

```
--------------------------------------------------------------------------------
JURADO, KATY          BORN:   MARIA CRISTINA JURADO GARCIA
                              JAN 16,'27 AT GUADALAJARA, MEXICO
     FATHER: LUIS JURADO
     COUSIN: EMILIO PORTES GIL, PRESIDENT OF MEXICO 1928-30
     COUSIN: LINDA CHRISTIAN, ACTRESS
     *** MARRIED:  '44 VICTOR VELAZQUEZ, ACTOR  (DIVORCED '49)
     SON:  '45 VICTOR HUGO VELAZQUEZ
     DAUGHTER:  '48 SANDRAMARIA CRISTINA VELAZQUEZ
     *** MARRIED:  '59 ERNEST BORGNINE, ACTOR  (DIVORCED '61)
     STEP-DAUGHTER: NANCY BORGNINE
     *** MARRIED:  '72 --, MARRIAGE REPORTED
     RESIDENCE: CUERNAVACA, MEXICO
     POSSESSION: THREE TIME ARIEL AWARD WINNER
     TALENT: ACTRESS
     CREDIT:  '51 THE BULLIGHTER AND THE LADY
     AA-NOM  SUP.ACT:  '54 BROKEN LANCE
     CREDIT:  '56 TRAPEZE
     CREDIT:  '66 SMOKY
     CREDIT:  '72 PAT GARRETT AND BILLY THE KID
```

KARLOFF, BORIS   BORN: WILLIAM HENRY PRATT
                            NOV 23,'87 AT LONDON, ENGLAND DIED IN '69
  GREAT-AUNT: ANNA HARRIET CRAWFORD, GOVERNESS TO KING OF SIAM
  FATHER: EDWARD PRATT
  MOTHER: ELIZA SARAH MILLARD
  STEP-SISTER: EMMA CAROLINE PRATT
  STEP-SISTER: ELIZA JULIA PRATT
  SISTER: JULIA HONORIA PRATT
  BROTHER: EDWARD MILLARD PRATT, CIVIL SERVANT IN INDIA
  BROTHER: GEORGE MARLOW PRATT, ACTOR, BUSINESSMAN
  BROTHER: CHARLES RARY PRATT, BUSINESSMAN IN BRAZIL
  BROTHER: FREDERICK GRENVILLE PRATT, CIVIL SERVANT IN INDIA
  BROTHER: DAVID CAMERON PRATT, BUSINESSMAN IN BRAZIL
  BROTHER: JOHN THOMAS PRATT, DIPLOMAT, AUTHOR
  BROTHER: RICHARD SEPTIMUS PRATT, DIPLOMAT
  STEP-BROTHER: EDWARD PRATT, JR. (DIED '50)
  *** MARRIED: '13 OLIVE DE WILTON, ACTRESS
  *** MARRIED: '23 HELEN SOULE (DIVORCED '28)
  *** MARRIED: '28 DOROTHY STINE (DIVORCED '46)
  DAUGHTER: '29 SARA JANE KARLOFF
  *** MARRIED: '46 EVELYN HELMORE
  RESIDENCE: LONDON, ENGLAND
  BIOGRAPHY: '75 DEAR BORIS, BY CYNTHIA LINDSAY
  TALENT: ACTOR
  CREDIT: '16 THE DUMB GIRL OF PORTICI
  CREDIT: '19 HIS MAJESTY THE AMERICAN
  CREDIT: '26 THE BELLS
  CREDIT: '29 THE FATAL WARNING, SERIES
  CREDIT: '31 FRNAKENSTEIN, SERIES
  CREDIT: '39 SON OF FRANKENSTEIN
  CREDIT: '45 THE BODY SNATCHER
  CREDIT: '68 THE CURSE OF THE CRIMSON ALTAR
  CREDIT: '72 HOUSE OF EVIL

KAYE, DANNY   BORN: DAVID DANIEL KOMINSKY
                         JAN 18,'13 AT BROOKLYN, NY
  FATHER: JACOB KOMINSKY, TAILOR
  MOTHER: CLARA NEMEROVSKY
  BROTHER: MAC KOMINSKY
  BROTHER: LAWRENCE KOMINSKY (DIED '69)
  *** MARRIED: '40 SYLVIA FINE, ACTRESS
  DAUGHTER: '46 DENA KAYE
  RESIDENCE: BEVERLY HILLS, CA
  BIOGRAPHY: '58 DANNY KAYE, BY KURT D. SINGER
  TALENT: ACTOR
  CREDIT: '44 UP IN ARMS, DEBUT
  CREDIT: '53 KNOCK ON WOOD
  AA-SPECIAL AWARD: '54 FOR HIS TALENTS AND SERVICE-AN HONORARY AWARD
  CREDIT: '56 THE COURT JESTER
  CREDIT: '69 THE MADWOMAN OF CHAILLOT

KEATON, BUSTER   BORN: JOSEPH FRANCIS KEATON, JR.
                            OCT 04,'95 AT PIQUA, KA DIED IN '66
  FATHER: JOE KEATON, ACTOR
  MOTHER: MYRA KEATON, ACTRESS
  SISTER: LOUISE KEATON
  BROTHER: HARRY KEATON

```
SISTER-IN-LAW: CONSTANCE TALMADGE, ACTRESS
SISTER-IN-LAW: NORMA TALMADGE, ACTRESS
*** MARRIED:  '21 NATALIE TALMADGE, ACTRESS, SCRIPT GIRL  (DIVORCED '32)
SON:  '22 JAMES KEATON
SON:  '23 ROBERT KEATON, ACTOR - ROBERT TALMADGE
*** MARRIED:  '33 MAE SCRIVEN  (DIVORCED '35)
*** MARRIED:  '40 ELEANOR KATHLEEN NORRIS, DANCER  (DIVORCED)
ROMANCE: BEATRICE LILLIE
FRIEND: FATTIE ARBUCKLE
FRIEND: NORMAN KERRY
RESIDENCE: BEVERLY HILLS, CA
BIOGRAPHY:  '66 KEATON, BY RUDI BLESH
TALENT: ACTOR-DIRECTOR
CREDIT:  '17 THE BUTCHER BOY
CREDIT:  '24 THE NAVIGATOR
CREDIT:  '33 WHAT, NO BEER?
CREDIT:  '43 FOREVER AND A DAY
CREDIT:  '53 THE AWAKENING
AA-SPECIAL AWARD:  '59 HONORARY AWARD FOR HIS UNIQUE TALENTS & 'IMMORTAL COMEDIES'
```

```
KEATON, DIANE          BORN:  DIANE HALL
                              JAN 05,'46 AT HIGHLAND PARK, CA
   FATHER: JACK HALL, CIVIL ENGINEER
   MOTHER: DOROTHY KEATON, PHOTOGRAPHER
   SISTER: DORRIE HALL, ARTIST
   SISTER: ROBIN HALL, NURSE
   BROTHER: RANDY HALL, POET
   ROMANCE: WOODY ALLEN, ACTOR, DIRECTOR, WRITER
   ROMANCE: MIKHAIL BARYSHNIKOV, DANCER, ACTOR
   ROMANCE: WARREN BEATTY, ACTOR
   RESIDENCE: NYC
   CREDIT:  '70 LOVERS AND OTHER STRANGERS, DEBUT
   CREDIT:  '75 PLAY IT AGAIN, SAM
   CREDIT:  '76 THE GODFATHER, PARTS 1 AND 2
   AA-WIN  ACTRESS:  '77 ANNIE HALL
   CREDIT:  '77 LOOKING FOR MR. GOODBAR
```

```
KEEL, HOWARD          BORN:  HAROLD CLIFFORD KEEL
                             APR 13,'17 AT GILLESPIE, IL
   *** MARRIED:  '43 ROSEMARY COOPER  (DIVORCED '48)
   *** MARRIED:  '49 HELEN ANDERSON  (DIVORCED '70)
   DAUGHTER:  '50 KAIJA LIANE KEEL
   SON:  '55 GUNNAR KEEL
   DAUGHTER:  '57 KRISTINE KEEL
   *** MARRIED:  '70 JUDY MAGAMOLL
   DAUGHTER:  '74 LESLIE GRACE KEEL
   TALENT: SINGER-ACTOR
   CREDIT:  '47 THE SMALL VOICE, DEBUT
   CREDIT:  '50 ANNIE GET YOUR GUN
   CREDIT:  '53 CALAMITY JANE
   CREDIT:  '54 SEVEN BRIDES FOR SEVEN BROTHERS
   CREDIT:  '66 WACO
   CREDIT:  '68 ARIZONA BUSHWHACKERS
```

KEELER, RUBY   BORN: ETHEL HILDA KEELER
                             AUG 25,'09 AT HALIFAX NOVA SCOTIA, CANADA
     FATHER: RALPH KEELER
     MOTHER: ELNORA LEAHY
     SISTER: MARJORIE KEELER
     SISTER: GERTRUDE KEELER
     *** MARRIED: '28 AL JOLSON (DIVORCED '40)
     ADOPTED SON: AL 'PETER' JOLSON, JR.
     *** MARRIED: '41 JOHN LOWE, JR. (DIED '69)
     DAUGHTER: '43 KATHLEEN LOWE
     DAUGHTER: '45 CHRISTINE LOWE
     SON: '46 JOHN LOWE, III
     DAUGHTER-IN-LAW: SHARON SMITH (MARRIED)
     DAUGHTER: '48 THERESA LOWE
     FRIEND: SARAH ROSE 'PATSY' KELLY, ACTRESS - CHILDHOOD FRIEND
     RESIDENCE: NEWPORT HARBOR, CA
     POSSESSION: GEORGE M. COHAN AWARD
     TALENT: ACTRESS-DANCER-GOLFER
     CREDIT: '33 42ND STREET
     CREDIT: '35 GO IN TO YOUR DANCE
     CREDIT: '37 READY WILLING AND ABLE
     CREDIT: '41 SWEETHEART OF THE CAMPUS
     CREDIT: '70 THE PHYNX

KEITH, BRIAN   BORN: ROBERT KEITH, JR.
                             NOV 14,'21 AT BAYONNE, NJ
     FATHER: ROBERT KEITH, ACTOR
     MOTHER: HELENA SHIPMAN
     *** MARRIED: '48 FRANCES HELM (DIVORCED '54)
     *** MARRIED: '54 JUDITH LONDON (DIVORCED)
     SON: '55 MICHAEL KEITH (DIED '63)
     DAUGHTER: '61 BARBARA KEITH
     DAUGHTER: '62 ELIZABETH KEITH
     SON: '63 RORY KEITH
     DAUGHTER: '64 MIMI KEITH
     *** MARRIED: '70 VICTORIA YOUNG
     SON: '70 ROBERT KEITH
     DAUGHTER: '71 DAISY KEITH
     RESIDENCE: HAWAII
     TALENT: ACTOR
     CREDIT: '52 ARROWHEAD, DEBUT
     CREDIT: '57 RUN OF THE ARROW
     CREDIT: '62 MOON PILOT
     CREDIT: '67 REFLECTIONS IN A GOLDEN EYE
     CREDIT: '72 SOMETHING BIG
     CREDIT: '78 HOOPER

KELLERMAN, SALLY   BORN: SALLY CLAIRE KELLERMAN
                             JUN 02,'41 AT LONG BEACH,CA
     FATHER: JOHN HELM KELLERMAN
     MOTHER: EDITH BAINE VAUGHN
     *** MARRIED: '70 RICHARD EDELSTEIN (DIVORCED '71)
     RESIDENCE: HOLLYWOOD HILLS, CA
     TALENT: ACTRESS
     CREDIT: '68 THE BOSTON STRANGLER
     CREDIT: '69 THE APRIL FOOLS
     AA-NOM SUP.ACT: '70 M*A*S*H

CREDIT: '72 THE LAST OF THE RED HOT LOVERS
CREDIT: '73 LOST HORIZON

KELLY, GENE   BORN: EUGENE CURRAN KELLY
                                 AUG 23,'12 AT PITTSBURGH,PA
    FATHER: JAMES PATRICK JOSEPH KELLY
    MOTHER: HARRIET CURRAN, ACTRESS
    SISTER: HARRIET 'JAY' KELLY
    SISTER: LOUISE KELLY
    BROTHER: JAMES KELLY, JR.
    BROTHER: FRED KELLY, PARTNER IN DANCE ACT
    *** MARRIED: '41 BETSY BLAIR, ACTRESS (DIVORCED '57)
    DAUGHTER: '42 KERRY KELLY
    *** MARRIED: '60 JEANNE COYNE, ACTRESS (DIED '73)
    SON: '62 TIMOTHY KELLY
    DAUGHTER: '63 BRIDGET KELLY
    RESIDENCE: BEVERLY HILLS, CA
    POSSESSION: FRENCH CHEVALIER-LEGION HONOR
    BIOGRAPHY: '74 GENE KELLY, BY CLIVE HIRSCHHORN
    TALENT: DANCER-ACTOR-CHOREOGRAPHER DIRECTOR
    CREDIT: '43 FOR ME AND MY GAL
    AA-NOM ACTOR: '45 ANCHORS AWEIGH
    AA-SPECIAL AWARD: '51 HONORARY AWARD OF APPRECIATION
    CREDIT: '58 MARJORIE MORNINGSTAR
    CREDIT: '73 FORTY CARATS

KELLY, GRACE   BORN: GRACE PATRICIA KELLY
                                 NOV 12,'28 AT PHILADELPHIA,PA
    FATHER: JOHN BRENDAN KELLY
    MOTHER: MARGARET MAJER
    SISTER: MARGARET 'PEGGY' KELLY
    SISTER: ELIZABETH ANN 'LIZANNE' KELLY
    BROTHER: JOHN B. 'KELL' KELLY
    UNCLE: WALTER C. KELLY, ACTOR-'THE VIRGINIA JUDGE'
    UNCLE: GEORGE KELLY, WRITER
    *** MARRIED: '56 PRINCE RAINER, III, HOUSE OF GRIMALDI
    DAUGHTER: '57 PRINCESS CAROLINE, LOUISE MARGUERITE GRIMALDI
    SON-IN-LAW: PHILIPPE JUNOT, MERCHANT BANKER (MARRIED '78)
    SON: '58 PRINCE ALBERT, ALEXANDRE LOUIS GRIMALDI
    DAUGHTER: '65 PRINCESS STEPHANIE, MARIE ELIZABETH GRIMALDI
    RESIDENCE: MONTE CARLO,MONACO
    POSSESSION: '49 CONTRACT AT M-G-M STUDIOS
    POSSESSION: FARM AT ROC AGEL, FRANCE
    BIOGRAPHY: '76 PRINCESS GRACE, BY GWEN ROBYNS
    TALENT: ACTRESS
    CREDIT: '52 HIGH NOON
    AA-NOM SUP.ACT: '53 MOGAMBO
    AA-WIN ACTRESS: '54 THE COUNTRY GIRL
    CREDIT: '56 HIGH SOCIETY

KENDALL, KAY   BORN: JUSTINE MCCARTHY KENDALL
                                 MAY 21,'26 AT HULL, YORKSHIRE, ENGLAND DIED IN '59
    GRANDMOTHER: MARIE KENDALL, ACTRESS
    FATHER: TERRY KENDALL, DANCER
    MOTHER: PAT, DANCER
    SISTER: KIM KENDALL
    *** MARRIED: '57 REX HARRISON, ACTOR
    STEP-SON: NOEL HARRISON

```
            STEP-SON: CAREY HARRISON
            TALENT: ACTRESS
            CREDIT:  '44 FIDDLERS THREE, DEBUT
            CREDIT:  '46 THE LONDON TOWN
            CREDIT:  '54 GENEVIEVE
            CREDIT:  '58 THE RELUCTANT DEBUTANTE
            CREDIT:  '59 ONCE MORE WITH FEELING
-------------------------------------------------------------------------------------------
KENNEDY, GEORGE
                           FEB 18,'26 AT NYC
            FATHER: GEORGE KENNEDY, SR., PIANIST, COMPOSER, CONDUCTOR
            MOTHER: HELEN MEADE, DANCER
            *** MARRIED:  '59 NORMA JEAN 'REVEL' WURMAN, SINGER
            DAUGHTER: '62 KARIANNE KENNEDY
            SON:  '65 CHRISTOPHER GEORGE KENNEDY
            RESIDENCE: SHERMAN OAKS, CA.
            TALENT: ACTOR
            CREDIT:  '60 LITTLE SHEPHERD OF KINGDOM COME - DEBUT
            CREDIT:  '63 CHARADE
            AA-WIN  SUP.ACT.:  '67 COOL HAND LUKE
            CREDIT:  '67 THE DIRTY DOZEN
            CREDIT:  '73 LOST HORIZON
-------------------------------------------------------------------------------------------
KERR, DEBORAH          BORN:  DEBORAH JANE KERR-TRIMMER
                              SEP 30,'21 AT HELENSBURGH,SCOTLAND
            FATHER: ARTHUR KERR-TRIMMER, ARCHITECT
            MOTHER: KATHLEEN ROSE SMALE
            BROTHER: EDMUND KERR-TRIMMER
            AUNT: PHYLLIS SMALE, DRAMA COACH
            *** MARRIED:  '45 ANTHONY BARTLEY  (DIVORCED '59)
            FATHER-IN-LAW: SIR CHARLES BARTLEY
            DAUGHTER:  '47 MELANIE JANE BARTLEY
            DAUGHTER:  '51 FRANCESCA BARTLEY
            *** MARRIED:  '60 PETER VIERTEL, WRITER  (DIVORCED '68)
            RESIDENCE: SWITZERLAND
            POSSESSION:  '47 BRISTOL GLASS AND ANTIQUE JEWELRY COLLECTIONS
            BIOGRAPHY:  '78 DEBORAH KERR, BY ERIC BRAUN
            TALENT: ACTRESS
            AA-NOM  ACTRESS:  '49 EDWARD, MY SON
            AA-NOM  ACTRESS:  '53 FROM HERE TO ETERNITY
            AA-NOM  ACTRESS:  '56 THE KING AND I
            AA-NOM  ACTRESS:  '57 HEAVEN KNOWS, MR. ALLISON
            AA-NOM  ACTRESS:  '58 SEPARATE TABLES
            AA-NOM  ACTRESS:  '60 THE SUNDOWNERS
-------------------------------------------------------------------------------------------
KERRY, NORMAN          BORN:  ARNOLD KAISER
                              JUN 16,'89 AT ROCHESTER, NY  DIED IN '56
            *** MARRIED:  '12 ROSINNE TRIPP  (DIVORCED '29)
            *** MARRIED:  '32 HELEN MARY WELLS  (DIVORCED '34)
            *** MARRIED:  '46 KAY ENGLISH
            FRIEND: BUSTER KEATON, ACTOR
            RESIDENCE: BEVERLY HILLS, CA
            TALENT: ACTOR
            CREDIT:  '16 MANHATTAN MADNESS
            CREDIT:  '24 CYTHEREA
            CREDIT:  '26 THE PHANTOM OF THE OPERA
            CREDIT:  '31 BACHELOR APARTMENTS
            CREDIT:  '41 TANKS A MILLION
```

KEYES, EVELYN
NOV 20,'17 AT PORT ARTHUR, TX
```
FATHER: --, DIED IN 1919
MOTHER: MAUDE
SISTER: --
SISTER: --
SISTER: --
BROTHER: SAMUEL KEYES
*** MARRIED:  '39 BARTON BAINBRIDGE  (SUICIDE '39)
*** MARRIED:  '44 CHARLES VIDOR, DIRECTOR  (DIVORCED '45)
*** MARRIED:  '46 JOHN HUSTON, ACTOR-DIRECTOR  (DIVORCED '50)
FATHER-IN-LAW: WALTER HUSTON, ACTOR
MOTHER-IN-LAW: RHEA GORE
ADOPTED SON: PAUL ALBERRAN 'PABLO' HUSTON
*** MARRIED:  '57 ARTIE SHAW, CLARINETIST, BANDLEADER
ROMANCE: ANTHONY QUINN
ROMANCE: KIRK DOUGLAS
FRIEND: MICHAEL TODD, PRODUCER
MEMOIRS:  '77 SCARLET OHARA'S YOUNGER SISTER
TALENT: ACTRESS
CREDIT:  '38 THE BUCCANEER, DEBUT
CREDIT:  '39 GONE WITH THE WIND
CREDIT:  '44 A THOUSAND AND ONE NIGHTS
CREDIT:  '46 THE JOLSON STORY
CREDIT:  '48 ENCHANTMENT
CREDIT:  '56 AROUND THE WORLD IN 80 DAYS
```

KILEY, RICHARD
BORN: RICHARD PAUL KILEY
MAR 31,'22 AT CHICAGO, IL
```
FATHER: LEO JOSEPH KILEY
MOTHER: LEONORE MCKENNA
*** MARRIED:  '48 MARY BELL WOOD  (DIVORCED '67)
DAUGHTER:  '49 KATHLEEN KILEY
DAUGHTER:  '50 DOROTHEA KILEY
DAUGHTER:  '51 ERIN KILEY
DAUGHTER:  '52 DIERDRE KILEY
SON:  '53 DAVID KILEY
SON:  '54 MICHAEL KILEY
*** MARRIED:  '68 PAT FERRIER
TALENT: ACTOR-SINGER
CREDIT:  '51 THE MOB
CREDIT:  '55 THE BLACKBOARD JUNGLE
CREDIT:  '58 SPANISH AFFAIR
CREDIT:  '69 PENDULUM
CREDIT:  '73 THE LITTLE PRINCE
```

KING KONG
JAN 01,'31 AT HOLLYWOOD, CA
```
FATHER: MERIAN C. COOPER, AUTHOR
ROMANCE: FAY WRAY
ROMANCE: JESSICA LANG
RESIDENCE: NYC
TALENT: ACTOR
CREDIT:  '33 KING KONG
CREDIT:  '33 SON OF KING KONG
CREDIT:  '76 KING KONG
```

KITT, EARTHA   BORN: EARTHA MAE KITT
                          JAN 26,'28 AT NORTH, SC
     FATHER: WILLIAM KITT, SHARE-CROPPER
     MOTHER: ANNA MAE RILEY, FARMER
     STEP-SISTER: ANNA PEARL KITT
     STEP-SISTER: ALMITA KITT
     *** MARRIED: '60 WILLIAM O. MCDONALD (DIVORCED '65)
     DAUGHTER: '61 KITT MCDONALD
     FRIEND: JAMES DEAN, ACTOR
     MEMOIRS: '76 ALONE WITH ME
     MEMOIRS: THURSDAY'S CHILD
     TALENT: ACTRESS-SINGER-DANCER
     COMMENT: MEMBER KATHERINE DUNCAN DANCE TROUPE
     CREDIT: '54 NEW FACES
     CREDIT: '57 ST. LOUIS BLUES
     CREDIT: '61 SAINT OF DEVIL'S ISLAND
     CREDIT: '65 SYNANON
     CREDIT: '71 UP THE CHASITY BELT
     CREDIT: '78 TIMBUKTU!, PLAY ON BROADWAY

KLUGMAN, JACK
                          APR 27,'22 AT PHILADEPHIA, PA
     *** MARRIED: '56 BRETT SOMERS, ACTRESS (SEPARATED '74)
     STEP-DAUGHTER: LESLIE SOMERS
     SON: '59 DAVID KLUGMAN
     SON: '62 ADAM KLUGMAN
     RESIDENCE: LOS AGNELES, CA
     TALENT: ACTOR
     CREDIT: '56 TIMETABLE
     CREDIT: '57 TWELVE ANGRY MEN
     CREDIT: '63 ACT ONE
     CREDIT: '69 GOODBYE COLUMBUS
     CREDIT: '71 WHO SAY'S I CAN'T RIDE A RAINBOW?

KOVACS, ERNIE
                          JAN 23,'19 AT TRENTON, NJ DIED IN '62
     FATHER: ANDREW J. KOVACS, TAVERN KEEPER
     MOTHER: MARY CHEBONICK
     BROTHER: THOMAS KOVACS
     *** MARRIED: '40 ELIZABETH SHOTWELL
     DAUGHTER: '41 BETTY KOVACS
     DAUGHTER: '49 KIP KOVACS
     *** MARRIED: '54 EDIE ADAMS
     DAUGHTER: '60 MIA KOVACS
     BIOGRAPHY: '78 THE ERNIE KOVACS PHILE, BY DAVID G. WALLEY
     TALENT: ACTOR
     CREDIT: '57 OPERATION MAD BALL
     CREDIT: '59 OUR MAN IN HAVANA
     CREDIT: '60 STRANGERS WHEN WE MET
     CREDIT: '61 FIVE GOLDEN HOURS
     CREDIT: '62 SAIL A CROOKED SHIP

KRISTOFFERSON, KRIS   BORN: KRISTOFFER KRISTOFFERSON
                                     JUN 22,'37 AT BROWNSVILLE, TX
    FATHER: --, AIR FORCE OFFICER
    SISTER: --, MARRIED ARMY OFFICER
    BROTHER: --, NAVY JET PILOT
    *** MARRIED: FRAN BEIR
    DAUGHTER: '62 TRACY KRISTOFFERSON
    SON: '69 KRIS KRISTOFFERSON, JR.
    *** MARRIED: '73 RITA COOLIDGE, SINGER
    FATHER-IN-LAW: RICHARD COOLIDGE, MINISTER
    SISTER-IN-LAW: PRISCILLA COOLIDGE, SINGER
    SISTER-IN-LAW: LINDA COOLIDGE, SINGER
    DAUGHTER: '74 CASEY KRISTOFFERSON
    ROMANCE: JANIS JOPLIN, SINGER
    ROMANCE: CARLY SIMON, SINGER
    ROMANCE: BARBRA STREISAND, ACTRESS, SINGER
    FRIEND: JON PETERS
    RESIDENCE: MALIBU
    TALENT: COMPOSER-SINGER-ACTOR HELICOPTER PILOT-US ARMY
    COMMENT: PHI BETA KAPPA KEY RHODES SCHOLAR-OXFORD
    CREDIT: '70 PAT GARRETT AND BILLY THE KID
    CREDIT: '72 CISCO PIKE
    CREDIT: '74 BLUME IN LOVE
    CREDIT: '75 ALICE DOESN'T LIVE HERE ANYMORE
    CREDIT: '76 A STAR IS BORN

LA MARR, BARBARA   BORN: REATHA WATSON
                                 JUL 28,'96 AT NORTH YAKIMA, WA   DIED IN '26
      FATHER: --, EDITOR
      *** MARRIED: '14 JACK LYTELL, COWBOY (DIED '14)
      *** MARRIED: '14 LAWRENCE CONVERSE, LAWYER-DIED IN JAIL (BIGAMY) (DIED '14)
      *** MARRIED: '16 PHIL AINSWORTH, ACTOR, DANCER (DIVORCED '17)
      *** MARRIED: '18 N. BERNARD 'BEN' DEELY, ACTOR (HER VAUDEVILLE PARTNER) (DIVORCED '22)
      *** MARRIED: '23 VIRGIL JACK DOUGHERTY, ACTOR
      ADOPTED SON: MARVIN CARVILLE LA MARR
      ROMANCE: BEN FINNEY
      FRIEND: ZASU PITTS, ACTRESS
      FRIEND: ADELA ROGERS ST. JOHNS, WRITER
      ENEMY: HERMAN ROTH, LAWYER SHE SUED FOR BLACKMAIL
      TALENT: ACTRESS, WRITER
      CREDIT: '21 DESPERATE TRAILS
      CREDIT: '22 THE PRISONER OF ZENDA
      CREDIT: '23 THE ETERNAL CITY
      CREDIT: '24 THY NAME IS WOMAN
      CREDIT: '25 THE GIRL FROM MONTMARTRE

LA PLANTE, LAURA
                                 NOV 01,'04 AT ST. LOUIS, MR
      MOTHER: LYDIA LA PLANTE
      *** MARRIED: '26 WILLIAM SEITER, DIRECTOR (DIVORCED '32)
      SON: '28 CHRIS SEITER
      *** MARRIED: '33 IRVING ASHER, PRODUCER
      SON: '39 ANTHONY ASHER
      DAUGHTER: '40 JILL ASHER
      RESIDENCE: PALM DESERT, CA
      TALENT: ACTRESS
      CREDIT: '21 THE OLD SWIMMING HOLE
      CREDIT: '27 THE CAT AND THE CANARY
      CREDIT: '35 WIDOW'S MIGHT
      CREDIT: '46 LITTLE MISTER JIM
      CREDIT: '57 SPRING REUNION

LA ROCQUE, ROD   BORN: RODERICK LA ROCQUE DE LA TOUR
                                 NOV 29,'98 AT CHICAGO, IL   DIED IN '69
      SISTER: MONIQUE LA ROCQUE DE LA TOUR
      UNCLE: WILLIAM LA ROCQUE
      *** MARRIED: '27 VILMA BANKY
      ROMANCE: POLA NEGRI
      RESIDENCE: BEVERLY HILLS, CA
      TALENT: ACTOR
      CREDIT: '17 EFFICIENCY EDGAR'S COURTSHIP
      CREDIT: '23 THE TEN COMMANDMENTS
      CREDIT: '29 LET US BE GAY
      CREDIT: '35 FRISCO WATERFRONT
      CREDIT: '41 MEET JOHN DOE

LADD, ALAN   BORN: ALAN WALBRIDGE LADD
                                 SEP 03,'13 AT HOT SPRINGS, AK   DIED IN '64
      FATHER: ALAN LADD, SR., AUDITOR
      MOTHER: INA RAWLEY
      STEP-FATHER: JAMES BEAVERS
      *** MARRIED: '30 MARJORIE JANE HARROLD (DIVORCED)
      SON: '37 ALAN LADD, JR.

```
*** MARRIED:  '42 EVELYN LEDERER, ACTRESS-SUE CAROL
DAUGHTER:  '43 ALANA LADD
SON:  '47 DAVID LADD
POSSESSION: JAGUAR FILM PRODUCTION CO.
TALENT: ACTOR
CREDIT:  '32 ONCE IN A LIFETIME
CREDIT:  '40 CAPTAIN CAUTION
CREDIT:  '48 WHISPERING SMITH
CREDIT:  '55 THE LONG GRAY LINE
CREDIT:  '64 THE CARPETBAGGERS
```

```
LAHR, BERT          BORN:  IRVING LAHRHEIM
                           AUG 13,'95 AT NYC  DIED IN '67
 *** MARRIED:  '37 MERCEDES DELPINO, VAUDEVILLE PARTNER  (ANNULLED '39)
SON:  '38 HERBERT LAHR
*** MARRIED:  '40 MILDRED SCHROEDER
SON:  '41 JOHN LAHR, WRITER
DAUGHTER:  '43 JANE LAHR
TALENT: ACTOR
CREDIT:  '31 FLYING HIGH
CREDIT:  '39 THE WIZARD OF OZ
CREDIT:  '44 MEET THE PEOPLE
CREDIT:  '62 TEN GIRLS AGO
CREDIT:  '68 THE NIGHT THEY RAIDED MINSKY'S
```

```
LAINE, FRANKIE          BORN:  FRANK PAUL LOVECCHIO
                               MAR 30,'13 AT CHICAGO,IL
FATHER: JOHN LOVECCHIO, BARBER
MOTHER: ANNA
BROTHER: JOSEPH LOVECCHIO
*** MARRIED:  '48 NELLINA GIOLUND  (DIVORCED '49)
*** MARRIED:  '50 NAN GREY, SINGER  (DIVORCED)
RESIDENCE: SHERMAN OAKS, CA
POSSESSION:  '32 WORLD'S RECORD-MARATHON DANCE CONTEST-3,501 HOURS
TALENT: ACTOR-SINGER
COMMENT: GREY HAD BEEN MARRIED TO RACE- JOCKIE JACKIE WESTROPE
CREDIT:  '50 WHEN YOU'RE SMILING
CREDIT:  '51 THE SUNNY SIDE OF THE STREET
CREDIT:  '52 RAINBOW ROUND MY SHOULDER
CREDIT:  '55 BRING YOUR SMILE ALONG
CREDIT:  '56 HE LAUGHED LAST
```

```
LAKE, ARTHUR          BORN:  ARTHUR SILVERLAKE
                             APR 17,'05 AT CORBIN,KT
FATHER: ARTHUR SILVERLAKE, SR., ACROBAT
MOTHER: EDITH GOODWIN, ACTRESS
SISTER: FLORENCE LAKE, ACTRESS
*** MARRIED:  '37 PATRICA VAN CLEVE
SPOUSE'S AUNT: MARION DAVIES, ACTRESS
DAUGHTER: MARION ROSE LAKE CANESSA
SON: ARTHUR PATRICK LAKE
RESIDENCE: SANTA MONICA, CA
TALENT: ACTOR
CREDIT:  '17 JACK AND THE BEANSTALK
CREDIT:  '27 THE IRRESISTIBLE LOVER
CREDIT:  '28 HAROLD TEEN
CREDIT:  '38 BLONDIE, SERIES
CREDIT:  '44 THREE IS A FAMILY
```

LAKE, VERONICA   BORN: CONSTANCE FRANCIS OCKELMAN
                              NOV 14,'19 AT BROOKLYN,NY DIED IN '73
FATHER: H.A. OCKELMAN, SAILOR
MOTHER: CONSTANCE CHARLOTTA TRIMBLE
STEP-FATHER: ANTHONY KEANE
*** MARRIED: '40 JOHN DETLIE, ART DIRECTOR (DIVORCED '43)
DAUGHTER: '42 ELAINE DETLIE
SON: '43 WILLIAM ANTHONY DETLIE
*** MARRIED: '44 ANDRE DE TOTH, DIRECTOR (DIVORCED '52)
SON: '45 MICHAEL DE TOTH
DAUGHTER: '48 DIANE DE TOTH
*** MARRIED: '55 JOSEPH ALLAN MCCARTHY (DIVORCED '59)
*** MARRIED: '62 RON HOUSE
*** MARRIED: '72 ROBERT CARLTON-MUNROE
RESIDENCE: NYC
POSSESSION: CONTRACT AT PARAMOUNT STUDIOS
MEMOIRS: '68 VERONICA
TALENT: ACTRESS
COMMENT: MADE PEEK-A-BOO HAIRDO FAMOUS
CREDIT: '39 ALL WOMEN HAVE SECRETS
CREDIT: '41 I WANTED WINGS
CREDIT: '47 VARIETY GIRL
CREDIT: '52 STRONGHOLD
CREDIT: '70 FLESH FEAST

LAMARR, HEDY   BORN: HEDWIG EVA MARIA KIESLER
                              NOV 09,'13 AT VIENNA, AUSTRIA
FATHER: EMIL KIESLER, BANKER
MOTHER: GERTRUDE
*** MARRIED: '33 FRITZ MANDL, INDUSTRIALIST (DIVORCED '37)
*** MARRIED: '39 GENE MARKEY, WRITER (DIVORCED '40)
STEP-DAUGHTER: MELINDA MARKEY
ADOPTED SON: JAMES MARKEY
*** MARRIED: '43 JOHN J. LODER, ACTOR (DIVORCED '48)
DAUGHTER: '45 DENISE LODER
SON: '47 ANTHONY LODER
*** MARRIED: '51 ERNEST 'TEDDY' STAUFFER, RESTAURATEUR (DIVORCED '52)
*** MARRIED: '53 W. HOWARD LEE, OIL MAN (DIVORCED '59)
*** MARRIED: '63 LEWIS BOLES, JR., LAWYER (DIVORCED '65)
FRIEND: REGINALD GARDINER, ACTOR
RESIDENCE: NYC
POSSESSION: '38 CONTRACT AT M-G-M STUDIOS
POSSESSION: ECSTASY BOUTIQUE NYC
MEMOIRS: '67 ECSTASY AND ME
TALENT: ACTRESS
CREDIT: '38 ALGIERS
CREDIT: '42 WHITE CARGO
CREDIT: '49 SAMSON AND DELILAH
CREDIT: '54 THE FACE THAT LAUNCHED A THOUSAND SHIPS
CREDIT: '57 THE FEMALE ANIMAL

LAMAS, FERNANDO   BORN: FERNANDO ALVARO LAMAS
                              JAN 09,'15 AT BUENOS AIRES, ARGENTINA
*** MARRIED: '40 PEARLA MUX, ACTRESS
*** MARRIED: '46 LYDIA BABACHI
DAUGHTER: '47 ALEJANDRE LAMAS
*** MARRIED: '54 ARLENE DAHL

SON: '58 LORENZO FERNANDO LAMAS
*** MARRIED: '63 ESTHER WILLIAMS
STEP-SON: BENJAMIN GAGE
STEP-DAUGHTER: SUSAN GAGE
STEP-SON: KIMBALL GAGE
ROMANCE: LANA TURNER
RESIDENCE: BEVERLY HILLS, CA
TALENT: ACTOR-DIRECTOR
COMMENT: KNOWN AS THE 'TROPICAL FERN'
CREDIT: '51 RICH, YOUNG AND PRETTY
CREDIT: '54 ROSE MARIE
CREDIT: '67 THE VIOLENT ONES
CREDIT: '69 100 RIFLES
CREDIT: '71 POWDER KEG
CREDIT: '78 THE CHEAP DETECTIVE

LAMOUR, DOROTHY   BORN: MARY LETA DOROTHY STANTON
                                DEC 10,'14 AT NEW ORLEANS, LA
STEP-FATHER: LAMBOUR
*** MARRIED: '35 HERBERT KAY, ORCHESTRA LEADER (DIVORCED '39)
*** MARRIED: '43 WILLIAM ROSS HOWARD
SON: '46 JOHN RIDGELY HOWARD
DAUGHTER-IN-LAW: DEBRA NELSON (MARRIED '73)
SON: '49 RICHARD HOWARD
ROMANCE: RANDOLPH SCOTT, ACTOR
TALENT: ACTRESS
COMMENT: MISS NEW ORLEANS OF 1931
CREDIT: '36 THE JUNGLE PRINCESS, DEBUT
CREDIT: '38 TROPIC HOLIDAY
CREDIT: '40 ROAD TO SINGAPORE, SERIES OF 'ROAD TO - ' TITLES
CREDIT: '63 DONOVAN'S REEF
CREDIT: '64 PAJAMA PARTY

LANCASTER, BURT   BORN: BURTON STEPHEN LANCASTER
                                NOV 02,'13 AT NYC
FATHER: JAMES LANCASTER
SISTER: JANE LANCASTER
SISTER: -- (DIED)
BROTHER: WILLIAM LANCASTER (DIED '55)
BROTHER: JAMES LANCASTER, JR., POLICEMAN (DIED '61)
*** MARRIED: '35 JUNE ERNST, CIRCUS PERFORMER (DIVORCED '36)
*** MARRIED: '46 NORMA ANDERSON (DIVORCED '69)
SON: '47 WILLIAM HENRY LANCASTER, ACTOR
SON: '49 JAMES STEVEN LANCASTER
DAUGHTER: '51 SUSAN ELIZABETH LANCASTER
DAUGHTER: '54 JOANNA MARI LANCASTER
DAUGHTER: '56 SIGHLE LANCASTER
FRIEND: NICK CRAVAT, PARTNER IN LANG & CRAVAT ACT
PARTNER: HAROLD HECHT, PRODUCER
PARTNER: JAMES HILL, PRODUCER, WRITER
RESIDENCE: BEVERLY HILLS, CA
POSSESSION: '49 CONTRACT AT WARNER BROTHERS
TALENT: ACROBAT-ACTOR
CREDIT: '46 THE KILLERS
AA-NOM ACTOR: '53 FROM HERE TO ETERNITY
AA-WIN ACTOR: '60 ELMER GANTRY
AA-NOM ACTOR: '62 BIRD MAN OF ALCATRAZ
CREDIT: '73 AIRPORT

LANCHESTER, ELSA   BORN: ELIZABETH SULLIVAN
                                 OCT 28,'02 AT LONDON, ENGLAND
    FATHER: JAMES SULLIVAN, ACCOUNTANT
    MOTHER: EDITH LANCHESTER
    BROTHER: --
    *** MARRIED: '29 CHARLES LAUGHTON, ACTOR (DIED '62)
    FRIEND: ISADORA DUNCAN, HER DANCE TEACHER
    RESIDENCE: PACIFIC PALISADES, CA
    MEMOIRS: CHARLES LAUGHTON AND I
    TALENT: ACTRESS
    CREDIT: '28 BLUEBOTTLES
    CREDIT: '35 THE BRIDE OF FRANKENSTEIN
    AA-NOM SUP.ACT: '49 COME TO THE STABLE
    AA-NOM SUP.ACT: '57 WITNESS FOR THE PROSECUTION
    CREDIT: '64 MARY POPPINS
    CREDIT: '71 WILLARD

LANGE, HOPE   BORN: HOPE ELISE ROSS LANGE
                            NOV 28,'33 AT REDDING RIDGE, CN
    FATHER: JOHN LANGE, MUSICIAN
    MOTHER: MINETTE BUDDECKE, ACTRESS
    *** MARRIED: '56 DON MURRAY (DIVORCED '61)
    SON: '57 CHRISTOPHER MURRAY
    DAUGHTER: '58 PATRICIA MURRAY
    *** MARRIED: '63 ALAN J. PAKULA, PRODUCER
    TALENT: ACTRESS
    CREDIT: '56 BUS STOP
    AA-NOM SUP.ACT: '57 PEYTON PLACE
    CREDIT: '59 THE BEST OF EVERYTHING
    CREDIT: '61 WILD IN THE COUNTRY
    CREDIT: '63 LOVE IS A BALL

LANGFORD, FRANCES
                            APR 04,'13 AT LAKELAND,FL
    FATHER: VASCO LANGFORD
    MOTHER: ANN NEWBERN, PIANIST
    *** MARRIED: '38 JON HALL, ACTOR (DIVORCED '55)
    *** MARRIED: '55 RALPH EVINRUDE, CHAIRMAN-EVINRUDE MOTOR CO.
    RESIDENCE: JENSEN BEACH, FL
    POSSESSION: FRANCES·LANGFORD OUTRIGGER RESORT, JENSEN BEACH, FL
    TALENT: SINGER-ACTRESS
    CREDIT: '35 EVERY NIGHT AT EIGHT
    CREDIT: '40 TOO MANY GIRLS
    CREDIT: '44 THE GIRL RUSH
    CREDIT: '52 NO TIME FOR TEARS
    CREDIT: '54 THE GLENN MILLER STORY

LANSBURY, ANGELA   BORN: ANGELA BRIGID LANSBURY
                                 OCT 16,'25 AT LONDON, ENGLAND
    FATHER: EDGAR LANSBURY, LUMBER MERCHANT
    MOTHER: MOYNA MACGILL, ACTRESS
    SISTER: ISOLDE LANSBURY
    BROTHER: BRUCE LANSBURY, PRODUCER-TWIN
    BROTHER: EDGAR LANSBURY, JR., PRODUCER-TWIN
    *** MARRIED: '45 RICHARD CROMWELL, ACTOR (DIVORCED '46)
    *** MARRIED: '49 PETER SHAW
    SON: '52 ANTHONY SHAW

```
        DAUGHTER:  '53 DIEDRE SHAW
        RESIDENCE: MALIBU, CA
        TALENT: ACTRESS
        AA-NOM  SUP.ACT:  '44 GASLIGHT
        AA-NOM  SUP.ACT:  '45 THE PICTURE OF DORIAN GRAY
        CREDIT:  '60 DARK AT THE TOP OF THE STAIRS
        AA-NOM  SUP.ACT:  '62 THE MANCHURIAN CANDIDATE
        CREDIT:  '71 BEDKNOBS AND BROOMSTICKS
----------------------------------------------------------------------------
LANZA, MARIO          BORN:  ALFRED ARNOLD COCCOZZA
                             JAN 31,'21 AT PHILADELPHIA,PA  DIED IN '59
        FATHER: ANTONIO COCCOZZA
        MOTHER: MARIA LANZA
        *** MARRIED:  '45 BETTY HICKS
        DAUGHTER:  '50 COLLEEN LANZA
        DAUGHTER:  '51 ELISA LANZA
        SON:  '52 DAMON LANZA
        SON:  '54 MARK LANZA
        FRIEND: KATHRYN GRAYSON
        POSSESSION:  '49 CONTRACT AT M-G-M STUDIOS DISPUTED IN 1952
        TALENT: ACTOR, TENOR
        CREDIT:  '49 THAT MIDNIGHT KISS
        CREDIT:  '51 THE GREAT CARUSO
        CREDIT:  '52 BECAUSE YOU'RE MINE
        CREDIT:  '56 SERENADE
        CREDIT:  '58 FOR THE FIRST TIME
----------------------------------------------------------------------------
LASSIE
                     JUN 08,'40 IN ENGLAND   BIRTHSIGN 'SIRIUS'
        FATHER: ERIC KNIGHT, AUTHOR
        STEP-FATHER: RUDD WEATHERWAX, TRAINER
        SON: LASSIE, II
        RESIDENCE: SAN FERNANDO VALLEY, CA
        TALENT: ACTOR
        CREDIT:  '42 LASSIE COME HOME
        CREDIT:  '45 SON OF LASSIE
        CREDIT:  '62 LASSIE'S GREAT ADVENTURE, LAST IN THE SERIES
----------------------------------------------------------------------------
LAUGHTON, CHARLES
                     JUL 01,'99 AT SCARBOROUGH, YORKS., ENGLAND  DIED IN '62
        FATHER: ROBERT LAUGHTON, INNKEEPER
        MOTHER: ELIZABETH CONLON, BARMAID
        BROTHER: TOM LAUGHTON
        BROTHER: FRANK LAUGHTON
        *** MARRIED:  '29 ELSA LANCHESTER, ACTRESS
        FRIEND: RAY BRADBURY, AUTHOR
        PARTNER: BERTOLD BRECHT, CO-AUTHOR OF PLAY 'GALILEO'
        RESIDENCE: SANTA MONICA, CA
        POSSESSION:  '31 CONTRACT AT PARAMOUNT PICTURES
        POSSESSION: MAYFLOWER FILM PRODUCTION CO.
        MEMOIRS: TELL ME A STORY
        TALENT: ACTOR-STORYTELLER-WRITER
        CREDIT:  '23 THE HUNCHBACK OF NOTRE DAME
        AA-WIN  ACTOR:  '32 THE PRIVATE LIFE OF HENRY VIII
        AA-NOM  ACTOR:  '35 MUTINY ON THE BOUNTY
        CREDIT:  '40 THEY KNEW WHAT THEY WANTED
        AA-NOM  ACTOR:  '57 WITNESS FOR THE PROSECUTION
        CREDIT:  '62 ADVISE AND CONSENT
```

LAUREL, STAN   BORN: ARTHUR STANLEY JEFFERSON
                             JUN 16,'90 AT ULVERSTON, LANCASHIRE, ENGLAND DIED IN '65
   *** MARRIED: RAEMOND WALBERN, ACTRESS
   *** MARRIED: '30 LOIS NELSON (DIVORCED '33)
   DAUGHTER: '31 LOIS LAUREL
   *** MARRIED: '35 VIRGINIA RUTH ROGERS (DIVORCED '37)
   *** MARRIED: '38 VIRGINIA RUTH ROGERS, RE-MARRIED (DIVORCED '39)
   *** MARRIED: '40 VERA ILLIANA, DANCER (DIVORCED '66)
   *** MARRIED: '46 IDA KITAEVA
   PARTNER: OLIVER HARDY
   RESIDENCE: SANTA MONICA, CA
   POSSESSION: BRONZE RAT - SYMBOL OF BRITISH WATER RATS CLUB
   BIOGRAPHY: COMEDY WORLD OF STAN LAUREL, BY JOHN MCCABE
   TALENT: ACTOR
   CREDIT: '26 PUTTING PANTS ON PHILIP
   CREDIT: '29 MEN O' WAR
   AA-SPECIAL AWARD: '33 THE MUSIC BOX SHORT SUBJECT
   CREDIT: '34 BABES IN TOYLAND
   CREDIT: '51 ATOLL K
   AA-SPECIAL AWARD: '60 HONORARY AWARD FOR 'CREATIVE' PIONEERING IN COMEDY'

LAURIE, PIPER   BORN: ROSETTA JACOBS
                             JAN 22,'32 AT DETROIT, MH
   FATHER: ALFRED JACOBS
   MOTHER: ROSETTA
   SISTER: SHERRE JACOBS
   *** MARRIED: '62 JOSEPH MORGENSTERN, JOURNALIST
   DAUGHTER: '71 ANNA GRACE MORGENSTERN
   RESIDENCE: WOODSTOCK, NY 250 YEAR OLD FARMHOUSE
   POSSESSION: '50 CONTRACT AT UNIVERSAL STUDIOS
   TALENT: ACTRESS
   CREDIT: '50 LOUISA, DEBUT
   CREDIT: '52 SON OF ALI BABA
   CREDIT: '55 AIN'T MISBEHAVIN'
   AA-NOM ACTRESS: '61 THE HUSTLER
   AA-NOM SUP.ACT: '76 CARRIE

LAWFORD, PETER   BORN: PETER AYLEN LAWFORD
                             SEP 07,'23 AT LONDON, ENGLAND
   FATHER: PETER SYDNEY ERNEST LAWFORD, ACTOR, LT. GENERAL, KNIGHT (DIED '53)
   MOTHER: LADY MAY
   COUSIN: BETTY LAWFORD, ACTRESS
   *** MARRIED: '54 PATRICIA KENNEDY (DIVORCED '66)
   BROTHER-IN-LAW: JOHN F. KENNEDY, SENATOR-THEN PRES. OF USA
   FATHER-IN-LAW: JOSEPH P. KENNEDY, EXECUTIVE, DIPLOMAT
   BROTHER-IN-LAW: ROBERT F. KENNEDY, SENATOR-THEN ATT.GEN OF USA
   BROTHER-IN-LAW: EDWARD KENNEDY, SENATOR
   SON: '55 CHRISTOPHER LAWFORD
   SON: '57 SYDNEY LAWFORD
   DAUGHTER: '59 VICTORIA FRANCES LAWFORD
   DAUGHTER: '61 ROBIN LAWFORD
   *** MARRIED: '71 MARY ROWAN (DIVORCED '73)
   FATHER-IN-LAW: DAN ROWAN, ACTOR
   *** MARRIED: '76 DEBORAH GOULD
   FRIEND: ROBERT F. KENNEDY
   FRIEND: FRANK SINATRA
   FRIEND: DEAN MARTIN

```
        FRIEND: MARILYN MONROE
        RESIDENCE: SANTA MONICA, CA
        RESIDENCE: NYC
        TALENT: ACTOR
        CREDIT:   '31 POOR OLD BILL
        CREDIT:   '38 LORD JEFF
        CREDIT:   '48 EASTER PARADE
        CREDIT:   '60 EXODUS
        CREDIT:   '65 HARLOW
        CREDIT:   '70 ONE MORE TIME
```

LAWRENCE, CAROL   BORN: CAROL MARIA LARAIA
                                 SEP 05,'32 AT MELROSE PARK,IL
```
        FATHER: MICHAEL LARAIA, INSURANCE BROKER
        MOTHER: ROSE MORENO
        BROTHER: JOSEPH LARAIA
        *** MARRIED:   '56 COSMO ALLEGRETTI, PUPPETEER  (ANNULLED '59)
        *** MARRIED:   '63 ROBERT GOULET
        FATHER-IN-LAW: JOSEPH GOULET
        MOTHER-IN-LAW: JEANETTE GAUTHIER
        STEP-DAUGHTER: NICOLETTE GOULET
        SON:   '64 CHRISTOPHER GOULET
        SON:   '66 MICHAEL GOULET
        TALENT: ACTRESS-SINGER
        CREDIT:   '54 NEW FACES
        CREDIT:   '61 WEST SIDE STORY
        CREDIT:   '62 A VIEW FROM THE BRIDGE
```

LAWRENCE, FLORENCE
                        1888 AT HAMILTON, ONTARIO, CANADA   DIED IN '38
```
        MOTHER: LOTTA LAURENCE
        *** MARRIED: HARRY SALTER
        FRIEND: CARL LAEMMLE
        PARTNER: ARTHUR JOHNSON
        RESIDENCE: LOS ANGELES, CA
        TALENT: ACTRESS
        COMMENT: KNOWN AS THE BIOGRAPH GIRL FOR THE BIOGRAPH FILM CO.
        COMMENT: KNOWN AS THE IMP GIRL FOR INDEPENDENT MOTION PICTURE CO.
        COMMENT: THE FIRST MOVIE 'STAR'
        CREDIT:   '08 A CALAMITOUS ELOPEMENT
        CREDIT:   '09 JONESY, SERIES
        CREDIT:   '10 THE ANGEL OF THE STUDIO
        CREDIT:   '14 A SINGULAR CYNIC
        CREDIT:   '24 GAMBLING WIVES
```

LAWRENCE, GERTRUDE   BORN: GERTRUD ALEXANDRA DAGMAR
                                   JUL 04,'98 AT LONDON, ENGLAND   DIED IN '52
```
        FATHER: ARTHUR LAWRENCE KLASEN, SINGER
        MOTHER: ALICE LOUISE BANKS, ACTRESS
        *** MARRIED:   '25 FRANCIS GORDON-HOWLEY (DIVORCED '27)
        DAUGHTER:   '26 PAMELA HOWLEY
        *** MARRIED:   '40 RICHARD ALDRICH
        RESIDENCE: NYC
        MEMOIRS: A STAR DANCED
        TALENT: ACTRESS-SINGER-DANCER
        CREDIT:   '29 THE BATTLE OF PARIS
        CREDIT:   '33 NO FUNNY BUSINESS
        CREDIT:   '36 MEN ARE NOT GODS
```

CREDIT: '50 THE GLASS MENAGERIE

LAWRENCE, STEVE   BORN: SIDNEY LIEBOWITZ
                              JUL 08,'35 AT BROOKLYN, NY
FATHER: MAX LIEBOWITZ, CANTOR
BROTHER: BERNARD LIEBOWITZ
*** MARRIED: '57 EYDIE GORME
BROTHER-IN-LAW: ROBERT GORME
FATHER-IN-LAW: NESSIM GORME, TAILOR
MOTHER-IN-LAW: FORTUNE
SISTER-IN-LAW: CORENE GORME
SON: '60 DAVID LAWRENCE
SON: '62 MICHAEL LAWRENCE
TALENT: ACTOR-SINGER
CREDIT: STAND UP AND BE COUNTED

LAYE, EVELYN
                         JUL 10,'00 AT LONDON, ENGLAND
FATHER: GILBERT LAYE
MOTHER: EVELYN FROUD
SISTER-IN-LAW: BEATRICE 'BINNIE' HALE-MUNRO, ACTRESS, SINGER
*** MARRIED: JOHN R. 'SONNIE' HALE-MUNRO, ACTOR-SINGER (DIVORCED)
*** MARRIED: FRANK LAWTON, ACTOR
RESIDENCE: LONDON, ENGLAND
MEMOIRS: BOO, TO MY FRIENDS
TALENT: ACTRESS-SINGER
CREDIT: '29 LUCK OF THE NAVY
CREDIT: '34 EVENSONG
CREDIT: '59 MAKE MINE A MILLION
CREDIT: '66 THEATRE OF DEATH
CREDIT: '71 SAY HELLO TO YESTERDAY

LEACHMAN, CLORIS
                         APR 30,'26 AT DES MOINES, IO
FATHER: --, LUMBER COMPANY MANAGER
SISTER: CLAIBORNE CARY, ACTRESS
*** MARRIED: '53 GEORGE ENGLUND, PRODUCER
SON: '53 ADAM ENGLUND
SON: '54 BRYAN ENGLUND
SON: '56 GEORGE ENGLUND, JR.
SON: '62 MORGAN ENGLUND
DAUGHTER: '66 DINAH ENGLUND
RESIDENCE: LOS ANGELES, CA
TALENT: ACTRESS
CREDIT: '56 THE RACK
CREDIT: '62 THE CHAPMAN REPORT
CREDIT: '69 BUTCH CASSIDY AND THE SUNDANCE, KID
AA-WIN SUP.ACT.: '71 THE LAST PICTURE SHOW
CREDIT: '73 MOTHER'S DAY

LEDERER, FRANCIS   BORN: FRANTISEK LEDERER
                              NOV 06,'02 AT PRAGUE, CZECHOSLOVAKIA
FATHER: JOSEPH LEDERER
MOTHER: ROSE ORNSTEIN
*** MARRIED: ADA NEJEDLY (DIVORCED '35)
*** MARRIED: '37 MARIA MARGARITA BOLADO, ACTRESS - MARGOT (DIVORCED '41)
*** MARRIED: '41 MARION IRVINE
RESIDENCE: CANOGA PARK, CA 'HONORARY MAYOR'

```
POSSESSION: CANOGA MISSION GALLERY
TALENT: ACTOR
CREDIT:  '34 THE PURSUIT OF HAPPINESS
CREDIT:  '39 CONFESSIONS OF A NAZI SPY
CREDIT:  '48 MILLION DOLLAR WEEKEND
CREDIT:  '56 LISBON
CREDIT:  '59 TERROR IS MAN
```

LEE, BRUCE   BORN: LI JUN FAN
```
                              NOV 27,'40 AT SAN FRANCISCO, CA   DIED IN '73
     FATHER: LI HOI CHUEN, OPERA PERFORMER  (DIED '65)
     MOTHER: GRACE LI
     SISTER: PHOEBE LI
     SISTER: AGNES LI
     BROTHER: ROBERT LI, SINGER
     BROTHER: PETER LI
     *** MARRIED:  '64 LINDA EMERY
     SON:  '65 BRANDON BRUCE LEE
     DAUGHTER: . '69 SHANNON LEE
     FRIEND: JAMES COBURN, ACTOR
     FRIEND: STEVE MCQUEEN, ACTOR
     FRIEND: LEE MARVIN, ACTOR
     FRIEND: SYLVIA WU, RESTAURATEUR
     PARTNER: RAYMOND CHOW, PRODUCER
     BIOGRAPHY:  '75 THE MAN ONLY I KNEW, BY LINDA LEE
     TALENT: ACTOR, WRITER, DIRECTOR
     COMMENT: 1ST STAGE NAME - LI SIU LOONG
     CREDIT:  '63 THE PHILOSOPHICAL ART OF SELF-DEFENSE-UNIVERSITY THESIS
     CREDIT:  '73 GAME OF DEATH
```

LEE, GYPSY ROSE   BORN: ROSE LOUISE HOVICK
```
                              JAN 09,'14 AT SEATTLE, WA   DIED IN '70
     FATHER: JOHN OLAV HOVICK, JOURNALIST
     MOTHER: ROSE
     SISTER: JUNE HAVOC, ACTRESS
     BROTHER-IN-LAW: WILLIAM SPIER
     *** MARRIED:  '37 ARNOLD R. MIZZY  (DIVORCED '41)
     *** MARRIED:  '42 ALEXANDER KIRKLAND
     SON:  '45 ERIK KIRKLAND PREMINGER, FATHER - OTTO PREMINGER
     ROMANCE: OTTO PREMINGER
     RESIDENCE: NYC AND HIGHLAND MILLS, NY
     POSSESSION: '37 CONTRACT AT 20TH CENTURY FOX
     MEMOIRS: GYPSY BASIS FOR PLAY
     TALENT: ACTRESS-DANCER
     CREDIT:  '36 ZIEGFELD FOLLIES OF 1936
     CREDIT:  '43 STAGE DOOR CANTEEN
     CREDIT:  '52 BABES IN BAGDAD
     CREDIT:  '63 THE STRIPPER
     CREDIT:  '66 THE TROUBLE WITH ANGELS
```

LEE, PEGGY   BORN: NORMA ENGSTROM
```
                              MAY 26,'20 AT JAMESTOWN,ND
     FATHER: MARVIN ENGSTROM, RAILROAD AGENT
     MOTHER: --  (DIED '24)
     *** MARRIED:  '43 DAVE BARBOUR, GUITARIST  (DIVORCED '51)
     DAUGHTER:  '44 NICKI BARBOUR
     *** MARRIED:  '55 BRAD DEXTER  (DIVORCED '56)
     *** MARRIED:  '56 DEWEY MARTIN  (DIVORCED '59)
```

```
*** MARRIED:  '64 JACK DEL RIO  (DIVORCED '64)
RESIDENCE: COLDWATER CANYON, LA, CA
POSSESSION: PEGGY LEE ENTERPRISES MUSIC PUBLISHING TV PRODUCTION
TALENT: ACTRESS-SINGER
CREDIT:  '50 MR. MUSIC
CREDIT:  '53 THE JAZZ SINGER
AA-NOM  SUP.ACT:  '55 PETE KELLY'S BLUES
```

LEIGH, JANET   BORN: JEANETTE HELEN MORRISON
                               JUL 26,'27 AT MERCED, CA
```
*** MARRIED:  '42 JOHN K. CARLYLE  (ANNULLED '42)
*** MARRIED:  '46 STANLEY REAMES, BANDLEADER  (DIVORCED '48)
*** MARRIED:  '51 TONY CURTIS, ACTOR  (DIVORCED '63)
DAUGHTER:  '56 KELLY LEE CURTIS
DAUGHTER:  '58 JAMIE LEIGH CURTIS
*** MARRIED:  '62 ROBERT BRANT, STOCK BROKER
POSSESSION:  '47 CONTRACT AT M-G-M STUDIOS UNTIL 1953
TALENT: ACTRESS
CREDIT:  '47 THE ROMANCE OF ROSIE RIDGE, DEBUT
CREDIT:  '49 THAT FORSYTHE WOMAN
CREDIT:  '53 HOUDINI
CREDIT:  '55 MY SISTER EILEEN
AA-NOM  SUP.ACT:  '60 PSYCHO
CREDIT:  '72 ONE IS A LONELY NUMBER
```

LEIGH, VIVIEN   BORN: VIVIEN MARY HARTLEY
                               NOV 05,'13 AT DARJEELING, INDIA DIED IN '67
```
FATHER: ERNEST RICHARD HARTLEY
MOTHER: GERTRUDE ROBINSON
*** MARRIED:  '32 HERBERT LEIGH HOLMAN, BARRISTER  (DIVORCED '37)
DAUGHTER:  '33 SUZANNE HOLMAN
*** MARRIED:  '40 LAURENCE OLIVIER  (DIVORCED '60)
STEP-SON: TARQUIN OLIVIER
STEP-SON: SIMON OLIVIER
ROMANCE: JOHN MERIVALE, ACTOR
ROMANCE: PETER FINCH, ACTOR
RESIDENCE: CHELSEA, LONDON, ENGLAND
BIOGRAPHY:  '77 VIVIEN LEIGH, BY ANNE EDWARDS
BIOGRAPHY:  '77 THE OLIVIERS, BY FELIX BARKER
TALENT: ACTRESS
CREDIT:  '34 THINGS ARE LOOKING UP
CREDIT:  '37 WATERLOO BRIDGE
AA-WIN  ACTRESS:  '39 GONE WITH THE WIND
CREDIT:  '48 ANNA KARENINA
AA-WIN  ACTRESS:  '51 A STREETCAR NAMED DESIRE
CREDIT:  '65 SHIP OF FOOLS
```

LEMMON, JACK   BORN: JOHN UHLER LEMMON, 3RD
                               FEB 08,'25 AT BOSTON, MS
```
FATHER: JOHN UHLER LEMMON, JR.
MOTHER: MILDRED LARUE NOEL
*** MARRIED:  '50 CYNTHIA STONE  (DIVORCED '56)
SON:  '54 CHRISTOPHER LEMMON
*** MARRIED:  '62 FELICIA FARR
DAUGHTER:  '66 COURTNEY LEMMON
TALENT: ACTOR-DIRECTOR
AA-WIN  SUP.ACT.:  '55 MISTER ROBERTS
AA-NOM  ACTOR:  '59 SOME LIKE IT HOT
```

```
AA-NOM  ACTOR:  '60 THE APARTMENT
AA-NOM  ACTOR:  '62 DAYS OF WINE AND ROSES
AA-WIN  ACTOR:  '73 SAVE THE TIGER
```

LENNON, JOHN
```
                      BORN:  JOHN WINSTON LENNON
                             OCT 09,'40 AT LIVERPOOL, ENGLAND
    FATHER: ALFRED LENNON
    MOTHER: JULIA
    AUNT: MARY 'MIMI' SMITH
    *** MARRIED:  '62 CYNTHIA POWELL
    SON:  '63 JOHN CHARLES JULIAN LENNON
    *** MARRIED:  '69 YOKO ONO
    SON:  '75 SEAN ONO LENNON
    PARTNER: GEORGE HARRISON, IN THE BEATLES & THE APPLE CO.
    PARTNER: PAUL MCCARTNEY, IN THE BEATLES & THE APPLE CO.
    PARTNER: RINGO STARR, IN THE BEATLES & THE APPLE CO.
    RESIDENCE: NYC
    MEMOIRS: IN HIS OWN WRITE
    TALENT: GUITARIST, COMPOSER, ACTOR
    CREDIT:  '64 A HARD DAY'S NIGHT, WITH BEATLES
    CREDIT:  '65 HELP!, WITH BEATLES
    CREDIT:  '67 HOW I WON THE WAR
```

LEVANT, OSCAR
```
                             DEC 27,'06 AT PITTSBURGH, PA   DIED IN '72
    FATHER: MAX LEVANT, JEWELER
    MOTHER: ANNE RADIN
    BROTHER: HARRY LEVANT
    BROTHER: HOWARD LEVANT
    BROTHER: BENJAMIN LEVANT
    *** MARRIED:  '32 BARBARA SMITH, DANCER  (DIVORCED '33)
    *** MARRIED:  '39 JUNE GILMARTIN, AKA JUNE GALE - ACTRESS,DANCER
    SISTER-IN-LAW: JOAN GALE, DANCER
    SISTER-IN-LAW: JANE GALE, DANCER
    DAUGHTER:  '40 MARCIA ANN LEVANT
    SON-IN-LAW: JEROME TALMER, JOURNALIST
    DAUGHTER:  '41 LORNA LEVANT
    DAUGHTER:  '42 AMANDA LEVANT
    SON-IN-LAW: CASEY CARMEL
    FRIEND: GEORGE GERSHWIN, COMPOSER
    FRIEND: IRA GERSHWIN, LYRICIST
    RESIDENCE: BEVERLY HILLS, CA
    MEMOIRS:  '68 THE UNIMPORTANCE OF BEING OSCAR
    TALENT: ACTOR, PIANIST, AUTHOR
    CREDIT:  '29 THE DANCE OF LIFE
    CREDIT:  '41 KISS THE BOYS GOODBYE
    CREDIT:  '45 RHAPSODY IN BLUE
    CREDIT:  '51 AN AMERICAN IN PARIS
    CREDIT:  '55 THE COBWEB
```

LEWIS, JERRY
```
                      BORN:  JOSEF LEVITCH
                             MAR 16,'26 AT NEWARK,NJ
    FATHER: DANIEL LEVITCH, SINGER
    MOTHER: RAE LEWIS, PIANIST
    *** MARRIED:  '44 PATTI PALMER, SINGER
    SON:  '45 GARY LEWIS, MUSICIAN  (MARRIED '67)
    DAUGHTER-IN-LAW: SARA JANE SUZARA
    SON:  '49 RONALD LEWIS
```

DAUGHTER-IN-LAW: GAIL
SON: '56 SCOTT LEWIS, PUBLICIST
SON: '57 CHRISTOPHER 'CHRIS' LEWIS
SON: '59 ANTHONY LEWIS
SON: '64 JOSEPH LEWIS
PARTNER: DEAN MARTIN
RESIDENCE: BEVERLY HILLS, CA HOUSE BUILT BY LOUIS B. MAYER
POSSESSION: NETWORK CINEMA CORP. FRANCHISING MINI-CINEMAS
MEMOIRS: '73 THE TOTAL FILM MAKER
TALENT: ACTOR
COMMENT: CHAIRMAN MUSCULAR DYSTROPHY CAMPAIGN SINCE 1950
CREDIT: '49 MY FRIEND IRMA
CREDIT: '53 THE STOOGE
CREDIT: '58 THE GEISHA BOY
CREDIT: '60 CINDERFELLA
CREDIT: '70 WHICH WAY TO THE FRONT?

LIBERACE   BORN: WLADZIU VALENTINO LIBERACE
                             MAY 16,'19 AT WEST ALLIS, WI
FATHER: SALVATORE LIBERACE, MUSICIAN
MOTHER: FRANCES LIBERACE
SISTER: ANN LIBERACE
BROTHER: GEORGE LIBERACE
BROTHER: RUDY LIBERACE
ROMANCE: JOANNE RID, DANCER
RESIDENCE: SHERMAN OAKS, CA
POSSESSION: '54 COLLECTION OF MINIATURE PIANOS
TALENT: PIANIST-ACTOR-ENTERTAINER
CREDIT: '49 EAST OF JAVA
CREDIT: '51 FOOTLIGHT VARIETIES
CREDIT: '55 SINCERELY YOURS
CREDIT: '65 THE LOVED ONE

LILLIE, BEATRICE   BORN: CONSTANCE SYLVIA MUNSTON
                             MAY 29,'94 AT TORONTO, ONTARIO,CANADA
FATHER: JOHN MUNSTON
MOTHER: LUCIE SHAW
SISTER: MURIEL MUNSTON
*** MARRIED: '20 SIR ROBERT PEEL (DIED '34)
SON: ROBERT PEEL, DIED 1942 IN ROYAL NAVY
RESIDENCE: NYC
MEMOIRS: EVERY OTHER INCH A LADY
TALENT: ACTRESS-SINGER
CREDIT: '26 EXIT SMILING
CREDIT: '29 SHOW OF SHOWS
CREDIT: '43 ON APPROVAL
CREDIT: '56 AROUND THE WORLD IN EIGHTY DAY
CREDIT: '67 THOROUGHLY MODERN MILLIE

LINDFORS, VIVECA   BORN: ELSA VIVECA TORSTEN LINDFORS
                             DEC 29,'20 AT UPPSALA, SWEDEN
FATHER: TORSTEN LINDFORS, PUBLISHER
MOTHER: KARIN DYMLING
*** MARRIED: '41 FOLKE ROGARD (DIVORCED '49)
DAUGHTER: '42 LENA ROGARD
SON: '43 JAN ROGARD
*** MARRIED: '49 DONALD SIEGEL, DIRECTOR (DIVORCED '53)
SON: '50 CHRISTOPHER SIEGEL

```
     *** MARRIED:  '54 GEORGE TABORI, WRITER  (DIVORCED '72)
     RESIDENCE: NYC
     POSSESSION:  '46 CONTRACT AT WARNER BROS.
     TALENT: ACTRESS
     COMMENT: CO-FOUNDER BERKSHIRE THEATRE
     CREDIT:  '48 NIGHT UNTO NIGHT
     CREDIT:  '48 ADVENTURES OF DON JUAN
     CREDIT:  '50 NO SAD SONGS FOR ME
     CREDIT:  '60 CAPTAIN DREYFUSS
     CREDIT:  '73 THE WAY WE WERE
     CREDIT:  '76 I AM A WOMAN, STAGE SHOW
---------------------------------------------------------------------------------------
LLOYD, HAROLD           BORN:  HAROLD CLAYTON LLOYD
                               APR 20,'89 AT BURCHARD,NB   DIED IN '71
     FATHER: J. DARSIE LLOYD, POOL HALL OWNER
     MOTHER: SARAH ELIZABETH FRASER
     BROTHER: GAYLORD LLOYD
     *** MARRIED:  '23 MILDRED DAVIS, ACTRESS  (DIED '69)
     SON:  '32 HAROLD LLOYD, JR.  (DIED '71)
     ADOPTED DAUGHTER: PEGGY LLOYD
     DAUGHTER: GLORIA LLOYD
     FRIEND: HAL ROACH, PRODUCER
     RESIDENCE: BENEDICT CANYON, BEVERLY HILLS CA
     MEMOIRS:  '28 AN AMERICAN COMEDY
     TALENT: ACTOR
     CREDIT:  '14 CURSES!
     CREDIT:  '15 PHUNPHILMS, SERIES
     CREDIT:  '18 LONESOME LUKE, SERIES
     CREDIT:  '47 MAD WEDNESDAY
     AA-SPECIAL AWARD:  '52 AN HONORARY AWARD TO A MASTER COMEDIAN AND GOOD CITIZEN
---------------------------------------------------------------------------------------
LOCKHART, GENE          BORN:  EUGENE LOCKHART
                               JUL 18,'91 AT LONDON, ONTARIO, CANADA   DIED IN '57
     FATHER: JOHN COATES LOCKHART, SINGER (TENOR)
     MOTHER: ELLEN DELANEY
     *** MARRIED:  '24 KATHLEEN ARTHUR, ACTRESS  (DIED '78)
     DAUGHTER:  '25 JUNE LOCKHART
     SON-IN-LAW: DR. JOHN FRANCIS MALONEY  (MARRIED '50)
     POSSESSION:  '10 CANADIAN 1 MILE SWIMMING CHAMP
     TALENT: ACTOR, WRITER, LYRICIST
     COMMENT: JOHN GIBSON LOCKHART, ANCESTOR WAS BIOGRAPHER OF SIR WALTER
             SCOTT
     COMMENT: WROTE SONG 'THE WORLD IS WAITING FOR THE SUNRISE'
     CREDIT:  '34 BY YOUR LEAVE
     AA-NOM  SUP.ACT:  '38 ALGIERS
     CREDIT:  '41 KEEPING COMPANY
     CREDIT:  '51 RHUBARB
     CREDIT:  '57 JEANNE EAGELS
---------------------------------------------------------------------------------------
LOCKHART, JUNE          BORN:  JUNE KATHLEEN LOCKHART
                               JUN 15,'25 AT NYC
     FATHER: GENE LOCKHART, ACTOR  (DIED '57)
     MOTHER: KATHLEEN ARTHUR, ACTRESS  (DIED '78)
     *** MARRIED:  '50 DR. JOHN FRANCIS MALONEY
     *** MARRIED:  '59 JOHN LINDSAY
     TALENT: ACTRESS
     CREDIT:  '40 ALL THIS AND HEAVEN TOO
     CREDIT:  '44 MEET ME IN ST. LOUIS
```

CREDIT: '45 KEEP YOUR POWDER DRY
CREDIT: '47 TIME LIMIT

LOLLOBRIGIDA, GINA
JUL 04,'28 AT SUBIACO, ITALY
FATHER: GIOVANNI LOLLOBRIGIDA, FURNITURE MANUFACTURER
MOTHER: GIUSEPPINA
*** MARRIED: '49 MIRKO SKOFIC (DIVORCED '68)
SON: '57 MIRKO SKOFIC, JR.
*** MARRIED: '69 GEORGE KAUFMAN
TALENT: ACTRESS
CREDIT: '52 THE WAYWARD WIFE
CREDIT: '53 BREAD, LOVE AND DREAMS
CREDIT: '58 WHERE THE HOT WINDS BLOW
CREDIT: '65 STRANGE BEDFELLOWS
CREDIT: '71 BAD MAN'S RIVER

LOMBARD, CAROLE   BORN: JANE ALICE PETERS
OCT 06,'08 AT FORT WAYNE, IN DIED IN '42
FATHER: FREDERICK C. PETERS
MOTHER: ELIZABETH KNIGHT
BROTHER: FREDERICK PETERS
BROTHER: STUART PETERS
*** MARRIED: '31 WILLIAM POWELL (DIVORCED '33)
*** MARRIED: '39 CLARK GABLE, ACTOR
ROMANCE: GEORGE RAFT
ROMANCE: ROBERT RISKIN, AUTHOR
ROMANCE: RUSS COLUMBO, SINGER
POSSESSION: '30 CONTRACT AT PARAMOUNT PICTURES
TALENT: ACTRESS
CREDIT: '21 THE PERFECT CRIME, DEBUT
CREDIT: '28 POWER
CREDIT: '32 NO MAN OF HER OWN
AA-NOM ACTRESS: '36 MY MAN GODFREY
CREDIT: '41 TO BE OR NOT TO BE

LONDON, JULIE   BORN: JULIE PECK
SEP 26,'26 AT SANTA ROSA, CA
FATHER: JACK PECK
MOTHER: JOSEPHINE TAYLOR
*** MARRIED: '47 JACK WEBB, ACTOR (DIVORCED '53)
DAUGHTER: '50 STACEY WEBB
DAUGHTER: '52 LISA WEBB
*** MARRIED: '59 BOBBY TROUPE, MUSICIAN
STEP-DAUGHTER: CYNTHIA TROUPE
STEP-DAUGHTER: RONNE TROUPE, ACTRESS
DAUGHTER: '62 KELLY TROUPE
SON: '63 JODY TROUPE, TWIN
SON: '63 REESE TROUPE, TWIN
RESIDENCE: ENCINO, CA
TALENT: ACTRESS-SINGER
CREDIT: '44 JUNGLE WOMAN
CREDIT: '51 THE FAT MAN
CREDIT: '58 MAN OF THE WEST
CREDIT: '60 THE THIRD VOICE
CREDIT: '62 THE GEORGE RAFT STORY

```
-------------------------------------------------------------------------------
LONG, RICHARD
                        DEC 27,'27 AT CHICAGO,IL   DIED IN '75
        FATHER: SHERMAN D. LONG, ARTIST
        MOTHER: DALE MCCORD
        SISTER: JANET LONG, TWIN - ARTIST
        SISTER: BARBARA LONG
        BROTHER-IN-LAW: JOHN THOMAS DIX, JR.
        BROTHER: JOHN LONG, TWIN
        BROTHER: ROBERT LONG
        BROTHER: PHILLIP LONG
        *** MARRIED:  '54 SUZAN BALL, ACTRESS  (DIED '55)
        *** MARRIED:  '57 MARA CORDAY, ACTRESS
        SON:  '57 CAREY LONG
        DAUGHTER:  '58 VALERIE LONG
        SON:  '60 GREGORY LONG
        RESIDENCE: LOS ANGELES, CA
        TALENT: ACTOR-DIRECTOR
        CREDIT:  '44 TOMORROW IS FOREVER
        CREDIT:  '47 THE EGG AND I
        CREDIT:  '54 SASKATCHEWAN
        CREDIT:  '59 HOME FROM THE HILL
        CREDIT:  '64 THE TENDERFOOT
-------------------------------------------------------------------------------
LONGET, CLAUDINE
                        JAN 29,'42 AT FRANCE
        FATHER: ROBERT LONGET
        MOTHER: ROLANDE DUMONT
        SISTER: DANIELLE LONGET
        *** MARRIED:  '61 ANDY WILLIAMS  (DIVORCED)
        DAUGHTER:  '64 NOELLE WILLIAMS
        SON:  '66 CHRISTIAN WILLIAMS
        SON:  '70 ROBERT WILLIAMS
        ROMANCE: VLADIMIR 'SPIDER' SAVITCH, SKI INSTRUCTOR  (DIED '76)
        RESIDENCE: ASPEN, CO
        TALENT: SINGER-FRENCH TEACHER FUTURE FARMER
        CREDIT:  '65 MCHALE'S NAVY, DEBUT
        CREDIT:  '67 THE PARTY
        CREDIT:  '68 THE SCAVENGERS
-------------------------------------------------------------------------------
LOREN, SOPHIA          BORN:  SOFIA VILLANI SCICOLONE
                        SEP 20,'32 AT NAPLES, ITALY
        FATHER: RICARDO SCICOLONE
        MOTHER: ROMILDA VILLANI, UNMARRIED
        SISTER: ANNA MARIA SCICOLONE
        BROTHER-IN-LAW: ROMANO MUSSOLINI  (MARRIED '62)
        *** MARRIED:  '57 CARLO PONTI, PRODUCER-MARRIED BY PROXY
        *** MARRIED:  '66 CARLO PONTI, REMARRIED
        SON:  '68 CARLO PONTI, JR.
        SON:  '73 EDOUARDO PONTI
        FRIEND: VITTORIO DE SICA, DIRECTOR
        RESIDENCE: PARIS, FRANCE
        BIOGRAPHY:  '76 SOPHIA, BY DONALD ZEE
        TALENT: ACTRESS
        CREDIT:  '53 AIDA
        CREDIT:  '58 HOUSEBOAT
        AA-WIN  ACTRESS:  '61 TWO WOMEN
        AA-NOM  ACTRESS:  '64 MARRIAGE ITALIAN STYLE
```

CREDIT: '72 MAN OF LA MANCHA
CREDIT: '78 FIREPOWER

LORRE, PETER
                    JUN 26,'04 AT ROSENBERG, HUNGARY DIED IN '64
    FATHER: ALOIS LORRE
    MOTHER: ELVIRA
    *** MARRIED: '33 CECILIE LVOVSKY (DIVORCED '45)
    *** MARRIED: '45 KAAREN VERNE (DIVORCED)
    *** MARRIED: '52 ANNA BRENNING
    DAUGHTER: '53 KATHRYN LORRE
    TALENT: ACTOR
    CREDIT: '31 'M'
    CREDIT: '31 WHITE DEMON
    CREDIT: '37 MR. MOTO, SERIES
    CREDIT: '48 CASBAH
    CREDIT: '59 THE BIG CIRCUS
    CREDIT: '66 THE TORN CURTAIN

LOVEJOY, FRANK   BORN: FRANK LOVEJOY, JR.
                          MAR 28,'12 AT NYC DIED IN '62
    FATHER: FRANK LOVEJOY, SR.
    MOTHER: DORA GARVEY
    *** MARRIED: FRANCES WILLIAMS, ACTRESS
    *** MARRIED: '40 JOAN BANKS, ACTRESS
    DAUGHTER: '41 JUDITH LOVEJOY
    SON: '42 STEPHEN LOVEJOY
    TALENT: ACTOR
    CREDIT: '48 BLACK BART
    CREDIT: '51 FORCE OF ARMS
    CREDIT: '52 THE HITCH HIKER
    CREDIT: '55 THE AMERICANO
    CREDIT: '58 THE GUNFIGHTER

LOVELACE, LINDA   BORN: LINDA SUSAN BORMAN
                           1949 AT BRYAN, TX
    *** MARRIED: '71 CHARLES TRAYNOR, PHOTOGRAPHER
    *** MARRIED: '76 LAWRENCE MARCIANO
    ROMANCE: DAVID WINTER, PRODUCER
    RESIDENCE: LOS ANGELES, CA
    POSSESSION: LOVELACE ENTERPRISES
    MEMOIRS: '73 INSIDE LINDA LOVELACE
    MEMOIRS: '74 THE INTIMATE DIARY OF LINDA LOVELACE
    TALENT: METHOD ACTRESS
    CREDIT: '71 DEEP THROAT
    CREDIT: '73 PAJAMA TOPS, STAGE SHOW
    CREDIT: '74 LINDA LOVELACE FOR PRESIDENT

LOY, MYRNA   BORN: MYRNA WILLIAMS
                      AUG 02,'05 AT RAIDERSBURG, MT
    FATHER: DAVID WILLIAMS, RANCHER
    MOTHER: DELLA JOHNSON
    BROTHER: DAVID WILLIAMS, JR.
    *** MARRIED: '36 ARTHUR HORNBLOW, JR., PRODUCER (DIVORCED '42)
    *** MARRIED: '42 JOHN HERTZ, JR. (DIVORCED '45)
    *** MARRIED: '46 GENE MARKEY, WRITER (DIVORCED '50)
    STEP-DAUGHTER: MELINDA MARKEY
    STEP-SON: JAMES MARKEY

```
*** MARRIED:   '52 HOWLAND SARGENT  (DIVORCED '60)
ROMANCE: RAMON NOVARRO
ROMANCE: WILLIAM POWELL
RESIDENCE: NYC
TALENT: ACTRESS
COMMENT: ADVISER ON FILMS TO UNESCO IN 1950
CREDIT:   '25 PRETTY LADIES
CREDIT:   '32 LOVE ME TONIGHT
CREDIT:   '34 THE THIN MAN
CREDIT:   '46 THE BEST YEARS OF OUR LIVES
CREDIT:   '60 MIDNIGHT LACE
CREDIT:   '69 THE AFRIL FOOLS
```

```
LUGOSI, BELA          BORN:  BELA LUGOSI BLASKO
                             OCT 20,'82 AT LUGOS, HUNGARY  DIED IN '56
   *** MARRIED:  '24 BEATRICE WEEKS  (DIVORCED)
   *** MARRIED:  '33 LILLIAN ARCH  (DIVORCED '53)
   SON:  '34 BELA LUGOSI, JR.
   *** MARRIED:  '55 HOPE LININGER
   BIOGRAPHY:  '76 LUGOSI:THE MAN BEHIND THE CAPE, BY ROBERT CREMER
   TALENT: ACTOR
   COMMENT: ADMITTED DRUG ADDICTION IN '55
   CREDIT:   '19 THE LAST OF THE MOHICANS
   CREDIT:   '29 THE THIRTEENTH CHAIR
   CREDIT:   '30 COUNT DRACULA
   CREDIT:   '39 NINOTCHKA
   CREDIT:   '40 FRANKENSTEIN, SERIES
   CREDIT:   '56 THE SHADOW CREEPS
```

```
LUKAS, PAUL           BORN:  PAUL LUKACS
                             MAY 26,'95 AT BUDAPEST, HUNGARY  DIED IN '71
   FATHER: JANOS LUKACS, ADVERTISING EXECUTIVE
   MOTHER: MARIA ZILAHY
   *** MARRIED:  '27 GIZELLA BENES  (DIED '62)
   *** MARRIED:  '63 ANNETTE DRIESENS
   TALENT: ACTOR
   CREDIT:   '16 MAN OF THE EARTH
   CREDIT:   '28 LOVES OF AN ACTRESS
   CREDIT:   '38 DINNER AT THE RITZ
   AA-WIN  ACTOR:  '43 WATCH ON THE RHINE
   CREDIT:   '58 THE ROOTS OF HEAVEN
   CREDIT:   '68 SOL MADRID
```

```
LUNT, ALFRED          BORN:  ALFRED LUNT, JR.
                             AUG 19,'92 AT MILWAUKEE, WI  DIED IN '77
   FATHER: ALFRED LUNT, SR.
   MOTHER: HARRIET WASHBORN BRIGGS
   *** MARRIED:  '22 LYNN FONTANNE, ACTRESS AND PARTNER
   FRIEND: HELEN HAYES, ACTRESS
   RESIDENCE: GENESEE DEPOT, WI
   TALENT: ACTOR
   CREDIT:   '23 BACKBONE
   CREDIT:   '25 LOVERS IN QUARANTINE
   CREDIT:   '26 SALLY OF THE SAWDUST
   AA-NOM  ACTOR:  '31 THE GUARDSMAN
   CREDIT:   '43 STAGE DOOR CANTEEN
   CREDIT:   '58 THE VISIT, STAGE PLAY
```

LUPINO, IDA
                        FEB 04,'18 AT LONDON, ENGLAND
        GRANDFATHER: GEORGE LUPINO, ACTOR, DANCER
        FATHER: STANLEY LUPINO, ACTOR
        MOTHER: CONSTANCE O'SHAY
        SISTER: RITA LUPINO, ACTRESS
        UNCLE: LUPINO LANE, ACTOR, DIRECTOR
        UNCLE: WALLACE LUPINO, ACTOR
        UNCLE: BARRY LUPINO, ACTOR
        UNCLE: MARK LUPINO, ACTOR
        *** MARRIED: '38 LOUIS HAYWARD, ACTOR (DIVORCED '45)
        *** MARRIED: '48 COLLIER YOUNG (DIVORCED '50)
        *** MARRIED: '52 HOWARD DUFF, ACTOR (DIVORCED '54)
        DAUGHTER: BRIDGET MARELIA DUFF
        RESIDENCE: SANTA MONICA, CA
        POSSESSION: '51 PARTNER IN FOUR STAR PROD. CO. WITH BOYER, NIVEN & POWELL
        TALENT: ACTRESS-DIRECTOR-PRODUCER
        COMMENT: A THEATRICAL FAMILY FOR THREE CENTURIES IN ENGLAND
        CREDIT: '33 HER FIRST AFFAIR
        CREDIT: '41 HIGH SIERRA
        CREDIT: '42 THE HARD WAY
        CREDIT: '52 BEWARE MY LOVELY
        CREDIT: '72 JUNIOR BONNER

LYNDE, PAUL   BORN: PAUL EDWARD LYNDE
                        JUN 13,'26 AT MT. VERNON,OH
        FATHER: HOY LYNDE
        MOTHER: SYLVIA BELL
        BROTHER: RICHARD LYNDE
        BROTHER: CORD LYNDE
        BROTHER: JOHN LYNDE
        TALENT: ACTOR
        CREDIT: '54 NEW FACES
        CREDIT: '63 BYE BYE BIRDIE
        CREDIT: '64 SEND ME NO FLOWERS
        CREDIT: '66 THE GLASS BOTTOM BOAT
        CREDIT: '68 HOW SWEET IT IS

LYNLEY, CAROL   BORN: CAROLYN LEE JONES
                        FEB 13,'41 AT NYC
        FATHER: CYRIL JONES
        MOTHER: FRANCES PELTCH
        *** MARRIED: MICHAEL SELSMAN
        DAUGHTER: '62 JILL VICTORIA SELSMAN
        FRIEND: FRED ASTAIRE, DANCER
        TALENT: ACTRESS
        CREDIT: '58 THE LIGHT IN THE FOREST
        CREDIT: '59 BLUE DENIM
        CREDIT: '64 THE PLEASURE SEEKERS
        CREDIT: '65 HARLOW
        CREDIT: '69 THE MALTESE BIPPY

```
------------------------------------------------------------------------------
LYON, SUE
                         JUL 10,'46 AT DAVENPORT,IO
   *** MARRIED:  '63 HAMPTON FANCHER  (DIVORCED)
   *** MARRIED:  '71 ROLAND HARRISON  (DIVORCED)
   DAUGHTER:  '72 SUSAN HARRISON
   *** MARRIED:  '73 COTTON ADAMSON, CONVICTED MURDERER-WED IN JAIL
   RESIDENCE: LOS ANGELES, CA
   TALENT: ACTRESS
   CREDIT:  '62 LOLITA
   CREDIT:  '64 NIGHT OF THE IGUANA
   CREDIT:  '67 THE FLIM FLAM MAN
   CREDIT:  '67 TONY ROME
   CREDIT:  '72 EVIL KNIEVEL
```

MACDONALD, JEANETTE   BORN: JEANETTE ANNA MACDONALD
                                    JUN 18,'01 AT PHILADELPHIA,PA   DIED IN '65
FATHER: DANIEL MACDONALD
MOTHER: ANNA MAY WRIGHT
SISTER: BLOSSOM MACDONALD, ACTRESS
SISTER: ELSIE MACDONALD, DANCER
*** MARRIED: '37 GENE RAYMOND, ACTOR
FATHER-IN-LAW: LEROY D. GUION
MOTHER-IN-LAW: MARY SMITH
ROMANCE: ROBERT RITCHIE
RESIDENCE: LOS ANGELES, CA
POSSESSION: '33 CONTRACT AT M-G-M UNTIL 1942
POSSESSION: '53 DOCTORATE IN MUSIC HON. DEGREE - ITHACA COLLEGE
TALENT: ACTRESS-SINGER
CREDIT: '29 THE LOVE PARADE
CREDIT: '35 NAUGHTY MARIETTA
CREDIT: '37 THE FIREFLY
CREDIT: '42 I MARRIED AN ANGEL
CREDIT: '49 THE SUN COMES UP

MACGRAW, ALI   BORN: ALICE MACGRAW
                            APR 01,'39 AT POUND RIDGE, NY
BROTHER: RICHARD MACGRAW
*** MARRIED: '60 ROBIN HOEN (DIVORCED '62)
*** MARRIED: '69 ROBERT EVANS, PRODUCER (DIVORCED '73)
SON: '71 JOSHUA EVANS
*** MARRIED: '73 STEVE MCQUEEN, ACTOR (SEPARATED '78)
STEP-DAUGHTER: TERRY MCQUEEN
STEP-SON: CHADWICK MCQUEEN
ROMANCE: ROBIN CLARK, ACTOR
RESIDENCE: MALIBU, CA
TALENT: ACTRESS-MODEL
CREDIT: '68 A LOVELY WAY TO DIE
CREDIT: '69 GOODBYE COLUMBUS
AA-NOM ACTRESS: '70 LOVE STORY
CREDIT: '72 GETAWAY
CREDIT: '78 PLAYERS

MACK, WILLARD   BORN: CHARLES W. MCLAUGHLIN
                             1873 AT MORRISBURG, ONTARIO, CANADA   DIED IN '34
*** MARRIED: '12 MARJORIE RAMBEAU, ACTRESS (DIVORCED '17)
*** MARRIED: '17 PAULINE FREDERICKS, ACTRESS (DIVORCED '20)
RESIDENCE: NYC
POSSESSION: COUNTRY HOME AT DARIEN, CONN.
TALENT: ACTOR, WRITER
COMMENT: BECAME ADDICTED TO ALCOHOL AND DRUGS
CREDIT: '16 ALOHA OE
CREDIT: '23 YOUR FRIEND AND MINE
CREDIT: '33 BROADWAY TO HOLLYWOOD

MACLAINE, SHIRLEY   BORN: SHIRLEY MACLEAN BEATTY
                                 APR 24,'34 AT RICHMOND,VA
FATHER: IRA O. BEATTY, ORCHESTRA CONDUCTOR
MOTHER: KATHLYN MACLEAN, DANCER
BROTHER: WARREN BEATTY, ACTOR
*** MARRIED: '54 STEVE PARKER (SEPARATED '77)
DAUGHTER: '55 STEPHANIE SACHIKO PARKER

FRIEND: BELLA ABZUG, POLITICIAN
POSSESSION: '78 AMERICAN GUILD OF VARIETY ARTISTS 'GEORGIE' AWARD
MEMOIRS: '70 DON'T FALL OFF THE MOUNTAIN
MEMOIRS: '75 YOU CAN GET THERE FROM HERE
TALENT: ACTRESS-AUTHOR
CREDIT: '55 THE TROUBLE WITH HARRY
AA-NOM ACTRESS: '58 SOME CAME RUNNING
AA-NOM ACTRESS: '60 THE APARTMENT
CREDIT: '62 THE CHILDREN'S HOUR
AA-NOM ACTRESS: '63 IRMA LA DOUCE
CREDIT: '68 SWEET CHARITY
AA-NOM ACTRESS: '77 THE TURNING POINT

MACMURRAY, FRED   BORN: FREDERICK MARTIN MACMURRAY
                           AUG 30,'08 AT KANKAKEE,IL
FATHER: FREDERICK MACMURRAY, VIOLINIST
MOTHER: MALETA MARTIN
*** MARRIED: '36 LILLIAN LAMONT, DANCER (DIED '53)
ADOPTED DAUGHTER: SUSAN MACMURRAY
ADOPTED SON: ROBERT MACMURRAY
*** MARRIED: '54 JUNE HAVER, ACTRESS
ADOPTED DAUGHTER: LAURIE MACMURRAY, TWIN
ADOPTED DAUGHTER: KATHARINE MACMURRAY, TWIN
TALENT: ACTOR
CREDIT: '34 FRIENDS OF MR. SWEENEY, DEBUT
CREDIT: '44 DOUBLE INDEMNITY
CREDIT: '54 THE CAINE MUTINY
CREDIT: '60 THE APARTMENT
CREDIT: '67 THE HAPPIEST MILLIONAIRE
CREDIT: '78 THE SWARM

MACRAE, GORDON
                           MAR 12,'21 AT EAST ORANGE,NJ
FATHER: 'WEE WILLIE' MAC RAE, ACTOR
*** MARRIED: SHEILA MACRAE, ACTRESS, SINGER (DIVORCED)
DAUGHTER: '45 MEREDITH MACRAE
DAUGHTER: '68 HEATHER MACRAE
SON-IN-LAW: GREG MULLAVEY
SON: '46 GORDON MACRAE, JR. (MARRIED '70)
DAUGHTER-IN-LAW: MEGAN HANDSCHUMAKER
*** MARRIED: '67 ELIZABETH SCHRAFFT
SON: BRUCE MACRAE
TALENT: ACTOR-SINGER
CREDIT: '49 LOOK FOR THE SILVER LINING
CREDIT: '51 STARLIFT
CREDIT: '55 OKLAHOMA!
CREDIT: '56 THE BEST THINGS IN LIFE ARE FREE
CREDIT: '56 CAROUSEL

MADISON, GUY   BORN: ROBERT MOSELEY
                           JAN 19,'22 AT BAKERSFIELD, CA
FATHER: BENJAMIN J. MOSELY
*** MARRIED: '49 GAIL RUSSELL, ACTRESS (DIVORCED '54)
*** MARRIED: '55 SHEILA CONNOLLY (DIVORCED '63)
DAUGHTER: '55 BRIDGET CATHERINE MADISON
DAUGHTER: '56 ERIN PATRICIA MADISON
DAUGHTER: '57 'DOLLY' MADISON
TALENT: ACTOR

```
CREDIT:   '44 SINCE YOU WENT AWAY, DEBUT
CREDIT:   '46 TILL THE END OF TIME
CREDIT:   '56 THE LAST FRONTIER
CREDIT:   '58 BULLWHIP
CREDIT:   '66 THE MYSTERY OF THUG ISLAND
```

MAGNANI, ANNA
                    MAR 07,'07 AT ALEXANDRIA, EGYPT DIED IN '73
```
FATHER: FRANCESCO MAGNANI
MOTHER: MARINA CASADEI
*** MARRIED:  '35 GEOFFREDO ALESSANDRINI, DIRECTOR
SON:  '42 LUCA ALESSANDRINI
ROMANCE: ROBERTO ROSSELLINI, DIRECTOR
TALENT: ACTRESS
CREDIT:  '34 THE BLIND WOMEN OF SORRENTO, DEBUT
CREDIT:  '45 OPEN CITY
AA-WIN  ACTRESS:  '55 THE ROSE TATTOO
AA-NOM  ACTRESS:  '57 WILD IS THE WIND
CREDIT:  '69 SECRET OF SANTA VITTORIA
```

MAIN, MARJORIE   BORN: MARY TOMLINSON
                            FEB 24,'90 AT ACTON,IN DIED IN '75
```
FATHER: SAMUEL JOSEPH TOMLINSON, MINISTER
MOTHER: MARY MCGAUGHEY
*** MARRIED:  '21 DR. STANLEY LEFEVRE KREBS  (DIED '35)
DAUGHTER:  '22 ANNABELLE KREBS
PARTNER: PERCY KILBRIDE, ACTOR
RESIDENCE: PALM SPRINGS, CA
POSSESSION:  '40 CONTRACT AT M-G-M RENEWED IN 1947
TALENT: ACTRESS
CREDIT:  '33 TAKE A CHANCE, DEBUT
CREDIT:  '41 A WOMAN'S FACE
AA-NOM  SUP.ACT:  '47 THE EGG AND I
CREDIT:  '49 MA AND PA KETTLE, SERIES
CREDIT:  '56 FRIENDLY PERSUASION
```

MALDEN, KARL   BORN: MALDEN SEKULOVICH
                          MAR 22,'14 AT GARY, IN
```
FATHER: PETER SEKULOVICH
MOTHER: MINNIE SEBERA
BROTHER: MILO SEKULOVICH
BROTHER: DANIEL SEKULOVICH
*** MARRIED: '38 MONA GRAHAM
DAUGHTER:  '48 MILA MALDEN
DAUGHTER:  '53 CARLA MALDEN
RESIDENCE: NYC
TALENT: ACTOR
CREDIT:  '40 THEY KNEW WHAT THEY WANTED
AA-WIN  SUP.ACT:  '51 A STREETCAR NAMED DESIRE
AA-NOM  SUP.ACT:  '54 ON THE WATERFRONT
CREDIT:  '60 THE GREAT IMPOSTER
CREDIT:  '69 PATTON
CREDIT:  '71 WILD ROVERS
```

```
--------------------------------------------------------------------------------
MALONE, DOROTHY          BORN:  DOROTHY MALONEY
                                JAN 30,'25 AT CHICAGO,IL
   *** MARRIED:  '59 JACQUES BERGERAC, ACTOR  (DIVORCED '64)
   DAUGHTER:  '60 MIMI BERGERAC
   DAUGHTER:  '61 DIANE BERGERAC
   *** MARRIED:  '69 ROBERT TOMARKIN, (ANNULLED '69)
   *** MARRIED:  '71 CHARLES H. BELL
   RESIDENCE: DALLAS, TX
   TALENT: ACTRESS
   CREDIT:  '43 FALCON AND THE CO-EDS
   CREDIT:  '50 CONVICTED
   CREDIT:  '54 PUSHOVER
   AA-WIN  SUP.ACT.:  '56 WRITTEN ON THE WIND
   CREDIT:  '63 BEACH PARTY
--------------------------------------------------------------------------------
MANSFIELD, JAYNE         BORN:  JAYNE PALMER
                                APR 19,'32 AT BRYN MAWR, PA   DIED IN '67
   *** MARRIED:  '50 PAUL MANSFIELD
   DAUGHTER:  '51 JAYNE MARIE MANSFIELD, ACTRESS
   *** MARRIED:  '58 MICHAEL HARGITAY, ACTOR, MR. UNIVERSE
   SON:  '58 MIKLOS HARGITAY
   SON:  '60 ZOL'TAN HARGITAY
   DAUGHTER:  '63 MARIA HARGITAY
   *** MARRIED:  '64 MATT CIMBER, DIRECTOR
   SON:  '65 ANTONIO CIMBER.
   ROMANCE: SAM BRODY
   RESIDENCE: HOLMBY HILLS, CA
   TALENT: ACTRESS
   COMMENT: MISS 40-21-35 1/2
   CREDIT:  '55 UNDERWATER
   CREDIT:  '56 ILLEGAL
   CREDIT:  '60 TOO HOT TO HANDLE
   CREDIT:  '64 PANIC BUTTON
   CREDIT:  '67 A GUIDE FOR THE MARRIED MAN
--------------------------------------------------------------------------------
MARCH,  FREDRIC          BORN:  ERNEST FREDRIC MCINTYRE BICKEL
                                AUG 31,'97 AT RACINE, WI   DIED IN '75
   FATHER: JOHN F. BICKEL, BUSINESSMAN
   MOTHER: CORA MARCHER
   SISTER: ELIZABETH BICKEL
   BROTHER: HAROLD BICKEL
   BROTHER: JOHN BICKEL
   *** MARRIED:  '24 ELLIS BAKER  (DIVORCED '27)
   *** MARRIED:  '27 FLORENCE ELDRIDGE, ACTRESS
   ADOPTED DAUGHTER: PENELOPE MARCH
   ADOPTED SON: ANTHONY MARCH
   RESIDENCE: NEW MILFORD,CN
   BIOGRAPHY:  '71 THE FILMS OF FREDRIC MARCH, BY LAWRENCE J. QUIRK
   TALENT: ACTOR
   AA-NOM  ACTOR:  '30 THE ROYAL FAMILY OF BROADWAY
   AA-WIN  ACTOR:  '31 DR. JEKYLL AND MR. HYDE
   AA-NOM  ACTOR:  '37 A STAR IS BORN
   CREDIT:  '39 LES MISERABLES
   AA-WIN  ACTOR:  '46 THE BEST YEARS OF OUR LIVES
   AA-NOM  ACTOR:  '51 DEATH OF A SALESMAN
```

MARSH, MAE   BORN: MARY WARNE MARSH
                              NOV 09,'95 AT MADRID, NM   DIED IN '68
    FATHER: CHARLES MARSH
    MOTHER: MARY WARNE
    SISTER: LOVEY MARSH
    SISTER: MARGARET MARSH, ACTRESS
    *** MARRIED: '18 LOUIS LEE ARMS, PUBLICIST
    DAUGHTER: MARY MARSH ARMS
    DAUGHTER: MARGUERITE LOUISE ARMS
    SON: BREWSTER ARMS, LAWYER
    RESIDENCE: HERMOSA BEACH, CA
    TALENT: ACTRESS
    COMMENT: KNOWN AS 'THE GOLDWYN GIRL'
    CREDIT: '12 MAN'S GENESIS
    CREDIT: '31 OVER THE HILL
    CREDIT: '48 THE SNAKEPIT
    CREDIT: '58 CRY TERROR
    CREDIT: '68 ARABELLA

MARSHALL, E. G.   BORN: EVERETT G. MARSHALL
                              JUN 18,'10 AT AWATONNA,MN
    FATHER: CHARLES G. MARSHALL
    MOTHER: HAZEL IRENE COBB
    *** MARRIED: '39 HELEN WOLF (DIVORCED '53)
    DAUGHTER: JILL MARSHALL
    SON: DEGEN MARSHALL
    TALENT: ACTOR
    CREDIT: '45 THE HOUSE ON 92ND STREET, DEBUT
    CREDIT: '55 PUSHOVER
    CREDIT: '57 TWELVE ANGRY MEN
    CREDIT: '66 THE CHASE
    CREDIT: '71 THE PURSUIT OF HAPPINESS

MARSHALL, HERBERT
                        MAY 23,'90 AT LONDON, ENGLAND   DIED IN '66
    *** MARRIED: '15 MOLLY MAITLAND (DIVORCED '28)
    *** MARRIED: '28 EDNA SARAH BEST, ACTRESS (DIVORCED '40)
    DAUGHTER: '29 SARAH BEST MARSHALL, ACTRESS
    *** MARRIED: '40 LEE RUSSELL (DIVORCED '46)
    DAUGHTER: '41 ANN MARSHALL
    *** MARRIED: '48 PATRICIA 'BOOTS' MALLORY, ACTRESS (DIED '58)
    *** MARRIED: '60 DEE KAHMANN
    TALENT: ACTOR
    CREDIT: '27 MUMSIE
    CREDIT: '39 ZAZA
    CREDIT: '42 THE MOON AND SIXPENCE
    CREDIT: '55 THE VIRGIN QUEEN
    CREDIT: '65 THE THIRD DAY

MARTIN, DEAN   BORN: DINO PAUL CROCETTI
                              JUN 17,'17 AT STEUBENVILLE,OH
    FATHER: GUY CROCETTI
    *** MARRIED: '40 BETTY MCDONALD (DIVORCED '49)
    DAUGHTER: '41 GAIL MARTIN
    SON-IN-LAW: PAUL POLENA (MARRIED '73)
    DAUGHTER: '42 DEANA MARTIN
    SON-IN-LAW: TERENCE GUERIN (MARRIED '69)

```
SON:  '43 CRAIG MARTIN
DAUGHTER:  '46 CLAUDIA MARTIN
SON-IN-LAW: KIEL MULLER  (MARRIED '69)
SON-IN-LAW: VINCENT LUCCHESI  (MARRIED '73)
*** MARRIED:  '49 JEANNE BIEGGERS, MODEL  (DIVORCED '69)
SON:  '51 DEAN 'DINO' MARTIN, JR.
DAUGHTER-IN-LAW: OLIVIA HUSSEY, ACTRESS
SON:  '53 RICCI MARTIN
DAUGHTER:  '56 GINA MARTIN
*** MARRIED:  '73 KATHY HAWN  (DIVORCED '76)
ROMANCE: PHYLLIS DAVIS, ACTRESS
PARTNER: JERRY LEWIS
POSSESSION: DINO'S LODGE, RESTAURANT IN LA
TALENT: SINGER-ACTOR
CREDIT:  '49 MY FRIEND IRMA
CREDIT:  '54 LIVING IT UP
CREDIT:  '64 KISS ME STUPID
CREDIT:  '68 HOW TO SAVE A MARRIAGE
CREDIT:  '69 AIRPORT
CREDIT:  '72 MATT HELM (SERIES)
```

```
MARTIN, MARY        BORN:  MARY VIRGINIA MARTIN
                           DEC 01,'13 AT WEATHERFORD,TX
    FATHER: PRESTON MARTIN, LAWYER
    MOTHER: JUNITA PRESSLEY
    *** MARRIED:  '35 BENJAMIN HAGMAN
    SON:  '36 LARRY HAGMAN, ACTOR
    *** MARRIED:  '40 RICHARD HALLIDAY, PRODUCER  (DIED '73)
    DAUGHTER:  '41 HELLER HALLIDAY
    SON-IN-LAW: BROMLEY DEMERITT, JR.  (MARRIED '73)
    RESIDENCE: NYC
    MEMOIRS: MY HEART BELONGS
    TALENT: ACTRESS-SINGER
    CREDIT:  '39 THE GREAT VICTOR HERBERT
    CREDIT:  '40 LOVE THY NEIGHBOR
    CREDIT:  '41 BIRTH OF THE BLUES
    CREDIT:  '42 HAPPY GO LUCKY
    CREDIT:  '53 MAIN STREET TO BROADWAY
```

```
MARTIN, TONY        BORN:  ALFRED MORRIS
                           DEC 25,'13 AT SAN FRANCISCO, CA
    FATHER: EDWARD MORRIS MARTIN
    MOTHER: HATTIE SMITH
    *** MARRIED:  '37 ALICE FAYE  (DIVORCED '40)
    BROTHER-IN-LAW: WILLIAM LEPPERT, TALENT AGENT
    *** MARRIED:  '48 CYD CHARISSE, DANCER
    STEP-SON: NICKY CHARISSE
    SON:  '50 TONY MARTIN, JR.
    MEMOIRS:  '76 THE TWO OF US
    TALENT: ACTOR
    CREDIT:  '36 SING, BABY, SING
    CREDIT:  '40 MUSIC IN MY HEART
    CREDIT:  '48 CASBAH
    CREDIT:  '53 HERE COME THE GIRLS
    CREDIT:  '57 LET'S BE HAPPY
```

MARVIN, LEE
                              FEB 19,'24 AT NYC
        FATHER: LAMONT W. MARVIN
        MOTHER: COURTNAY
        BROTHER: ROBERT MARVIN
        *** MARRIED: '51 BETTY EDELING (DIVORCED '67)
        SON: '52 CHRISTOPHER MARVIN
        DAUGHTER: '54 COURTENAY MARVIN
        DAUGHTER: '56 CYNTHIA MARVIN
        DAUGHTER: '58 CLAUDIA MARVIN
        *** MARRIED: '70 PAMELA FREELEY
        ROMANCE: MICHELLE TRIOLA MARVIN
        RESIDENCE: MALIBU,CA
        TALENT: ACTOR
        CREDIT: '51 YOU'RE IN THE NAVY NOW
        CREDIT: '55 NOT AS A STRANGER
        CREDIT: '57 ATTACK
        AA-WIN ACTOR: '65 CAT BALLOU
        CREDIT: '73 THE ICEMAN COMETH

MARX, CHICO   BORN: LEONARD MARX
                              MAR 22,'87 AT NYC DIED IN '61
        FATHER: SAMUEL MARX, TAILOR
        MOTHER: MINNIE SCHOENBERG
        BROTHER: ZEPPO MARX
        BROTHER: HARPO MARX
        BROTHER: GROUCHO MARX
        BROTHER: GUMMO MARX
        SISTER-IN-LAW: RUTH JOHNSON
        SISTER-IN-LAW: KATHERINE MARVIS
        SISTER-IN-LAW: EDEN HARTFORD
        SISTER-IN-LAW: SUSAN FLEMING
        SISTER-IN-LAW: MARIAN BENDA
        SISTER-IN-LAW: BARBARA BLAKELY
        NIECE: MIRIAM MARX
        NIECE: KAY MARX
        NIECE: MINNIE MARX, TWIN
        NIECE: MELINDA MARX
        NEPHEW: ARTHUR MARX, WRITER
        NEPHEW: ROBERT MARX
        NEPHEW: TIMOTHY MARX
        NEPHEW: WILLIAM MARX, PIANIST
        NEPHEW: ALEXANDER MARX
        NEPHEW: JAMES MARX, TWIN
        UNCLE: AL SHEAN
        *** MARRIED: '10 BETTY KARP
        DAUGHTER: '11 MAXINE MARX
        *** MARRIED: '58 MARY DIVITHAS
        TALENT: ACTOR
        CREDIT: '29 THE COCONUTS, MARX BROTHERS
        CREDIT: '30 ANIMAL CRACKERS, MARX BROTHERS
        CREDIT: '31 MONKEY BUSINESS, MARX BROTHERS
        CREDIT: '33 DUCK SOUP, MARX BROTHERS
        CREDIT: '35 A NIGHT AT THE OPERA, HARPO, CHICO, GROUCHO

```
--------------------------------------------------------------------------------
MARX, GROUCHO        BORN:  JULIUS HENRY MARX
                           OCT 02,'90 AT NYC  DIED IN '77
     FATHER: SAMUEL MARX, TAILOR
     MOTHER: MINNIE SCHOENBERG
     BROTHER: ZEPPO MARX
     BROTHER: CHICO MARX
     BROTHER: HARPO MARX
     BROTHER: GUMMO MARX
     SISTER-IN-LAW: BETTY KARP
     SISTER-IN-LAW: MARY DIVITHAS
     SISTER-IN-LAW: MARIAN BENDA
     SISTER-IN-LAW: BARBARA BLAKELY
     NIECE: MAXINE MARX
     NIECE: KAY MARX
     NIECE: MINNIE MARX, TWIN
     NEPHEW: ROBERT MARX
     NEPHEW: TIMOTHY MARX
     NEPHEW: WILLIAM MARX, PIANIST
     NEPHEW: ALEXANDER MARX
     NEPHEW: JAMES MARX, TWIN
     UNCLE: AL SHEAN, COMIC-PARTNER OF ED GALLAGHER
     *** MARRIED:  '20 RUTH JOHNSON  (DIVORCED '42)
     SON:  '25 ARTHUR MARX, WRITER
     DAUGHTER-IN-LAW: IRENE KAHN  (MARRIED)
     DAUGHTER:  '32 MIRIAM MARX
     *** MARRIED:  '45 KATHERINE MARVIS  (DIVORCED '51)
     DAUGHTER:  '45 MELINDA MARX
     SON-IN-LAW: MACK GILBERT  (MARRIED '68)
     *** MARRIED:  '54 EDEN HARTFORD  (DIVORCED '70)
     GRANDSON:  '50 ANDREW MARX
     FRIEND: NAT PERRIN, WRITER
     FRIEND: ERIN FLEMING
     RESIDENCE: BEVERLY HILLS, CA
     MEMOIRS:  '64 MEMOIRS OF A MANGY LOVER
     MEMOIRS:  '76 THE GROUCHO PHILE
     MEMOIRS: BEDS
     TALENT: ACTOR
     CREDIT:  '47 YOU BET YOUR LIFE, TV & RADIO QUIZ SHOW
     CREDIT:  '51 DOUBLE DYNAMITE
     CREDIT:  '68 SKIDOO
     AA-SPECIAL AWARD:  '73 HONORARY AWARD FOR 'BRILLIANT CREATIVITY' IN COMEDY
--------------------------------------------------------------------------------
MARX, GUMMO         BORN:  MILTON MARX
                           1893 AT NYC  DIED IN '77
     FATHER: SAMUEL MARX, TAILOR
     MOTHER: MINNIE SCHOENBERG
     BROTHER: ZEPPO MARX
     BROTHER: CHICO MARX
     BROTHER: HARPO MARX
     BROTHER: GROUCHO MARX
     SISTER-IN-LAW: BETTY KARP
     SISTER-IN-LAW: MARY DIVITHAS
     SISTER-IN-LAW: SUSAN FLEMING
     SISTER-IN-LAW: MARIAN BENDA
     SISTER-IN-LAW: BARBARA BLAKELY
     SISTER-IN-LAW: RUTH JOHNSON
     SISTER-IN-LAW: KATHERINE MARVIS
```

SISTER-IN-LAW: EDEN HARTFORD
NIECE: MAXINE MARX
NIECE: MIRIAM MARX
NIECE: MINNIE MARX, TWIN
NIECE: MELINDA MARX
NEPHEW: ARTHUR MARX
NEPHEW: TIMOTHY MARX
NEPHEW: WILLIAM MARX, PIANIST
NEPHEW: ALEXANDER MARX
NEPHEW: JAMES MARX, TWIN
UNCLE: AL SHEAN
*** MARRIED: HELEN
DAUGHTER: KAY MARX
SON: ROBERT MARX
RESIDENCE: PALM SPRINGS, CA
TALENT: ACTOR, AGENT
COMMENT: LEFT THE ACT IN EARLY '30'S

MARX, HARPO   BORN: ADOLPH ARTHUR MARX
                              NOV 23,'88 AT NYC DIED IN '64
FATHER: SAMUEL MARX, TAILOR
MOTHER: MINNIE SCHOENBERG
BROTHER: ZEPPO MARX
BROTHER: CHICO MARX
BROTHER: GROUCHO MARX
BROTHER: GUMMO MARX
SISTER-IN-LAW: BETTY KARP
SISTER-IN-LAW: MARY DIVITHAS
SISTER-IN-LAW: MARIAN BENDA
SISTER-IN-LAW: BARBARA BLAKELY
SISTER-IN-LAW: RUTH JOHNSON
SISTER-IN-LAW: KATHERINE MARVIS
SISTER-IN-LAW: EDEN HARTFORD
NIECE: MAXINE MARX
NIECE: KAY MARX
NIECE: MIRIAM MARX
NIECE: MELINDA MARX
NEPHEW: ARTHUR MARX, WRITER
NEPHEW: ROBERT MARX
UNCLE: AL SHEAN, COMIC
*** MARRIED: '36 SUSAN FLEMING
ADOPTED SON: WILLIAM MARX, PIANIST
ADOPTED SON: ALEXANDER MARX
ADOPTED DAUGHTER: MINNIE MARX, TWIN
ADOPTED SON: JAMES MARX, TWIN
RESIDENCE: BEVERLY HILLS, CA
POSSESSION: '48 PRIMITIVE PAINTINGS COLLECTION
MEMOIRS: HARPO SPEAKS!
TALENT: ACTOR
CREDIT: TOO MANY KISSES, DEBUT

MARX, ZEPPO   BORN: HERBERT MARX
                              FEB 25,'01 AT NYC
FATHER: SAMUEL MARX, TAILOR
MOTHER: MINNIE SCHOENBERG
BROTHER: CHICO MARX
BROTHER: HARPO MARX
BROTHER: GROUCHO MARX

```
BROTHER: GUMMO MARX
SISTER-IN-LAW: BETTY KARP
SISTER-IN-LAW: MARY DIVITHAS
SISTER-IN-LAW: SUSAN FLEMING
SISTER-IN-LAW: RUTH JOHNSON
SISTER-IN-LAW: KATHERINE MARVIS
SISTER-IN-LAW: EDEN HARTFORD
NIECE: MAXINE MARX
NIECE: KAY MARX
NIECE: MIRIAM MARX
NIECE: MINNIE MARX, TWIN
NIECE: MELINDA MARX
NEPHEW: ARTHUR MARX
NEPHEW: ROBERT MARX
NEPHEW: WILLIAM MARX, PIANIST
NEPHEW: ALEXANDER MARX
NEPHEW: JAMES MARX, TWIN
UNCLE: AL SHEAN, COMIC
*** MARRIED:  '27 MARIAN BENDA  (DIVORCED '54)
BROTHER-IN-LAW: ALLAN 'PINKY' MILLER
SON:  '28 TIMOTHY MARX
*** MARRIED:  '59 BARBARA BLAKELY  (DIVORCED)
RESIDENCE: PALM SPRINGS, CA
TALENT: ACTOR
COMMENT: LEFT ACT AFTER 'DUCK SOUP'
```

MASON, JAMES   BORN: JAMES NEVILLE MASON
                                  MAY 15,'09 AT HUDDERSFIELD, YORKS., ENGLAND
```
FATHER: JOHN MASON
MOTHER: MABEL HATTERSLEY GAUNT
*** MARRIED:  '40 PAMELA OSTRER, ACTRESS - PAMELA KELLINO  (DIVORCED '64)
DAUGHTER:  '48 PORTLAND MASON
SON:  '49 ALEXANDER MORGAN MASON
*** MARRIED:  '71 CLARISSA KAYE
FRIEND: PORTLAND HOFFA
RESIDENCE: CLARENS, LAKE GENEVA, SWITZERLAND
POSSESSION:  '47 COLLECTION OF PUSSYCATS
POSSESSION: FARM IN HERTFORDSHIRE, ENGLAND
MEMOIRS: THE CATS IN OUR LIVES
TALENT: ACTOR
CREDIT:  '35 LATE EXTRA
CREDIT:  '49 CAUGHT
AA-NOM  ACTOR:  '54 A STAR IS BORN
AA-NOM  SUP.ACT:  '66 GEORGY GIRL
CREDIT:  '78 HEAVEN CAN WAIT
```

MASON, MARSHA
                          APR 03,'43 AT ST. LOUIS, MR
```
FATHER: JAMES 'JIM' MASON
*** MARRIED:  '73 NEIL SIMON, PLAYRIGHT
RESIDENCE: LOS ANGELES, CA
TALENT: ACTRESS
CREDIT:  '72 BLUME IN LOVE, DEBUT
AA-NOM  ACTRESS:  '73 CINDERELLA LIBERTY
AA-NOM  ACTRESS:  '77 THE GOODBYE GIRL
CREDIT:  '78 THE CHEAP DETECTIVE
CREDIT:  '79 PROMISES IN THE DARK
```

MASON, PAMELA   BORN: PAMELA OSTRER
                                  MAR 10,'18 AT WESTGATE, ENGLAND
     FATHER: ISADORE OSTRER
     MOTHER: HELEN SPEAR MORGAN
     *** MARRIED: ROY KELLINO
     *** MARRIED: '40 JAMES MASON, ACTOR (DIVORCED '64)
     DAUGHTER: '48 PORTLAND MASON
     SON: '49 ALEXANDER MORGAN MASON
     TALENT: WRITER-ACTRESS
     COMMENT: AKA PAMELA KELLINO
     CREDIT: '36 THE LUCK OF THE DEVIL, DEBUT
     CREDIT: '38 I MET A MURDERER
     CREDIT: '44 THEY WERE SISTERS
     CREDIT: '46 THE UPTURNED GLASS
     CREDIT: '51 LADY POSSESSED

MASSEY, ILONA   BORN: ILONA HAJMASSY
                                  JUL 05,'12 AT BUDAPEST,HUNGARY
     FATHER: FRANCIS HAJMASSY
     MOTHER: LIDIA KISS
     *** MARRIED: NICHOLAS SZAVOZD (DIVORCED)
     *** MARRIED: '41 ALAN CURTIS, ACTOR (DIVORCED '42)
     *** MARRIED: '52 CHARLES WALKER (DIVORCED '55)
     *** MARRIED: '55 GENERAL DONALD S. DAWSON
     ROMANCE: MICHAEL WHALEN, ACTOR
     RESIDENCE: BETHESDA, MD
     TALENT: SINGER-ACTRESS ANTI-COMMUNIST
     CREDIT: '37 ROSALIE
     CREDIT: '41 INTERNATIONAL LADY
     CREDIT: '47 END OF THE RAINBOW
     CREDIT: '50 LOVE HAPPY
     CREDIT: '59 JET OVER THE ATLANTIC

MASSEY, RAYMOND   BORN: RAYMOND HART MASSEY
                                    AUG 30,'96 AT TORONTO,ONTARIO,CANADA
     FATHER: CHESTER D. MASSEY
     MOTHER: ANNA VINCENT
     BROTHER: VINCENT MASSEY, GOVERNMENT OFFICER
     *** MARRIED: '21 MARGERY HILDA FREMANTLE (DIVORCED '29)
     FATHER-IN-LAW: ADMIRAL SIR SIDNEY FREMANTLE, NAVY OFFICER
     SON: '22 GEOFFREY MASSEY
     *** MARRIED: '29 ADRIENNE ALLEN (DIVORCED '39)
     DAUGHTER: '30 ANNA MASSEY
     SON: '31 DANIEL MASSEY
     *** MARRIED: '39 DOROTHY LUDINGTON
     RESIDENCE: NYC
     TALENT: ACTOR
     CREDIT: '31 THE SPECKLED BAND
     AA-NOM ACTOR: '40 ABE LINCOLN IN ILLINOIS
     CREDIT: '41 DANGEROUSLY THEY LIVE
     CREDIT: '55 EAST OF EDEN
     CREDIT: '68 MACKENNA'S GOLD

MASTROIANNI, MARCELLO
                              SEP 28,'24 AT FROSINONE, ITALY
  FATHER: OTTONE MASTROIANNI, CARPENTER
  MOTHER: IDA IROLLE
  *** MARRIED: '50 FLORA CARABELLA
  DAUGHTER: '51 BARBARA MASTROIANNI
  DAUGHTER: '72 CHIARA-CHARLOTTE DENEUVE
  ROMANCE: CATHERINE DENEUVE
  RESIDENCE: ROME, ITALY
  TALENT: ACTOR
  CREDIT: '49 SUNDAY IN AUGUST
  CREDIT: '59 LA DOLCE VITA
  AA-NOM ACTOR: '62 DIVORCE - ITALIAN STYLE
  CREDIT: '67 THE STRANGER
  CREDIT: '70 LEO THE LAST
  AA-NOM ACTOR: '77 A SPECIAL DAY

MATTHAU, WALTER   BORN: WALTER MATTHOW
                              OCT 01,'20 AT NYC
  FATHER: MILTON MATUSCHANSKAYASKY, AKA MATTHOW
  MOTHER: ROSE BEROLSKY
  BROTHER: HENRY MATTHOW
  *** MARRIED: '48 GRACE GERALDINE JOHNSON (DIVORCED '58)
  SON: '49 DAVID MATTHAU
  DAUGHTER: '50 JENNIFER MATTHAU
  *** MARRIED: '59 CAROL GRACE MARCUS SAROYAN
  SON: '60 CHARLES MATTHAU
  STEP-SON: ARAN SAROYAN
  PARTNER: TONY RANDALL
  POSSESSION: CLASSICAL MUSIC COLLECTION
  TALENT: ACTOR
  CREDIT: '55 THE KENTUCKIAN
  AA-WIN SUP.ACT.: '66 THE FORTUNE COOKIE
  CREDIT: '68 THE ODD COUPLE
  AA-NOM ACTOR: '71 KOTCH
  AA-NOM ACTOR: '75 THE SUNSHINE BOYS

MATURE, VICTOR   BORN: VICTOR JOHN MATURE
                              JAN 29,'16 AT LOUISVILLE, KT
  FATHER: M. G. MATURE
  MOTHER: CLARA
  *** MARRIED: '38 FRANCES CHARLES, ACTRESS-FRANCES EVANS (DIVORCED '40)
  *** MARRIED: '41 MARTHA STEPHENSON KEMP (DIVORCED '43)
  *** MARRIED: '48 DOROTHY STEPHEN BERRY (DIVORCED '55)
  *** MARRIED: '59 ADRIANNE JOY URWICK
  *** MARRIED: '74 LOREY
  DAUGHTER: '75 VICTORIA MATURE, HIS FIRST CHILD
  RESIDENCE: RANCHO SANTA FE, CA
  TALENT: ACTOR
  COMMENT: KNOWN AS 'THE HUNK'
  CREDIT: '39 THE HOUSEKEEPER'S DAUGHTER
  CREDIT: '46 MY DARLING CLEMENTINE
  CREDIT: '53 THE ROBE
  CREDIT: '66 AFTER THE FOX
  CREDIT: '72 EVERY LITTLE CROOK AND NANNY

MAXWELL, MARILYN   BORN: MARVEL MARILYN MAXWELL
                          AUG 03,'22 AT CLARINDA, IO DIED IN '72
*** MARRIED: '44 JOHN CONTE, ACTOR (DIVORCED '46)
*** MARRIED: '49 ANDERS MCINTYRE (DIVORCED '50)
*** MARRIED: '54 JEROME 'JERRY' DAVIS, WRITER (DIVORCED '60)
SON: '56 MATTHEW PAUL DAVIS
FRIEND: ROCK HUDSON
TALENT: SINGER-ACTRESS
CREDIT: '42 SWING FEVER
CREDIT: '54 OFF LIMITS
CREDIT: '58 ROCK-A-BYE-BABY
CREDIT: '62 CRITIC'S CHOICE
CREDIT: '64 STAGECOACH TO HELL

MAY, ELAINE   BORN: ELAINE BERLIN
                     APR 21,'32 AT PHILADELPHIA,PA
FATHER: JOHN BERLIN, ACTOR
*** MARRIED: '52 MARVIN MAY
DAUGHTER: '53 JEAN BESLIN MAY
*** MARRIED: '60 SHELDON HARNICK
*** MARRIED: '63 DR. REUBEN FINE
PARTNER: MIKE NICHOLS
TALENT: ACTRESS-WRITER-DIRECTOR
CREDIT: '67 LUV
CREDIT: '67 ENTER LAUGHING
CREDIT: '71 A NEW LEAF - ACTED, WROTE,DIRECTED
CREDIT: '72 SUCH GOOD FRIENDS, WROTE

MAYER, LOUIS B.   BORN: LAZARUS MAYER
                         JUL 04,'85 AT DEMRE, LITHUANIA DIED IN '57
FATHER: JACOB MAYER
MOTHER: SARAH
SISTER: YETTA MAYER
SISTER: IDA MAYER
BROTHER-IN-LAW: JACK CUMMINGS, PRODUCER
BROTHER: RUDOLPH 'RUDY' MAYER
BROTHER: JERRY G. MAYER
*** MARRIED: '04 MARGARET SHENBERG
DAUGHTER: '05 EDITH MAYER
SON-IN-LAW: WILLIAM GOETZ, PRODUCER
DAUGHTER: '07 IRENE MAYER
SON-IN-LAW: DAVID O. SELZNICK, PRODUCER
*** MARRIED: '48 LORENA DANKER
FRIEND: JEAN HOWARD
FRIEND: HERBERT HOOVER
PARTNER: IRVING THALBERG
PARTNER: MARCUS LOEW
RESIDENCE: SANTA MONICA, CA
BIOGRAPHY: '75 MAYER AND THALBERG, BY SAMUEL MARX
TALENT: EXECUTIVE
AA-SPECIAL AWARD: '50 HONORARY AWARD FOR DISTINGUISH SERVICE TO THE FILM INDUSTRY

```
----------------------------------------------------------------------------------------
MAYO, VIRGINIA          BORN:  VIRGINIA JONES
                               NOV 30,'20 AT ST. LOUIS, MR
  *** MARRIED:  '47 MICHAEL O'SHEA, ACTOR  (DIED '73)
  DAUGHTER:  '53 MARY O'SHEA
  RESIDENCE: LOS ANGELES, CA
  POSSESSION:  '48 CONTRACT AT WARNER BROS.
  TALENT: ACTRESS
  CREDIT:  '44 UP IN ARMS
  CREDIT:  '49 THE GIRL FROM JONES BEACH
  CREDIT:  '56 CONGO CROSSING
  CREDIT:  '65 YOUNG FURY
----------------------------------------------------------------------------------------
MAZURKI, MIKE           BORN:  MIKHAIL MAZURWSKI
                               DEC 25,'09 AT TARNOPAL, AUSTRIA
  *** MARRIED:  '45 JEANETTE BRIGGS
  *** MARRIED:  '68 SYLVIA WEINBLATT
  TALENT: WRESTLER-ACTOR
  CREDIT:  '41 THE SHANGHAI GESTURE, DEBUT
  CREDIT:  '47 UNCONQUERED
  CREDIT:  '56 DAVY CROCKETT
  CREDIT:  '63 DONOVAN'S REEF
  CREDIT:  '66 SEVEN WOMEN
----------------------------------------------------------------------------------------
MCCALLUM, DAVID
                               SEP 19,'33 AT GLASGOW, SCOTLAND
  *** MARRIED:  '57 JILL IRELAND, ACTRESS  (DIVORCED)
  FATHER-IN-LAW: JOHN ALFRED IRELAND
  MOTHER-IN-LAW: DOROTHY CONNOLL EBORN
  SON:  '58 PAUL MCCALLUM
  SON:  '59 JASON MCCALLUM
  SON:  '60 VALENTINE MCCALLUM
  *** MARRIED:  '67 KATE CARPENTER, MODEL
  RESIDENCE: SANTA MONICA, CA
  TALENT: ACTOR
  CREDIT:  '50 PRELUDE TO FAME
  CREDIT:  '58 VIOLENT PLAYGROUND
  CREDIT:  '62 BILLY BUDD
  CREDIT:  '63 THE GREAT ESCAPE
  CREDIT:  '70 THE RAVINE
----------------------------------------------------------------------------------------
MCCAMBRIDGE, MERCEDES   BORN:  CARLOTTA MERCEDES MCCAMBRIDGE
                               MAR 17,'18 AT JOLIET, IL
  FATHER: JOHN PATRICK MCCAMBRIDGE
  MOTHER: MARIE MAHAFFRY
  *** MARRIED:  '40 WILLIAM FIFIELD  (DIVORCED '46)
  SON:  '41 JON FIFIELD
  *** MARRIED:  '50 FLETCHER MARKLE  (DIVORCED '62)
  MEMOIRS:  '61 THE TWO OF US
  TALENT: ACTRESS
  AA-WIN  SUP.ACT.:  '49 ALL THE KING'S MEN
  CREDIT:  '54 JOHNNY GUITAR
  AA-NOM  SUP.ACT:  '56 GIANT
  CREDIT:  '59 SUDDENLY LAST SUMMER
  CREDIT:  '69 WOMEN
```

MCCARTNEY, PAUL   BORN: JAMES PAUL MCCARTNEY
                             JUN 18,'42 AT LIVERPOOL, ENGLAND
    FATHER: JAMES MCCARTNEY, SALESMAN
    MOTHER: --, NURSE
    STEP-SISTER: RUTH MCCARTNEY, SINGER
    BROTHER: MICHAEL MCCARTNEY
    *** MARRIED: '69 LINDA EASTMAN
    DAUGHTER: '69 MARY MCCARTNEY
    DAUGHTER: '71 STELLA MCCARTNEY
    SON: '77 JAMES LOUIS MCCARTNEY
    PARTNER: GEORGE HARRISON, IN THE BEATLES & THE APPLE CO.
    PARTNER: JOHN LENNON, IN THE BEATLES & THE APPLE CO.
    PARTNER: RINGO STARR, IN THE BEATLES & THE APPLE CO.
    RESIDENCE: WEYBRIDGE, ENGLAND
    TALENT: GUITARIST, COMPOSER, ACTOR
    CREDIT: '64 A HARD DAY'S NIGHT, WITH BEATLES
    CREDIT: '65 HELP!, WITH BEATLES

MCCOY, "COLONEL" TIM
                             APR 10,'91 AT SAGINAW, MH
    FATHER: --, POLICE CHIEF
    *** MARRIED: '10 AGNES MILLER (DIVORCED '28)
    SON: '11 RONALD MCCOY
    SON: '12 TERENCE MICHAEL MCCOY
    *** MARRIED: '45 INGA ARVAD, JOURNALIST (DIED '73)
    SON: '47 TIMOTHY MCCOY
    RESIDENCE: NOGALES, AR
    MEMOIRS: '77 TIM MCCOY REMEMBERS THE WEST
    TALENT: ACTOR
    COMMENT: AKA - HIGH EAGLE OF THE ARAPHAHOE INDIAN TRIBE
    COMMENT: LT. COLONEL IN U.S. ARMY WAS EARNED RANK
    CREDIT: '26 WAR PAINT
    CREDIT: '31 THE FIGHTING FOOL
    CREDIT: '32 TEXAS CYCLONE
    CREDIT: '34 HELL BENT FOR LOVE
    CREDIT: '65 REQUIEM FOR A GUNFIGHTER

MCCREA, JOEL
                             NOV 05,'05 AT LOS ANGELES
    *** MARRIED: '33 FRANCES DEE, ACTRESS
    SON: '34 JODY MCCREA, ACTOR
    SON: '35 DAVID MCCREA, RANCHER
    SON: '55 PETER MCCREA
    ROMANCE: CONSTANCE BENNETT
    ROMANCE: GLORIA SWANSON
    ROMANCE: DOROTHY MACKAILL
    FRIEND: CECIL B. DE MILLE
    FRIEND: WILL ROGERS
    RESIDENCE: RANCH IN CAMARILLO,CA
    TALENT: ACTOR
    COMMENT: NATIONAL COWBOY HALL OF FAME PRESIDENT
    CREDIT: '23 PENROD AND SAM
    CREDIT: '32 BIRD OF PARADISE
    CREDIT: '42 THE PALM BEACH STORY
    CREDIT: '55 STRANGER ON HORSEBACK
    CREDIT: '62 RIDE THE HIGH COUNTRY

```
-------------------------------------------------------------------
MCDANIEL,  HATTIE
                      JUN 10,'95 AT WICHITA, KA   DIED IN '52
    FATHER: REV. HENRY MCDANIEL, MINISTER
    MOTHER: SUSAN HOLBERT
    *** MARRIED:  '41 J. LLOYD CRAWFORD  (DIED)
    *** MARRIED:  '49 LARRY C. WILLIAMS  (DIVORCED '50)
    TALENT: ACTRESS
    CREDIT:  '32 THE GOLDEN WEST
    CREDIT:  '36 SHOWBOAT
    AA-WIN  SUP.ACT.:  '39 GONE WITH THE WIND
    CREDIT:  '43 THANK YOUR LUCKY STARS
    CREDIT:  '49 THE BIG WHEEL
-------------------------------------------------------------------
MCDONALD,  MARIE         BORN:  CORA MARIE FRYE
                             1923 AT BURGIN,KT   DIED IN '65
    GRANDMOTHER: MARIA MOULLNER, OPERA SINGER
    FATHER: EVERETT FRYE
    MOTHER: MARIE MCDONALD, SR., SHOWGIRL
    STEP-SISTER: ROSE TUBONI
    STEP-SISTER: ELEANOR TUBONI
    *** MARRIED:  '42 VICTOR ORSATTI, AGENT  (DIVORCED '47)
    BROTHER-IN-LAW: FRANK ORSATTI, AGENT, ENTREPRENEUR
    BROTHER-IN-LAW: ALBERT ORSATTI, AGENT
    BROTHER-IN-LAW: ERNEST ORSATTI, AGENT
    *** MARRIED:  '47 HARRY KARL, SHOE MERCHANT  (DIVORCED '54)
    ADOPTED DAUGHTER: DENISE KARL
    ADOPTED SON: HARRISON KARL
    *** MARRIED:  '55 HARRY KARL, REMARRIED  (DIVORCED '58)
    DAUGHTER:  '56 TINA MARIE KARL
    *** MARRIED:  '59 LOU BASS  (DIVORCED)
    *** MARRIED:  '62 EDWARD CALLAHAN  (DIVORCED)
    *** MARRIED:  '63 DONALD TAYLOR
    RESIDENCE: ENCINO, CA
    TALENT: SINGER-ACTRESS
    COMMENT: KNOWN AS 'THE BODY'
    CREDIT:  '41 IT STARTED WITH EVE
    CREDIT:  '47 LIVING IN A BIG WAY
    CREDIT:  '49 TELL IT TO THE JUDGE
    CREDIT:  '59 GEISHA BOY
    CREDIT:  '63 PROMISES, PROMISES
-------------------------------------------------------------------
MCDOWALL,  RODDY         BORN:  RODERICK ANDREW MCDOWALL
                             SEP 17,'28 AT LONDON, ENGLAND
    FATHER: THOMAS MCDOWALL
    MOTHER: WINIFRED CORCORAN
    SISTER: VIRGINIA MCDOWALL
    RESIDENCE: NYC
    POSSESSION:  '60 TONY AWARD-SUPPORTING ACTOR IN THE FIGHTING COCK
    TALENT: ACTOR-PHOTOGRAPHER
    CREDIT:  '37 SCRUFFY
    CREDIT:  '43 LASSIE COME HOME
    CREDIT:  '50 BIG TIMBER
    CREDIT:  '62 CLEOPATRA
    CREDIT:  '68 PLANET OF THE APES
```

MCGUIRE, DOROTHY   BORN: DOROTHY HACKETT MCGUIRE
                                     JUN 14,'18 AT OMAHA,NB
     FATHER: THOMAS JOHNSON MCGUIRE
     MOTHER: ISABELLE FLAHERTY
     *** MARRIED: '43 JOHN SWOPE
     DAUGHTER: '44 MARY 'TOPO' SWOPE, ACTRESS
     SON: '45 MARK SWOPE
     RESIDENCE: BEVERLY HILLS, CA
     TALENT: ACTRESS
     CREDIT: '43 CLAUDIA
     AA-NOM ACTRESS: '47 GENTLEMAN'S AGREEMENT
     CREDIT: '54 THREE COINS IN A FOUNTAIN
     CREDIT: '63 SUMMER MAGIC
     CREDIT: '71 FLIGHT OF THE DOVES

MCLAGLEN, VICTOR
                         DEC 11,'83 AT TUNBRIDGE WELLS, KENT, ENGLAND   DIED IN '59
     FATHER: RT. REV. ANDREW MCLAGLEN, BISHOP OF CLAREMONT
     SISTER: LILLIAN MARION MCLAGLEN (DIED '55)
     BROTHER: LEOPOLD MCLAGLEN, ACTOR, JIU-JITSU CHAMPION
     BROTHER: FRED MCLAGLEN
     BROTHER: SYDNEY MCLAGLEN
     BROTHER: ARTHUR MCLAGLEN, SCULPTOR
     BROTHER: LEWIS MCLAGLEN
     BROTHER: CLIFFORD MCLAGLEN, ACTOR
     BROTHER: CYRIL MCLAGLEN, ACTOR
     BROTHER: KENNETH MCLAGLEN
     SISTER-IN-LAW: MARIAN LORD, ACTRESS (MARRIED '31)
     *** MARRIED: '19 ENID LAMONT (DIED '42)
     FATHER-IN-LAW: CHARLES LAMONT, ADMIRAL AND CHIEF OF THE CLAN
     DAUGHTER: '20 SHEILA MCLAGLEN
     SON: '21 ANDREW MCLAGLEN, DIRECTOR
     *** MARRIED: '43 SUZANNE M. BRUEGGEMANN (DIVORCED '48)
     *** MARRIED: '48 MARGARET PUMPHREY
     STEP-SON: MARSHALL PUMPHREY, JR.
     RESIDENCE: LAGUNA, CA
     POSSESSION: '30 CONTRACT AT 20TH CENTURY FOX
     MEMOIRS: '34 EXPRESS TO HOLLYWOOD
     TALENT: ACTOR APPEARED IN 150 FILMS
     COMMENT: BOXING CHAMPION EASTERN CANADA
     CREDIT: '20 THE CALL OF THE ROAD
     AA-WIN ACTOR: '35 THE INFORMER
     AA-NOM SUP.ACT: '52 THE QUIET MAN
     CREDIT: '59 SEA FURY

MCQUEEN, STEVE   BORN: TERRENCE STEPHEN MCQUEEN
                                   MAR 24,'30 AT SLATER, MR
     FATHER: WILLIAM MCQUEEN
     MOTHER: JULIA CRAWFORD
     *** MARRIED: '56 NEILE ADAMS (DIVORCED '72)
     DAUGHTER: '59 TERRY MCQUEEN
     SON: '60 CHADWICK MCQUEEN
     *** MARRIED: '73 ALI MACGRAW, ACTRESS-MODEL (SEPARATED '78)
     STEP-SON: JOSHUA EVANS
     RESIDENCE: MALIBU, CA
     BIOGRAPHY: '72 STAR ON WHEELS, BY WILLIAM NOLAN
     TALENT: ACTOR,TANK DRIVER FOR U.S. MARINES

```
          CREDIT:   '56 HATFUL OF RAIN, DEBUT
          CREDIT:   '60 THE MAGNIFICENT SEVEN
          AA-NOM  ACTOR:  '66 THE SAND PEBBLES
          CREDIT:   '68 BULLITT
          CREDIT:   '72 PAPILLON
          CREDIT:   '78 AN ENEMY OF THE PEOPLE
------------------------------------------------------------------------------------------
MEADOWS, AUDREY          BORN:   AUDREY COTTER
                                 1929 AT WUCHANG, CHINA
          FATHER: FRANCIS MEADOWS COTTER, EPISCOPAL MISSIONARY
          MOTHER: IDA MILLER TAYLOR
          SISTER: JAYNE MEADOWS, ACTRESS
          BROTHER-IN-LAW: MILTON KRIMS
          BROTHER-IN-LAW: STEVE ALLEN
          BROTHER: FRANCIS COTTER, JR.
          BROTHER: G. EDWARD COTTER, EXECUTIVE-CONTINENTAL AIRLINES
          NEPHEW: WILLIAM CHRISTOPHER ALLEN
          *** MARRIED:  '56 RANDOLPH RAUSE
          *** MARRIED:  '61 ROBERT F. SIX, EXECUTIVE-CONTINENTAL AIRLINES
          TALENT: ACTRESS-SINGER
          CREDIT:   '62 THAT TOUCH OF MINK
          CREDIT:   '63 TAKE HER SHE'S MINE
          CREDIT:   '67 ROSIE
------------------------------------------------------------------------------------------
MEADOWS, JAYNE          BORN:   JANE COTTER
                                SEP 27,'26 AT WUCHANG, CHINA
          FATHER: FRANCIS MEADOWS COTTER, EPISCOPAL MISSIONARY
          MOTHER: IDA MILLER TAYLOR
          SISTER: AUDREY MEADOWS, ACTRESS-SINGER
          BROTHER-IN-LAW: RANDOLPH RAUSE, EXECUTIVE-CONTINENTAL AIRLINES
          BROTHER: FRANCIS COTTER, JR.
          BROTHER: G. EDWARD COTTER, EXECUTIVE-CONTINENTAL AIRLINES
          *** MARRIED: MILTON KRIMS
          *** MARRIED:  '54 STEVE ALLEN, PERFORMER, AUTHOR, MUSICIAN
          FATHER-IN-LAW: CARROLL ALLEN, VAUDEVILLIAN
          MOTHER-IN-LAW: ISABELLE DONOHU, AKA - BELLE MONTROSE
          STEP-SON: STEVE ALLEN, JR.
          STEP-SON: BRIAN ALLEN
          STEP-SON: DAVID ALLEN
          SON:    '57 WILLIAM CHRISTOPHER ALLEN
          POSSESSION: COLLECTION OF EARRINGS
          TALENT: ACTRESS
          CREDIT:   '46 UNDERCURRENT
          CREDIT:   '47 DARK DELUSION
          CREDIT:   '48 LUCK OF THE IRISH
          CREDIT:   '48 ENCHANTMENT
          CREDIT:   '60 COLLEGE CONFIDENTIAL
------------------------------------------------------------------------------------------
MEEKER, RALPH           BORN:   RALPH RATHGEBER, JR.
                                NOV 21,'20 AT MINNEAPOLIS, MN
          FATHER: RALPH RATHGEBER
          MOTHER: MAGNHILD SENOVIA HAAVIG
          *** MARRIED:  '64 SALOME JENS
          RESIDENCE: NYC
          TALENT: ACTOR
          CREDIT:   '51 TERESA, DEBUT
          CREDIT:   '55 KISS ME DEADLY
          CREDIT:   '58 PATHS OF GLORY
```

```
CREDIT:  '67 THE DIRTY DOZEN
CREDIT:  '71 THE ANDERSON TAPES
```

MELCHIOR, LAURITZ   BORN: LAURITZ LEBRECHT HOMMEL
                                MAR 20,'90 AT COPENHAGEN,DENMARK DIED IN '73
```
    FATHER: MELCHIOR, VOICE TEACHER
    MOTHER: JOLIE MOELLER  (DIED '90)
    SISTER: AGGE MELCHIOR
    SISTER: BODIL MELCHIOR
    *** MARRIED: '20 INGER NATHANSEN  (DIED '24)
    SON:  '21 IB JORGEN MELCHIOR, DIRECTOR
    DAUGHTER-IN-LAW: BERLE CLEO BALDON
    DAUGHTER:  '22 BIRTE INGER MELCHIOR
    *** MARRIED:  '25 MARIA HACKER, ACTRESS  (DIED '63)
    *** MARRIED:  '64 MARY MARKHAM  (DIVORCED '66)
    GRANDSON:  '43 LEIF LAURITZ MELCHIOR
    GRANDDAUGHTER:  '47 HELLE BIRTE MELCHIOR
    FRIEND: SIEGFRIED WAGNER
    RESIDENCE: BEVERLY HILLS, CA
    POSSESSION: THE ORDER OF DANNEBROG CROSS
    TALENT: TENOR-ACTOR
    CREDIT:  '13 I PAGLIACCI, DEBUT IN OPERA
    CREDIT:  '45 THRILL OF ROMANCE, DEBUT IN FILMS
    CREDIT:  '46 TWO SISTERS FROM BOSTON
    CREDIT:  '47 THIS TIME FOR KEEPS
    CREDIT:  '48 LUXURY LINER
    CREDIT:  '53 THE STARS ARE SINGING
```

MENJOU, ADOLPHE   BORN: ADOLPHE JEAN MENJOU
                                FEB 18,'90 AT PITTSBURGH, PA DIED IN '63
```
    FATHER: ALBERT MENJOU, HOTEL MANAGER
    MOTHER: NORA JOYCE
    BROTHER: HENRY MENJOU
    COUSIN: JAMES JOYCE, WRITER
    *** MARRIED:  '19 KATHERINE TINSLEY  (DIVORCED '27)
    *** MARRIED:  '28 KATHRYN CARVER, ACTRESS-KATHRYN HILL  (DIVORCED '33)
    *** MARRIED:  '34 VERREE TEASDALE
    ADOPTED SON: PETER ADOLPHE MENJOU
    RESIDENCE: BEVERLY HILLS, CA
    MEMOIRS:  '52 IT TOOK NINE TAILORS
    TALENT: ACTOR
    COMMENT: REPUTATION OF BEING HOLLYWOOD'S BEST-DRESSED MAN
    CREDIT:  '16 BLUE ENVELOPE
    CREDIT:  '25 THE SWAN
    AA-NOM  ACTOR:  '30 THE FRONT PAGE
    CREDIT:  '40 TURNABOUT
    CREDIT:  '50 TO PLEASE A LADY
    CREDIT:  '60 POLLYANNA
```

MERCOURI, MELINA
                         OCT 18,'25 AT ATHENS, GREECE
```
    GRANDFATHER: --, MAYOR OF ATHENS FOR 30 YEARS
    FATHER: STAMATIS MERCOURI, LEGISLATOR, GOVT. MINISTER
    MOTHER: IRENE ELIOPOULOS
    *** MARRIED:  '42 PANAYIOTIS HAROKOPOS
    *** MARRIED:  '66 JULES DASSIN, ACTOR-DIRECTOR
    STEP-DAUGHTER: JULIE DASSIN
    STEP-DAUGHTER: RICHELLE DASSIN
```

STEP-SON: JOSEPH DASSIN
MEMOIRS: I WAS BORN GREEK
TALENT: ACTRESS
CREDIT: '54 STELLA
CREDIT: '56 HE WHO MUST DIE
AA-NOM ACTRESS: '60 NEVER ON SUNDAY
CREDIT: '64 TOPKAPI
CREDIT: '71 PROMISE AT DAWN
CREDIT: '78 A DREAM OF PASSION

MEREDITH, BURGESS   BORN: BURGESS GEORGE MEREDITH
                                     NOV 16,'08 AT CLEVELAND,OH
FATHER: WILLIAM GEORGE MEREDITH, DOCTOR
MOTHER: IDA BETH BURGESS.
*** MARRIED: '32 HELEN DERBY (DIVORCED '35)
*** MARRIED: '36 MARGARET PERRY (DIVORCED '38)
*** MARRIED: '43 PAULETTE GODDARD (DIVORCED '48)
*** MARRIED: '49 KAJA SUNDSTEN
SON: '50 JONATHAN MEREDITH
DAUGHTER: '52 TALA BETH MEREDITH
FRIEND: BRENDA VACCARO, ACTRESS
RESIDENCE: ROCKLAND COUNTY, NY
TALENT: ACTOR
CREDIT: '36 WINTERSET
CREDIT: '45 THE STORY OF G. I. JOE
CREDIT: '53 THE GAY ADVENTURE
CREDIT: '67 HURRY SUNDOWN
AA-NOM SUP.ACT: '75 THE DAY OF THE LOCUST
AA-NOM SUP.ACT: '76 ROCKY

MERMAN, ETHEL   BORN: ETHEL AGNES ZIMMERMANN
                                 JAN 16,'09 AT ASTORIA,NY
FATHER: EDWARD ZIMMERMAN
MOTHER: AGNES
*** MARRIED: '40 WILLIAM B. SMITH, AGENT (DIVORCED '41)
*** MARRIED: '41 ROBERT D. LEVITT (DIVORCED '52)
DAUGHTER: '42 ETHEL LEVITT
SON: '43 ROBERT LEVITT, JR.
*** MARRIED: '53 ROBERT F. SIX, EXECUTIVE-CONTINENTAL AIRLINES (DIVORCED '60)
*** MARRIED: '64 ERNEST BORGNINE, ACTOR (DIVORCED '64)
STEP-DAUGHTER: NANCY BORGNINE
RESIDENCE: NYC
POSSESSION: IMPRESSIONIST ART COLLECTION
MEMOIRS: '56 WHO COULD ASK FOR ANYTHING MORE?
TALENT: ACTRESS-SINGER
CREDIT: '30 FOLLOW THE LEADER
CREDIT: '38 ALEXANDER'S RAGTIME BAND
CREDIT: '43 STAGE DOOR CANTEEN
CREDIT: '53 CALL ME MADAM
CREDIT: '65 THE ART OF LOVE

MERRILL, DINA   BORN: NADINIA HUTTON
                                 DEC 09,'25 AT NYC
FATHER: E. F. HUTTON, FINANCIER
MOTHER: MARJORIE POST, POST CEREALS HEIRESS
COUSIN: BARBARA HUTTON, WOOLWORTH'S STORES HEIRESS
*** MARRIED: '46 STANLEY M. RUMBOUGH, JR. (DIVORCED '66)
SON: '47 STANLEY D. RUMBOUGH

DAUGHTER: '48 NINA RUMBOUGH
*** MARRIED: '66 CLIFF ROBERTSON, ACTOR
STEP-DAUGHTER: STEPHANIE ROBERTSON
DAUGHTER: '68 HEATHER ROBERTSON
TALENT: ACTRESS
CREDIT: '57 THE DESK SET
CREDIT: '63 THE COURTSHIP OF EDDIE'S FATHER
CREDIT: '64 THE PLEASURE SEEKERS
CREDIT: '65 I'LL TAKE SWEDEN
CREDIT: '73 RUN WILD

MERRILL, GARY
                        AUG 02,'15 AT HARTFORD, CN
*** MARRIED: BARBARA LEEDS (DIVORCED '50)
*** MARRIED: '50 BETTE DAVIS, ACTRESS (DIVORCED '60)
ADOPTED SON: MICHAEL MERRILL
ADOPTED DAUGHTER: MARGOT MERRILL
RESIDENCE: CAPE ELIZABETH LIGHTHOUSE
TALENT: ACTOR
CREDIT: '44 WINGED VICTORY
CREDIT: '50 ALL ABOUT EVE
CREDIT: '56 BERMUDA AFFAIR
CREDIT: '66 DESTINATION INNER SPACE
CREDIT: '68 THE POWER

MILES, SARAH
                        DEC 31,'41 AT INGATESTONE,ENGLAND
FATHER: JOHN MILES, ENGINEER
SISTER: VANESSA MILES
BROTHER: CHRISTOPHER MILES, DIRECTOR
*** MARRIED: '67 ROBERT BOLT, PLAYWRIGHT (DIVORCED '75)
SON: '67 THOMAS BOLT
TALENT: ACTRESS
CREDIT: '62 TERM OF TRIAL
CREDIT: '66 BLOW UP
AA-NOM ACTRESS: '70 RYAN'S DAUGHTER
CREDIT: '72 LADY CAROLINE LAMB
CREDIT: '73 THE MAN WHO LOVED CAT DANCING

MILES, VERA   BORN: VERA MAY RALSTON
                        AUG 23,'30 AT BOISE CITY, OK
*** MARRIED: '49 ROBERT MILES (DIVORCED '54)
DAUGHTER: '50 DEBORAH MILES
DAUGHTER: '52 KELLY MILES
*** MARRIED: '54 GORDON SCOTT, ACTOR (DIVORCED '59)
SON: '57 MICHAEL SCOTT
*** MARRIED: '60 KEITH LARSEN, ACTOR (DIVORCED)
SON: '60 ERIK LARSEN
*** MARRIED: '73 BOB JONES, DIRECTOR
CREDIT: '50 TWO TICKETS TO BRADWAY, DEBUT
CREDIT: '60 PSYCHO
CREDIT: '68 THE GREEN BERETS

```
-----------------------------------------------------------------------------------
MILLAND, RAY          BORN:    REGINALD TRUSCOTT-JONES
                               JAN 03,'08 AT NEATH, GLAMORGAN, WALES
    MOTHER: ELIZABETH TRUSCOTT-JONES
    STEP-FATHER: ALFRED MULLANE
    *** MARRIED: '31 MURIEL WEBSTER, SHOWGIRL
    SON:  '40 DANIEL DAVID MILLAND
    DAUGHTER:  '41 VICTORIA FRANCESCA MILLAND
    POSSESSION: '34 CONTRACT AT PARAMOUNT PICTURES
    MEMOIRS:  '74 WIDE EYED IN BABYLON
    TALENT: ACTOR
    COMMENT: 1ST STAGE NAME-JACK MILLAND
    CREDIT:  '31 BACHELOR FATHER, AMERICAN DEBUT
    AA-WIN  ACTOR: '45 THE LOST WEEKEND
    CREDIT:  '54 DIAL M FOR MURDER
    CREDIT:  '70 LOVE STORY
    CREDIT:  '72 THE THING WITH TWO HEADS
-----------------------------------------------------------------------------------
MILLER, ANN          BORN:   LUCILLE ANN COLLIER
                             APR 12,'19 AT CHIRENO, TX
    FATHER: JOHN ALFRED COLLIER, LAWYER
    MOTHER: CLARA EMMA BIRDWELL
    *** MARRIED:  '46 REESE L. MILNER  (DIVORCED '47)
    SON:  '47 DOUGLAS MILNER
    *** MARRIED:  '58 WILLIAM MOSS  (DIVORCED '61)
    *** MARRIED:  '62 ARTHUR CAMERON  (ANNULLED '62)
    FRIEND: CONRAD NICHOLSON HILTON, SR., HOTELMAN
    RESIDENCE: LOS ANGELES, CA
    MEMOIRS: MILLER'S HIGH LIFE
    TALENT: ACTRESS,DANCER
    CREDIT:  '38 YOU CAN'T TAKE IT WITH YOU
    CREDIT:  '43 REVEILLE WITH BEVERLY
    CREDIT:  '49 ON THE TOWN
    CREDIT:  '53 KISS ME KATE
    CREDIT:  '56 THE OPPOSITE SEX
-----------------------------------------------------------------------------------
MILLER, MARVIN          BORN:   MARVIN MUELLER
                                JUL 18,'13 AT ST. LOUIS,MR
    MOTHER: TERESA KIEMAST  (DIED '51)
    *** MARRIED:  '38 ELIZABETH DAWSON, ARTIST
    SON:  '42 ANTHONY DAWSON MILLER
    DAUGHTER:  '52 MELISSA MILLER
    GRANDSON:  '62 KEVIN CHRISTOPHER MILLER
    RESIDENCE: LOS ANGELES, CA
    TALENT: ACTOR-AUTHOR
    CREDIT:  '45 JOHNNY ANGEL
    CREDIT:  '47 THE HIGH WINDOW
    CREDIT:  '47 INTRIGUE
    CREDIT:  '53 OFF LIMITS
    CREDIT:  '54 THE SHANGHAI STORY
-----------------------------------------------------------------------------------
MILLS, HAYLEY          BORN:   HAYLEY CATHERINE VIVIAN MILLS
                               APR 18,'46 AT LONDON, ENGLAND
    FATHER: JOHN MILLS, ACTOR
    MOTHER: MARY HAYLEY BELL, ACTRESS
    SISTER: JULIET MILLS, ACTRESS
    BROTHER: JOHN MILLS, JR.
    *** MARRIED:  '71 ROY BOULTING, PRODUCER
```

```
SON:  '76 CRISPIAN BOULTING
ROMANCE: LEIGH LAWSON, ACTOR
POSSESSION: COLLECTION OF FIGURINES WITH EMPHASIS OF HORSES
BIOGRAPHY:  '69 WHAT SHALL WE DO TOMORROW?, BY MARY HAYLEY BELL
TALENT: ACTRESS
CREDIT:  '59 TIGER BAY, DEBUT
AA-SPECIAL AWARD:  '60 MINIATURE STATUETTE FOR HER PERFORMANCE IN 'POLLYANNA'
CREDIT:  '61 THE PARENT TRAP
CREDIT:  '65 THE MOONSPINNERS
CREDIT:  '72 ENDLESS NIGHT
```

MILLS, JOHN   BORN: JOHN LEWIS ERNEST WATTS MILLS
                         FEB 22,'08 AT NORTH ELMHAM, NORFOLK, ENGLAND
```
    FATHER: LEWIS MILLS, SCHOOL TEACHER AND HEADMASTER
    MOTHER: EDITH BAKER
    SISTER: ANNETTE MILLS
    *** MARRIED: AILEEN RAYMOND
    *** MARRIED:  '41 MARY HAYLEY BELL, ACTRESS
    DAUGHTER:  '46 HAYLEY MILLS, ACTRESS
    SON-IN-LAW: ROY BOULTING, PRODUCER  (MARRIED '74)
    DAUGHTER:  '48 JULIET MILLS, ACTRESS  (MARRIED)
    SON-IN-LAW: MICHAEL MIKLENDA, BLDG. CONTRACTOR
    SON: JOHN MILLS, JR.
    GRANDSON:  '76 CRISPIAN BOULTING
    RESIDENCE: LONDON, ENGLAND
    POSSESSION:  '61 COMMANDER OF BRITISH EMPIRE- HONOR
    POSSESSION: FARM IN COUNTRY NEAR LONDON
    BIOGRAPHY:  '69 WHAT SHALL WE DO TOMORROW?  BY MARY HAYLEY BELL
    TALENT: ACTOR-PRODUCER-DIRECTOR
    CREDIT:  '32 THE MIDSHIPMAID
    CREDIT:  '45 THE WAY TO THE STARS
    CREDIT:  '53 HOBSON'S CHOICE
    CREDIT:  '66 THE FAMILY WAY
    AA-WIN  SUP.ACT.:  '70 RYAN'S DAUGHTER
```

MIMIEUX, YVETTE
                         JAN 08,'39 AT LOS ANGELES, CA
```
    FATHER: RENE A. MIMIEUX
    MOTHER: CARMEN MONTEMAYOR
    *** MARRIED:  '72 STANLEY DONEN, WRITER-PRODUCER
    ROMANCE: FREDRIC E. MYROW, MUSICIAN
    TALENT: ACTRESS
    CREDIT:  '60 THE TIME MACHINE, DEBUT
    CREDIT:  '62 THE LIGHT IN THE PIAZZA
    CREDIT:  '65 JOY IN THE MORNING
    CREDIT:  '67 THE CAPER OF THE GOLDEN BULLS
    CREDIT:  '73 THE NEPTUNE FACTOR
```

MINEO, SAL   BORN: SALVATORE MINEO
                        JAN 10,'39 AT NYC DIED IN '76
```
    FATHER: SALVATORE MINEO, SR.
    MOTHER: JOSEPHINE
    SISTER: SARINA MINEO
    BROTHER: MICHAEL MINEO
    ROMANCE: TINA LOUISE, ACTRESS
    ROMANCE: SUSAN LADIN
    RESIDENCE: LOS ANGELES, CA
    POSSESSION:  '58 SPEEDBOAT NAMED 'BIMBO II'
```

TALENT: ACTOR
AA-NOM SUP.ACT: '55 REBEL WITHOUT A CAUSE
CREDIT: '55 SIX BRIDGES TO CROSS
AA-NOM SUP.ACT: '60 EXODUS
CREDIT: '59 THE GENE KRUPA STORY
CREDIT: '66 KRAKATOA
CREDIT: '71 ESCAPE FROM THE PLANET OF THE APES

MINNELLI, LIZA   BORN: LIZA MAY MINNELLI
                            MAY 12,'46 AT LOS ANGELES, CA
GRANDFATHER: FRANK AVENT GUMM, SINGER
GRANDMOTHER: MINA GENNELL, ACTRESS, SINGER, DANCER
GRANDMOTHER: ETHEL MARION MILNE, PIANIST
FATHER: VINCENTE MINNELLI, PRODUCER
MOTHER: JUDY GARLAND, ACTRESS-SINGER
STEP-FATHER: SID LUFT
STEP-FATHER: MARK HERRIN, ACTOR
STEP-FATHER: MICKEY DEAMS, CLUB MANAGER
STEP-MOTHER: GEORGETTE MAGNANI
STEP-MOTHER: DENISE GIGANTI
STEP-SISTER: LORNA LUFT
STEP-SISTER: CHRISTIANA NINA MINNELLI
STEP-BROTHER: JOEY LUFT
AUNT: DOROTHY VIRGINA GUMM
AUNT: MARY JANE SUZANNE GUMM
*** MARRIED: '67 PETER ALLEN, SINGER (DIVORCED '72)
*** MARRIED: '74 JOHN JOSEPH 'JACK' HALEY, JR., PRODUCER
BIOGRAPHY: '75 LIZA!, BY JAMES R. PARRISH
TALENT: ACTRESS
CREDIT: '68 CHARLEY BUBBLES
AA-NOM ACTRESS: '69 THE STERILE CUCKOO
AA-WIN ACTRESS: '72 CABARET
CREDIT: '75 LUCKY LADY
CREDIT: '77 NEW YORK, NEW YORK

MIRANDA, CARMEN   BORN: MARIA DA CARMO MIRANDA DACUNHA
                            FEB 09,'04 AT MARCO CANAVEZES, PORTUGAL DIED IN '55
FATHER: JOSE PINTO CUNHA
MOTHER: MARIA EMILIA MIRANDA
SISTER: AURORA CUNHA, SINGER
*** MARRIED: '47 DAVID SEBASTIAN
RESIDENCE: BEVERLY HILLS, CA
TALENT: ACTRESS, DANCER, SINGER
COMMENT: KNOWN AS THE 'BRAZILIAN BOMBSHELL'
CREDIT: '40 DOWN ARGENTINE WAY, DEBUT
CREDIT: '43 THE GANG'S ALL HERE
CREDIT: '45 DOLL FACE
CREDIT: '50 NANCY GOES TO RIO
CREDIT: '53 SCARED STIFF

MITCHUM, ROBERT   BORN: ROBERT CHARLES DURAN MITCHUM
                            AUG 06,'17 AT BRIDGEPORT,CN
FATHER: JAMES MITCHUM, RAILROAD WORKER
MOTHER: ANNE
SISTER: JULIE MITCHUM, NIGHTCLUB ENTERTAINER
BROTHER: JOHN MITCHUM
*** MARRIED: '40 DOROTHY SPENCER
DAUGHTER: PETRINE MITCHUM

```
SON: JIM MITCHUM, ACTOR
SON: CHRIS MITCHUM
RESIDENCE: FARM IN MARYLAND
TALENT: ACTOR
AA-NOM  SUP.ACT:  '45 G. I. JOE
CREDIT:  '49 THE BIG STEAL
CREDIT:  '54 SHE COULDN'T SAY NO
CREDIT:  '60 THE SUNDOWNERS
CREDIT:  '62 TWO FOR THE SEASAW
CREDIT:  '70 RYAN'S DAUGHTER
```

MITZI THE DOLPHIN   BORN: MITZI DOLPHINA DOLPHIS
                           JAN 01,'49 AT WATERBED, ATLANTIC OCEAN DIED IN '71
```
RESIDENCE: GRASSY KEY, FL
TALENT: ACTRESS
CREDIT:  '63 FLIPPER, FILM & TV SERIES
```

MIX, TOM   BORN: THOMAS EDWIN MIX
                         JAN 06,'80 AT DRIFTWOOD, PA DIED IN '40
```
FATHER: EDWIN E. MIX, LUMBERMAN
MOTHER: ELIZABETH SMITH
SISTER: EMMA MIX
SISTER: ESTHER MIX
BROTHER: HARRY MIX  (DIED '90)
*** MARRIED:  '02 GRACE I. ALLIN, TEACHER  (ANNULLED '03)
*** MARRIED:  '05 KITTY JEWEL PERRINE  (DIVORCED '07)
*** MARRIED:  '09 OLIVE STOKES, RODEO RIDER  (DIVORCED '17)
DAUGHTER:  '13 RUTH JANE MIX
*** MARRIED:  '18 VICTORIA FORDE, ACTRESS  (DIVORCED '30)
DAUGHTER:  '22 THOMASINA MIX
*** MARRIED:  '32 MABEL HUBBELL WARD, ACROBAT
PARTNER: TONY, HIS HORSE
RESIDENCE: PACOIMA, CA
MEMOIRS:  '23 THE WEST OF YESTERDAY
BIOGRAPHY:  '72 THE LIFE AND LEGEND, BY PAUL E. MIX
TALENT: ACTOR, US MARSHAL
CREDIT:  '10 THE FEUD
CREDIT:  '18 WESTERN BLOOD
CREDIT:  '25 THE BEST BAD MAN
CREDIT:  '31 THE GALLOPING GHOST, SERIES
CREDIT:  '43 DAREDEVILS OF THE WEST
```

MONROE, MARILYN   BORN: NORMA JEAN BAKER
                                JUN 01,'26 AT LOS ANGELES, CA DIED IN '62
```
FATHER: EDWARD MORTENSEN
MOTHER: GLADYS BAKER MONROE, FILM EDITOR
STEP-SISTER: BERNICE BAKER
STEP-BROTHER: JACK BAKER
*** MARRIED:  '44 JIM DOUGHERTY  (DIVORCED '46)
*** MARRIED:  '54 JOE DIMAGGIO, BASEBALL PLAYER  (DIVORCED '55)
*** MARRIED:  '56 ARTHUR MILLER, PLAYWRIGHT  (DIVORCED '61)
FRIEND: JACK GORDEAN, AGENT
FRIEND: JOSEPH M. SCHENCK, PRODUCER
RESIDENCE: BEVERLY HILLS, CA
POSSESSION:  '55 MARILYN MONROE FILM PROD. CO.
POSSESSION:  '58 DAVID DI DONATELLO AWARD - ITALIAN FILM ACADEMY
BIOGRAPHY:  '69 NORMA JEAN, BY FRED LAWRENCE GUILES
TALENT: MODEL-ACTRESS
```

```
CREDIT:   '48 DANGEROUS YEARS
CREDIT:   '50 ALL ABOUT EVE
CREDIT:   '56 BUS STOP
CREDIT:   '59 SOME LIKE IT HOT
CREDIT:   '61 THE MISFITS
```

MONTALBAN, RICARDO
                            NOV 25,'20 AT MEXICO CITY, MEXICO
```
BROTHER: CARLOS MONTALBAN, ACTOR
*** MARRIED:  '44 GEORGIANNA YOUNG, ACTRESS
BROTHER-IN-LAW: JACK YOUNG
SISTER-IN-LAW: LORETTA YOUNG, ACTRESS
SISTER-IN-LAW: POLLY ANN YOUNG, ACTRESS
SISTER-IN-LAW: ELIZABETH JANE YOUNG, ACTRESS - SALLY BLANE
SON:  '47 MARK MONTALBAN
DAUGHTER:  '49 LAURA MONTALBAN
DAUGHTER:  '52 ANITA MONTALBAN
SON: VICTOR MONTALBAN
POSSESSION:  '47 CONTACT AT M-G-M
TALENT: ACTOR
CREDIT:   '47 FIESTA
CREDIT:   '50 BATTLEGROUND
CREDIT:   '54 LATIN LOVERS
CREDIT:   '57 SAYONARA
CREDIT:   '68 SWEET CHARITY
```

MONTGOMERY, ELIZABETH
                            APR 15,'33 AT LOS ANGELES, CA
```
FATHER: ROBERT MONTGOMERY, ACTOR
MOTHER: ELIZABETH BRYAN ALLEN
STEP-MOTHER: ELIZABETH GRANT HARKNESS
BROTHER: ROBERT MONTGOMERY, JR.
*** MARRIED:  '54 FREDERIC GALLATIN CAMMANN  (DIVORCED '55)
*** MARRIED:  '57 GIG YOUNG, ACTOR  (DIVORCED '63)
*** MARRIED:  '63 WILLIAM ASHER  (DIVORCED '74)
SON:  '64 WILLIAM ASHER, JR.
SON:  '65 ROBERT ASHER
DAUGHTER:  '69 REBECCA ELIZABETH ASHER
RESIDENCE: MALIBU, CA
TALENT: ACTRESS
CREDIT:  '55 THE COURT MARTIAL OF BILLY MITCHELL
CREDIT:  '63 JOHNNY COOL
CREDIT:  '63 WHO'S BEEN SLEEPING IN MY BED?
CREDIT: BEWITCHED, TV SERIES
```

MONTGOMERY, GEORGE   BORN: GEORGE MONTGOMERY LETZ
                                AUG 29,'16 AT BRADY,MT
```
FATHER: GEORGE G. LETZ
MOTHER: DENA
SISTER: ROSE LETZ
SISTER: LYDA LETZ
SISTER: EDA LETZ
SISTER: MARY LETZ
SISTER: OLGA LETZ
BROTHER: MATTHEW LETZ
BROTHER: MAURICE LETZ
BROTHER: SAMUEL LETZ
BROTHER: JAMES LETZ  (DIED '68)
```

```
        BROTHER: NICHOLAS LETZ
        BROTHER: MICHAEL LETZ
        BROTHER: WILLIAM LETZ
        *** MARRIED:  '43 DINAH SHORE  (DIVORCED '62)
        DAUGHTER:  '48 MELISSA ANN MONTGOMERY
        SON-IN-LAW: DAVID LEE BURK  (MARRIED '69)
        SON-IN-LAW: MARK HIME
        GRANDDAUGHTER:  '74 JENNIFER TRINITY HIME
        GRANDSON:  '76 ADAM HIME
        ADOPTED SON: JOHN DAVID MONTGOMERY
        ROMANCE: GLORIA VANDERBILT
        ROMANCE: GINGER ROGERS
        ROMANCE: KAY WILLIAMS
        ROMANCE: KATHRYN GRAYSON
        ROMANCE: HEDY LAMARR, ACTRESS
        FRIEND: GARY COOPER, ACTOR
        FRIEND: ROBERT TAYLOR, ACTOR
        RESIDENCE: LOS ANGELES, CA
        POSSESSION:  '39 CONTRACT AT 20TH CENTURY FOX
        POSSESSION:  '57 MONT PRODUCTIONS, INC
        POSSESSION: RANCH IN MONTANA
        TALENT: ACTOR, PRODUCER, DIRECTOR, WRITER, SCULPTOR, ARCHITECT
        CREDIT:  '42 TEN GENTLEMEN FROM WEST POINT
        CREDIT:  '42 CHINA GIRL
        CREDIT:  '43 CONEY ISLAND
        CREDIT:  '57 BLACK PATCH, ACTED, PRODUCED, WROTE
        CREDIT:  '62 THE STEEL CLAW, ACTED, PRODUCED, WROTE,DIRECT
        CREDIT:  '69 STRANGERS AT SUNRISE
-------------------------------------------------------------------------------
MONTGOMERY, ROBERT      BORN:  HENRY MONTGOMERY, JR.
                               MAY 21,'04 AT BEACON, NY
        FATHER: HENRY MONTGOMERY
        MOTHER: MARY WEED BERNARD
        *** MARRIED:  '28 ELIZABETH BRYAN ALLEN  (DIVORCED '50)
        SON:  '30 ROBERT MONTGOMERY, JR.
        DAUGHTER:  '33 ELIZABETH MONTGOMERY, ACTRESS
        SON-IN-LAW: FREDERIC GALLATIN CAMMANN  (MARRIED '54)
        SON-IN-LAW: GIG YOUNG, ACTOR  (MARRIED '57)
        SON-IN-LAW: WILLIAM ASHER  (MARRIED '63)
        *** MARRIED:  '50 ELIZABETH GRANT HARKNESS
        GRANDSON:  '64 WILLIAM ASHER, JR.
        GRANDSON:  '65 ROBERT ASHER
        GRANDDAUGHTER:  '69 REBECCA ELIZABETH ASHER
        FRIEND: DWIGHT DAVID EISENHOWER
        RESIDENCE: NYC
        POSSESSION:  '29 CONTRACT AT M-G-M
        POSSESSION: FARM IN PUTNAM COUNTY, NY
        TALENT: ACTOR-DIRECTOR-PRODUCER
        COMMENT: PRESIDENT OF LINCOLN CENTER REPERTORY CO.
        COMMENT: SCREEN ACTORS GUILD PRESIDENT 1935
        CREDIT:  '29 UNTAMED
        CREDIT:  '31 PRIVATE LIVES
        AA-NOM  ACTOR:  '37 NIGHT MUST FALL
        AA-NOM  ACTOR:  '41 HERE COMES MR. JORDAN
        CREDIT:  '49 ONCE MORE MY DARLING
```

MOORE, COLLEEN   BORN: KATHLEEN MORRISON
                         AUG 19,'00 AT PORT HURON, MH
    FATHER: CHARLES MORRISON
    MOTHER: AGNES KELLY
    BROTHER: CLEVE MORRISON
    UNCLE: WALTER HOVEY, EDITOR OF THE CHICAGO TRIBUNE
    *** MARRIED: '23 JOHN MCCORMACK (DIVORCED '30)
    *** MARRIED: '32 ALBERT P. SCOTT (DIVORCED '34)
    *** MARRIED: '37 HOMER P. HARGRAVE (DIED '66)
    STEP-DAUGHTER: JUDY HARGRAVE
    STEP-SON: HOMER HARGRAVE, JR.
    ROMANCE: KING LOUIS WALLIS VIDOR, DIRECTOR
    FRIEND: RONALD REAGAN
    RESIDENCE: PASO ROBLES, CA
    MEMOIRS: '68 SILENT STAR
    TALENT: ACTRESS
    COMMENT: DOLLHOUSE ON DISPLAY IN CHICAGO MUSEUM
    CREDIT: '17 THE BAD BOY
    CREDIT: '23 FLAMING YOUTH
    CREDIT: '25 SO BIG
    CREDIT: '28 LILAC TIME
    CREDIT: '29 WHY BE GOOD?

MOORE, CONSTANCE
                       JAN 18,'20 AT SIOUX CITY, IO
    STEP-FATHER: J. G. SMITH
    *** MARRIED: '39 JOHN MASCHIO, AGENT
    DAUGHTER: '42 MARY CONSTANCE 'GINA' MASCHIO
    SON: '47 MICHAEL MASCHIO
    RESIDENCE: BEVERLY HILLS, CA
    POSSESSION: '44 CONTRACT AT RKO
    TALENT: ACTRESS, SINGER
    CREDIT: '38 STATE POLICE
    CREDIT: '42 BY JUPITER, STAGE SHOW
    CREDIT: '44 SHOW BUSINESS
    CREDIT: '45 DELIGHTFULLY DANGEROUS
    CREDIT: '47 HIT PARADE OF 1947

MOORE, MARY TYLER
                       DEC 29,'36 AT BROOKLYN,NY
    FATHER: GEORGE TYLER MOORE, SOUTHERN CALIF. GAS CO. EXEC.
    MOTHER: MARJORIE HACKETT
    SISTER: ELIZABETH ANN MOORE (DIED '78)
    BROTHER: JOHN MOORE
    *** MARRIED: '60 RICHARD MEEKER
    SON: '61 RICHARD MEEKER, JR.
    *** MARRIED: '63 GRANT TINKER, TV EXECUTIVE
    TALENT: ACTRESS
    CREDIT: '67 THOROUGHLY MODERN MILLIE
    CREDIT: '68 WHAT'S SO BAD ABOUT FEELING GOOD?
    CREDIT: '68 DON'T JUST STAND THERE
    CREDIT: '69 CHANGE OF HABIT
    CREDIT: '70 RUN A CROOKED MILE

MOORE, ROGER
OCT 14,'28 AT LONDON, ENGLAND
FATHER: GEORGE MOORE, POLICEMAN
MOTHER: LILLIAN POPE
*** MARRIED: DOORN VAN STEYN (DIVORCED '53)
*** MARRIED: '53 DOROTHY SQUIRES, SINGER
*** MARRIED: '69 LUISA MATTIOLI
DAUGHTER: DEBORAH MOORE
SON: GEOFFREY MOORE
SON: CHRISTIAN MOORE
RESIDENCE: BUCKINGHAMSHIRE, ENGLAND
TALENT: ACTOR
CREDIT: '54 THE LAST TIME I SAW PARIS
CREDIT: '55 DIANE
CREDIT: '61 GOLD OF THE SEVEN SAINTS
CREDIT: '73 LIVE AND LET DIE
CREDIT: '77 THE SPY WHO LOVED ME

MOORE, TERRY   BORN: HELEN KOFORD
JAN 07,'29 AT LOS ANGELES, CA
MOTHER: LUELLA BICKMORE
*** MARRIED: '51 GLENN DAVIS, FOOTBALL PLAYER (DIVORCED '52)
*** MARRIED: '56 EUGENE C. MCGRATH (DIVORCED '58)
*** MARRIED: '59 STUART CRAMER (DIVORCED '70)
SON: '60 STUART CRAMER, IV
SON: '61 GRANT LAMAR CRAMER
ROMANCE: HOWARD HUGHES
ROMANCE: GLENN FORD, ACTOR
RESIDENCE: BRENTWOOD, CA
TALENT: ACTRESS
COMMENT: PRESIDENT OF THE NORTH STAR AIRCRAFT COMPANY
CREDIT: '43 THE MURDER IN THORNTON SQUARE
AA-NOM SUP.ACT: '52 COME BACK, LITTLE SHEBA
CREDIT: '53 THE SUNNY SIDE OF THE STREET
CREDIT: '59 A PRIVATE'S AFFAIR
CREDIT: '65 TOWN TAMER

MOOREHEAD, AGNES   BORN: AGNES ROBERTSON MOOREHEAD
DEC 06,'06 AT CLINTON, MS DIED IN '74
FATHER: REV. JOHN HENDERSON MOOREHEAD
MOTHER: MARY MILDRED MCCAULEY
*** MARRIED: '30 JOHN GRIFFITH LEE, ACTOR (DIVORCED '52)
ADOPTED SON: SEAN LEE
*** MARRIED: '53 ROBERT GIST, ACTOR (DIVORCED '58)
RESIDENCE: VILLA AGNESE BEVERLY HILLS, CA
POSSESSION: LANDGRANT FAMILY FARM IN OHIO
POSSESSION: CONTRACT AT M-G-M, 1943-50
BIOGRAPHY: '76 A VERY PRIVATE PERSON, BY DR. WARREN SHERK
TALENT: ACTRESS
CREDIT: '41 CITIZEN KANE, DEBUT
AA-NOM SUP.ACT: '42 THE MAGNIFICENT AMBERSONS
AA-NOM SUP.ACT: '44 MRS. PARKINGTON
AA-NOM SUP.ACT: '48 JOHNNY BELINDA
AA-NOM SUP.ACT: '64 HUSH. . .HUSH SWEET CHARLOTTE

```
-----------------------------------------------------------------------------------
MORAN, LOIS           BORN:  LOIS DARLINGTON DOWLING
                             MAR 01,'07 AT PITTSBURGH, PA
  *** MARRIED:  '35 CLARENCE M. YOUNG, COLONEL
  SON:  '36 TIMOTHY YOUNG
  ROMANCE: F. SCOTT FITZGERALD
  ROMANCE: DOUGLAS MONTGOMERY
  RESIDENCE: SEDONA, AR
  TALENT: ACTRESS
  CREDIT:  '25 LOVE HUNGRY
  CREDIT:  '27 THE WHIRLWIND OF YOUTH
  CREDIT:  '30 THE DANCERS
  CREDIT:  '31 THE MEN IN HER LIFE
  CREDIT:  '38 STELLA DALLAS
-----------------------------------------------------------------------------------
MORAN, POLLY          BORN:  PAULINE THERESA MORAN
                             JUN 28,'83 AT CHICAGO, IL  DIED IN '52
  FATHER: THOMAS MORAN
  MOTHER: MILDRED FRANCES KELLY
  *** MARRIED:  '33 MARTIN MALONE, ATTORNEY
  ADOPTED SON: JOHN M. MALONE
  RESIDENCE: LAGUNA BEACH, CA
  TALENT: ACTRESS
  COMMENT: BILLED AS 'THAT SOMEWHAT DIFFERENT COMEDIENNE '
  CREDIT:  '15 POLITICS, DEBUT IN 1915
  CREDIT:  '29 CAUGHT SHORT
  CREDIT:  '33 ALICE IN WONDERLAND
  CREDIT:  '41 PETTICOAT POLITICS
  CREDIT:  '49 ADAM'S RIB
-----------------------------------------------------------------------------------
MOREAU, JEANNE
                             JAN 03,'28 AT PARIS, FRANCE
  FATHER: ANATOLE DESIRE MOREAU, RESTAURATEUR
  MOTHER: KATHLEEN BUCKLEY, FOLIES BERGERE DANCER
  SISTER: MICHELE MOREAU
  *** MARRIED:  '49 JEAN-LOUIS RICHARD  (DIVORCED '51)
  SON:  '49 JEROME RICHARD
  *** MARRIED:  '66 TEODORO RUBANIS  (DIVORCED)
  *** MARRIED:  '77 WILLIAM FRIEDKIN, DIRECTOR
  TALENT: ACTRESS
  CREDIT:  '55 THE SHE-WOLVES
  CREDIT:  '59 THE LOVERS
  CREDIT:  '61 JULES ET JIM
  CREDIT:  '65 VIVA MARIA
  CREDIT:  '70 ALEX IN WONDERLAND
-----------------------------------------------------------------------------------
MORENO, ANTONIO       BORN:  ANTONIO MONTEAGUADO Y MORENO
                             SEP 26,'86 AT MADRID, SPAIN  DIED IN '66
  FATHER: JUAN MORENO, SPANISH ARMY SERGEANT
  *** MARRIED:  '23 DAISY CANFIELD  (DIED '33)
  STEP-DAUGHTER: ELIZABETH DANZIGER, AKA BETH MORENO
  STEP-DAUGHTER: DAISY DANZIGER, AKA DAISY MORENO
  STEP-SON: ROBERT C. DANZIGER, AKA ROBERT MORENO
  ROMANCE: EDITH STOREY, ACTRESS
  FRIEND: WILLIAM DESMOND TAYLOR, ACTOR, DIRECTOR  (DIED '22)
  RESIDENCE: CRESTMOUNT, MORENO HIGHLANDS, LOS ANGELES, CA
  POSSESSION:  '14 CONTRACT AT VITAGRAPH FILM CO.
  TALENT: ACTOR
```

```
CREDIT:   '12 THE VOICE OF THE MILLION
CREDIT:   '23 MY AMERICAN WIFE
CREDIT:   '36 THE BOHEMIAN GIRL
CREDIT:   '47 CAPTAIN FROM CASTILLE
CREDIT:   '55 THE SEARCHERS
```

MORENO, RITA   BORN: ROSITA DOLORES ALVERIO
                             DEC 11,'31 AT HUMACHAO,PUERTO RICO
```
MOTHER: ROSA ALVERIO
STEP-FATHER: EDWARD MORENO
STEP-BROTHER: DENNIS MORENO
*** MARRIED:  '65 LEONARD GORDON, CARDIOLOGIST
DAUGHTER:   '66 FERNANDA LU GORDON
ROMANCE: GEORGE HORMEL, MEAT PACKER
ROMANCE: MARLON BRANDO, ACTOR
RESIDENCE: NYC
TALENT: ACTRESS-DANCER-SINGER
COMMENT: NICKNAME - RITA THE CHEETAH
CREDIT:   '50 PAGAN LOVE SONG
CREDIT:   '56 THE KING AND I
AA-WIN  SUP.ACT.:  '61 WEST SIDE STORY
CREDIT:   '69 POPI
CREDIT:   '71 CARNAL KNOWLEDGE
```

MORGAN, FRANK   BORN: FRANCIS PHILLIP WUPPERMANN
                             JUN 01,'90 AT NYC   DIED IN '49
```
FATHER: GEORGE WUPPERMANN
BROTHER: RALPH KUHNER WUPPERMANN, ACTOR - RALPH MORGAN  (DIED '56)
SISTER-IN-LAW: GRACE ARNOLD, ACTRESS
NIECE: CLAUDIA MORGAN, ACTRESS
*** MARRIED:  '14 ALMA MULLER
SON:   '16 GEORGE MORGAN
POSSESSION: THE ANGOSTURA-WUPPERMANN CORP. DISTRIBUTORS OF BITTERS
TALENT: ACTOR
COMMENT: WON 1947 HONOLULU RACE ON HIS SAILBOAT DOLPHIN
COMMENT: WROTE ENCYCLOPAEDIA BRITANNICA DEFINITION OF ACTOR/4500 WORDS
CREDIT:   '17 MODERN CINDERELLA
AA-NOM  ACTOR:  '34 AFFAIRS OF CELLINI
CREDIT:   '39 THE WIZARD OF OZ, (TITLE ROLE)
AA-NOM  SUP.ACT:  '42 TORTILLA FLAT
CREDIT:   '50 KEY TO THE CITY
```

MORGAN, MICHELE   BORN: SIMONE ROUSSEL
                               FEB 29,'20 AT PARIS, FRANCE
```
*** MARRIED:  '42 WILLIAM MARSHALL, PRODUCER  (DIVORCED '49)
SON:  '46 MICHAEL MARSHALL
*** MARRIED:  '50 HENRI VIDAL, ACTOR  (DIED '59)
MEMOIRS:  '76 IF I TALK OF HER
TALENT: ACTRESS
CREDIT:   '41 JOAN OF PARIS
CREDIT:   '48 THE FALLEN IDOL
CREDIT:   '51 THE SEVEN DEADLY SINS
CREDIT:   '60 THE MIRROR HAS TWO FACES
CREDIT:   '68 BENJAMIN
CREDIT:   '78 CAT AND MOUSE
```

```
-------------------------------------------------------------------------------
MORLEY, ROBERT
                        MAY 29,'08 AT WILTSHIRE, ENGLAND
    FATHER: ROBERT WILTON MORLEY, ARMY OFFICER
    MOTHER: GERTRUDE EMILY FASS
    *** MARRIED:  '40 JOAN BUCKMASTER
    BROTHER-IN-LAW: JOHN BUCKMASTER, ACTOR
    MOTHER-IN-LAW: GLADYS COOPER, ACTRESS
    SON:  '41 SHERIDAN MORLEY
    DAUGHTER:  '44 ANNABEL MORLEY
    GRANDDAUGHTER:  '70 ALEXIS MORLEY
    RESIDENCE: 'FAIRMAN'S COTTAGE', WARGRAVE, BERKSHIRE, ENGLAND
    MEMOIRS:  '66 ROBERT MORLEY, RESPONSIBLE GENTLEMAN
    MEMOIRS:  '67 A RELUCTANT AUTOBIOGRAPHY
    TALENT: ACTOR
    AA-NOM  SUP.ACT:  '38 MARIE ANTOINETTE
    CREDIT:  '40 MAJOR BARBARA
    CREDIT:  '53 GILBERT AND SULLIVAN
    CREDIT:  '66 WAY WAY OUT
    CREDIT:  '73 THEATRE OF BLOOD
-------------------------------------------------------------------------------
MOSTEL, ZERO          BORN:  SAMUEL JOEL MOSTEL
                        FEB 28,'15 AT BROOKLYN, NY  DIED IN '77
    FATHER: ISRAEL MOSTEL
    MOTHER: CELIA DUCHS
    *** MARRIED: KATHRYN HARKIN, DANCER
    SON: JOSHUA MOSTEL
    SON: TOBIAS MOSTEL
    RESIDENCE: NYC
    POSSESSION: PERUVIAN TEXTILES COLLECTION
    POSSESSION: PRE-COLUMBIAN ART COLLECTION
    TALENT: ACTOR
    CREDIT:  '50 PANIC IN THE STREETS
    CREDIT:  '51 THE ENFORCER
    CREDIT:  '66 A FUNNY THING HAPPENED ON THE  WAY TO THE FORUM
    CREDIT:  '68 THE PRODUCERS
    CREDIT:  '72 THE HOT ROCK
-------------------------------------------------------------------------------
MUNI, PAUL            BORN:  MUNI WEISENFREUND
                        SEP 22,'95 AT LWOW, POLAND  DIED IN '67
    FATHER: PHILIP WEISENFREUND
    MOTHER: SALLY WEISBERG
    *** MARRIED:  '21 BELLA FINKLE
    RESIDENCE: NYC
    POSSESSION:  '32 CONTRACT AT WARNER BROTHERS
    BIOGRAPHY:  '74 ACTOR - THE LIFE & TIMES OF PM, BY JEROME LAWRENCE
    TALENT: ACTOR
    AA-NOM  ACTOR:  '28 THE VALIANT DEBUT
    AA-NOM  ACTOR:  '32 I AM A FUGITIVE FROM A CHAIN  GANG
    AA-WIN  ACTOR:  '36 THE STORY OF LOUIS PASTEUR
    AA-NOM  ACTOR:  '37 THE LIFE OF EMILE ZOLA
    AA-NOM  ACTOR:  '59 THE LAST ANGRY MAN
```

MURPHY, AUDIE   BORN: AUDIE LEON MURPHY
                              JUN 20,'24 AT KINGSTON,TX   DIED IN '71
     FATHER: EMMETT BERRY MURPHY
     MOTHER: JOSIE BELL KILLIAN
     SISTER: ELIZABETH CORINNE MURPHY
     SISTER: ARIEL JUNE MURPHY
     SISTER: ONETA MURPHY (DIED '19)
     SISTER: J. W. MURPHY (DIED '20)
     SISTER: VEDA NADINE MURPHY
     SISTER: BEATRICE 'BILLIE' MURPHY
     BROTHER: CHARLES EMMETT 'BUCK' MURPHY
     BROTHER: VERNON MURPHY (DIED '19)
     BROTHER: RICHARD HOUSTON MURPHY (DIED '54)
     BROTHER: EUGENE PORTER MURPHY
     BROTHER: JOSEPH PRESTON MURPHY (DIED '68)
     *** MARRIED: '49 ACTRESS-WANDA HENDRIX (DIVORCED '51)
     *** MARRIED: '51 PAMELA ARCHER
     SON: '52 TERRY MICHAEL MURPHY
     SON: '54 JAMES SHANNON MURPHY
     MEMOIRS: TO HELL AND BACK
     BIOGRAPHY: '75 AMERICAN SOLDIER, BY HAROLD SIMPSON
     TALENT: ACTOR
     COMMENT: TWELVE AUNTS & UNCLES ON EACH SIDE OF HIS FAMILY
     CREDIT: '48 BEYOND GLORY
     CREDIT: '55 TO HELL AND BACK
     CREDIT: '63 SHOWDOWN
     CREDIT: '69 A TIME FOR DYING

MURPHY, GEORGE   BORN: GEORGE LLOYD MURPHY
                              JUL 04,'02 AT NEW HAVEN, CN
     FATHER: MICHAEL MURPHY, COACH ATHLETE
     MOTHER: NORA LONG
     *** MARRIED: '26 JULIETTE HENKEL, DANCE PARTNER-JULIETTE JOHNSON (DIED '73)
     SON: '38 DENNIS MICHAEL MURPHY
     DAUGHTER: '43 MELISSA ELAINE MURPHY
     FRIEND: LOUIS B. MAYER
     RESIDENCE: BEVERLY HILLS, CA
     POSSESSION: SILVER BUFFALO HIGHEST BOY SCOUT AWARD
     MEMOIRS: '70 SAY . . . DIDN'T YOUR USE TO BE GEORGE MURPHY?
     TALENT: ACTOR-POLITICIAN
     COMMENT: ELECTED US SENATOR , CALIFORNIA 1966-72
     CREDIT: '34 KID MILLIONS, DEBUT
     CREDIT: '41 RISE AND SHINE
     CREDIT: '47 THE BIG CITY
     AA-SPECIAL AWARD: '50 HONORARY AWARD FOR SERVICES TO THE FILM INDUSTRY
     CREDIT: '52 WALK EAST ON BEACON

MURRAY, KEN   BORN: DON COURT
                              JUL 14,'03 AT NYC
     SISTER: DOROTHY COURT
     *** MARRIED: CHARLOTTE (DIVORCED '34)
     SON: '44 KEN MURRAY,JR.
     *** MARRIED: '48 BETTE LOU WALTERS
     DAUGHTER: '52 PAMELA MURRAY
     DAUGHTER: '54 JANE MURRAY
     SON: CORT MURRAY
     RESIDENCE: BEVERLY HILLS, CA

MEMOIRS: LIFE ON A POGO STICK
TALENT: ACTOR, AUTHOR
CREDIT: '29 HALF MARRIAGE
CREDIT: '41 A NIGHT AT EARL CARROLL'S
CREDIT: '42 BLACKOUTS, STAGE SHOW
AA-SPECIAL AWARD: '47 BILL AND COO
CREDIT: '66 FOLLOW ME BOYS

MURRAY, MAE   BORN: MARIE ADRIENNE KOENIG
                          APR 10,'85 AT PORTSMOUTH, VA DIED IN '65
*** MARRIED: '08 WILLIAM MORRIS SCHWENKER, JR.
*** MARRIED: '16 JAMES JAY O'BRIEN
*** MARRIED: '25 ROBERT Z. LEONARD, ACTOR, DIRECTOR (DIVORCED '26)
*** MARRIED: '26 PRINCE DAVID M'DIVANI (DIVORCED '33)
BROTHER-IN-LAW: PRINCE SERGE M'DIVANI (DIED '36)
SON: '27 KORAN DAVID M'DIVANI, AKA DANIEL MICHAEL CUNNING
DAUGHTER-IN-LAW: PATRICIA ANN MALONEY (MARRIED '50)
ROMANCE: JOSE SALACETOS
PARTNER: JOAQUIN ELIZONDO, ACTOR, DANCING PARTNER
RESIDENCE: LOS ANGELES, CA
POSSESSION: '15 CONTRACT WITH THE FAMOUS PLAYERS-LASKY
MEMOIRS: '59 THE SELF ENCHANTED
TALENT: ACTRESS-DANCER
COMMENT: AKA THE GIRL WITH THE BEE-STUNG LIPS
CREDIT: '16 TO HAVE AND TO HOLD, DEBUT IN 1916
CREDIT: '18 HER BODY IN BOND
CREDIT: '23 JAZZMANIA
CREDIT: '25 THE MERRY WIDOW
CREDIT: '31 HIGH STAKES

NAGEL, CONRAD
MAR 16,'97 AT KEOKUK, IO DIED IN '70
FATHER: FRANK NAGEL, MUSIC TEACHER
MOTHER: FRANCES MURPHY
*** MARRIED: RUTH HELMS (DIVORCED)
*** MARRIED: LYNN MERRICK
TALENT: ACTOR
CREDIT: '18 LITTLE WOMEN
CREDIT: '27 QUALITY STREET
CREDIT: '31 EAST LYNNE
CREDIT: '45 FOREVER YOURS
CREDIT: '59 THE MAN WHO UNDERSTOOD WOMEN

NAISH, J. CARROLL   BORN: JOSEPH PATRICK CARROLL NAISH
JAN 21,'00 AT NYC DIED IN '73
FATHER: PATRICK SARSFIELD NAISH
MOTHER: CATHERINE MORAN
*** MARRIED: '28 GLADYS HEARNEY
DAUGHTER: '29 CAROL ELAINE NAISH
RESIDENCE: BEVERLY HILLS, CA
TALENT: ACTOR
COMMENT: JOHN NAISH - GREAT GRANDFATHER LORD CHANCELLOR OF IRELAND
CREDIT: '30 GOOD INTENTIONS
CREDIT: '35 LITTLE BIG SHOT
AA-NOM SUP.ACT: '43 SAHARA
AA-NOM SUP.ACT: '45 A MEDAL FOR BENNY
CREDIT: '57 THE YOUNG DON'T CRY

NALDI, NITA   BORN: ANITA DONNA DOOLEY
APR 04,'99 AT NYC DIED IN '61
*** MARRIED: '30 J. SEARLE BARCLAY (DIED)
FRIEND: DIANA BARRYMORE
RESIDENCE: HOTEL WENTWORTH, TIME SQUARE, NYC - FOR 25 YEARS
TALENT: ACTRESS
CREDIT: '20 DR. JEKYLL AND MR. HYDE
CREDIT: '22 BLOOD AND SAND
CREDIT: '23 THE TEN COMMANDMENTS
CREDIT: '25 COBRA
CREDIT: '28 WHAT PRICE BEAUTY?

NATWICK, MILDRED
JUN 19,'08 AT BALTIMORE, MD
FATHER: JOSEPH NATWICK
MOTHER: MILDRED DAWES
RESIDENCE: NYC
TALENT: ACTRESS
COMMENT: NEVER MARRIED
CREDIT: '40 THE LONG VOYAGE HOME
CREDIT: '50 CHEAPER BY THE DOZEN
CREDIT: '55 THE TROUBLE WITH HARRY
AA-NOM SUP.ACT: '67 BAREFOOT IN THE PARK
CREDIT: '69 THE MALTESE BIPPY

NAZIMOVA   BORN: ALLA NAZIMOVA LEWTON
                       JUN 04,'76 AT YALTA, RUSSIA   DIED IN '45
   SISTER: NINA LEWTON
   NEPHEW: VAL LEWTON, AKA VLADIMIR IVAN LEVENTON (DIED '51)
   *** MARRIED: '03 PAUL ORLENOFF, ACTOR
   ROMANCE: CHARLES BRYANT, ACTOR, DIRECTOR
   FRIEND: DAGMAR GODOWSKY, ACTRESS
   RESIDENCE: LOS ANGELES, CA
   TALENT: ACTRESS-DANCER
   COMMENT: OWNED THE GARDEN OF ALLAH HOTEL IN HOLLYWOOD
   COMMENT: FAMILY MIGRATED FROM SPAIN CHANGING NAME FROM LAVENDERA
   CREDIT: '16 WAR BRIDES, DEBUT IN 1916
   CREDIT: '21 CAMILLE
   CREDIT: '23 SALOME
   CREDIT: '35 SINCE YOU WENT AWAY
   CREDIT: '44 THE BRIDGE OF SAN LUIS REY

NEAGLE, ANNA   BORN: FLORENCE MARJORIE ROBERTSON
                      OCT 20,'04 AT FOREST GATE, LONDON, ENGLAND   DIED IN '66
   FATHER: HERBERT WILLIAM ROBERTSON
   MOTHER: FLORENCE NEAGLE, ACTRESS
   BROTHER: STUART ROBERTSON, SINGER
   BROTHER: ALAN ROBERTSON
   *** MARRIED: ROSS ALEXANDER, ACTOR
   *** MARRIED: '43 HERBERT WILCOX, PRODUCER-DANCER
   TALENT: ACTRESS-PRODUCER
   COMMENT: 1952-COMMANDER OF THE BRITISH EMPIRE
   CREDIT: '32 GOOD NIGHT VIENNA
   CREDIT: '33 BITTERSWEET
   CREDIT: '48 SPRING IN PARK LANE
   CREDIT: '51 THE LADY AND THE TRAMP
   CREDIT: '59 THE LADY IS A SQUARE

NEAL, PATRICIA   BORN: PATRICIA LOUISE NEAL
                      JAN 20,'26 AT PACKARD, KT
   FATHER: WILLIAM BURDETTE NEAL
   MOTHER: EURA MILDRED PETREY
   SISTER: MARGARET NEAL
   BROTHER: PETER NEAL
   *** MARRIED: '53 ROALD DAHL, WRITER
   SON: '60 THEODORE MATTHEW ROALD DAHL
   DAUGHTER: '64 OPHELIA MAGDALENE DAHL
   DAUGHTER: '65 LUCILLE NEAL DAHL
   DAUGHTER: OLIVIA TWENTY DAHL (DIED '62)
   DAUGHTER: TESSA SOPHIA DAHL
   ROMANCE: GARY COOPER
   FRIEND: LILLIAN HELLMAN, WRITER
   BIOGRAPHY: '69 PAT AND ROALD, BY BARRY FARRELL
   TALENT: ACTRESS
   CREDIT: '49 THE FOUNTAINHEAD
   CREDIT: '57 A FACE IN THE CROWD
   AA-WIN ACTRESS: '63 HUD
   AA-NOM ACTRESS: '68 THE SUBJECT WAS ROSES
   CREDIT: '71 THE HOMECOMING

NEFF, HILDEGARDE   BORN: HILDEGARDE KNEFF
                                DEC 28,'25 AT ULM, GERMANY
    *** MARRIED: '62 DAVID CAMERON·
    DAUGHTER: '68 CHRISTINA CAMERON
    RESIDENCE: SALZBURG, AUSTRIA
    MEMOIRS: '71 THE GIFT HORSE
    TALENT: ACTRESS-AUTHOR
    CREDIT: '46 THE MURDERS ARE AMONGST US
    CREDIT: '51 DECISION BEFORE DAWN
    CREDIT: '53 THE MAN BETWEEN
    CREDIT: '63 AND SO TO BED
    CREDIT: '68 THE LOST CONTINENT

NEGRI, POLA   BORN: APPOLONIA CHALUPEC
                            DEC 30,'97 AT LIPNO, POLAND
    FATHER: GEORGES CHALUPEC
    MOTHER: ELEANORA VON KIELESEWSKA
    *** MARRIED: '19 COUNT EUGEN DOMSKI (DIVORCED '20)
    *** MARRIED: '27 PRINCE SERGE M'DIVANI, DIED PLAYING IN A POLO MATCH (DIED '36)
    BROTHER-IN-LAW: PRINCE DAVID M'DIVANI
    ROMANCE: CHARLES CHAPLIN, ACTOR
    ROMANCE: RUDOLPH VALENTINO, ACTOR
    ROMANCE: ROD LA ROCQUE, ACTOR
    FRIEND: ERNST LUBITSCH, DIRECTOR
    RESIDENCE: SAN ANTONIO, TX
    MEMOIRS: '70 MEMOIRS OF A STAR
    TALENT: ACTRESS
    COMMENT: MEMBER OF THE IMPERIAL RUSSIAN BALLET CO.
    CREDIT: '23 BELLA DONNA, DEBUT
    CREDIT: '24 FORBIDDEN PARADISE
    CREDIT: '31 A WOMAN COMMANDS
    CREDIT: '43 HI DIDDLE, HI DIDDLE
    CREDIT: '64 THE MOON SPINNERS

NELSON, BARRY   BORN: ROBERT NEILSEN
                            APR 16,'20 AT OAKLAND, CA
    FATHER: TRYGVE NEILSEN
    MOTHER: LISBET CHRISTOPHISON
    *** MARRIED: '51 TERESA CELLI
    TALENT: ACTOR
    CREDIT: '42 CHINA CARAVAN
    CREDIT: '51 THE MAN WITH MY FACE
    CREDIT: '63 MARY MARY
    CREDIT: '69 AIRPORT
    CREDIT: '72 PETE 'N TILLIE

NELSON, GENE   BORN: EUGENE BERG
                            MAR 24,'20 AT SEATTLE, WA
    FATHER: LEE BERG (DIED '52)
    MOTHER: LENORE NELSON
    *** MARRIED: '42 MIRIAM FRANKLIN, DANCER (DIVORCED '56)
    SON: '47 ALAN CHRISTOPHER NELSON, FILM EDITOR
    *** MARRIED: '58 MARILYN MORGEN
    SON: '62 DOUGLAS NELSON
    DAUGHTER: '66 VICTORIA LEANDRA NELSON
    ROMANCE: PIPER LAURIE
    ROMANCE: JANE POWELL

FRIEND: JUNE HAVER, ACTRESS
POSSESSION: '76 NELSON PRODUCTION CO.
TALENT: DANCER-ACTOR-DIRECTOR
CREDIT: '50 THE DAUGHTER OF ROSIE O'GRADY, DEBUT
CREDIT: '51 TEA FOR TWO
CREDIT: '52 LULLABY OF BROADWAY
CREDIT: '55 OKLAHOMA!
CREDIT: '62 20,000 EYES

NELSON, OZZIE   BORN: OSWALD GEORGE NELSON
                              MAR 20,'07 AT JERSEY CITY, NJ   DIED IN '75
    FATHER: GEORGE WALDUMAR NELSON
    MOTHER: ETHEL IRENE ORR
    BROTHER: ALFRED NELSON
    *** MARRIED: '35 HARRIET HILLIARD, ACTRESS
    FATHER-IN-LAW: ROY SNYDER, ACTOR-AKA ROY HILLIARD
    SON: '36 DAVID NELSON
    DAUGHTER-IN-LAW: JUNE BLAIR, ACTRESS (MARRIED '64)
    SON: '40 RICK NELSON, ACTOR, SINGER
    DAUGHTER-IN-LAW: KRISTIN HARMON (MARRIED '63)
    GRANDDAUGHTER: '63 TRACY KRISTIN NELSON
    GRANDSON: '67 ERIC NELSON, JR., TWIN
    GRANDSON: '68 MATTHEW NELSON, TWIN
    GRANDSON: '69 GUNNAR NELSON
    RESIDENCE: LOS ANGELES, CA
    TALENT: ACTOR
    CREDIT: '41 SWEETHEART OF THE CAMPUS
    CREDIT: '44 HI, GOOD LOOKIN
    CREDIT: '45 PEOPLE ARE FUNNY
    CREDIT: '52 HERE COME THE NELSONS
    CREDIT: '68 THE IMPOSSIBLE YEARS

NELSON, RICK   BORN: ERIC HILLIARD NELSON
                             MAY 08,'40 AT TEANECK, NJ
    FATHER: OZZIE NELSON, ACTOR
    MOTHER: HARRIET HILLIARD, ACTRESS
    BROTHER: DAVID NELSON, ACTOR
    SISTER-IN-LAW: JUNE BLAIR, ACTRESS (MARRIED '64)
    *** MARRIED: '63 KRISTIN HARMON
    FATHER-IN-LAW: TOM HARMON, SPORTS ANNOUNCER
    DAUGHTER: '63 TRACY KRISTIN NELSON
    SON: '67 ERIC NELSON, JR., TWIN
    SON: '67 MATTHEW NELSON, TWIN
    SON: '69 GUNNAR NELSON
    TALENT: ACTOR-SINGER
    CREDIT: '52 HERE COME THE NELSONS
    CREDIT: '59 RIO BRAVO
    CREDIT: '60 THE WACKIEST SHIP
    CREDIT: '65 LOVE AND KISSES

NESBIT, EVELYN   BORN: EVELYN FLORENCE NESBIT
                               1885 AT TARENTUM, PA DIED IN '67
    *** MARRIED: '05 HARRY K. THAW (DIVORCED '16)
    SON: '12 RUSSELL THAW
    *** MARRIED: '18 VIRGIL JAMES MONTANI, ACTOR, BOXER-JACK CLIFFORD (DIVORCED '33)
    ROMANCE: STANFORD WHITE, ARCHITECT, KILLED BY HER HUSBAND IN 1906
    RESIDENCE: LOS ANGELES, CA
    BIOGRAPHY: '75 RAGTIME, BY E. L. DOCTOROW

```
TALENT: ACTRESS
COMMENT: 'THE GIRL IN THE RED SWING'
COMMENT: MODEL FOR CHARLES GIBSON'S PAINTING 'THE ETERNAL QUESTION'
CREDIT: THREADS OF DESTINY
CREDIT: THE HIDDEN WOMAN
```

```
NEWMAN, PAUL          BORN:  PAUL L. NEWMAN
                             JAN 26,'25 AT CLEVELAND, OH
    FATHER: ARTHUR NEWMAN, OWNED SPORTING GOODS STORE
    MOTHER: THERESA FETZER
    UNCLE: JOE NEWMAN, JOURNALIST
    *** MARRIED:  '47 JACQUELINE WITTE, ACTRESS  (DIVORCED '56)
    SON:  '50 SCOTT NEWMAN, ACTOR
    DAUGHTER:  '51 SUSAN NEWMAN
    DAUGHTER:  '52 STEPHANIE NEWMAN
    *** MARRIED:  '58 JOANNE WOODWARD, ACTRESS
    DAUGHTER:  '59 ELEANOR NEWMAN
    DAUGHTER:  '60 MELISSA NEWMAN
    DAUGHTER:  '61 CARA NEWMAN
    FRIEND: BARBRA STREISAND
    FRIEND: SIDNEY POITIER
    FRIEND: STEVE MCQUEEN
    RESIDENCE: WESTPORT, CN
    POSSESSION:  '54 CONTRACT AT WARNER BROS.
    TALENT: ACTOR-DIRECTOR-AUTOMOBILE RACER
    CREDIT:  '54 THE SILVER CHALICE
    AA-NOM  ACTOR:  '58 CAT ON A HOT TIN ROOF
    AA-NOM  ACTOR:  '61 THE HUSTLER
    AA-NOM  ACTOR:  '63 HUD
    AA-NOM  ACTOR:  '67 COOL HAND LUKE
    CREDIT:  '69 BUTCH CASSIDY AND THE SUNDANCE KID
    CREDIT:  '75 THE STING
```

```
NICHOLS, MIKE          BORN:  MICHAEL IGOR PESCHKOWSKY
                             NOV 06,'31 AT BERLIN, GERMANY
    GRANDFATHER: GUSTAV LANDAUER, POLITICIAN
    GRANDMOTHER: HEDWIG LACHMANN
    FATHER: PAUL PESCHKOWSKY, PHYSICIAN
    BROTHER: --
    *** MARRIED: PAT SCOT, SINGER  (DIVORCED)
    *** MARRIED: MARGO CALLAS  (DIVORCED)
    *** MARRIED: ANNABEL, WRITER
    DAUGHTER:  '65 DAISY NICHOLS
    SON:  '74 MAX NICHOLS
    DAUGHTER:  '76 JENNY NICHOLS
    ROMANCE: GLORIA STEINEM
    PARTNER: ELAINE MAY
    RESIDENCE: CONNECTICUT 60 ACRE FARM
    TALENT: ACTOR-DIRECTOR-PRODUCER BREEDER OF ARABIAN HORSES
    AA-NOM  DIRECTOR:  '66 WHO'S AFRAID OF VIRGINIA WOOLF ?
    AA-WIN  DIRECTOR:  '67 THE GRADUATE
    CREDIT:  '70 CATCH 22, DIRECTED
    CREDIT:  '71 CARNAL KNOWLEDGE, DIRECTED
    CREDIT:  '73 THE DAY OF THE DOLPHIN, DIRECTED
```

```
------------------------------------------------------------------------
NICHOLSON,  JACK
                        APR 22,'37 AT NEPTUNE, NJ
    FATHER: JOHN NICHOLSON, SIGN PAINTER
    MOTHER: ETHEL MAY
    SISTER: --
    SISTER: --
    *** MARRIED:  '61 SANDRA KNIGHT  (DIVORCED '66)
    DAUGHTER:  '63 JENNIFER NICHOLSON
    ROMANCE: MICHELLE PHILLIPS - ACTRESS, SINGER
    ROMANCE: ANGELICA HUSTON
    TALENT: ACTOR
    AA-NOM  SUP.ACT:  '69 EASY RIDER
    AA-NOM  ACTOR:  '70 FIVE EASY PIECES
    AA-NOM  ACTOR:  '73 THE LAST DETAIL
    AA-NOM  ACTOR:  '74 CHINATOWN
    AA-WIN  ACTOR:  '75 ONE FLEW OVER THE CUCKOO'S  NEST
------------------------------------------------------------------------
NIVEN,  DAVID           BORN:   JAMES DAVID GRAHAM NIVEN
                        MAR 01,'10 AT LONDON, ENGLAND
    FATHER: WILLIAM GRAHAM NIVEN, MILITARY OFFICER  (DIED '15)
    MOTHER: HENRIETTE DEGACHER, LADY COMYN PLATT
    *** MARRIED:  '40 PRIMULA ROLLO, DIED PLAYING A PARTY GAME  (DIED '46)
    SON:  '42 JAMES NIVEN
    SON:  '45 DAVID NIVEN, JR.
    *** MARRIED:  '48 HJORDIS TERSMEDEN
    DAUGHTER: KRISTINA NIVEN
    DAUGHTER: FIONA NIVEN
    ROMANCE: VIRGINIA BRUCE
    ROMANCE: SIMONE SIMON
    ROMANCE: NORMA SHEARER
    FRIEND: GILBERT ROLAND
    FRIEND: ERROL FLYNN
    RESIDENCE: VEVEY, SWITZERLAND
    RESIDENCE: ST. JEAN, CAP FERRAT, FRANCE
    POSSESSION:  '51 PARTNER IN FOUR STAR PROD. CO. WITH LUPINO, BOYER & POWELL
    MEMOIRS:  '74 THE MOON'S A BALLOON
    MEMOIRS:  '76 BRING ON THE EMPTY HORSES
    TALENT: ACTOR-AUTHOR-BRITISH ARMY COLONEL
    CREDIT:  '35 BARBARY COAST
    CREDIT:  '40 RAFFLES
    AA-WIN  ACTOR:  '58 SEPARATE TABLES
    CREDIT:  '64 THE PINK PANTHER
    CREDIT:  '70 THE STATUE
------------------------------------------------------------------------
NOLAN,  LLOYD
                        AUG 11,'02 AT SAN FRANCISCO
    FATHER: JAMES NOLAN
    MOTHER: MARGARET SHEA
    *** MARRIED:  '33 MEL ELFRID
    DAUGHTER:  '40 MELINDA JOYCE NOLAN
    SON:  '42 JAY NOLAN
    RESIDENCE: BRENTWOOD, CA
    POSSESSION: RANCH NEAR CAMARILLO, CALIF.
    TALENT: ACTOR
    CREDIT:  '35 STOLEN HARMONY
    CREDIT:  '44 A TREE GROWS IN BOOKLYN
    CREDIT:  '58 PEYTON PLACE
```

CREDIT: '68 ICE STATION ZEBRA
CREDIT: '69 AIRPORT

NORMAND, MABEL   BORN: MABEL ETHELREID NORMAND
                               NOV 10,'94 AT ATLANTA, GA DIED IN '30
    FATHER: CLAUDE GEORGE NORMAND
    MOTHER: MARY DRURY
    SISTER: GLADYS NORMAND
    BROTHER: CLAUDE NORMAND, JR.
    *** MARRIED: '26 LEW CODY, ACTOR, PRODUCER
    ROMANCE: MACK SENNETT, PRODUCER
    ROMANCE: WILLIAM DESMOND TAYLOR, DIRECTOR
    FRIEND: ANNA Q. NILSSON, ACTRESS
    TALENT: ACTRESS
    COMMENT: HER MARRIAGE WAS A PARTY GAG AND WAS NEVER CONSUMMATED
    CREDIT: '11 THE UNVEILING, FILM DEBUT-1911
    CREDIT: '12 MABEL & FATTY (ARBUCKLE), SERIES
    CREDIT: '18 SIS HOPKINS
    CREDIT: '20 PECK'S BAD GIRL
    CREDIT: '23 OH, MABEL, BEHAVE!

NORTH, SHEREE   BORN: DAWN BETHEL
                               JAN 17,'30 AT LOS ANGELES
    *** MARRIED: '50 FRED BESSIRE
    DAUGHTER: '51 DAWN BESSIRE
    *** MARRIED: '55 JOHN (BUD) FREEMAN
    *** MARRIED: '58 DR. GREGORY SOMMER
    DAUGHTER: '59 ERICA SOMMER
    TALENT: ACTRESS
    CREDIT: '51 EXCUSE MY DUST
    CREDIT: '55 HOW TO BE VERY VERY POPULAR
    CREDIT: '58 MARDI GRAS
    CREDIT: '69 THE GYPSY MOTHS
    CREDIT: '73 CHARLEY VARRICK

NOVAK, KIM   BORN: MARILYN PAULINE NOVAK
                               FEB 13,'33 AT CHICAGO,IL
    FATHER: JOSEPH A. NOVAK
    MOTHER: BLANCHE KRAL
    SISTER: ARLENE NOVAK
    *** MARRIED: '65 RICHARD JOHNSON, ACTOR (DIVORCED '66)
    *** MARRIED: '76 ROBERT MALLORY, VETERINARIAN
    RESIDENCE: MONTERREY, CA
    POSSESSION: '54 CONTRACT AT COLUMBIA PICTURES
    TALENT: ACTRESS
    CREDIT: '54 PUSHOVER, DEBUT
    CREDIT: '56 PICNIC
    CREDIT: '58 VERTIGO
    CREDIT: '62 THE NOTORIOUS LANDLADY
    CREDIT: '65 MOLL FLANDERS

NOVARRO, RAMON   BORN: JOSE RAMON GIL SAMANIEGOS
                               FEB 06,'99 AT DURANGO, MEXICO DIED IN '68
    FATHER: M. N. SAMANIEGOS, DENTIST
    MOTHER: ELENOR GAVILAN
    SISTER: CARMEN SAMANIEGOS, DANCER
    SISTER: LUZ SAMANIEGOS
    SISTER: LENORE SAMANIEGOS, NUN

BROTHER: MARIANO SAMANIEGOS, DENTIST
BROTHER: EDUARDO SAMANIEGOS, ARCHITECT
BROTHER: JOSE SAMANIEGOS, CHEMIST
BROTHER: ANTONIO SAMANIEGOS, FILM TECHNICIAN
COUSIN: DOLORES DEL RIO, ACTRESS
ROMANCE: MYRNA LOY, ACTRESS
FRIEND: ALICE TERRY, ACTRESS (MRS. REX INGRAM)
FRIEND: ELSIE JANIS
RESIDENCE: LOS ANGELES, CA
POSSESSION: '22 CONTRACT WITH REX INGRAM'S CO.
TALENT: ACTOR-DANCER-VIOLINIST
CREDIT: '19 THE GOAT, DEBUT IN 1919
CREDIT: '26 BEN-HUR
CREDIT: '35 THE NIGHT IS YOUNG
CREDIT: '49 THE BIG STEAL
CREDIT: '60 HELLER IN PINK TIGHTS

NOVELLO, IVOR   BORN: DAVID IVOR NOVELLO DAVIES
                         JAN 15,'93 AT CARDIFF, WALES   DIED IN '51
FATHER: DAVID DAVIES, ACCOUNTANT
MOTHER: CLARA NOVELLO, SINGER, MUSIC TEACHER
STEP-SISTER: MARIE NOVELLO DAVIES
FRIEND: ARTHUR MORGAN, ACTOR AND HIS CHAUFFEUR
BIOGRAPHY: '51 MAN OF THE THEATRE, BY PETER NOBLE
TALENT: ACTOR, WRITER
COMMENT: WROTE SONG 'KEEP THE HOMEFIRES BURNING' IN 1915
CREDIT: '21 CARNIVAL
CREDIT: '28 WHEN THE BOYS LEAVE HOME
CREDIT: '35 THE PHANTOM FIEND

O'BRIEN, EDMOND
                              SEP 10,'15 AT NYC
    FATHER: JAMES O'BRIEN
    MOTHER: AGNES BALDWIN
    *** MARRIED: '41 NANCY KELLY (DIVORCED '42)
    *** MARRIED: '48 OLGA SAN JUAN, ACTRESS
    DAUGHTER: '49 MARIA O'BRIEN
    SON-IN-LAW: MICHAEL ANDERSON, ACTOR
    DAUGHTER: '50 BRIDGET O'BRIEN
    SON-IN-LAW: TOM BELCHER, DIRECTOR
    SON: '62 BRENDAN O'BRIEN
    RESIDENCE: LOS ANGELES, CA
    TALENT: ACTOR
    CREDIT: '39 THE HUNCHBACK OF NOTRE DAME
    CREDIT: '47 A DOUBLE LIFE
    AA-WIN SUP.ACT.: '54 THE BAREFOOT CONTESSA
    AA-NOM SUP.ACT: '64 SEVEN DAYS IN MAY
    CREDIT: '69 THE LOVE GOD

O'BRIEN, MARGARET   BORN: ANGELA MAXINE O'BRIEN
                              JAN 15,'37 AT SAN DIEGO, CA
    FATHER: LAWRENCE O'BRIEN, CIRCUS PERFORMER (DIED '36)
    MOTHER: GLADYS FLORES (DIED '58)
    STEP-FATHER: DON SYLVIO, BAND LEADER
    AUNT: MARISSA FLORES, DANCER, ACTRESS
    *** MARRIED: '59 HAROLD R. ALLEN, ARTIST (DIVORCED '69)
    *** MARRIED: '74 ROY THORSEN
    DAUGHTER: '76 MARA TOLENE THORSEN
    ROMANCE: JULIO TIJER, PERUVIAN PRODUCER
    RESIDENCE: BEVERLY HILLS, CA
    POSSESSION: PERUVIAN & SPANISH ART COLLECTION
    MEMOIRS: MY DIARY
    TALENT: ACTRESS
    CREDIT: '41 BABES ON BROADWAY
    CREDIT: '43 LOST ANGEL
    AA-SPECIAL AWARD: '44 AN HONORARY MINIATURE STATUE 'OUTSTANDING CHILD ACTRESS'
    CREDIT: '49 LITTLE WOMEN
    CREDIT: '56 GLORY
    CREDIT: '60 HELLER IN PINK TIGHTS

O'BRIEN, PAT   BORN: WILLIAM JOSEPH PATRICK O'BRIEN
                              NOV 11,'99 AT MILWAUKEE,WI
    FATHER: WILLIAM O'BRIEN, SR.
    MOTHER: MARGARET MCGOVERN
    *** MARRIED: '31 ELOISE TAYLOR
    ADOPTED DAUGHTER: MAVOURNEEN O'BRIEN
    ADOPTED DAUGHTER: BRIGID O'BRIEN
    ADOPTED SON: PATRICK O'BRIEN, JR.
    ADOPTED SON: TERENCE O'BRIEN
    DAUGHTER: KATHLEEN O'BRIEN
    FRIEND: SPENCER TRACY
    RESIDENCE: 'TARA' IN BRENTWOOD, CALIF.
    MEMOIRS: '63 WIND ON MY BACK
    TALENT: ACTOR
    CREDIT: '31 THE FRONT PAGE
    CREDIT: '38 BOY MEETS GIRL
    CREDIT: '43 HIS BUTLER'S SISTER

```
     CREDIT:  '52 JUBILEE TRAIL
     CREDIT:  '59 SOME LIKE IT HOT
---------------------------------------------------------------------------------------------------
O'CONNELL, ARTHUR
                              MAR 29,'08 AT NYC
     FATHER: MICHAEL O'CONNELL
     MOTHER: JULIA BYRNE
     *** MARRIED:  '62 ANN HALL DUNLOP
     TALENT: ACTOR
     CREDIT:  '42 LAW OF THE JUNGLE
     AA-NOM  SUP.ACT:  '55 PICNIC
     AA-NOM  SUP.ACT:  '59 ANATOMY OF A MURDER
     CREDIT:  '65 YOUR CHEATING HEART
     CREDIT:  '72 THE POSEIDON ADVENTURE
---------------------------------------------------------------------------------------------------
O'CONNOR,  CAROLL
                              AUG 02,'22 AT NYC
     FATHER: EDWARD JOSEPH O'CONNOR, LAWYER
     MOTHER: ELSIE PATRICIA
     BROTHER: HUGH  O'CONNOR
     *** MARRIED:  '45 PATSY FAYE
     *** MARRIED:  '51 NANCY FIELDS
     ADOPTED SON: HUGH O'CONNOR
     RESIDENCE: WESTWOOD, CA
     POSSESSION: '78 THE GINGER MAN RESTAURANT IN BEVERLY HILLS
     TALENT: ACTOR, AUTHOR, POLITICIAN
     CREDIT:  '61 BY LOVE POSSESSED
     CREDIT:  '63 CLEOPATRA
     CREDIT:  '67 POINT BLANK
     CREDIT:  '70 ALL IN THE FAMILY, TV SERIES
---------------------------------------------------------------------------------------------------
O'CONNOR,  DONALD          BORN:  DONALD DAVID DIXON O'CONNOR
                              AUG 28,'25 AT CHICAGO, IL
     FATHER: JOHN EDWARD O'CONNOR, CIRCUS STRONG MAN
     MOTHER: EFFIE IRENE CRANE, CIRCUS ACROBAT
     BROTHER: JACK O'CONNOR, DANCER  (DIED '55)
     BROTHER: BILL O'CONNOR
     *** MARRIED:  '44 GWEN CARTER, ACTRESS  (DIVORCED '54)
     DAUGHTER:  '46 DONNA O'CONNOR
     SON-IN-LAW: JEFF THOMAS, SINGER  (MARRIED '67)
     *** MARRIED:  '56 GLORIA NOBLE
     BROTHER-IN-LAW: BILLY WILKERSON, PUBLISHER
     DAUGHTER:  '57 ALICIA O'CONNOR
     SON:  '60 DONALD FREDERICK O'CONNOR
     SON:  '62 KEVIN O'CONNOR
     RESIDENCE: BRENTWOOD, CA
     POSSESSION:  '38 CONTRACT AT PARAMOUNT PICTURES
     POSSESSION:  '60 RIVERSIDE HOTEL IN RENO, NEV.
     TALENT: ACTOR
     CREDIT:  '38 SING YOU SINNERS
     CREDIT:  '49 FRANCIS, SERIES
     CREDIT:  '51 THE BUSTER KEATON STORY
     CREDIT:  '52 SINGIN' IN THE RAIN
     CREDIT:  '65 THAT FUNNY FEELING
```

O'HARA, MAUREEN   BORN: MAUREEN FITZSIMMONS
                                   AUG 17,'20 AT DUBLIN, IRELAND
     FATHER: CHARLES FITZSIMMONS
     MOTHER: MARGUERITE LILLBURN, ACTRESS, SINGER
     SISTER: BRIDGET FITZSIMMONS
     *** MARRIED: '38 GEORGE HANLEY BROWN, DIRECTOR (ANNULLED '41)
     *** MARRIED: '41 WILL PRICE, DIRECTOR (DIVORCED '53)
     DAUGHTER: '44 BRONWYN FITZSIMMONS PRICE
     *** MARRIED: '68 CHARLES F. BLAIR, JR., AIR FORCE OFFICER, PILOT (DIED '78)
     FRIEND: JOHN WAYNE
     RESIDENCE: CHRISTIANSTAD VIRGIN ISLANDS
     POSSESSION: ANTILLES AIR BOATS CO. VICE PRESIDENT
     TALENT: ACTRESS
     CREDIT: '39 JAMAICA INN, DEBUT
     CREDIT: '42 THE BLACK SWAN
     CREDIT: '46 DO YOU LOVE ME
     CREDIT: '56 EVERYTHING BUT THE TRUTH
     CREDIT: '70 HOW DO I LOVE THEE

O'HERLIHY, DAN   BORN: DANIEL O'HERLIHY
                                   MAY 01,'19 AT WEXFORD, IRELAND
     FATHER: JOHN O'HERLIHY, CIVIL SERVANT
     MOTHER: ELLEN HANTON
     SISTER: MARGUERITE O'HERLIHY
     BROTHER: MICHAEL O'HERLIHY, SET DESIGNER
     *** MARRIED: '45 ELSA BENNETT, ACTRESS
     SISTER-IN-LAW: OLGA BENNETT
     SON: '46 OLWEN O'HERLIHY
     DAUGHTER: '48 PATRICIA O'HERLIHY
     SON: '51 GAVIN O'HERLIHY
     SON: '53 CORMAC O'HERLIHY
     SON: '55 LORCAN PATRICK O'HERLIHY
     RESIDENCE: MALIBU, CA
     RESIDENCE: KILLINEY BAY, IRELAND
     TALENT: ACTOR
     COMMENT: MEMBER INSTITUTES OF BRITISH & IRISH ARCHITECTS
     CREDIT: '46 ODD MAN OUT
     AA-NOM ACTOR: '54 ADVENTURES OF ROBINSON CRUSOE
     CREDIT: '58 HOME BEFORE DARK
     CREDIT: '69 WATERLOO
     CREDIT: '74 THE TAMARIND SEED

O'KEEFE, DENNIS   BORN: EDWARD VANES 'BUD' FLANAGAN
                                   MAR 29,'08 AT FORT MADISON, IO DIED IN '68
     FATHER: EDWARD VANES FLANAGAN, SR., ACTOR
     MOTHER: CHARLOTTE EDWARDS, ACTRESS
     SISTER: HORTENSE FLANAGAN
     *** MARRIED: '40 STEPHANIE BERINDE CARROLL, ACTRESS - STEFFI DUNA
     STEP-DAUGHTER: JULIENA LAFAYE CARROLL
     SON: '43 EDWARD JAMES FLANAGAN O'KEEFE
     RESIDENCE: BEVERLY HILLS, CA
     TALENT: ACTOR, AUTHOR
     COMMENT: EARLY STAGE NAME - LARRY DOYLE
     COMMENT: PEN NAME - JONATHAN RICKS
     CREDIT: '39 THAT'S RIGHT, YOU'RE WRONG
     CREDIT: '45 THE AFFAIRS OF SUSAN
     CREDIT: '47 DISHONORED LADY

```
CREDIT:  '53 THE FAKE
CREDIT:  '58 GRAFT AND CORRUPTION
```

O'NEAL, RYAN   BORN: PATRICK RYAN O'NEILL
                                 APR 20,'41 AT LOS ANGELES, CA
```
     FATHER: CHARLES O'NEILL
     MOTHER: PATRICIA CALLAGHAN
     BROTHER: KEVIN O'NEILL, ACTOR
     *** MARRIED:  '63 JOANNA MOORE, ACTRESS  (DIVORCED '66)
     DAUGHTER:  '63 TATUM O'NEAL, ACTRESS
     SON:  '64 GRIFFIN PATRICK O'NEAL
     *** MARRIED:  '67 LEIGH TAYLOR-YOUNG, ACTRESS  (DIVORCED)
     SON:  '67 PATRICK O'NEAL
     ROMANCE: URSULA ANDRESS
     ROMANCE: JACQUELINE BISSET
     ROMANCE: ANGELICA HUSTON
     ROMANCE: ANOUK AIMEE
     RESIDENCE: MALIBU, CA
     TALENT: ACTOR
     CREDIT:  '69 THE BIG BOUNCE
     AA-NOM  ACTOR:  '70 LOVE STORY
     CREDIT:  '72 WHAT'S UP DOC
     CREDIT:  '73 PAPER MOON
     CREDIT:  '75 NICKELODEON
     CREDIT:  '78 THE DRIVER
```

O'NEILL, JENNIFER
                              FEB 20,'48 AT RIO DE JANEIRO, BRAZIL
```
     GRANDFATHER: OSCAR O'NEILL, BANK PRESIDENT
     FATHER: OSCAR O'NEILL, JR.
     MOTHER: IRENE POPE
     *** MARRIED:  '66 DEED ROSSITER  (DIVORCED '72)
     DAUGHTER:  '67 AIMEE ROSSITER
     *** MARRIED:  '73 JOSEPH KOSTER
     *** MARRIED:  '75 NICHOLAS DE NOIA, CHOREOGRAPHER
     *** MARRIED:  '78 JEFF BARRY, SONGWRITER
     ROMANCE: HERB ALLEN, FINANCIER
     ROMANCE: ELLIOT GOULD, ACTOR
     RESIDENCE: BEDFORD VILLAGE, NY
     TALENT: ACTRESS
     CREDIT:  '70 RIO LOBO
     CREDIT:  '71 SUCH GOOD FRIENDS
     CREDIT:  '71 SUMMER OF '42
     CREDIT:  '72 THE CAREY TREATMENT
     CREDIT:  '74 THE REINCARNATION OF PETER PROUD
     CREDIT:  '78 CARAVANS
```

O'SULLIVAN, MAUREEN   BORN: MAUREEN PAULA O'SULLIVAN
                                      MAY 17,'11 AT BOYLE, ROSCOMMON, IRELAND
```
     FATHER: CHARLES O'SULLIVAN, ARMY OFFICER
     *** MARRIED:  '36 JOHN VILLIERS FARROW, DIRECTOR  (DIED '63)
     SON:  '39 MICHAEL FARROW  (DIED '58)
     DAUGHTER:  '46 MIA FARROW, ACTRESS
     SON-IN-LAW: FRANK SINATRA, SINGER, ACTOR  (MARRIED '66)
     SON-IN-LAW: ANDRE PREVIN, CONDUCTOR
     DAUGHTER: PRUDENCE FARROW
     DAUGHTER: TERESA FARROW
     DAUGHTER: STEPHANIE FARROW
```

```
      SON: PATRICK FARROW
      SON: JOHN FARROW, JR.
      ROMANCE: ROBERT RYAN, ACTOR  (DIED '73)
      GRANDDAUGHTER:  '70 GIGI PREVIN
      GRANDSON:  '74 KYM LARK PREVIN
      GRANDSON: MATTHEW PHINEAS PREVIN, TWIN
      GRANDSON: SASCHA VILLIERS PREVIN, TWIN
      FRIEND: VIVIEN LEIGH, SCHOOLMATES IN LONDON
      FRIEND: F. SCOTT FITZGERALD
      RESIDENCE: NYC
      POSSESSION: WEDIQUETTE BRIDAL SERVICES-EXECUTIVE DIRECTOR
      TALENT: ACTRESS
      CREDIT:  '30 SO THIS IS LONDON, DEBUT
      CREDIT:  '34 TARZAN, SERIES
      CREDIT:  '48 THE BIG CLOCK
      CREDIT:  '53 ALL I DESIRE
      CREDIT:  '65 NEVER TOO LATE
---------------------------------------------------------------------------
O'TOOLE, PETER          BORN:  PETER SEAMUS O'TOOLE
                               AUG 02,'33 AT CONNEMARA, IRELAND
      FATHER: PATRICK JOSEPH O'TOOLE
      MOTHER: CONSTANCE
      SISTER: PATRICIA O'TOOLE
      *** MARRIED:  '59 SIAN PHILLIPS, ACTRESS
      DAUGHTER:  '60 CATHERINE 'KATE' O'TOOLE
      DAUGHTER:  '63 PATRICIA 'PAT' O'TOOLE
      FRIEND: H. A. L. 'HARRY' CRAIG, WRITER, ANARCHIST, POET
      PARTNER: JULES BUCK, PRODUCER
      RESIDENCE: HAMPSTEAD, LONDON
      POSSESSION: SPEED RECORD FOR BEER DRINKING AT DIRTY DICK'S PUB, DUBLIN
      TALENT: ACTOR
      AA-NOM  ACTOR:  '62 LAWRENCE OF ARABIA
      AA-NOM  ACTOR:  '64 BECKET
      AA-NOM  ACTOR:  '68 THE LION IN WINTER
      AA-NOM  ACTOR:  '69 GOODBYE, MR. CHIPS
      AA-NOM  ACTOR:  '72 THE RULING CLASS
---------------------------------------------------------------------------
OAKIE, JACK          BORN:  LEWIS DELANEY OFFIELD
                            NOV 12,'03 AT SEDALIA, MR  DIED IN '78
      *** MARRIED:  '36 VENITA VARDEN, ACTRESS  (DIVORCED '38)
      *** MARRIED:  '45 VICTORIA HORNE
      ROMANCE: FRANCES DEE
      FRIEND: GRETA GARBO, ACTRESS
      RESIDENCE: NORTHRIDGE, CA
      POSSESSION: AFGHAN HOUND SHOWDOGS
      TALENT: ACTOR
      CREDIT:  '27 FINDERS KEEPERS, DEBUT
      CREDIT:  '33 IF I HAD A MILLION
      AA-NOM  SUP.ACT:  '40 THE GREAT DICTATOR
      CREDIT:  '50 LAST OF THE BUCCANEERS
      CREDIT:  '62 LOVER COME BACK
---------------------------------------------------------------------------
OBERON, MERLE          BORN:  ESTELLE MERLE O'BRIEN THOMPSON
                              FEB 19,'11 AT TASMANIA, AUSTRALIA
      FATHER: JOHN THOMPSON, ARMY OFFICER  (DIED '10)
      MOTHER: CONSTANCE CHARLOTTE
      *** MARRIED:  '39 ALEXANDER KORDA, PRODUCER  (DIVORCED '45)
      *** MARRIED:  '45 LUCIEN BALLARD, BY PROXY  (DIVORCED '49)
```

```
      *** MARRIED:  '57 BRUNO PAGLIAI  (DIVORCED '73)
      ADOPTED SON: BRUNO PAGLIAI, JR.
      ADOPTED DAUGHTER: FRANCESCA PAGLIAI
      *** MARRIED:  '75 ROBERT WOLDERS, ACTOR
      RESIDENCE: MALIBU,CA
      TALENT: ACTRESS
      CREDIT:  '31 SERVICES FOR LADIES
      AA-NOM  ACTRESS: '35 THE DARK ANGEL
      CREDIT:  '39 WUTHERING HEIGHTS
      CREDIT:  '45 THIS LOVE OF OURS
      CREDIT:  '46 TEMPTATION
      CREDIT:  '63 OF LOVE AND DESIRE
------------------------------------------------------------------------------------------
OLAND, WARNER          BORN:   JOHAN WARNER OLAND
                               OCT 03,'80 AT UMEA, SWEDEN  DIED IN '38
      FATHER: JONAS OLAND
      MOTHER: MARIA
      BROTHER: CARL OLAND
      *** MARRIED:  '08 EDITH SHEARN, ACTRESS  (SEPARATED '37)
      FRIEND: KEYE LUKE, ACTOR
      POSSESSION: ISLAND IN GULF OF CALIFORNIA & FARM IN MASSACHUSETTS
      TALENT: ACTOR
      CREDIT:  '09 JEWELS OF THE MADONNA, DEBUT
      CREDIT:  '23 HIS CHILDREN'S CHILDREN
      CREDIT:  '27 THE JAZZ SINGER
      CREDIT:  '31 CHARLIE CHAN, STAR IN SERIES
      CREDIT:  '35 WEREWOLF OF LONDON
------------------------------------------------------------------------------------------
OLIVIER, LAURENCE          BORN:   LAURENCE KERR OLIVIER
                                   MAY 22,'07 AT DORKING, SURREY, ENGLAND
      FATHER: REV. GERARD KERR OLIVIER
      MOTHER: AGNES LOUISE CROCKENDEN  (DIED '19)
      BROTHER: RICHARD  OLIVIER
      *** MARRIED: '30 JILL ESMOND  (DIVORCED '40)
      MOTHER-IN-LAW: EVA MOORE, ACTRESS
      SON:  '31 TARQUIN OLIVIER
      SON:  '32 SIMON OLIVIER
      *** MARRIED:  '40 VIVIEN LEIGH, ACTRESS  (DIVORCED '60)
      STEP-DAUGHTER: SUZANNE HOLMAN
      *** MARRIED:  '62 JOAN PLOWRIGHT, ACTRESS
      SON:  '63 RICHARD OLIVIER
      SON:  '64 TAMSIN OLIVIER
      POSSESSION:  '31 CONTRACT AT RKO STUDIOS
      POSSESSION:  '47 KNIGHTHOOD
      BIOGRAPHY:  '77 THE OLIVIERS, BY FELIX BARKER
      TALENT: ACTOR, PRODUCER, DIRECTOR
      AA-NOM  ACTOR:  '39 WUTHERING HEIGHTS
      AA-NOM  ACTOR:  '40 REBECCA
      AA-NOM  ACTOR:  '46 HENRY V
      AA-SPECIAL AWARD:  '46 HONORING HIS WORK ON 'HENRY V' AS ACTOR, PRODUCER & DIRECTOR
      AA-WIN  ACTOR:  '48 HAMLET
      AA-NOM  DIRECTOR:  '48 HAMLET
      AA-NOM  ACTOR:  '56 RICHARD III
      AA-NOM  ACTOR:  '60 THE ENTERTAINER
      AA-NOM  ACTOR:  '65 OTHELLO
      AA-NOM  ACTOR:  '72 SLEUTH
      AA-NOM  SUP.ACT:  '76 MARATHON MAN
```

OWEN, REGINALD   BORN: JOHN REGINALD OWEN
                        AUG 05,'87 AT WHEATHAMPSTEAD, ENGLAND DIED IN '72
FATHER: J. FENWICK OWEN
*** MARRIED: '08 LYDIA BILBROOKE (DIVORCED '23)
*** MARRIED: '34 BILLEY EDISE (DIED '56)
*** MARRIED: '56 BARBARA HAVEMAN
FRIEND: FLORENZ ZIEGFELD
RESIDENCE: BEVERLY HILLS, CA
TALENT: ACTOR
CREDIT: '29 THE LETTER, DEBUT
CREDIT: '36 TROUBLE FOR TWO
CREDIT: '42 WHITE CARGO
CREDIT: '58 THE YOUNG INVADERS
CREDIT: '68 ROSIE

```
-------------------------------------------------------------------------------------------------
PACINO, AL           BORN:  ALFRED JAMES 'SONNY' PACINO
                            APR 25,'39 AT NYC
     GRANDFATHER: JAMES GERARD
     GRANDMOTHER: KATE
     FATHER: SALVATORE PACINO
     MOTHER: ROSE GERARD
     *** MARRIED:  '76 JOANNE-ALEX SKYLAR, MARRIAGE HOAX REPORTED JAN.'76
     ROMANCE: JILL CLAYBURGH, ACTRESS
     ROMANCE: SUSAN TYRELL, ACTRESS
     ROMANCE: TUESDAY WELD, ACTRESS
     ROMANCE: CAROL KANE, ACTRESS
     ROMANCE: MARTHE KELLER, ACTRESS
     FRIEND: LEE STRASBERG, ACTING COACH
     POSSESSION: OBIE AWARD FOR PERFORMANCE - THE INDIAN WANTS THE BRONX
     POSSESSION: TONY AWARD FOR PERFORMANCE - DOES A TIGER WEAR A NECKTIE?
     TALENT: ACTOR
     CREDIT:  '71 THE PANIC IN NEEDLE PARK
     AA-NOM  SUP.ACT:  '72 THE GODFATHER
     AA-NOM  ACTOR:  '73 SERPICO
     CREDIT: '73 SCARECROW
     AA-NOM  ACTOR:  '74 THE GODFATHER PART II
     AA-NOM  ACTOR:  '75 DOG DAY AFTERNOON
-------------------------------------------------------------------------------------------------
PAGE, GERALDINE         BORN:  GERALDINE SUE PAGE
                              NOV 22,'24 AT KIRKSVILLE, MR
     FATHER: LEON ELWIN PAGE
     MOTHER: EDNA PEARL MAIZE
     BROTHER: DONALD PAGE
     *** MARRIED: --, ACTOR  (DIED)
     *** MARRIED:  '54 ALEXANDER SCHNEIDER, VIOLINIST  (DIVORCED '57)
     *** MARRIED:  '63 RIP TORN, ACTOR
     STEP-DAUGHTER: DANAE TORN
     DAUGHTER:  '64 ANGELICA TORN
     SON:  '65 ANTHONY TORN, TWIN
     SON:  '65 JONATHAN TORN, TWIN
     RESIDENCE: THE TORN PAGE, GREENWICH VILLAGE, NYC
     TALENT: ACTRESS
     AA-NOM  SUP.ACT:  '53 HONDO
     AA-NOM  ACTRESS:  '61 SUMMER AND SMOKE
     AA-NOM  ACTRESS:  '62 SWEET BIRD OF YOUTH
     AA-NOM  SUP.ACT:  '66 YOU'RE A BIG BOY NOW
     AA-NOM  SUP.ACT:  '72 PETE 'N' TILLIE
-------------------------------------------------------------------------------------------------
PAGET, DEBRA          BORN:  DEBRALEE GRIFFIN
                            AUG 19,'33 AT DENVER, CO
     FATHER: FRANK GRIFFIN
     MOTHER: MARGARET GIBSON
     SISTER: TEALA LORING GRIFFIN
     SISTER: LISA GAYE GRIFFIN
     SISTER: MARGARET GRIFFIN
     BROTHER: RUELL SHAYNE GRIFFIN
     *** MARRIED:  '58 DAVID STREET, ACTOR, SINGER  (DIVORCED '58)
     *** MARRIED:  '60 BUDD BOETTICHER, WRITER  (DIVORCED '61)
     *** MARRIED:  '62 LOUIS C. KUNG, OILMAN
     RESIDENCE: HOUSTON, TX
     TALENT: ACTRESS
     CREDIT:  '48 CRY OF THE CITY
```

```
CREDIT:  '54 PRINCE VALIANT
CREDIT:  '56 LOVE ME TENDER
CREDIT:  '62 TALES OF TERROR
CREDIT:  '64 THE HAUNTED PALACE
```

PAIGE, JANIS   BORN: DONNA MAE TJADEN
                                 SEP 16,'22 AT TACOMA, WA
```
*** MARRIED:  '47 FRANK MARTINELLI  (DIVORCED '50)
*** MARRIED:  '56 ARTHUR STANDER  (DIVORCED '57)
*** MARRIED:  '62 RAY GILBERT, COMPOSER  (DIED '76)
STEP-DAUGHTER: JOANNE GILBERT
RESIDENCE: HOLLYWOOD HILLS, CA
TALENT: ACTRESS-SINGER
CREDIT:  '44 HOLLYWOOD CANTEEN, DEBUT
CREDIT:  '48 ROMANCE ON THE HIGH SEAS
CREDIT:  '57 PAJAMA GAME
CREDIT:  '61 PLEASE DON'T EAT THE DAISIES
CREDIT:  '67 WELCOME TO HARD TIMES
```

PALANCE, JACK   BORN: JOHN PALAHNUIK, JR.
                                 FEB 18,'20 AT LATTIMER, PA
```
FATHER: JOHN PALAHNUIK
MOTHER: ANN GRAMIAK
*** MARRIED:  '49 VIRGINIA BAKER  (DIVORCED '66)
DAUGHTER:  '50 HOLLY PALANCE
DAUGHTER:  '51 BROOK GABRIELLE PALANCE
SON:  '55 CODY JOHN PALANCE
POSSESSION:  '75 FARM IN PENNSYLVANIA
TALENT: ACTOR
CREDIT:  '50 PICNIC IN THE STREETS
AA-NOM  SUP.ACT:  '52 SUDDEN FEAR
AA-NOM  SUP.ACT:  '53 SHANE
CREDIT:  '61 ATTILA THE HUN
CREDIT:  '66 THE PROFESSIONALS
CREDIT:  '73 OKLAHOMA CRUDE
```

PALMER, BETSY   BORN: PATRICIA BETSY HRUNEK
                                 NOV 01,'29 AT EAST CHICAGO, IND
```
FATHER: RUDOLPH V. HRUNEK
*** MARRIED:  '54 DR. VINCENT MERENDINO  (DIVORCED '74)
DAUGHTER:  '62 MISSIE MERENDINO
TALENT: ACTRESS
CREDIT:  '55 THE LONG GRAY LINE
CREDIT:  '55 QUEEN BEE
CREDIT:  '57 THE TIN STAR
CREDIT:  '59 THE LAST ANGRY MAN
CREDIT:  '59 IT COULD HAPPEN TO JANE
```

PALMER, LILLI   BORN: MARIA LILLI PEISER
                                 MAY 24,'14 AT POSEN, GERMANY
```
FATHER: ALFRED PEISER, PHYSICIAN
MOTHER: ROSE LISSMANN, ACTRESS
SISTER: IRENE PEISER
*** MARRIED:  '43 REX HARRISON, ACTOR  (DIVORCED '57)
STEP-SON: NOEL HARRISON
SON:  '44 CAREY HARRISON
*** MARRIED:  '57 CARLOS THOMPSON, ACTOR
RESIDENCE: GSTAAD, SWITZERLAND
```

```
RESIDENCE: COSTA DEL SOL, SPAIN
MEMOIRS:   '76 CHANGE LOBSTERS AND DANCE
TALENT: ACTRESS
CREDIT:   '34 CRIME UNLIMITED
CREDIT:   '46 CLOAK AND DAGGER
CREDIT:   '52 THE FOURPOSTER
CREDIT:   '69 DE SADE
CREDIT:   '71 MURDERS IN THE RUE MORGUE
CREDIT:   '78 THE RED RAVEN, AUTOBIOGRAPHIC NOVEL
```

PAPAS, IRENE   BORN: IRENE LELEKOS
```
                           MAR 09,'26 AT CORINTH, GREECE
FATHER: STAVROS LELEKOS
MOTHER: ELENI
*** MARRIED:  '47 ALKIS PAPAS  (DIVORCED '51)
*** MARRIED:  '57 JOSE KOHN  (ANNULLED '57)
TALENT: ACTRESS
CREDIT:   '51 NECRIPOLITIA (LOST ANGELS), DEBUT
CREDIT:   '56 THE POWER AND THE PRIZE
CREDIT:   '62 ELECTRA
CREDIT:   '64 ZORBA THE GREEK
CREDIT:   '68 Z
CREDIT:   '76 IPHIGENIA
```

PARKER, ELEANOR
```
                           JUN 26,'22 AT CEDARVILLE, OH
FATHER: LESTER K. PARKER, TEACHER
SISTER: --
BROTHER: --
*** MARRIED:  '43 FRED LOSEE, DENTIST  (DIVORCED '44)
*** MARRIED:  '46 BERT FRIEDLOB, PRODUCER  (DIVORCED '53)
DAUGHTER:  '48 SUSAN FRIEDLOB
DAUGHTER:  '50 SHARON FRIEDLOB
SON:  '52 RICHARD FRIEDLOB
*** MARRIED:  '56 PAUL CLEMENS, ARTIST  (DIVORCED '64)
DAUGHTER:  '57 PAUL CLEMENS, JR.
*** MARRIED:  '66 RAYMOND HIRSCH
TALENT: ACTRESS
CREDIT:   '43 MISSION TO MOSCOW
AA-NOM  ACTRESS:  '50 CAGED
AA-NOM  ACTRESS:  '51 DETECTIVE STORY
AA-NOM  ACTRESS:  '55 INTERRUPTED MELODY
CREDIT:   '62 MADISON AVENUE
```

PARKER, FESS   BORN: FESS PARKER, JR.
```
                           AUG 16,'25 AT FT. WORTH, TX
FATHER: FESS PARKER, SR.
MOTHER: MACKIE ALLEN
*** MARRIED:  '60 MARCELLA RINEHART
SON:  '61 FESS PARKER, III
DAUGHTER:  '64 ASHLEY ALLEN PARKER
RESIDENCE: SANTA BARBARA, CA
POSSESSION:  '56 CONTRACT AT DISNEY STUDIOS-FIRST ADULT CONTRACT HOLDER
TALENT: ACTOR
CREDIT:   '52 UNTAMED FRONTIER, DEBUT
CREDIT:   '55 DAVY CROCKETT, SERIES
CREDIT:   '57 OLD YELLER
CREDIT:   '62 HELL IS FOR HEROS
```

CREDIT: '66 SMOKY

PARKER, JEAN   BORN: LOIS STEPHANIE ZELINSKA
                                AUG 11,'12 AT BUTTE, MT
   *** MARRIED: '36 GEORGE MACDONALD (DIVORCED '40)
   *** MARRIED: '41 DOUGLAS DAWSON, RADIO COMMENTATOR (DIVORCED '43)
   *** MARRIED: '44 CURTIS BROTTIER, ALSO KNOWN AS CURTIS GROTTER (DIVORCED '49)
   *** MARRIED: '51 ROBERT LOWERY HANKS, ACTOR - ROBERT LOWERY (DIVORCED '58)
   SON: '52 ROBERT LOWERY HANKS, JR.
   ROMANCE: ROBERT DONAT
   RESIDENCE: EAGLE ROCK, CA
   TALENT: ACTRESS
   COMMENT: AKA LOIS MAE GREEN
   CREDIT: '33 LITTLE WOMEN
   CREDIT: '40 BEYOND TOMORROW
   CREDIT: '42 ONE BODY TOO MANY
   CREDIT: '54 BLACK TUESDAY
   CREDIT: '65 APACHE UPRISING

PARKER, SUZY   BORN: CECELIA PARKER
                                OCT 28,'34 AT SAN ANTONIO,TX
   FATHER: GEORGE LOFTON PARKER
   MOTHER: ELIZABETH
   SISTER: DORIAN LEIGH PARKER
   BROTHER-IN-LAW: IDDO BEN-GURION, WRITER
   *** MARRIED: '55 PIERRE LASALLE (DIVORCED '61)
   DAUGHTER: '59 GEORGIA LASALLE
   *** MARRIED: '63 BRADFORD DILLMAN, ACTOR
   STEP-DAUGHTER: PAMELA DILLMAN
   STEP-SON: JEFFREY DILLMAN
   DAUGHTER: '65 DINAH DILLMAN
   SON: '67 CHRISTOPHER PARKER DILLMAN
   TALENT: ACTRESS, MODEL
   CREDIT: '57 KISS THEM FOR ME, DEBUT
   CREDIT: '58 TEN NORTH FREDERICK
   CREDIT: '59 THE BEST OF EVERYTHING
   CREDIT: '61 THE DECEPTION
   CREDIT: '66 CHAMBER OF HORRORS

PARKS, LARRY   BORN: SAMUEL KLAUSMAN
                                DEC 13,'14 AT OLATHE, KA DIED IN '75
   *** MARRIED: '44 BETTY GARRETT, ACTRESS
   SON: '50 GARRETT PARKS
   SON: '51 ANDREW PARKS
   RESIDENCE: HOLLYWOOD, CA
   TALENT: ACTOR
   COMMENT: RECEIVED SUBPOENA IN 1951 TO APPEAR BEFORE HOUSE
            UN-AMERICAN ACTIVITIES COMMITTEE
            INVESTIGATING COMMUNISM
   CREDIT: '41 MYSTERY SHIP
   CREDIT: '45 COUNTER ATTACK
   AA-NOM ACTOR: '46 THE JOLSON STORY
   CREDIT: '52 LOVE IS BETTER THAN EVER
   CREDIT: '63 FREUD

PARSONS, ESTELLE
                          NOV 20,'27 AT MARBLEHEAD, MS
    FATHER: EBEN PARSONS, LAWYER
    MOTHER: ELINOR MATTSON, COURT REPORTER
    *** MARRIED: '53 RICHARD GEHMAN, AUTHOR 'THE HAPHAZARD GOURMET' (DIVORCED '58)
    DAUGHTER: MARTHA GEHMAN, TWIN
    DAUGHTER: ABBIE GEHMAN, TWIN
    ROMANCE: JACK LEMMON
    ROMANCE: PETER ZIMROTH, PROFESSOR OF LAW AT NYU
    RESIDENCE: NYC
    POSSESSION: FARM IN UPSTATE NEW YORK
    TALENT: ACTRESS
    AA-WIN SUP.ACT.: '67 BONNIE AND CLYDE
    AA-NOM SUP.ACT: '68 RACHEL, RACHEL
    CREDIT: '69 I NEVER SANG FOR MY FATHER
    CREDIT: '70 I WALK THE LINE
    CREDIT: '73 TWO PEOPLE

PARSONS, LOUELLA O.   BORN: LOUELLA OETTINGER
                                AUG 06,'81 AT FREEPORT, IL DIED IN '72
    FATHER: JOSHUA OETTINGER
    MOTHER: HELEN STINE
    SISTER: FLORENCE OETTINGER
    BROTHER: EDWIN OETTINGER
    BROTHER: FRED OETTINGER
    BROTHER: RAE OETTINGER
    COUSIN: MAGGIE ETTINGER, PUBLICIST
    *** MARRIED: JOHN PARSONS, REAL ESTATE MAN
    *** MARRIED: CAPT. JACK MCCAFFREY, RIVER BOAT CAPTAIN
    DAUGHTER: '06 HARRIET PARSONS, WRITER-PRODUCER
    *** MARRIED: '30 DR. HARRY W. MARTIN (DIED '51)
    ROMANCE: PETER J. BRADY, BANKER
    ROMANCE: JIMMY MCHUGH, COMPOSER
    FRIEND: WM. R. HEARST
    FRIEND: HEDDA HOPPER
    RESIDENCE: BEVERLY HILLS, CA
    RESIDENCE: MARSONS FARM
    MEMOIRS: THE GAY ILLITERATE
    TALENT: ACTRESS, JOURNALIST
    CREDIT: '37 HOLLYWOOD HOTEL
    CREDIT: '46 WITHOUT RESERVATIONS
    CREDIT: '51 STARLIFT

PAVAN, MARISA   BORN: MARIA-LUISA PIERANGELI
                                JUN 19,'32 AT CAGLIARI, SARDINIA, ITALY
    SISTER: PIER ANGELI, TWIN
    SISTER: PATRICIA PIERANGELI
    BROTHER-IN-LAW: VIC DAMONE, SINGER
    BROTHER-IN-LAW: ARMANDO TRAVAJOLI
    NEPHEW: PERRY ROCCO LUIGI DAMONE
    NEPHEW: HOWARD ANDREA TRAVAJOLI
    *** MARRIED: '56 JEAN-PIERRE AUMONT, ACTOR (DIVORCED '65)
    SON: '57 JEAN-CLAUDE AUMONT
    SON: '58 PATRICK AUMONT
    *** MARRIED: '69 JEAN-PIERRE AUMONT, REMARRIED
    ROMANCE: VIC DAMONE
    RESIDENCE: PARIS, FRANCE

```
POSSESSION: FARMHOUSE IN IBIZA, BALEARES, SPAIN
TALENT: ACTRESS
CREDIT:  '52 WHAT PRICE GLORY, DEBUT
AA-NOM  SUP.ACT:  '55 THE ROSE TATTOO
CREDIT:  '59 SOLOMON AND SHEBA
CREDIT:  '59 JOHN PAUL JONES
```

PAYNE, JOHN
```
                        MAY 23,'12 AT ROANOKE, VA
    MOTHER: IDA SCHAEFER
    BROTHER: PETER PAYNE
    BROTHER: WILLIAM PAYNE
    *** MARRIED:  '37 ANNE SHIRLEY, ACTRESS  (DIVORCED '43)
    DAUGHTER:  '40 JULIE ANNE PAYNE
    *** MARRIED:  '45 GLORIA DE HAVEN, ACTRESS  (DIVORCED '50)
    FATHER-IN-LAW: CARTER DE HAVEN
    MOTHER-IN-LAW: FLORA PARKER, ACTRESS
    DAUGHTER:  '45 KATHLEEN PAYNE
    SON:  '48 THOMAS PAYNE
    *** MARRIED:  '53 ALEXANDRA 'SANDY' CURTIS
    POSSESSION: MONTANA RANCH
    TALENT: ACTOR
    CREDIT:  '36 DODSWORTH, DEBUT
    CREDIT:  '41 REMEMBER THE DAY
    CREDIT:  '48 LARCENY
    CREDIT:  '56 THE BOSS
    CREDIT:  '68 THEY RAN FOR THEIR LIVES
```

PECK, GREGORY
```
                    BORN:  ELDRED GREGORY PECK
                        APR 05,'16 AT LA JOLLA, CA
    FATHER: GREGORY PECK, SR., DRUGGIST
    MOTHER: BERNICE AYRES
    *** MARRIED: KATHERINE CORNELL
    *** MARRIED:  '42 GRETA RICE KONEN, HAIRDRESSER  (DIVORCED '54)
    SON:  '44 STEPHEN PECK
    SON:  '46 JONATHAN PECK, JOURNALIST  (SUICIDE '75)
    SON:  '49 CAREY PECK
    *** MARRIED:  '55 VERONIQUE PASSANI
    SON:  '56 ANTHONY PECK
    DAUGHTER:  '58 CECELIA PECK
    TALENT: ACTOR, PRODUCER
    AA-NOM  ACTOR:  '45 THE KEYS OF THE KINGDOM
    AA-NOM  ACTOR:  '46 THE YEARLING
    AA-NOM  ACTOR:  '47 GENTLEMAN'S AGREEMENT
    AA-NOM  ACTOR:  '49 TWELVE O'CLOCK HIGH
    AA-WIN  ACTOR:  '62 TO KILL A MOCKINGBIRD
    CREDIT:  '77 MACARTHUR
```

PEPPARD, GEORGE
```
                        OCT 01,'33 AT DETROIT, MH
    FATHER: GEORGE PEPPARD, SR.
    MOTHER: VERNELLE ROHRER, SINGER
    *** MARRIED:  '54 HELEN DAVIES  (DIVORCED '65)
    SON:  '55 BRADFORD DAVIES PEPPARD
    DAUGHTER:  '56 JULIE LOUISE PEPPARD
    *** MARRIED:  '66 ELIZABETH ASHLEY, ACTRESS
    SON:  '68 CHRISTOPHER PEPPARD
    *** MARRIED:  '75 SHERRY BOUCHER
```

```
RESIDENCE: NYC
RESIDENCE: BEVERLY HILLS, CA
TALENT: ACTOR
CREDIT:    '57 THE STRANGE ONE
CREDIT:    '61 BREAKFAST AT TIFFANY'S
CREDIT:    '66 THE BLUE MAX
CREDIT:    '69 THE EXECUTIONER
CREDIT:    '71 ONE MORE TIME
CREDIT:    '78 FIVE DAYS FROM HOME
```

```
PERKINS,  TONY         BORN:  ANTHONY PERKINS
                              APR 04,'32 AT NYC
    FATHER: OSGOOD PERKINS, ACTOR  (DIED '37)
    MOTHER: JANET RANE
    BROTHER-IN-LAW: JAMES RANDALL, PRODUCER
    NEPHEW: STARLITE RANDALL
    *** MARRIED:  '73 BARENTHIA 'BERRY' BERENSON, MODEL
    SON:  '74 OSGOOD ROBERT PERKINS
    SON:  '76 ELVIS BROOKE PERKINS
    SISTER-IN-LAW: MARISA BERENSON, MODEL-ACTRESS
    ROMANCE: NORMA MOORE, ACTRESS
    RESIDENCE: NYC
    POSSESSION:  '58 TONY AWARD FOR STAGE PLAY,LOOK HOMEWARD, ANGEL
    POSSESSION:  '72 MURRAY - A COLLIE DOG - BEST MAN AT HIS WEDDING
    TALENT: ACTOR, WRITER, DIRECTOR
    CREDIT:  '53 THE ACTRESS, DEBUT
    AA-NOM  SUP.ACT:  '56 FRIENDLY PERSUASION
    CREDIT:  '60 PSYCHO
    CREDIT:  '68 PRETTY POISON
    CREDIT:  '72 PLAY IT AS IT LAYS
```

```
PERREAU,  GIGI         BORN:  GHISLAINE PERREAU
                              FEB 06,'41 AT LOS ANGELES, CA
    FATHER: ROBERT PERREAU
    SISTER: JANINE PERREAU
    BROTHER: RICHARD MILES
    BROTHER: PETER MILES
    *** MARRIED:  '60 FRANK GALLO, OF GALLO VINEYARDS  (DIVORCED '68)
    SON:  '61 TONY GALLO
    DAUGHTER:  '64 GINA GALLO
    *** MARRIED:  '70 GENE DE RUELLE
    DAUGHTER:  '71 DANIELLE DE RUELLE
    SON:  '72 KEITH DE RUELLE
    RESIDENCE: STUDIO CITY, CA
    TALENT: ACTRESS
    CREDIT:  '43 MADAME CURIE, DEBUT
    CREDIT:  '47 SONG OF LOVE
    CREDIT:  '51 ANYBODY SEEN MY GAL?
    CREDIT:  '58 WILD HERITAGE
    CREDIT:  '61 LOOK IN ANY WINDOW
```

```
PETERS,  JEAN          BORN:  ELIZABETH JEAN PETERS
                              OCT 15,'26 AT CANTON, OH
    *** MARRIED:  '54 STUART CRAMER  (DIVORCED '56)
    *** MARRIED:  '57 HOWARD HUGHES  (DIVORCED '71)
    *** MARRIED:  '71 STANLEY HOUGH
    POSSESSION:  '47 CONTRACT AT 20TH CENTURY FOX
    POSSESSION: REC'D HOTEL IN HUGHES DIVORCE
```

TALENT: ACTRESS
CREDIT: '47 CAPTAIN FROM CASTILLE
CREDIT: '49 IT HAPPENS EVERY SPRING
CREDIT: '53 PICKUP ON SOUTH STREET
CREDIT: '54 THREE COINS IN A FOUNTAIN
CREDIT: '55 A MAN CALLED PETER

PHILLIPS, MICHELLE   BORN: HOLLY MICHELLE GILLIAM
                                       1944
FATHER: -- POSTAL EMPLOYEE
MOTHER: -- (DIED '49)
*** MARRIED: '61 JOHN PHILLIPS, SINGER - MAMAS AND PAPAS GROUP (DIVORCED '69)
STEP-DAUGHTER: MACKENZIE PHILLIPS, ACTRESS
DAUGHTER: '68 CHYNA PHILLIPS
*** MARRIED: '69 DENNIS HOPPER, ACTOR
*** MARRIED: '78 ROBERT STEPHEN BIRCH, RADIO EXECUTIVE
ROMANCE: JACK NICHOLSON, ACTOR
ROMANCE: WARREN BEATTY, ACTOR
RESIDENCE: BEVERLY HILLS, CA
TALENT: ACTRESS, SINGER
CREDIT: '60 MAMAS AND PAPAS, FOLK MUSIC AND ROCK GROUP
CREDIT: '69 THE LAST MOVIE
CREDIT: '74 DILLINGER
CREDIT: '77 VALENTINO

PICKENS, SLIM   BORN: LOUIS BERT LINDLEY, JR.
                                  JUN 29,'19 AT KINGSBERG, CA
*** MARRIED: MARGARET
DAUGHTER: DARYLE ANN PICKENS
DAUGHTER: MARGARET LOUISE PICKENS
SON: THOMAS MICHAEL PICKENS
RESIDENCE: THOUSAND OAKS, CA
TALENT: ACTOR-COWBOY
CREDIT: '53 THE SUN SHINES BRIGHT
CREDIT: '56 THE GREAT LOCOMOTIVE CHASE
CREDIT: '63 DR. STRANGELOVE
CREDIT: '67 ROUGH NIGHT IN JERICHO
CREDIT: '72 THE COWBOYS
CREDIT: '78 THE SWARM

PICKFORD, MARY   BORN: GLADYS MARY SMITH
                                   APR 08,'93 AT TORONTO ONTARIO, CANADA
FATHER: JOHN CHARLES SMITH
MOTHER: CHARLOTTE HENNESSEY
SISTER: LOTTIE SMITH, ACTRESS - LOTTIE PICKFORD (DIED '36)
BROTHER: JACK SMITH, ACTOR - JACK PICKFORD (DIED '33)
SISTER-IN-LAW: OLIVE THOMAS, ACTRESS (SUICIDE '20)
SISTER-IN-LAW: MARILYN MILLER, ACTRESS (DIVORCED)
*** MARRIED: '11 OWEN MOORE, ACTOR (DIVORCED '17)
BROTHER-IN-LAW: MATT MOORE, ACTOR
*** MARRIED: '17 DOUGLAS FAIRBANKS, ACTOR (DIVORCED '35)
STEP-SON: DOUGLAS FAIRBANKS, JR., ACTOR-PRODUCER
*** MARRIED: '36 CHARLES 'BUDDY' ROGERS, ACTOR
ADOPTED DAUGHTER: GWYNNE SMITH, AFTER SISTER LOTTIE SMITH DIED
ADOPTED DAUGHTER: ROXANNE PICKFORD ROGERS
ADOPTED SON: RONALD PICKFORD ROGERS
FRIEND: DAVID BELASCO, PRODUCER
PARTNER: DOUGLAS FAIRBANKS, UNITED ARTISTS CO.

```
        PARTNER: D.W. GRIFFITH, UNITED ARTISTS CO.
        RESIDENCE: PICKFAIR, BEVERLY HILLS, CA
        MEMOIRS:  '55 SUNSHINE & SHADOW
        TALENT: ACTRESS, PRODUCER, AUTHOR
        CREDIT:  '09 HER FIRST BISCUITS
        CREDIT:  '17 REBECCA OF SUNNYBROOK FARM
        CREDIT:  '19 POLLYANNA
        CREDIT:  '21 LITTLE LORD FAUNTLEROY
        AA-WIN  ACTRESS:  '28 COQUETTE
        AA-SPECIAL AWARD:  '75 HONORARY AWARD FOR HER UNIQUE CONTRIBUTIONS TO FILM
```

PIDGEON, WALTER   BORN: WALTER DAVID PIDGEON
```
                             SEP 23,'97 AT EAST ST. JOHN,NEW BRUNSWICK, CANADA
        FATHER: CALEB BURPEE PIDGEON, HABERDASHER
        BROTHER: DAVID PIDGEON
        BROTHER: CHARLES PIDGEON
        *** MARRIED:  '22 EDNA PICKLES, ARTIST  (DIED '23)
        DAUGHTER: '23 EDNA VERNE PIDGEON
        *** MARRIED:  '30 RUTH WALKER
        RESIDENCE: BEL AIR, LOS ANGELES, CA
        TALENT: ACTOR-SINGER
        CREDIT:  '26 MANNEQUIN
        CREDIT:  '39 NICK CARTER, MASTER DETECTIVE
        AA-NOM  ACTOR:  '42 MRS. MINIVER
        AA-NOM  ACTOR:  '43 MADAME CURIE
        CREDIT:  '62 ADVISE AND CONSENT
        CREDIT:  '73 THE NEPTUNE FACTOR
```

PINZA, EZIO   BORN: EZIO FORTUNATO PINZA
```
                             MAY 18,'89 AT ROME, ITALY  DIED IN '57
        FATHER: CESARE PINZA
        MOTHER: CLELIA BULGARELLI
        *** MARRIED:  '01 AUGUST CASSINELLI
        DAUGHTER:  '02 CLAUDIA PINZA
        *** MARRIED:  '40 DORIS LEAK
        DAUGHTER:  '41 CELIA PINZA
        DAUGHTER:  '42 GLORIA PINZA
        SON:  '43 EZIO PIETRO PINZA
        RESIDENCE: STAMFORD, CT
        MEMOIRS: AUTOBIOGRAPHY:EZIO PINZA
        TALENT: ACTOR-SINGER
        CREDIT:  '47 CARNEGIE HALL
        CREDIT:  '50 MR. IMPERIUM
        CREDIT:  '51 SLIGHTLY DISHONORABLE
        CREDIT:  '53 TONIGHT WE SING
```

PITTS, ZASU   BORN: ELIZA SUSAN PITTS
```
                             JAN 03,'98 AT PARSONS, KA  DIED IN '63
        *** MARRIED:  '21 THOMAS GALLERY  (DIVORCED '32)
        DAUGHTER:  '22 ANN GALLERY
        ADOPTED SON: MARVIN CARVILLE LA MARR, AKA DONALD MICHAEL GALLERY
        DAUGHTER-IN-LAW: JOYCE REYNOLDS, ACTRESS
        *** MARRIED:  '33 EDWARD WOODALL
        FRIEND: BARBARA LA MARR, ACTRESS
        PARTNER: THELMA TODD, IN ACT 'TODD & PITTS'
        TALENT: ACTRESS
        CREDIT:  '17 THE LITTLE PRINCESS
        CREDIT:  '26 MONTE CARLO, RE-MAKE IN 1926
```

CREDIT: '33 THEY JUST HAD TO GET MARRIED
CREDIT: '43 LET'S FACE IT
CREDIT: '63 THE THRILL OF IT ALL

PLESHETTE, SUZANNE
                         JAN 31,'37 AT NYC
FATHER: EUGENE PLESHETTE, FILM EXHIBITOR
MOTHER: GERALDINE, DANCER
*** MARRIED: '64 TROY DONAHUE, ACTOR (DIVORCED '64)
*** MARRIED: '68 THOMAS JOSEPH GALLAGHER, III, AKA THE IRISH PRINCE
RESIDENCE: BEVERLY HILLS, CA
POSSESSION: '72 THE BEDSIDE MANOR LINEN CO.
TALENT: ACTRESS, POET
CREDIT: '58 GEISHA BOY
CREDIT: '63 THE BIRDS
CREDIT: '65 A RAGE TO LIVE
CREDIT: '68 THE POWER
CREDIT: '69 SUPPOSE THEY GAVE A WAR AND NOBODY CAME

PLUMMER, CHRISTOPHER
                         DEC 13,'29 AT TORONTO, ONTARIO, CANADA
FATHER: JOHN PLUMMER
MOTHER: ISABELLA MARY ABBOTT
*** MARRIED: '56 TAMMY GRIMES, ACTRESS (DIVORCED '60)
DAUGHTER: '57 AMANDA PLUMMER
*** MARRIED: '62 PATRICIA LEWIS, JOURNALIST (DIVORCED '68)
*** MARRIED: '70 ELAINE TAYLOR, ACTRESS
RESIDENCE: DARIEN, CONNECTICUT
TALENT: ACTOR
CREDIT: '58 STAGE STRUCK
CREDIT: '65 THE SOUND OF MUSIC
CREDIT: '69 LOCK UP YOUR DAUGHTERS
CREDIT: '70 WATERLOO
CREDIT: '73 THE PHYX
CREDIT: '78 INTERNATIONAL VELVET

POITIER, SIDNEY
                         FEB 20,'24 AT MIAMI, FL
FATHER: REGINALD POITIER
MOTHER: EVELYN OUTTEN
*** MARRIED: '50 JUANITA HARDY, DANCER (DIVORCED)
DAUGHTER: '51 BEVERLY POITIER
DAUGHTER: '52 PAMELA POITIER
DAUGHTER: '53 SHERRY POITIER
*** MARRIED: '76 JOANNA SHIMKUS
FRIEND: PAUL NEWMAN
FRIEND: BARBRA STREISAND
RESIDENCE: BAHAMAS
BIOGRAPHY: '69 THE LONG JOURNEY, BY CAROLYN H. EWERS
TALENT: ACTOR-DIRECTOR
CREDIT: '50 NO WAY OUT
CREDIT: '55 THE BLACKBOARD JUNGLE
AA-NOM ACTOR: '58 THE DEFIANT ONES
AA-WIN ACTOR: '63 LILIES OF THE FIELD
CREDIT: '67 IN THE HEAT OF THE NIGHT
CREDIT: '73 A WARM DECEMBER
CREDIT: '78 A PIECE OF THE ACTION, ACTOR AND DIRECTOR

```
--------------------------------------------------------------------------------
POWELL, DICK          BORN:  RICHARD E. POWELL
                             NOV 14,'04 AT MOUNTAIN VIEW, AK   DIED IN '63
     FATHER: EWING POWELL
     MOTHER: SALLIE THOMPSON
     BROTHER: HOWARD POWELL
     *** MARRIED:  '25 MILDRED MAUND  (DIVORCED '33)
     *** MARRIED:  '36 JOAN BLONDELL, ACTRESS  (DIVORCED '44)
     BROTHER-IN-LAW: EDWARD BLONDELL, CAMERMAN
     FATHER-IN-LAW: EDDIE BLONDELL, ACTOR
     MOTHER-IN-LAW: KATHRYN CAIN, ACTRESS
     SISTER-IN-LAW: GLORIA BLONDELL, ACTRESS
     STEP-SON: NORMAN SCOTT BARNES
     DAUGHTER:   '38 ELLEN POWELL
     *** MARRIED:  '45 JUNE ALLYSON
     ADOPTED DAUGHTER: PAMELA POWELL
     SON:  '50 RICHARD KEITH POWELL, JR.
     ROMANCE: MARY BRIAN, ACTRESS
     POSSESSION:  '51 PARTNER IN FOUR STAR PROD. CO. WITH BOYER, LUPINO & NIVEN
     TALENT: ACTOR
     CREDIT:  '31 STREET SCENE
     CREDIT:  '36 STAGE STRUCK
     CREDIT:  '40 CHRISTMAS IN JULY
     CREDIT:  '49 MRS. MIKE
     CREDIT:  '54 SUSAN SLEPT HERE
--------------------------------------------------------------------------------
POWELL, ELEANOR          BORN:  ELEANOR TORREY POWELL
                                NOV 21,'12 AT SPRINGFIELD, MS
     FATHER: CLARENCE POWELL  (DIED '13)
     MOTHER: BLANCHE
     *** MARRIED:  '43 GLENN FORD, ACTOR  (DIVORCED '60)
     SON:  '45 PETER FORD
     RESIDENCE: BEVERLY HILLS, CA
     POSSESSION: CRESTVIEW ESCROW FIRM
     TALENT: DANCER, ACTRESS, MINISTER
     CREDIT:  '36 BORN TO DANCE
     CREDIT:  '41 LADY BE GOOD
     CREDIT:  '43 I DOOD IT
     CREDIT:  '43 THOUSANDS CHEER
     CREDIT:  '50 THE DUCHESS OF IDAHO
--------------------------------------------------------------------------------
POWELL, JANE          BORN:  SUZANNE BURCE
                             APR 01,'29 AT PORTLAND, OR
     FATHER: PAUL BURCE
     MOTHER: EILEEN
     *** MARRIED:  '49 GEARY A. STEFFEN, II, ICE SKATER  (DIVORCED '54)
     SON:  '51 GEARY A. STEFFEN, III
     DAUGHTER:  '52 SUZANNE ILEEN STEFFEN
     *** MARRIED:  '54 PAT NERNEY, AUTOMOBILE DEALER  (DIVORCED '63)
     DAUGHTER:  '55 LINDSAY AVERILL NERNEY
     *** MARRIED:  '65 JAMES FITZGERALD, PUBLICITY MAN
     ROMANCE: GENE NELSON
     FRIEND: KATHRYN GRAYSON, ACTRESS
     RESIDENCE: PACIFIC PALISADES, CA
     TALENT: ACTRESS, SINGER
     CREDIT:  '44 SONG OF THE OPEN ROAD, DEBUT
     CREDIT:  '51 RICH, YOUNG AND PRETTY
     CREDIT:  '54 DEEP IN MY HEART
```

CREDIT: '57 THE GIRL MOST LIKELY
CREDIT: '58 THE FEMALE ANIMAL

POWELL, WILLIAM   BORN: WILLIAM HORATIO POWELL
                                    JUL 29,'92 AT PITTSBURGH, PA
   FATHER: HORATIO WARREN POWELL, ACCOUNTANT
   MOTHER: NETTIE MANILA BRADY
   *** MARRIED: '15 EILEEN WILSON, ACTRESS (DIVORCED '31)
   SON: '25 WILLIAM DAVID POWELL (SUICIDE '68)
   *** MARRIED: '31 CAROLE LOMBARD, ACTRESS (DIVORCED '33)
   *** MARRIED: '40 DIANA LEWIS, ACTRESS
   ROMANCE: MYRNA LOY, ACTRESS
   ROMANCE: JEAN HARLOW, ACTRESS
   FRIEND: MYRON SELZNICK, AGENT
   FRIEND: RONALD COLMAN, ACTOR
   RESIDENCE: PALM SPRINGS, CA
   TALENT: ACTOR
   CREDIT: '22 SHERLOCK HOLMES, DEBUT
   AA-NOM ACTOR: '34 THE THIN MAN
   AA-NOM ACTOR: '36 MY MAN GODFREY
   AA-NOM ACTOR: '47 LIFE WITH FATHER
   CREDIT: '55 MISTER ROBERTS

POWER, TYRONE   BORN: TYRONE EDMUND POWER
                                    MAY 05,'13 AT CINCINNATI, OH DIED IN '58
   FATHER: FREDERICK TYRONE EDMOND POWER, ACTOR
   MOTHER: HELEN EMMA REAUME, ACTRESS & DRAMA COACH
   *** MARRIED: '39 SUZANNE CARPENTIER, ACTRESS KNOWN AS ANNABELLA (DIVORCED '48)
   STEP-DAUGHTER: ANNE POWER (MARRIED '54)
   SON-IN-LAW: OSKAR WERNER, ACTOR
   *** MARRIED: '49 LINDA CHRISTIAN, ACTRESS (DIVORCED '55)
   DAUGHTER: '49 ROMINA POWER, ACTRESS
   DAUGHTER: '53 TARYN POWER, ACTRESS
   *** MARRIED: '58 DEBORAH MINARDOS, ACTRESS
   SON: '59 TYRONE POWER, 3RD
   ROMANCE: JANET GAYNOR, ACTRESS
   ROMANCE: SONJA HENIE, ICE SKATER-ACTRESS
   FRIEND: DON AMECHE, ACTRESS
   FRIEND: CHARLES BOYER, ACTOR
   POSSESSION: NEWPORTER SAILBOAT - KETCH
   TALENT: ACTOR
   CREDIT: '32 TOM BROWN OF CULVER
   CREDIT: '37 CAFE METROPOLE
   CREDIT: '41 BLOOD AND SAND
   CREDIT: '47 THE CAPTAIN FROM CASTILE
   CREDIT: '57 THE SUN ALSO RISES

POWERS, MALA   BORN: MARY ELLEN POWERS
                                    DEC 29,'21 AT SAN FRANCISCO, CA
   FATHER: GEORGE POWERS, DRAMATIC COACH
   MOTHER: DELL
   *** MARRIED: '54 MONTE VANTON
   SON: '57 VERNON VANTON
   *** MARRIED: '70 M. HUGHES MILLER, PUBLISHER
   RESIDENCE: TOLUCA LAKE, CA
   TALENT: ACTRESS
   CREDIT: '41 TOUGH AS THEY COME
   CREDIT: '55 RAGE AT DAWN

```
CREDIT:  '57 THE STORM RIDER
CREDIT:  '69 DADDY'S GONE A-HUNTING
CREDIT:  '72 DOOMSDAY
```

PREMINGER, OTTO
DEC 05,'06 AT VIENNA, AUSTRIA

```
*** MARRIED: MARION MILL
*** MARRIED: MARY GARDNER  (DIVORCED '60)
DAUGHTER:  '21 VICTORIA PREMINGER, TWIN
SON:  '21 MARK PREMINGER, TWIN
ROMANCE: GYPSY ROSE LEE
SON:  '45 ERIK KIRKLAND PREMINGER, MOTHER-GYPSY ROSE LEE
*** MARRIED:  '60 PATRICIA HOPE BRYCE
ENEMY: MICHAEL RENNIE, ACTOR
MEMOIRS: PREMINGER
TALENT: ACTOR, LAWYER, DIRECTOR
CREDIT:  '42 THE PIED PIPER
CREDIT:  '43 THEY GOT ME COVERED
AA-NOM  DIRECTOR:  '44 LAURA
AA-NOM  DIRECTOR:  '63 THE CARDINAL
```

PRENTISS, PAULA
BORN: PAULINE RAGUSA
MAR 04,'39 AT SAN ANTONIO, TX

```
FATHER: THOMAS J. RAGUSA
MOTHER: PAULINE GARDNER
SISTER: ANN GARDNER RAGUSA
*** MARRIED:  '60 RICHARD BENJAMIN, ACTOR
SON:  '74 ROSS THOMAS BENJAMIN
TALENT: ACTRESS
CREDIT:  '60 WHERE THE BOYS ARE
CREDIT:  '61 THE HONEYMOON MACHINE
CREDIT:  '62 MAN'S FAVORITE SPORT
CREDIT:  '63 THE WORLD OF HENRY ORIENT
CREDIT:  '65 WHAT'S NEW, PUSSYCAT?
CREDIT:  '67 HE AND SHE, TV SERIES
```

PRESLE, MICHELINE
BORN: MICHELINE CHASSAGNE
AUG 22,'22 AT PARIS, FRANCE

```
FATHER: ROBERT CHASSAGNE
*** MARRIED:  '46 WILLIAM MARSHALL, PRODUCER  (DIVORCED)
STEP-SON: MICHAEL MARSHALL
POSSESSION:  '49 CONTRACT AT 20TH CENTURY FOX
TALENT: ACTRESS
CREDIT:  '38 PARADISE LOST
CREDIT:  '50 UNDER MY SKIN
CREDIT:  '55 NAPOLEON
CREDIT:  '60 BLIND DATE
CREDIT:  '67 KING OF HEARTS
```

PRESLEY, ELVIS
BORN: ELVIS ARON PRESLEY
JAN 08,'35 AT TUPELO,MP DIED IN '77

```
FATHER: VERNON ELVIS PRESLEY
MOTHER: GLADYS LOVE  (DIED '58)
BROTHER: JESS GARON PRESLEY, TWIN  (DIED '35)
*** MARRIED:  '67 PRISCILLA BEAULIEU  (DIVORCED '73)
DAUGHTER:  '68 LISA MARIE PRESLEY
ROMANCE: NATALIE WOOD, ACTRESS
ROMANCE: GINGER ALDEN, MODEL
```

```
FRIEND: THOMAS A. PARKER, MANAGER
RESIDENCE: MEMPHIS, TN
POSSESSION: COLLECTION OF AUTOMOBILES
BIOGRAPHY:  '71 ELVIS, BY JERRY HOPKINS
TALENT: SINGER-ACTOR
CREDIT:  '56 LOVE ME TENDER
CREDIT:  '57 JAIL HOUSE ROCK
CREDIT:  '64 KISSIN' COUSINS
CREDIT:  '67 EASY COME EASY GO
CREDIT:  '70 THE TROUBLE WITH GIRLS
```

PRESTON, ROBERT

```
                    BORN:  ROBERT PRESTON MESERVEY
                           JUN 08,'18 AT NEWTON,MS
FATHER: FRANK W. MESERVEY
MOTHER: RUTH REA
BROTHER: FRANK MESERVEY
*** MARRIED:  '40 KAY FELTUS, ACTRESS-CATHERINE CRAIG
FATHER-IN-LAW: ROY FELTUS, THEATRE OWNER
RESIDENCE: GREENWICH, CN
POSSESSION:  '58 2 MOVIE THEATRES IN INDIANA
POSSESSION: CONTRACT AT PARAMOUNT PICTURES
TALENT: ACTOR-SINGER
CREDIT:  '39 UNION PACIFIC, DEBUT
CREDIT:  '49 THE LADY GAMBLES
CREDIT:  '52 FACE TO FACE
CREDIT:  '62 THE MUSIC MAN
CREDIT:  '63 ALL THE WAY HOME
```

PRICE, VINCENT

```
                    MAY 27,'11 AT ST. LOUIS, MR
FATHER: VINCENT LEONARD PRICE
MOTHER: MARGUERITE COBB WILCOX
SISTER: HARRIET PRICE
SISTER: LAURA LOUISE PRICE
BROTHER: JAMES PRICE
*** MARRIED:  '38 EDITH BARRETT, ACTRESS  (DIVORCED '48)
SON:  '39 VINCENT B. PRICE, JOURNALIST
*** MARRIED:  '49 MARY GRANT  (DIVORCED '72)
DAUGHTER:  '62 MARY VICTORIA PRICE
*** MARRIED:  '74 CORAL BROWNE, ACTRESS
MEMOIRS:  '59 I LIKE WHAT I KNOW
TALENT: ACTOR-ART COLLECTOR
CREDIT:  '38 SERVICE DELUXE
CREDIT:  '47 THE WEB
CREDIT:  '58 THE FLY
CREDIT:  '64 THE RAVEN
CREDIT:  '69 TROUBLE WITH GIRLS
```

PROWSE, JULIET

```
                    SEP 25,'37 AT BOMBAY, INDIA
FATHER: REGINALD PROWSE
MOTHER: PHYLLIS DOONE
STEP-FATHER: GEORGE POLTE
BROTHER: CLIVE PROWSE
*** MARRIED:  '69 EDDIE JAMES
*** MARRIED:  '72 JOHN MCCOOK
SON:  '72 SETH MCCOOK
ROMANCE: SERGIO FADINI, DANCING PARTNER
```

ROMANCE: FRANK SINATRA
POSSESSION: '62 CONTRACT AT 20TH CENTURY FOX
TALENT: DANCER
CREDIT: '59 CAN CAN
CREDIT: '60 G. I. BLUES
CREDIT: '61 THE FIERCEST HEART
CREDIT: '66 RUN FOR YOUR WIFE

PRYOR, RICHARD
DEC 01,'40 AT PEORIA, IL

GRANDMOTHER: MARIE BRYANT
FATHER: -- (DIED '70)
MOTHER: -- (DIED '69)
SON: '62 RICHARD PRYOR, JR.
*** MARRIED: '67 MAXINE (DIVORCED)
DAUGHTER: '67 ELIZABETH ANNE PRYOR
DAUGHTER: '70 RAIN PRYOR
*** MARRIED: '77 DEBORAGH MCGUIRE, MODEL
DAUGHTER: RENEE
ROMANCE: PAM GRIER, ACTRESS
FRIEND: JULIETTE WHITTAKER
RESIDENCE: NORTHRIDGE, CA
POSSESSION: '76 CONTRACT AT UNIVERSAL
POSSESSION: HONORARY DEGREE - SAN JOSE STATE COLLEGE - BLACK STREET HISTORY
TALENT: ACTOR, WRITER
CREDIT: '66 BUSY BODY
CREDIT: '73 LADY SINGS THE BLUES
CREDIT: '76 SILVER STREAK
CREDIT: '77 GREASED LIGHTNING
CREDIT: '78 THE WIZ

PURDOM, EDMUND
DEC 19,'32 AT WELWYN GARDEN CITY, ENGLAND

FATHER: C. B. PURDOM, AUTHOR, CRITIC, PRODUCER
MOTHER: LILIAN ANTONIA CUTLAR
*** MARRIED: '51 TITA PHILLIPS, BALLERINA (DIVORCED '56)
DAUGHTER: '52 LILIAN PURDOM
DAUGHTER: '54 MARINA PURDOM
*** MARRIED: '57 ALICIA DARR (DIVORCED '61)
*** MARRIED: '62 LINDA CHRISTIAN, ACTRESS (DIVORCED '63)
STEP-DAUGHTER: ROMINA POWER, ACTRESS
STEP-DAUGHTER: TARYN POWER, ACTRESS
TALENT: ACTOR
CREDIT: '53 TITANIC
CREDIT: '54 THE EGYPTIAN
CREDIT: '60 THE COSSACKS
CREDIT: '64 THE YELLOW ROLLS ROYCE
CREDIT: '69 THE MAN IN THE GOLDEN MASK

QUINN, ANTHONY   BORN: ANTHONY RUDOLPH OAXACA QUINN
                                 APR 21,'15 AT CHIHUAHUA, MEXICO
    FATHER: FRANK QUINN
    MOTHER: MANUELA 'NELLIE' OAXACA
    SISTER: STELLA QUINN
    *** MARRIED: '37 KATHERINE DE MILLE, ACTRESS (DIVORCED '65)
    FATHER-IN-LAW: CECIL B. DE MILLE, PRODUCER
    MOTHER-IN-LAW: CONSTANCE ADAMS, ACTRESS
    SON: '38 CHRISTOPHER QUINN, DROWNED- (DIED '41)
    DAUGHTER: '41 CHRISTINA QUINN
    DAUGHTER: '42 KATHLEEN QUINN, ACTRESS
    SON-IN-LAW: PAUL COLWELL, DIRECTOR (MARRIED)
    SON: '45 DUNCAN QUINN, ACTOR
    DAUGHTER: '52 VALENTINA QUINN
    SON: '63 FRANCESCO QUINN, MOTHER-ADDOLARI
    DAUGHTER: '64 DANIELE QUINN, MOTHER-ADDOLARI
    *** MARRIED: '65 JOLANDA ADDOLARI
    SON: '66 LORENZO QUINN
    FRIEND: AIMEE SEMPLE MCPHERSON
    RESIDENCE: RIDGEFIELD, CONN. & PACIFIC PALISADES, CALIF.
    POSSESSION: FRENCH MODERN ART COLLECTION
    POSSESSION: FARM AT OJAI, CA
    MEMOIRS: '72 THE ORIGINAL SIN
    TALENT: ACTOR, DIRECTOR
    AA-WIN SUP.ACT.: '52 VIVA ZAPATA!
    AA-WIN SUP.ACT.: '56 LUST FOR LIFE
    AA-NOM ACTOR: '57 WILD IS THE WIND
    AA-NOM ACTOR: '64 ZORBA THE GREEK
    CREDIT: '77 THE GREEK TYCOON

```
-------------------------------------------------------------------------------
RAFFERTY, FRANCES              JUN 26,'22 AT SIOUX CITY,IO
     FATHER: MAXWELL A. RAFFERTY
     BROTHER: MAXWELL RAFFERTY, JR., POLITICIAN & EDUCATOR
     *** MARRIED: TOM BAKER, WRITER
     SON:  '50 KEVIN BAKER
     DAUGHTER:  '52 BRIDGET BAKER
     FRIEND: ALEXIS SMITH, ACTRESS
     TALENT: ACTRESS
     CREDIT:  '42 SEVEN SWEETHEARTS
     CREDIT:  '44 DRAGON SEED
     CREDIT:  '48 LADY AT MIDNIGHT
     CREDIT:  '52 RODEO
     CREDIT:  '54 THE SHANGHAI STORY
     CREDIT: SEVEN SWEETHEARTS
-------------------------------------------------------------------------------
RAFT, GEORGE         BORN:  GEORGE RANFT
                            SEP 27,'95 AT NYC
     FATHER: CONRAD RANFT
     MOTHER: EVA GLOCKNER
     SISTER: CATHERINE RANFT
     BROTHER: ANTHONY RANFT
     BROTHER: MICHAEL RANFT
     BROTHER: JOSEPH RANFT
     BROTHER: WILLIAM RANFT
     *** MARRIED:  '16 GRAYCE MULROONEY, (REPORTED BUT NOT VERIFIED)
     ROMANCE: BETTY GRABLE
     ROMANCE: CAROLE LOMBARD, ACTRESS
     ROMANCE: VIRGINIA PINE
     FRIEND: RUDOLPH VALENTINO, ACTOR
     RESIDENCE: CENTURY CITY, LA, CA
     BIOGRAPHY:  '73 THE GEORGE RAFT FILE, BY PARISH & WHITNEY
     TALENT: ACTOR-DANCER
     CREDIT:  '29 QUEEN OF THE NIGHT CLUBS
     CREDIT:  '34 ALL OF ME
     CREDIT:  '48 INTRIGUE
     CREDIT:  '59 SOME LIKE IT HOT
     CREDIT:  '72 HAMMERSMITH
-------------------------------------------------------------------------------
RAINER, LUISE
                    JAN 12,'10 AT VIENNA, AUSTRIA
     *** MARRIED:  '37 CLIFFORD ODETS, WRITER  (DIVORCED '40)
     *** MARRIED:  '45 ROBERT KNITTEL,   PUBLISHER
     DAUGHTER:  '46 PATRICIA KNITTEL
     FRIEND: WILLIAM POWELL, ACTOR
     RESIDENCE: LONDON, ENGLAND
     TALENT: ACTRESS
     CREDIT:  '35 ESCAPADE
     AA-WIN  ACTRESS:  '36 THE GREAT ZIEGFELD
     AA-WIN  ACTRESS:  '37 THE GOOD EARTH
     CREDIT:  '38 THE TOY WIFE
     CREDIT:  '43 HOSTAGES
```

RAINS, CLAUDE   BORN: WILLIAM CLAUDE RAINS
                                NOV 10,'89 AT LONDON, ENGLAND DIED IN '67
    FATHER: FREDERICK WILLIAM RAINS, ACTOR
    MOTHER: EMILY ELIZA COX
    *** MARRIED: '13 ISABEL JEANS, ACTRESS (DIVORCED)
    *** MARRIED: '20 MARIE HEMINGWAY (DIVORCED '20)
    *** MARRIED: '24 BEATRIX THOMPSON (DIVORCED '35)
    *** MARRIED: '35 FRANCES PROPPER (DIVORCED '59)
    DAUGHTER: '36 JENNIFER RAINS
    *** MARRIED: '59 AGI JAMBOR
    *** MARRIED: '60 ROSEMARY CLARK
    RESIDENCE: DOWNINGTON, PA.
    TALENT: ACTOR
    CREDIT: '33 THE INVISIBLE MAN, DEBUT IN 1933
    AA-NOM SUP.ACT: '39 MR. SMITH GOES TO WASHINGTON
    AA-NOM SUP.ACT: '43 CASABLANCA
    AA-NOM SUP.ACT: '44 MR. SKEFFINGTON
    AA-NOM SUP.ACT: '46 NOTORIOUS

RALSTON, VERA HRUBA   BORN: VERA HRUBA
                                JUN 12,'19 AT PRAGUE, CZECHOSZOVAKIA
    FATHER: RUDOLF HRUBA, JEWELER
    MOTHER: MARIE
    BROTHER: RUDOLF HRUBA, JR., PRODUCER - RUDOLF RALSTON
    *** MARRIED: '52 HERBERT J. YATES (DIED '66)
    *** MARRIED: '73 CHARLES ALVA
    RESIDENCE: SANTA BARBARA, CA
    TALENT: ICE SKATER-ACTRESS
    COMMENT: SILVER MEDAL 1936 OLYMPICS
    COMMENT: KNOWN AS THE QUEEN OF THE 'B' MOVIES
    CREDIT: '42 ICE CAPADES
    CREDIT: '45 DAKOTA
    CREDIT: '46 MURDER IN THE MUSIC HALL
    CREDIT: '53 FAIR WIND TO JAVA
    CREDIT: '57 ACCUSED OF MURDER

RANDALL, TONY   BORN: ANTHONY L. RANDALL
                                FEB 26,'20 AT TULSA, OK
    FATHER: --, ART DEALER
    MOTHER: FRANCES MARIE RIZZO
    *** MARRIED: '42 FLORENCE MITCHELL
    RESIDENCE: NYC
    TALENT: ACTOR
    COMMENT: COLLECTOR OF MODERN ART, OPERA RECORDINGS & ANTIQUES
    CREDIT: '57 OH MEN OH WOMEN
    CREDIT: '59 PILLOW TALK
    CREDIT: '61 LET'S MAKE LOVE
    CREDIT: '63 ISLAND OF LOVE
    CREDIT: '68 HELLO DOWN THERE

RATHBONE, BASIL   BORN: PHILIP ST. JOHN BASIL RATHBONE
                                JUN 13,'92 AT JOHANNESBURG, SOUTH AFRICA DIED IN '67
    FATHER: EDGAR PHILIP RATHBONE
    MOTHER: BARBARA ANN GEORGE
    *** MARRIED: '14 ETHEL MARION FORMAN
    SON: '15 RODION RATHBONE
    *** MARRIED: '26 IDA BERGER FITZMAURICE, WRITER-OUIDA BERGERE

DAUGHTER: '27 CYNTHIA BARBARA RATHBONE
RESIDENCE: NYC
MEMOIRS: '62 IN AND OUT OF CHARACTER
TALENT: ACTOR
CREDIT: '21 INNOCENT
AA-NOM SUP.ACT: '36 ROMEO AND JULIET
AA-NOM SUP.ACT: '38 IF I WERE KING
CREDIT: '67 HILLBILLIES IN THE HAUNTED HOUSE
CREDIT: SHERLOCK HOLMES SERIES

RATOFF, GREGORY
APR 20,'93 AT PETROGRAD, RUSSIA   DIED IN '61

MOTHER: SOPHIE
*** MARRIED: '22 EUGENIE LEONTOVICH (DIVORCED '49)
*** MARRIED: '50 MARIA KOSTES, SINGER
RESIDENCE: LOS ANGELES, CA
TALENT: ACTOR-DIRECTOR
CREDIT: '32 MELODY OF LIFE
CREDIT: '41 ADAM HAD FOUR SONS
CREDIT: '50 ALL ABOUT EVE
CREDIT: '60 EXODUS

RAY, ALDO   BORN: ALDO DARE
SEP 25,'26 AT PEN ARGYL, PA
*** MARRIED: '54 JEAN MARIE DONNELL, AKA JEFF DONNELL - ACTRESS (DIVORCED '56)
*** MARRIED: '60 JOHANNA BENNETT
POSSESSION: '51 CONTRACT AT COLUMBIA STUDIOS
TALENT: ACTOR
CREDIT: '51 MY TRUE STORY
CREDIT: '53 LET'S DO IT AGAIN
CREDIT: '58 THE NAKED AND THE DEAD
CREDIT: '65 SYLVIA
CREDIT: '68 THE GREEN BERETS

RAYE, MARTHA   BORN: MARGARET THERESA YVONNE REED
AUG 27,'08 AT BUTTE, MT
FATHER: PETER REED, VAUDEVILLIAN
MOTHER: MABEL HOOPER, VAUDEVILLIAN
*** MARRIED: '37 HAMILTON 'BUD' WESTMORE, COSMETICIAN (DIVORCED '38)
*** MARRIED: '38 DAVID ROSE, MUSICIAN (DIVORCED '40)
*** MARRIED: '41 NEAL LANG, HOTEL MAN (DIVORCED '41)
*** MARRIED: '44 NICK CONDOS, DANCER (DIVORCED '53)
DAUGHTER: '44 MELODYE CONDOS
*** MARRIED: '54 THOMAS BEGLEY, DANCER (DIVORCED '56)
*** MARRIED: '58 ROBERT O'SHEA, HER BODYGUARD (DIVORCED '62)
RESIDENCE: MIAMI BEACH & NASSAU IN THE BAHAMAS & BEL AIR, CA
POSSESSION: MOTOR YACHT
TALENT: ACTRESS-SINGER
CREDIT: '36 RHYTHM ON THE RANGE, DEBUT
CREDIT: '41 HELLZAPOPPIN'
CREDIT: '43 PIN-UP GIRL
CREDIT: '62 JUMBO
CREDIT: '70 PUFNSTUF

RAYMOND, GENE   BORN: RAYMOND GUION
                               AUG 13,'08 AT NYC
    FATHER: LEROY D. GUION
    MOTHER: MARY SMITH
    *** MARRIED: '37 JEANETTE MACDONALD, ACTRESS (DIED '65)
    FATHER-IN-LAW: DANIEL MACDONALD
    MOTHER-IN-LAW: ANNA MAY WRIGHT
    SISTER-IN-LAW: BLOSSOM MACDONALD, ACTRESS
    SISTER-IN-LAW: ELSIE MACDONALD, DANCER
    *** MARRIED: '74 ADA HEES
    FRIEND: JANE WYMAN
    RESIDENCE: LOS ANGELES, CA
    TALENT: ACTOR
    CREDIT: '31 PERSONAL MAID, DEBUT
    CREDIT: '37 THAT GIRL FROM PARIS
    CREDIT: '41 SMILING THROUGH
    CREDIT: '55 HIT THE DECK
    CREDIT: '64 THE BEST MAN

REAGAN, RONALD   BORN: RONALD WILSON REAGAN
                               FEB 06,'00 AT TAMPICO, IL
    FATHER. JOHN EDWARD REAGAN
    MOTHER: NELLIE WILSON
    BROTHER: J. NEIL REAGAN
    *** MARRIED: '40 JANE WYMAN, ACTRESS (DIVORCED '48)
    ADOPTED SON: MICHAEL REAGAN
    DAUGHTER: '42 MAUREEN REAGAN
    *** MARRIED: '52 NANCY DAVIS, ACTRESS
    DAUGHTER: '52 PATRICIA REAGAN
    SON: '58 RONALD REAGAN, JR.
    RESIDENCE: PACIFIC PALISADES, CA
    POSSESSION: RANCH NEAR MALIBU, CA
    MEMOIRS: '65 WHERE'S THE REST OF ME?
    TALENT: ACTOR-POLITICIAN
    CREDIT: '37 LOVE IS ON THE AIR
    CREDIT: '38 ACCIDENTS WILL HAPPEN
    CREDIT: '49 THE HASTY HEART
    CREDIT: '54 LAW AND ORDER
    CREDIT: '64 THE KILLERS

REDDY, HELEN
                         OCT 25,'42 AT MELBOURNE, AUSTRALIA
    FATHER: MAX REDDY, WRITER-ACTOR
    MOTHER: STELLA LAMOND, ACTRESS
    SISTER: ANTONIA LAMOND REDDY
    *** MARRIED: '60 --, MUSICIAN (DIVORCED)
    *** MARRIED: '65 JEFF WALD
    DAUGHTER: '66 TRACY WALD
    SON: '67 JORDAN WALD
    RESIDENCE: HOLLYWOOD HILLS, CA
    POSSESSION: '74 IMAGE AWARD OF THE NAACP
    TALENT: SINGER-ACTRESS
    CREDIT: '46 FAMILY THEATRE ACT, DEBUT ON STAGE
    CREDIT: '72 I AM WOMAN, RECORDING
    CREDIT: '75 AIRPORT 75, DEBUT IN FILMS

```
-------------------------------------------------------------------------------
REDFORD, ROBERT          BORN:  CHARLES ROBERT REDFORD, JR.
                                AUG 18,'37 AT SANTA MARIA, CA
    FATHER: CHARLES REDFORD
    MOTHER: MARTHA HART
    BROTHER: WILLIAM REDFORD
    *** MARRIED:  '58 LOLA VAN WANGEMEN
    DAUGHTER: AMY REDFORD
    DAUGHTER: SHAUNA REDFORD
    SON: SCOTT REDFORD
    SON: JAIMIE REDFORD
    RESIDENCE: MONTANA
    POSSESSION: SUNDANCE, UTAH, SKI RESORT
    BIOGRAPHY:  '75 THE SUPERSTAR NOBODY KNOWS, BY DAVID HANNA
    TALENT: ACTOR-AUTHOR-PRODUCER
    CREDIT:  '62 WARHUNT
    CREDIT:  '66 THE CHASE
    CREDIT:  '67 BAREFOOT IN THE PARK
    CREDIT:  '70 BUTCH CASSIDY AND THE SUNDANCE, KID
    AA-NOM  ACTOR:  '73 THE STING
    CREDIT:  '73 THE WAY WE WERE
    CREDIT:  '76 ALL THE PRESIDENT'S MEN
-------------------------------------------------------------------------------
REDGRAVE, LYNN          BORN:  LYNN RACHEL REDGRAVE
                                MAR 08,'43 AT LONDON, ENGLAND
    FATHER: MICHAEL REDGRAVE, ACTOR
    MOTHER: RACHEL KEMPSON
    SISTER: VANESSA REDGRAVE, ACTRESS
    BROTHER-IN-LAW: TONY RICHARDSON, DIRECTOR
    BROTHER: COLIN REDGRAVE
    *** MARRIED:  '67 JOHN CLARKE
    SON:  '68 BENJAMIN CLARKE
    DAUGHTER:  '70 KELLY CLARKE
    TALENT: ACTRESS
    CREDIT:  '63 TOM JONES
    AA-NOM  ACTRESS:  '66 GEORGY GIRL
    CREDIT:  '67 SMASHING TIME
    CREDIT:  '71 KILLER FROM YUMA
    CREDIT:  '72 EVERYTHING YOU ALWAYS WANTED TO KNOW ABOUT SEX
-------------------------------------------------------------------------------
REDGRAVE, MICHAEL          BORN:  MICHAEL SCUDAMORE REDGRAVE
                                  MAR 20,'08 AT BRISTOL, ENGLAND
    FATHER: ROY REDGRAVE
    MOTHER: MARGARET SCUDAMORE
    *** MARRIED:  '35 RACHEL KEMPSON
    FATHER-IN-LAW: ERIC WILLIAM EDWARD KEMPSON, HEADMASTER ROYAL NAVY COLLEGE
    SON:  '36 COLIN REDGRAVE
    DAUGHTER:  '37 VANESSA REDGRAVE, ACTRESS
    SON-IN-LAW: TONY RICHARDSON, DIRECTOR
    DAUGHTER:  '43 LYNN REDGRAVE, ACTRESS
    SON-IN-LAW: JOHN CLARKE  (MARRIED '67)
    GRANDDAUGHTER:  '63 NATASHA RICHARDSON
    GRANDDAUGHTER:  '65 JOELY KIM RICHARDSON
    GRANDSON:  '68 BENJAMIN CLARKE
    GRANDDAUGHTER:  '70 KELLY CLARKE
    POSSESSION:  '52 KNIGHTHOOD
    POSSESSION:  '57 REDGRAVE FILM PRODUCTION CO.
    MEMOIRS:  '55 THE ACTOR'S WAYS AND MEANS
```

```
TALENT: ACTOR-AUTHOR
CREDIT:  '36 SECRET AGENT
CREDIT:  '46 THE CAPTIVE HEART
AA-NOM  ACTOR:  '47 MOURNING BECOMES ELECTRA
CREDIT:  '61 THE INNOCENTS
CREDIT:  '70 NICHOLAS AND ALEXANDER
```

REDGRAVE, VANESSA

```
                         JAN 30,'37 AT LONDON, ENGLAND
FATHER: MICHAEL REDGRAVE, ACTOR
MOTHER: RACHEL KEMPSON
SISTER: LYNN REDGRAVE, ACTRESS
BROTHER-IN-LAW: JOHN CLARKE
BROTHER: COLIN REDGRAVE
NIECE: KELLY CLARKE
*** MARRIED:  '62 TONY RICHARDSON, DIRECTOR  (DIVORCED '67)
DAUGHTER:  '63 NATASHA RICHARDSON
DAUGHTER:  '65 JOELY KIM RICHARDSON
ROMANCE: FRANCO NERO, ACTOR
SON:  '69 CARLO NERO, FATHER - FRANCO NERO
TALENT: ACTRESS
CREDIT:  '58 BEHIND THE MASK
AA-NOM  ACTRESS:  '66 MORGAN!
CREDIT:  '66 BLOW UP
AA-NOM  ACTRESS:  '68 ISADORA
AA-NOM  ACTRESS:  '71 MARY, QUEEN OF SCOTS
AA-WIN  SUP.ACT.: '77 JULIA
```

REED, DONNA   BORN: DONNA BELLE MULLENGER

```
                         JAN 27,'21 AT DENISON, IO
FATHER: WILLIAM R. MULLENGER
MOTHER: HAZEL
*** MARRIED:  '43 WILLIAM TUTTLE, MAKEUP MAN  (DIVORCED '45)
*** MARRIED:  '45 TONY OWEN, AGENT-PRODUCER  (DIVORCED '71)
DAUGHTER:  '47 PENNY OWEN
DAUGHTER:  '48 MARY ANN OWEN
SON:  '49 TONY OWEN, JR.
SON:  '50 TIMOTHY OWEN
*** MARRIED:  '74 GROVER ASMUS, COLONEL
RESIDENCE: BEVERLY HILLS, CA
TALENT: ACTRESS
COMMENT: 1ST STAGE NAME DONNA ADAMS
CREDIT:  '41 BABES ON BROADWAY
CREDIT:  '43 THE HUMAN COMEDY
CREDIT:  '46 IT'S A WONDERFUL LIFE
AA-WIN  SUP.ACT.:  '53 FROM HERE TO ETERNITY
CREDIT:  '60 PEPE
```

REED, OLIVER

```
                    FEB 13,'38 AT WIMBLEDON, ENGLAND
FATHER: PETER REED, JOURNALIST
SISTER: TRACY REED, ACTRESS
BROTHER: DAVID REED, AGENT
BROTHER: SIMON REED, PUBLICIST
UNCLE: SIR CAROL REED, DIRECTOR
*** MARRIED:  '60 KATHERINE BYRNE  (DIVORCED '70)
SON:  '62 MARK REED
DAUGHTER:  '70 SARAH REED
```

```
ROMANCE: JACQUELINE DARRELL, BALLERINA
RESIDENCE: SURREY, ENGLAND
TALENT: ACTOR
CREDIT:  '59 BEAT GIRL, DEBUT
CREDIT:  '68 OLIVER!
CREDIT:  '71 THE DEVILS OF LOUDON
CREDIT:  '73 THE THREE MUSKETEERS
CREDIT:  '75 TOMMY
```

REEVES, STEVE
```
                      JAN 21,'26 AT GLASGOW, MT
*** MARRIED:  '63 COUNTESS LINA CZARTJAWICZ
ROMANCE: LIANA ORFEI, ACTRESS
RESIDENCE: BERNE, SWITZERLAND
POSSESSION: HORSE RANCH NEAR SAN DIEGO, CA
TALENT: ACTOR
COMMENT: TITLES: MR. PACIFIC MR. AMERICA, MR. WORLD,
         MR. UNIVERSE
CREDIT:  '59 HERCULES
CREDIT:  '60 HERCULES UNCHAINED
CREDIT:  '63 DUEL OF THE TITANS
CREDIT:  '63 THE SLAVE
CREDIT:  '63 THE PIRATE PRINCE
```

REID, WALLACE
```
                  BORN:  WILLIAM WALLACE REID
                      APR 15,'91 AT ST. LOUIS, MR  DIED IN '23
FATHER: JAMES HALLECK REID, ACTOR
MOTHER: BERTHA BELLE WESTBROOKE
*** MARRIED:  '13 DOROTHY DAVENPORT, ACTRESS
BROTHER-IN-LAW: ARTHUR RANKIN, ACTOR
FATHER-IN-LAW: HARRY DAVENPORT, ACTOR, DIRECTOR
MOTHER-IN-LAW: PHYLLIS RANKIN, ACTRESS
SISTER-IN-LAW: ANN DAVENPORT, ACTRESS
SISTER-IN-LAW: KATE DAVENPORT, ACTRESS
SON:  '17 WILLIAM WALLACE REID, JR., ACTOR
RESIDENCE: LOS ANGELES, CA
TALENT: ACTOR
COMMENT: DRUG ADDICTION CAUSED DEATH
CREDIT:  '11 THE DEERSLAYER
CREDIT:  '15 BIRTH OF A NATION
CREDIT:  '18 RUGGLES OF RED GAP
CREDIT:  '22 THIRTY DAYS
```

REINER, CARL
```
                      MAR 20,'22 AT BRONX, NY
FATHER: IRVING REINER
MOTHER: BESSIE MATHIAS
BROTHER: CHARLES REINER
*** MARRIED:  '43 ESTELLE LEBOST, ARTIST
SON:  '46 ROB REINER, ACTOR
DAUGHTER-IN-LAW: PENNY MARSHALL, ACTRESS
DAUGHTER: SYLVIA A. REINER
SON: LUCAS REINER
RESIDENCE: LOS ANGELES, CA AND SCARSDALE, NY
TALENT: ACTOR, WRITER, PRODUCER, DIRECTOR
CREDIT:  '59 HAPPY ANNIVERSARY
CREDIT:  '61 GIDGET GOES HAWAIAN
CREDIT:  '65 THE ART OF LOVE
```

```
    CREDIT:  '67 A GUIDE FOR THE MARRIED MAN
    CREDIT:  '69 THE COMIC
    CREDIT:  '78 'OH, GOD!', DIRECTOR
```

REMICK, LEE   BORN: LEE ANN REMICK
                                DEC 14,'35 AT QUINCY, MS
```
    FATHER: FRANK E. REMICK, DEPARTMENT STORE OWNER
    MOTHER: MARGARET WALDO, ACTRESS - PATRICIA REMICK
    BROTHER: BRUCE REMICK
    *** MARRIED:  '57 WILLIAM COLLERAN  (DIVORCED '69)
    SON:  '61 MATTHEW COLLERAN
    DAUGHTER:  '62 KATE COLLERAN
    *** MARRIED:  '70 WILLIAM R. GOWENS
    POSSESSION: ANTIQUES COLLECTION
    TALENT: ACTRESS
    CREDIT:  '57 A FACE IN THE CROWD, DEBUT
    CREDIT:  '59 ANATOMY OF A MURDER
    AA-NOM  ACTRESS:  '62 DAYS OF WINE AND ROSES
    CREDIT:  '68 NO WAY TO TREAT A LADY
    CREDIT:  '70 LOOT
```

RENALDO, DUNCAN   BORN: RENAULT RENALDO DUNCAN
                                   APR 23,'04 AT CAMDEN,NJ
```
    *** MARRIED:  '39 LEA ROSENBLATT
    *** MARRIED:  '56 AUDREY MADALENE LEONARD
    DAUGHTER: STEPHANIE RENALDO
    SON: JEREMY RENALDO
    SON: RICHARD RENALDO
    SON: EDWIN RENALDO
    FRIEND: PAT O'BRIEN
    PARTNER: LEO CARILLO
    RESIDENCE: RANCHO MI AMIGO, SANTA BARBARA CA
    POSSESSION: 2 HORSES NAMED DIABLO
    TALENT: ACTOR, WRITER, PRODUCER ARTIST
    CREDIT:  '28 CLOTHES MAKE THE WOMAN
    CREDIT:  '43 FOR WHOM THE BELL TOLLS
    CREDIT:  '44 THE CISCO KID, MOVIES AND TV SERIES
    CREDIT:  '49 WE WERE STRANGERS
    CREDIT:  '59 ZORRO RIDES AGAIN
```

RENNIE, MICHAEL
                          AUG 29,'09 AT BRADFORD, YORKSHIRE, ENGLAND DIED IN '71
```
    FATHER: JAMES RENNIE
    MOTHER: EDITH DOBBIE
    *** MARRIED:  '50 MARGARET MCGRATH, ACTRESS  (DIVORCED '60)
    DAUGHTER:  '53 DAVID RENNIE
    ROMANCE: MARY GARDNER
    TALENT: ACTOR
    CREDIT:  '37 GANG WAY
    CREDIT:  '46 CAESAR AND CLEOPATRA
    CREDIT:  '53 THE ROBE
    CREDIT:  '60 THE LOST WORLD
    CREDIT:  '69 KRAKATOA - EAST OF JAVA
```

REYNOLDS, BURT
                          FEB 11,'35 IN GEORGIA
   FATHER: BURTON 'BURT' REYNOLDS, SHERIFF
   *** MARRIED: '63 JUDY CARNE, ACTRESS (DIVORCED '65)
   ROMANCE: DINAH SHORE, ACTRESS
   ROMANCE: INGER STEVENS, ACTRESS
   ROMANCE: CHRIS EVERT, TENNIS PLAYER
   ROMANCE: SALLY FIELD, ACTRESS
   RESIDENCE: RANCH IN FLORIDA
   MEMOIRS: '76 BURT REYNOLDS MAGGIE DOYLE
   TALENT: ACTOR
   CREDIT: '61 ANGEL BABY
   CREDIT: '69 SAM WHISKEY
   CREDIT: '69 PLAYGIRL MAGAZINE - 1ST MALE NUDE CENTERFOLD
   CREDIT: '72 DELIVERANCE
   CREDIT: '75 NICKELODEON
   CREDIT: '77 SMOKEY AND THE BANDIT

REYNOLDS, DEBBIE   BORN: MARY FRANCES REYNOLDS
                          APR 11,'32 AT EL PASO, TX
   FATHER: RAYMOND F. REYNOLDS
   MOTHER: MAXENE
   BROTHER: WILLIAM REYNOLDS, MAKE-UP MAN
   *** MARRIED: '55 EDDIE FISHER, ACTOR-SINGER (DIVORCED '59)
   DAUGHTER: '56 CARRIE FISHER, ACTRESS
   SON: '58 TODD FISHER
   *** MARRIED: '60 HARRY KARL, SHOE MERCHANT (DIVORCED '75)
   STEP-DAUGHTER: DENISE KARL
   STEP-SON: HARRISON KARL
   STEP-DAUGHTER: TINA MARIE KARL
   ROMANCE: ROBERT WAGNER
   FRIEND: MICHAEL TODD, PRODUCER
   FRIEND: ELIZABETH TAYLOR, ACTRESS
   RESIDENCE: BEVERLY HILLS, CA
   POSSESSION: MISS BURBANK, CA IN 1948
   POSSESSION: HARMON PRODUCTIONS
   MEMOIRS: '63 IF I KNEW THEN
   TALENT: ACTRESS-SINGER
   CREDIT: '48 JUNE BRIDE
   CREDIT: '52 SINGIN' IN THE RAIN
   CREDIT: '56 BUNDLE OF JOY
   CREDIT: '61 THE SECOND TIME AROUND
   AA-NOM ACTRESS: '64 THE UNSINKABLE MOLLY BROWN
   CREDIT: '67 DIVORCE AMERICAN STYLE

RICHARDSON, RALPH   BORN: RALPH DAVID RICHARDSON
                          DEC 19,'02 AT CHELTENHAM, GLOS., ENGLAND
   FATHER: ARTHUR RICHARDSON, ART MASTER
   MOTHER: LYDIA RUSSELL
   BROTHER: CHRISTOPHER RICHARDSON
   BROTHER: AMBROSE RICHARDSON
   *** MARRIED: '24 MURIEL HEWITT (DIED '42)
   *** MARRIED: '44 MERIM FORBES
   SON: '45 CHARLES DAVID RICHARDSON
   RESIDENCE: HAMPSTEAD, LONDON, ENGLAND
   TALENT: ACTOR
   COMMENT: KNIGHTHOOD IN 1947 - HONORS LIST

CREDIT: '33 THE GHOUL
CREDIT: '38 THE DIVORCE OF LADY X
AA-NOM SUP.ACT: '49 THE HEIRESS
CREDIT: '57 THE PASSIONATE STRANGER
CREDIT: '73 O LUCKY MAN

RIGG, DIANA
                    JUL 20,'38 AT DONCASTER, YORKSHIRE, ENGLAND
FATHER: LOUIS RIGG
MOTHER: BERYL HELLIWELL
*** MARRIED: '73 MENACHEM GUEFFEN, ARTIST
ROMANCE: PHILIP SAVILLE, DIRECTOR
RESIDENCE: BARNES, ENGLAND
POSSESSION: FINCA IN IBIZA, BALEARES,SPAIN
TALENT: ACTRESS
CREDIT: '68 A MIDSUMMER NIGHT'S DREAM
CREDIT: '69 ON HER MAJESTY'S SECRET SERVICE
CREDIT: '71 THE HOSPITAL
CREDIT: '73 THEATRE OF BLOOD

RIN TIN TIN
                    SEP 15,'16 AT SAINT MIHIEL, LORRAINE, FRANCE DIED IN '32
*** MARRIED: NANETTE
SON: RIN TIN TIN, JR., ACTOR
FRIEND: HAL B. WALLIS, HIS PRESS AGENT
FRIEND: LEE DUNCAN, TRAINER
FRIEND: DARRYL F. ZANUCK, WRITER, PRODUCER
ENEMY: STRONGHEART
RESIDENCE: RIVERSIDE, CA
BIOGRAPHY: '49 THE RIN TIN TIN STORY, BY JAMES W. ENGLISH
TALENT: ACTOR
CREDIT: '22 THE MAN FROM HELL'S RIVER
CREDIT: '25 CLASH OF THE WOLVES
CREDIT: '28 RINTY OF THE DESERT
CREDIT: '29 MILLION DOLLAR COLLAR
CREDIT: '31 LIGHTNING WARRIOR, SERIES

RITTER, TEX   BORN: MAURICE WOODWARD
                    JAN 12,'05 AT MURVAUL, TX DIED IN '74
*** MARRIED: '41 DOROTHY FAY SOUTHWORTH, ACTRESS
SON: '47 JONATHAN RITTER, ACTOR
SON: '49 THOMAS RITTER
FRIEND: JOHNNY BOND, BIOGRAPHER
RESIDENCE: NASHVILLE, TN
TALENT: ACTOR COUNTRY MUSICIAN
COMMENT: RAN FOR US SENATE IN 1970
CREDIT: '36 SONG OF THE GRINGO
CREDIT: '45 FLAMING BULLETS
CREDIT: '52 HIGH NOON, RECORDED TITLE SONG
CREDIT: '66 GIRL FROM TOBACCO ROW

RITTER, THELMA   BORN: THELMA ADELE RITTER
                    FEB 14,'05 AT BROOKLYN,NY DIED IN '69
FATHER: CHARLES RITTER, BARITONE
MOTHER: LUCY HALE
*** MARRIED: '27 JOSEPH A. MORAN
SON: '37 JOSEPH ANTHONY MORAN
DAUGHTER: '40 MONICA MORAN

RESIDENCE: FOREST HILLS, LONG ISLAND, NY
POSSESSION: ENCYCLOPAEDIA BRITANNICA SET - WON ON SHOW 'INFORMATION PLEASE'
TALENT: ACTRESS
AA-NOM SUP.ACT: '50 ALL ABOUT EVE
AA-NOM SUP.ACT: '51 THE MATING SEASON
AA-NOM SUP.ACT: '52 WITH A SONG IN MY HEART
AA-NOM SUP.ACT: '53 PICKUP ON SOUTH STREET
AA-NOM SUP.ACT: '59 PILLOW TALK
AA-NOM SUP.ACT: '62 BIRD MAN OF ALCATRAZ

ROBARDS, JR., JASON

BORN: JASON NELSON ROBARDS, JR.
JUL 26,'22 AT CHICAGO, IL
FATHER: JASON ROBARDS, SR., ACTOR
MOTHER: HOPE GLANVILLE
*** MARRIED: '46 ELEANOR PITMAN (DIVORCED '58)
DAUGHTER: '47 SARA LOUISE ROBARDS
SON: '48 JASON ROBARDS, III
SON: '49 DAVID ROBARDS
*** MARRIED: '59 RACHEL TAYLOR (DIVORCED)
*** MARRIED: '61 LAUREN BACALL, ACTRESS (DIVORCED '69)
STEP-DAUGHTER: LESLIE HOWARD BOGART
STEP-SON: STEPHEN BOGART
SON: '62 SAM ROBARDS
*** MARRIED: '70 LOIS O'CONNOR
DAUGHTER: '72 SHANNON ROBARDS
SON: '74 JAKE ROBARDS
TALENT: ACTOR
CREDIT: '59 BY LOVE POSSESSED
CREDIT: '66 A THOUSAND CLOWNS
CREDIT: '72 THE WAR BETWEEN WOMEN AND MEN
CREDIT: '73 PLAY IT AS IT LAYS
AA-NOM SUP.ACT: '76 ALL THE PRESIDENT'S MEN
AA-WIN SUP.ACT.: '77 JULIA

ROBERTS, RACHEL

SEP 20,'27 AT LLANDDEWIRYDUCH, WALES
FATHER: RICHARD RHYS ROBERTS, MINISTER (DIED '65)
MOTHER: RACHEL ANN
*** MARRIED: ALAN DOBIE
*** MARRIED: '62 REX HARRISON (DIVORCED '71)
STEP-SON: NOEL HARRISON
STEP-SON: CAREY HARRISON
ROMANCE: DARREN RAMIREZ
ROMANCE: VALENTINE MAYER
TALENT: ACTRESS-SINGER
CREDIT: '52 VALLEY OF SONG
CREDIT: '57 THE GOOD COMPANIONS
AA-NOM ACTRESS: '63 THIS SPORTING LIFE
CREDIT: '71 WILD ROVERS
CREDIT: '73 O LUCKY MAN

ROBERTSON, CLIFF

BORN: CLIFFORD PARKER ROBERTSON, III
SEP 09,'25 AT LA JOLLA, CA
FATHER: CLIFFORD ROBERTSON
MOTHER: ANDREE (DIED '27)
*** MARRIED: '57 CYNTHIA STONE
DAUGHTER: '59 STEPHANIE ROBERTSON
*** MARRIED: '66 DINA MERRILL, ACTRESS

```
        DAUGHTER:  '68 HEATHER ROBERTSON
        TALENT: ACTOR-DIRECTOR
        CREDIT:  '55 PICNIC, DEBUT
        CREDIT:  '63 MY SIX LOVES
        CREDIT:  '64 THE BEST MAN
        CREDIT:  '67 THE HONEY POT
        AA-WIN  ACTOR:  '68 CHARLY
-------------------------------------------------------------------------------
ROBERTSON, DALE        BORN:  DAYLE LYMOINE ROBERTSON
                              JUL 14,'23 AT OKLAHOMA CITY, OK
        FATHER: MELVIN ROBERTSON
        BROTHER: ROXY ROBERTSON
        BROTHER: CHESTER ROBERTSON
        *** MARRIED:  '51 JACQUELINE WILSON  (DIVORCED '54)
        DAUGHTER:  '52 ROCHELLE ROBERTSON
        *** MARRIED:  '56 MARY MURPHY  (ANNULLED '57)
        *** MARRIED:  '59 LULA MAE HARDING
        ADOPTED DAUGHTER: REBEL LEE ROBERTSON
        RESIDENCE: RANCH NEAR TUCSON, ARIZONA
        TALENT: ACTOR
        CREDIT:  '49 FIGHTING MAN OF THE PLAINS, DEBUT
        CREDIT:  '52 LYDIA BAILEY
        CREDIT:  '56 A DAY OF FURY
        CREDIT:  '63 LAW OF THE LAWLESS
        CREDIT:  '65 BLOOD ON THE ARROW
-------------------------------------------------------------------------------
ROBESON, PAUL          BORN:  PAUL LEROY BUSTILL ROBESON
                              APR 09,'98 AT PRINCETON, NJ  DIED IN '76
        FATHER: WILLIAM DREW ROBESON, MINISTER
        MOTHER: MARIA LOUISA BUSTILL  (DIED '04)
        SISTER: MARION ROBESON
        BROTHER: WILLIAM DREW ROBESON, JR., DOCTOR
        BROTHER: REEVE 'REED' ROBESON
        BROTHER: BENJAMIN ROBESON, MINISTER
        *** MARRIED:  '21 ESLANDA CARDOZO GOODE  (DIED '65)
        SON:  '27 PAUL 'PAULI' ROBESON, JR.
        RESIDENCE: HARLEM, NYC
        RESIDENCE: PHILADELPHIA, PA
        BIOGRAPHY:  '74 LIFE AND TIMES, BY VIRGINIA HAMILTON
        TALENT: SINGER, ACTOR, FOOTBALL PLAYER, LAWYER
        COMMENT: PHI BETA KAPPA RUTGERS UNIVERSITY
        COMMENT: 1952-STALIN PEACE PRIZE
        CREDIT:  '33 THE EMPEROR JONES
        CREDIT:  '36 SHOWBOAT
        CREDIT:  '38 KING SOLOMON'S MINES
        CREDIT:  '39 THE PROUD VALLEY
-------------------------------------------------------------------------------
ROBINSON, EDWARD G.      BORN:  EMANUEL GOLDENBERG
                              DEC 12,'93 AT BUCHAREST, ROMANIA  DIED IN '73
        FATHER: MORRIS GOLDENBERG
        MOTHER: SARAH GUTTMAN
        BROTHER: ZACKERY GOLDENBERG
        BROTHER: JACK GOLDENBERG
        BROTHER: OSCAR GOLDENBERG
        BROTHER: WILLIE GOLDENBERG
        BROTHER: MAX GOLDENBERG, DENTIST
        *** MARRIED:  '27 GLADYS LLOYD, ARTIST  (DIVORCED '56)
        SON:  '33 EDWARD G. 'MANNY' ROBINSON, JR, ACTOR  (DIED '74)
```

```
*** MARRIED:  '58 JANE ADLER
GRANDDAUGHTER:  '60 FRANCESCA ROBINSON
RESIDENCE: BEVERLY HILLS, CA
MEMOIRS: ALL MY YESTERDAYS
BIOGRAPHY:  '58 MY FATHER - MY SON, BY EDWARD G. ROBINSON, JR.
TALENT: ACTOR,ART COLLECTOR
CREDIT:  '23 THE BRIGHT SHAWL
CREDIT:  '30 LITTLE CAESAR
CREDIT:  '43 FLESH AND FANTASY
CREDIT:  '52 ACTORS AND SIN
CREDIT:  '67 GRAND SLAM
AA-SPECIAL AWARD:  '72 HONORARY AWARD TO 'A RENAISSANCE MAN'
CREDIT:  '72 SOYLENT GREEN
```

ROGERS, GINGER   BORN: VIRGINIA KATHERINE MCMATH
```
                             JUL 16,'11 AT INDEPENDENCE, MR
   FATHER: WILLIAM EDDINS MCMATH
   MOTHER: LELA HAWORTH, AKA LELA OWENS - STAGE MOTHER  (DIED '77)
   STEP-FATHER: JOHN LOGAN ROGERS
   COUSIN: RITA HAYWORTH, ACTRESS
   COUSIN: EDUARDO CANSINO, JR., ACTOR
   *** MARRIED:  '29 JACK CULPEPPER, STAGE PERFORMER  (DIVORCED '31)
   *** MARRIED:  '33 LEW AYRES, ACTOR  (DIVORCED '40)
   *** MARRIED:  '42 JACK BRIGGS  (DIVORCED '49)
   *** MARRIED:  '53 JACQUES BERGERAC, ACTOR  (DIVORCED '57)
   *** MARRIED:  '61 WILLIAM MARSHALL, PRODUCER  (DIVORCED '72)
   STEP-SON: MICHAEL MARSHALL
   ROMANCE: ROBERT RISKIN, WRITER
   ROMANCE: MERVYN LEROY, DIRECTOR
   PARTNER: FRED ASTAIRE
   RESIDENCE: PALM SPRINGS, CA
   POSSESSION:  '30 CONTRACT AT PARAMOUNT PICTURES
   POSSESSION: RANCH AT ROGUE RIVER, OR
   BIOGRAPHY:  '75 GINGER ROGERS, BY PATRICK MCGILLIGAN
   TALENT: DANCER-ACTRESS
   COMMENT: FASHION CONSULTANT J. C. PENNEY STORES
   CREDIT:  '30 YOUNG MAN OF MANHATTAN
   CREDIT:  '35 TOP HAT
   AA-WIN  ACTRESS:  '40 KITTY FOYLE
   CREDIT:  '48 IT HAD TO BE YOU
   CREDIT:  '57 OH MEN, OH WOMEN
   CREDIT:  '65 THE CONFESSION
```

ROGERS, ROY   BORN: LEONARD SLYE
```
                             NOV 05,'12 AT DUCK RUN, OH
   FATHER: ANDREW E. SLYE
   MOTHER: MATTIE MARTHA WOMACH
   SISTER: MARY SLYE
   *** MARRIED:  '36 ARLENE WILKINS  (DIED '46)
   DAUGHTER:  '37 CHERYL DARLENE ROGERS
   DAUGHTER:  '38 LINDA LOU ROGERS
   DAUGHTER:  '39 MARION ROGERS
   SON:  '40 ROY ROGERS, JR.
   SON:  '41 SCOTT WARD ROGERS
   *** MARRIED:  '47 DALE EVANS, ACTRESS
   STEP-SON: THOMAS FOX, JR.
   DAUGHTER:  '48 ROBIN ROGERS  (DIED)
   SON: '49 JOHN ROGERS
```

```
        DAUGHTER:  '50 MARY LITTLE DOE ROGERS
        DAUGHTER:  '51 MARION ROGERS
        DAUGHTER:  '52 DEBORAH ROGERS  (DIED)
        PARTNER: TRIGGER, ACTOR  (DIED '65)
        RESIDENCE: VICTORVILLE, CA
        TALENT: SINGER-ACTOR
        CREDIT:  '38 UNDER WESTERN SKYS
        CREDIT:  '44 THE MAN FROM MUSIC MOUNTAIN
        CREDIT:  '47 ROLL ON TEXAS MOON
        CREDIT:  '51 TRAIL OF ROBIN HOOD
        CREDIT:  '53 PALS OF THE GOLDEN WEST
-------------------------------------------------------------------------------
ROGERS, WILL           BORN:  WILLIAM PENN ADAIR ROGERS
                              NOV 04,'79 AT OLAGAH, INDIAN TERRITORY  DIED IN '35
        FATHER: CLEM VANN ROGERS
        MOTHER: MARY SCHRIMPSHER
        *** MARRIED:  '08 BETTY BLAKE
        SON:  '12 WILL ROGERS, JR., ACTOR
        DAUGHTER: MARY ROGERS
        SON: JAMES ROGERS
        FRIEND: WILEY POST, ACTOR, AVIATOR  (DIED '35)
        TALENT: ACTOR-HUMORIST
        COMMENT: ELECTED MAYOR, BEVERLY HILLS, CA
        CREDIT:  '18 LAUGHING BILL HYDE
        CREDIT:  '21 BOYS WILL BE BOYS
        CREDIT:  '21 GUILE OF WOMEN
        CREDIT:  '30 HAPPY DAYS
        CREDIT:  '35 DOUBTING THOMAS
-------------------------------------------------------------------------------
ROLAND, GILBERT         BORN:  LUIS ANTONIO DAMASCO DEALONSO
                              DEC 11,'05 AT JUAREZ, MEXICO
        FATHER: FRANCISCO ALONSO, BULLFIGHTER
        MOTHER: CONSUELO BOTANA
        BROTHER: CHICO ALONSO, DIRECTOR
        *** MARRIED:  '41 CONSTANCE BENNETT, ACTRESS  (DIVORCED '46)
        FATHER-IN-LAW: RICHARD BENNETT, ACTOR
        SISTER-IN-LAW: JOAN BENNETT, ACTRESS
        SISTER-IN-LAW: BARBARA BENNETT, ACTRESS
        STEP-SON: PETER BENNETT PLANT
        DAUGHTER:  '42 GYL CHRISTINA ROLAND
        DAUGHTER:  '43 LORINDA ALONZO ROLAND
        *** MARRIED:  '54 GUILLERMINA CANTU
        ROMANCE: CLARA BOW, ACTRESS
        ROMANCE: NORMA TALMADGE
        TALENT: ACTOR
        CREDIT:  '25 THE PLASTIC AGE, DEBUT
        CREDIT:  '33 SHE DONE HIM WRONG
        CREDIT:  '49 WE WERE STRANGERS
        CREDIT:  '52 THE BAD AND THE BEAUTIFUL
        CREDIT:  '73 RUN WILD
-------------------------------------------------------------------------------
ROMAN, RUTH
                              DEC 23,'23 AT BOSTON, MS
        FATHER: ANTHONY ROMAN, CARNIVAL BARKER
        MOTHER: MARY
        SISTER: EVE ROMAN
        SISTER: ANNA ROMAN
        *** MARRIED:  '40 JACK FLAXMAN  (DIVORCED '41)
```

*** MARRIED: '50 MORTIMER HALL, PUBLISHER (DIVORCED '55)
MOTHER-IN-LAW: DOROTHY SCHIFF, PUBLISHER
SON: '52 RICHARD HALL
*** MARRIED: '56 BUDD B. MOSS, AGENT (ANNULLED '60)
ROMANCE: HUGH O'BRIAN, ACTOR
ROMANCE: BILL WALSH, CARTOONIST
RESIDENCE: BRENTWOOD, CA
POSSESSION: '49 CONTRACT AT WARNER BROS.
TALENT: ACTRESS
COMMENT: SURVIVOR OF THE SINKING SHIP ANDREA DORIA IN 1956
CREDIT: '44 LADIES COURAGEOUS
CREDIT: '51 STRANGERS ON A TRAIN
CREDIT: '58 BITTER VICTORY
CREDIT: '65 LOVE HAS MANY FACES
CREDIT: '72 THE BABY

ROMANOFF, "PRINCE" MICHAEL   BORN: HARRY F. GEGUZONOFF
                                           FEB 21,'90 AT VILNA, LITHUANIA   DIED IN '71
*** MARRIED: '48 GLORIA LISTER
RESIDENCE: BEVERLY HILLS, CA
POSSESSION: ROMANOFF'S RESTAURANTS IN BEVERLY HILLS & PALM SPRINGS
TALENT: ACTOR, RESTAURATEUR
COMMENT: AKA HARRY GERGUSON OF CHICAGO, ILLINOIS
COMMENT: 'PRINCE' MICHAEL ALEXANDROVICH DMITRI OBOLENSKY ROMANOFF
CREDIT: '48 ARCH OF TRIUMPH
CREDIT: '53 PARIS MODEL
CREDIT: '64 GOODBYE, CHARLIE
CREDIT: '67 CAPRICE

ROMERO, CESAR   BORN: CAESAR JULIUS 'BUTCH' ROMERO
                              FEB 15,'07 AT NYC
GRANDFATHER: JOSE JULIAN MARTI, REVOLUTIONARY, POET
FATHER: CAESAR JULIUS ROMERO (DIED '51)
MOTHER: MARIA MANTILLA MARTI, SINGER (DIED '62)
SISTER: GRACIELA ROMERO
SISTER: MARIA TERESA ROMERO
BROTHER: EDUARDO S. ROMERO
UNCLE: BOLIVAR SIMON ROMERO
UNCLE: FRANKLIN BENJAMIN ROMERO
UNCLE: NELSON HORATIO ROMERO
FRIEND: TYRONE POWER
FRIEND: JOAN CRAWFORD
PARTNER: LIZ HIGGINS, DANCER
POSSESSION: '72 RESTAURANT 'CAPPUCINO' IN L.A.
TALENT: DANCER, ACTOR
CREDIT: '35 METROPOLITAN, DEBUT
CREDIT: '39 THE RETURN OF THE CISCO KID
CREDIT: '51 HAPPY GO LUCKY
CREDIT: '69 A TALENT FOR LOVING
CREDIT: '72 NOW YOU SEE HIM, NOW YOU DON'T

ROONEY, MICKEY   BORN: JOE YULE, JR.
                               SEP 23,'22 AT BROOKLYN, NY
FATHER: JOE YULE, VAUDEVILLE ACTOR
MOTHER: NELL CARTER
*** MARRIED: '42 AVA GARDNER, ACTRESS (DIVORCED '43)
*** MARRIED: '44 BETTY JANE RASE (DIVORCED '49)
SON: '44 MICKEY ROONEY, JR.

```
        DAUGHTER-IN-LAW: MERCY MONTELLO  (MARRIED '69)
        SON:  '47 TIMOTHY ROONEY
        *** MARRIED:  '49 MARTHA VICKERS - ACTRESS  (DIVORCED '51)
        SON:  '49 THEODORE ROONEY
        *** MARRIED:  '52 ELAINE MAHNKEN  (DIVORCED '59)
        *** MARRIED:  '59 BARBARA ANN THOMASEN  (DIVORCED)
        DAUGHTER:  '59 KELLY ANN ROONEY
        DAUGHTER:  '60 KERRY ROONEY
        SON:  '61 KYLE ROONEY
        DAUGHTER:  '62 KIMMY SUE ROONEY
        *** MARRIED:  '66 MARGARET LANG  (DIVORCED '67)
        *** MARRIED:  '69 CAROLYN HOCKETT
        *** MARRIED:  '78 JANICE DARLENE CHAMBERLAIN, SINGER
        FRIEND: JUDY GARLAND, ACTRESS
        RESIDENCE: WESTLAKE VILLAGE, CA
        MEMOIRS:  '65-I. E.
        TALENT: ACTOR
        COMMENT: EARLY STAGENAME WAS MCGUIRE ROONEY
        AA-SPECIAL AWARD:  '38 AN HONORARY MINIATURE AWARD
        CREDIT:  '38 LOVE FINDS ANDY HARDY
        AA-NOM  ACTOR:  '39 BABES IN ARMS
        AA-NOM  ACTOR:  '43 THE HUMAN COMEDY
        AA-NOM  SUP.ACT:  '56 THE BOLD AND THE BRAVE
        CREDIT:  '69 THE COMIC
```

ROSENBLOOM, "SLAPSY" MAXIE   BORN: MAXWELL ROSENBLOOM
                                            OCT 01,'03 AT NYC DIED IN '76

```
        MOTHER: --, DANCER
        *** MARRIED:  '39 MURIEL FALDER, CHILD PSYCHOLOGIST  (DIVORCED '45)
        ROMANCE: ELIZABETH CAMPBELL
        FRIEND: ADDISON 'JACK' RANDALL, ACTOR
        RESIDENCE: HOLLYWOOD PLAZA HOTEL
        POSSESSION:  '39 CONTRACT AT COLUMBIA`PICTURES
        TALENT: ACTOR, BOXER
        COMMENT: WORLD LIGHT HEAVYWEIGHT BOXING CHAMPION 1930-34
        CREDIT:  '33 MR. BROADWAY
        CREDIT:  '48 HAZARD
        CREDIT:  '51 MR. UNIVERSE
        CREDIT:  '55 ABBOTT AND COSTELLO MEET THE  KEYSTONE KOPS
        CREDIT:  '59 THE BEAT GENERATION
```

ROSS, DIANA
                              MAR 26,'44 AT DETROIT, MH
```
        GRANDFATHER: WILLIAM MOTON, MINISTER
        FATHER: FRED EARLL ROSS
        MOTHER: ERNESTINE
        SISTER: RITA ROSS, ACTRESS
        BROTHER: ARTHUR ROSS
        BROTHER: FRED ROSS
        BROTHER: CHICO ROSS
        *** MARRIED:  '71 ROBERT SILBERSTEIN  (DIVORCED '77)
        DAUGHTER:  '71 RHONDA SUZANNE SILBERSTEIN
        DAUGHTER:  '72 TRACEE JOY SILBERSTEIN
        DAUGHTER:  '75 CHUDNEY LANE SILBERSTEIN
        FRIEND: ARTHUR ASHE, TENNIS PLAYER
        PARTNER: MARY WILSON, IN GROUP PRIMETTES & SUPREMES
        PARTNER: FLORENCE BALLARD, IN GROUP PRIMETTES & SUPREMES  (DIED '76)
        PARTNER: CINDY BIRDSONG, IN GROUP SUPREMES
```

PARTNER: BERRY GORDY, FOUNDED MOTOWN RECORDS
RESIDENCE: BEVERLY HILLS, CA
BIOGRAPHY: '78 SUPREME LADY, BY CONNIE BERMAN
TALENT: SINGER, ACTRESS
AA-NOM ACTRESS: '72 LADY SINGS THE BLUES
CREDIT: '74 MAHOGANY
CREDIT: '78 THE WIZ

ROSS, KATHARINE
                              JAN 29,'42 AT LOS ANGELES, CA
FATHER: DUDLEY ROSS, NAVY OFFICER
MOTHER: KATHARINE
*** MARRIED: --, PRODUCER
*** MARRIED: '66 JOEL FRABRANI, ACTOR (DIVORCED '67)
*** MARRIED: '74 GAETANO LISI, CHAUFFEUR
*** MARRIED: '78 BILL STEVENSON, GUITARIST
ROMANCE: CASEY TIBBS, RODEO PERFORMER
ROMANCE: CLAIR HUFFAKER, WRITER
ROMANCE: CONRAD HALL, PHOTOGRAPHER
RESIDENCE: MALIBU, CA
POSSESSION: '68 CONTRACT AT UNIVERSAL STUDIOS FOR 7 YEARS - ENDED IN '71
TALENT: ACTRESS
AA-NOM SUP.ACT: '67 THE GRADUATE
CREDIT: '67 GAMES
CREDIT: '69 TELL THEM WILLIE BOY IS HERE
CREDIT: '69 BUTCH CASSIDY AND THE SUNDANCE KID
CREDIT: '70 FOOLS
CREDIT: '78 THE SWARM

ROTH, LILLIAN   BORN: LILLIAN RUTSTEIN
                              DEC 13,'10 AT BOSTON, MS
FATHER: ARTHUR RUTSTEIN
MOTHER: KATHERINE SILVERMAN
SISTER: ANN RUTSTEIN, ACTRESS - ANN ROTH
*** MARRIED: WILLIAM C. SCOTT (DIVORCED)
*** MARRIED: DAVID LYONS (DIED)
*** MARRIED: WILLIAM RICHARDS (DIVORCED)
*** MARRIED: BENJAMIN SHALLECK (DIVORCED)
*** MARRIED: EUGENE WEINER (DIVORCED)
*** MARRIED: EDWARD GOLDMAN (DIVORCED)
*** MARRIED: MARK HARRIS (DIVORCED)
*** MARRIED: THOMAS B. MCGUIRE (DIVORCED '64)
ROMANCE: HERBERT OSHINSKY (DIED)
RESIDENCE: NYC
MEMOIRS: I'LL CRY TOMORROW
MEMOIRS: BEYOUND MY WORTH
TALENT: ACTRESS-SINGER-AUTHOR
CREDIT: '20 THE LOVE PARADE
CREDIT: '30 MADAM SATAN
CREDIT: '31 ANIMAL CRACKERS
CREDIT: '33 LADIES THEY TALK ABOUT
CREDIT: '33 TAKE A CHANCE

ROWLANDS, GENA   BORN: VIRGINIA CATHRYN ROWLANDS
                           JUN 19,'36 AT CAMBRIA, WI
   FATHER: EDWIN MERWIN ROWLANDS, WISCONSIN STATE SENATOR
   MOTHER: MARY ALLEN NEAL
   *** MARRIED: '54 JOHN CASSAVETES, ACTOR, DIRECTOR
   DAUGHTER: '65 ALEXANDRA CASSAVETES
   SON: '67 NICHOLAS CASSAVETES
   DAUGHTER: '70 ZOE CASSAVETES
   RESIDENCE: HOLLYWOOD HILLS, CA
   TALENT: ACTRESS
   CREDIT: '58 THE HIGH COST OF LOVING
   CREDIT: '62 LONELY ARE THE BRAVE
   CREDIT: '69 THE HAPPY ENDING
   CREDIT: '71 MINNIE AND MOSKOWITZ
   AA-NOM ACTRESS: '74 A WOMAN UNDER THE INFLUENCE

RUGGLES, CHARLES   BORN: CHARLES SHERMAN RUGGLES
                           FEB 08,'86 AT LOS ANGELES, CA   DIED IN '70
   BROTHER: WESLEY RUGGLES, ACTOR, DIRECTOR (DIED '72)
   *** MARRIED: ADELE ROWLAND, ACTRESS (DIVORCED)
   *** MARRIED: '42 MARION SHIELDS LA BARBA
   PARTNER: MARY BOLAND, ACTRESS
   RESIDENCE: PACIFIC PALISADES, CA
   POSSESSION: RUGGLES KENNELS AND CHICKEN FARM
   TALENT: ACTOR
   CREDIT: '15 REFORM CANDIDATE, DEBUT
   CREDIT: '30 CHARLEY'S AUNT
   CREDIT: '35 RUGGLES OF RED GAP
   CREDIT: '46 THE PERFECT MARRIAGE
   CREDIT: '58 THE PLEASURE OF HIS COMPANY, STAGE AND FILM
   CREDIT: '66 FOLLOW ME, BOYS

RUSH, BARBARA
                           JAN 04,'27 AT DENVER, CO
   FATHER: ROY L. RUSH
   MOTHER: MARGUERITE
   *** MARRIED: '50 JEFFERY HUNTER, ACTOR (DIVORCED '54)
   SON: '52 CHRISTOPHER HUNTER
   *** MARRIED: '59 WARREN COWAN
   DAUGHTER: '63 CLAUDIA COWAN
   *** MARRIED: '70 JAMES GRUZALSKI
   TALENT: ACTRESS
   CREDIT: '51 THE FIRST LEGION
   CREDIT: '55 CAPTAIN LIGHTFOOT
   CREDIT: '60 STRANGERS WHEN WE MEET
   CREDIT: '67 HOMBRE
   CREDIT: '74 SUPERDAD

RUSSELL, JANE   BORN: ERNESTINE JANE RUSSELL
                           JUN 21,'21 AT BEMIDJI, MN
   FATHER: REV. ROY WILLIAM RUSSELL
   MOTHER: GERALDINE JACOBI
   BROTHER: THOMAS RUSSELL
   BROTHER: KENNETH RUSSELL
   BROTHER: JAMES RUSSELL
   BROTHER: WALLACE RUSSELL
   *** MARRIED: '43 BOB WATERFIELD, FOOTBALL PLAYER (DIVORCED '67)

ADOPTED SON: THOMAS WATERFIELD
ADOPTED DAUGHTER: TRACY WATERFIELD
ADOPTED SON: ROBERT WATERFIELD, JR.
*** MARRIED: '68 ROGER BARRETT, DIED 3 MONTHS AFTER MARRIAGE (DIED '68)
*** MARRIED: '74 JOHN PEOPLES
FRIEND: HOWARD HUGHES
FRIEND: CLARK GABLE
FRIEND: MARILYN MONROE,
POSSESSION: '40 7 YEAR CONTRACT WITH HOWARD HUGHES - RENEWED
POSSESSION: '55 20 YEAR CONTRACT WITH HOWARD HUGHES
MEMOIRS: AUTOBIOGRAPHY OF JANE RUSSELL
TALENT: ACTRESS
COMMENT: SERVED AS OFFICER OF ADOPTION AGENCY - WAIF
CREDIT: '40 THE OUTLAW, DEBUT
CREDIT: '48 THE PALEFACE
CREDIT: '54 THE FRENCH LINE
CREDIT: '55 GENTLEMEN MARRY BRUNETTES
CREDIT: '57 THE FUZZY PINK NIGHTGOWN
CREDIT: '66 WACO

RUSSELL, ROSALIND
                              JUN 04,'08 AT WATERBURY, CN DIED IN '76
FATHER: JAMES RUSSELL, SR., LAWYER
MOTHER: CLARA MCKNIGHT, VOGUE MAGAZINE EDITOR
SISTER: CLARA RUSSELL
SISTER: MARY JANE RUSSELL
BROTHER: JAMES RUSSELL, JR.
BROTHER: JOHN RUSSELL
*** MARRIED: '41 FREDERICK BRISSON, PRODUCER
FATHER-IN-LAW: CARL BRISSON PETERSEN, ACTOR, ENTERTAINER
SON: '43 LANCE BRISSON
DAUGHTER-IN-LAW: PATRICIA MORROW, ACTRESS
ROMANCE: JAMES STEWART
RESIDENCE: BEVERLY HILLS, CA
POSSESSION: PH.D. UNIVERSITY OF PORTLAND FINE ARTS
MEMOIRS: '77 LIFE IS A BANQUET
TALENT: ACTRESS
CREDIT: '34 THE PRESIDENT VANISHES
AA-NOM ACTRESS: '42 MY SISTER EILEEN
AA-NOM ACTRESS: '46 SISTER KENNY
AA-NOM ACTRESS: '47 MOURNING BECOMES ELECTRA
AA-NOM ACTRESS: '58 AUNTIE MAME

RUTHERFORD, ANN   BORN: THERESE ANN RUTHERFORD
                              NOV 02,'17 AT TORONTO, ONTARIO, CANADA
FATHER: JOHN D. RUTHERFORD, OPERA SINGER
MOTHER: LUCILLE MANSFIELD, ACTRESS
SISTER: JUDITH ARLEN, ACTRESS
*** MARRIED: '42 DAVID MAY, RETAILER (DIVORCED '53)
ADOPTED DAUGHTER: GLORIA MAY
*** MARRIED: '53 WILLIAM DOZIER, TV PRODUCER
STEP-DAUGHTER: DEBORAH LESLIE DOZIER
RESIDENCE: BEVERLY HILLS, CA
TALENT: ACTRESS
CREDIT: '38 LOVE FINDS ANDY HARDY
CREDIT: '40 PRIDE AND PREJUDICE
CREDIT: '47 THE SECRET LIFE OF WALTER MITTY
CREDIT: '72 THEY ONLY KILL THEIR MASTERS

RUTHERFORD, MARGARET   BORN: MARGARET TAYLOR RUTHERFORD
                                    MAY 11,'92 AT LONDON, ENGLAND   DIED IN '72
     FATHER: WILLIAM RUTHERFORD BENN
     MOTHER: FLORENCE NICHOLSON
     *** MARRIED: '45 J. B. STRINGER DAVIS
     POSSESSION: '61 OFFICER-ORDER OF BRITISH EMPIRE
     BIOGRAPHY: '56 MARGARET RUTHERFORD, BY ERIC KEOWN
     TALENT: ACTRESS
     CREDIT: '36 TALK OF THE DEVIL
     CREDIT: '45 BLITHE SPIRIT
     CREDIT: '51 THE MAGIC BOX
     AA-WIN SUP.ACT.: '63 THE V.I.P.S
     CREDIT: '68 ARABELLA

RYAN, ROBERT   BORN: ROBERT BUSHNELL RYAN
                              NOV 11,'09 AT CHICAGO,IL   DIED IN '73
     FATHER: TIMOTHY A. RYAN
     MOTHER: MABEL BUSHNELL
     BROTHER: JONATHAN RYAN (DIED '13)
     *** MARRIED: '39 JESSICA CADWALADER
     SON: '46 TIMOTHY RYAN
     SON: '48 CHENEY RYAN
     DAUGHTER: '51 LISA RYAN
     RESIDENCE: NYC
     POSSESSION: BEVERLY HILLS OFFICE BUILDING
     TALENT: ACTOR
     CREDIT: '40 GOLDEN GLOVES
     AA-NOM SUP.ACT: '47 CROSSFIRE
     CREDIT: '52 THEY CLASH BY NIGHT
     CREDIT: '62 BILLY BUDD
     CREDIT: '73 THE ICEMAN COMETH

```
--------------------------------------------------------------------------------
SABU          BORN:  SABU DASTAGIR
                     MAR 15,'24 AT KARAPUR, MYSORE, INDIA  DIED IN '63
   *** MARRIED:  '48 MARILYN COOPER, ACTRESS
SON:  '51 PAUL DASTAGIR
DAUGHTER:  '57 JASMIN DASTAGIR
BIOGRAPHY:  '37 ELEPHANT DANCE, BY FRANCES HUBBARD FLAHERTY
TALENT: ACTOR
CREDIT:  '37 ELEPHANT BOY
CREDIT:  '40 THE THIEF OF BAGHDAD
CREDIT:  '42 THE JUNGLE BOOK
CREDIT:  '54 HELLO, ELEPHANT
CREDIT:  '64 A TIGER WALKS
--------------------------------------------------------------------------------
SAINT CYR, LILI          BORN:  MARIE VAN SCHAAK
                                JUN 03,'17 AT MINNEAPOLIS, MN
   FATHER: EDWARD VAN SCHAAK
   MOTHER: IDELLA
   *** MARRIED: CORDELL MILNE, MOTORCYCLE RACER
   *** MARRIED: RICHARD HUBERT, WAITER
   *** MARRIED: PAUL VALENTINE, DANCER, SINGER  (DIVORCED '49)
   *** MARRIED:  '50 ARMANDO ORSINI
   *** MARRIED:  '55 TED JORDAN
   *** MARRIED:  '59 JOSEPH A. ZOMAR
   RESIDENCE: HOLLYWOOD HILLS, CA
   TALENT: ACTRESS-ECDYSIAST
   CREDIT:  '58 THE NAKED AND THE DEAD
   CREDIT:  '58 I, MOBSTER
   CREDIT: SON OF SINBAD
--------------------------------------------------------------------------------
SAINT JAMES, SUSAN          BORN:  SUSAN MILLER
                                   AUG 14,'46 AT LOS ANGELES, CA
   FATHER: CHARLES DANIEL MILLER
   MOTHER: CONSTANCE GEIGER
   *** MARRIED:  '67 RICHARD NEUBERT, WRITER  (DIVORCED '68)
   *** MARRIED:  '71 TOM LUCAS
   DAUGHTER:  '72 SUNSHINE LUCAS
   SON:  '73 HARMONY LUCAS
   ENEMY: ROCK HUDSON
   POSSESSION:  '66 CONTRACT AT UNIVERSAL STUDIOS
   POSSESSION:  '76 NO HUNTING CLUB PRODUCTION CO.
   TALENT: ACTRESS
   CREDIT:  '68 WHERE ANGELS GO TROUBLE FOLLOWS
--------------------------------------------------------------------------------
SAINT JOHN, JILL          BORN:  JILL OPPENHEIM
                                 AUG 19,'40 AT LOS ANGELES, CA
   *** MARRIED:  '57 NEIL DUBIN
   *** MARRIED:  '60 LANCE REVENTLOW
   *** MARRIED:  '67 JACK JONES, SINGER
   FATHER-IN-LAW: ALLAN JONES
   MOTHER-IN-LAW: IRENE HERVEY
   FRIEND: HENRY KISSINGER
   RESIDENCE: ASPEN, CO
   TALENT: ACTRESS
   CREDIT:  '59 SUMMER LOVE
   CREDIT:  '63 WHO'S BEEN SLEEPING IN MY BED?
   CREDIT:  '67 TONY ROME
   CREDIT:  '71 DIAMONDS ARE FOREVER
```

CREDIT: '71 MCMILLAN AND WIFE, TV SERIES
CREDIT: '77 OUTLAW BLUES

SAINT, EVA MARIE
                              JUL 04,'24 AT EAST ORANGE,NJ
FATHER: JOHN MERLE SAINT (DIED '73)
MOTHER: EVA MARIE RICE
SISTER: ADELAIDE SAINT
*** MARRIED: '51 JEFFREY HAYDEN, TV DIRECTOR, PRODUCER
SON: '55 DARRELL HAYDEN
DAUGHTER: '58 LAURETTE HAYDEN
RESIDENCE: NYC
TALENT: ACTRESS
AA-WIN SUP.ACT.: '54 ON THE WATERFRONT
CREDIT: '56 THAT CERTAIN FEELING
CREDIT: '60 EXODUS
CREDIT: '62 ALL FALL DOWN
CREDIT: '69 LOVING

SANDERS, GEORGE
                    JUL 03,'06 AT ST. PETERSBURG, RUSSIA   DIED IN '72
FATHER: HENRY SANDERS, ROPE MANUFACTURER
MOTHER: MARGARET KILBE, HORTICULTURIST
BROTHER: THOMAS CHARLES SANDERS, ACTOR - TOM CONWAY (DIED '67)
*** MARRIED: '40 ELSIE M. POOLE, ACTRESS- SUSAN LARSEN (DIVORCED '47)
*** MARRIED: '49 ZSA ZSA GABOR (DIVORCED '54)
SISTER-IN-LAW: MAGDA GABOR
SISTER-IN-LAW: EVA GABOR, ACTRESS
*** MARRIED: '58 BENITA HUME (DIED '67)
STEP-DAUGHTER: JULIET COLMAN
*** MARRIED: '70 MAGDA GABOR
SISTER-IN-LAW: ZSA ZSA GABOR, ACTRESS
STEP-DAUGHTER: FRANCESCA HILTON
SISTER-IN-LAW: EVA GABOR, ACTRESS
MEMOIRS: MEMOIRS OF A PROFESSIONAL CAD
TALENT: ACTOR
COMMENT: OWNED THE CAD CO.-SAUSAGE MFGS
CREDIT: '29 STRANGE CARGO, DEBUT
CREDIT: '39 THE OUTSIDER
CREDIT: '44 THE PORTRAIT OF DORIAN GRAY
AA-WIN SUP.ACT.: '50 ALL ABOUT EVE
CREDIT: '59 SOLOMON AND SHEBA
CREDIT: '72 PSYCHOMANIA

SANDS, TOMMY   BORN: THOMAS ADRIAN SANDS
                              AUG 27,'35 AT CHICAGO,IL
FATHER: BENNY SANDS, PIANIST
MOTHER: GRACE
STEP-BROTHER: EDWARD DEAN
*** MARRIED: '60 NANCY SINATRA, SINGER, ACTRESS (DIVORCED '65)
FATHER-IN-LAW: FRANK SINATRA, SINGER, ACTOR
*** MARRIED: '73 SHEILA WALLACE
RESIDENCE: HONOLULU, HA
POSSESSION: '57 CONTRACT AT 20TH CENTURY FOX
TALENT: ACTOR, SINGER, GUITARIST
CREDIT: '57 SING BOY SING
CREDIT: '60 BABES IN TOYLAND
CREDIT: '65 NONE BUT THE BRAVE

```
        CREDIT:   '70 THE LONGEST DAY
-----------------------------------------------------------------------------------------------------
SARRAZIN, MICHAEL          BORN:   JACQUES MICHEL ANDRE SARRAZIN
                                   MAY 22,'40 AT QUEBEC CITY, QUEBEC
     FATHER: BERNARD SARRAZIN, ATTORNEY
     MOTHER: ENID SCOTT
     ROMANCE: JACQUELINE BISSET, ACTRESS
     POSSESSION:  '69 CONTACT AT UNIVERSAL STUDIOS
     TALENT: ACTOR
     CREDIT:   '67 THE FLIM FLAM MAN
     CREDIT:   '69 THEY SHOOT HORSES, DON'T THEY?
     CREDIT:   '71 SOMETIMES A GREAT NOTION
     CREDIT:   '74 THE REINCARNATION OF PETER PROUD
-----------------------------------------------------------------------------------------------------
SAVALAS, TELLY            BORN:   ARISTOTLE SAVALAS
                                  JAN 21,'24 AT GARDEN CITY, NY
     FATHER: NICHOLAS CONSTANTINE SAVALAS
     MOTHER: CHRISTINA KAPSALLIS
     SISTER: KATHERINE SAVALAS
     BROTHER: CONSTANTINE 'GUS' SAVALAS, FOREIGN SERVICE OFFICER
     BROTHER: DEMOSTHENES 'GEORGE' SAVALAS, ACTOR
     BROTHER: PRAXITELES 'TED' SAVALAS, TEACHER
     *** MARRIED:  '50 CATHERINE  (DIVORCED)
     *** MARRIED:  '60 MARILYNN GARDNER
     DAUGHTER:  '61 CHRISTINA SAVALAS
     DAUGHTER:  '62 PENELOPE SAVALAS
     DAUGHTER:  '63 CANDACE SAVALAS
     SON:  '73 NICHOLAS SAVALAS
     *** MARRIED:  '74 SALLY ADAMS, ACTRESS
     BIOGRAPHY:  '75 TELLY SAVALAS, BY MARSHA DALY
     TALENT: ACTOR
     AA-NOM  SUP.ACT:  '62 BIRD MAN OF ALCATRAZ
     CREDIT:   '65 THE BATTLE OF THE BULGE
     CREDIT:   '68 THE SCALPHUNTERS
     CREDIT:   '71 PRETTY MAIDS ALL IN A ROW
     CREDIT:   '73 KOJAK, TV SERIES
-----------------------------------------------------------------------------------------------------
SCHEIDER, ROY
                          NOV 10,'35 AT ORANGE, NJ
     *** MARRIED: CYNTHIA, FILM EDITOR
     DAUGHTER:  '64 MAXIMILIA SCHEIDER
     RESIDENCE: NYC
     POSSESSION:  '76 PARTNER-JOE ALLEN RESTAURANTS NY, LONDON, PARIS, LOS ANGELES
     TALENT: ACTOR
     CREDIT:   '64 THE CURSE OF THE LIVING CORPSE
     AA-NOM  SUP.ACT:  '71 THE FRENCH CONNECTION
     CREDIT:   '71 KLUTE
     CREDIT:   '75 JAWS
     CREDIT:   '77 THE DEEP
-----------------------------------------------------------------------------------------------------
SCHELL, MARIA            BORN:   MARIA MARGRETHE ANNA SCHELL
                                 JAN 15,'26 AT VIENNA, AUSTRIA
     FATHER: HERMANN FERDINAND SCHELL, WRITER
     MOTHER: MARGARETHE NOE VON NORDBERG, ACTRESS
     SISTER: IMMY SCHELL
     BROTHER: KARL SCHELL, ACTOR
     BROTHER: MAXIMILIAN SCHELL, ACTOR
     *** MARRIED:  '57 HORST HACHLER
```

```
SON:  '62 OLIVER CHRISTIAN HACHLER
*** MARRIED:  '66 VEIT RELINS
RESIDENCE: FARMHOUSE IN BAVARIA
TALENT: ACTRESS
CREDIT:  '51 THE MAGIC BOX
CREDIT:  '58 THE BROTHERS KARAMAZOV
CREDIT:  '61 CIMARRON
```

SCHELL, MAXIMILIAN
```
                          DEC 08,'30 AT VIENNA, AUSTRIA
FATHER: HERMANN FERDINAND SCHELL, WRITER
MOTHER: MARGARETHE NOE VON NORDBERG, ACTRESS
SISTER: MARIA SCHELL, ACTRESS
SISTER: IMMY SCHELL
BROTHER: KARL SCHELL, ACTOR
ROMANCE: NANCY KWAN, ACTRESS
ROMANCE: SORAYA ESFANDIARY PAHLAVI, PRINCESS OF IRAN
POSSESSION:  '74 GOLDEN BOWL AWARD (GERMAN)
TALENT: ACTOR-DIRECTOR
CREDIT:  '58 THE YOUNG LIONS
AA-WIN  ACTOR:  '61 JUDGMENT AT NUREMBERG
CREDIT:  '64 TOPKAPI
CREDIT:  '68 THE CASTLE
AA-NOM  ACTOR:  '75 THE MAN IN THE GLASS BOOTH
AA-NOM  SUP.ACT: '77  JULIA
```

SCHILDKRAUT, JOSEPH
```
                          MAR 22,'95 AT VIENNA, AUSTRIA  DIED IN '64
FATHER: RUDOLPH SCHILDKRAUT, ACTOR
MOTHER: ERNA WEINSTEIN
*** MARRIED:  '23 ELISE BARTLETT, ACTRESS  (DIVORCED '31)
*** MARRIED:  '32 MARIE MCKAY  (DIED '62)
*** MARRIED:  '63 LENORA ROGERS
RESIDENCE: NYC
POSSESSION:      COLLECTION OF RARE BOOKS
MEMOIRS:  '59 MY FATHER AND I
TALENT: ACTOR
CREDIT:  '22 ORPHANS OF THE STORM
AA-WIN  SUP.ACT.:  '37 THE LIFE OF EMILE ZOLA
CREDIT:  '46 MONSIEUR BEAUCAIRE
CREDIT:  '59 THE DIARY OF ANNE FRANK
CREDIT:  '65 THE GREATEST STORY EVER TOLD
```

SCHNEIDER, ROMY   BORN: ROSE MARIE ALBACH-RETTY
```
                          SEP 23,'38 AT VIENNA, AUSTRIA
GRANDMOTHER: ROSA ALBACH-RETTY, ACTRESS
FATHER: WOLF ALBACH-RETTY, ACTOR
MOTHER: MAGDA SCHNEIDER, ACTRESS
BROTHER: WOLF ALBACH-RETTY
*** MARRIED:  '66 HARRY MAYER HAUBENSTOCK, PRODUCER
*** MARRIED:  '75 DANIEL BIASINI
FRIEND: PETER O'TOOLE
TALENT: ACTRESS
CREDIT:  '58 THE STORY OF VICKIE
CREDIT:  '62 BOCCACCIO 70
CREDIT:  '65 WHAT'S NEW PUSSYCAT?
CREDIT:  '72 THE ASSASSINATION OF TROTSKY
CREDIT:  '78 A WOMAN AT HER WINDOW
```

SCOFIELD, PAUL   BORN: DAVID SCOFIELD
                              JAN 21, '22 AT HURSTPIERPOINT, SUSSEX, ENGLAND
   *** MARRIED: '44 JOY PARKER, ACTRESS
   RESIDENCE: BALCOMBE, SUSSEX, ENGLAND
   TALENT: ACTOR
   CREDIT: '55 THAT LADY
   CREDIT: '64 THE TRAIN
   AA-WIN ACTOR: '66 A MAN FOR ALL SEASONS
   CREDIT: '71 BARTLEBY
   CREDIT: '73 A DELICATE BALANCE

SCOTT, GEORGE C.   BORN: GEORGE CAMPBELL SCOTT
                              OCT 18, '27 AT WISE, VA
   FATHER: GEORGE D. SCOTT, MINER
   MOTHER: -- (DIED '31)
   *** MARRIED: CAROLYN HUGHES, ACTRESS
   *** MARRIED: PATRICIA REED, SINGER, ACTRESS
   *** MARRIED: '60 COLLEEN DEWHURST, ACTRESS (DIVORCED '65)
   SON: '61 ALEXANDER SCOTT
   SON: '62 CAMPBELL SCOTT
   *** MARRIED: '67 COLLEEN DEWHURST, REMARRIED (DIVORCED '72)
   *** MARRIED: '72 TRISH VAN DEVERE, ACTRESS
   RESIDENCE: SOUTH SALEM, NY
   TALENT: ACTOR-DIRECTOR
   CREDIT: '58 THE HANGING TREE, DEBUT
   AA-NOM SUP.ACT: '59 ANATOMY OF A MURDER
   AA-NOM SUP.ACT: '61 THE HUSTLER
   AA-WIN ACTOR: '70 PATTON
   AA-NOM ACTOR: '71 THE HOSPITAL
   CREDIT: '75 THE HINDENBURG

SCOTT, GORDON   BORN: GORDON M. WERSCHKUL
                              AUG 03, '27 AT PORTLAND, OR
   *** MARRIED: '54 VERA MILES, ACTRESS (DIVORCED '59)
   STEP-DAUGHTER: KELLY MILES
   STEP-DAUGHTER: DEBORAH MILES
   SON: '57 MICHAEL SCOTT
   TALENT: FIREMAN, COWBOY, LIFEGUARD, ACTOR
   CREDIT: '55 TARZAN'S HIDDEN JUNGLE
   CREDIT: '64 ARM OF FIRE
   CREDIT: '66 THE TRAMPLERS

SCOTT, RANDOLPH   BORN: GEORGE RANDOLPH SCOTT
                              JAN 23, '03 AT ORANGE, VA
   FATHER: GEORGE SCOTT
   MOTHER: LUCY CRANE
   *** MARRIED: '26 MARION DUPONT SOMERVILLE
   *** MARRIED: '44 PATRICIA STILLMAN
   ADOPTED SON: CHRISTOPHER SCOTT
   ADOPTED DAUGHTER: SANDRA SCOTT
   ROMANCE: VIVIENNE GAY
   ROMANCE: VIRGINIA CHERRILL
   RESIDENCE: BEVERLY HILLS, CA
   TALENT: ACTOR
   CREDIT: '31 SKY BRIDE, DEBUT
   CREDIT: '36 LAST OF THE MOHICANS
   CREDIT: '46 BADMAN'S TERRITORY

```
CREDIT:  '54 THE BOUNTY HUNTER
CREDIT:  '62 RIDE THE HIGH COUNTRY
```

SCOTT, ZACHARY   BORN: ZACHARY THOMSON SCOTT
                                    FEB 24,'14 AT AUSTIN,TX   DIED IN '65
```
*** MARRIED:  '35 ELAINE ANDERSON  (DIVORCED '49)
SON:   '36 WAVERLY SCOTT
*** MARRIED:  '52 RUTH FORD
DAUGHTER:  '53 SHELLEY SCOTT
TALENT: ACTOR
CREDIT:  '44 MASK OF DEMETRIOUS, DEBUT
CREDIT:  '47 STALLION ROAD
CREDIT:  '53 LET'S MAKE IT LEGAL
CREDIT:  '56 BANDIDO
CREDIT:  '62 IT'S ONLY MONEY
```

SEBERG, JEAN   BORN: JEAN DOROTHY SEBERG
                                    NOV 13,'38 AT MARSHALLTOWN,IO
```
*** MARRIED:  '58 FRANCOIS MOREUIL
*** MARRIED:  '63 ROMAIN GARY, NOVELIST
*** MARRIED:  '72 DENNIS BERRY, DIRECTOR
TALENT: ACTRESS
CREDIT:  '57 SAINT JOAN, WON TITLE ROLE IN CONTEST
CREDIT:  '60 BREATHLESS
CREDIT:  '64 LILITH
CREDIT:  '69 PAINT YOUR WAGON
CREDIT:  '74 THE DEAD OF SUMMER
```

SEGAL, GEORGE
                                    FEB 13,'34 AT GREAT NECK,NY
```
FATHER: GEORGE SEGAL, SR.
MOTHER: FANNY BODKIN
BROTHER: --, WRITER
*** MARRIED:  '56 MARION SOBOL
DAUGHTER:  '57 ELIZABETH SEGAL
DAUGHTER:  '58 PATRICIA SEGAL
PARTNER: PATRICIA SCOTT, PARTNER IN MUSICAL ACT
TALENT: ACTOR-DIRECTOR
CREDIT:  '62 THE LONGEST DAY
CREDIT:  '65 KING RAT
AA-NOM  SUP.ACT:  '66 WHO'S AFRAID OF VIRGINIA WOOLF?
CREDIT:  '70 THE OWL AND THE PUSSYCAT
CREDIT:  '70 WHERE'S POPPA?
CREDIT:  '73 A TOUCH OF CLASS
```

SELLERS, PETER
                                    SEP 08,'25 AT SOUTHSEA, ENGLAND
```
FATHER: WILLIAM SELLERS, PIANIST
MOTHER: AGNES MARKS
*** MARRIED:  '51 ANNE HOWE, ACTRESS  (DIVORCED '64)
DAUGHTER:  '52 SARAH JANE PETERS SELLERS
SON:  '53 MICHAEL PETER ANTHONY SELLERS
*** MARRIED:  '64 BRITT EKLAND, ACTRESS  (DIVORCED '69)
DAUGHTER:  '65 VICTORIA SELLERS
*** MARRIED:  '70 MIRANDA QUARRY  (DIVORCED '74)
*** MARRIED:  '77 LYNNE FREDERICK, ACTRESS
POSSESSION: GIANT MECHANICAL ELEPHANT
TALENT: ACTOR-DIRECTOR
```

```
CREDIT:    '55 THE LADY KILLERS
CREDIT:    '59 THE MOUSE THAT ROARED
CREDIT:    '63 THE PINK PANTHER, SERIES
AA-NOM  ACTOR:  '64 DR. STRANGELOVE
CREDIT:    '68 I LOVE YOU ALICE B. TOKLAS
CREDIT:    '73 SOFT BEDS, HARD BATTLES
CREDIT:    '78 THE PRISONER OF ZENDA
```

SENNETT, MACK   BORN: MICHAEL SINNOTT
                          JAN 17,'80 AT RICHMOND, QUEBEC, CANADA   DIED IN '60
```
FATHER: JOHN FRANCIS SINNOTT
MOTHER: CATHERINE FOY
SISTER: MARY SINNOTT
BROTHER: JOHN SINNOTT
BROTHER: GEORGE SINNOTT
ROMANCE: MABEL NORMAND, ACTRESS
POSSESSION: MACK SENNETT STUDIO GLENDALE, CA
MEMOIRS:   '54 KING OF COMEDY
TALENT: ACTOR, PRODUCER, DIRECTOR
COMMENT: CREATED THE 'KEYSTONE KOPS'
CREDIT:    '08 BALKED AT THE ALTAR
CREDIT:    '13 THE MISTAKEN MASHER
CREDIT:    '21 MOLLY O
AA-SPECIAL AWARD:   '37 A SPECIAL AWARD TO THAT MASTER OF FUN AND COMEDY GENIUS.
```

SHARIF, OMAR   BORN: MICHEL SHAHOUB
                          APR 10,'32 AT ALEXANDRIA, EGYPT
```
FATHER: JOSEPH SHAHOUB, TIMBER MERCHANT
MOTHER: CLAIRE SAADA
*** MARRIED:  '56 FATEN HAMAMA
SON:  '57 TAREK SHARIF
*** MARRIED:  '77 SOHAIR RAMZI
TALENT: ACTOR, BRIDGE PLAYER
AA-NOM  SUP.ACT:  '62 LAWRENCE OF ARABIA
CREDIT:    '65 GENGHIS KHAN
CREDIT:    '69 CHE!
CREDIT:    '73 THE TAMARIND SEED
CREDIT:    '75 JUGGERNAUT
```

SHAW, ARTIE   BORN: ABRAHAM ISAAC ARSHAWSKY
                          MAY 23,'10 AT NYC
```
FATHER: HARRY ARSHAWSKY
MOTHER: SARAH STRAUSS
*** MARRIED:  '30 MARGARET ALLEN (DIVORCED)
*** MARRIED:  '40 LANA TURNER, ACTRESS  (DIVORCED '42)
*** MARRIED:  '42 ELIZABETH KERN  (DIVORCED '45)
FATHER-IN-LAW: JEROME KERN, COMPOSER
SON:  '43 STEVEN KERN SHAW
*** MARRIED:  '45 AVA GARDNER, ACTRESS  (DIVORCED '46)
*** MARRIED:  '46 KATHLEEN WINSOR
*** MARRIED:  '52 DORIS DOWLING  (DIVORCED '56)
SON:  '53 JONATHAN DOWLING SHAW
*** MARRIED:  '57 EVELYN KEYES, ACTRESS
STEP-SON: PAUL ALBERRAN 'PABLO' HUSTON
ROMANCE: JUDY GARLAND, ACTRESS
RESIDENCE: NYC
MEMOIRS: THE TROUBLE WITH CINDERELLA
MEMOIRS: I LOVE YOU, I HATE YOU, DROP DEAD
```

TALENT: BANDLEADER,ACTOR,PRODUCER SAXOPHONIST
COMMENT: KNOWN AS 'THE KING OF SWING'
CREDIT: DANCING CO-ED
CREDIT: SECOND CHORUS

SHAW, ROBERT
AUG 09,'27 AT LIVERPOOL, LANCS., ENGLAND DIED IN '78
FATHER: THOMAS SHAW, PHYSICIAN
MOTHER: DOREEN AVERY, NURSE
SISTER: ELIZABETH SHAW
SISTER: JOANNA SHAW
SISTER: WENDY SHAW
BROTHER: ALEXANDER SHAW
*** MARRIED: '52 JENNIFER BOURKE
DAUGHTER: '54 PENNY SHAW
*** MARRIED: '64 MARY URE, ACTRESS (DIED '75)
DAUGHTER: '65 HANNAH SHAW
ADOPTED SON: CHARLES JANSEN SHAW
*** MARRIED: '75 VIRGINIA DEWITT JANSEN
SON: '76 THOMAS SHAW
RESIDENCE: TOURMAKEADY, IRELAND
TALENT: ACTOR, AUTHOR
CREDIT: '55 THE DAM BUSTERS
AA-NOM SUP.ACT: '66 A MAN FOR ALL SEASONS
CREDIT: '72 YOUNG WINSTON
CREDIT: '75 JAWS
CREDIT: '78 AVALANCHE EXPRESS

SHEARER, NORMA   BORN: EDITH NORMA SHEARER
AUG 10,'04 AT MONTREAL, QUEBEC, CANADA
FATHER: ANDREW SHEARER
MOTHER: EDITH FISHER
SISTER: ATHOLE SHEARER
BROTHER-IN-LAW: HOWARD HAWKS, PRODUCER
BROTHER: DOUGLAS SHEARER, SOUND ENGINEER
*** MARRIED: '27 IRVING THALBERG, PRODUCER (DIED '37)
FATHER-IN-LAW: WILLIAM THALBERG
MOTHER-IN-LAW: HENRIETTA HEYMAN
SISTER-IN-LAW: SYLVIA THALBERG, WRITER
SON: '30 IRVING THALBERG, JR.
DAUGHTER: '35 KATHARINE THALBERG
*** MARRIED: '42 MARTIN ARROUGE, SKI INSTRUCTOR
FRIEND: GEORGE RAFT, ACTOR
RESIDENCE: SANTA BARBARA, CA
TALENT: MODEL-ACTRESS
AA-NOM ACTRESS: '29 THEIR OWN DESIRE
AA-WIN ACTRESS: '29 THE DIVORCEE
AA-NOM ACTRESS: '30 A FREE SOUL
AA-NOM ACTRESS: '34 THE BARRETTS OF WIMPOLE STREET
AA-NOM ACTRESS: '36 ROMEO AND JULIET
AA-NOM ACTRESS: '38 MARIE ANTOINETTE

SHEPHERD, CYBILL
FEB 18,'50 AT MEMPHIS, TN
FATHER: WILLIAM JENNINGS SHEPHERD
MOTHER: PATRICIA
ROMANCE: PETER BOGDANOVICH, DIRECTOR
TALENT: MODEL-ACTRESS

CREDIT: '72 THE LAST PICTURE SHOW
CREDIT: '73 DAISY MILLER
CREDIT: '74 AT LONG LAST LOVE
CREDIT: '76 TAXI DRIVER
CREDIT: '77 SPECIAL DELIVERY

SHERIDAN, ANN   BORN: CLARA LOU SHERIDAN
                          FEB 21,'15 AT DENTON,TX   DIED IN '67
FATHER: GEORGE W. SHERIDAN
MOTHER: LULA STEWART WARREN
SISTER: KITTY SHERIDAN
SISTER: MABEL SHERIDAN
SISTER: PAULINE SHERIDAN
BROTHER-IN-LAW: LEO R. KENT
BROTHER-IN-LAW: ROBERT E. DAY
BROTHER-IN-LAW: C. H. ROWTON
BROTHER: GEORGE SHERIDAN, JR.
*** MARRIED: '36 EDWARD NORRIS (DIVORCED '39)
*** MARRIED: '42 GEORGE BRENT, ACTOR (DIVORCED '43)
*** MARRIED: '56 JAMES OWENS
*** MARRIED: '66 SCOTT MCKAY, ACTOR
ROMANCE: STEVE HANNAGAN, PUBLICIST
RESIDENCE: LOS ANGELES, CA
POSSESSION: '35 CONTRACT AT PARAMOUNT STUDIOS
POSSESSION: '56 18 POODLES
POSSESSION: BEST DRESSED WOMAN AWARD
TALENT: ACTRESS
COMMENT: THE OOMPH GIRL
CREDIT: '27 CASEY AT THE BAT
CREDIT: '35 ENTER MADAME
CREDIT: '40 THEY DRIVE BY NIGHT
CREDIT: '50 STELLA
CREDIT: '57 WOMAN AND THE HUNTER

SHIRE, TALIA   BORN: TALIA ROSE COPPOLA
                          1947 AT NYC
GRANDFATHER: FRANCESCO PENNINO
FATHER: CARMINE COPPOLA, COMPOSER
MOTHER: ITALIA PENNINO
BROTHER: AUGUST COPPOLA, NOVELIST
BROTHER: FRANCIS FORD COPPOLA, DIRECTOR
SISTER-IN-LAW: ELEANOUR NEIL, DECORATOR
NIECE: GLO COPPOLA
NIECE: SOFIA COPPOLA
NEPHEW: MARK COPPOLA
NEPHEW: ROMAN COPPOLA
*** MARRIED: '70 DAVID SHIRE, COMPOSER
SON: '75 MATTHEW ORLANDO SHIRE
RESIDENCE: SHERMAN OAKS, CA
TALENT: ACTRESS
AA-NOM SUP.ACT: '74 THE GODFATHER PART II
AA-NOM ACTRESS: '76 ROCKY

```
SHIRLEY, ANNE          BORN:  DAWN EVELYEEN PARIS
                              APR 17,'19 AT NYC
     FATHER: HARRY PARIS, MILKMAN  (DIED '24)
     MOTHER: MARY 'MIMI' MERCER, SINGER
     *** MARRIED:  '37 JOHN PAYNE, ACTOR  (DIVORCED '42)
     DAUGHTER:  '40 JULIE ANNE PAYNE
     *** MARRIED:  '45 ADRIAN SCOTT  (DIVORCED '49)
     *** MARRIED:  '49 CHARLES LEDERER, WRITER  (DIED '76)
     SPOUSE'S AUNT: MARION DAVIES, ACTRESS
     SON:  '50 DANIEL DAVIES LEDERER
     RESIDENCE: MALIBU, CA
     POSSESSION: PUSSYCAT COLLECTION
     TALENT: ACTRESS
     COMMENT: KNOWN AS DAWN O'DAY CHILD ACTRESS WHO BEGAN
              WORKING AT 18 MONTHS AS A MODEL, RETIRED AT AGE 25 YEARS
     CREDIT:  '35 ANNE OF GREEN GABLES, SOURCE OF STAGENAME
     AA-NOM  SUP.ACT:  '37 STELLA DALLAS
     CREDIT:  '40 ANNE OF WINDY POPLARS
     CREDIT:  '41 ALL THAT MONEY CAN BUY
     CREDIT:  '44 FAREWELL MY LOVELY
```

```
SHORE, DINAH           BORN:  FRANCES ROSE SHORE
                              MAR 01,'17 AT WINCHESTER, TN
     FATHER: S. A. SHORE
     MOTHER: ANNA STEIN
     SISTER: BESS SHORE
     *** MARRIED:  '43 GEORGE MONTGOMERY, ACTOR  (DIVORCED '62)
     DAUGHTER:  '48 MELISSA ANN MONTGOMERY  (MARRIED '69)
     SON-IN-LAW: DAVID LEE BURK, ACTOR
     SON-IN-LAW: MARK HIME
     ADOPTED SON: JOHN DAVID MONTGOMERY
     *** MARRIED:  '63 MAURICE SMITH  (DIVORCED '64)
     ROMANCE: BURT REYNOLDS, ACTOR
     GRANDDAUGHTER:  '74 JENNIFER TRINITY HIME
     GRANDSON:  '76 ADAM HIME
     FRIEND: JIM STAFFORD, SINGER
     RESIDENCE: BEVERLY HILLS, CA
     TALENT: ACTRESS, SINGER
     CREDIT:  '43 THANK YOUR LUCKY STARS
     CREDIT:  '45 BELLE OF THE YUKON
     CREDIT:  '51 TV SERIES AND SPECIALS
     CREDIT:  '52 AARON SLICK FROM PUNKIN CRICK
     CREDIT:  '57 THE DINAH SHORE SHOW, TV TALK SHOW
```

```
SIDNEY, SYLVIA         BORN:  SOPHIA KOSOW
                              AUG 08,'10 AT NYC
     FATHER: VICTOR KOSOW
     MOTHER: REBECCA SAPERSTEIN
     STEP-FATHER: SIGMUND SIDNEY, DOCTOR
     *** MARRIED:  '35 BENNETT CERF, EDITOR  (DIVORCED '36)
     *** MARRIED:  '38 LUTHER ADLER, ACTOR  (DIVORCED '47)
     DAUGHTER:  '39 JODY ADLER
     *** MARRIED:  '47 CARLTON W. ALSOP  (DIVORCED '50)
     RESIDENCE: NYC
     TALENT: ACTRESS
     CREDIT:  '29 THRU DIFFERENT EYES
     CREDIT:  '37 YOU ONLY LIVE ONCE
```

```
CREDIT:   '45 BLOOD ON THE SUN
CREDIT:   '55 VIOLENT SATURDAY
AA-NOM  SUP.ACT:  '73 SUMMER WISHES, WINTER DREAMS
```

SIGNORET, SIMONE　　　　　BORN: SIMONE-HENRIETTE KAMINKER
```
                              MAR 25,'21 AT WIESBADEN, GERMANY
    FATHER: ANDRE KAMINKER, ARMY OFFICER
    MOTHER: GEORGETTE SIGNORET
    BROTHER: --
    BROTHER: --
    *** MARRIED:  '46 YVES ALLEGRET, DIRECTOR  (DIVORCED '49)
    BROTHER-IN-LAW: MARC ALLEGRET, DIRECTOR  (DIED '73)
    DAUGHTER:  '47 CATHERINE ALLEGRET
    *** MARRIED:  '51 YVES MONTAND, ACTOR
    FATHER-IN-LAW: LUIGI LIVI, BROOMMAKER
    MOTHER-IN-LAW: LOUISE MONTAND
    RESIDENCE: PARIS, FRANCE
    TALENT: ACTRESS
    CREDIT:  '42 BOLERO
    AA-WIN  ACTRESS:  '59 ROOM AT THE TOP
    AA-NOM  ACTRESS:  '65 SHIP OF FOOLS
    CREDIT:  '68 THE SEAGULL
    CREDIT:  '74 THE CONFESSION
    CREDIT:  '78 MME. ROSA
```

SILVERS, PHIL　　　　　BORN: PHILIP SILVERSMITH
```
                          MAY 11,'11 AT BROOKLYN, NY
    FATHER: SAUL SILVERSMITH
    MOTHER: SARAH
    *** MARRIED:  '45 JO-CARROLL DENNISON, MISS AMERICA OF 1942  (DIVORCED '50)
    *** MARRIED:  '56 EVELYN PATRICK, ACTRESS  (DIVORCED '66)
    DAUGHTER:  '57 TRACEY EDITH SILVERS
    DAUGHTER:  '58 NANCY ELIZABETH SILVERS
    DAUGHTER:  '61 CATHERINE SILVERS, TWIN
    DAUGHTER:  '61 CANDICE SILVERS, TWIN
    DAUGHTER:  '65 LOREY LOCKE SILVERS
    RESIDENCE: LOS ANGELES, CA
    POSSESSION:  '75 CONTRACT AT COLUMBIA PICTURES
    MEMOIRS:  '73 THIS LAUGH IS ON ME
    TALENT: ACTOR
    CREDIT:  '41 TOM, DICK AND HARRY, DEBUT
    CREDIT:  '44 COVER GIRL
    CREDIT:  '50 SUMMER STOCK
    CREDIT:  '63 IT'S A MAD MAD MAD MAD WORLD
    CREDIT:  '74 THE BOATNIKS
```

SIMMONS, JEAN　　　　　BORN: JEAN MERILYN SIMMONS
```
                          JAN 31,'29 AT CROUCH HILL, LONDON, ENGLAND
    FATHER: CHARLES SIMMONS
    MOTHER: WINIFRED ADA LOVELAND
    SISTER: --
    SISTER: --
    BROTHER: --
    *** MARRIED:  '50 STEWART GRANGER, ACTOR  (DIVORCED '60)
    STEP-SON: JAIME GRANGER
    STEP-SON: LINDSAY GRANGER
    DAUGHTER:  '56 TRACY GRANGER
    *** MARRIED:  '60 RICHARD BROOKS, WRITER, DIRECTOR
```

DAUGHTER: '61 KATE BROOKS
TALENT: ACTRESS
CREDIT: '44 KISS THE BRIDE GOODBYE
AA-NOM SUP.ACT: '48 HAMLET
CREDIT: '56 GUYS AND DOLLS
CREDIT: '60 ELMER GANTRY
AA-NOM ACTRESS: '69 THE HAPPY ENDING

SINATRA, FRANK   BORN: FRANCIS ALBERT SINATRA
                            DEC 12,'15 AT HOBOKEN,NJ
FATHER: MARTIN ANTHONY SINATRA, PRIZEFIGHTER-MARTY O'BRIEN
MOTHER: NATALIE 'DOLLY' GARAVANTI
*** MARRIED: '39 NANCY BARBATO (DIVORCED '51)
DAUGHTER: '40 NANCY SINATRA, SINGER
SON-IN-LAW: TOMMY SANDS, ACTOR, SINGER, GUITARIST (MARRIED '60)
SON: '44 FRANK SINATRA, JR.
DAUGHTER: '48 CHRISTINE SINATRA
SON-IN-LAW: WES FARRELL
*** MARRIED: '51 AVA GARDNER, ACTRESS (DIVORCED '57)
*** MARRIED: '66 MIA FARROW, ACTRESS (DIVORCED '70)
MOTHER-IN-LAW: MAUREEN O'SULLIVAN, ACTRESS
*** MARRIED: '76 BARBARA BLAKELY
ROMANCE: DOROTHY PROVINE
ROMANCE: LANA TURNER,
ROMANCE: LADY ADELE BEATTY
ROMANCE: MARILYN MAXWELL
ROMANCE: JULIET PROUSE
RESIDENCE: PALM SPRINGS, CA
TALENT: SINGER, ACTOR
CREDIT: '41 LAS VEGAS NIGHTS
AA-WIN SUP.ACT.: '53 FROM HERE TO ETERNITY
AA-NOM ACTOR: '55 THE MAN WITH THE GOLDEN ARM
CREDIT: '65 NONE BUT THE BRAVE
CREDIT: '70 DIRTY DINGUS MAGEE

SKELTON, RED   BORN: RICHARD BERNARD SKELTON
                          JUL 18,'10 AT VINCENNES, IN
FATHER: JOSEPH SKELTON, CIRCUS CLOWN
MOTHER: IDA MAE
*** MARRIED: '32 EDNA STILLWELL, WRITER (DIVORCED '43)
*** MARRIED: '45 GEORGIA MAUREEN DAVIS, MODEL (DIVORCED '71)
DAUGHTER: '47 VALENTINA SKELTON
SON-IN-LAW: CARLOS JOSE ALONSO (MARRIED '69)
SON: '48 RICHARD SKELTON (DIED '58)
*** MARRIED: '73 LOTHIAN TOLAND
RESIDENCE: BEVERLY HILLS, CA
POSSESSION: '47 COLLECTION OF PIPES
TALENT: ACTOR
CREDIT: '38 HAVING WONDERFUL TIME, DEBUT
CREDIT: '42 WHISTLING IN DIXIE
CREDIT: '43 WHISTLING IN BROOKLYN
CREDIT: '50 THREE LITTLE WORDS
CREDIT: '57 PUBLIC PIGEON NUMBER ONE

```
------------------------------------------------------------------------------
SLEZAK, WALTER          BORN:   WALTER LEO SLEZAK
                                MAY 03,'02 AT VIENNA, AUSTRIA
      FATHER: LEO SLEZAK, OPERA SINGER
      MOTHER: ELSE WERTHEIM
      SISTER: MARGARETE SLEZAK, ACTRESS  (DIED '53)
      *** MARRIED:  '43 JOHANNA VAN RIJN, OPERA SINGER
      DAUGHTER:  '44 ERICA SLEZAK
      DAUGHTER:  '45 INGRID SLEZAK
      SON:  '46 LEO LAURITZ WALTER SLEZAK
      FRIEND: LAURITZ MELCHIOR
      MEMOIRS:  '62 WHAT TIME'S THE NEXT SWAN?
      TALENT: ACTOR
      CREDIT:  '42 ONCE UPON A HONEYMOON
      CREDIT:  '54 WHITE WITCH DOCTOR
      CREDIT:  '61 COME SEPTEMBER
      CREDIT:  '71 BLACK BEAUTY
------------------------------------------------------------------------------
SMITH, C. AUBREY        BORN:   CHARLES AUBREY SMITH
                                JUL 21, 1863 AT LONDON, ENGLAND  DIED IN 1948
      FATHER: CHARLES JOHN SMITH, DOCTOR
      MOTHER: SARAH ANN CLODE
      *** MARRIED:  '96 ISABEL MARY SCOTT WOOD
      DAUGHTER: HONOR BERYL CLODE SMITH
      FRIEND: BORIS KARLOFF
      RESIDENCE: BEVERLY HILLS, CA
      POSSESSION:  '38 ORDER OF THE BRITISH EMPIRE
      POSSESSION:  '44 KNIGHTHOOD
      TALENT: ACTOR
      COMMENT: CHAMPION CRICKET PLAYER OF SOUTHERN CALIFORNIA
      CREDIT:  '15 BUILDER OF BRIDGES
      CREDIT:  '22 FLAMES OF PASSION
      CREDIT:  '33 MORNING GLORY
      CREDIT:  '40 WATERLOO BRIDGE
      CREDIT:  '49 LITTLE WOMEN
------------------------------------------------------------------------------
SMITH, MAGGIE           BORN:   MARGARET SMITH
                                DEC 28,'34 AT ILFORD, ESSEX, ENGLAND
      FATHER: NATHANIEL SMITH
      MOTHER: MARGARET LITTLE HUTTON
      *** MARRIED:  '67 ROBERT STEPHANS
      SON:  '67 CHRISTOPHER STEPHANS
      SON:  '69 TOBY STEPHANS
      POSSESSION:  '70 NAMED  COMMANDER OF BRITISH EMPIRE IN HONORS LIST
      TALENT: ACTRESS
      CREDIT:  '58 NOWHERE TO GO
      CREDIT:  '63 THE VIP'S
      AA-NOM  SUP.ACT:  '65 OTHELLO
      AA-WIN  ACTRESS:  '69 THE PRIME OF MISS JEAN BRODIE
      AA-NOM  ACTRESS:  '72 TRAVELS WITH MY AUNT
      CREDIT:  '78 DEATH ON THE NILE
------------------------------------------------------------------------------
SMITH, ROGER
                                DEC 18,'34 AT SOUTH GATE, CA
      FATHER: DALLAS SMITH
      MOTHER: LEONE
      *** MARRIED:  '56 VICTORIA SHAW
      DAUGHTER:  '57 TRACEY SMITH
```

```
SON:     '58 JORDAN SMITH
SON:     '62 DALLAS THOMAS SMITH
*** MARRIED:   '67 ANN-MARGRET, SINGER, ACTRESS
FATHER-IN-LAW: GUSTAV OLSSON
MOTHER-IN-LAW: ANNA ARONSON
RESIDENCE: BEVERLY HILLS, CA
TALENT: ACTOR
CREDIT:  '56 THE YOUNG REBELS
CREDIT:  '57 OPERATION MAD BALL
CREDIT:  '59 AUNTIE MAME
CREDIT:  '59 NEVER STEAL ANYTHING SMALL
CREDIT:  '68 ROGUES GALLERY
```

```
SNODGRESS, CARRIE          BORN:  CAROLINE SNODGRESS
                                  OCT 27,'45 AT PARK RIDGE, IL
FATHER: HARRY A. SNODGRESS, JR.
BROTHER: HARRY A. SNODGRESS, III
BROTHER: MELVIN SNODGRESS
BROTHER: JOHN SNODGRESS
SON:   '73 ZEKE SNODGRESS, FATHER - NEIL YOUNG
ROMANCE: NEIL YOUNG
TALENT: ACTRESS
AA-NOM ACTRESS:   '70 DIARY OF A MAD HOUSEWIFE
CREDIT: RABBIT, RUN
```

```
SOMERS, SUZANNE            BORN:  SUZANNE MAHONEY
                                  1948 AT SAN BRUNO, CA
FATHER: 'DUCKY' MAHONEY, BASEBALL PLAYER
MOTHER: MARION, MEDICAL SECRETARY
*** MARRIED:   '65 BRUCE SOMMERS  (DIVORCED '66)
SON:    '65 BRUCE SOMMERS, JR.
*** MARRIED:   '77 ALAN HAMEL
RESIDENCE: MARINA DEL REY, CA
TALENT: ACTRESS
CREDIT:  '73 AMERICAN GRAFFITI
CREDIT:  '77 THREE'S COMPANY, TV SERIES
CREDIT:  '78 ZUMA BEACH, TV SPECIAL
```

```
SOMMER, ELKE              BORN:  ELKE SCHLETZ
                                 NOV 05,'41 AT BERLIN, GERMANY
FATHER: --, MINISTER  (DIED '55)
MOTHER: RENATE
*** MARRIED:   '64 JOE HYAMS, JOURNALIST
STEP-DAUGHTER: BONNIE HYAMS
STEP-SON: JAY HYAMS
STEP-SON: CHRISTOPHER HYAMS
ROMANCE: KURT FRINGS, AGENT
RESIDENCE: HOLMBY HILLS, CA
TALENT: ACTRESS, ARTIST
COMMENT: MISS VIAREGGIO, ITALY OF 1959-BEAUTY CONTEST WINNER
CREDIT:  '60 DON'T BOTHER TO KNOCK
CREDIT:  '63 THE PRIZE
CREDIT:  '66 THE VENETIAN AFFAIR
CREDIT:  '68 THE WICKED DREAMS OF PAULA SCHULTZ
CREDIT:  '71 ZEPPELIN
```

```
--------------------------------------------------------------------------------
SOTHERN, ANN          BORN:  HARRIETTE LAKE
                             JAN 22,'09 AT VALLEY CITY, ND
    FATHER: WALTER J. LAKE
    MOTHER: ANNETTE YDE-LAKE, SINGER
    SISTER: MARION LAKE
    SISTER: BONNIE LAKE, SINGER
    COUSIN: SIMON LAKE, DESIGNED FIRST SUBMARINE
    *** MARRIED:  '36 ROGER PRYOR, ACTOR  (DIVORCED '42)
    FATHER-IN-LAW: ARTHUR PRYOR, BANDLEADER
    *** MARRIED:  '43 ROBERT STERLING, ACTOR  (DIVORCED '49)
    DAUGHTER: '44 PATRICIA 'TISHA' STERLING, ACTRESS
    SON-IN-LAW: LAL BAUM, REALTOR
    GRANDDAUGHTER: HEIDI BAUM
    FRIEND: RICHARD EGAN, ACTOR
    RESIDENCE: BEVERLY HILLS, CA
    POSSESSION: COLLECTION OF TRANSOCEANIC AIR MAIL ENVELOPES
    POSSESSION: COLLECTION OF PORCELAIN AND CHINA ANIMALS
    TALENT: ACTRESS
    CREDIT:  '34 LET'S FALL IN LOVE, DEBUT
    CREDIT:  '39 MAISIE, SERIES
    CREDIT:  '41 LADY BE GOOD
    CREDIT:  '49 A LETTER TO THREE WIVES
    CREDIT:  '64 THE BEST MAN
    CREDIT:  '78 THE MANITOU
--------------------------------------------------------------------------------
SPACEK, SISSY         BORN:  MARY ELIZABETH SPACEK
                             DEC 25,'50 AT QUITMAN, TX
    FATHER: ED SPACEK
    MOTHER: VIRGINIA
    BROTHER: ED SPACEK, JR.
    BROTHER: ROBERT SPACEK  (DIED)
    COUSIN: RIP TORN, ACTOR
    *** MARRIED:  '74 JACK FISK, DIRECTOR
    RESIDENCE: TOPANGA, CA
    TALENT: ACTRESS
    CREDIT:  '72 PRIME CUT, DEBUT IN 1972
    CREDIT:  '74 BADLANDS
    AA-NOM  ACTRESS:  '76 CARRIE
    CREDIT:  '77 THREE WOMEN, WON N.Y. FILM CRITICS AWARD
    CREDIT:  '78 VERNA, U.S.O. GIRL, TV SHOW
--------------------------------------------------------------------------------
STACK, ROBERT         BORN:  ROBERT MODINI
                             JAN 13,'19 AT LOS ANGELES, CA
    FATHER: JAMES LANGFORD STACK
    MOTHER: ELIZABETH WOOD
    *** MARRIED:  '56 ROSEMARY BOWE
    DAUGHTER: '57 ELIZABETH LANGFORD STACK
    SON: '58 CHARLES ROBERT STACK
    TALENT: ACTOR
    CREDIT:  '39 FIRST LOVE
    CREDIT:  '48 A DATE WITH JUDY
    AA-NOM  SUP.ACT:  '56 WRITTEN ON THE WIND
    CREDIT:  '58 THE GIFT OF LOVE
    CREDIT:  '67 THE CORRUPT ONES
```

STALLONE, SYLVESTER   BORN: MICHAEL SYLVESTER STALLONE
                                        JUL 06,'46 AT NYC
FATHER: FRANK STALLONE, HAIR DRESSER
MOTHER: JACQUELINE, SHOWGIRL
BROTHER: FRANK STALLONE, JR., SINGER
*** MARRIED: '70 SASHA
SON: '76 SAGE MOON BLOOD STALLONE
RESIDENCE: LOS ANGELES, CA
TALENT: ACTOR-WRITER-ARTIST
CREDIT: '73 THE LORDS OF FLATBUSH
AA-NOM ACTOR: '76 ROCKY
CREDIT: '77 PEACOCK ALLEY, NOVEL
CREDIT: '78 F.I.S.T.

STANWYCK, BARBARA   BORN: RUBY STEVENS
                                     JUL 16,'07 AT BROOKLYN,NY
FATHER: BYRON STEVENS, SAILOR (DIED '09)
MOTHER: CATHERINE MCGEE (DIED '11)
SISTER: MILDRED STEVENS, SHOWGIRL
BROTHER: BYRON E. STEVENS, ACTOR (DIED '64)
*** MARRIED: '28 FRANK FAY, ACTOR (DIVORCED '35)
SON: ANTHONY FAY
ADOPTED SON: DION FAY
*** MARRIED: '39 ROBERT TAYLOR, ACTOR (DIVORCED '52)
RESIDENCE: BEVERLY HILLS, CA
POSSESSION: '47 COLLECTION OF 1ST EDITION BOOKS
TALENT: ACTRESS
CREDIT: '29 LOCKED DOOR, DEBUT
AA-NOM ACTRESS: '37 STELLA DALLAS
AA-NOM ACTRESS: '41 BALL OF FIRE
AA-NOM ACTRESS: '44 DOUBLE INDEMNITY
AA-NOM ACTRESS: '48 SORRY, WRONG NUMBER

STAPLETON, JEAN   BORN: JEANNE MURRAY
                                   JAN 19,'23 AT NYC
FATHER: JOSEPH E. MURRAY
MOTHER: MARIE STAPLETON, SINGER
BROTHER: JOHN STAPLETON
*** MARRIED: '57 WILLIAM PUTCH
DAUGHTER: '59 PAMELA PUTCH
SON: '61 JOHN PUTCH
RESIDENCE: WEST LOS ANGELES AND CALEDONIA STATE PARK, PA.
TALENT: ACTRESS
CREDIT: '58 DAMN YANKEES
CREDIT: '60 BELLS ARE RINGING
CREDIT: '61 SOMETHING WILD
CREDIT: '67 UP THE DOWN STAIRCASE
CREDIT: ALL IN THE FAMILY, TV SERIES

STAPLETON, MAUREEN
                             JUN 21,'25 AT TROY, NY
FATHER: JOHN P. STAPLETON
MOTHER: IRENE WALSH
*** MARRIED: '49 MAX ALLENTUCK (DIVORCED '59)
SON: '50 DANIEL ALLENTUCK
DAUGHTER: '54 KATHARINE ALLENTUCK
TALENT: ACTRESS

```
AA-NOM  SUP.ACT:  '58 LONELYHEARTS
CREDIT:  '60 THE FUGITIVE KIND
CREDIT:  '62 BYE BYE BIRDIE
AA-NOM  SUP.ACT:  '70 AIRPORT
CREDIT:  '70 PLAZA SUITE
```

STARR, RINGO   BORN: RICHARD STARKEY
                              JUL 07,'40 AT LIVERPOOL, ENGLAND
```
FATHER: HARRY STARKEY
MOTHER: ELSIE GRAVES
*** MARRIED:  '65 MAUREEN COX, HAIRDRESSER
SON:  '65 ZAK STARR
ROMANCE: NANCY ANDREWS
PARTNER: RORY STORME, OF THE HURRICANES
PARTNER: GEORGE HARRISON, IN THE BEATLES & THE APPLE CO.
PARTNER: JOHN LENNON, IN THE BEATLES & THE APPLE CO.
PARTNER: PAUL MCCARTNEY, IN THE BEATLES & THE APPLE CO.
RESIDENCE: LONDON, ENGLAND
POSSESSION: COLLECTION OF RINGS
TALENT: PERCUSSIONIST, ACTOR
CREDIT:  '64 A HARD DAY'S NIGHT, WITH BEATLES
CREDIT:  '65 HELP!, WITH BEATLES
CREDIT:  '68 CANDY
CREDIT:  '70 THE MAGIC CHRISTIAN
CREDIT:  '73 THAT'LL BE THE DAY
```

STEIGER, ROD   BORN: RODNEY STEPHEN STEIGER
                              APR 14,'25 AT WEST HAMPTON,NY
```
FATHER: FREDERICK STEIGER
MOTHER: LORRAINE DRIVER
*** MARRIED:  '52 SALLY GRACIE  (DIVORCED '54)
*** MARRIED:  '59 CLAIRE BLOOM, ACTRESS  (DIVORCED '69)
DAUGHTER:  '60 ANNA JUSTINE STEIGER
*** MARRIED:  '73 SHERRY NELSON, SECRETARY
RESIDENCE: NYC
POSSESSION: MODERN ART COLLECTION
TALENT: ACTOR
AA-NOM  SUP.ACT:  '54 ON THE WATERFRONT
CREDIT:  '56 THE UNHOLY WIFE
AA-NOM  ACTOR:  '65 THE PAWNBROKER
AA-WIN  ACTOR:  '67 IN THE HEAT OF THE NIGHT
CREDIT:  '70 WATERLOO
CREDIT:  '78 F.I.S.T.
```

STERLING, JAN   BORN: JANE STERLING ADRIANCE
                              APR 03,'23 AT NYC
```
*** MARRIED:  '41 JOHN MERIVALE, ACTOR  (DIVORCED '48)
*** MARRIED:  '50 PAUL DOUGLAS, ACTOR  (DIED '59)
STEP-DAUGHTER: MARGARET DOUGLAS
SON:  '55 ADAM DOUGLAS
ROMANCE: SAM WANAMAKER
TALENT: ACTRESS
CREDIT:  '48 JOHNNY BELINDA, DEBUT
CREDIT:  '51 ACE IN THE HOLE
AA-NOM  SUP.ACT:  '54 THE HIGH AND THE MIGHTY
CREDIT:  '56 THE HARDER THEY FALL
CREDIT:  '61 LOVE IN A GOLDFISH BOWL
```

```
STERLING, ROBERT        BORN:  WILLIAM JOHN HART
                               NOV 13,'17 AT NEW CASTLE, PA
    FATHER: WALTER S. HART, BASEBALL PLAYER
    *** MARRIED:  '43 ANN SOTHERN, ACTRESS  (DIVORCED '49)
    DAUGHTER:  '44 PATRICIA 'TISHA' STERLING, ACTRESS
    SON-IN-LAW: LAL BAUM, REALTOR
    *** MARRIED:  '51 ANNE JEFFRIES, ACTRESS
    SON: JEFFREYS STERLING
    SON: ROBERT STERLING, JR.
    SON: TYLER STERLING
    GRANDDAUGHTER: HEIDI BAUM
    FRIEND: GENE TIERNEY
    RESIDENCE: WESTWOOD, CA
    TALENT: ACTOR, COMPUTER SCIENTIST
    CREDIT:  '39 ONLY ANGELS HAVE WINGS
    CREDIT:  '46 THE SECRET HEART
    CREDIT:  '51 THUNDER IN THE DUST
    CREDIT:  '61 RETURN TO PEYTON PLACE
-------------------------------------------------------------------------
STEVENS, INGER          BORN:  INGER STENSLAND
                               OCT 18,'34 AT STOCKHOLM, SWEDEN  DIED IN '70
    BROTHER: CARL STENSLAND
    *** MARRIED:  '55 ANTHONY SOGLIO  (DIVORCED '57)
    *** MARRIED:  '61 IKE JONES, PRODUCER
    ROMANCE: BURT REYNOLDS, ACTOR
    RESIDENCE: HOLLYWOOD HILLS, CA
    TALENT: ACTRESS
    CREDIT:  '57 MAN ON FIRE, DEBUT
    CREDIT:  '58 THE WORLD THE FLESH AND THE DEVIL
    CREDIT:  '63 THE FARMER'S DAUGHTER, TV SERIES
    CREDIT:  '67 A GUIDE FOR THE MARRIED MAN
    CREDIT:  '69 A DREAM OF KINGS
-------------------------------------------------------------------------
STEWART, ANITA          BORN:  ANNA MARIE STEWART
                               FEB 07,'95 AT BROOKLYN, NY  DIED IN '61
    FATHER: WILLIAM STEWART, BUSINESSMAN
    MOTHER: MARTHA
    SISTER: LUCILLE LEE STEWART, ACTRESS
    BROTHER-IN-LAW: RALPH INCE, WRITER, DIRECTOR, ACTOR
    BROTHER: GEORGE STEWART, ACTOR  (DIED '46)
    *** MARRIED:  '18 RUDOLPH CAMERON, ACTOR, DIRECTOR  (DIVORCED '28)
    *** MARRIED:  '29 GEORGE PEABODY CONVERSE, SPORTSMAN  (DIVORCED '46)
    FRIEND: THOMAS INCE, PRODUCER (SISTER'S RELATIVE)
    RESIDENCE: BEVERLY HILLS, CA
    TALENT: ACTRESS
    CREDIT:  '12 THE WOOD VIOLET, DEBUT
    CREDIT:  '14 THE PAINTED WORLD
    CREDIT:  '15 THE GODESS
    CREDIT:  '21 PLAYTHINGS OF DESTINY
    CREDIT:  '25 NEVER THE TWAIN SHALL MEET
-------------------------------------------------------------------------
STEWART, JAMES          BORN:  JAMES MAITLAND STEWART
                               MAY 20,'08 AT INDIANA, PA
    FATHER: ALEXANDER MAITLAND STEWART
    MOTHER: EMILY ELIZABETH PEABODY
    *** MARRIED:  '49 GLORIA HATRICK MCLEAN
    DAUGHTER:  '51 KELLY STEWART, TWIN
```

```
DAUGHTER:  '51 JUDY STEWART, TWIN
*** MARRIED:  '58 MARY FRENCH
SON: MICHAEL STEWART
SON: RONALD STEWART  (DIED)
ROMANCE: MARGARET SULLAVAN
FRIEND: HENRY FONDA, ACTOR
FRIEND: JOSHUA LOGAN, DIRECTOR
RESIDENCE: BEVERLY HILLS, CA
BIOGRAPHY:  '70 THE FILMS OF JAMES STEWART, BY KENNETH D. JONES
TALENT: ACTOR
COMMENT: GENERAL, US AIR FORCE, RESERVE
AA-NOM  ACTOR:  '39 MR. SMITH GOES TO WASHINGTON
AA-WIN  ACTOR:  '40 THE PHILADELPHIA STORY
AA-NOM  ACTOR:  '46 IT'S A WONDERFUL LIFE
AA-NOM  ACTOR:  '50 HARVEY
AA-NOM  ACTOR:  '59 ANATOMY OF A MURDER
```

STOCKWELL, DEAN
```
                         MAR 05,'36 AT LOS ANGELES, CA
FATHER: HARRY STOCKWELL, ACTOR
MOTHER: NINA OLIVETTE, ACTRESS  (DIED '71)
BROTHER: GUY STOCKWELL, ACTOR
*** MARRIED:  '61 MILLIE PERKINS, ACTRESS  (DIVORCED '63)
TALENT: ACTOR
CREDIT:  '45 ANCHORS AWEIGH
CREDIT:  '48 THE BOY WITH GREEN HAIR
CREDIT:  '59 COMPULSION
CREDIT:  '62 LONG DAY'S JOURNEY INTO NIGHT
CREDIT:  '74 THE LONERS
```

STONE, FRED   BORN: FREDERICK ANDREW STONE
```
                     AUG 19, 1873 AT VALMONT, CO   DIED IN '59
FATHER: LEWIS PRESTON STONE
MOTHER: CLARA JOHNSTON
*** MARRIED:  '04 ALLENE CRATER, ACTRESS
DAUGHTER:  '05 DOROTHY STONE, ACTRESS
DAUGHTER:  '15 CAROL STONE, ACTRESS
SON-IN-LAW: ROBERT W. MCCAHON  (MARRIED)
DAUGHTER:  '16 PAULA STONE, ACTRESS
SON-IN-LAW: MICHAEL SLOAN  (MARRIED)
PARTNER: DAVID MONTGOMERY
MEMOIRS:  '45 ROLLING STONE
TALENT: ACTOR-DANCER
COMMENT: PRES. NATIONAL VAUDEVILLE ARTISTS ASSOCIATION
CREDIT:  '18 THE GOAT
CREDIT:  '24 BROADWAY AFTER DARK
CREDIT:  '36 THE FARMER IN THE DELL
CREDIT:  '40 THE WESTERNER
```

STONE, LEWIS   BORN: LEWIS SHEPARD STONE
```
                     NOV 15, 1879 AT WORCESTER, MS   DIED IN '53
FATHER: BERTRAND MCDONALD STONE
MOTHER: LUCILLE PHILENA
AUNT: BESS, CO-FOUNDER BOSTON OPERA CO.
AUNT: AGNES, CO-FOUNDER BOSTON OPERA CO.
AUNT: MARY, CO-FOUNDER BOSTON OPERA CO.
*** MARRIED: MARGARET LANGHAM  (DIED)
*** MARRIED:  '20 FLORENCE PRYOR, ACTRESS - FLORENCE OAKLEY  (DIVORCED '29)
```

```
*** MARRIED:  '30 HAZEL ELIZABETH WOLF
DAUGHTER: VIRGINIA STONE
DAUGHTER: BARBARA STONE
FRIEND: CHARLES RUGGLES
RESIDENCE: LOS ANGELES, CA
POSSESSION: YACHTS 'SERENA' AND 'PHANTOM'
POSSESSION: CONTRACT AT M-G-M FROM 1924-53
TALENT: ACTOR
CREDIT:  '15 HONOR ALTAR, DEBUT
AA-NOM  ACTOR:  '28 THE PATRIOT
CREDIT:  '52 THE PRISONER OF ZENDA, REMAKE OF 1922 FILM
CREDIT: YOU'RE ONLY YOUNG ONCE, ANDY HARDY SERIES
CREDIT: THREE IN LOVE
CREDIT: GRAND HOTEL
-----------------------------------------------------------------------------------
STORM, GALE          BORN:  JOSEPHINE COTTLE
                            APR 05,'21 AT BLOOMINGTON, TX
*** MARRIED:  '41 LEE BONNELL, PRODUCER
SON:  '42 PHILLIP BONNELL
SON:  '44 PETER BONNELL
SON:  '46 PAUL BONNELL
DAUGHTER:  '56 SUSANNA BONNELL
POSSESSION: SHOWTIME PRODUCTIONS
TALENT: ACTRESS
CREDIT:  '39 TOM BROWN'S SCHOOLDAYS
CREDIT:  '43 NEARLY EIGHTEEN
CREDIT:  '49 ABANDONED
CREDIT:  '61 MY LITTLE MARGIE, TV SERIES
CREDIT:  '70 WOMAN OF THE NORTH COUNTRY
-----------------------------------------------------------------------------------
STREISAND, BARBRA          BORN:  BARBARA JOAN STREISAND
                                 APR 24,'42 AT BROOKLYN, NY
FATHER: EMANUEL STREISAND, EDUCATOR
MOTHER: DIANE ROSEN
STEP-FATHER: LOUIS KIND
STEP-SISTER: ROSALIND KIND
BROTHER: SHELDON STREISAND
*** MARRIED:  '63 ELLIOT GOULD, ACTOR  (DIVORCED)
SON:  '66 JOSHUA GOULD
ROMANCE: JON PETERS, HAIRDRESSER & PRODUCER
RESIDENCE: MALIBU, CA
POSSESSION:  '77 AMERICAN GUILD OF VARIETY ARTI STS 'GEORGIE' AWARD
BIOGRAPHY:  '75 THE GREATEST STAR, BY RENE JORDON
TALENT: ACTRESS, SINGER
AA-WIN  ACTRESS:  '68 FUNNY GIRL
CREDIT:  '69 FUNNY LADY
CREDIT:  '70 THE OWL AND THE PUSSYCAT
CREDIT:  '72 UP THE SANDBOX
AA-NOM  ACTRESS:  '73 THE WAY WE WERE
CREDIT:  '76 A STAR IS BORN
-----------------------------------------------------------------------------------
SULLAVAN, MARGARET          BORN:  MARGARET BROOKE SULLAVAN
                                  MAY 16,'09 AT NORFOLK,VA  DIED IN '60
FATHER: CORNELIUS HANCOCK SULLAVAN
MOTHER: GARLAND COUNCIL
STEP-SISTER: LEWISE WINSTON
BROTHER: 'SONNY' SULLAVAN, LAWYER
*** MARRIED:  '31 HENRY FONDA, ACTOR  (DIVORCED '32)
```

```
*** MARRIED:   '34 WILLIAM WYLER, DIRECTOR  (DIVORCED '36)
*** MARRIED:   '37 LELAND HAYWARD, AGENT  (DIVORCED '47)
DAUGHTER:  '37 BROOKE HAYWARD, MODEL, ACTRESS, BIOGRAPHER
SON-IN-LAW: MICHAEL THOMAS
DAUGHTER:  '39 BRIDGET HAYWARD
SON:  '42 WILLIAM 'BILL' HAYWARD
*** MARRIED:  '50 KENNETH WAGG
ROMANCE: JAMES STEWART, ACTOR
GRANDSON: JEFF THOMAS
GRANDSON: WILLIAM THOMAS
RESIDENCE: NEW HAVEN,CN
TALENT: ACTRESS
CREDIT:   '34 SO RED THE ROSE
CREDIT:   '35 THE GOOD FAIRY
AA-NOM  ACTRESS:  '38 THREE COMRADES
CREDIT:   '43 CRY HAVOC
CREDIT:   '50 NO SAD SONGS FOR ME
```

SUTHERLAND, DONALD
```
                            JUL 17,'34 AT ST. JOHN, NEW BRUNSWICK, CAN
*** MARRIED:  '66 SHIRLEY DOUGLAS, ACTRESS  (DIVORCED '71)
DAUGHTER:  '66 RACHEL SUTHERLAND
SON:  '66 KIEFER SUTHERLAND
SON:  '74 ROEG RACETTE SUTHERLAND
ROMANCE: FRANCINE RACETTE
RESIDENCE: PARIS, FRANCE
TALENT: ACTOR
CREDIT:   '65 DR. TERROR'S HOUSE OF HORRORS
CREDIT:   '67 THE DIRTY DOZEN
CREDIT:   '70 M.A.S.H.
CREDIT:   '71 JOHNNY GOT HIS GUN
CREDIT:   '71 KLUTE
CREDIT:   '76 CASANOVA
CREDIT:   '78 ANIMAL HOUSE
```

SWANSON, GLORIA   BORN: GLORIA JOSEPHINE MAY SWANSON
```
                         MAR 27,'99 AT CHICAGO,IL
FATHER: JOSEPH THEODORE SWANSON
MOTHER: ADELAIDE KLANOWSKI
STEP-FATHER: CHARLES E. WOODRUFF
*** MARRIED:   '16 WALLACE BEERY, ACTOR  (DIVORCED '18)
*** MARRIED:   '20 HERBERT K. SOMBORN, RESTAURATEUR-THE BROWN DERBY  (DIVORCED '23)
DAUGHTER:  '21 GLORIA SOMBORN
SON:  '22 JOSEPH P. SOMBORN
ADOPTED SON: JOSEPH P. SWANSON
*** MARRIED:   '25 MARQUIS HENRI DE LA FALAISE  DE LA COUDRAY  (DIVORCED '31)
*** MARRIED:   '31 MICHAEL FARMER  (DIVORCED '34)
DAUGHTER:  '32 MICHELE BRIDGET FARMER
SON-IN-LAW: ROBERT AMON
*** MARRIED:   '45 WILLIAM M. DAVEY  (DIVORCED '45)
*** MARRIED:   '76 WILLIAM DUFTY
FRIEND: CECIL B. DE MILLE, PRODUCER
```

RESIDENCE: CROTON-ON-HUDSON, NY AND 5TH AVE, NYC, APARTMENT
POSSESSION: 'GOWNS BY GLORIA' CLOTHING CO.
TALENT: ACTRESS
CREDIT: '19 FOR BETTER, FOR WORSE
AA-NOM ACTRESS: '27 SADIE THOMPSON
AA-NOM ACTRESS: '29 THE TRESPASSER
AA-NOM ACTRESS: '50 SUNSET BOULEVARD
CREDIT: '62 NERO'S MISTRESS, AKA NERO'S BIG WEEKEND

```
-----------------------------------------------------------------------------------------------
TALBOT, LYLE          BORN:   LYSLE HENDERSON
                              FEB 08,'02 AT PITTSBURGH,PA
     FATHER: EDWARD HENDERSON
     MOTHER: FLORENCE TALBOT
     *** MARRIED:  '37 MARJORIE CRAMER
     *** MARRIED:  '42 TOMMY ADAMS
     *** MARRIED:  '46 KEVIN MCCLURE, ACTRESS  (DIVORCED '46)
     *** MARRIED:  '49 MARGARET CAROL EPPLE
     SON:  '49 STEPHEN TALBOT
     SON:  '52 DAVID TALBOT
     DAUGHTER:  '53 CYNTHIA TALBOT
     DAUGHTER:  '55 MARGARET TALBOT
     *** MARRIED:  '72 FRANCES NEAL, ACTRESS
     STEP-DAUGHTER: VANA HEFLIN
     STEP-DAUGHTER: CATHLEEN HEFLIN
     STEP-SON: TRACY NEAL HEFLIN
     RESIDENCE: STUDIO CITY, CA
     POSSESSION:  '31 CONTRACT AT WARNER BROS
     TALENT: ACTOR
     CREDIT:  '32 LOVE IS A RACKET
     CREDIT:  '38 ONE WILD NIGHT
     CREDIT:  '44 UP IN ARMS
     CREDIT:  '56 THE GREAT MAN
     CREDIT:  '60 SUNRISE AT CAMPOBELLO
-----------------------------------------------------------------------------------------------
TALMADGE, CONSTANCE
                              APR 19,'99 AT BROOKLYN, NY  DIED IN '73
     FATHER: FREDERICK TALMADGE
     MOTHER: MARGARET, STAGE MOTHER
     SISTER: NORMA TALMADGE
     SISTER: NATALIE TALMADGE, ACTRESS
     BROTHER-IN-LAW: JOSEPH M. SCHENCK, PRODUCER
     BROTHER-IN-LAW: GEORGE JESSEL, ACTOR
     BROTHER-IN-LAW: DR. CARVEL JAMES
     BROTHER-IN-LAW: BUSTER KEATON, ACTOR
     NEPHEW: JAMES KEATON
     NEPHEW: ROBERT KEATON, ACTOR - ROBERT TALMADGE
     *** MARRIED:  '21 JOHN PIALOGLOU
     *** MARRIED:  '23 ALISTAIR MCINTOSH  (DIVORCED '27)
     *** MARRIED:  '29 TOWNSEND NETCHER
     *** MARRIED:  '39 WALTER M. GIBLIN, FINANCIER  (DIED '64)
     *** MARRIED:  '65 WILLIAM COLLIER, JR.
     FRIEND: AILEEN PRINGLE, ACTRESS
     FRIEND: IRVING BERLIN
     RESIDENCE: LOS ANGELES, CA
     RESIDENCE: NYC
     TALENT: ACTRESS
     CREDIT:  '14 IN BRIDAL ATTIRE
     CREDIT:  '16 THE MATRIMANIAC
     CREDIT:  '22 THE PRIMITIVE LOVER
     CREDIT:  '27 VENUS OF VENICE
     CREDIT:  '29 VENUS
```

TALMADGE, NORMA
                        MAY 26,'97 AT NIAGARA FALLS, NY DIED IN '57
    FATHER: FREDERICK TALMADGE
    MOTHER: MARGARET
    SISTER: CONSTANCE TALMADGE, ACTRESS
    SISTER: NATALIE TALMADGE, ACTRESS
    BROTHER-IN-LAW: JOHN PIALOGLOU
    BROTHER-IN-LAW: ALISTAIR MCINTOSH
    BROTHER-IN-LAW: TOWNSEND NETCHER
    BROTHER-IN-LAW: WALTER M. GIBLIN
    BROTHER-IN-LAW: BUSTER KEATON
    NEPHEW: JAMES KEATON
    NEPHEW: ROBERT KEATON, ACTOR - ROBERT TALMADGE
    *** MARRIED: '17 JOSEPH M. SCHENCK, PRODUCER (DIVORCED)
    BROTHER-IN-LAW: NICHOLAS M. SCHENCK, EXECUTIVE
    *** MARRIED: '34 GEORGE JESSEL, ACTOR
    FATHER-IN-LAW: JOSEPH AARON JESSEL, PLAYWRIGHT
    MOTHER-IN-LAW: CHARLOTTE SCHWARTZ
    *** MARRIED: '46 DR. CARVEL JAMES
    ROMANCE: EDWIN JUSTIN MAYER
    ROMANCE: GILBERT ROLAND, WHILE MAKING CAMILLE
    TALENT: ACTRESS
    CREDIT: '10 A DIXIE MOTHER
    CREDIT: '14 SUNSHINE AND SHADOWS
    CREDIT: '23 WITHIN THE LAW
    CREDIT: '27 CAMILLE
    CREDIT: '30 DUBARRY, WOMAN OF PASSION

TAMBLYN, RUSS
                        DEC 30,'34 AT LOS ANGELES, CA
    FATHER: EDWARD TAMBLYN, ACTOR (DIED '57)
    MOTHER: SALLY TRIPPLET
    BROTHER: WARREN TAMBLYN
    BROTHER: LAWRENCE TAMBLYN
    *** MARRIED: '56 VENETIA STEVENSON (DIVORCED '57)
    *** MARRIED: '60 ELIZABETH KEMPTON
    TALENT: ACTOR, DANCER
    CREDIT: '50 FATHER OF THE BRIDE
    CREDIT: '54 SEVEN BRIDES FOR SEVEN BROTHERS
    AA-NOM SUP.ACT: '57 PEYTON PLACE
    CREDIT: '61 WEST SIDE STORY
    CREDIT: '70 THE LAST MOVIE

TANDY, JESSICA
                        JUN 07,'09 AT LONDON, ENGLAND
    FATHER: HARRY TANDY
    MOTHER: JESSIE HELEN HORSPOOL
    BROTHER: MICHAEL TANDY
    BROTHER: EDWARD TANDY
    *** MARRIED: '32 JACK HAWKINS (DIVORCED '40)
    DAUGHTER: '33 SUSAN HAWKINS
    *** MARRIED: '42 HUME CRONYN
    SON: '43 CHRISTOPHER CRONYN
    DAUGHTER: '45 TANDY CRONYN
    RESIDENCE: NYC
    POSSESSION: ISLAND IN THE BAHAMAS
    TALENT: ACTRESS

```
CREDIT:   '44 THE SEVENTH CROSS
CREDIT:   '48 FOREVER AMBER
CREDIT:   '58 THE LIGHT IN THE FOREST
CREDIT:   '63 THE BIRDS
```

TATE, SHARON

                              1943 AT DALLAS, TX DIED IN '69
```
    FATHER: PAUL J. TATE
    MOTHER: DORIS
    SISTER: DEBORAH ANN TATE
    SISTER: PATRICIA GAYE TATE
    *** MARRIED:  '68 ROMAN POLANSKI, DIRECTOR
    FRIEND: JAY SEBRING, HAIRSTYLIST
    TALENT: ACTRESS
    CREDIT:  '63 THE WHEELER DEALERS
    CREDIT:  '67 VALLEY OF THE DOLLS
    CREDIT:  '69 THE HOUSE OF SEVEN JOYS
```

TAYLOR, ELIZABETH   BORN: ELIZABETH ROSEMOND TAYLOR
                              FEB 27,'32 AT LONDON, ENGLAND
```
    FATHER: FRANCIS TAYLOR, ART DEALER
    MOTHER: SARA WARMBRODT, ACTRESS
    BROTHER: HOWARD TAYLOR
    *** MARRIED:  '50 CONRAD NICHOLSON HILTON, JR.  (DIVORCED '51)
    FATHER-IN-LAW: CONRAD NICHOLSON HILTON, SR., HOTEL OWNER
    *** MARRIED:  '52 MICHAEL WILDING  (DIVORCED '57)
    SON:  '53 MICHAEL HOWARD WILDING, JR.
    DAUGHTER-IN-LAW: BETH CLUTTER  (MARRIED '70)
    DAUGHTER-IN-LAW: JOHANNA LYKKE-DAHN  (MARRIED '70)
    SON:  '55 CHRISTOPHER EDWARD WILDING
    *** MARRIED:  '57 MICHAEL TODD, PRODUCER-BORN AVROM GOLDBOGEN  (DIED '58)
    DAUGHTER:  '57 ELIZABETH FRANCES TODD
    STEP-SON: MICHAEL TODD, JR.
    *** MARRIED:  '59 EDDIE FISHER  (DIVORCED '64)
    STEP-DAUGHTER: CARRIE FISHER, ACTRESS
    STEP-SON: TODD FISHER
    ADOPTED DAUGHTER: MARIA-PETRA FISHER
    *** MARRIED:  '64 RICHARD BURTON  (DIVORCED '74)
    STEP-DAUGHTER: JESSICA BURTON
    STEP-DAUGHTER: KATE BURTON
    *** MARRIED:  '75 RICHARD BURTON, REMARRIED  (DIVORCED '76)
    *** MARRIED:  '76 JOHN WILLIAM WARNER, JR.
    ROMANCE: GLENN DAVIS, FOOTBALL PLAYER
    GRANDDAUGHTER:  '71 LEYLA WILDING
    GRANDDAUGHTER:  '75 NAOMI WILDING
    RESIDENCE: GSTAAD, SWITZERLAND
    RESIDENCE: MIDDLEBURG, VIRGINIA
    POSSESSION:  '77 THE GREAT LADY AWARD OF THE GOVERNMENT OF PUERTO RICO
    POSSESSION: PICASSO PAINTING 'LA FAMILLE'
    BIOGRAPHY:  '77 RICHARD AND ELIZABETH, BY DAVID & ROBBINS
    TALENT: ACTRESS-EQUESTRIAN
    CREDIT:  '44 LASSIE COME HOME, DEBUT
    AA-NOM  ACTRESS:  '57 RAINTREE COUNTY
    AA-NOM  ACTRESS:  '58 CAT ON A HOT TIN ROOF
    AA-NOM  ACTRESS:  '59 SUDDENLY  LAST SUMMER
    AA-WIN  ACTRESS:  '60 BUTTERFIELD 8
    AA-WIN  ACTRESS:  '66 WHO'S AFRAID OF VIRGINIA WOOLF?
```

TAYLOR, ROBERT   BORN: SPANGLER ARLINGTON BROUGH
                                 AUG 05,'11 AT FILLEY, NB DIED IN '69
    FATHER: SPANGLER A. BROUGH, PHYSICIAN
    MOTHER: RUTH ADELIA STANHOPE
    *** MARRIED: '39 BARBARA STANWYCK, ACTRESS (DIVORCED '52)
    *** MARRIED: '54 URSULA THIESS, ACTRESS (DIVORCED '69)
    STEP-DAUGHTER: MANUELA THIESS
    STEP-SON: MICHAEL THIESS, ACTOR (DIED '69)
    SON: '55 TERENCE TAYLOR
    DAUGHTER: '59 TESSA TAYLOR
    ROMANCE: IRENE HERVEY, ACTRESS
    FRIEND: DICK POWELL, ACTOR
    FRIEND: LOUIS B. MAYER, EXECUTIVE
    POSSESSION: '52 MODEL RACING CAR COLLECTION
    POSSESSION: '52 6 PASSENGER PLANE
    TALENT: ACTOR
    CREDIT: '34 ANDY HARDY
    CREDIT: '37 WATERLOO BRIDGE
    CREDIT: '41 BILLY THE KID
    CREDIT: '52 IVANHOE
    CREDIT: '63 GUNS OF WYOMING
    CREDIT: '68 DEVIL MAY CARE

TAYLOR, ROD   BORN: RODNEY TAYLOR
                              JAN 11,'29 AT SYDNEY, AUSTRALIA
    FATHER: WILLIAM STUART TAYLOR
    MOTHER: MONA STEWART
    *** MARRIED: PEGGY WILLIAMS, MODEL (DIVORCED)
    *** MARRIED: '63 MARY HILEM, MODEL (DIVORCED '69)
    SISTER-IN-LAW: JO ANNE HILEM
    DAUGHTER: '64 FELICIA RODERICA TAYLOR
    ROMANCE: ANITA EKBERG, ACTRESS
    FRIEND: ROBERT WALKER, ACTOR
    RESIDENCE: BEVERLY HILLS, CA
    POSSESSION: '55 CONTRACT AT M-G-M
    POSSESSION: '66 YACHT- ZACA PREV. OWNER-ERROL FLYNN
    POSSESSION: '72 RODLOR PRODUCTIONS
    TALENT: ACTOR
    CREDIT: '56 THE CATERED AFFAIR
    CREDIT: '63 THE VIP'S
    CREDIT: '67 HOTEL
    CREDIT: '73 TRADER HORN

TEMPLE, SHIRLEY   BORN: SHIRLEY JANE TEMPLE
                                  APR 23,'28 AT SANTA MONICA, CA
    FATHER: GEORGE FRANCIS TEMPLE, BANKER
    MOTHER: GERTRUDE CREIGER
    BROTHER: JOHN TEMPLE
    BROTHER: GEORGE TEMPLE
    *** MARRIED: '45 JOHN AGAR, ACTOR (DIVORCED '49)
    DAUGHTER: '47 LINDA SUSAN AGAR
    *** MARRIED: '50 CHARLES A. BLACK
    SON: '52 CHARLES ALDEN BLACK
    DAUGHTER: '54 LORI ALDEN BLACK
    RESIDENCE: SAN FRANCISCO, CA
    MEMOIRS: '45 MY YOUNG LIFE
    TALENT: ACTRESS

```
CREDIT:   '32 THE RED-HAIRED ALIBI
AA-SPECIAL AWARD:   '34 AN HONORARY MINIATURE AWARD
CREDIT:   '34 LITTLE MISS MARKER
CREDIT:   '37 HEIDI
CREDIT:   '40 THE BLUE BIRD
CREDIT:   '49 A KISS FOR CORLISS
```

TERRY-THOMAS   BORN: THOMAS TERRY HOAR STEVENS
```
                          JUL 14,'11 AT LONDON, ENGLAND
   FATHER: ERNEST FREDERICK STEVENS
   MOTHER: ELLEN ELIZABETH HOAR
   SISTER: MARY STEVENS
   BROTHER: JOHN STEVENS
   BROTHER: WILLIAM STEVENS
   BROTHER: RICHARD STEVENS
   *** MARRIED:   '38 IDA PATLAWSKY, DANCER  (DIVORCED '62)
   *** MARRIED:   '63 BELINDA CUNNINGHAM
   SON:   '64 TIMOTHY 'TIGER' STEVENS
   RESIDENCE: QUEENS GATE, LONDON, ENGLAND
   POSSESSION: 150 FANCY WAISTCOATS
   MEMOIRS:   '59 FILLING THE GAP
   TALENT: ACTOR
   CREDIT:   '56 THE PRIVATE'S PROGRESS
   CREDIT:   '60 SCHOOL FOR SCOUNDRELS
   CREDIT:   '65 HOW TO MURDER YOUR WIFE
   CREDIT:   '71 THE ABOMINABLE DR. PHIBES
```

THATCHER, TORIN
```
                          JAN 15,'05 AT BOMBAY, INDIA
   FATHER: TORIN JAMES BLAIR THATCHER
   MOTHER: EDITH RACHEL BATTY
   *** MARRIED:   '39 MILDRED DANIEL  (DIED '50)
   SON:   '49 PHILLIP TORIN THATCHER
   *** MARRIED:   '52 ANNE MARIE WOLFE, ACTRESS- ANNE LE BORGNE
   FRIEND: BURT LANCASTER, ACTOR
   RESIDENCE: LOS ANGELES, CA
   TALENT: ACTOR
   CREDIT:   '34 GENERAL JOHN REGAN, DEBUT
   CREDIT:   '40 MAJOR BARBARA
   CREDIT:   '46 GREAT EXPECTATIONS
   CREDIT:   '57 WITNESS FOR THE PROSECUTION
   CREDIT:   '66 THE KING'S PIRATE
```

THAXTER, PHYLLIS   BORN: PHYLLIS ST. FELIX THAXTER
```
                          NOV 20,'20 AT PORTLAND, ME
   FATHER: SIDNEY THAXTER, JUDGE
   MOTHER: --, ACTRESS
   *** MARRIED:   '44 JAMES T. AUBREY, EXECUTIVE  (DIVORCED '62)
   DAUGHTER:   '45 SCHUYLER AUBREY
   SON-IN-LAW: ILYA SALKIND, PRODUCER
   SON:   '53 JAMES W. AUBREY
   *** MARRIED:   '63 GILBERT LEA
   RESIDENCE: NYC
   RESIDENCE: CUMBERLAND, ME
   TALENT: ACTRESS
   CREDIT:   '44 THIRTY SECONDS OVER TOKYO, DEBUT
   CREDIT:   '47 TENTH AVENUE ANGEL
   CREDIT:   '51 COME FILL THE CUP
```

CREDIT: '54 WOMEN'S PRISON
CREDIT: '64 THE WORLD OF HENRY ORIENT

THOMAS, DANNY   BORN: AMOS JACOBS
                              JAN 06,'14 AT DEERFIELD, MH
   FATHER: CHARLES JACOBS
   MOTHER: MARGARET CHRISTEN SIMON
   BROTHER: THOMAS JACOBS
   *** MARRIED: '36 ROSE MARIE CASSANITI
   DAUGHTER: '38 MARGARET JULIA 'MARLO' THOMAS, ACTRESS
   SON-IN-LAW: DAVID GEFFEN
   DAUGHTER: '48 THERESA CECILIA 'TERRE' THOMAS
   SON-IN-LAW: LARRY GORDON
   SON: CHARLES ANTHONY THOMAS
   RESIDENCE: BEVERLY HILLS, CA
   TALENT: ACTOR
   CREDIT: '47 THE UNFINISHED DANCE
   CREDIT: '51 CALL ME MISTER
   CREDIT: '53 THE JAZZ SINGER
   CREDIT: '54 TV SERIES

THUNDERCLOUD, CHIEF   BORN: VICTOR DANIELS
                                  APR 12,'89 AT MUSKOGEE,OK DIED IN '55
   *** MARRIED: FRANCES DELMAR, SINGER, DANCER
   RESIDENCE: VENTURA, CA
   TALENT: COWBOY, BOXER, ACTOR
   COMMENT: SCOTT T. WILLIAMS AKA CHIEF THUNDERCLCUD #2
   COMMENT: WILLIAMS DISTANTLY RELATED TO CHIEF PCNTIAC OF OTTAWA TRIBE
   CREDIT: '39 GERONIMO
   CREDIT: '44 BUFFALO BILL, SERIES
   CREDIT: '49 AMBUSH, SERIES
   CREDIT: '51 SANTA FE, SERIES

TIBBETT, LAWRENCE   BORN: LAWRENCE MERVIL TIBBET
                                NOV 16,'96 AT BAKERSFIELD, CA DIED IN '60
   FATHER: WILLIAM EDWARD TIBBET, POLICE OFFICER
   MOTHER: FRANCES ELLEN MACKENZIE
   *** MARRIED: '16 GRACE M. SMITH (DIVORCED '31)
   SON: '18 LAWRENCE TIBBETT, TWIN
   SON: '18 RICHARD TIBBETT, TWIN
   *** MARRIED: '32 JENNIE MARSTON ADAMS BURGARD
   SON: '33 MICHAEL TIBBETT
   ROMANCE: LUPE VELEZ, ACTRESS
   RESIDENCE: BEVERLY HILLS, CA
   TALENT: BARITONE, ACTOR
   AA-NOM ACTOR: '29 THE ROGUE SONG
   CREDIT: '30 ROGUE SONG
   CREDIT: '31 THE PRODIGAL
   CREDIT: '35 METROPOLITAN
   CREDIT: '36 UNDER YOUR SPELL

TIERNEY, GENE   BORN: GENE ELIZA TIERNEY
                              NOV 20,'20 AT BROOKLYN, NY
   FATHER: HOWARD SHERWOOD TIERNEY
   MOTHER: BELLE TAYLOR
   SISTER: PATRICIA TIERNEY
   BROTHER: HOWARD TIERNEY, JR.
   *** MARRIED: '41 OLEG CASSINI, FASHION DESIGNER (DIVORCED '52)

```
BROTHER-IN-LAW: IGOR CASSINI, COLUMNIST-CHOLLY KNICKERBOCKER
DAUGHTER:  '43 DARIA CASSINI
DAUGHTER:  '44 CHRISTINA CASSINI
*** MARRIED:  '60 W. HOWARD LEE, OILMAN
ROMANCE: ROBERT STERLING, ACTOR
ROMANCE: PRINCE ALY KHAN
RESIDENCE: HOUSTON, TX
TALENT: ACTRESS
CREDIT:  '40 HUDSON'S BAY
CREDIT:  '44 LAURA
AA-NOM  ACTRESS:  '45 LEAVE HER TO HEAVEN
CREDIT:  '48 WHIRLPOOL
CREDIT:  '54 THE EGYPTIAN
CREDIT:  '64 THE PLEASURE SEEKERS
```

TIERNEY, LAWRENCE
                              MAR 15,'19 AT BROOKLYN, NY
```
FATHER: LAWRENCE A. TIERNEY
MOTHER: MARIAN A. CROWLEY
BROTHER: EDWARD TIERNEY
BROTHER: GERALD TIERNEY, ACTOR - SCOTT BRADY
TALENT: TRACK STAR & ACTOR
COMMENT: 14 ARRESTS FOR DRINKING AND ASSAULTS
CREDIT:  '45 DILLINGER
CREDIT:  '47 SAN QUENTIN
CREDIT:  '51 THE HOODLUM
CREDIT:  '71 SUCH GOOD FRIENDS
```

TIFFIN, PAMELA   BORN: PAMELA WONSO
                           OCT 13,'42 AT OKLAHOMA CITY, OK
```
FATHER: STANLEY WONSO
MOTHER: GRACE IRENE TIFFIN
*** MARRIED:  '62 CLAY FELKER, PUBLISHER  (DIVORCED '71)
RESIDENCE: NYC
POSSESSION:  '58 6 PAIRS OF CONTACT LENSES
TALENT: MODEL - ACTRESS
CREDIT:  '60 SUMMER AND SMOKE
CREDIT:  '65 THE HALLELUJAH TRAIL
CREDIT:  '68 KISS THE OTHER SHEIK
CREDIT:  '69 VIVA MAX
```

TONE, FRANCHOT   BORN: STANISLAUS PASCAL F. TONE
                           FEB 27,'05 AT NIAGARA FALLS, NY DIED IN '68
```
FATHER: FRANK JEROME TONE, PRES. CARBORUNDUM CO.
MOTHER: GERTRUDE FRANCHOT
BROTHER: JEROME TONE
*** MARRIED:  '35 JOAN CRAWFORD, ACTRESS  (DIVORCED '39)
*** MARRIED:  '41 JEAN WALLACE, ACTRESS  (DIVORCED '48)
SON:  '42 THOMAS JEFFERSON TONE
SON:  '43 PASCAL F. TONE
*** MARRIED:  '51 BARBARA PAYTON, ACTRESS  (DIVORCED '52)
*** MARRIED:  '56 DOLORES DORN-HEFT, ACTRESS  (DIVORCED '59)
FRIEND: JEAN DALRYMPLE
FRIEND: JOAN CRAWFORD, ACTRESS
ENEMY: TOM NEAL
RESIDENCE: NYC
RESIDENCE: POINT COMFORT, CANADA
TALENT: ACTOR
```

```
COMMENT: PHI BETA KAPPA KEY CORNELL 1927
CREDIT:  '32 THE WISER SEX
AA-NOM  ACTOR:  '35 MUTINY ON THE BOUNTY
CREDIT:  '41 VIRGINIA
CREDIT:  '48 EVERY GIRL SHOULD BE MARRIED
CREDIT:  '51 HERE COMES THE GROOM
CREDIT:  '68 THE HIGH COMMISSIONER
```

TOOMEY, REGIS
AUG 13,'02 AT PITTSBURGH, PA

```
FATHER: FRANCIS X. TOOMEY
MOTHER: MARIE
SISTER: OTHELIA TOOMEY
SISTER: SARAH TOOMEY
BROTHER: ORD TOOMEY
*** MARRIED:  '25 KATHRYN SCOTT
RESIDENCE: BRENTWOOD, CA
POSSESSION: COLLECTION OF PIPES
TALENT: ACTOR
COMMENT: MADE OVER 250 FILMS
CREDIT:  '29 FRAMED
CREDIT:  '35 G-MEN
CREDIT:  '46 THE BIG SLEEP
CREDIT:  '55 GUYS AND DOLLS
CREDIT:  '67 PETER GUNN
```

TORME, MEL   BORN: MELVIN HOWARD TORME
SEP 13,'25 AT CHICAGO, IL

```
FATHER: WILLIAM TORME
MOTHER: BETTY SOPKIN
*** MARRIED:  '49 CANDY TOXTON, AKA-SUSAN PERRY  (DIVORCED '55)
SON:  '53 STEVEN TORME, AKA STEVE MARCH, SINGER
DAUGHTER:  '55 MISSY TORME
*** MARRIED:  '56 ARLENE MILES  (DIVORCED '65)
STEP-DAUGHTER: TAMI MILES
SON:  '59 TRACY TORME
*** MARRIED:  '66 JANETTE SCOTT, ACTRESS  (DIVORCED '77)
MOTHER-IN-LAW: THORA HIRD, ACTRESS
DAUGHTER:  '69 DAISY ANN TORME
SON:  '73 JAMES SCOTT TORME
FRIEND: STEVE ALLEN
RESIDENCE: LOS ANGELES, CA
TALENT: SINGER,ACTOR,COMPOSER
CREDIT:  '43 HIGHER AND HIGHER, DEBUT
CREDIT:  '50 THE DUCHESS OF IDAHO
CREDIT:  '59 THE BIG OPERATOR
CREDIT:  '64 THE PATSY
```

TORN, RIP   BORN: ELMORE TORN, JR.
FEB 06,'31 AT TEMPLE, TX

```
FATHER: ELMORE TORN
MOTHER: THELMA SPACEK
COUSIN: SISSY SPACEK, ACTRESS
*** MARRIED: ANN WEDGEWORTH  (DIVORCED)
DAUGHTER:  '60 DANAE TORN
*** MARRIED:  '63 GERALDINE PAGE, ACTRESS
DAUGHTER:  '64 ANGELICA TORN
SON:  '65 ANTHONY TORN, TWIN
```

```
        SON:   '65 JONATHAN TORN, TWIN
        RESIDENCE: NYC
        TALENT: ACTOR
        CREDIT:  '56 BABY DOLL
        CREDIT:  '61 KING OF KINGS
        CREDIT:  '66 YOU'RE A BIG BOY NOW
        CREDIT:  '69 TROPIC OF CANCER
-------------------------------------------------------------------------------
TRACY, SPENCER            BORN:   SPENCER BONAVENTURE TRACY
                                  APR 05,'00 AT MILWAUKEE, WI   DIED IN '67
        FATHER: JOHN EDWARD TRACY
        MOTHER: CAROLINE BROWN
        BROTHER: CARROLL TRACY
        *** MARRIED:  '23 LOUISE TREADWELL, ACTRESS
        SON:   '24 JOHN TRACY, ARTIST
        DAUGHTER:  '32 LOUISE TRACY
        ROMANCE: KATHARINE HEPBURN, ACTRESS
        ROMANCE: LORETTA YOUNG, ACTRESS
        FRIEND: PAT O'BRIEN, SCHOOLMATE AT MARQUETTE UNIV.
        BIOGRAPHY:  '69 SPENCER TRACY, BY LARRY SWINDELL
        TALENT: ACTOR
        COMMENT: ENDOWED THE JOHN TRACY CLINIC FOR THE DEAF
        AA-NOM  ACTOR:  '36 SAN FRANCISCO
        AA-WIN  ACTOR:  '37 CAPTAINS COURAGEOUS
        AA-WIN  ACTOR:  '38 BOYS TOWN
        AA-NOM  ACTOR:  '50 FATHER OF THE BRIDE
        AA-NOM  ACTOR:  '55 BAD DAY AT BLACK ROCK
        AA-NOM  ACTOR:  '58 THE OLD MAN AND THE SEA
        AA-NOM  ACTOR:  '60 INHERIT THE WIND
        AA-NOM  ACTOR:  '61 JUDGMENT AT NUREMBERG
        AA-NOM  ACTOR:  '67 GUESS WHO'S COMING TO DINNER
-------------------------------------------------------------------------------
TRAVOLTA, JOHN
                          FEB 18,'54 AT ENGLEWOOD, NJ
        FATHER: SALVATORE TRAVOLTA, TIRE DEALER
        MOTHER: HELEN BURKE, ACTRESS, DRAMA TEACHER
        SISTER: MARGARET TRAVOLTA, ACTRESS
        SISTER: ELLEN TRAVOLTA, ACTRESS
        SISTER: ANN TRAVOLTA, ACTRESS
        BROTHER: SAM TRAVOLTA, SINGER
        BROTHER: JOE TRAVOLTA, SINGER, BARTENDER
        ROMANCE: DIANA HYLAND, ACTRESS  (DIED '76)
        RESIDENCE: LOS ANGELES, CA
        POSSESSION: MODEL AIRPLANE COLLECTION
        TALENT: ACTOR, SINGER, DANCER
        CREDIT:  '73 WELCOME BACK KOTTER, TV SERIES
        CREDIT:  '76 CARRIE
        CREDIT:  '76 THE BOY IN THE PLASTIC BUBBLE
        AA-NOM  ACTOR:  '77 SATURDAY NIGHT FEVER
        CREDIT:  '78 GREASE
        CREDIT:  '78 AMERICAN GIGOLO
-------------------------------------------------------------------------------
TREVOR, CLAIRE            BORN:   CLAIRE WEMLINGER
                                  MAR 18,'09 AT NYC
        FATHER: NOEL B. WEMLINGER
        SISTER: MAUDE WEMLINGER
        SISTER: MILDRED WEMLINGER
        SISTER: MABEL WEMLINGER
```

BROTHER: MALCOLM 'BYRON' WEMLINGER
*** MARRIED: '38 CLARK ANDREWS (DIVORCED '42)
*** MARRIED: '43 CYLOS DUNSMOOR (DIVORCED '47)
SON: '44 CHARLES DUNSMOOR
*** MARRIED: '48 MILTON BREN
SON: '49 DONALD BREN
SON: '50 PETER BREN
RESIDENCE: NEWPORT BEACH, CA
TALENT: ACTRESS
CREDIT: '33 LIFE IN THE RAW, DEBUT
AA-NOM SUP.ACT: '37 DEAD END
AA-WIN SUP.ACT.: '48 KEY LARGO
AA-NOM SUP.ACT: '54 THE HIGH AND THE MIGHTY
CREDIT: '65 HOW TO MURDER YOUR WIFE

TRUEX, ERNEST
                         SEP 19,'89 AT RICH HILL,MR DIED IN '73
*** MARRIED: JULIA MILLS (DIED)
*** MARRIED: MARY JANE BARRETT (DIVORCED '39)
SON: '34 BARRETT TRUEX
*** MARRIED: '41 SYLVIA FIELD, ACTRESS
STEP-DAUGHTER: SALLY MOFFET
SON: PHILIP TRUEX
SON: JAMES TRUEX
RESIDENCE: FALLBROOK, CA
TALENT: ACTOR
CREDIT: '33 WHISTLING IN THE DARK
CREDIT: '40 CHRISTMAS IN JULY
CREDIT: '48 ALWAYS TOGETHER
CREDIT: '56 THE LEATHER SAINT
CREDIT: '65 FLUFFY

TRYON, TOM
                    JAN 14,'26 AT HARTFORD, CN
FATHER: ARTHUR LANE TRYON, HABERDASHER
MOTHER: ELIZABETH LESTER
*** MARRIED: '56 ANN NOYES (DIVORCED '58)
RESIDENCE: NYC
TALENT: ACTOR-NOVELIST
COMMENT: FAMILY ANCESTOR-WILLIAM TRYON,GOVERNOR-NORTH CAROLINA & NY
CREDIT: '55 THE SCARLET HOUR
CREDIT: '63 THE CARDINAL
CREDIT: '65 THE GLORY GUYS
CREDIT: '71 THE OTHER, NOVEL
CREDIT: '76 CROWNED HEADS, NOVEL

TUCKER, FORREST   BORN: FORREST MEREDITH TUCKER
                         FEB 12,'19 AT PLAINFIELD, IN
FATHER: FORREST A. TUCKER
MOTHER: DORIS P. HERINGLAKE
*** MARRIED: '40 SANDRA JOLLEY
DAUGHTER: '41 PAMELA BROOKE JOLLEY TUCKER
*** MARRIED: '50 MARILYN JOHNSON (DIED '60)
*** MARRIED: '61 MARILYN FISH
DAUGHTER: '62 CYNTHIA TUCKER
TALENT: ACTOR
CREDIT: '40 THE WESTERNER, DEBUT
CREDIT: '50 SANDS OF IWO JIMA

```
         CREDIT:  '58 AUNTIE MAME
         CREDIT:  '68 THE NIGHT THEY RAIDED MINSKY'S
         CREDIT:  '72 CANCEL MY RESERVATION
------------------------------------------------------------------------
TUCKER, SOPHIE          BORN:  SONIA KALISH
                               JAN 13,'84 AT BOSTON, MS OR RUSSIA   DIED IN '66
         FATHER: CHARLES KALISH, RESTAURATEUR
         *** MARRIED: FRANK WESTPHAL
         *** MARRIED:  '01 LOUIS TUCK  (DIVORCED)
         SON:  '02 BERT TUCK
         *** MARRIED:  '20 ALBERT LACKERMAN  (DIVORCED '32)
         FRIEND: TED LEWIS, BANDLEADER
         POSSESSION: OWNER CARLTON TERRACE & LAKE ROAD INN - CLEVELAND, OHIO
         MEMOIRS: SOME OF THESE DAYS
         TALENT: ACTRESS
         COMMENT: KNOWN AS THE 'LAST OF THE RED-HOT MAMAS'
         CREDIT:  '29 HONKY TONK
         CREDIT:  '34 GAY LOVE
         CREDIT:  '37 THOROUGHBREDS DON'T CRY
         CREDIT:  '44 FOLLOW THE BOYS
------------------------------------------------------------------------
TUFTS, SONNY            BORN:  BOWEN CHARLESTON TUFTS, III
                               JUL 16,'11 AT BOSTON, MS   DIED IN '70
         FATHER: BOWEN CHARLESTON TUFTS, II  (DIED '35)
         MOTHER: OCTAVIA  (DIED '57)
         BROTHER: DAVID ALBERT TUFTS
         *** MARRIED:  '38 BARBARA DARE, DANCER  (DIVORCED '51)
         ROMANCE: BARBARA ATKINS, DANCER
         ROMANCE: MARJORIE VON, DANCER
         ROMANCE: NANCY HEINZ
         RESIDENCE: LOS ANGELES, CA
         TALENT: ACTOR-SINGER
         CREDIT:  '39 AMBUSH
         CREDIT:  '45 DUFFY'S TAVERN
         CREDIT:  '53 CAT-WOMEN OF THE MOON
         CREDIT:  '67 COTTONPICKIN' CHICKENPICKERS
------------------------------------------------------------------------
TURNER, LANA            BORN:  JULIA JEAN MILDRED FRANCES
                               FEB 08,'20 AT WALLACE, ID
         FATHER: VIRGIL TURNER, DANCER
         MOTHER: MILDRED COWAN
         *** MARRIED:  '40 ARTIE SHAW, BAND LEADER  (DIVORCED '42)
         *** MARRIED:  '43 STEPHEN CRANE, ACTOR-RESTAURATEUR  (DIVORCED '44)
         DAUGHTER:  '44 CHERYL CRANE
         *** MARRIED:  '48 HENRY J. (BOB) TOPPING  (DIVORCED '52)
         *** MARRIED:  '53 LEX BARKER, ACTOR  (DIVORCED '57)
         STEP-DAUGHTER: LYNNE ALEXANDER BARKER
         STEP-SON: ALEXANDER BARKER
         *** MARRIED:  '60 FRED MAY  (DIVORCED '62)
         *** MARRIED:  '65 ROBERT EATON  (DIVORCED '69)
         *** MARRIED:  '69 RONALD DANTE  (DIVORCED '72)
         ROMANCE: JOHNNY STOMPANATO, DIED '58 FROM KNIFE WOUNDS
                          INFLICTED BY CHERYL CRANE
         ROMANCE: FERNANDO LAMAS, ACTOR
         ROMANCE: TONY MARTIN, SINGER
         RESIDENCE: SANTA MONICA, CA
```

```
POSSESSION: LANA TURNER MINI-SPAS
TALENT: ACTRESS
COMMENT: THE 'SWEATER GIRL'
CREDIT:  '37 A STAR IS BORN
CREDIT:  '44 MARRIAGE IS A PRIVATE AFFAIR
AA-NOM ACTRESS:  '57 PEYTON PLACE
CREDIT:  '61 BY LOVE POSSESSED
CREDIT:  '74 PERSECUTION
```

TUSHINGHAM, RITA
```
                         MAR 14,'42 AT LIVERPOOL, ENGLAND
FATHER: JOHN TUSHINGHAM, GROCER
MOTHER: ENID
BROTHER: PETER TUSHINGHAM
BROTHER: COLIN TUSHINGHAM
*** MARRIED:  '62 TERENCE BICKNELL, CAMERAMAN
DAUGHTER:  '64 DONNA BICKNELL
PARTNER: DESMOND DAVIS, DIRECTOR
TALENT: ACTRESS
CREDIT:  '61 A TASTE OF HONEY, DEBUT
CREDIT:  '64 THE GIRL WITH GREEN EYES
CREDIT:  '69 THE GURU
CREDIT:  '70 THE BED SITTING ROOM
```

TWIGGY   BORN: LESLIE HORNBY
```
                    SEP 19,'49 AT LONDON, ENGLAND
FATHER: WILLIAM NORMAN HORNBY, CARPENTER
MOTHER: HELEN REEMAN
SISTER: VIVIAN HORNBY
SISTER: SHIRLEY HORNBY
*** MARRIED:  '77 MICHAEL WITNEY, ACTOR
ROMANCE: JUSTIN DE VILLENEUVE, HER MANAGER
TALENT: MODEL,ACTRESS, SINGER
CREDIT:  '71 THE BOYFRIEND, DEBUT
CREDIT:  '74 'W'
```

TYSON, CICELY
```
                    DEC 19,'39 AT NYC
FATHER: WILLIAM TYSON, CARPENTER
MOTHER: THEODOSIA
SISTER: EMILY TYSON
ROMANCE: MILES DAVIS, MUSICIAN
ROMANCE: PAUL WINFIELD, ACTOR
RESIDENCE: NYC
POSSESSION:  '78 WOMAN OF THE YEAR AWARD BY THE LADIES' HOME JOURNAL
TALENT: ACTRESS
AA-NOM ACTRESS:  '72 SOUNDER
CREDIT: A MAN CALLED ADAM
CREDIT: THE COMEDIANS
CREDIT: THE HEART IS A LONELY HUNTER
CREDIT: THE BLUE BEARD
```

```
---------------------------------------------------------------------------------------------------------------
ULLMAN, LIV          BORN:  LIV JOHANNE ULLMANN
                            DEC 16,'39 AT TOKYO, JAPAN
     FATHER: VIGGO ULLMANN
     MOTHER: JANA LUND
     *** MARRIED:  '60 JAPPE STANG, PSYCHIATRIST   (DIVORCED '65)
     DAUGHTER:  '65 LINN ULLMAN, FATHER-BERGMAN
     ROMANCE: INGMAR BERGMAN, DIRECTOR
     MEMOIRS:  '76 CHANGING
     TALENT: ACTRESS
     CREDIT:  '59 THE WAYWARD GIRL
     CREDIT:  '65 PERSONA
     CREDIT:  '71 POPE JOAN
     AA-NOM  ACTRESS:  '72 THE EMIGRANTS
     AA-NOM  ACTRESS:  '76 FACE TO FACE
---------------------------------------------------------------------------------------------------------------
USTINOV, PETER          BORN:  PETER ALEXANDER USTINOV
                               APR 15,'21 AT LONDON, ENGLAND
     FATHER: IONA USTINOV, JOURNALIST
     MOTHER: NADIA BENOIS, ARTIST
     *** MARRIED:  '40 ISOLDE DENHAM
     DAUGHTER:  '41 TAMARA USTINOV
     *** MARRIED:  '54 SUZANNE CLOUTIER
     SON:  '56 IGOR USTINOV
     DAUGHTER:  '59 PAVIA USTINOV
     *** MARRIED:  '72 HELENE DU LAU D'ALLEMAN, PRESS AGENT
     RESIDENCE: LONDON, ENGLAND
     MEMOIRS:  '77 DEAR ME
     TALENT: ACTOR, WRITER, PRODUCER DIRECTOR
     CREDIT:  '40 MEIN KAMPF
     CREDIT:  '49 PRIVATE ANGELO
     AA-NOM  SUP.ACT:  '51 QUO VADIS
     AA-WIN  SUP.ACT.:  '60 SPARTACUS
     AA-WIN  SUP.ACT.:  '64 TOPKAPI
     CREDIT:  '72 HAMMERSMITH IS OUT
```

VACCARO, BRENDA
                         NOV 18,'39 AT BROOKLYN, NY
    FATHER: MARIO VACCARO
    MOTHER: CHRISTINE PAVIA
    *** MARRIED: '65 MARTIN FRIED
    *** MARRIED: '77 WILLIAM BISHOP, ATTORNEY
    ROMANCE: MICHAEL DOUGLAS
    TALENT: ACTRESS
    CREDIT: '69 MIDNIGHT COWBOY
    CREDIT: '71 SUMMERTREE
    CREDIT: '73 HONOR THY FATHER
    AA-NOM SUP.ACT: '75 JACQUELINE SUSANN'S ONCE IS NOT ENOUGH

VALENTINO, RUDOLPH
                       MAY 06,'95 AT CASTELLANETA, PUGLIA, ITALY   DIED IN '26
    FATHER: GIOVANNI GUGLIELMI, ROYAL ITALIAN CAVALRY OFFICER
    MOTHER: BEATRICE GABRIELLA BARBIN
    SISTER: BEATRICE GUGLIELMI
    SISTER: MARIA GUGLIELMI
    BROTHER: ALBERTO GUGLIELMI
    *** MARRIED: '20 JEAN ACKER, ACTRESS (DIVORCED '22)
    *** MARRIED: '23 WINIFRED SHAUNESSEY, AKA NATASHA RAMBOVA-ACTRESS (DIVORCED '25)
    FATHER-IN-LAW: RICHARD HUDNUT
    ROMANCE: POLA NEGRI, ACTRESS
    FRIEND: JUNE MATHIS
    FRIEND: JULIO SAMMARCELLI
    RESIDENCE: 'THE FALCON'S LAIR' IN BEVERLY HILLS, CA
    TALENT: ACTOR
    COMMENT: OWNED MOTOR YACHT 'PHEONIX'
    COMMENT: REAL NAME: RODOLFO ALFONZO RAFFAELO PIERRE FILIBERT
            GUGLIELMI DI VALENTINO D'ANTONGUOLLA
    CREDIT: '14 MY OFFICIAL WIFE
    CREDIT: '20 THE MARRIED VIRGIN
    CREDIT: '21 THE SHEIK
    CREDIT: '22 THE ISLE OF LOVE
    CREDIT: '26 SON OF THE SHEIK

VALLEE, RUDY   BORN: HUBERT PRIOR VALLEE
                         JUL 28,'01 AT ISLAND POND, VT
    FATHER: CHARLES ALPHONSE VALLEE
    MOTHER: KATHERINE LYNCH
    SISTER: KATHLEEN VALLEE
    BROTHER: WILLIAM VALLEE, WRITER
    *** MARRIED: '28 LEONIE CAUCHOIS (ANNULLED '28)
    *** MARRIED: '31 FAY WEBB (DIVORCED '36)
    *** MARRIED: '43 JANE GREER, ACTRESS (DIVORCED '45)
    *** MARRIED: '49 ELEANOR KATHLEEN NORRIS
    PARTNER: LESLIE CHARTERIS, AUTHOR
    RESIDENCE: LOS ANGELES,CA
    POSSESSION: '29 VILLA VALLEE NIGHTCLUB, NYC
    POSSESSION: SAINT ENTERPRISES, INC.
    POSSESSION: RUE DE VALLEE STREET SIGN
    MEMOIRS: I DIGRESS
    TALENT: SINGER, BANDLEADER, ACTOR
    CREDIT: '29 THE VAGABOND LOVER, DEBUT
    CREDIT: '38 GOLD DIGGERS IN PARIS
    CREDIT: '47 THE BACHELOR AND THE BOBBYSOXER

CREDIT: '55 GENTLEMEN MARRY BRUNETTES
CREDIT: '68 LIVE A LITTLE, LOVE A LITTLE

VALLI, ALIDA   BORN: ALIDA MARIA ALTENBURGER
                               MAY 31,'21 AT POLA, ISTRIA, ITALY
   *** MARRIED: '44 OSCAR DE MEJO, PIANIST COMPOSER (DIVORCED '52)
   SON: '45 CARLO DE MEJO
   SON: '50 LORENZO DE MEJO
   FRIEND: PIERO PICCIONI
   RESIDENCE: FRASCHETTI, ITALY
   TALENT: ACTRESS
   CREDIT: '47 THE PARADINE CASE
   CREDIT: '49 THE THIRD MAN
   CREDIT: '62 OPHELIA
   CREDIT: '67 OEPIDUS REX

VAN CLEEF, LEE
                               JAN 09,'25 AT SOMERVILLE, NJ
   FATHER: C. LEROY VAN CLEEF, ACCOUNTANT
   MOTHER: --, SINGER
   *** MARRIED: '43 JOAN
   DAUGHTER: DEBORAH VAN CLEEF
   SON: ALAN VAN CLEEF
   RESIDENCE: SAN FERNANDO VALLEY, CA
   POSSESSION: '73 LVC MUSIC CO.
   TALENT: ACTOR
   CREDIT: '52 HIGH NOON
   CREDIT: '58 GUNS, GIRLS AND GANGSTERS
   CREDIT: '66 DAY OF ANGER
   CREDIT: '70 EL CONDOR

VAN DOREN, MAMIE   BORN: JOAN LUCILLE OLANDER
                               FEB 06,'33 AT ROWENA,SD
   *** MARRIED: '55 RAY ANTHONY
   SON: '56 PETER ANTHONY
   *** MARRIED: '66 LEE MEYERS
   *** MARRIED: '72 ROSS MCCLINTOCH (ANNULLED)
   TALENT: SINGER-ACTRESS
   CREDIT: '53 FORBIDDEN, DEBUT
   CREDIT: '55 THE SECOND GREATEST SEX
   CREDIT: '58 TEACHER'S PET
   CREDIT: '66 THE NAVY VS. THE NIGHT MONSTERS

VAN DYKE, DICK
                               DEC 18,'25 AT WEST PLAINS, MR
   FATHER: L. W. VAN DYKE
   MOTHER: HAZEL
   BROTHER: JERRY VAN DYKE, ACTOR
   *** MARRIED: '48 MARJORIE WILLETT
   SON: '50 CHRISTIAN VAN DYKE
   SON: '52 BARRY VAN DYKE
   DAUGHTER: '55 STACEY VAN DYKE
   DAUGHTER: '62 CARRIE BETH VAN DYKE
   GRANDDAUGHTER: '74 JESSICA LEE VAN DYKE
   FRIEND: BYRON PAUL, PERSONAL MANAGER
   RESIDENCE: LOS ANGELES, CA
   POSSESSION: '66 RADIO STATION- KXIV - PHOENIX
   TALENT: ACTOR

CREDIT: '63 BYE BYE BIRDIE
CREDIT: '64 MARY POPPINS
CREDIT: '68 CHITTY CHITTY BANG BANG
CREDIT: '71 COLD TURKEY
CREDIT: '76 THE COMEDIANS

VAN FLEET, JO
                          DEC 30,'19 AT OAKLAND, CA
FATHER: HUGH VAN FLEET
MOTHER: CATHERINE GARDNER
*** MARRIED: '46 WILLIAM BALES
SON: '47 MICHAEL BALES
TALENT: ACTRESS
AA-WIN SUP.ACT.: '55 EAST OF EDEN
CREDIT: '60 WILD RIVER
CREDIT: '68 COOL HAND LUKE
CREDIT: '72 THE GANG THAT COULDN'T SHOOT STRAIGHT

VAN, BOBBY
                          DEC 06,'30 AT BRONX, NY
FATHER: HARRY KING
*** MARRIED: DIANE GARRETT
*** MARRIED: '68 ELAINE JOYCE
RESIDENCE: BEVERLY HILLS, CA
TALENT: ACTOR-DANCER
CREDIT: '52 BECAUSE YOU'RE MINE
CREDIT: '53 KISS ME KATE
CREDIT: '73 LOST HORIZON

VANCE, VIVIAN   BORN: VIVIAN JONES
                          JUL 26,'12 AT CHERRYVALE, KA
FATHER: ROBERT A. JONES
MOTHER: MAE RAGEN
*** MARRIED: '41 PHILIP OBER (DIVORCED '59)
*** MARRIED: '61 JOHN DODDS, EDITOR
RESIDENCE: NYC
TALENT: ACTRESS
CREDIT: '50 THE SECRET FURY
CREDIT: '53 I LOVE LUCY, TV SERIES
CREDIT: '65 THE GREAT RACE

VARSI, DIANE   BORN: DIANE MARIE ANTONIA VARSI
                          FEB 23,'38 AT SAN FRANCISCO, CA
FATHER: RUSSELL VARSI, FLORIST
MOTHER: BEATRICE DEMERCHANT
SISTER: GAIL VARSI
*** MARRIED: '55 --, (NAME HAS BEEN SUPPRESSED) (ANNULLED '55)
*** MARRIED: '56 JAMES DICKSON, PRODUCER (DIVORCED '58)
SON: '56 SHAWN MICHAEL VARSI, (FATHER'S NAME SUPPRESSED)'
*** MARRIED: '61 MICHAEL HAUSMAN
DAUGHTER: '63 WILLOW HAUSMAN
*** MARRIED: '67 RUSSELL PARKER
RESIDENCE: BENNINGTON, VERMONT
POSSESSION: '56 CONTRACT AT 20TH CENTURY FOX
TALENT: ACTRESS
AA-NOM SUP.ACT: '57 PEYTON PLACE
CREDIT: '58 TEN NORTH FREDERICK
CREDIT: '59 COMPULSION

```
CREDIT:  '68 WILD IN THE STREETS
CREDIT:  '71 JOHNNY GOT HIS GUN
```

VAUGHN, ROBERT   BORN: ROBERT FRANCIS VAUGHN
                              NOV 22,'32 AT NYC
```
     FATHER: GERALD WALTER VAUGHN, ACTOR
     MOTHER: MARCELLA FRANCES GAUDEL, ACTRESS
     *** MARRIED:  '74 LINDA STAAB, ACTRESS
     ROMANCE: JOYCE JAMESON
     RESIDENCE: HOLLYWOOD HILLS, CA
     MEMOIRS: ONLY VICTIMS
     TALENT: ACTOR
     CREDIT:  '58 TEENAGE CAVEMAN
     AA-NOM  SUP.ACT:  '59 THE YOUNG PHILADELPHIANS
     CREDIT:  '64 THE MAN FROM U.N.C.L.E., TV SERIES
     CREDIT:  '68 BULLITT
     CREDIT:  '71 THE STATUE
```

VELEZ, LUPE   BORN: MARIA GUADALUPE VILLALOBOS
                              JUL 18,'08 AT SAN LUIS POTOSI, MEXICO   DIED IN '44
```
     FATHER: JACOB VILLALOBOS, ARMY OFFICER
     MOTHER: REMEDIOS VELEZ, OPERA SINGER
     SISTER: MERCEDES VILLALOBOS VELEZ
     SISTER: JOSEFINA VILLALOBOS VELEZ
     BROTHER: EMIGDIO VILLALOBOS VELEZ
     *** MARRIED:  '33 JOHNNY WEISSMULLER, ACTOR  (DIVORCED '38)
     ADOPTED DAUGHTER: JUANA VELEZ, HER SISTER JOSEFINA'S DAUGHTER
     ROMANCE: GARY COOPER, ACTOR
     FRIEND: CONTESSA DOROTHY DI FRASSO
     FRIEND: BEATRICE VERDUGO, EMPLOYED AS HER SECRETARY
     POSSESSION: CHIHUAHUA SHOW DOGS
     TALENT: ACTRESS
     CREDIT:  '40 MEXICAN SPITFIRE, SERIES
     CREDIT:  '43 REDHEAD
     CREDIT: THE GAUCHO
     CREDIT: LADY OF THE PAVEMENTS
     CREDIT: HOT PEPPER
```

VENUTA, BENAY
                      JAN 27,'11 AT SAN FRANCISCO, CA
```
     *** MARRIED:  '36 KENNETH KELLY, DOCTOR  (DIVORCED '38)
     *** MARRIED:  '39 ARMAND S. DEUTSCH  (DIVORCED '50)
     DAUGHTER:  '41 PATRICIA DEUTSCH
     DAUGHTER:  '43 DEBORAH DEUTSCH
     *** MARRIED:  '51 FRED CLARK, ACTOR  (DIVORCED '63)
     RESIDENCE: NYC
     POSSESSION: PRE-COLUMBIAN & MODERN ART COLLECTION
     TALENT: ACTRESS
```

VERA-ELLEN   BORN: VERA-ELLEN WESTMEYER ROHE
                              FEB 16,'26 AT CINCINNATI, OH
```
     FATHER: MARTIN F. ROHE, PIANO TUNER
     MOTHER: ALMA WESTMEYER
     *** MARRIED:  '45 ROBERT HIGHTOWER, DANCER  (DIVORCED '46)
     *** MARRIED:  '54 VICTOR ROTHSCHILD  (DIVORCED '66)
     TALENT: ACTRESS, SINGER, DANCER
     CREDIT:  '44 BILLY ROSE'S CASA MANANA CLUB
     CREDIT:  '45 WONDER MAN, DEBUT
```

```
CREDIT:   '49 ON THE TOWN
CREDIT:   '53 CALL ME MADAM
CREDIT:   '57 LET'S BE HAPPY
```

VERDON, GWEN   BORN: GWYNETH EVELYN VERDON
                              JAN 13,'26 AT LOS ANGELES, CA
```
FATHER: JOSEPH VERDON
MOTHER: GERTRUDE STANDRING, DANCER
*** MARRIED:  '42 JAMES HENAGHAN  (DIVORCED '47)
*** MARRIED:  '50 O'FARRELL
SON:  '51 JAMES O'FARRELL
*** MARRIED:  '60 BOB FOSSE, DIRECTOR
POSSESSION: TONY AWARD FOR PERFORMANCE IN CAN-CAN
TALENT: ACTRESS-DANCER
CREDIT:   '51 ON THE RIVIERA
CREDIT:   '51 DAVID AND BATHSHEBA
CREDIT:   '51 MEET ME AFTER THE SHOW
CREDIT:   '53 THE FARMER TAKES A WIFE
CREDIT:   '58 DAMN YANKEES
```

VERDUGO, ELENA
                          APR 20,'25 AT LOS ANGELES, CA
```
MOTHER: BEATRICE VERDUGO
*** MARRIED:  '46 CHARLES MARION  (DIVORCED '56)
SON:  '47 RICHARD ANTHONY MARION
*** MARRIED:  '72 DR. CHARLES ROSEWELL
TALENT: ACTRESS
CREDIT:   '40 DOWN ARGENTINE WAY
CREDIT:   '47 SONG OF SCHEHERAZADE
CREDIT:   '52 THIEF OF DAMASCUS
CREDIT:   '68 HOW SWEET IT IS
```

VOIGHT, JON
                      DEC 29,'38 AT NYC
```
FATHER: ELMER VOIGHT, PRO GOLFER
MOTHER: BARBARA CAMP
BROTHER: BARRY VOIGHT, GEOLOGIST
BROTHER: JAMES WESLEY VOIGHT, AKA CHIP TAYLOR-ENTERTAINER
*** MARRIED:  '62 LAURI PETERS
*** MARRIED:  '71 MARCELLINE BERTRAND
SON:  '72 JAMES HAVEN VOIGHT
RESIDENCE: BRENTWOOD, LA, CA
TALENT: ACTOR, WRITER
CREDIT:   '67 THE HOUR OF THE GUN
AA-NOM  ACTOR:  '69 MIDNIGHT COWBOY
CREDIT:   '72 DELIVERANCE
CREDIT:   '75 THE ODESSA FILE
CREDIT:   '78 COMING HOME
```

VON FURSTENBURG, BETSY   BORN: SEE COMMENT
                              AUG 16,'31 AT WESTPHALIA, GERMANY
```
FATHER: COUNT FRANZ VON FURSTENBURG
MOTHER: ELIZABETH JOHNSON
*** MARRIED:  '54 GUY VINCENT DE LA MAIXONEUVE  (DIVORCED)
DAUGHTER:  '55 CAROLINE DE LA MAIXONEUVE
ROMANCE: CONRAD NICHOLSON HILTON, JR.
POSSESSION: '52 CONTRACT AT M-G-M STUDIOS
TALENT: ACTRESS
```

COMMENT: ELIZABETH CAROLINE MARIA FELICITAS VON FURSTENBURG HEDRINGEN
CREDIT: WOMEN WITHOUT NAMES
CREDIT: SKIRTS AHOY!

VON STROHEIM, ERICH   BORN: ERICH STROHEIM VON NORDENWALD
                                         SEP 22,'86 AT VIENNA, AUSTRIA   DIED IN '57
FATHER: FREDERICK 'BENNO' NORDENWALD, COLONEL - SIXTH DRAGOONS
MOTHER: JOHANNA VON BONDY, LADY-IN-WAITING AUSTRIAN COURT
BROTHER: BRUNO VON NORDENWALD
*** MARRIED: MARGUERITE KNOX (DIED)
*** MARRIED: '15 MAY JONES
SON: '16 ERICH VON STROHEIM, JR.
*** MARRIED: '30 VALERIE MARGUERITE GERMONPREZ
SON: '31 JOSEF ERICH VON STROHEIM
*** MARRIED: '43 SHEILA DARCY
ROMANCE: DENISE VERNAC, ACTRESS
RESIDENCE: CHATEAU MAUREPAS, SEINE ET OISE, FRANCE
TALENT: DIRECTOR ACTOR
COMMENT: THE MAN YOU LOVE TO HATE
CREDIT: '19 BLIND HUSBANDS
CREDIT: '21 FOOLISH WIVES
CREDIT: '30 FRIENDS AND LOVERS
CREDIT: '41 SO ENDS OUR NIGHT
AA-NOM SUP.ACT: '50 SUNSET BOULEVARD

VON SYDOW, MAX   BORN: MAX CARL ADOLPH VON SYDOW
                                   APR 10,'29 AT LUND, SWEDEN
FATHER: CARL WILHELM VON SYDOW
MOTHER: GRETA RAPPE
*** MARRIED: '51 KERATIN OLIN, ACTRESS
SON: '52 CLAS WILHELM VON SYDOW
SON: '53 PER HENRIK VON SYDOW
RESIDENCE: STOCKHOLM, SWEDEN
TALENT: ACTOR
CREDIT: '51 MISS JULIE
CREDIT: '59 THE FACE
CREDIT: '69 THE KREMLIN LETTER
CREDIT: '73 THE EXORCIST
CREDIT: '77 MARCH OR DIE

WAGGONER, LYLE   BORN: LYLE WESLEY WAGGONER
                                  APR 13,'35 AT KANSAS CITY, KA
    FATHER: MYRON WAGGONER
    MOTHER: MARIE
    *** MARRIED: '60 SHARON ADELAIDE KENNEDY
    SON: '68 JASON KENNEDY WAGGONER
    SON: '69 BEAU JUSTIN WAGGONER
    RESIDENCE: SAN FERNANDO VALLEY, CA
    TALENT: ACTOR
    COMMENT: ELECTED MAYOR OF ENCINO, CA 1976
    CREDIT: '72 LOST IN SPACE, TV SERIES
    CREDIT: '77 WONDER WOMAN, TV SERIES

WAGNER, ROBERT   BORN: ROBERT WAGNER, JR.
                                  FEB 10,'30 AT DETROIT, MH
    FATHER: ROBERT WAGNER, SR.
    *** MARRIED: '56 NATALIE WOOD, ACTRESS (DIVORCED '62)
    *** MARRIED: '63 MARION MARSHALL (DIVORCED '71)
    DAUGHTER: '64 KATHERINE WAGNER
    *** MARRIED: '72 NATALIE WOOD, ACTRESS
    STEP-DAUGHTER: NATASHA GREGSON
    DAUGHTER: '74 COURTNEY BROOKE WAGNER
    ROMANCE: DEBBIE REYNOLDS
    POSSESSION: '76 YACHT 'SPLENDOUR'
    TALENT: ACTOR
    CREDIT: '50 HALLS OF MONTEZUMA, DEBUT
    CREDIT: '56 A KISS BEFORE DYING
    CREDIT: '59 ALL THE FINE YOUNG CANNIBALS
    CREDIT: '66 THE BIGGEST BUNDLE OF ALL
    CREDIT: '69 WINNING

WALKER, CLINT   BORN: NORMAN E. WALKER
                                  MAY 30,'27 AT HARTFORD, IL
    FATHER: PAUL ARNOLD WALKER
    SISTER: LUCILLE NEOMA WALKER, TWIN
    *** MARRIED: '48 VERNA LUCILLE GARVER
    DAUGHTER: '50 VALERIE JEAN WALKER
    *** MARRIED: '74 GISELLE CAMILLE D'ARC
    POSSESSION: '60 YACHT 'MANA KUA'
    TALENT: ACTOR
    CREDIT: '57 FORT DOBBS
    CREDIT: '60 YELLOWSTONE KELLY
    CREDIT: '66 NIGHT OF THE GRIZZLY
    CREDIT: '67 THE DIRTY DOZEN
    CREDIT: '69 THE GREAT BANK ROBBERY

WALKER, ROBERT   BORN: ROBERT HUDSON WALKER
                                  OCT 13,'14 AT SALT LAKE CITY, UT   DIED IN '51
    FATHER: HORACE WALKER
    MOTHER: ZELLA MCQUARRIE
    BROTHER: WALTER WALKER
    BROTHER: WAYNE WALKER
    BROTHER: RICHARD WALKER
    *** MARRIED: '39 JENNIFER JONES, ACTRESS (DIVORCED '45)
    SON: '40 ROBERT WALKER, JR., ACTOR
    SON: '41 MICHAEL WALKER
    *** MARRIED: '48 BARBARA FORD

SPOUSE'S UNCLE: FRANCIS FORD
FATHER-IN-LAW: SEAN ALOYSIUS O'FEENEY, DIRECTOR AKA JOHN FORD
TALENT: ACTOR
CREDIT: '39 WINTER CARNIVAL
CREDIT: '44 THIRTY SECONDS OVER TOKYO
CREDIT: '48 ONE TOUCH OF VENUS
CREDIT: '51 STRANGERS ON A TRAIN
CREDIT: '52 MY SON JOHN

WALLACH, ELI

                    DEC 07,'15 AT BROOKLYN, NY
FATHER: ABRAHAM WALLACH
MOTHER: BERTHA SCHORR
*** MARRIED: '48 ANNE JACKSON
SON: '51 PETER DOUGLAS WALLACH
DAUGHTER: '55 ROBERTA LEE WALLACH
DAUGHTER: '58 KATHERINE BEATRICE WALLACH
FRIEND: LEE STRASBERG
RESIDENCE: GREENWICH VILLAGE, NY
TALENT: ACTOR
CREDIT: '56 BABY DOLL, DEBUT
CREDIT: '61 THE MISFITS
CREDIT: '67 THE TIGER MAKES OUT
CREDIT: '68 HOW TO SAVE A MARRIAGE
CREDIT: '71 ROMANCE OF A HORSE THIEF

WALTER, JESSICA

                    JAN 31,'40 AT BROOKLYN, NY
FATHER: DAVID WALTER, CELLIST
*** MARRIED: '66 ROSS BOWMAN (SEPARATED '76)
DAUGHTER: '72 BROOKE BOWMAN
TALENT: ACTRESS
CREDIT: '64 LILITH
CREDIT: '66 THE GROUP
CREDIT: '67 GRAND PRIX
CREDIT: '69 NUMBER ONE
CREDIT: '71 PLAY MISTY FOR ME

WARDEN, JACK

                    SEP 18,'20 AT NEWARK, NJ
FATHER: JOHN F. WARDEN
MOTHER: LAURA COSTELLA
*** MARRIED: VANDA DUPRE, ACTRESS
SON: '62 CHRISTOPHER WARDEN
RESIDENCE: MALIBU, CA
TALENT: ACTOR
COMMENT: FOUGHT IN WELTERWEIGHT BOXING MATCHES AS JOHNNY COSTELLO
CREDIT: '53 FROM HERE TO ETERNITY
CREDIT: '57 TWELVE ANGRY MEN
CREDIT: '65 MIRAGE
CREDIT: '73 BILLY TWO HATS
AA-NOM SUP.ACT: '75 SHAMPOO
CREDIT: '78 HEAVEN CAN WAIT

WARFIELD, WILLIAM   BORN: WILLIAM CEASAR WARFIELD
                                  JAN 20,'20 AT HELENA, AK
    FATHER: ROBERT ELZA WARFIELD
    MOTHER: BERTHA MCCAMERY
    *** MARRIED: '52 LEONTYNE PRICE, SINGER (DIVORCED '72)
    TALENT: ACTOR-SINGER
    CREDIT: '51 SHOWBOAT
    CREDIT: '52 PORGY AND BESS
    CREDIT: CALL ME MISTER
    CREDIT: THE GREEN PASTURES

WARHOL, ANDY
                          AUG 06,'28 AT PITTSBURGH, PA
    FATHER: JAMES WARHOL
    MOTHER: JULIA VON
    BROTHER: PAUL WARHOL
    BROTHER: JOHN WARHOL
    FRIEND: NICO
    FRIEND: MARIO MONTEZ
    FRIEND: INGRID SUPERSTAR
    TALENT: ACTOR, DIRECTOR, ARTIST
    CREDIT: '63 SLEEP
    CREDIT: '64 BLOW JOB
    CREDIT: '65 HARLOT
    CREDIT: '66 THE CHELSEA GIRLS
    CREDIT: '69 F**K, OR (BLUE MOVIE)

WATERS, ETHEL
                          OCT 31,'00 AT CHESTER, PA   DIED IN '77
    FATHER: JOHN WESLEY WATERS
    MOTHER: LOUISA TAR ANDERSON
    *** MARRIED: --, MARRIED AT AGE 12 1/2 (DIVORCED)
    *** MARRIED: EDDIE MALLORY (DIVORCED)
    FRIEND: COUNT BASIE, MUSICIAN
    FRIEND: BILLY GRAHAM, EVANGELIST
    RESIDENCE: LOS ANGELES, CA
    MEMOIRS: '51 TO ME IT'S WONDERFUL
    MEMOIRS: '72 HIS EYE IS ON THE SPARROW
    TALENT: SINGER, ACTRESS
    CREDIT: '29 ON WITH THE SHOW
    CREDIT: '42 TALES OF MANHATTAN
    AA-NOM SUP.ACT: '49 PINKY
    CREDIT: '52 MEMBER OF THE WEDDING
    CREDIT: '59 THE SOUND AND THE FURY

WAYNE, DAVID   BORN: DAVID WAYNE MCMEEKAN
                              JAN 30,'14 AT TRAVERSE CITY,MH
    FATHER: DAVID JAMES MCMEEKAN
    MOTHER: HELEN MASON
    *** MARRIED: '40 JANE GORDON TRIX, ACTRESS
    DAUGHTER: '41 MELINDA WAYNE, TWIN
    DAUGHTER: '41 SUSAN WAYNE, TWIN
    SON: '42 TIMOTHY WAYNE
    RESIDENCE: WESTPORT, CN
    TALENT: ACTOR
    CREDIT: '49 ADAM'S RIB
    CREDIT: '52 WAIT TILL THE SUN SHINES NELLIE

```
        CREDIT:  '57 THE THREE FACES OF EVE
        CREDIT:  '60 THE BIG GAMBLE
        CREDIT:  '70 THE ANDROMEDA STRAIN
```

WAYNE, JOHN　　　　BORN: MARION MICHAEL MORRISON
```
                         MAY 26,'07 AT WINTERSET, IO
        FATHER: CLYDE MORRISON, PHARMICIST
        MOTHER: MARY BROWN
        BROTHER: ROBERT MORRISON
        *** MARRIED:  '32 JOSEPHINE SAENZ, DAUGHTER PANAMANIAN DIPLOMAT  (DIVORCED '44)
        SON:  '34 MICHAEL A. MORRISON, AKA MICHAEL WAYNE-PRODUCER
        SON:  '39 PATRICK MORRISON, ACTOR
        DAUGHTER:  '40 ANTONIA MORRISON
        DAUGHTER:  '41 MELINDA MORRISON
        *** MARRIED:  '46 ESPERANZA 'CHATA' BAUER, ACTRESS  (DIVORCED '53)
        *** MARRIED:  '54 PILAR PALLETT, DAUGHTER OF A PERUVIAN SENATOR
        DAUGHTER:  '55 AISSA MORRISON
        SON:  '62 ETHAN MORRISON
        DAUGHTER:  '66 MARISA MORRISON
        FRIEND: TOM MIX, ACTOR
        FRIEND: PATRICIA STACY, SECRETARY
        FRIEND: YAKIMA CANUTT
        RESIDENCE: NEWPORT BEACH, CA
        POSSESSION:  '52 BATJAC FILM PRODUCTION CO.
        POSSESSION: CATTLE RANCH, STANFIELD, ARIZO NA
        BIOGRAPHY:  '71 DUKE, BY MIKE TOMKIN
        TALENT: ACTOR
        COMMENT: FOOTBALL TEAM TACKLE USC
        CREDIT:  '29 SALUTE
        CREDIT:  '39 STAGECOACH
        AA-NOM  ACTOR:  '49 SANDS OF IWO JIMA
        CREDIT:  '54 THE HIGH AND THE MIGHTY
        AA-WIN  ACTOR:  '69 TRUE GRIT
        CREDIT:  '73 CAHILL
```

WEAVER, DENNIS
```
                         JUN 04,'24 AT JOPLIN, MR
        *** MARRIED:  '45 GERALDINE STOVELL
        SON:  '48 RICHARD WEAVER, FILM EDITOR, ACTOR  (MARRIED '75)
        DAUGHTER-IN-LAW: ALICE ORNSTEIN
        SON:  '53 ROBERT WEAVER
        SON:  '59 RUSTIN WEAVER, ACTOR
        RESIDENCE: ENCINO, CA
        POSSESSION:  '60 EMMY AWARD FOR GUNSMOKE TV SERIES
        POSSESSION:  '77 CABIN AT LAKE ARROWHEAD, CA
        POSSESSION: DANDY MIKE AND COSMIC PRINCE - RACE HORSES
        TALENT: ACTOR, DIRECTOR
        COMMENT: PRESIDENT, SCREEN ACTORS GUILD ELECTED IN 1973
        CREDIT:  '52 THE RAIDERS
        CREDIT:  '55 SEVEN ANGRY MEN
        CREDIT:  '58 TOUCH OF EVIL
        CREDIT:  '66 DUEL AT DIABLO
        CREDIT:  '70 MCCLOUD, TV SERIES
```

WEBB, CLIFTON   BORN: WEBB PARMALEE HOLLENBECK
                                  NOV 09,'91 AT INDIANAPOLIS, IN DIED IN '66
   MOTHER: MABELLE HOLLENBECK
   RESIDENCE: BEVERLY HILLS, CA
   RESIDENCE: GREENWICH, CONNECTICUT
   POSSESSION: '44 CONTRACT AT 20TH CENTURY FOX
   TALENT: ACTOR
   CREDIT: '20 POLLY WITH A PAST
   AA-NOM SUP.ACT: '44 LAURA
   AA-NOM SUP.ACT: '46 THE RAZOR'S EDGE
   AA-NOM ACTOR: '48 SITTING PRETTY
   CREDIT: '62 SATAN NEVER SLEEPS

WEBB, JACK   BORN: JACK RANDOLPH WEBB
                               APR 02,'20 AT SANTA MONICA, CA
   FATHER: SAMUEL CHESTER WEBB
   MOTHER: MARGARET SMITH
   *** MARRIED: '47 JULIE LONDON (DIVORCED '54)
   DAUGHTER: '50 STACEY WEBB
   DAUGHTER: '52 LISA WEBB
   *** MARRIED: '55 DOROTHY TOWNE (DIVORCED '57)
   *** MARRIED: '58 JACKIE LOUGHERY (DIVORCED '64)
   TALENT: ACTOR, PRODUCER, DIRECTOR
   CREDIT: '50 THE MAN
   CREDIT: '54 DRAGNET
   CREDIT: '55 PETE KELLY'S BLUES
   CREDIT: '57 THE D. I.
   CREDIT: '62 THE LAST TIME I SAW ARCHIE

WEISSMULLER, JOHNNY   BORN: PETER JOHN WEISSMULLER
                                        JUN 02,'04 AT WINDBER, PA
   *** MARRIED: CAMILLA LOUIER
   *** MARRIED: '30 BOBBE ARNST, SINGER (DIVORCED '32)
   *** MARRIED: '33 LUPE VELEZ, ACTRESS (DIVORCED '38)
   *** MARRIED: '39 BERYL SCOTT (DIVORCED '43)
   DAUGHTER: '39 WENDY WEISSMULLER
   SON: '40 JOHN WEISSMULLER, JR.
   DAUGHTER: '42 HEIDI WEISSMULLER
   *** MARRIED: '48 ALLENE GATES, GOLFER (DIVORCED '62)
   *** MARRIED: '63 MARIA BROCK MANDELL
   RESIDENCE: FORT LAUDERDALE, FL
   MEMOIRS: WATER, WORLD & WEISSUMULLER
   TALENT: SWIMMER-ACTOR
   COMMENT: WON 5 OLYMPIC GOLD MEDALS WON 67 WORLD RECORDS
   COMMENT: SWIMMING 52 NATIONAL RECORDS
   CREDIT: '32 TARZAN THE APE MAN, SERIES
   CREDIT: '42 JUNGLE JIM, SERIES
   CREDIT: '46 SWAMP FIRE
   CREDIT: '70 THE PHYNX

WELCH, RAQUEL   BORN: RAQUEL TEJADA
                                  SEP 05,'40 AT CHICAGO, IL
   FATHER: ARMAND TEJADA
   MOTHER: JOSEPHINE HALL
   *** MARRIED: '59 JAMES WESTLEY WELCH (DIVORCED '65)
   SON: '60 DAMON WELCH
   DAUGHTER: '62 TAHNEE WELCH

```
*** MARRIED:  '67 PATRICK CURTIS, ACTOR, PRODUCER  (DIVORCED '71)
FRIEND: BARRY FROST, MANAGER
RESIDENCE: BEVERLY HILLS, CA
POSSESSION:  '67 CURTWELL, INC
TALENT: MODEL, ACTESS
CREDIT:  '64 ROUSTABOUT
CREDIT:  '69 MYRA BRECKINRIDGE
CREDIT:  '72 KANSAS CITY BOMBER
CREDIT:  '73 THE THREE MUSKETEERS
CREDIT:  '75 MOTHER,JUGS, AND SPEED
----------------------------------------------------------------------------------------------
WELD, TUESDAY          BORN:  SUSAN KER WELD
                              AUG 27,'43 AT NYC
   FATHER: LATHROP MOTLEY WELD
   MOTHER: AILEEN KER, MODEL
   SISTER: SALLY WELD
   BROTHER: DAVID WELD
   *** MARRIED:  '65 CLAUDE HARZ  (DIVORCED '71)
   DAUGHTER:  '66 NATASHA HARZ
   *** MARRIED:  '75 DUDLEY MOORE, ACTOR
   SON:  '76 PATRICK MOORE
   TALENT: ACTRESS
   CREDIT:  '56 ROCK, ROCK, ROCK
   CREDIT:  '62 WILD IN THE COUNTRY
   CREDIT:  '68 PRETTY POISON
   CREDIT:  '73 PLAY IT AS IT LAYS
   AA-NOM SUP.ACT:  '77 LOOKING FOR MR. GOODBAR
----------------------------------------------------------------------------------------------
WELLES, ORSON          BORN:  GEORGE ORSON WELLES
                              MAY 06,'15 AT KENOSHA, WI
   FATHER: RICHARD HEAD WELLES, INVENTOR
   MOTHER: BEATRICE IVES, PIANIST, POLITICAL SUFFRAGETTE
   BROTHER: RICHARD WELLES
   *** MARRIED:  '34 VIRGINIA NICHOLSON  (DIVORCED '40)
   SON:  '38 CHRISTOPHER WELLES
   *** MARRIED:  '43 RITA HAYWORTH, ACTRESS  (DIVORCED '47)
   BROTHER-IN-LAW: EDUARDO CANSINO, JR., ACTOR
   FATHER-IN-LAW: EDUARDO CANSINO, DANCER
   MOTHER-IN-LAW: VOLGA HAWORTH, DANCER
   DAUGHTER:  '44 REBECCA WELLES
   *** MARRIED:  '55 PAOLA MARI
   DAUGHTER:  '56 BEATRICE WELLES
   FRIEND: CHARLES LEDERER, WRITER
   FRIEND: PETER BOGDANOVICH, PRODUCER
   FRIEND: GEORGE 'SHORTY' CHIRELLO, ACTOR, COOK AND HIS CHAUFFEUR
   RESIDENCE: LOS ANGELES, CA
   POSSESSION:  '37 MERCURY THEATRE GROUP PARTNER-JOHN HOUSEMAN
   POSSESSION:  '39 CONTRACT AT R.K.O STUDIOS
   BIOGRAPHY:  '73 ORSON WELLES, BY PETER BOGDANOVICH
   TALENT: WRITER DIRECTOR-ACTOR
   AA-NOM  ACTOR:  '41 CITIZEN KANE
   AA-NOM  DIRECTOR:  '41 CITIZEN KANE
   CREDIT:  '48 MACBETH
   CREDIT:  '49 THE THIRD MAN
   AA-SPECIAL AWARD:  '70 HONORARY AWARD FOR SUPERLATIVE ARTISTRY AND VERSATILITY
   CREDIT:  '74 THE FAKE
```

WERNER, OSKAR   BORN: OSKAR JOSEPH BSCHLIESSMAYER
                           NOV 13,'22 AT VIENNA, AUSTRIA
   FATHER: OSKAR BSCHLIESSMAYER
   MOTHER: STEFANIE KAROLINE ZELTA
   *** MARRIED: '46 ELISABETH KALLINA, ACTRESS (DIVORCED '50)
   DAUGHTER: '47 ELEANORE WERNER
   *** MARRIED: '54 ANNE POWER
   FATHER-IN-LAW: TYRONE POWER, ACTOR
   MOTHER-IN-LAW: SUZANNE CARPENTIER, KNOWN AS ANNABELLA-ACTRESS
   RESIDENCE: VADUZ, LICHTENSTEIN
   TALENT: ACTOR-DIRECTOR
   CREDIT: '49 EROICA
   CREDIT: '61 JULES AND JIM
   AA-NOM ACTOR: '65 SHIP OF FOOLS
   CREDIT: '66 FARHENHEIT 451
   CREDIT: '68 INTERLUDE

WEST, MAE
                         AUG 17,'92 AT BROOKLYN,NY
   FATHER: JOHN PATRICK WEST, HEAVYWEIGHT BOXER
   MOTHER: MATILDA DELKER-DOLGER
   SISTER: BEVERLY WEST
   BROTHER: JOHN EDWIN WEST
   *** MARRIED: '11 FRANK WALLACE (DIVORCED '43)
   POSSESSION: '32 CONTRACT AT PARAMOUNT
   POSSESSION: BEACH HOUSE AT SANTA MONICA, CA
   MEMOIRS: '56 GOODNESS HAD NOTHING TO DO WITH IT
   MEMOIRS: THE CONSTANT SINNER
   MEMOIRS: DIAMOND LIL
   TALENT: ACTRESS-AUTHOR
   COMMENT: MAE WEST LIFE-SAVING JACKET NAMED IN HER HONOR
   CREDIT: '32 NIGHT AFTER NIGHT, DEBUT
   CREDIT: '33 SHE DONE HIM WRONG
   CREDIT: '39 MY LITTLE CHICKADEE
   CREDIT: '43 THE HEATS ON
   CREDIT: '70 MYRA BECKINRIDGE

WHITE, PEARL   BORN: PEARL FAY WHITE
                         MAR 04,'89 AT GREEN RIDGE, MR DIED IN '39
   FATHER: EDWARD G. WHITE
   MOTHER: ELIZABETH HOUSE
   SISTER: OPAL WHITE, DIED AGED 3 - DIPHTHERIA
   SISTER: GRACE WHITE
   BROTHER: GEORGE WHITE
   BROTHER: FRED WHITE
   *** MARRIED: '07 VICTOR SUTHERLAND, ACTOR (DIVORCED '14)
   *** MARRIED: '18 WALLACE MCCUTCHEON (DIVORCED '21)
   ROMANCE: THEODORE COZZIKA
   FRIEND: BLANCHE RUBENSTEIN, ACTRESS
   RESIDENCE: BAYSIDE, LONG ISLAND, NY
   RESIDENCE: GAZERAN, RAMBOUILLET, FRANCE
   MEMOIRS: '19 JUST ME
   TALENT: ACTRESS
   CREDIT: '12 MAYBLOSSOM
   CREDIT: '14 THE EXPLOITS OF ELAINE, SERIES
   CREDIT: '15 THE PERILS OF PAULINE, SERIES
   CREDIT: '24 PARISIAN NIGHTS

CREDIT: '25 THE PERILS OF PARIS

WHITING, MARGARET
                              JUL 22,'24 AT DETROIT,MH
   FATHER: RICHARD WHITING, COMPOSER (DIED '39)
   SISTER: BARBARA WHITING
   *** MARRIED: HUBBELL ROBINSON (DIVORCED)
   *** MARRIED: '50 LOUIS BUSCH, KNOWN AS JOE 'FINGERS' CARR (DIVORCED '53)
   DAUGHTER: '51 DEBORAH BUSCH
   *** MARRIED: '58 JOHN RICHARD MOORE (DIVORCED '61)
   TALENT: SINGER-ACTRESS
   CREDIT: '56 FRESH FROM PARIS
   CREDIT: UNDERWORLD INFORMER

WHITMAN, STUART   BORN: STUART MAXWELL WHITMAN
                              FEB 01,'29 AT SAN FRANCISCO,CA
   *** MARRIED: '52 PATRICIA LALONDE (DIVORCED '66)
   SON: '53 ANTHONY WHITMAN
   SON: '54 MICHAEL WHITMAN
   DAUGHTER: '56 LINDA WHITMAN
   SON: '58 SCOTT WHITMAN
   *** MARRIED: '66 CAROLINE DOUBIS
   TALENT: ACTOR
   CREDIT: '52 WHEN WORLDS COLLIDE
   CREDIT: '58 TEN NORTH FREDERICK
   AA-NOM ACTOR: '61 THE MARK
   CREDIT: '65 SANDS OF KALAHARI
   CREDIT: '71 CAPTAIN APACHE

WHITMORE, JAMES   BORN: JAMES ALLEN WHITMORE, JR.
                              OCT 01,'21 AT WHITE PLAINS, NY
   FATHER: JAMES A. WHITMORE, CIVIC OFFICIAL
   MOTHER: FLORENCE BELLE CRANE
   *** MARRIED: '47 NANCY MYGATT
   SON: '48 JAMES WHITMORE, III
   SON: '50 STEPHEN WHITMORE
   SON: '52 DANIEL WHITMORE
   *** MARRIED: '71 AUDRA LINDLEY
   TALENT: ACTOR
   AA-NOM SUP.ACT: '49 BATTLEGROUND
   CREDIT: '53 KISS ME KATE
   CREDIT: '60 WHO WAS THAT LADY?
   CREDIT: '68 PLANET OF THE APES
   AA-NOM ACTOR: '75 GIVE 'EM HELL, HARRY!

WHITTY, DAME MAY
                         JUN 19,'65 AT LIVERPOOL, ENGLAND DIED IN '48
   GRANDFATHER: MICHAEL JAMES WHITTY, PUBLISHER
   FATHER: ALFRED WHITTY, JOURNALIST
   MOTHER: MARY L. ASHTON
   DAUGHTER: '05 MARGARET WEBSTER, DIRECTOR (DIED '73)
   *** MARRIED: '92 BEN WEBSTER,   ACTOR (DIED '47)
   RESIDENCE: BEVERLY HILLS, CA
   POSSESSION: ORDER OF THE BRITISH EMPIRE - HONORS LIST OF 1918
   TALENT: ACTRESS
   AA-NOM SUP.ACT: '37 NIGHT MUST FALL
   CREDIT: '38 THE LADY VANISHES
   AA-NOM SUP.ACT: '42 MRS. MINIVER

CREDIT: '44 THE WHITE CLIFFS OF DOVER
CREDIT: '47 GREEN DOLPHIN STREET

WIDMARK, RICHARD
                          DEC 26,'14 AT SUNRISE, MN
FATHER: CARL H. WIDMARK, SALESMAN
MOTHER: ETHEL MAE BARR
BROTHER: DONALD WIDMARK
*** MARRIED: '42 JEAN HAZELWOOD
DAUGHTER: ANNE WIDMARK (MARRIED '69)
SON-IN-LAW: SANDY KOUFAX, BASEBALL PLAYER
RESIDENCE: BRENTWOOD, CA
POSSESSION: FARM NEAR SANTA BARBARA, CA
TALENT: ACTOR
AA-NOM SUP.ACT: '47 KISS OF DEATH
CREDIT: '55 A PRIZE OF GOLD
CREDIT: '65 THE BEDFORD INCIDENT
CREDIT: '69 A TALENT FOR LOVING
CREDIT: '72 WHEN THE LEGENDS DIE
CREDIT: '78 THE SWARM

WILDE, CORNEL
                          OCT 13,'15 AT NYC
FATHER: LOUIS BELA WILDE
MOTHER: RENEE VID
*** MARRIED: '38 PATRICIA KNIGHT (DIVORCED '51)
DAUGHTER: '43 WENDY WILDE
*** MARRIED: '51 JEAN WALLACE, ACTRESS
STEP-SON: THOMAS JEFFERSON TONE
STEP-SON: PASCAL F. TONE
TALENT: ACTOR-DIRECTOR
CREDIT: '40 LADY WITH RED HAIR
AA-NOM ACTOR: '45 A SONG TO REMEMBER
CREDIT: '47 FOREVER AMBER
CREDIT: '66 THE NAKED PREY
CREDIT: '71 NO BLADE OF GRASS

WILDER, GENE   BORN: GERALD SILBERMAN
                          JUN 11,'34 AT MILWAUKEE, WI
FATHER: WILLIAM J. SILBERMAN
MOTHER: JEANNE BAER
*** MARRIED: '67 MARY JOAN SCHULTZ
ADOPTED DAUGHTER: KATHARINE ANASTASIA WILDER
ROMANCE: TERRI GARR
RESIDENCE: LOS ANGELES, CA
TALENT: ACTOR
CREDIT: '67 BONNIE AND CLYDE
AA-NOM SUP.ACT: '68 THE PRODUCERS
CREDIT: '71 WILLY WONKA AND THE CHOCOLATE FACTORY
CREDIT: '75 YOUNG FRANKENSTEIN
CREDIT: '76 SILVER STREAK

WILDING, MICHAEL
                          JUL 23,'12 AT WESTCLIFF, ESSEX, ENGLAND
FATHER: HENRY WILDING
MOTHER: ETHEL THOMPSON
*** MARRIED: '37 KAY YOUNG (DIVORCED '52)
*** MARRIED: '52 ELIZABETH TAYLOR, ACTRESS (DIVORCED '57)

```
SON:    '53 MICHAEL HOWARD WILDING, JR.
DAUGHTER-IN-LAW: BETH CLUTTER  (MARRIED '70)
DAUGHTER-IN-LAW: JOHANNA LYKKE-DAHN
SON:    '55 CHRISTOPHER EDWARD WILDING
*** MARRIED:  '58 SUSAN NELL
*** MARRIED:  '64 MARGARET LEIGHTON, ACTRESS
GRANDDAUGHTER:  '71 LEYLA WILDING
GRANDDAUGHTER:  '75 NAOMI WILDING
RESIDENCE: CHICHESTER, ENGLAND
TALENT: ACTOR
CREDIT:   '35 WEDDING GROUP
CREDIT:   '47 AN IDEAL HUSBAND
CREDIT:   '57 DANGER WITHIN
CREDIT:   '68 THE SWEET RIDE
CREDIT:   '72 LADY CAROLINE LAMB
```

WILLIAMS, ANDY
```
                        DEC 03,'30 AT WALL LAKE, IO
    FATHER: JAY EMERSON WILLIAMS
    MOTHER: FLORENCE FINLEY
    SISTER: JANE WILLIAMS
    BROTHER: RICHARD WILLIAMS
    BROTHER: ROBERT WILLIAMS
    BROTHER: DONALD WILLIAMS
    *** MARRIED:  '61 CLAUDINE LONGET, SINGER  (DIVORCED '75)
    DAUGHTER:  '63 NOELLE WILLIAMS
    SON:   '65 CHRISTIAN WILLIAMS
    SON:   '70 ROBERT WILLIAMS
    ROMANCE: LAURIE WRIGHT
    POSSESSION: '60 COLLECTION OF MODERN ART
    TALENT: ACTOR-SINGER
    COMMENT: WILLIAMS BROTHERS SINGERS
    CREDIT: SOMETHING IN THE WIND
    CREDIT: I'D RATHER BE RICH
```

WILLIAMS, ESTHER   BORN: ESTHER JANE WILLIAMS
```
                        AUG 08,'23 AT INGLEWOOD, CA
    FATHER: LOU WILLIAMS, ARTIST
    MOTHER: BULA
    SISTER: MAUREEN WILLIAMS
    *** MARRIED:  '41 LEONARD KOVNER  (DIVORCED '44)
    *** MARRIED:  '45 BEN GAGE, RADIO ANNOUNCER  (DIVORCED '57)
    SON:   '49 BENJAMIN GAGE
    SON:   '50 KIMBALL GAGE
    DAUGHTER:  '53 SUSAN GAGE
    *** MARRIED:  '63 FERNANDO LAMAS
    STEP-DAUGHTER: ALEJANDRE LAMAS
    STEP-SON: LORENZO FERNANDO LAMAS
    ROMANCE: JEFF CHANDLER, ACTOR
    RESIDENCE: SANTA MONICA, CA
    TALENT: SWIMMER-ACTRESS
    COMMENT: STAGE 30 AT MGM SPECIALLY DESIGNED WATERTANK
    CREDIT:   '42 THRILL OF A ROMANCE, DEBUT
    CREDIT:   '52 MILLION DOLLAR MERMAID
    CREDIT:   '53 DANGEROUS WHEN WET
    CREDIT:   '61 THE BIG SHOW
```

WILLIAMS, GUINN "BIG BOY"
APR 26,'99 AT DECATUR, TX   DIED IN '62
```
FATHER: GUINN WILLIAMS, SR., CONGRESSMAN
MOTHER: MINNIE LEE
SISTER: MINNIE LEE WILLIAMS
SISTER: LUCILLE WILLIAMS
*** MARRIED: DOROTHY
SON: MALCOLM WILLIAMS, ACTOR
ROMANCE: MARY PHILBIN, ACTRESS
RESIDENCE: SAN FERNANDO VALLEY, CA
POSSESSION: RANCH AT SPOFFORD, TEXAS
TALENT: ACTOR, POLITICIAN
COMMENT: ELECTED TO U.S. CONGRESS FROM TEXAS
CREDIT:  '29 NOAHS ARK
CREDIT:  '42 MR. WISE GUY
CREDIT:  '44 THIRTY SECONDS OVER TOKYO
CREDIT:  '55 THE OUTLAW'S DAUGHTER
CREDIT:  '62 THE COMANCHEROS
```

WILLS, CHILL
JUL 18,'03 AT SEAGOVILLE, TX
```
*** MARRIED:  '28 BETTY CHAPPELLE  (DIED '71)
DAUGHTER:  '39 JILL WILLS
SON:  '42 WILL WILLS
*** MARRIED:  '73 NOVADEEN GOOGE  (DIVORCED '74)
RESIDENCE: ENCINO, CA
POSSESSION: GRAIN CO. & STEAK HOUSE CHAIN
TALENT: ACTOR
CREDIT:  '40 BOOM TOWN
CREDIT:  '48 RAW DEAL
CREDIT:  '53 CITY THAT NEVER SLEEPS
AA-NOM SUP.ACT:  '60 THE ALAMO
CREDIT:  '62 THE DEADLY COMPANIONS
```

WILSON, MARIE   BORN: KATHERINE ELIZABETH WILSON
DEC 30,'17 AT ANAHEIM, CA DIED IN '72
```
*** MARRIED: NICK GRINDE, DIRECTOR  (DIVORCED)
*** MARRIED: ALAN NIXON, ACTOR  (DIVORCED)
*** MARRIED:  '51 BOB FALLON, DIRECTOR
SON: GREGSON FALLON
FRIEND: KEN MURRAY, ACTOR-WRITER
TALENT: ACTRESS
CREDIT:  '36 SATAN MET A LADY
CREDIT:  '40 BOY MEETS GIRL
CREDIT:  '49 MY FRIEND IRMA
CREDIT:  '54 MARRY ME AGAIN
CREDIT:  '62 MR. HOBBS TAKES A VACATION
```

WINCHELL, WALTER   BORN: WALTER WINCHEL
APR 07,'97 AT NYC   DIED IN '72
```
FATHER: JACOB WINECHEL, AKA - JAKE WINCHEL
MOTHER: JANETTE BAKST
BROTHER: ALGERNON WINCHEL
*** MARRIED:  '17 MARIE 'RITA' GREEN, VAUDEVILLE PARTNER  (DIVORCED '18)
*** MARRIED:  '19 JUNE MAGEE  (DIED '70)
DAUGHTER:  '27 EILEEN JEAN 'WALDA' WINCHELL, ACTRESS - TONI EDEN
SON-IN-LAW: WILLIAM F. LAWLESS, DESIGNER
```

```
SON-IN-LAW: HYATT VON DEHN, HOTELMAN  (MARRIED '55)
SON:  '36 WALTER WINCHELL, JR.  (SUICIDE '69)
DAUGHTER-IN-LAW: EVA ANNELIES
ADOPTED DAUGHTER: GLORIA WINCHELL  (DIED)
GRANDDAUGHTER: KENYA ALISE WINCHELL
GRANDDAUGHTER: MARY ELIZABETH VON DEHN
GRANDSON: OWEN REED WINCHELL
FRIEND: ROSE BIGMAN, SECRETARY FOR 40 YEARS
PARTNER: GEORGE JESSEL, ACTOR
RESIDENCE: SCOTTSDALE, AR & NYC
MEMOIRS:  '75 WINCHELL EXCLUSIVE
TALENT: ACTOR, JOURNALIST
COMMENT: FOUNDED DAMON RUNYON CANCER FUND IN 1946
CREDIT:  '37 LOVE AND HISSES
CREDIT: WAKE UP AND LIVE
```

```
WINDSOR, CLAIRE          BORN:  OLGA VIOLA CRONK
                         APR 14,'97 AT CAWKER CITY, KA   DIED IN '72
MOTHER: ROSELLA  (DIED '50)
SISTER: NELLIE MAE CRONK
*** MARRIED:  '17 DAVID WILLIS BOWES  (DIVORCED '20)
SON:  '18 WILLIAM W. BOWES, AKA - WILLIAM WINDSOR
*** MARRIED:  '25 BERT LYTELL, ACTOR, DIRECTOR  (DIVORCED '27)
BROTHER-IN-LAW: WILFRED LYTELL, ACTOR
ROMANCE: ANTHONY J. TSAKLAKIS, LAWYER
ROMANCE: PHILIP MORGAN HAYWARD PLANT
ROMANCE: ALFRED C. READ, JR., FINANCIER
ROMANCE: THOMAS F. MANVILLE, JR., ABESTOS MANUFACTURING HEIR
ROMANCE: ERSKINE GWYNNE VANDERBILT
FRIEND: CHARLES 'BUDDY' ROGERS
FRIEND: DAGMAR GODOWSKY, ACTRESS
ENEMY: MARIAN YOUNG READ
POSSESSION:  '22 CONTRACT WITH SAM GOLDWYN
POSSESSION: FISHING BOAT 'CONQUEST'
TALENT: ACTRESS
CREDIT: THE MODERN FLAPPER
CREDIT: RICH MEN'S WIVES
CREDIT: WHAT WIVES WANT
CREDIT: DANCE MADNESS
CREDIT: THE LITTLE JOURNEY
```

```
WINDSOR, MARIE          BORN:  EMILY MARIE BERTELSON
                        DEC 11,'17 AT MARYVALE,UT  DIED IN '72
*** MARRIED:  '47 TED STEELE  (DIED '47)
*** MARRIED:  '54 JACK HUPP
SON:  '55 RICHARD HUPP
TALENT: ACTRESS
COMMENT: WON MISS UTAH BEAUTY CONTEST
CREDIT:  '41 ALL AMERICAN COED, DEBUT
CREDIT:  '51 THE NARROW MARGIN
CREDIT:  '57 THE UNHOLY WIFE
CREDIT:  '66 CHAMBER OF HORRORS
CREDIT:  '73 WEDNESDAY MORNING
```

WINKLER, HENRY
OCT 30,'45 AT NYC
FATHER: HARRY WINKLER
MOTHER: ILSE
SISTER: BEATRICE WINKLER
*** MARRIED: '78 STACEY WEITZMAN, PUBLICIST
RESIDENCE: HOLLYWOOD HILLS, CA
POSSESSION: '70 M.A. DEGREE - YALE UNIVERSITY
POSSESSION: '77 GOLDEN GLOBE AWARD FOR HAPPY DAYS - TV SERIES
TALENT: ACTOR
CREDIT: '74 THE LORDS OF FLATBUSH
CREDIT: '77 HEROES

WINTERS, JONATHAN   BORN: JONATHAN HARSHMAN WINTERS
NOV 11,'25 AT DAYTON, OH
FATHER: JONATHAN HARSHMAN
MOTHER: ALICE KILGORE RODGERS WINTERS
*** MARRIED: '48 EILEEN ANN SCHAUDER
SON: '50 JONATHAN 'JAY' WINTERS
DAUGHTER: '56 LUCINDA KELLEY WINTERS
MEMOIRS: THE IRON CLOWN
TALENT: ACTOR, ARTIST
CREDIT: '63 IT'S A MAD, MAD, MAD, MAD WORLD, DEBUT
CREDIT: '65 THE LOVED ONE
CREDIT: '66 THE RUSSIANS ARE COMING
CREDIT: '67 OH DAD POOR DAD
CREDIT: '69 VIVA MAX

WINTERS, SHELLEY   BORN: SHIRLEY SCHRIFT
AUG 18,'22 AT ST. LOUIS, MR
FATHER: JOHAN SCHRIFT, CLOTHING DESIGNER
MOTHER: ROSE WINTER, OPERA SINGER
SISTER: BLANCHE SCHRIFT
*** MARRIED: '42 MACK MEYER, TEXTILE SALESMAN (DIVORCED '48)
*** MARRIED: '52 VITTORIO GASSMAN, ACTOR (DIVORCED '54)
DAUGHTER: '53 VITTORIA GASSMAN
*** MARRIED: '57 ANTHONY FRANCIOSA, ACTOR (DIVORCED '60)
ROMANCE: FARLEY GRANGER, ACTOR
FRIEND: BERT MARX, AGENT
POSSESSION: '43 COLUMBIA PICTURES CONTRACT
TALENT: ACTRESS
CREDIT: '44 SHE'S A SOLDIER, TOO
AA-NOM ACTRESS: '51 A PLACE IN THE SUN
AA-WIN SUP.ACT.: '59 THE DIARY OF ANNE FRANK
AA-WIN SUP.ACT.: '65 A PATCH OF BLUE
AA-NOM SUP.ACT: '72 THE POSEIDON ADVENTURE

WINWOOD, ESTELLE
JAN 24,'83 AT LEIGH, LANCS., ENGLAND
FATHER: GEORGE GOODWIN
MOTHER: ROSALIE ELLIS
BROTHER-IN-LAW: EDMUND GWENN, ACTOR
*** MARRIED: '01 ARTHUR CHESNEY (DIVORCED)
*** MARRIED: '19 FRANCIS BARLOW BRADLEY (DIED '29)
*** MARRIED: '30 GUTHRIE MCCLINTIC
*** MARRIED: '45 ROBERT BARTON HENDERSON
FRIEND: TALLULAH BANKHEAD, ACTRESS

```
          RESIDENCE: MT. KISCO, NY
          TALENT: ACTRESS
          CREDIT:  '34 THE HOUSE OF TRENT
          CREDIT:  '56 THE SWAN
          CREDIT:  '58 ALIVE AND KICKING
          CREDIT:  '62 NOTORIOUS LANDLADY
          CREDIT:  '68 THE PRODUCERS
------------------------------------------------------------------------
WOOD, NATALIE        BORN:  NATASHA ZACHARENKO
                            JUL 20,'38 AT SAN FRANCISCO, CA
          FATHER: NICHOLAS GURDIN, SET & STAGE DESIGNER
          MOTHER: MARCI KULEFF, BALLET DANCER
          SISTER: LANA WOOD, ACTRESS
          *** MARRIED:  '57 ROBERT WAGNER  (DIVORCED '62)
          *** MARRIED:  '69 RICHARD GREGSON
          DAUGHTER:  '70 NATASHA GREGSON
          *** MARRIED:  '72 ROBERT WAGNER
          STEP-DAUGHTER: KATHERINE WAGNER
          DAUGHTER:  '74 COURTNEY BROOKE WAGNER
          TALENT: ACTRESS
          CREDIT:  '43 HAPPY LAND
          AA-NOM  SUP.ACT:  '55 REBEL WITHOUT A CAUSE
          AA-NOM  ACTRESS:  '61 SPLENDOR IN THE GRASS
          CREDIT:  '61 WEST SIDE STORY
          AA-NOM  ACTRESS:  '63 LOVE WITH THE PROPER STRANGER
          CREDIT:  '69 BOB AND CAROL AND TED AND ALICE
------------------------------------------------------------------------
WOOD, PEGGY         BORN:  MARGARET PEGGY WOOD
                           FEB 09,'92 AT BROOKLYN, NY  DIED IN '78
          FATHER: EUGENE WOOD
          MOTHER: MARY GARDNER
          *** MARRIED: JOHN VAN ALSTYN WEAVER, AUTHOR  (DIED '38)
          SON:  '28 DAVID WEAVER
          *** MARRIED:  '41 WILLIAM HENRY WALLING, ARMY OFFICER  (DIED '73)
          RESIDENCE: STAMFORD, CN
          RESIDENCE: NYC
          MEMOIRS: HOW YOUNG YOU LOOK
          TALENT: ACTRESS, SINGER, AUTHOR
          CREDIT:  '19 ALMOST A HUSBAND
          CREDIT:  '34 ANDY HARDY
          CREDIT:  '49 MAMA, TV SERIES
          CREDIT:  '60 THE STORY OF RUTH
          AA-NOM  SUP.ACT:  '65 THE SOUND OF MUSIC
------------------------------------------------------------------------
WOODPECKER, WOODY
                           JAN 01,'41 AT PINEWOOD STUDIOS
          FATHER: WALTER LANTZ
          FRIEND: CHILLY WILLY
          RESIDENCE: WESTWOOD, CA
          TALENT: ACTOR
          CREDIT: AUTOBIOGRAPHICAL SERIES
------------------------------------------------------------------------
WOODWARD, JOANNE     BORN:  JOANNE GIGNILLIAT WOODWARD
                           FEB 27,'30 AT THOMASVILLE, GE
          FATHER: WADE WOODWARD, PUBLISHER
          MOTHER: ELINOR TRIMMIER
          BROTHER: WADE WOODWARD, JR., ARCHITECT
          *** MARRIED:  '58 PAUL NEWMAN, ACTOR
```

STEP-DAUGHTER: SUSAN NEWMAN
STEP-SON: SCOTT NEWMAN, ACTOR
DAUGHTER: '59 ELEANOR NEWMAN
STEP-DAUGHTER: STEPHANIE NEWMAN
DAUGHTER: '60 MELISSA NEWMAN
DAUGHTER: '61 CARA NEWMAN
RESIDENCE: WESTPORT, CN
POSSESSION: '54 7 YEAR CONTRACT AT 20TH
TALENT: ACTRESS
AA-WIN ACTRESS: '57 THE THREE FACES OF EVE
CREDIT: '60 FROM THE TERRACE
CREDIT: '63 A NEW KIND OF LOVE
AA-NOM ACTRESS: '68 RACHEL, RACHEL
AA-NOM ACTRESS: '73 SUMMER WISHES, WINTER DREAMS
CREDIT: '78 THE END

WOOLLEY, MONTY   BORN: EDGAR MONTILLION WOOLLEY
                      AUG 17,'88 AT HOTEL BRISTOL, NYC DIED IN '63
FATHER: WILLIAM EDGAR WOOLEY, OWNER OF HOTEL BRISTOL
MOTHER: JESSIE ARMS
BROTHER: JAMES WOOLLEY (DIED '58)
FRIEND: COLE PORTER, MUSICIAN, CLASSMATE AT YALE
FRIEND: GERTRUDE WILLIAMS
RESIDENCE: SARATOGA SPRINGS, NY
POSSESSION: FOLIO OF ORIGINAL PRINTING OF SHAKESPEARE'S PLAYS
TALENT: ACTOR, PROFESSOR
CREDIT: '37 LIVE, LOVE AND LEARN
AA-NOM ACTOR: '42 THE PIED PIPER
CREDIT: '43 HOLY MATRIMONY
AA-NOM SUP.ACT: '44 SINCE YOU WENT AWAY
CREDIT: '46 NIGHT AND DAY, PLAYED AUTOBIOGRAPHICAL ROLE
CREDIT: '55 KISMET
CREDIT: '59 THE MAN WHO CAME TO DINNER

WRAY, FAY
                SEP 10,'07 AT RANCH 'WRAYLAND' ALBERTA, CANADA
SISTER: WILLOW WRAY
*** MARRIED: '29 JOHN MONK SAUNDERS, WRITER (DIVORCED '38)
DAUGHTER: '30 SUSAN SAUNDERS
*** MARRIED: '42 ROBERT RISKIN, WRITER (DIED '55)
DAUGHTER: '43 VICKI RISKIN
SON: '44 ROBERT RISKIN, JR.
*** MARRIED: '71 STANFORD ROTHENBERG, NEUROSURGEON
RESIDENCE: LOS ANGELES, CA
TALENT: ACTRESS
CREDIT: '28 STREET OF SIN
CREDIT: '33 KING KONG
CREDIT: '41 ADAM HAD FOUR SONS
CREDIT: '53 SMALL TOWN GIRL
CREDIT: '56 CRIME OF PASSION

WYATT, JANE   BORN: JANE WADDINGTON WYATT
                   AUG 10,'12 AT CAMPGAW, NJ
FATHER: CHRISTOPHER BILLOP WYATT
MOTHER: EUPHEMIA WADDINGTON
*** MARRIED: '35 EDGAR B. WARD
SON: '37 CHRISTOPHER WARD
SON: '43 MICHAEL WARD

```
RESIDENCE: LOS ANGELES, CA
TALENT: ACTRESS
CREDIT:   '34 ONE MORE RIVER
CREDIT:   '41 KISSES FOR BREAKFAST
CREDIT:   '50 OUR VERY OWN
CREDIT:   '65 NEVER TOO LATE
CREDIT:   '73 TOM SAWYER, TV MOVIE
--------------------------------------------------------------------------------
WYMAN, JANE          BORN:   SARAH JANE FULKS
                             JAN 04,'14 AT ST. JOSEPH, MR
    FATHER: R. D. FULKS, POLITICIAN
    MOTHER: EMMA REISE
    *** MARRIED:   '37 MYRON FUTTERMAN  (DIVORCED '38)
    *** MARRIED:   '40 RONALD REAGAN, ACTOR  (DIVORCED '48)
    SON:   '41 MICHAEL REAGAN
    DAUGHTER:   '42 MAUREEN REAGAN
    *** MARRIED:   '52 FRED KARGER, BANDLEADER  (DIVORCED '54)
    *** MARRIED:   '61 FRED KARGER, REMARRIED
    RESIDENCE: BEVERLY HILLS, CA
    TALENT: ACTRESS
    CREDIT:   '37 GOLD DIGGERS OF 1937
    AA-NOM  ACTRESS:   '46 THE YEARLING
    AA-WIN  ACTRESS:   '48 JOHNNY BELINDA
    AA-NOM  ACTRESS:   '51 THE BLUE VEIL
    AA-NOM  ACTRESS:   '54 THE MAGNIFICENT OBSESSION
--------------------------------------------------------------------------------
WYNN, ED             BORN:   ISAIAH EDWIN LEOPOLD
                             NOV 09,'86 AT PHILADELPHIA, PA   DIED IN '66
    FATHER: JOSEPH LEOPOLD
    MOTHER: MINNIE
    *** MARRIED:   '14 HILDA KEENAN, ACTRESS  (DIVORCED '37)
    SON:   '16 KEENAN WYNN, ACTOR
    *** MARRIED:   '37 FRIEDA MIERS, SHOWGIRL  (DIVORCED '39)
    *** MARRIED:   '46 DOROTHY ELIZABETH NESBITT
    RESIDENCE: HOLLYWOOD, CA
    BIOGRAPHY:   '59 ED WYNN'S SON, BY KEENAN WYNN
    TALENT: ACTOR-WRITER-DIRECTOR
    CREDIT:   '27 RUBBER HEELS
    CREDIT:   '33 THE CHIEF
    CREDIT:   '43 STAGE DOOR CANTEEN
    AA-NOM  SUP.ACT:   '59 THE DIARY OF ANNE FRANK
    CREDIT:   '67 THE GNOME MOBILE
--------------------------------------------------------------------------------
WYNN, KEENAN         BORN:   FRANCIS XAVIER ALOYSIUS KEENAN-WYNN
                             JUL 27,'16 AT NYC
    FATHER: ED WYNN, ACTOR
    MOTHER: HILDA KEENAN, ACTRESS
    STEP-MOTHER: FRIEDA MIERS
    STEP-MOTHER: DOROTHY ELIZABETH NESBITT
    *** MARRIED:   '38 EVE ABBOTT, ACTRESS  (DIVORCED '46)
    SON:   '41 EDMUND WYNN
    SON:   '45 TRACY WYNN
    DAUGHTER-IN-LAW: KRISTIN WASSGREN, MISS SWEDEN
    *** MARRIED:   '49 BETTY JANE BUTLER  (DIVORCED '53)
    *** MARRIED:   '54 SHARLEY JEAN HUDSON
    DAUGHTER:   '55 HILDA WYNN
    DAUGHTER:   '60 EDWYNNA WYNN
    FRIEND: VAN JOHNSON, ACTOR
```

MEMOIRS: AUTOBIOGRAPHY: ED WYNN'S SON
TALENT: ACTOR
CREDIT: '45 UNDER THE CLOCK
CREDIT: '53 KISS ME KATE
CREDIT: '63 DR. STRANGELOVE
CREDIT: '67 THE WAR WAGON
CREDIT: '73 THE LOVE BUG RIDES AGAIN

WYNTER, DANA   BORN: DAGMAR WINTER
                                  JUN 08,'30 AT LONDON, ENGLAND
FATHER: PETER WINTER, DOCTOR
MOTHER: FREDRIQUE SPENCER-MARCUS
*** MARRIED: '56 GREGSON BAUTZER, ATTORNEY (SEPARATED '64)
SON: '60 MARK RAGAN BAUTZER
FRIEND: CHARLES FELDMAN, AGENT, PRODUCER
POSSESSION: '55 CONTACT AT 20TH CENTURY FOX
POSSESSION: COTTAGE IN COUNTY WICKLOW, IRELAND
TALENT: ACTRESS
CREDIT: '51 WHITE CORRIDORS
CREDIT: '55 THE VIEW FROM POMPEY'S HEAD
CREDIT: '57 VALUE
CREDIT: '60 SINK THE BISMARK
CREDIT: '69 AIRPORT
CREDIT: '70 SANTEE

```
------------------------------------------------------------------------
YORK, MICHAEL          BORN:  MICHAEL YORK JOHNSON
                              MAR 27,'42 AT FULMER, ENGLAND
    FATHER: JOSEPH GWYNNE JOHNSON
    MOTHER: FLORENCE EDITH CHOWN
    *** MARRIED:  '68 PATRICIA MCCALLUM, PHOTOGRAPHER
    RESIDENCE: KNIGHTSBRIDGE, LONDON, ENGLAND
    TALENT: ACTOR
    CREDIT:  '67 THE TAMING OF THE SHREW
    CREDIT:  '68 ROMEO AND JULIET
    CREDIT:  '72 CABARET
    CREDIT:  '73 LOST HORIZON
    CREDIT:  '76 LOGAN'S RUN
------------------------------------------------------------------------
YORK, SUSANNAH         BORN:  SUSANNAH YOLANDE FLETCHER
                              JAN 09,'41 AT LONDON, ENGLAND
    *** MARRIED:  '60 MICHAEL WELLS, ACTOR
    DAUGHTER:  '72 SASHA WELLS
    SON:  '73 ORLANDO WELLS
    RESIDENCE: CHELSEA, LONDON, ENGLAND
    TALENT: ACTRESS
    CREDIT:  '60 TUNES OF GLORY, DEBUT
    CREDIT:  '63 TOM JONES
    CREDIT:  '66 A MAN FOR ALL SEASONS
    AA-NOM  SUP.ACT:  '69 THEY SHOOT HORSES, DON'T THEY?
    CREDIT:  '72 IMAGES
------------------------------------------------------------------------
YOUNG, GIG             BORN:  BYRON ELLSWORTH BARR
                              NOV 04,'17 AT ST. CLOUD, MN   DIED IN '78
    FATHER: JOHN EARL BARR
    MOTHER: EMMA DINGMANE
    BROTHER: DONALD BARR
    *** MARRIED:  '39 SHEILA STAPLER  (DIVORCED '47)
    *** MARRIED:  '50 SOPHIE ROSENSTEIN  (DIED '52)
    *** MARRIED:  '57 ELIZABETH MONTGOMERY, ACTRESS  (DIVORCED '63)
    FATHER-IN-LAW: ROBERT MONTGOMERY, ACTOR
    MOTHER-IN-LAW: ELIZABETH BRYAN ALLEN
    *** MARRIED:  '63 ELAINE WHITMAN, AKA- ELAINE WILLIAMS  (DIVORCED '66)
    DAUGHTER:  '64 JENNIFER YOUNG
    *** MARRIED:  '78 KIM SCHMIDT (DIED '78)
    TALENT: ACTOR
    CREDIT:  '40 MISBEHAVING HUSBANDS
    AA-NOM  SUP.ACT:  '51 COME FILL THE CUP
    AA-NOM  SUP.ACT:  '58 TEACHER'S PET
    AA-WIN  SUP.ACT.:  '69 THEY SHOOT HORSES, DON'T THEY?
    CREDIT:  '70 LOVERS AND OTHER STRANGERS
------------------------------------------------------------------------
YOUNG, LORETTA         BORN:  GRETCHEN MICHAELA YOUNG
                              JAN 06,'13 AT SALT LAKE CITY, UT
    FATHER: JOHN EARL YOUNG
    MOTHER: GLADYS ROYAL
    SISTER: POLLY ANN YOUNG, ACTRESS
    STEP-SISTER: GEORGIANNA YOUNG, ACTRESS
    SISTER: ELIZABETH JANE YOUNG, ACTRESS - SALLY BLANE
    BROTHER-IN-LAW: RICARDO MONTALBAN, ACTOR
    BROTHER-IN-LAW: NORMAN FOSTER, DIRECTOR
    BROTHER: JACK YOUNG
    *** MARRIED:  '30 GRANT WITHERS  (ANNULLED '31)
```

```
*** MARRIED:  '40 THOMAS H. A. LEWIS  (DIVORCED '69)
ADOPTED DAUGHTER: JANE LEWIS
ADOPTED DAUGHTER: JUDY LEWIS
SON:  '45 CHRISTOPHER LEWIS
SON:  '49 PETER LEWIS
ROMANCE: CLARK GABLE, ACTOR
ROMANCE: RICHARD CORTEZ, ACTOR
ROMANCE: GEORGE BRENT, ACTOR
ROMANCE: JOSEPH MANKIEWICZ, DIRECTOR
RESIDENCE: BEVERLY HILLS, CA
POSSESSION: COLLECTION OF RELIGIOUS ART & JEWELRY
MEMOIRS:  '62 THE THINGS I HAD TO LEARN
TALENT: ACTRESS
CREDIT:  '28 LAUGH CLOWN LAUGH, DEBUT
CREDIT:  '37 LADIES IN LOVE
AA-WIN  ACTRESS:  '47 THE FARMER'S DAUGHTER
AA-NOM  ACTRESS:  '49 COME TO THE STABLE
CREDIT:  '52 BECAUSE OF YOU
```

YOUNG, ROBERT   BORN: ROBERT GEORGE YOUNG
                                  FEB 22,'07 AT CHICAGO, IL
```
FATHER: THOMAS YOUNG, CARPENTER
MOTHER: MARGARET FYFE
BROTHER: JOSEPH YOUNG
*** MARRIED:  '33 ELIZABETH LOUISE HENDERSON, ACTRESS-BETTY HENDERSON
DAUGHTER:  '33 CAROL YOUNG
DAUGHTER:  '37 BARBARA QUEEN YOUNG
DAUGHTER:  '43 ELIZABETH LOUISE YOUNG
DAUGHTER:  '45 KATHLEEN JOY YOUNG
DAUGHTER:  '59 CAROL YOUNG
FRIEND: OTTO KRUGER, ACTOR
POSSESSION: RANCH NEAR CARMEL, CALIFORNIA
TALENT: ACTOR
CREDIT:  '32 THE BLACK CAMEL, DEBUT
CREDIT:  '41 LADY BE GOOD
CREDIT:  '54 FATHER KNOWS BEST, TV SERIES
CREDIT:  '69 MARCUS WELBY, M.D., TV SERIES
CREDIT:  '72 ALL MY DARLING DAUGHTERS
```

ZETTERLING, MAI
                          MAY 27,'25 AT VASTERAAS, SWEDEN
    FATHER: JOEL ZETTERLING
    MOTHER: LINNEA MARIA TORNBLOM
    *** MARRIED: TUTTE LEMKOW
    *** MARRIED: '58 DAVID HUGHES
    RESIDENCE: LONDON, ENGLAND
    RESIDENCE: ARLES, FRANCE
    TALENT: ACTRESS-DIRECTOR
    COMMENT: MEMBER SWEDISH ROYAL THEATRE COMPANY - 1942-1947
    CREDIT: '43 FRENZY
    CREDIT: '47 FRIEDA
    CREDIT: '55 A PRIZE OF GOLD
    CREDIT: '64 LOVING COUPLES, DIRECTOR
    CREDIT: '66 NIGHT GAMES, DIRECTOR/BASED ON HER BOOK

ZIMBALIST, JR., EFREM
                          NOV 30,'23 AT NYC
    FATHER: EFREM ZIMBALIST, VIOLINIST
    MOTHER: ALMA GLUCK, SOPRANO
    *** MARRIED: '45 EMILY MCNAIR (DIED '50)
    DAUGHTER: '45 NANCY ZIMBALIST
    SON: '46 EFREM ZIMBALIST, III
    *** MARRIED: '56 LORANDA STEPHANIE SPAULDING
    DAUGHTER: '56 STEPHANIE ZIMBALIST, JR., ACTRESS
    *** MARRIED: '72 LORANDA STEPHANIE SPAULDING, REMARRIED
    RESIDENCE: ENCINO, CA
    TALENT: ACTOR
    CREDIT: '50 HOUSE OF STRANGERS
    CREDIT: '57 BAND OF ANGELS
    CREDIT: '61 BY LOVE POSSESSED
    CREDIT: '62 THE CHAPMAN REPORT
    CREDIT: '67 WAIT UNTIL DARK

THE SUPPORTING CAST

(A CROSS-REFERENCE SYSTEM)

AADLAND, BEVERLY
    FLYNN, ERROL
ABBERTSON, EDITH
    FRANCIS, ANNE
ABBOTT, BUD
    COSTELLO, LOU
ABBOTT, DIAHNNE
    DE NIRO, ROBERT
ABBOTT, EVE
    JOHNSON, VAN
    WYNN, KEENAN
ABBOTT, FLORENCE 'BABE'
    ABBOTT, BUD
ABBOTT, GEORGE
    EWELL, TOM
ABBOTT, HARRY
    ABBOTT, BUD
ABBOTT, ISABELLA MARY
    PLUMMER, CHRISTOPHER
ABBOTT, JR., HARRY
    ABBOTT, BUD
ABBOTT, JUDITH ANN
    EWELL, TOM
ABBOTT, OLIVE VICTORIA
    ABBOTT, BUD
ABBOTT, RAE VICTORIA
    ABBOTT, BUD
ABBOTT, WILLIAM HARRY 'BUD'
    ABBOTT, BUD
ABELOFF, DR. ROBT.
    FRANCIS, ANNE
ABELOFF, ELIZABETH JANE
    FRANCIS, ANNE
ABZUG, BELLA
    MACLAINE, SHIRLEY
ACHA, LOLITA DE
    ARNAZ, DESI
ACKER, JEAN
    VALENTINO, RUDOLPH
ACKERMAN, BETTYE LOUISE
    JAFFE, SAM
ADAMS, ADA
    ADAMS, EDIE
ADAMS, ALLYSON LEE
    ADAMS, NICK
ADAMS, ANDREW D.
    ADAMS, NICK
ADAMS, CONSTANCE
    DE MILLE, C. B.
    QUINN, ANTHONY
ADAMS, EDIE
    KOVACS, ERNIE
ADAMS, JEB STUART
    ADAMS, NICK
ADAMS, MELANIE ELAINE
    COMO, PERRY
ADAMS, NEILE
    MCQUEEN, STEVE

ADAMS, PERLINA
    COLE, NAT 'KING'
ADAMS, SALLY
    SAVALAS, TELLY
ADAMS, SHIRLEE MAE
    FONDA, HENRY
    FONDA, JANE
    FONDA, PETER
ADAMS, TOMMY
    TALBOT, LYLE
ADAMSCHOCK, PETER
    ADAMS, NICK
ADAMSON, COTTON
    LYON, SUE
ADDOLARI, JOLANDA
    QUINN, ANTHONY
ADLER, FRIEDEL
    BERGMAN, INGRID
ADLER, JANE
    ROBINSON, EDWARD G.
ADLER, JODY
    SIDNEY, SYLVIA
ADLER, LOU
    EKLAND, BRITT
    FABARES, SHELLEY
ADLER, LUTHER
    SIDNEY, SYLVIA
ADRIAN, GILBERT
    GAYNOR, JANET
ADRIAN, ROBIN
    GAYNOR, JANET
AGAR, JOHN
    TEMPLE, SHIRLEY
AGAR, JOHN G.
    AGAR, JOHN
AGAR, LINDA SUSAN
    AGAR, JOHN
    TEMPLE, SHIRLEY
AGAR, MARTIN DAVID
    AGAR, JOHN
AGAR, 3RD, JOHN GEORGE
    AGAR, JOHN
AGEE, JANE CAMERON
    BROLIN, JAMES
AHERNE, BRIAN
    DE HAVILLAND, OLIVIA
    FONTAINE, JOAN
AHERNE, ELANA
    AHERNE, BRIAN
AHERNE, PATRICK
    AHERNE, BRIAN
AHERNE, WILLIAM DE LACY
    AHERNE, BRIAN
AIMEE, ANOUK
    FINNEY, ALBERT
    O'NEAL, RYAN
AINSWORTH, PHIL
    LA MARR, BARBARA

AITKEN, BLANCHE HOPE
    HYDE WHITE, WILFRED
ALBACH-RETTY, ROSA
    SCHNEIDER, ROMY
ALBACH-RETTY, WOLF
    SCHNEIDER, ROMY
ALBERGHETTI, CARLA
    ALBERGHETTI, ANNA MARIA
ALBERGHETTI, DANIELE
    ALBERGHETTI, ANNA MARIA
ALBERGHETTI, DANIELLE
    ALBERGHETTI, ANNA MARIA
ALBERGHETTI, PAOLO
    ALBERGHETTI, ANNA MARIA
ALBERT, EDWARD
    ALBERT, EDDIE
ALBERT, MARISA
    ALBERT, EDDIE
ALBERT, PRINCE
    KELLY, GRACE
ALBRIGHT, JOHN PAUL
    ALBRIGHT, LOLA
ALBRIGHT, LOLA
    CARSON, JACK
ALDA, ALAN
    ALDA, ROBERT
ALDA, ANTHONY
    ALDA, ALAN
    ALDA, ROBERT
ALDA, BEATRICE
    ALDA, ALAN
    ALDA, ROBERT
ALDA, ELIZABETH
    ALDA, ALAN
    ALDA, ROBERT
ALDA, EVE
    ALDA, ALAN
    ALDA, ROBERT
ALDA, ROBERT
    ALDA, ALAN
ALDEN, GINGER
    PRESLEY, ELVIS
ALDERMAN, CLARA DE ROULHAC
    BLACKMER, SIDNEY
ALDRICH, RICHARD
    LAWRENCE, GERTRUDE
ALESSANDRINI, GEOFFREDO
    MAGNANI, ANNA
ALESSANDRINI, LUCA
    MAGNANI, ANNA
ALEXANDER, ARLETTE
    BISSET, JACQUELINE
ALEXANDER, JASON
    ALEXANDER, JANE
ALEXANDER, ROBERT
    ALEXANDER, JANE
ALEXANDER, ROSS
    NEAGLE, ANNA

ALEXANDER, WILLIAM
    BURSTYN, ELLEN
ALI, MOHAMMED
    FETCHIT, STEPIN
ALLAWAY, EDNA
    CHASE, ILKA
ALLEGRET, CATHERINE
    SIGNORET, SIMONE
ALLEGRET, MARC
    SIGNORET, SIMONE
ALLEGRET, YVES
    SIGNORET, SIMONE
ALLEGRETTI, COSMO
    LAWRENCE, CAROL
ALLEN, ADRIENNE
    MASSEY, RAYMOND
ALLEN, BRIAN
    ALLEN, STEVE
    MEADOWS, JAYNE
ALLEN, CARROLL
    ALLEN, STEVE
    MEADOWS, JAYNE
ALLEN, DAVID
    ALLEN, STEVE
    MEADOWS, JAYNE
ALLEN, EDWARD
    ALLEN, GRACIE
ALLEN, ELIZABETH BRYAN
    MONTGOMERY, ELIZABETH
    MONTGOMERY, ROBERT
    YOUNG, GIG
ALLEN, FRED
    HALEY, JACK
ALLEN, GRACIE
    BURNS, GEORGE
ALLEN, HAROLD R.
    O'BRIEN, MARGARET
ALLEN, HERB
    O'NEILL, JENNIFER
ALLEN, JR., STEVE
    ALLEN, STEVE
    MEADOWS, JAYNE
ALLEN, LESLIE
    CURTIS, TONY
ALLEN, LORRAINE
    CUGAT, XAVIER
ALLEN, MACKIE
    PARKER, FESS
ALLEN, MARGARET
    SHAW, ARTIE
ALLEN, PETER
    MINNELLI, LIZA
ALLEN, ROBERT
    ALLEN, FRED
ALLEN, STEVE
    MEADOWS, AUDREY
    MEADOWS, JAYNE

ALLEN, STEVE
    TORME, MEL
ALLEN, VALERIE
    DONAHUE, TROY
ALLEN, WILLIAM CHRISTOPHER
    ALLEN, STEVE
    MEADOWS, AUDREY
    MEADOWS, JAYNE
ALLEN, WOODY
    KEATON, DIANE
ALLENTUCK, DANIEL
    STAPLETON, MAUREEN
ALLENTUCK, KATHARINE
    STAPLETON, MAUREEN
ALLENTUCK, MAX
    STAPLETON, MAUREEN
ALLEY, CHERYL
    HOWARD, RON
ALLIN, GRACE I.
    MIX, TOM
ALLMAN, ELIJAH BLUE
    CHER
ALLMAN, GREGG
    CHER
ALLYSON, JUNE
    POWELL, DICK
ALMOND, MATTHEW JAMES
    BUJOLD, GENEVIEVE
ALMOND, PAUL
    BUJOLD, GENEVIEVE
ALMQUIST, MARGARET ELLEN
    DAY, DENNIS
ALONSO, CARLOS JOSE
    SKELTON, RED
ALONSO, CHICO
    BENNETT, CONSTANCE
    ROLAND, GILBERT
ALONSO, FRANCISCO
    ROLAND, GILBERT
ALSOP, CARLTON W.
    SIDNEY, SYLVIA
ALVA, CHARLES
    RALSTON, VERA HRUBA
ALVERIO, ROSA
    MORENO, RITA
AMECHE, BONNIE
    AMECHE, DON
AMECHE, CONSTANCE
    AMECHE, DON
AMECHE, DON
    POWER, TYRONE
AMECHE, FELIX
    AMECHE, DON
AMECHE, JIM
    AMECHE, DON
AMECHE, JR., DOMINIC 'DON'
    AMECHE, DON

AMECHE, KATHERINE
    AMECHE, DON
AMECHE, LONNIE
    AMECHE, DON
AMECHE, THOMAS
    AMECHE, DON
AMES, ADRIENNE
    CABOT, BRUCE
AMES, DOROTHY J.
    CABOT, BRUCE
AMES, JR., LEON
    AMES, LEON
AMES, RACQUEL
    HALL, JON
AMES, SHELLEY
    AMES, LEON
AMON, ROBERT
    SWANSON, GLORIA
AMSTERDAM, CATHY
    AMSTERDAM, MOREY
AMSTERDAM, GEOFFREY
    AMSTERDAM, MOREY
AMSTERDAM, MAX
    AMSTERDAM, MOREY
ANDERSEN, VIA
    HERSHOLT, JEAN
ANDERSON, BIG ED
    ANDERSON, EDDIE 'ROCHESTER'
ANDERSON, CORNELIUS
    ANDERSON, EDDIE 'ROCHESTER'
ANDERSON, DAVID
    ANDERSON, EDDIE 'ROCHESTER'
ANDERSON, EDMOND
    ANDERSON, EDDIE 'ROCHESTER'
ANDERSON, ELAINE
    SCOTT, ZACHARY
ANDERSON, ETHEL FOGG
    CLIFT, MONTGOMERY
ANDERSON, EVANGELA
    ANDERSON, EDDIE 'ROCHESTER'
ANDERSON, HELEN
    KEEL, HOWARD
ANDERSON, LOUISA TAR
    WATERS, ETHEL
ANDERSON, MARY
    ANDERSON, EDDIE 'ROCHESTER'
ANDERSON, MICHAEL
    O'BRIEN, EDMOND
ANDERSON, NORMA
    LANCASTER, BURT
ANDERSON, STEPHANIE
    ANDERSON, EDDIE 'ROCHESTER'
ANDERSON, WILLIAM
    ANDERSON, EDDIE 'ROCHESTER'
ANDERSSON, GERD
    ANDERSSON, BIBI
ANDERSSON, JOSEF
    ANDERSSON, BIBI

ANDRESS, CHARLOTTE
    ANDRESS, URSULA
ANDRESS, ERICA
    ANDRESS, URSULA
ANDRESS, GISELA
    ANDRESS, URSULA
ANDRESS, HEINZ
    ANDRESS, URSULA
ANDRESS, KATHI
    ANDRESS, URSULA
ANDRESS, ROLF
    ANDRESS, URSULA
ANDRESS, URSULA
    BELMONDO, JEAN-PAUL
    DEAN, JAMES
    DEREK, JOHN
    O'NEAL, RYAN
ANDREWS, CHARLES FORREST
    ANDREWS, DANA
ANDREWS, CHRIS
    ANDREWS, JULIE
ANDREWS, CLARK
    TREVOR, CLAIRE
ANDREWS, DAVID
    ANDREWS, DANA
ANDREWS, DONALD
    ANDREWS, JULIE
ANDREWS, KATHRYN
    ANDREWS, DANA
ANDREWS, LAVERNE
    ANDREWS, MAXENE
    ANDREWS, PATRICIA
ANDREWS, LESLIE
    ARLISS, GEORGE
ANDREWS, MAXENE
    ANDREWS, LAVERNE
    ANDREWS, PATRICIA
ANDREWS, NANCY
    STARR, RINGO
ANDREWS, PATRICIA
    ANDREWS, LAVERNE
    ANDREWS, MAXENE
ANDREWS, PETER
    ANDREWS, LAVERNE
    ANDREWS, MAXENE
    ANDREWS, PATRICIA
ANDREWS, STEPHEN
    ANDREWS, DANA
ANDREWS, SUSAN
    ANDREWS, DANA
ANDREWS, TED
    ANDREWS, JULIE
ANGELI, PIER
    AUMONT, JEAN-PIERRE
    DAMONE, VIC
    DEAN, JAMES
    PAVAN, MARISA

ANKA, PAUL
    HEATHERTON, JOEY
ANKER, JULIAN
    ARTHUR, JEAN
ANNELIES, EVA
    WINCHELL, WALTER
ANSARA, MATTHEW MICHAEL
    EDEN, BARBARA
ANSARA, MICHAEL
    EDEN, BARBARA
ANSON, LAURA
    ARBUCKLE, FATTY
ANTHONY, PETER
    VAN DOREN, MAMIE
ANTHONY, RAY
    VAN DOREN, MAMIE
AOKI, TSURA
    HAYAKAWA, SESSUE
APPERLEY, SARAH IDA
    BRUCE, VIRGINIA
    CLAIRE, INA
    GILBERT, JOHN
ARBUCKLE, FATTIE
    KEATON, BUSTER
ARBUCKLE, WILLIAM GOODRICH
    ARBUCKLE, FATTY
ARCH, LILLIAN
    DONLEVY, BRIAN
    LUGOSI, BELA
ARCHER, PAMELA
    MURPHY, AUDIE
ARIAS, DHANI
    HARRISON, GEORGE
ARIAS, OLIVIA
    HARRISON, GEORGE
ARKIN, ADAM
    ARKIN, ALAN
ARKIN, ANTHONY
    ARKIN, ALAN
ARKIN, DAVID I.
    ARKIN, ALAN
ARKIN, MATTHEW
    ARKIN, ALAN
ARLEN, JUDITH
    RUTHERFORD, ANN
ARLISS-ANDREWS, WILLIAM
    ARLISS, GEORGE
ARLISS, CHARLES
    ARLISS, GEORGE
ARLISS, DAISY
    ARLISS, GEORGE
ARLISS, FRED
    ARLISS, GEORGE
ARMENDARIZ, CARMEN
    ARMENDARIZ, PEDRO
ARMENDARIZ, FRANCISCO
    ARMENDARIZ, PEDRO

ARMENDARIZ, JR., PEDRO
    ARMENDARIZ, PEDRO
ARMENDARIZ, SR., PEDRO
    ARMENDARIZ, PEDRO
ARMS, BREWSTER
    MARSH, MAE
ARMS, JESSIE
    WOOLLEY, MONTY
ARMS, LOUIS LEE
    MARSH, MAE
ARMS, MARGUERITE LOUISE
    MARSH, MAE
ARMS, MARY MARSH
    MARSH, MAE
ARMSTRONG, BEATRICE
    ARMSTRONG, LOUIS
ARMSTRONG, MARY
    FORD, FRANCIS
ARMSTRONG, WILLIE
    ARMSTRONG, LOUIS
ARNAUDT, FRANCESCA JUANA SOFIA
    CABOT, BRUCE
ARNAZ, DESI
    BALL, LUCILLE
ARNAZ, II, DESIDERIO ALBERTO
    ARNAZ, DESI
ARNAZ, JR., DESI
    ARNAZ, DESI
    BALL, LUCILLE
ARNAZ, LUCIE
    ARNAZ, DESI
    BALL, LUCILLE
ARNESS, CRAIG
    ARNESS, JAMES
ARNESS, JENNY LEE
    ARNESS, JAMES
ARNESS, ROLF
    ARNESS, JAMES
ARNOLD, DOROTHY JANE
    ARNOLD, EDWARD
ARNOLD, ELIZABETH ORLANDO
    ARNOLD, EDWARD
ARNOLD, ELLIOT
    JOHNS, GLYNIS
ARNOLD, GRACE
    MORGAN, FRANK
ARNOLD, JR., WILLIAM EDWARD
    ARNOLD, EDWARD
ARNST, BOBBE
    WEISSMULLER, JOHNNY
ARNSTEIN, FRANCES
    BRICE, FANNY
ARNSTEIN, NICKY
    BRICE, FANNY
ARNSTEIN, WILLIAM JULES
    BRICE, FANNY
ARONSON, ANNA
    ANN-MARGRET

ARONSON, ANNA
    SMITH, ROGER
ARROUGE, MARTIN
    SHEARER, NORMA
ARSHAWSKY, HARRY
    SHAW, ARTIE
ARTHUR, GEORGE K.
    ARTHUR, JEAN
ARTHUR, KATHLEEN
    LOCKHART, GENE
    LOCKHART, JUNE
ARVAD, INGA
    MCCOY, 'COLONEL' TIM
ARVIDSON, LINDA
    GRIFFITH, D. W.
ASHE, ARTHUR
    ROSS, DIANA
ASHER, ANTHONY
    LA PLANTE, LAURA
ASHER, IRVING
    LA PLANTE, LAURA
ASHER, JERRY
    CRAWFORD, JOAN
ASHER, JILL
    LA PLANTE, LAURA
ASHER, JR., WILLIAM
    MONTGOMERY, ELIZABETH
    MONTGOMERY, ROBERT
ASHER, MORRIS DAVID
    ASNER, EDWARD
ASHER, REBECCA ELIZABETH
    MONTGOMERY, ELIZABETH
    MONTGOMERY, ROBERT
ASHER, ROBERT
    MONTGOMERY, ELIZABETH
    MONTGOMERY, ROBERT
ASHER, WILLIAM
    MONTGOMERY, ELIZABETH
    MONTGOMERY, ROBERT
ASHERSON, RENEE
    DONAT, ROBERT
ASHLEY, ELIZABETH
    PEPPARD, GEORGE
ASHLEY, LADY SYLVIA HAWKES
    CABOT, BRUCE
    FAIRBANKS, DOUGLAS
    FAIRBANKS, JR., DOUGLAS
    GABLE, CLARK
ASHROW, DR. DAVID
    ALLYSON, JUNE
ASHTON, MARY L.
    WHITTY, DAME MAY
ASMUS, GROVER
    REED, DONNA
ASNER, KATHRYN
    ASNER, EDWARD
ASNER, LIZA
    ASNER, EDWARD

ASNER, MATTHEW
    ASNER, EDWARD
ASTAIRE, ADELE
    ASTAIRE, FRED
ASTAIRE, AVA
    ASTAIRE, FRED
ASTAIRE, FRED
    LYNLEY, CAROL
    ROGERS, GINGER
ASTAIRE, JR., FRED
    ASTAIRE, FRED
ASTIN, ALLEN
    ASTIN, JOHN
    DUKE, PATTY
ASTIN, ALLEN VARLEY
    ASTIN, JOHN
ASTIN, DAVID
    ASTIN, JOHN
    DUKE, PATTY
ASTIN, JOHN
    DUKE, PATTY
ASTIN, MACKENZIE
    ASTIN, JOHN
    DUKE, PATTY
ASTIN, SEAN
    ASTIN, JOHN
ASTIN, THOMAS
    ASTIN, JOHN
    DUKE, PATTY
ASTOR, MARY
    BARRYMORE, JOHN
ASUNSOLO, JESUS MARTINEZ
    DEL RIO, DOLORES
ASZBERGER, MME.
    GIELGUD, JOHN
ATKINS, BARBARA
    TUFTS, SONNY
AUBREY, JAMES T.
    THAXTER, PHYLLIS
AUBREY, JAMES W.
    THAXTER, PHYLLIS
AUBREY, SCHUYLER
    THAXTER, PHYLLIS
AUER, ANTHONY
    AUER, MISCHA
AUER, LEOPOLD
    AUER, MISCHA
AUER, ZOE
    AUER, MISCHA
AUMONT, FRANCOIS
    AUMONT, JEAN-PIERRE
AUMONT, JEAN-CLAUDE
    ANGELI, PIER
    AUMONT, JEAN-PIERRE
    PAVAN, MARISA
AUMONT, JEAN-PIERRE
    ANGELI, PIER

AUMONT, JEAN-PIERRE
    PAVAN, MARISA
AUMONT, MARIA CHRISTINE
    AUMONT, JEAN-PIERRE
AUMONT, PATRICK
    ANGELI, PIER
    AUMONT, JEAN-PIERRE
    PAVAN, MARISA
AURNESS, PETER
    ARNESS, JAMES
AURNESS, ROLF C.
    ARNESS, JAMES
AUSTERLITZ, FREDERIC
    ASTAIRE, FRED
AUTRY, DELBERT
    AUTRY, GENE
AUTRY, DUDLEY (DOUG)
    AUTRY, GENE
AUTRY, GENE
    BURNETTE, SMILEY
AUTRY, VELDA
    AUTRY, GENE
AUTRY, WILLIAM T.
    AUTRY, GENE
AUTRY, WILMA
    AUTRY, GENE
AVALLONE, NICOLAS
    AVALON, FRANKIE
AVALON, ANTHONY
    AVALON, FRANKIE
AVALON, DINA MARY
    AVALON, FRANKIE
AVALON, JOSEPH
    AVALON, FRANKIE
AVALON, JR., FRANK
    AVALON, FRANKIE
AVALON, LAURA
    AVALON, FRANKIE
AVERY, DOREEN
    SHAW, ROBERT
AYRES, BERNICE
    PECK, GREGORY
AYRES, JUSTIN BRET
    AYRES, LEW
AYRES, LEW
    GAYNOR, JANET
    ROGERS, GINGER
AZNAOURIAN, MISHA
    AZNAVOUR, CHARLES
AZNAVOUR, PATRICIA
    AZNAVOUR, CHARLES
AZNAVOUR, PATRICK
    AZNAVOUR, CHARLES
BABACHI, LYDIA
    LAMAS, FERNANDO
BABBITT, ART
    CHAMPION, MARGE

BACAL, NATALIE WEINSTEIN
    BACALL, LAUREN
BACALL, LAUREN
    BOGART, HUMPHREY
    ROBARDS, JR., JASON
BACHARACH, BERT
    DICKINSON, ANGIE
BACHARACH, BURT
    DICKINSON, ANGIE
BACHARACH, LEA 'NIKKI'
    DICKINSON, ANGIE
BACKUS, RUSSELL GOULD
    BACKUS, JIM
BAER, JACOB HENRY 'BUDDY'
    BAER, JR., MAX
BAER, JEANNE
    WILDER, GENE
BAER, MAX
    BAER, JR., MAX
BAGUENO, TERESA
    ITURBI, JOSE
BAILEY, BILL
    BAILEY, PEARL
BAILEY, DAVID
    DENEUVE, CATHERINE
BAILEY, EURA
    BAILEY, PEARL
BAILEY, HENRY
    BAILEY, PEARL
BAILEY, JOSEPH JAMES
    BAILEY, PEARL
BAILEY, VIRGINIA
    BAILEY, PEARL
BAINBRIDGE, BARTON
    KEYES, EVELYN
BAINTER, CHARLES FRANCIS
    BAINTER, FAY
BAKALYAR, BEATRICE
    FRANCIOSA, ANTHONY
BAKER, ANN
    GREENSTREET, SYDNEY
BAKER, BERNICE
    MONROE, MARILYN
BAKER, BRIDGET
    RAFFERTY, FRANCES
BAKER, EDITH
    MILLS, JOHN
BAKER, ELLIS
    MARCH, FREDRIC
BAKER, JACK
    MONROE, MARILYN
BAKER, KEVIN
    RAFFERTY, FRANCES
BAKER, SOPHIE
    BUTTONS, RED
BAKER, TOM
    RAFFERTY, FRANCES

BAKER, VIRGINIA
    BAKER, CARROLL
    PALANCE, JACK
BAKER, WILLIAM
    BAKER, CARROLL
BAKER, WILLIAM H.
    BOOTH, SHIRLEY
BAKSH, SHAKIRA
    CAINE, MICHAEL
BAKST, JANETTE
    WINCHELL, WALTER
BALDINI, ANNA
    CARUSO, ENRICO
BALDON, BERLE CLEO
    MELCHIOR, LAURITZ
BALDWIN, AGNES
    O'BRIEN, EDMOND
BALDWIN, EVELYN MARJORIE
    GRIFFITH, D. W.
BALES, MICHAEL
    VAN FLEET, JO
BALES, WILLIAM
    VAN FLEET, JO
BALFE, VERONICA
    COOPER, GARY
BALL, FRED
    BALL, LUCILLE
BALL, HENRY
    BALL, LUCILLE
BALL, LUCILLE
    ARNAZ, DESI
BALL, SUZAN
    LONG, RICHARD
BALLARD, FLORENCE
    ROSS, DIANA
BALLARD, LUCIEN
    OBERON, MERLE
BALSAM, ADAM
    BALSAM, MARTIN
BALSAM, ALBERT
    BALSAM, MARTIN
BALSAM, TALIA
    BALSAM, MARTIN
BALSAM, ZOE
    BALSAM, MARTIN
BANCROFT, ANNE
    BROOKS, MEL
BANKHEAD, EUGENIA
    BANKHEAD, TALLULAH
BANKHEAD, JOHN H.
    BANKHEAD, TALLULAH
BANKHEAD, TALLULAH
    BARRYMORE, ETHEL
    WINWOOD, ESTELLE
BANKHEAD, WILLIAM BROCKMAN
    BANKHEAD, TALLULAH
BANKS, ALICE LOUISE
    LAWRENCE, GERTRUDE

BANKS, JOAN
    LOVEJOY, FRANK
BANKSTON, EVALENE
    GORCEY, LEO
BANKY, VILMA
    COLMAN, RONALD
    LA ROCQUE, ROD
BANNISTER, HARRY
    HARDING, ANN
BANNISTER, JANE
    HARDING, ANN
BANO, AL
    CHRISTIAN, LINDA
BARBATO, NANCY
    SINATRA, FRANK
BARBIN, BEATRICE GABRIELLA
    VALENTINO, RUDOLPH
BARBOUR, DAVE
    LEE, PEGGY
BARBOUR, NICKI
    LEE, PEGGY
BARCLAY, J. SEARLE
    NALDI, NITA
BARDOT, BRIGITTE
    BELMONDO, JEAN-PAUL
BARDOT, LOUIS
    BARDOT, BRIGITTE
BARDOT, MIJANOU
    BARDOT, BRIGITTE
BARKER, ALEXANDER
    BARKER, LEX
    DAHL, ARLENE
    TURNER, LANA
BARKER, CHRISTOPHER
    BARKER, LEX
BARKER, GREGORY
    HAYWARD, SUSAN
BARKER, JESS
    HAYWARD, SUSAN
BARKER, LEX
    DAHL, ARLENE
    TURNER, LANA
BARKER, LYNNE ALEXANDER
    BARKER, LEX
    DAHL, ARLENE
    TURNER, LANA
BARKER, TIMOTHY
    HAYWARD, SUSAN
BARNES, BINNIE
    BROWN, JOE E.
BARNES, GEORGE
    BLONDELL, JOAN
BARNES, NORMAN SCOTT
    ALLYSON, JUNE
    BLONDELL, JOAN
    POWELL, DICK
BARNETT, MABEL
    COOPER, GLADYS

BARNHART, AGNES
    HYER, MARTHA
BARON, LITA
    CALHOUN, RORY
BAROUH, PIERRE
    AIMEE, ANOUK
BARR, DONALD
    YOUNG, GIG
BARR, ETHEL MAE
    WIDMARK, RICHARD
BARR, JOHN EARL
    YOUNG, GIG
BARRETT, EDITH
    PRICE, VINCENT
BARRETT, ELETHA
    FINCH, PETER
BARRETT, JANE
    BAXTER, WARNER
BARRETT, MARY JANE
    TRUEX, ERNEST
BARRETT, ROGER
    RUSSELL, JANE
BARRIE, SIR JAMES
    BARRIE, WENDY
BARRIE, SIR JAMES MATTHEW
    BARRIE, WENDY
BARRY, FREDERIC JAMES
    BARRY, GENE
BARRY, JEFF
    O'NEILL, JENNIFER
BARRY, JOAN
    CHAPLIN, CHARLES
BARRY, LIZA
    BARRY, GENE
BARRY, MICHAEL
    BARRY, GENE
BARRYMORE, DIANA
    BARRYMORE, ETHEL
    BARRYMORE, JOHN
    BARRYMORE, JR., JOHN
    BARRYMORE, LIONEL
    COSTELLO, DOLORES
    NALDI, NITA
BARRYMORE, DOLORES ETHEL MAE
    BARRYMORE, ETHEL
    BARRYMORE, JOHN
    BARRYMORE, JR., JOHN
    BARRYMORE, LIONEL
    COSTELLO, DOLORES
BARRYMORE, DOROTHY BLYTH
    BARRYMORE, JR., JOHN
BARRYMORE, ETHEL
    BARRYMORE, JOHN
    BARRYMORE, LIONEL
    COSTELLO, DOLORES
BARRYMORE, JOHN
    ASTOR, MARY

BARRYMORE, JOHN
    BARRYMORE, ETHEL
    BARRYMORE, JR., JOHN
    BARRYMORE, LIONEL
    COSTELLO, DOLORES
    FLYNN, ERROL
BARRYMORE, JOHN BLYTH
    BARRYMORE, JR., JOHN
BARRYMORE, JR., JOHN
    BARRYMORE, ETHEL
    BARRYMORE, JOHN
    BARRYMORE, LIONEL
    COSTELLO, DOLORES
BARRYMORE, LIONEL
    BARRYMORE, ETHEL
    BARRYMORE, JOHN
    BARRYMORE, JR., JOHN
    COSTELLO, DOLORES
    GABLE, CLARK
BARRYMORE, MAURICE
    BARRYMORE, ETHEL
    BARRYMORE, JOHN
    BARRYMORE, LIONEL
    COSTELLO, DOLORES
BARRYMORE, SECOND, ETHEL
    BARRYMORE, ETHEL
    BARRYMORE, JOHN
    BARRYMORE, JR., JOHN
    BARRYMORE, LIONEL
BARTHELMESS, ALFRED
    BARTHELMESS, RICHARD
BARTHELMESS, MARY HAY
    BARTHELMESS, RICHARD
BARTHELMESS, STEWART
    BARTHELMESS, RICHARD
BARTHOLOMEW, CELIA
    BARTHOLOMEW, FREDDIE
BARTHOLOMEW, FREDERICK ROBERT
    BARTHOLOMEW, FREDDIE
BARTHOLOMEW, KATHLEEN MILLICENT
    BARTHOLOMEW, FREDDIE
BARTLETT, DUSTY
    HUNTER, JEFFREY
BARTLETT, ELISE
    SCHILDKRAUT, JOSEPH
BARTLETT, HALL
    FLEMING, RHONDA
BARTLEY, ANTHONY
    KERR, DEBORAH
BARTLEY, FRANCESCA
    KERR, DEBORAH
BARTLEY, MELANIE JANE
    KERR, DEBORAH
BARTLEY, SIR CHARLES
    KERR, DEBORAH
BARTOK, EVA
    BARRYMORE, JR., JOHN

BARYSHNIKOV, MIKHAIL
    KEATON, DIANE
BASEHART, GAYLA
    BASEHART, RICHARD
BASEHART, HARRY T.
    BASEHART, RICHARD
BASEHART, JENNA
    BASEHART, RICHARD
BASEHART, JOHN
    BASEHART, RICHARD
BASIE, COUNT
    WATERS, ETHEL
BASQUETTE, GLADYS
    CHAMPION, MARGE
BASQUETTE, LINA
    CHAMPION, MARGE
BASS, LOU
    MCDONALD, MARIE
BASSEY, SHIRLEY
    FINCH, PETER
BATES, DOROTHY
    BEGLEY, ED
BATES, HAROLD ARTHUR
    BATES, ALAN
BATTLER, ANNE
    COSTELLO, LOU
BATTY, EDITH RACHEL
    THATCHER, TORIN
BAUER, ESPERANZA 'CHATA'
    WAYNE, JOHN
BAUM, FLORENCE
    BROOKS, MEL
BAUM, HEIDI
    SOTHERN, ANN
    STERLING, ROBERT
BAUM, LAL
    SOTHERN, ANN
    STERLING, ROBERT
BAUMGARNER, CHARLES
    GARNER, JAMES
BAUMGARNER, JACK
    GARNER, JAMES
BAUMGARNER, WELDON
    GARNER, JAMES
BAUTZER, GREGSON
    WYNTER, DANA
BAUTZER, MARK RAGAN
    WYNTER, DANA
BAXTER, ANNE
    HODIAK, JOHN
BAXTER, EDWIN F.
    BAXTER, WARNER
BAXTER, KENNETH STUART
    BAXTER, ANNE
    HODIAK, JOHN
BAYNE, BEVERLY
    BUSHMAN, FRANCIS X.

BEAN, JACK
    GAYNOR, MITZI
BEATON, CECIL
    DIETRICH, MARLENE
    GARBO, GRETA
BEATTY, IRA O.
    BEATTY, WARREN
    MACLAINE, SHIRLEY
BEATTY, LADY ADELE
    SINATRA, FRANK
BEATTY, WARREN
    CARON, LESLIE
    CHRISTIE, JULIE
    COLLINS, JOAN
    KEATON, DIANE
    MACLAINE, SHIRLEY
    PHILLIPS, MICHELLE
BEAULIEU, PRISCILLA
    PRESLEY, ELVIS
BEAVERS, JAMES
    LADD, ALAN
BECK, PATSY
    CHANEY, JR., LON
BECKERMAN, CECILE
    BOONE, RICHARD
BEDELL, LEW
    BARRYMORE, JR., JOHN
BEDOS, GUY
    BELMONDO, JEAN-PAUL
BEEDLE, WILLIAM FRANKLIN
    HOLDEN, WILLIAM
BEERY, CAROL ANN
    BEERY, WALLACE
BEERY, JR., NOAH
    BEERY, WALLACE
    JONES, BUCK
BEERY, NOAH
    BEERY, WALLACE
BEERY, WALLACE
    SWANSON, GLORIA
BEERY, WILLIAM
    BEERY, WALLACE
BEGLEY, HELENE
    BEGLEY, ED
BEGLEY, JR., ED
    BEGLEY, ED
BEGLEY, MARTIN
    BEGLEY, ED
BEGLEY, MAUREEN K.
    BEGLEY, ED
BEGLEY, MICHAEL JOSEPH
    BEGLEY, ED
BEGLEY, THOMAS
    RAYE, MARTHA
BEGLEY, THOMAS ALLENE
    BEGLEY, ED
BEHRS, PATRICIA
    DEREK, JOHN

BEIDERBECKE, BIX
    CARMICHAEL, HOAGY
BEIR, FRAN
    KRISTOFFERSON, KRIS
BELAFONTE, ADRIENNE
    BELAFONTE, HARRY
BELAFONTE, DAVID
    BELAFONTE, HARRY
BELAFONTE, GINA
    BELAFONTE, HARRY
BELAFONTE, HAROLD GEORGE
    BELAFONTE, HARRY
BELAFONTE, SHARI
    BELAFONTE, HARRY
BELASCO, DAVID
    PICKFORD, MARY
BELCHER, ERNEST
    CHAMPION, GOWER
    CHAMPION, MARGE
BELCHER, TOM
    O'BRIEN, EDMOND
BELGE, BURHAN
    GABOR, EVA
    GABOR, ZSA ZSA
BELINE, ROSELLE
    COMO, PERRY
BELL, CHARLES H.
    MALONE, DOROTHY
BELL, MARGARETTE
    CORTEZ, RICARDO
BELL, MARY
    HOLDEN, WILLIAM
BELL, MARY HAYLEY
    MILLS, HAYLEY
    MILLS, JOHN
BELL, REX
    BOW, CLARA
BELL, SYLVIA
    LYNDE, PAUL
BELLAMY, CHARLES REXFORD
    BELLAMY, RALPH
BELLAMY, LYNN
    BELLAMY, RALPH
BELLAMY, RALPH
    FARRELL, CHARLES
BELLAMY, WILLARD
    BELLAMY, RALPH
BELLO, MARINO
    HARLOW, JEAN
BELLSON, DEE DEE JEAN
    BAILEY, PEARL
BELLSON, LOUIS
    BAILEY, PEARL
BELLSON, TONY
    BAILEY, PEARL
BELMONDO, FLORENCE
    BELMONDO, JEAN-PAUL

BELMONDO, SR., JEAN-PAUL
    BELMONDO, JEAN-PAUL
BEN-GURION, IDDO
    DILLMAN, BRADFORD
    PARKER, SUZY
BENCHLEY, CHARLES HENRY
    BENCHLEY, ROBERT
BENCHLEY, JR., ROBERT J.
    BENCHLEY, ROBERT
BENCHLEY, NATHANIEL GODDARD
    BENCHLEY, ROBERT
BENCHLEY, NATHANIEL ROBERT
    BENCHLEY, ROBERT
BENCHLEY, PETER BRADFORD
    BENCHLEY, ROBERT
BENDA, MARIAN
    MARX, CHICO
    MARX, GROUCHO
    MARX, GUMMO
    MARX, HARPO
    MARX, ZEPPO
BENDIX, LORRAINE
    BENDIX, WILLIAM
BENDIX, OSCAR 'MAX'
    BENDIX, WILLIAM
BENDIX, STEPHANIE
    BENDIX, WILLIAM
BENEDETTO, JOHN
    BENNETT, TONY
BENES, GIZELLA
    LUKAS, PAUL
BENET, BRENDA
    BIXBY, BILL
BENJAMIN, DOROTHY
    CARUSO, ENRICO
BENJAMIN, RICHARD
    PRENTISS, PAULA
BENJAMIN, ROSS THOMAS
    BENJAMIN, RICHARD
    PRENTISS, PAULA
BENN, WILLIAM RUTHERFORD
    RUTHERFORD, MARGARET
BENNETT, ANTONIA
    BENNETT, TONY
BENNETT, BARBARA
    BENNETT, CONSTANCE
    BENNETT, JOAN
    BENNETT, RICHARD
    ROLAND, GILBERT
BENNETT, CONSTANCE
    BENNETT, JOAN
    BENNETT, RICHARD
    MCCREA, JOEL
    ROLAND, GILBERT
BENNETT, D'ANDREA
    BENNETT, TONY
BENNETT, DAEGAL
    BENNETT, TONY

BENNETT, ELSA
    O'HERLIHY, DAN
BENNETT, GEORGE W.
    BENNETT, RICHARD
BENNETT, JOAN
    BENNETT, CONSTANCE
    BENNETT,. RICHARD
    FLYNN, ERROL
    ROLAND, GILBERT
BENNETT, JOANNA
    BENNETT, TONY
BENNETT, JOHANNA
    RAY, ALDO
BENNETT, OLGA
    O'HERLIHY, DAN
BENNETT, RICHARD
    BENNETT, CONSTANCE
    BENNETT, JOAN
    ROLAND, GILBERT
BENNY, JACK
    ALLEN, FRED
    ANDERSON, EDDIE 'ROCHESTER'
    COOPER, GARY
    HALEY, JACK
BENNY, JOAN NAOMI
    BENNY, JACK
BENOIS, NADIA
    USTINOV, PETER
BENSON, MARGARET
    HARRISON, REX
BERENGER, JOSANNE MARIANNA
    BRANDO, MARLON
BERENSON, BARENTHIA 'BERRY'
    PERKINS, TONY
BERENSON, MARISA
    PERKINS, TONY
BERG, LEE
    NELSON, GENE
BERGEN, CANDICE
    BERGEN, EDGAR
BERGEN, CONSTANCE
    ARDEN, EVE
BERGEN, EDGAR
    BERGEN, CANDICE
    CANOVA, JUDY
BERGEN, EDWARD G.
    ARDEN, EVE
BERGEN, ELIZABETH
    ARDEN, EVE
BERGEN, KRIS EDGAR
    BERGEN, CANDICE
    BERGEN, EDGAR
BERGER, JOSEF
    BERGER, SENTA
BERGERAC, DIANE
    MALONE, DOROTHY
BERGERAC, JACQUES
    MALONE, DOROTHY

BERGERAC, JACQUES
    ROGERS, GINGER
BERGERAC, MIMI
    MALONE, DOROTHY
BERGMAN, INGMAR
    ULLMANN, LIV
BERGMAN, JUSTUS
    BERGMAN, INGRID
BERGREN, JOHN
    BERGEN, CANDICE
    BERGEN, EDGAR
BERKELEY, GERTRUDE
    BERKELEY, BUSBY
BERLE, MILTON
    CASSIDY, JACK
BERLE, VICTORIA
    BERLE, MILTON
BERLE, WILLIAM
    BERLE, MILTON
BERLIN, IRVING
    TALMADGE, CONSTANCE
BERLIN, JOHN
    MAY, ELAINE
BERLINGER, MOSES
    BERLE, MILTON
BERLINGER, ROSALIND
    BERLE, MILTON
BERMAN, JOSHUA
    BERMAN, SHELLEY
BERMAN, NATHAN
    BERMAN, SHELLEY
BERMAN, RACHEL
    BERMAN, SHELLEY
BERN, PAUL
    GILBERT, JOHN
    HARLOW, JEAN
BERNARD, EDOUARD
    BERNHARDT, SARAH
BERNARD, JEANNE
    BERNHARDT, SARAH
BERNARD, MARY WEED
    MONTGOMERY, ROBERT
BERNARD, REGINE
    BERNHARDT, SARAH
BERNARDI, ADAM
    BERNARDI, HERSHEL
BERNARDI, BERNARD
    BERNARDI, HERSHEL
BERNARDI, BERYL
    BERNARDI, HERSHEL
BERNARDI, ROBIN
    BERNARDI, HERSHEL
BERNHARD, HARVEY
    HOLDEN, WILLIAM
BEROLSKY, ROSE
    MATTHAU, WALTER
BERRY, DENNIS
    SEBERG, JEAN

BERRY, DOROTHY STEPHEN
    MATURE, VICTOR
BERTOLINI, LYDIA
    BRAZZI, ROSSANO
BERTON, PIERRE
    BERNHARDT, SARAH
BERTRAND, MARCELLINE
    VOIGHT, JON
BESSANT, DON
    CHRISTIE, JULIE
BESSIRE, DAWN
    NORTH, SHEREE
BESSIRE, FRED
    NORTH, SHEREE
BEST, EDNA SARAH
    MARSHALL, HERBERT
BETLIE, JOHN
    LAKE, VERONICA
BEVERLY, HELEN
    COBB, LEE J.
BEY, TURHAN
    CHRISTIAN, LINDA
BIASINI, DANIEL
    SCHNEIDER, ROMY
BICKEL, ELIZABETH
    MARCH, FREDRIC
BICKEL, HAROLD
    MARCH, FREDRIC
BICKEL, JOHN
    MARCH, FREDRIC
BICKEL, JOHN F.
    MARCH, FREDRIC
BICKFORD, DORIS
    BICKFORD, CHARLES
BICKFORD, DOROTHY
    BICKFORD, CHARLES
BICKFORD, ESTHER
    BICKFORD, CHARLES
BICKFORD, JONATHAN
    BICKFORD, CHARLES
BICKFORD, LORETUS
    BICKFORD, CHARLES
BICKFORD, REX
    BICKFORD, CHARLES
BICKFORD, RUTH
    BICKFORD, CHARLES
BICKFORD, THOMAS
    BICKFORD, CHARLES
BICKFORD, WILLIAM
    BICKFORD, CHARLES
BICKMORE, LUELLA
    MOORE, TERRY
BICKNELL, DONNA
    TUSHINGHAM, RITA
BICKNELL, TERENCE
    TUSHINGHAM, RITA
BIEGGERS, JEANNE
    MARTIN, DEAN

BORGNINE, SHARON
    BORGNINE, ERNEST
BORGOLO, COUNT FRANCESCO DI
    ANDRESS, URSULA
BOSELLI, ANNA
    BORGNINE, ERNEST
BOSELLI, COUNT PAOLO
    BORGNINE, ERNEST
BOTANA, CONSUELO
    ROLAND, GILBERT
BOTTOMS, BARTHOLOMEW
    BOTTOMS, TIMOTHY
BOTTOMS, BEN
    BOTTOMS, TIMOTHY
BOTTOMS, JAMES 'BUD'
    BOTTOMS, TIMOTHY
BOTTOMS, JOSEPH
    BOTTOMS, TIMOTHY
BOTTOMS, SAM
    BOTTOMS, TIMOTHY
BOUCHER, SHERRY
    PEPPARD, GEORGE
BOULTING, CRISPIAN
    MILLS, HAYLEY
    MILLS, JOHN
BOULTING, ROY
    MILLS, HAYLEY
    MILLS, JOHN
BOURKE, JENNIFER
    SHAW, ROBERT
BOW, CLARA
    COOPER, GARY
    ROLAND, GILBERT
BOW, ROBERT
    BOW, CLARA
BOWE, ROSEMARY
    STACK, ROBERT
BOWES, DAVID WILLIS
    WINDSOR, CLAIRE
BOWES, WILLIAM W.
    WINDSOR, CLAIRE
BOWMAN, BROOKE
    WALTER, JESSICA
BOWMAN, ROSS
    WALTER, JESSICA
BOYD, CHARLES W.
    BOYD, WILLIAM
BOYD, MARTHA
    BOYD, STEPHEN
BOYD, PATTI
    HARRISON, GEORGE
BOYD, WILLIAM
    HAYES, GABBY
BOYER, CHARLES
    POWER, TYRONE
BOYER, MAURICE
    BOYER, CHARLES

BOYER, MICHAEL
    BOYER, CHARLES
BRABIN, CHARLES
    BARA, THEDA
BRADBURY, RAY
    LAUGHTON, CHARLES
BRADFORD, MARJORIE
    BENCHLEY, ROBERT
BRADLEY, FRANCIS BARLOW
    WINWOOD, ESTELLE
BRADLEY, GRACE
    BOYD, WILLIAM
BRADY, ALICE
    GABLE, CLARK
    HOPPER, HEDDA
BRADY, NETTIE MANILA
    POWELL, WILLIAM
BRADY, PETER J.
    PARSONS, LOUELLA O.
BRADY, SADIE
    COCA, IMOGENE
BRANDO, CHEYENNE 'TARITA'
    BRANDO, MARLON
BRANDO, CHRISTIAN DEVI
    BRANDO, MARLON
BRANDO, FRANCES
    BRANDO, MARLON
BRANDO, JOCELYN
    BRANDO, MARLON
BRANDO, MARLON
    ANDRESS, URSULA
    MORENO, RITA
BRANDO, MIKO
    BRANDO, MARLON
BRANDO, REBECCA
    BRANDO, MARLON
BRANDO, SR., MARLON
    BRANDO, MARLON
    FONDA, HENRY
BRANT, ROBERT
    LEIGH, JANET
BRAZIER, ALICE
    COOPER, GARY
BRAZZI, ADELMO
    BRAZZI, ROSSANO
BRAZZI, FRANCA
    BRAZZI, ROSSANO
BRAZZI, OSCAR
    BRAZZI, ROSSANO
BRECHT, BERTOLD
    LAUGHTON, CHARLES
BREGMAN, BARRY
    HALEY, JACK
BREGMAN, LOUIS 'BUDDY'
    ALBERGHETTI, ANNA MARIA
    HALEY, JACK
BREGMAN, MARTIN
    PACINO, AL

BREN, DONALD
    TREVOR, CLAIRE
BREN, MILTON
    TREVOR, CLAIRE
BREN, PETER
    TREVOR, CLAIRE
BRENNAN, ARTHUR WELLS
    BRENNAN, WALTER
BRENNAN, JR., WALTER
    BRENNAN, WALTER
BRENNAN, RUTH
    BRENNAN, WALTER
BRENNAN, WILLIAM JOHN
    BRENNAN, WALTER
BRENNING, ANNA
    LORRE, PETER
BRENT, EVELYN
    COOPER, GARY
BRENT, GEORGE
    CHATTERTON, RUTH
    SHERIDAN, ANN
    YOUNG, LORETTA
BRETT, JEREMY
    BATES, ALAN
BREWER, SUSAN
    FONDA, HENRY
    FONDA, JANE
    FONDA, PETER
BRIAN, MARY
    POWELL, DICK
BRIDGES, BEAU
    BRIDGES, JEFF
    BRIDGES, LLOYD
BRIDGES, JEFF
    BRIDGES, LLOYD
BRIDGES, LLOYD
    BRIDGES, JEFF
BRIDGES, LUCINDA
    BRIDGES, JEFF
    BRIDGES, LLOYD
BRIGGS, EARL F.
    BRUCE, VIRGINIA
BRIGGS, HARRIET WASHBORN
    LUNT, ALFRED
BRIGGS, JACK
    ROGERS, GINGER
BRIGGS, JEANETTE
    MAZURKI, MIKE
BRIGGS, STANLEY
    BRUCE, VIRGINIA
BRINKMAN, CHRISTOPHER
    CRAIN, JEANNE
BRINKMAN, JEANINE
    CRAIN, JEANNE
BRINKMAN, LISABETTE
    CRAIN, JEANNE
BRINKMAN, MARIA
    CRAIN, JEANNE

BRINKMAN, MICHAEL ANTHONY
    CRAIN, JEANNE
BRINKMAN, PAUL
    CRAIN, JEANNE
BRINKMAN, PAUL FREDERICK
    CRAIN, JEANNE
BRINKMAN, TIMOTHY
    CRAIN, JEANNE
BRISKIN, CANDICE
    HUTTON, BETTY
BRISKIN, LINDSAY
    HUTTON, BETTY
BRISKIN, TED
    HUTTON, BETTY
BRISSON, FREDERICK
    RUSSELL, ROSALIND
BRISSON, LANCE
    RUSSELL, ROSALIND
BRITE, DENNIS R.
    FOCH, NINA
BRITE, SCHUYLER DIRK
    FOCH, NINA
BRITT, MAY
    DAVIS, JR., SAMMY
BRODERICK, HELEN
    CRAWFORD, BRODERICK
BRODERICK, WILLIAM E.
    CRAWFORD, BRODERICK
BRODY, SAM
    MANSFIELD, JAYNE
BROKAW, FRANCES DE VILLERS
    FONDA, HENRY
    FONDA, JANE
    FONDA, PETER
BROLIN, JESS
    BROLIN, JAMES
BROLIN, JOSH
    BROLIN, JAMES
BROMFIELD, JOHN
    CALVET, CORINNE
BRONSON, ANTHONY
    BRONSON, CHARLES
    IRELAND, JILL
BRONSON, CHARLES
    IRELAND, JILL
BRONSON, SUZANNE
    BRONSON, CHARLES
    IRELAND, JILL
BRONSON, ZULEIKA
    BRONSON, CHARLES
    IRELAND, JILL
BROOKMAN, KITTY
    BROOKS, MEL
BROOKS, EDWARD
    BANCROFT, ANNE
    BROOKS, MEL
BROOKS, KATE
    SIMMONS, JEAN

BROOKS, MAXIMILIAN
    BANCROFT, ANNE
    BROOKS, MEL
BROOKS, MEL
    BANCROFT, ANNE
BROOKS, NICHOLAS
    BANCROFT, ANNE
    BROOKS, MEL
BROOKS, PHYLLIS
    GRANT, CARY
BROOKS, RICHARD
    SIMMONS, JEAN
BROOKS, STEFANIE
    BANCROFT, ANNE
    BROOKS, MEL
BROTTIER, CURTIS
    PARKER, JEAN
BROUGH, SPANGLER A.
    TAYLOR, ROBERT
BROWN, CAROLINE
    TRACY, SPENCER
BROWN, CLARENCE
    GARBO, GRETA
BROWN, DONALD
    BROWN, JOE E.
BROWN, FRANCIS VAN ARNUUM
    HAYES, HELEN
BROWN, GEORGE HANLEY
    O'HARA, MAUREEN
BROWN, GEORGE STANFORD
    DALY, JAMES
BROWN, HARRIET
    BRIDGES, LLOYD
BROWN, HORACE M.
    DAVIES, MARION
BROWN, JANET
    DICKINSON, ANGIE
BROWN, JOE LEROY
    BROWN, JOE E.
BROWN, KATHRYN FRANCES
    BROWN, JOE E.
BROWN, MARGARET PEARL
    DARNELL, LINDA
BROWN, MARY
    WAYNE, JOHN
BROWN, MARY ELIZABETH ANN
    BROWN, JOE E.
BROWN, MARYLOU
    DICKINSON, ANGIE
BROWN, MATHIAS
    BROWN, JOE E.
BROWN, NORTON S.
    CHASE, ILKA
BROWN, RICHARD
    GABOR, EVA
    GABOR, ZSA ZSA
BROWNE, CORAL
    PRICE, VINCENT

BROWNE, JOAN
    ALDA, ALAN
    ALDA, ROBERT
BRU, JUAN CUGAT DE
    CUGAT, XAVIER
BRU, MYRIAM
    BUCHHOLZ, HORST
BRUCE, JENNIFER
    BRUCE, NIGEL
BRUCE, NIGEL
    COOPER, GLADYS
BRUCE, PAULINE
    BRUCE, NIGEL
BRUCE, SIR MICHAEL WALLER
    BRUCE, NIGEL
BRUCE, SIR WILLIAM WALLER
    BRUCE, NIGEL
BRUCE, VIRGINIA
    GILBERT, JOHN
    NIVEN, DAVID
BRUDERLIN, HENRY
    BROLIN, JAMES
BRUEGGEMANN, SUZANNE M.
    MCLAGLEN, VICTOR
BRYAN, HELEN
    DURYEA, DAN
BRYANT, CHARLES
    NAZIMOVA
BRYANT, MARIE
    PRYOR, RICHARD
BRYCE, PATRICIA HOPE
    PREMINGER, OTTO
BRYNER, BORIS
    BRYNNER, YUL
BRYNNER, II, YUL 'ROCKY'
    BRYNNER, YUL
BRYNNER, MELODY
    BRYNNER, YUL
BRYNNER, MIA
    BRYNNER, YUL
BRYNNER, VERA
    BRYNNER, YUL
BRYNNER, VICTORIA
    BRYNNER, YUL
BRYSON, WINIFRED
    BAXTER, WARNER
BSCHLIESSMAYER, OSKAR
    WERNER, OSKAR
BUCH, PATRICIA
    BENNETT, TONY
BUCHHOLTZ, HEIDI
    BUCHHOLZ, HORST
BUCHHOLZ, BEATRICE
    BUCHHOLZ, HORST
BUCHHOLZ, CHRISTOPHER
    BUCHHOLZ, HORST
BUCHINSKY, JOHN
    BRONSON, CHARLES

BUCK, GENE
    DAVIES, MARION
BUCK, JULES
    O'TOOLE, PETER
BUCKLEY, KATHLEEN
    MOREAU, JEANNE
BUCKMASTER, HERBERT J.
    COOPER, GLADYS
BUCKMASTER, JOAN
    COOPER, GLADYS
    MORLEY, ROBERT
BUCKMASTER, JOHN
    COOPER, GLADYS
    MORLEY, ROBERT
BUDDECKE, MINETTE
    LANGE, HOPE
BUHL, LAURA
    GAYNOR, JANET
BUJAC, ADELE DE
    CABOT, BRUCE
BUJAC, JENNIFER DE
    CABOT, BRUCE
BUJOLD, FERMIN
    BUJOLD, GENEVIEVE
BULGARELLI, CLELIA
    PINZA, EZIO
BULIFANT, JOYCE
    HAYES, HELEN
BURCE, PAUL
    POWELL, JANE
BURGARD, JENNIE MARSTON ADAMS
    TIBBETT, LAWRENCE
BURGES, MIGUEL
    CRISTAL, LINDA
BURGESS, IDA BETH
    MEREDITH, BURGESS
BURGIN, BARBARA
    BERGEN, POLLY
BURGIN, WILLIAM
    BERGEN, POLLY
BURK, DAVID LEE
    MONTGOMERY, GEORGE
    SHORE, DINAH
BURKE, HELEN
    TRAVOLTA, JOHN
BURKE, WILLIAM
    BURKE, BILLIE
BURNETT, CHRISTINE
    BURNETT, CAROL
BURNETT, JODY
    BURNETT, CAROL
BURNETTE, BRIAN
    BURNETTE, SMILEY
BURNETTE, CAROLYN
    BURNETTE, SMILEY
BURNETTE, LINDA
    BURNETTE, SMILEY

BURNETTE, REV. GEORGE
    BURNETTE, SMILEY
BURNETTE, STEPHEN
    BURNETTE, SMILEY
BURNS, GEORGE
    ALLEN, GRACIE
    HALEY, JACK
BURNS, ROLAND JON
    ALLEN, GRACIE
    BURNS, GEORGE
BURNS, SANDRA JEAN
    ALLEN, GRACIE
    BURNS, GEORGE
BURNS, WILLIAM
    CANOVA, JUDY
BURR, MICHAEL EVAN
    BURR, RAYMOND
BURR, MINERVA SMITH
    BURR, RAYMOND
BURR, SR., WILLIAM JOHNSTON
    BURR, RAYMOND
BURR, WILLIAM JOHNSTON
    BURR, RAYMOND
BURSTYN, JEFFERSON
    BURSTYN, ELLEN
BURSTYN, NEIL
    BURSTYN, ELLEN
BURTON, BOB
    COCA, IMOGENE
BURTON, JESSICA
    BURTON, RICHARD
    TAYLOR, ELIZABETH
BURTON, KATE
    BURTON, RICHARD
    TAYLOR, ELIZABETH
BURTON, PHILIP
    BURTON, RICHARD
BURTON, RICHARD
    TAYLOR, ELIZABETH
BURTON, SKIP
    BLACK, KAREN
BURWELL, OLIVE
    GILBERT, JOHN
BUSBY, AMY
    BERKELEY, BUSBY
BUSCH, DEBORAH
    WHITING, MARGARET
BUSCH, LOUIS
    BLAIR, JANET
    WHITING, MARGARET
BUSH, FRANCES CLEVELAND
    CHANEY, JR., LON
    CHANEY, LON
BUSHMAN, BRUCE
    BUSHMAN, FRANCIS X.
BUSHMAN, JOHN
    BUSHMAN, FRANCIS X.

BUSHMAN, JOSEPHINE
  BUSHMAN, FRANCIS X.
BUSHMAN, LEONORE
  BUSHMAN, FRANCIS X.
BUSHMAN, RALPH
  BUSHMAN, FRANCIS X.
BUSHMAN, RICHARD STANBURY
  BUSHMAN, FRANCIS X.
BUSHMAN, VIRGINIA
  BUSHMAN, FRANCIS X.
BUSHNELL, MABEL
  RYAN, ROBERT
BUSTILL, MARIA LOUISA
  ROBESON, PAUL
BUTLER, BETTY JANE
  WYNN, KEENAN
BUTTONS, AMY
  BUTTONS, RED
BUTTS, ROBERT DALE
  EVANS, DALE
BUYDENS, ANNE
  DOUGLAS, KIRK
  DOUGLAS, MICHAEL
BUZZI, ED
  BUZZI, RUTH
BUZZI, HAROLD
  BUZZI, RUTH
BYINGTON, EDWIN LEE
  BYINGTON, SPRING
BYRD, MARGUERITE
  BELAFONTE, HARRY
BYRNE, ANNE
  HOFFMAN, DUSTIN
BYRNE, JULIA
  O'CONNELL, ARTHUR
BYRNE, KATHERINE
  REED, OLIVER
CAAN, ARTHUR
  CAAN, JAMES
CAAN, BARBARA
  CAAN, JAMES
CAAN, RONALD
  CAAN, JAMES
CAAN, SCOTT ANDREW
  CAAN, JAMES
CAAN, TARA ALISA
  CAAN, JAMES
CABOT, ALPHONSINE
  CABOT, BRUCE
CABOT, BRUCE MICHAEL
  CABOT, BRUCE
CABRE, MARIO
  GARDNER, AVA
CADWALADER, JESSICA
  RYAN, ROBERT
CAESAR, MAX
  CAESAR, SID

CAESAR, MICHELE ANDREA
  CAESAR, SID
CAESAR, SID
  COCA, IMOGENE
CAGNEY, BILL
  CAGNEY, JAMES
CAGNEY, CATHLEEN
  CAGNEY, JAMES
CAGNEY, EDDIE
  CAGNEY, JAMES
CAGNEY, GRACE
  CAGNEY, JAMES
CAGNEY, HARRY
  CAGNEY, JAMES
CAGNEY, JAMES FRANCIS
  CAGNEY, JAMES
CAGNEY, JEANNE
  CAGNEY, JAMES
CAGNEY, JIMMY
  CAGNEY, JAMES
CAGNEY, ROBERT
  CAGNEY, JAMES
CAIN, KATHRYN
  BLONDELL, JOAN
  POWELL, DICK
CAINE, DOMINIQUE
  CAINE, MICHAEL
CALDERON, MARTITA VALENTINA
  DE HAVILLAND, OLIVIA
  FONTAINE, JOAN
CALDWELL, F. M.
  BARTHELMESS, RICHARD
CALDWELL, MARY HAY
  BARTHELMESS, RICHARD
CALDWELL, VIOLA
  BAXTER, WARNER
CALHERN, LOUIS
  CHASE, ILKA
CALHOUN, CINDY FRANCES
  CALHOUN, RORY
CALHOUN, EDNA
  HORNE, LENA
CALHOUN, LORRIE MARIE
  CALHOUN, RORY
CALHOUN, RORYE
  CALHOUN, RORY
CALHOUN, TAMI ELIZABETH
  CALHOUN, RORY
CALL, FLORA
  DISNEY, WALT
CALLAGHAN, PATRICIA
  O'NEAL, RYAN
CALLAHAN, EDWARD
  MCDONALD, MARIE
CALLAS, MARGO
  NICHOLS, MIKE
CALPASS, KATHERINE
  DISNEY, WALT

CALVET, MICHAEL
  CALVET, CORINNE
CAMBRIDGE, ALEXANDER
  CAMBRIDGE, GODFREY
CAMBRIDGE, RUTH
  EBSEN, BUDDY
CAMERON, ARTHUR
  MILLER, ANN
CAMERON, CHRISTINA
  NEFF, HILDEGARDE
CAMERON, DAVID
  NEFF, HILDEGARDE
CAMERON, RUDOLPH
  STEWART, ANITA
CAMMANN, FREDERIC GALLATIN
  MONTGOMERY, ELIZABETH
  MONTGOMERY, ROBERT
CAMP, BARBARA
  VOIGHT, JON
CAMPBELL, ELIZABETH
  ROSENBLOOM,'SLAPSIE' MAXIE
CAMPBELL, LORI
  CABOT, BRUCE
CAMPBELL, WEBSTER
  GRIFFITH, CORINNE
CANDOLI, CAROLYN
  ADAMS, EDIE
  HUTTON, BETTY
CANDOLI, PETE
  ADAMS, EDIE
  HUTTON, BETTY
CANESSA, MARION ROSE LAKE
  LAKE, ARTHUR
CANFIELD, DAISY
  MORENO, ANTONIO
CANNON, DYAN
  GRANT, CARY
CANOVA, DIANE 'ANNE'
  CANOVA, JUDY
CANOVA, JOE
  CANOVA, JUDY
CANOVA, LEO 'PETE'
  CANOVA, JUDY
CANSINO, EDUARDO
  HAYMES, DICK
  HAYWORTH, RITA
  WELLES, ORSON
CANSINO, JR., EDUARDO
  HAYWORTH, RITA
  ROGERS, GINGER
  WELLES, ORSON
CANSINO, VERNON
  HAYWORTH, RITA
CANTOR, EDNA
  CANTOR, EDDIE
CANTOR, JANET
  CANTOR, EDDIE

CANTOR, MARILYN
  CANTOR, EDDIE
CANTOR, MARJORIE
  CANTOR, EDDIE
CANTOR, NATALIE
  CANTOR, EDDIE
CANTU, GUILLERMINA
  ROLAND, GILBERT
CANUTT, YAKIMA
  WAYNE, JOHN
CARABELLA, FLORA
  MASTROIANNI, MARCELLO
CAREWE, EDWIN
  DEL RIO, DOLORES
CAREY, ANNA THERESE
  CAREY, MACDONALD
CAREY, EDITH
  HARRISON, REX
CAREY, ELLEN
  CAREY, HARRY
CAREY, JR., HARRY
  CAREY, HARRY
CAREY, JR., MACDONALD
  CAREY, MACDONALD
CAREY, LISA
  CAREY, MACDONALD
CAREY, LYNN
  CAREY, MACDONALD
CAREY, PAUL GORDON
  CAREY, MACDONALD
CAREY, STEVEN
  CAREY, MACDONALD
CARILLO, LEO
  RENALDO, DUNCAN
CARLISLE, BEATRICE
  CHAMPION, GOWER
CARLSON, CARL
  HENIE, SONJA
CARLTON-MUNROE, ROBERT
  LAKE, VERONICA
CARLTON, ALMA OSBORNE
  JOLSON, AL
CARLYLE, JOHN K.
  LEIGH, JANET
CARMEL, CASEY
  LEVANT, OSCAR
CARMICHAEL, HOAGY BIX
  CARMICHAEL, HOAGY
CARMICHAEL, HOWARD CLYDE
  CARMICHAEL, HOAGY
CARMICHAEL, RANDY BOB
  CARMICHAEL, HOAGY
CARNE, JUDY
  REYNOLDS, BURT
CARNEY, BRIAN
  CARNEY, ART
CARNEY, EDWARD
  CARNEY, ART

CHAPLIN, CHARLES
    GODDARD, PAULETTE
    NEGRI, POLA
CHAPLIN, CHARLES SPENCER
    CHAPLIN, CHARLES
CHAPLIN, CHRISTOPHER
    CHAPLIN, CHARLES
    CHAPLIN, GERALDINE
CHAPLIN, EUGENE
    CHAPLIN, CHARLES
    CHAPLIN, GERALDINE
CHAPLIN, GERALDINE
    CHAPLIN, CHARLES
CHAPLIN, III, CHARLES SPENCER
    CHAPLIN, GERALDINE
    GODDARD, PAULETTE
CHAPLIN, JANE
    CHAPLIN, CHARLES
    CHAPLIN, GERALDINE
CHAPLIN, JOSEPHINE
    CHAPLIN, CHARLES
    CHAPLIN, GERALDINE
CHAPLIN, MICHAEL
    CHAPLIN, CHARLES
    CHAPLIN, GERALDINE
CHAPLIN, SHANE
    CHAPLIN, CHARLES
    CHAPLIN, GERALDINE
CHAPLIN, SYDNEY
    CHAPLIN, CHARLES
CHAPLIN, SYDNEY EARLE
    CHAPLIN, CHARLES
    CHAPLIN, GERALDINE
    GODDARD, PAULETTE
CHAPLIN, VICTORIA
    CHAPLIN, CHARLES
    CHAPLIN, GERALDINE
CHAPLIN, 3RD, CHARLES SPENCER
    CHAPLIN, CHARLES
CHAPMAN, VIRGINIA
    ARNESS, JAMES
CHAPPELLE, BETTY
    WILLS, CHILL
CHARISSE, CYD
    ASTAIRE, FRED
    MARTIN, TONY
CHARISSE, NICKY
    CHARISSE, CYD
    MARTIN, TONY
CHARISSE, NICO
    CHARISSE, CYD
CHARLES, FRANCES
    MATURE, VICTOR
CHARLOTTE, CONSTANCE
    OBERON, MERLE
CHARLTON, LILLA
    HESTON, CHARLTON

CHARRIER, JACQUES
    BARDOT, BRIGITTE
CHARRIER, NICOLAS JACQUES
    BARDOT, BRIGITTE
CHARTERIS, LESLIE
    VALLEE, RUDY
CHASE, BARRIE
    ASTAIRE, FRED
CHASE, FRANK D.
    CHASE, ILKA
CHASE, ILKA
    CALHERN, LOUIS
CHASSAGNE, ROBERT
    PRESLE, MICHELINE
CHATTERTON, WALTER
    CHATTERTON, RUTH
CHAUCHOIN, CHARLES
    COLBERT, CLAUDETTE
CHAUCHOIN, GEORGE
    COLBERT, CLAUDETTE
CHEBONICK, MARY
    KOVACS, ERNIE
CHEKHOV, ANTON
    CHEKHOV, MICHAEL
CHEKOV, XENIA J.
    CHEKHOV, MICHAEL
CHERRILL, VIRGINIA
    GRANT, CARY
    SCOTT, RANDOLPH
CHERRY, HELEN MARY
    HOWARD, TREVOR
CHERRY, NETTIE
    ALLEN, WOODY
CHESNEY, ARTHUR
    WINWOOD, ESTELLE
CHEVALIER, CHARLES
    CHEVALIER, MAURICE
CHEVALIER, PAUL
    CHEVALIER, MAURICE
CHEVALIER, VICTOR CHARLES
    CHEVALIER, MAURICE
CHILDS, DORIS SELLERS
    BOND, WARD
CHIRELLO, GEORGE 'SHORTY'
    WELLES, ORSON
CHOW, RAYMOND
    LEE, BRUCE
CHOWN, FLORENCE EDITH
    YORK, MICHAEL
CHRISTIAN, LINDA
    JURADO, KATY
    POWER, TYRONE
    PURDOM, EDMUND
CHRISTIE, JULIE
    BEATTY, WARREN
CHRISTOPHISON, LISBET
    NELSON, BARRY

CHUEN, LI HOI
    LEE, BRUCE
CHURCHILL, DIANA
    JOHNS, GLYNIS
CHWATT, IDA
    BUTTONS, RED
CHWATT, JOSEF
    BUTTONS, RED
CHWATT, MICHAEL
    BUTTONS, RED
CILENTO, DIANE
    CONNERY, SEAN
CIMBER, ANTONIO
    MANSFIELD, JAYNE
CIMBER, MATT
    MANSFIELD, JAYNE
CINTRON, MARIA PROVIDENCIA
    FERRER, JOSE
CISNEROS, EMILY
    CARRADINE, JOHN
CLAIRE, CORA B. LIEURANCE
    CLAIRE, INA
CLAIRE, INA
    GILBERT, JOHN
CLARK, BRADLEY
    CLARK, DICK
CLARK, CANDY
    BRIDGES, JEFF
CLARK, CYNTHIA
    CLARK, DICK
CLARK, DWAYNE
    CLARK, DICK
CLARK, FRED
    VENUTA, BENAY
CLARK, III, RICHARD AUGUSTUS
    CLARK, DICK
CLARK, LESLIE
    CLARK, PETULA
CLARK, RICHARD AUGUSTUS
    CLARK, DICK
CLARK, ROBIN
    MACGRAW, ALI
CLARK, ROSEMARY
    RAINS, CLAUDE
CLARKE, BENJAMIN
    REDGRAVE, LYNN
    REDGRAVE, MICHAEL
CLARKE, JOHN
    REDGRAVE, LYNN
    REDGRAVE, MICHAEL
    REDGRAVE, VANESSA
CLARKE, KELLY
    REDGRAVE, LYNN
    REDGRAVE, MICHAEL
    REDGRAVE, VANESSA
CLARKE, LOIS
    GARNER, JAMES

CLARKE, LYDIA
    HESTON, CHARLTON
CLAYBURGH, JILL
    PACINO, AL
CLAYTON, G. VERNER
    CLAYTON, JAN
    HAYDEN, RUSSELL
CLAYTON, JAN
    HAYDEN, RUSSELL
CLAYTON, LOU
    DURANTE, JIMMY
CLEGHORN, HELEN
    BYINGTON, SPRING
CLEMENS, JR., PAUL
    PARKER, ELEANOR
CLEMENS, PAUL
    PARKER, ELEANOR
CLEMENTS, STANLEY
    GRAHAME, GLORIA
CLEVE, PATRICA VAN
    LAKE, ARTHUR
CLIFFORD, HANNAH
    BEGLEY, ED
CLIFT, JR., WILLIAM BROOKS
    CLIFT, MONTGOMERY
CLIFT, ROBERTA 'ETHEL'
    CLIFT, MONTGOMERY
CLIFT, WILLIAM BROOKS
    CLIFT, MONTGOMERY
CLODE, SARAH ANN
    SMITH, C. AUBREY
CLOONEY, ANDREW
    CLOONEY, ROSEMARY
CLOONEY, ELIZABETH
    CLOONEY, ROSEMARY
CLOONEY, GAIL
    CLOONEY, ROSEMARY
CLOONEY, NICHOLAS
    CLOONEY, ROSEMARY
CLOONEY, ROSEMARY
    FERRER, JOSE
CLOUTIER, SUZANNE
    USTINOV, PETER
CLUTTER, BETH
    TAYLOR, ELIZABETH
    WILDING, MICHAEL
COBB, ANTHONY
    COBB, LEE J.
COBB, BENJAMIN JACOB
    COBB, LEE J.
COBB, GERALD
    COBB, LEE J.
COBB, HAZEL IRENE
    MARSHALL, E.G.
COBB, JULIE
    COBB, LEE J.
COBB, VINCENT
    COBB, LEE J.

COBURN, IV, JAMES
    COBURN, JAMES
COBURN, JAMES
    LEE, BRUCE
COBURN, LISA
    COBURN, JAMES
COBURN, MOSES DOUVILLE
    COBURN, CHARLES
COBURN, SR., JAMES
    COBURN, JAMES
COCA, IMOGENE
    CAESAR, SID
COCA, JOSE FERNANDEZ Y
    COCA, IMOGENE
COCCOZZA, ANTONIO
    LANZA, MARIO
COCHRAN, XANDRA
    COCHRAN, STEVE
CODY, LEW
    NORMAND, MABEL
COLE, CAROL
    COLE, NAT 'KING'
COLE, STEPHANIE NATALIE MARIA
    COLE, NAT 'KING'
COLES, EDWARD
    COLE, NAT 'KING'
COLLERAN, KATE
    REMICK, LEE
COLLERAN, MATTHEW
    REMICK, LEE
COLLERAN, WILLIAM
    REMICK, LEE
COLLIER, JOHN ALFRED
    MILLER, ANN
COLLIER, JR., WILLIAM
    TALMADGE, CONSTANCE
COLLINS, ALANA
    HAMILTON, GEORGE
COLLINS, CATHLEEN
    DEREK, JOHN
COLLINS, CHARLES
    CRISTAL, LINDA
COLLINS, JACQUELINE
    COLLINS, JOAN
COLLINS, JR., WILLIAM
    COLLINS, JOAN
COLLINS, WILLIAM
    COLLINS, JOAN
COLMAN, CHARLES
    COLMAN, RONALD
COLMAN, JULIET
    COLMAN, RONALD
    HUME, BENITA
    SANDERS, GEORGE
COLMAN, RONALD
    BANKY, VILMA
    HUME, BENITA

COLMAN, RONALD
    POWELL, WILLIAM
COLT, ETHEL BARRYMORE
    BARRYMORE, ETHEL
    BARRYMORE, JOHN
    BARRYMORE, JR., JOHN
    BARRYMORE, LIONEL
COLT, JOHN DREW
    BARRYMORE, ETHEL
    BARRYMORE, JOHN
    BARRYMORE, JR., JOHN
    BARRYMORE, LIONEL
COLT, RUSSELL GRISWOLD
    BARRYMORE, ETHEL
    BARRYMORE, JOHN
    BARRYMORE, LIONEL
COLT, SAMUEL PEABODY
    BARRYMORE, ETHEL
    BARRYMORE, JOHN
    BARRYMORE, JR., JOHN
    BARRYMORE, LIONEL
COLUMBO, RUSS
    LOMBARD, CAROLE
COLWELL, PAUL
    QUINN, ANTHONY
COMBS, LORETTA BARNETT
    AGAR, JOHN
COMDEN, BARRY
    DAY, DORIS
COMDEN, BETTY
    HOLLIDAY, JUDY
COMO, DAVID
    COMO, PERRY
COMO, MELANIE ROSELLE
    COMO, PERRY
COMO, PERRY
    ANGELI, PIER
COMO, PIETRO
    COMO, PERRY
COMO, RONALD
    COMO, PERRY
COMO, TERRI
    COMO, PERRY
CONDOS, MELODYE
    RAYE, MARTHA
CONDOS, NICK
    RAYE, MARTHA
CONLON, ELIZABETH
    LAUGHTON, CHARLES
CONN, EVA
    BARRY, GENE
CONNERY, GIOVANNA
    CONNERY, SEAN
CONNERY, JASON
    CONNERY, SEAN
CONNERY, JOSEPH
    CONNERY, SEAN

CONNOLLY, JOHN
    JONES, JAMES EARL
CONNOLLY, SHEILA
    MADISON, GUY
CONNORS, JEFFREY
    CONNORS, CHUCK
CONNORS, KEVIN
    CONNORS, CHUCK
CONNORS, MICHAEL
    CONNORS, CHUCK
CONNORS, STEVEN
    CONNORS, CHUCK
CONSIDINE, JOHN
    BENNETT, JOAN
CONTE, JOHN
    MAXWELL, MARILYN
CONTE, MARK
    CONTE, RICHARD
CONTE, PASQUALE
    CONTE, RICHARD
CONVERSE, GEORGE PEABODY
    STEWART, ANITA
CONVERSE, LAWRENCE
    LA MARR, BARBARA
CONWAY, JACK
    BUSHMAN, FRANCIS X.
CONWELL, MARY ELIZABETH
    FARNUM, DUSTIN
    FARNUM, WILLIAM
COOGAN, CHRISTOPHER FENTON
    COOGAN, JACKIE
COOGAN, JACKIE
    GRABLE, BETTY
COOGAN, JOANN DOLLIVER
    COOGAN, JACKIE
COOGAN, JOHN ANTHONY
    COOGAN, JACKIE
COOGAN, JOHN HENRY
    COOGAN, JACKIE
COOGAN, LESLIE DIANE
    COOGAN, JACKIE
COOLIDGE, LINDA
    KRISTOFFERSON, KRIS
COOLIDGE, PRISCILLA
    KRISTOFFERSON, KRIS
COOLIDGE, RICHARD
    KRISTOFFERSON, KRIS
COOLIDGE, RITA
    KRISTOFFERSON, KRIS
COOPER, ARTHUR
    COOPER, GARY
COOPER, CHARLES F.
    COOPER, GLADYS
COOPER, CHARLES HENRY
    COOPER, GARY
COOPER, CHRISTINA
    COOPER, JACKIE

COOPER, GARY
    BOW, CLARA
    MONTGOMERY, GEORGE
    NEAL, PATRICIA
    VELEZ, LUPE
COOPER, GLADYS
    BRUCE, NIGEL
    MORLEY, ROBERT
COOPER, JACKIE
    GRANVILLE, BONITA
COOPER, JOHN
    COOPER, JACKIE
COOPER, JOHN ANTHONY
    COOPER, JACKIE
COOPER, JULIE
    COOPER, JACKIE
COOPER, MARIA VERONICA
    COOPER, GARY
COOPER, MARILYN
    SABU
COOPER, MERIAN C.
    KING KONG
COOPER, ROSEMARY
    KEEL, HOWARD
COOPER, RUSSELL
    COOPER, JACKIE
COPPOLA, AUGUST
    SHIRE, TALIA
COPPOLA, CARMINE
    SHIRE, TALIA
COPPOLA, FRANCIS FORD
    SHIRE, TALIA
COPPOLA, GLO
    SHIRE, TALIA
COPPOLA, MARK
    SHIRE, TALIA
COPPOLA, ROMAN
    SHIRE, TALIA
COPPOLA, SOFIA
    SHIRE, TALIA
CORBETT, JULIA
    HUSSEY, RUTH
CORCORAN, WINIFRED
    MCDOWALL, RODDY
CORD, DAMION
    CORD, ALEX
CORDAY, MARA
    LONG, RICHARD
COREY, BONNIE ALICE ELSIE
    COREY, WENDELL
COREY, JENNIFER JULIA
    COREY, WENDELL
COREY, JONATHAN WENDELL
    COREY, WENDELL
COREY, LUCY ROBIN
    COREY, WENDELL
COREY, MILTON ROTHWELL
    COREY, WENDELL

COREY, RONALD
    COREY, WENDELL
CORNELL, KATHERINE
    PECK, GREGORY
CORRELL, BARBARA JOAN
    CORRELL, CHARLES
CORRELL, CHARLES
    GOSDEN, FREEMAN
CORRELL, DOROTHY ALYCE
    CORRELL, CHARLES
CORRELL, JOHN JOSEPH
    CORRELL, CHARLES
CORRELL, JOSEPH BOLAND
    CORRELL, CHARLES
CORRELL, JR., CHARLES JAMES
    CORRELL, CHARLES
CORRELL, RICHARD THOMAS
    CORRELL, CHARLES
CORTESA, VALENTINA
    BASEHART, RICHARD
CORTEZ, HELEN
    CORTEZ, RICARDO
CORTEZ, RICHARD
    YOUNG, LORETTA
CORY, ALICIA
    BOTTOMS, TIMOTHY
COSBY, ANNA
    COSBY, BILL
COSBY, ENNIS WILLIAM
    COSBY, BILL
COSBY, ENSA
    COSBY, BILL
COSBY, ERIKE RANEE
    COSBY, BILL
COSBY, ERINN CHARLENE
    COSBY, BILL
COSBY, EVIN HARRAH
    COSBY, BILL
COSBY, WILLIAM
    COSBY, BILL
COSDEN, JR., JOSHUA
    GABOR, EVA
    GABOR, ZSA ZSA
COSGROVE, RUTH
    BERLE, MILTON
COSNER, ARDANELLE
    CARRADINE, JOHN
COSTELLA, LAURA
    WARDEN, JACK
COSTELLO, CAROLE LOU
    COSTELLO, LOU
COSTELLO, CHRISTINE
    COSTELLO, LOU
COSTELLO, DOLORES
    BARRYMORE, ETHEL
    BARRYMORE, JOHN
    BARRYMORE, JR., JOHN

COSTELLO, DOLORES
    BARRYMORE, LIONEL
COSTELLO, HELENE
    BARRYMORE, JOHN
    BARRYMORE, JR., JOHN
    COSTELLO, DOLORES
COSTELLO, JR., LOU
    COSTELLO, LOU
COSTELLO, LOU
    ABBOTT, BUD
COSTELLO, MAURICE
    BARRYMORE, JOHN
    BARRYMORE, JR., JOHN
    COSTELLO, DOLORES
COSTELLO, PATRICIA
    COSTELLO, LOU
COTTEN, JUDITH KIP
    COTTEN, JOSEPH
COTTER, FRANCIS MEADOWS
    MEADOWS, AUDREY
    MEADOWS, JAYNE
COTTER, G. EDWARD
    MEADOWS, AUDREY
    MEADOWS, JAYNE
COTTER, JR., FRANCIS
    ALLEN, STEVE
    MEADOWS, AUDREY
    MEADOWS, JAYNE
COTTON, SR., JOSEPH
    COTTEN, JOSEPH
COULTER, THERON 'JOHN'
    BENNETT, CONSTANCE
    BENNETT, JOAN
COUNCIL, GARLAND
    SULLAVAN, MARGARET
COURT, DOROTHY
    MURRAY, KEN
COURTENAY, THOMAS HENRY
    COURTENAY, TOM
COURTLAND, JEROME
    BERGEN, POLLY
COURTNEY, FLORENCE
    JESSEL, GEORGE
COWAN, CLAUDIA
    RUSH, BARBARA
COWAN, MILDRED
    TURNER, LANA
COWAN, WARREN
    RUSH, BARBARA
COWARD, ARTHUR SABIN
    COWARD, NOEL
COWARD, NOEL
    DIETRICH, MARLENE
COWL, JANE
    GABLE, CLARK
COX, EMILY ELIZA
    RAINS, CLAUDE

COX, MAUREEN
    STARR, RINGO
COX, WALLY
    BRANDO, MARLON
COYNE, JEANNE
    KELLY, GENE
COZZIKA, THEODORE
    WHITE, PEARL
CRABBE, CAREN
    CRABBE, BUSTER
CRABBE, CULLEN 'CUFFY'
    CRABBE, BUSTER
CRABBE, ELIZABETH
    HARDING, ANN
CRABBE, SUSAN
    CRABBE, BUSTER
CRAIG, ELI
    FIELD, SALLY
CRAIG, H. A. L. 'HARRY'
    O'TOOLE, PETER
CRAIG, PETER
    FIELD, SALLY
CRAIG, STEVE
    FIELD, SALLY
CRAIN, GEORGE A.
    CRAIN, JEANNE
CRAIN, RITA
    CRAIN, JEANNE
CRAMER, GRANT LAMAR
    MOORE, TERRY
CRAMER, IV, STUART
    MOORE, TERRY
CRAMER, MARJORIE
    TALBOT, LYLE
CRAMER, STUART
    MOORE, TERRY
    PETERS, JEAN
CRAMTON, HARRY CLYDE
    EVERETT, CHAD
CRANE, CHERYL
    BARKER, LEX
    TURNER, LANA
CRANE, EFFIE IRENE
    O'CONNOR, DONALD
CRANE, FLORENCE BELLE
    WHITMORE, JAMES
CRANE, LUCY
    SCOTT, RANDOLPH
CRANE, STEPHEN
    TURNER, LANA
CRATER, ALLENE
    STONE, FRED
CRAVAT, NICK
    LANCASTER, BURT
CRAWFORD, 'SCOOP'
    EMERSON, FAYE
CRAWFORD, ANNA HARRIET
    KARLOFF, BORIS

CRAWFORD, CATHARINE
    CRAWFORD, JOAN
CRAWFORD, CHRISTINA
    CRAWFORD, JOAN
CRAWFORD, CHRISTOPHER
    CRAWFORD, BRODERICK
CRAWFORD, CYNTHIA
    CRAWFORD, JOAN
CRAWFORD, J. LLOYD
    MCDANIEL, HATTIE
CRAWFORD, JOAN
    FAIRBANKS, JR., DOUGLAS
    GABLE, CLARK
    ROMERO, CESAR
    TONE, FRANCHOT
CRAWFORD, JULIA
    MCQUEEN, STEVE
CRAWFORD, KELLY
    CRAWFORD, BRODERICK
CRAWFORD, KIM
    CRAWFORD, BRODERICK
CRAWFORD, WILLIAM
    EMERSON, FAYE
CRAYNE, DANNI
    FRANCISCUS, JAMES
    JANSSEN, DAVID
CREIGER, GERTRUDE
    TEMPLE, SHIRLEY
CREIGHTON, CLEVA
    CHANEY, JR., LON
    CHANEY, LON
CREIGHTON, LOUISE
    BURNETT, CAROL
CRENNA, DOMENICK
    CRENNA, RICHARD
CRENNA, JR., RICHARD
    CRENNA, RICHARD
CRENNA, MARIA
    CRENNA, RICHARD
CRENNA, SEANA
    CRENNA, RICHARD
CRICHTON, JUDY
    FURNESS, BETTY
CRISTAL, LINDA
    CHAMPION, GOWER
CRISTALDI, FRANCO
    CARDINALE, CLAUDIA
CRISTALDI, PATRICK FRANK
    CARDINALE, CLAUDIA
CRISTILLO, ANTHONY SEBASTIAN
    COSTELLO, LOU
CRISTILLO, MARIE THERESA
    COSTELLO, LOU
CRISTILLO, SEBASTIAN
    COSTELLO, LOU
CROCETTI, GUY
    MARTIN, DEAN

CROCKENDEN, AGNES LOUISE
    OLIVIER, LAURENCE
CROLINS, MINA
    GLEASON, JAMES 'JIMMY'
CROMWELL, RICHARD
    LANSBURY, ANGELA
CRONK, NELLIE MAE
    WINDSOR, CLAIRE
CRONYN, CHRISTOPHER
    CRONYN, HUME
    TANDY, JESSICA
CRONYN, HUME
    TANDY, JESSICA
CRONYN, TANDY
    CRONYN, HUME
    TANDY, JESSICA
CROSBY, BOB
    CROSBY, BING
CROSBY, CATHERINE
    CROSBY, BING
CROSBY, CHRISTOPHER
    CROSBY, BING
CROSBY, DENNIS MICHAEL
    CROSBY, BING
CROSBY, EVERETT
    CROSBY, BING
CROSBY, GARY EVAN
    CROSBY, BING
CROSBY, HARRY LOWE
    CROSBY, BING
CROSBY, HOWARD LINDSAY
    CROSBY, BING
CROSBY, III, HARRY LILLIS
    CROSBY, BING
CROSBY, LAWRENCE
    CROSBY, BING
CROSBY, MARY FRANCES
    CROSBY, BING
CROSBY, MARY ROSE
    CROSBY, BING
CROSBY, NATHANIEL PATRICK
    CROSBY, BING
CROSBY, PHILIP LANG
    CROSBY, BING
CROSBY, THEODORE
    CROSBY, BING
CROUCH, JACKIE JEAN
    CHER
CROWLEY, MARIAN A.
    TIERNEY, LAWRENCE
CUDAHY, MICHAEL
    CRAWFORD, JOAN
CUGAT, ALBERT
    CUGAT, XAVIER
CUGAT, FRANCIS
    CUGAT, XAVIER
CUGAT, HENRY
    CUGAT, XAVIER

CUGAT, REGINA
    CUGAT, XAVIER
CUKOR, GEORGE
    HEPBURN, KATHARINE
CULP, JASON
    CULP, ROBERT
CULP, JOSEPH
    CULP, ROBERT
CULP, JOSHUA
    CULP, ROBERT
CULP, RACHEL
    CULP, ROBERT
CULPEPPER, JACK
    ROGERS, GINGER
CUMMINGS, ANTHONY
    CUMMINGS, ROBERT
CUMMINGS, CHARLES
    CUMMINGS, ROBERT
CUMMINGS, CHARLES CLARENCE
    CUMMINGS, ROBERT
CUMMINGS, JACK
    MAYER, LOUIS B.
CUMMINGS, LAUREL
    CUMMINGS, ROBERT
CUMMINGS, MARY MELINDA
    CUMMINGS, ROBERT
CUMMINGS, MICHELLE HELENE
    CUMMINGS, ROBERT
CUMMINGS, ROBERT RICHARD
    CUMMINGS, ROBERT
CUMMINGS, SHARON PATRICIA
    CUMMINGS, ROBERT
CUNARD, GRACE
    FORD, FRANCIS
CUNHA, AURORA
    MIRANDA, CARMEN
CUNHA, JOSE PINTO
    MIRANDA, CARMEN
CUNNINGHAM, BELINDA
    TERRY-THOMAS
CURLY, ELLEN
    HALEY, JACK
CURRAN, HARRIET
    KELLY, GENE
CURTIS, ALAN
    MASSEY, ILONA
CURTIS, ALEXANDRA
    CURTIS, TONY
CURTIS, ALEXANDRA 'SANDY'
    PAYNE, JOHN
CURTIS, ALLEGRA
    CURTIS, TONY
CURTIS, BENJAMIN
    CURTIS, TONY
CURTIS, JAMIE LEIGH
    CURTIS, TONY
    LEIGH, JANET

CURTIS, KELLY LEE
    CURTIS, TONY
    LEIGH, JANET
CURTIS, NICHOLAS
    CURTIS, TONY
CURTIS, PATRICK
    WELCH, RAQUEL
CURTIS, TONY
    LEIGH, JANET
CUTLAR, LILIAN ANTONIA
    PURDOM, EDMUND
CZARTJAWICZ, COUNTESS LINA
    REEVES, STEVE
D'ABRUZZO, ANN
    ALDA, ALAN
    ALDA, ROBERT
D'ABRUZZO, VINCENT
    ALDA, ALAN
    ALDA, ROBERT
D'ALLEMAN, HELENE DU LAU
    USTINOV, PETER
D'ARC, GISELLE CAMILLE
    WALKER, CLINT
D'ARRAST, HENRI D'ABBADIE
    BOARDMAN, ELEANOR
DAHL, ARLENE
    BARKER, LEX
    LAMAS, FERNANDO
DAHL, LUCILLE NEAL
    NEAL, PATRICIA
DAHL, OLIVIA TWENTY
    NEAL, PATRICIA
DAHL, OPHELIA MAGDALENE
    NEAL, PATRICIA
DAHL, ROALD
    NEAL, PATRICIA
DAHL, RUDOLPH
    DAHL, ARLENE
DAHL, TESSA
    HOLLOWAY, STANLEY
DAHL, TESSA SOPHIA
    NEAL, PATRICIA
DAHL, THEODORE MATTHEW ROALD
    NEAL, PATRICIA
DAILEY, 3RD, DAN
    DAILEY, DAN
DALRYMPLE, JEAN
    TONE, FRANCHOT
DALTON, JAMES
    DRESSLER, MARIE
DALY, CYNTHIA ANN
    DALY, JAMES
DALY, DAVID
    DALY, JAMES
DALY, GLYNN
    DALY, JAMES
DALY, JOSEPH
    BERGMAN, INGRID

DALY, MARY ELLEN
    DALY, JAMES
DALY, PEGEEN
    DALY, JAMES
DALY, PERCIFER
    DALY, JAMES
DALY, TIMOTHY
    DALY, JAMES
DALY, TYNE
    DALY, JAMES
DAMALA, JACQUES
    BERNHARDT, SARAH
DAMALA, MAURICE
    BERNHARDT, SARAH
DAMITA, LILI
    FLYNN, ERROL
DAMITA, PIERRE
    DAMITA, LILI
DAMONE, ANDREA
    DAMONE, VIC
DAMONE, DANIELLA
    DAMONE, VIC
DAMONE, MAMIE
    DAMONE, VIC
DAMONE, PERRY ROCCO LUIGI
    ANGELI, PIER
    DAMONE, VIC
    PAVAN, MARISA
DAMONE, VIC
    ANGELI, PIER
    COMO, PERRY
    PAVAN, MARISA
DAMONE, VICTORIA CATHERINE
    DAMONE, VIC
DANA, BARBARA
    ARKIN, ALAN
DANESE, SHERRA LYNN
    FALK, PETER
DANIEL, MILDRED
    THATCHER, TORIN
DANIELE, MAELY
    BARTHOLOMEW, FREDDIE
DANIELS, MELVILLE
    DANIELS, BEBE
DANKER, LORENA
    MAYER, LOUIS B.
DANTE, RONALD
    TURNER, LANA
DANZIGER, DAISY
    MORENO, ANTONIO
DANZIGER, ELIZABETH
    MORENO, ANTONIO
DANZIGER, ROBERT C.
    MORENO, ANTONIO
DARCEL, DENISE
    CALVET, CORINNE
DARCY, SHEILA
    VON STROHEIM, ERICH

DARE, BARBARA
    TUFTS, SONNY
DARIN, BOBBY
    DEE, SANDRA
DARIN, DODD MITCHELL CASSOTTO
    DARIN, BOBBY
    DEE, SANDRA
DARLING, GERTRUDE
    BENCHLEY, ROBERT
DARNELL, CALVIN ROY
    DARNELL, LINDA
DARNELL, MONTE MALOYA
    DARNELL, LINDA
DARNELL, UNDEEN
    DARNELL, LINDA
DARR, ALICIA
    PURDOM, EDMUND
DARRELL, JACQUELINE
    REED, OLIVER
DARREN, ANTHONY
    DARREN, JAMES
DARREN, CHRISTIAN
    DARREN, JAMES
DARREN, JOHN
    DARPEN, JAMES
DARREN, JR., JAMES
    DARREN, JAMES
DASSIN, JOSEPH
    DASSIN, JULES
    MERCOURI, MELINA
DASSIN, JULES
    MERCOURI, MELINA
DASSIN, JULIE
    DASSIN, JULES
    MERCOURI, MELINA
DASSIN, RICHELLE
    DASSIN, JULES
    MERCOURI, MELINA
DASSIN, SAMUEL
    DASSIN, JULES
DASTAGIR, JASMIN
    SABU
DASTAGIR, PAUL
    SABU
DAUPHIN, NORMA
    CAREY, MACDONALD
DAVENPORT, AILEEN
    HOLBROOK, HAL
DAVENPORT, ANN
    HART, WILLIAM S.
    REID, WALLACE
DAVENPORT, DOROTHY
    HART, WILLIAM S.
    REID, WALLACE
DAVENPORT, HARRY
    HART, WILLIAM S.
    REID, WALLACE

DAVENPORT, KATE
    HART, WILLIAM S.
    REID, WALLACE
DAVEY, WILLIAM M.
    SWANSON, GLORIA
DAVID, CHARLES HENRI
    DURBIN, DEANNA
DAVID, PETER
    DURBIN, DEANNA
DAVIES, DAVID
    NOVELLO, IVOR
DAVIES, HELEN
    PEPPARD, GEORGE
DAVIES, MARIE NOVELLO
    NOVELLO, IVOR
DAVIES, MARION
    CHASE, ILKA
    CLAIRE, INA
    LAKE, ARTHUR
    SHIRLEY, ANNE
DAVIS, BARBARA
    DAVIS, BETTE
DAVIS, BETTE
    MERRILL, GARY
DAVIS, DESMOND
    TUSHINGHAM, RITA
DAVIS, FRANCIS
    HOLM, CELESTE
DAVIS, GEORGIA MAUREEN
    SKELTON, RED
DAVIS, GLENN
    MOORE, TERRY
    TAYLOR, ELIZABETH
DAVIS, HARLOW MORRELL
    DAVIS, BETTE
DAVIS, J. B. STRINGER
    RUTHERFORD, MARGARET
DAVIS, JAY
    DURBIN, DEANNA
DAVIS, JEFF
    DAVIS, JR., SAMMY
DAVIS, JEROME 'JERRY'
    MAXWELL, MARILYN
DAVIS, MARK
    DAVIS, JR., SAMMY
DAVIS, MATTHEW PAUL
    MAXWELL, MARILYN
DAVIS, MILDRED
    LLOYD, HAROLD
DAVIS, MILES
    TYSON, CICELY
DAVIS, NANCY
    REAGAN, RONALD
DAVIS, PHYLLIS
    MARTIN, DEAN
DAVIS, RAMONA
    DAVIS, JR., SAMMY

DAVIS, SR., SAMMY
    DAVIS, JR., SAMMY
DAVIS, TRACEY
    DAVIS, JR., SAMMY
DAWES, MILDRED
    NATWICK, MILDRED
DAWSON, DOUGLAS
    PARKER, JEAN
DAWSON, ELIZABETH
    MILLER, MARVIN
DAWSON, GARY
    DORS, DIANA
DAWSON, GENERAL DONALD S.
    MASSEY, ILONA
DAWSON, MARK
    DORS, DIANA
DAWSON, RICHARD 'DICKIE'
    DORS, DIANA
DAY, DENNIS
    BLYTH, ANN
DAY, ELIAS
    DAY, LARAINE
DAY, ROBERT E.
    SHERIDAN, ANN
DE COPPET, PAULINE
    BARA, THEDA
DE CROISSET, JACQUELINE
    BRYNNER, YUL
DE HAVEN, CARTER
    DE HAVEN, GLORIA
    PAYNE, JOHN
DE HAVEN, GLORIA
    PAYNE, JOHN
DE HAVEN, JR., CARTER
    DE HAVEN, GLORIA
DE HAVEN, MARJORIE
    DE HAVEN, GLORIA
DE HAVILLAND, OLIVIA
    AHERNE, BRIAN
    FLYNN, ERROL
    FONTAINE, JOAN
DE HAVILLAND, WALTER AUGUSTUS
    DE HAVILLAND, OLIVIA
    FONTAINE, JOAN
DE LAURENTIIS, ALFREDO
    DE LAURENTIIS, DINO
DE MILLE, CECIL B.
    GOLDWYN, SAMUEL
    MCCREA, JOEL
    QUINN, ANTHONY
    SWANSON, GLORIA
DE MILLE, CECILIA HOYT
    DE MILLE, C. B.
DE MILLE, HENRY CHURCHILL
    DE MILLE, C. B.
DE MILLE, JOHN
    DE MILLE, C. B.

DE MILLE, KATHERINE
    DE MILLE, C. B.
    QUINN, ANTHONY
DE MILLE, RICHARD
    DE MILLE, C. B.
DE MILLE, WILLIAM
    DE MILLE, C. B.
DE NIRO, SR., ROBERT
    DE NIRO, ROBERT
DE SICA, VITTORIO
    LOREN, SOPHIA
DEAL, NANCY ANN
    GREENE, LORNE
DEAMS, MICKEY
    GARLAND, JUDY
    MINNELLI, LIZA
DEAN, EDWARD
    SANDS, TOMMY
DEAN, JAMES
    ADAMS, NICK
    ANDRESS, URSULA
    ANGELI, PIER
    KITT, EARTHA
DEAN, WINTON
    DEAN, JAMES
DEANE, DORIS
    ARBUCKLE, FATTY
DEE, FRANCES
    MCCREA, JOEL
    OAKIE, JACK
DEE, SANDRA
    DARIN, BOBBY
DEELY, N. BERNARD 'BEN'
    LA MARR, BARBARA
DEGACHER, HENRIETTE
    NIVEN, DAVID
DEIBEL, KAY
    AVALON, FRANKIE
DEL COMPOS, ANTHONY
    ASTOR, MARY
DEL COMPOS, MANUEL
    ASTOR, MARY
DEL RIO, DOLORES
    COOPER, GARY
    NOVARRO, RAMON
DEL RIO, JACK
    LEE, PEGGY
DEL RIO, JAIME
    DEL RIO, DOLORES
DELANEY, ELLEN
    LOCKHART, GENE
DELDRIDGE, ALICE
    BELLAMY, RALPH
DELKER-DOLGER, MATILDA
    WEST, MAE
DELMAR, FRANCES
    THUNDERCLOUD, CHIEF

DELPINO, MERCEDES
    LAHR, BERT
DEMERCHANT, BEATRICE
    VARSI, DIANE
DEMERITT, JR., BROMLEY
    MARTIN, MARY
DEMPSEY, JACK
    DANIELS, BEBE
DEMPSTER, CAROL
    FIELDS, W.C.
DEMSKY, HARRY DANIELOVITCH
    DOUGLAS, KIRK
DENEUVE, CATHERINE
    MASTROIANNI, MARCELLO
DENEUVE, CHIARA-CHARLOTTE
    DENEUVE, CATHERINE
    MASTROIANNI, MARCELLO
DENEUVE, CHRISTIAN
    DENEUVE, CATHERINE
DENHAM, ISOLDE
    USTINOV, PETER
DENITZ, ANNE
    EDDY, NELSON
DENNIS, FRANK
    DENNIS, SANDY
DENNIS, JACK
    DENNIS, SANDY
DENNISON, JO-CARROLL
    SILVERS, PHIL
DENNY, BARBARA
    DENNY, REGINALD
DENNY, JOAN
    DENNY, REGINALD
DENNY, JR., REGINALD
    DENNY, REGINALD
DENNY, W. H.
    DENNY, REGINALD
DERBY, HELEN
    MEREDITH, BURGESS
DEREK, JOHN
    ANDRESS, URSULA
DEREK, RUSSELL ANDRE
    ANDRESS, URSULA
    DEREK, JOHN
DEREK, SEAN CATHERINE
    ANDRESS, URSULA
    DEREK, JOHN
DETLIE, ELAINE
    LAKE, VERONICA
DETLIE, WILLIAM ANTHONY
    LAKE, VERONICA
DETRICH, ELIZABETH
    DIETRICH, MARLENE
DEULOFEO, MINGALL
    CUGAT, XAVIER
DEUTSCH, ARMAND S.
    VENUTA, BENAY

DEUTSCH, DEBORAH
    VENUTA, BENAY
DEUTSCH, PATRICIA
    VENUTA, BENAY
DEVI, KAMALA
    CONNORS, CHUCK
DEVINE, DENNIS
    DEVINE, ANDY
DEVINE, TIMOTHY
    DEVINE, ANDY
DEVINE, TOD
    DEVINE, ANDY
DEWELL, MICHAEL
    FOCH, NINA
DEWHURST, COLLEEN
    SCOTT, GEORGE C.
DEXTER, BRAD
    LEE, PEGGY
DI FRASSO, CONTESSA DOROTHY
    COOPER, GARY
    VELEZ, LUPE
DIBOS, PIERRE
    CALVET, CORINNE
DICKINSON, GENE
    DICKINSON, ANGIE
DICKSON, JAMES
    VARSI, DIANE
DIETRICH, LOUIS ERICH OTTO
    DIETRICH, MARLENE
DIETRICH, MARLENE
    FAIRBANKS, JR., DOUGLAS
    GILBERT, JOHN
DILL, DIANA
    DOUGLAS, KIRK
    DOUGLAS, MICHAEL
DILLER, III, PETER
    DILLER, PHYLLIS
DILLER, PERRY
    DILLER, PHYLLIS
DILLER, SALLY
    DILLER, PHYLLIS
DILLER, SHERWOOD ANDERSON
    DILLER, PHYLLIS
DILLER, STEPHANIE
    DILLER, PHYLLIS
DILLER, SUZANNE
    DILLER, PHYLLIS
DILLMAN, BRADFORD
    PARKER, SUZY
DILLMAN, CHRISTOPHER PARKER
    DILLMAN, BRADFORD
    PARKER, SUZY
DILLMAN, DEAN
    DILLMAN, BRADFORD
DILLMAN, DINAH
    DILLMAN, BRADFORD
    PARKER, SUZY

DILLMAN, JEFFREY
    DILLMAN, BRADFORD
    PARKER, SUZY
DILLMAN, PAMELA
    DILLMAN, BRADFORD
    PARKER, SUZY
DILLON, BARBARA
    GIELGUD, JOHN
DILLON, JOSEPHINE
    GABLE, CLARK
DIMAGGIO, JOE
    MONROE, MARILYN
DINAPOLI, MILDRED
    BANCROFT, ANNE
    BROOKS, MEL
DINGMANE, EMMA
    YOUNG, GIG
DISNEY, DIANE MARIE
    DISNEY, WALT
DISNEY, ELIAS
    DISNEY, WALT
DISNEY, ROY O.
    DISNEY, WALT
DISNEY, SHARON MAE
    DISNEY, WALT
DIVITHAS, MARY
    MARX, CHICO
    MARX, GROUCHO
    MARX, GUMMO
    MARX, HARPO
    MARX, ZEPPO
DIX, JR., JOHN THOMAS
    LONG, RICHARD
DOBBIE, EDITH
    RENNIE, MICHAEL
DOBIE, ALAN
    ROBERTS, RACHEL
DODDS, JOHN
    VANCE, VIVIAN
DOER, BETTY REED
    HALE, ALAN
DOETLER, FRANCES
    GABLE, CLARK
DOLLIVER, LILLIAN RITA
    COOGAN, JACKIE
DOMERGUE, FAITH
    HUGHES, HOWARD
DOMSKI, COUNT EUGEN
    NEGRI, POLA
DONAHUE, TROY
    PLESHETTE, SUZANNE
DONAHUE, WOOLWORTH
    BARRIE, WENDY
DONALDSON, MAUREEN
    GRANT, CARY
DONAT, ERNST EMILE
    DONAT, ROBERT

DONAT, ROBERT
    PARKER, JEAN
DONEN, STANLEY
    MIMIEUX, YVETTE
DONLEVY, JUDITH
    DONLEVY, BRIAN
DONNELL, JEAN MARIE
    RAY, ALDO
DONOHU, ISABELLE
    ALLEN, STEVE
    MEADOWS, JAYNE
DONOVAN, KING
    COCA, IMOGENE
DONOVAN, WARD
    DILLER, PHYLLIS
DOONE, PHYLLIS
    PROWSE, JULIET
DORLEAC, FRANCOISE
    DENEUVE, CATHERINE
DORLEAC, MAURICE
    DENEUVE, CATHERINE
DORN-HEFT, DOLORES
    TONE, FRANCHOT
DOTTI, ANDREA
    HEPBURN, AUDREY
DOTTI, LUCA
    HEPBURN, AUDREY
DOUBIS, CAROLINE
    WHITMAN, STUART
DOUGHERTY, JIM
    MONROE, MARILYN
DOUGHERTY, VIRGIL JACK
    LA MARR, BARBARA
DOUGLAS, ADAM
    STERLING, JAN
DOUGLAS, ANTHONY
    DOUGLAS, KIRK
    DOUGLAS, MICHAEL
DOUGLAS, ERIC
    DOUGLAS, KIRK
    DOUGLAS, MICHAEL
DOUGLAS, GREGORY
    DOUGLAS, MELVYN
DOUGLAS, JOEL
    DOUGLAS, KIRK
    DOUGLAS, MICHAEL
DOUGLAS, JR., MELVYN
    DOUGLAS, MELVYN
DOUGLAS, KIRK
    DOUGLAS, MICHAEL
    KEYES, EVELYN
DOUGLAS, MARGARET
    DOUGLAS, PAUL
    STERLING, JAN
DOUGLAS, MARY HELEN
    DOUGLAS, MELVYN
DOUGLAS, MICHAEL
    DOUGLAS, KIRK

DOUGLAS, MICHAEL
    VACCARO, BRENDA
DOUGLAS, PAUL
    STERLING, JAN
DOUGLAS, PETER
    DOUGLAS, KIRK
    DOUGLAS, MICHAEL
DOUGLAS, PIERRE GAHAGAN 'PETER'
    DOUGLAS, MELVYN
DOUGLAS, SHIRLEY
    SUTHERLAND, DONALD
DOUGLAS, VINCENT
    DOUGLAS, KIRK
    DOUGLAS, MICHAEL
DOUGLASS, KINGMAN
    ASTAIRE, FRED
DOURAS, BERNARD J.
    DAVIES, MARION
DOURAS, CHARLES
    DAVIES, MARION
DOURAS, ETHEL
    DAVIES, MARION
DOURAS, IRENE
    DAVIES, MARION
DOURAS, ROSE MARIE
    DAVIES, MARION
DOUVAN, EUGENE
    DEE, SANDRA
DOVE, BILLIE
    HUGHES, HOWARD
DOWLING, DORIS
    SHAW, ARTIE
DOWNEY, MORTON
    BENNETT, CONSTANCE
    BENNETT, JOAN
DOZIER, DEBORAH LESLIE
    DE HAVILLAND, OLIVIA
    FONTAINE, JOAN
    RUTHERFORD, ANN
DOZIER, WILLIAM
    DE HAVILLAND, OLIVIA
    FONTAINE, JOAN
    RUTHERFORD, ANN
DRAI, VICTOR
    BISSET, JACQUELINE
DRAKE, BETSY
    GRANT, CARY
DREW, GEORGIANA
    BARRYMORE, ETHEL
    BARRYMORE, JOHN
    BARRYMORE, JR., JOHN
    BARRYMORE, LIONEL
    COSTELLO, DOLORES
DREW, JOHN
    BARRYMORE, ETHEL
    BARRYMORE, JOHN
    BARRYMORE, LIONEL

DREW, SIDNEY
    BARRYMORE, ETHEL
    BARRYMORE, JOHN
    BARRYMORE, LIONEL
DREYFUSS, CATHERINE
    DREYFUSS, RICHARD
DREYFUSS, LOREN
    DREYFUSS, RICHARD
DREYFUSS, SR., RICHARD
    DREYFUSS, RICHARD
DRIESENS, ANNETTE
    LUKAS, PAUL
DRIMMER, ERIC
    GABOR, EVA
    GABOR, ZSA ZSA
DRIVER, LORRAINE
    STEIGER, ROD
DRIVER, PERRY MARCUS
    DILLER, PHYLLIS
DROUGHT, ETHEL ADELAIDE
    HYDE WHITE, WILFRED
DRU, JOANNE
    HAYMES, DICK
    IRELAND, JOHN
DRURY, MARY
    NORMAND, MABEL
DRYDEN, WHEELER
    CHAPLIN, CHARLES
DUBIN, NEIL
    SAINT JOHN, JILL
DUBOIS, SHERRY
    HACKETT, BUDDY
DUCHS, CELIA
    MOSTEL, ZERO
DUESLER, RUTH
    ARNESS, JAMES
DUFF, BRIDGET MARELIA
    DUFF, HOWARD
    LUPINO, IDA
DUFF, CARLTON
    DUFF, HOWARD
DUFF, DOUGLAS
    DUFF, HOWARD
DUFF, HOWARD
    LUPINO, IDA
DUFTY, WILLIAM
    SWANSON, GLORIA
DUKE, ANGIER BIDDLE
    DAVIES, MARION
DUKE, CAROL
    DUKE, PATTY
DUKE, JOHN
    DUKE, PATTY
DUKE, PATTY
    ASTIN, JOHN
DUKE, RAYMOND
    DUKE, PATTY

DUKE, SEAN
    DUKE, PATTY
DUKENFIELD, ADELE
    FIELDS, W.C.
DUKENFIELD, ELSIE MAE
    FIELDS, W.C.
DUKENFIELD, JAMES C.
    FIELDS, W.C.
DUKENFIELD, LEROY
    FIELDS, W.C.
DUKENFIELD, WALTER
    FIELDS, W.C.
DUMONT, ROLANDE
    LONGET, CLAUDINE
DUNAWAY, JOHN
    DUNAWAY, FAYE
DUNBAR, DOROTHY
    BAER, JR., MAX
DUNCAN, ISADORA
    LANCHESTER, ELSA
DUNCAN, LEE
    RIN TIN TIN
DUNCAN, MANCIL
    DUNCAN, SANDY
DUNCAN, ROBIN
    DUNCAN, SANDY
DUNFEE, JACK
    HUME, BENITA
DUNLAP, JENNIE
    GABLE, CLARK
DUNLOP, ANN HALL
    O'CONNELL, ARTHUR
DUNN, CHARLES
    DUNNE, IRENE
DUNN, ETTA
    BERKELEY, BUSBY
DUNN, JOSEPH JOHN
    DUNNE, IRENE
DUNNING, A. SCHUYLER
    HOLM, CELESTE
DUNNING, DANIEL
    HOLM, CELESTE
DUNSMOOR, CHARLES
    TREVOR, CLAIRE
DUNSMOOR, CYLOS
    TREVOR, CLAIRE
DUNSTAN, DOROTHY
    GIBSON, HOOT
DUPRE, VANDA
    WARDEN, JACK
DURAND, AUGUSTINE LOUISE
    BOYER, CHARLES
DURANTE, ALBERT
    DURANTE, JIMMY
DURANTE, BARTHOLOMEW
    DURANTE, JIMMY
DURANTE, CE CE ALICIA
    DURANTE, JIMMY

DURANTE, LILIAN
    DURANTE, JIMMY
DURANTE, MICHAEL
    DURANTE, JIMMY
DURBIN, EDITH
    DURBIN, DEANNA
DURBIN, JAMES
    DURBIN, DEANNA
DURFEE, MINTA
    ARBUCKLE, FATTY
DUROCHER, LEO
    DAY, LARAINE
DURYEA, PETER
    DURYEA, DAN
DURYEA, RICHARD
    DURYEA, DAN
DURYEA, RICHARD HEWLETT
    DURYEA, DAN
DUSICK, MICHELLE LEE
    FARENTINO, JAMES
DUSSART, GHISLAIN
    BARDOT, BRIGITTE
DUVIVIER, DENISE
    FLYNN, ERROL
DYMLING, KARIN
    LINDFORS, VIVECA
EARLE, DOROTHY
    HAYES, GABBY
EASTMAN, LINDA
    MCCARTNEY, PAUL
EASTWOOD, ALISON
    EASTWOOD, CLINT
EASTWOOD, CLINT
    BROLIN, JAMES
    GARNER, JAMES
EASTWOOD, CLINTON
    EASTWOOD, CLINT
EASTWOOD, JEANNE
    EASTWOOD, CLINT
EASTWOOD, KYLE CLINTON
    EASTWOOD, CLINT
EATON, MABEL
    FARNUM, DUSTIN
    FARNUM, WILLIAM
EATON, ROBERT
    TURNER, LANA
EBORN, DOROTHY CONNOLL
    IRELAND, JILL
    MCCALLUM, DAVID
EBSEN, ALIX
    EBSEN, BUDDY
EBSEN, BONNIE
    EBSEN, BUDDY
EBSEN, CATHERINE
    EBSEN, BUDDY
EBSEN, CHRISTIAN
    EBSEN, BUDDY

EBSEN, DUSTIN
  EBSEN, BUDDY
EBSEN, ELIZABETH 'LIBBY'
  EBSEN, BUDDY
EBSEN, HELGA
  EBSEN, BUDDY
EBSEN, KIRSTEN
  EBSEN, BUDDY
EBSEN, NORMA
  EBSEN, BUDDY
EBSEN, SUSANNAH
  EBSEN, BUDDY
EBSEN, VILMA
  EBSEN, BUDDY
EDDINGTON, NORA
  FLYNN, ERROL
  HAYMES, DICK
EDDY, NELSON
  HARLOW, JEAN
EDDY, WILLIAM DARIUS
  EDDY, NELSON
EDELING, BETTY
  MARVIN, LEE
EDELSTEIN, RICHARD
  KELLERMAN, SALLY
EDISE, BILLEY
  OWEN, REGINALD
EDWARDS, BLAKE
  ANDREWS, JULIE
EDWARDS, CHARLOTTE
  O'KEEFE, DENNIS
EDWARDS, EDWARD
  EDWARDS, CLIFF
EDWARDS, GEORGE CLIFTON
  EDWARDS, CLIFF
EGAN, RICHARD
  SOTHERN, ANN
EGGAR, JACK
  EGGAR, SAMANTHA
EGGAR, RALPH A. J.
  EGGAR, SAMANTHA
EHRLICH, HELEN
  IVES, BURL
EILERS, SALLY
  GIBSON, HOOT
EISENHOWER, DWIGHT DAVID
  MONTGOMERY, ROBERT
EKBERG, ANITA
  TAYLOR, ROD
EKBERG, GUSTAV
  EKBERG, ANITA
EKLAND, BRITT
  SELLERS, PETER
EKLAND, NICOLAI
  EKLAND, BRITT
ELDRIDGE, FLORENCE
  MARCH, FREDRIC

ELFRID, MEL
  NOLAN, LLOYD
ELIOPOULOS, IRENE
  MERCOURI, MELINA
ELIZABETH, MARY
  DAY, DENNIS
  GARDNER, AVA
ELIZONDO, JOAQUIN
  MURRAY, MAE
ELKINS, HILLIARD
  BLOOM, CLAIRE
ELLINGTON, MARIE
  COLE, NAT 'KING'
ELLIOTT, MARY
  CUMMINGS, ROBERT
ELLIS, ROSALIE
  WINWOOD, ESTELLE
EMERSON, LAWRENCE L.
  EMERSON, FAYE
EMERSON, OLIVE
  ARNOLD, EDWARD
EMERY, BARBARA NICHOLAI
  BANKHEAD, TALLULAH
EMERY, JOHN
  BANKHEAD, TALLULAH
  BENNETT, JOAN
EMERY, LINDA
  LEE, BRUCE
ENGLAND, CHESTER B.
  CANOVA, JUDY
ENGLAND, JULIETA
  CANOVA, JUDY
ENGLISH, KAY
  KERRY, NORMAN
ENGLUND, ADAM
  LEACHMAN, CLORIS
ENGLUND, BRYAN
  LEACHMAN, CLORIS
ENGLUND, DINAH
  LEACHMAN, CLORIS
ENGLUND, GEORGE
  LEACHMAN, CLORIS
ENGLUND, JR., GEORGE
  LEACHMAN, CLORIS
ENGLUND, MORGAN
  LEACHMAN, CLORIS
ENGSTROM, MARVIN
  LEE, PEGGY
ENKE, SHELDON A.
  ADAMS, EDIE
ENOS, GEORGE
  BERKELEY, BUSBY
ENOS, SR., WILLIAM
  BERKELEY, BUSBY
ENRICO, HELEN
  FARENTINO, JAMES
EPLING, MARY LEE
  FAIRBANKS, JR., DOUGLAS

EPPLE, MARGARET CAROL
  TALBOT, LYLE
ERCOLANI, WILLIAM
  DARREN, JAMES
ERNST, HUGH 'BUD'
  FURNESS, BETTY
ERNST, JUNE
  LANCASTER, BURT
ESMOND, JILL
  OLIVIER, LAURENCE
ETTINGER, MAGGIE
  PARSONS, LOUELLA O.
EVANS, ALICE
  EVANS, ROBERT
EVANS, ANNA
  BROWN, JOE E.
EVANS, ARCHIBALD
  EVANS, ROBERT
EVANS, CHARLES
  EVANS, ROBERT
EVANS, DALE
  ROGERS, ROY
EVANS, JOSHUA
  EVANS, ROBERT
  MACGRAW, ALI
  MCQUEEN, STEVE
EVANS, LINDA
  DEREK, JOHN
EVANS, PAULINE ALICE
  FAWCETT-MAJORS, FARRAH
EVANS, ROBERT
  GRAYSON, KATHRYN
  MACGRAW, ALI
EVERETT, KATHERINE KERRIE
  EVERETT, CHAD
EVERETT, SHANNON KIMBERLY
  EVERETT, CHAD
EVERT, CHRIS
  REYNOLDS, BURT
EVINRUDE, RALPH
  LANGFORD, FRANCES
EWELL, TAYLOR ALLEN
  EWELL, TOM
FABARES, JAMES
  FABARES, SHELLEY
FABARES, NANETTE 'SMOKEY'
  FABARES, SHELLEY
  FABRAY, NANETTE
FABARES, RAOUL
  FABRAY, NANETTE
FABARES, SHELLEY
  FABRAY, NANETTE
FABRAY, NANETTE
  FABARES, SHELLEY
FADINI, SERGIO
  PROWSE, JULIET
FAGAN, JOSEPH
  CLAIRE, INA

FAIR, ELINOR
  BOYD, WILLIAM
FAIRBANKS, DAPHNE
  FAIRBANKS, JR., DOUGLAS
FAIRBANKS, DOUGLAS
  FAIRBANKS, JR., DOUGLAS
  GOLDWYN, SAMUEL
  PICKFORD, MARY
FAIRBANKS, ELLA ADELAIDE MARSH
  FAIRBANKS, DOUGLAS
FAIRBANKS, JOHN
  FAIRBANKS, DOUGLAS
FAIRBANKS, JR., DOUGLAS
  CRAWFORD, JOAN
  DIETRICH, MARLENE
  FAIRBANKS, DOUGLAS
  PICKFORD, MARY
FAIRBANKS, MELISSA
  FAIRBANKS, JR., DOUGLAS
FAIRBANKS, VICTORIA
  FAIRBANKS, JR., DOUGLAS
FALAISE, MARQUIS HENRI DE LA
  BENNETT, CONSTANCE
  BENNETT, JOAN
  BENNETT, RICHARD
  SWANSON, GLORIA
FALDER, MURIEL
  ROSENBLOOM, 'SLAPSIE' MAXIE
FALK, JACQUELINE
  FALK, PETER
FALK, JR., HENRY
  DUKE, PATTY
FALK, KATHERINE
  FALK, PETER
FALK, MICHAEL
  FALK, PETER
FALKENSTEIN, SOPHIE
  CAAN, JAMES
FALLON, BOB
  WILSON, MARIE
FALLON, GREGSON
  WILSON, MARIE
FANCHER, HAMPTON
  LYON, SUE
FARENTINO, ANTHONY
  FARENTINO, JAMES
FARENTINO, DAVID MICHAEL
  FARENTINO, JAMES
FARENTINO, JAMES
  ASHLEY, ELIZABETH
FARINOLA, ELAINE
  DAMONE, VIC
FARINOLA, PEARL
  DAMONE, VIC
FARINOLA, ROCCO
  DAMONE, VIC
FARINOLA, SANDRA
  DAMONE, VIC

FARINOLA, TERESA
    DAMONE, VIC
FARMER, MICHAEL
    SWANSON, GLORIA
FARMER, MICHELE BRIDGET
    SWANSON, GLORIA
FARNSWORTH, ARTHUR
    DAVIS, BETTE
FARNSWORTH, ELIZABETH
    DOUGLAS, PAUL
FARNUM, ADELE
    FARNUM, DUSTIN
    FARNUM, WILLIAM
FARNUM, DUSTIN
    FARNUM, WILLIAM
FARNUM, ESTELLE
    FARNUM, DUSTIN
    FARNUM, WILLIAM
FARNUM, GREENLEAF D.
    FARNUM, DUSTIN
    FARNUM, WILLIAM
FARNUM, JR., WILLIAM
    FARNUM, WILLIAM
FARNUM, MARSHALL
    FARNUM, DUSTIN
    FARNUM, WILLIAM
FARNUM, WILLIAM
    FARNUM, DUSTIN
FARR, FELICIA
    LEMMON, JACK
FARRELL, CHARLES
    GAYNOR, JANET
FARRELL, DAVIS
    FARRELL, CHARLES
FARRELL, HELEN
    CARNEY, ART
FARRELL, WES
    SINATRA, FRANK
FARROW, JOHN VILLIERS
    FARROW, MIA
    O'SULLIVAN, MAUREEN
FARROW, JR., JOHN
    FARROW, MIA
    O'SULLIVAN, MAUREEN
FARROW, MIA
    O'SULLIVAN, MAUREEN
    SINATRA, FRANK
FARROW, MICHAEL
    FARROW, MIA
    O'SULLIVAN, MAUREEN
FARROW, PATRICK
    FARROW, MIA
    O'SULLIVAN, MAUREEN
FARROW, PRUDENCE
    FARROW, MIA
    O'SULLIVAN, MAUREEN
FARROW, STEPHANIE
    FARROW, MIA

FARROW, STEPHANIE
    O'SULLIVAN, MAUREEN
FARROW, TERESA
    FARROW, MIA
    O'SULLIVAN, MAUREEN
FASS, GERTRUDE EMILY
    MORLEY, ROBERT
FAULK, MABEL
    CARROLL, DIAHANN
FAVOR, RUTH
    DAVIS, BETTE
FAWCETT, JAMES WILLIAM
    FAWCETT-MAJORS, FARRAH
FAWCETT, THERESA DIANNE
    FAWCETT-MAJORS, FARRAH
FAY, ANTHONY
    STANWYCK, BARBARA
FAY, DION
    STANWYCK, BARBARA
FAY, FRANK
    STANWYCK, BARBARA
FAYE, ALICE
    HARRIS, PHIL
    MARTIN, TONY
FAYE, PATSY
    O'CONNOR, CARROLL
FAZENDA, ANTHONY
    FAZENDA, LOUISE
FAZENDA, JOSEPH A.
    FAZENDA, LOUISE
FAZENDA, MAY
    FAZENDA, LOUISE
FAZENDA, ULYSSES
    FAZENDA, LOUISE
FELDMAN, CHARLES
    WYNTER, DANA
FELKER, CLAY
    TIFFIN, PAMELA
FELSING, WILHELMINA ELIZABETH
    DIETRICH, MARLENE
FELTON, KATE
    FIELDS, W.C.
FELTUS, KAY
    PRESTON, ROBERT
FELTUS, ROY
    PRESTON, ROBERT
FERGUSON, KATHERINE
    IRELAND, JOHN
FERNANDES, EMILIO
    ARMENDARIZ, PEDRO
FERRER, CHRIS
    FERRER, MEL
    HEPBURN, AUDREY
FERRER, DR. JOSE
    FERRER, MEL
FERRER, GABRIEL
    CLOONEY, ROSEMARY

FERRER, GABRIEL
    FERRER, JOSE
FERRER, JOSE
    CLOONEY, ROSEMARY
FERRER, LETICIA THYRA
    FERRER, JOSE
FERRER, MARIA
    CLOONEY, ROSEMARY
    FERRER, JOSE
FERRER, MARK
    FERRER, MEL
    HEPBURN, AUDREY
FERRER, MEL
    HEPBURN, AUDREY
FERRER, MELA
    FERRER, MEL
    HEPBURN, AUDREY
FERRER, MIGUEL
    CLOONEY, ROSEMARY
    FERRER, JOSE
FERRER, MONSITA
    CLOONEY, ROSEMARY
    FERRER, JOSE
FERRER, PEPA
    FERRER, MEL
    HEPBURN, AUDREY
FERRER, RAFAEL
    FERRER, JOSE
FERRER, RAPHAEL
    CLOONEY, ROSEMARY
    FERRER, JOSE
FERRER, SEAN
    FERRER, MEL
    HEPBURN, AUDREY
FERRIER, PAT
    KILEY, RICHARD
FETZER, THERESA
    NEWMAN, PAUL
FIELD, MARGARET 'MAGGIE'
    FIELD, SALLY
FIELD, PRINCESS
    FIELD, SALLY
FIELD, SALLY
    REYNOLDS, BURT
FIELD, SYLVIA
    TRUEX, ERNEST
FIELD, VIRGINIA
    DOUGLAS, PAUL
FIELDS, EVERETT
    FIELDS, W.C.
FIELDS, FREDDIE
    BERGEN, POLLY
FIELDS, GRACIE
    BANKS, MONTAGUE 'MONTY'
FIELDS, III, WILLIAM CLAUDE
    FIELDS, W.C.
FIELDS, JR., WILLIAM CLAUDE
    FIELDS, W.C.

FIELDS, KATHY
    BERGEN, POLLY
FIELDS, NANCY
    O'CONNOR, CARROLL
FIELDS, PAMELA
    BERGEN, POLLY
FIELDS, PETER
    BERGEN, POLLY
FIELDS, RONALD J.
    FIELDS, W.C.
FIELDS, SHEP
    BERGEN, POLLY
FIELDS, W.C.
    BROWN, JOE E.
FIFIELD, JON
    MCCAMBRIDGE, MERCEDES
FIFIELD, WILLIAM
    MCCAMBRIDGE, MERCEDES
FINA, JULIA
    CONTE, RICHARD
FINCH, ANITA
    FINCH, PETER
FINCH, CHARLES
    FINCH, PETER
FINCH, DIANA
    FINCH, PETER
FINCH, PETER
    LEIGH, VIVIEN
FINCH, SAMANTHA
    FINCH, PETER
FINCHER, FAITH
    DE HAVEN, GLORIA
FINCHER, HARRY
    DE HAVEN, GLORIA
FINCHER, RICHARD
    DE HAVEN, GLORIA
FINDER, JENNY
    AMSTERDAM, MOREY
FINE, SYLVIA
    KAYE, DANNY
FINKLE, BELLA
    MUNI, PAUL
FINKLEA, ERNEST
    CHARISSE, CYD
FINLEY, FLORENCE
    WILLIAMS, ANDY
FINNEY, ALBERT
    AIMEE, ANOUK
    EGGAR, SAMANTHA
FINNEY, BEN
    LA MARR, BARBARA
FINNEY, SIMON
    FINNEY, ALBERT
FINNEY, SR., ALBERT
    FINNEY, ALBERT
FISH, MARILYN
    TUCKER, FORREST

FISHER, ALICIA GLADYS
   FINCH, PETER
FISHER, CARRIE
   FISHER, EDDIE
   REYNOLDS, DEBBIE
   TAYLOR, ELIZABETH
FISHER, EDDIE
   REYNOLDS, DEBBIE
   TAYLOR, ELIZABETH
FISHER, EDITH
   SHEARER, NORMA
FISHER, JOELY
   FISHER, EDDIE
FISHER, JOSEPH
   FISHER, EDDIE
FISHER, MARIA-PETRA
   BURTON, RICHARD
   FISHER, EDDIE
   TAYLOR, ELIZABETH
FISHER, PAULINE
   GAYNOR, MITZI
FISHER, RAE
   ABBOTT, BUD
FISHER, TODD
   FISHER, EDDIE
   REYNOLDS, DEBBIE
   TAYLOR, ELIZABETH
FISHER, TRICIA LEIGH
   FISHER, EDDIE
FISK, JACK
   SPACEK, SISSY
FISS, ANNA
   CORRELL, CHARLES
FITE, ELIZABETH
   GOSDEN, FREEMAN
FITZGERALD, EDWARD
   FITZGERALD, GERALDINE
FITZGERALD, F. SCOTT
   MORAN, LOIS
   O'SULLIVAN, MAUREEN
FITZGERALD, JAMES
   POWELL, JANE
FITZGERALD, WALLACE
   HUDSON, ROCK
FITZMAURICE, IDA BERGER
   RATHBONE, BASIL
FITZSIMMONS, BRIDGET
   O'HARA, MAUREEN
FITZSIMMONS, CHARLES
   O'HARA, MAUREEN
FLADUME, JOSEPHINE
   BUSHMAN, FRANCIS X.
FLAHERTY, ISABELLE
   MCGUIRE, DOROTHY
FLANAGAN, HORTENSE
   O'KEEFE, DENNIS
FLANAGAN, MARGARET ELIZABETH
   BRENNAN, WALTER

FLANAGAN, SR., EDWARD VANES
   O'KEEFE, DENNIS
FLAXMAN, JACK
   ROMAN, RUTH
FLEMING, ERIN
   MARX, GROUCHO
FLEMING, SUSAN
   MARX, CHICO
   MARX, GUMMO
   MARX, HARPO
   MARX, ZEPPO
FLETCHER, BRAMWELL
   BARRYMORE, JOHN
FLORES, GLADYS
   O'BRIEN, MARGARET
FLORES, MARISSA
   O'BRIEN, MARGARET
FLORSHEIM, MARY
   JONES, ALLAN
FLOWERTON, CONSUELO
   FOCH, NINA
FLYNN, ARLETTA
   FLYNN, ERROL
FLYNN, DEIDRE
   FLYNN, ERROL
   HAYMES, DICK
FLYNN, ERROL
   ABBOTT, BUD
   BENNETT, JOAN
   CHRISTIAN, LINDA
   DAMITA, LILI
   NIVEN, DAVID
FLYNN, RORY
   FLYNN, ERROL
   HAYMES, DICK
FLYNN, SEAN LESLIE
   DAMITA, LILI
   FLYNN, ERROL
FLYNN, THEODORE THOMSON
   DAMITA, LILI
   FLYNN, ERROL
FOCH, DIRK
   FOCH, NINA
FOGELSON, ELIJAH 'BUDDY'
   GARSON, GREER
FOLEY, SHIRLEY
   BOONE, PAT
FONDA, AMY
   FONDA, HENRY
   FONDA, JANE
   FONDA, PETER
FONDA, BRIDGET
   FONDA, HENRY
   FONDA, JANE
   FONDA, PETER
FONDA, HARRIET
   FONDA, HENRY

FONDA, HENRY
   BOND, WARD
   FONDA, JANE
   FONDA, PETER
   STEWART, JAMES
   SULLAVAN, MARGARET
FONDA, JANE
   FONDA, HENRY
   FONDA, PETER
FONDA, JAYNE
   FONDA, HENRY
FONDA, JUSTIN
   FONDA, HENRY
   FONDA, JANE
   FONDA, PETER
FONDA, PETER
   FONDA, HENRY
   FONDA, JANE
   HOPPER, DENNIS
FONDA, WM. BRACE
   FONDA, HENRY
FONTAINE, GEORGE M.
   DE HAVILLAND, OLIVIA
   FONTAINE, JOAN
FONTAINE, JOAN
   AHERNE, BRIAN
   DE HAVILLAND, OLIVIA
FONTAINE, JOHN FORREST
   CALVET, CORINNE
FONTANNE, LYNN
   LUNT, ALFRED
FORBES, BRENDA
   CHATTERTON, RUTH
FORBES, MARY TAYLOR
   CHATTERTON, RUTH
FORBES, MERIM
   RICHARDSON, RALPH
FORBES, RALPH
   CHATTERTON, RUTH
FORD, ALBERT
   BOOTH, SHIRLEY
FORD, BARBARA
   FORD, FRANCIS
   WALKER, ROBERT
FORD, FRANCIS
   WALKER, ROBERT
FORD, GLENN
   GARLAND, JUDY
   MOORE, TERRY
   POWELL, ELEANOR
FORD, JR., FRANCIS
   FORD, FRANCIS
FORD, NEWTON
   FORD, GLENN
FORD, PETER
   FORD, GLENN
   POWELL, ELEANOR

FORD, PHILIP
   FORD, FRANCIS
FORD, ROBERT
   FORD, FRANCIS
FORD, RUTH
   SCOTT, ZACHARY
FORDE, VICTORIA
   MIX, TOM
FOREST, STEVE
   ANDREWS, DANA
FORMAN, ETHEL MARION
   RATHBONE, BASIL
FORMAN, MILOS
   ANDERSSON, BIBI
FORSYTHE, BROOKE
   FORSYTHE, JOHN
FORSYTHE, DALL
   FORSYTHE, JOHN
FORSYTHE, PAGE
   FORSYTHE, JOHN
FORWOOD, ANTHONY
   JOHNS, GLYNIS
FORWOOD, GARETH
   JOHNS, GLYNIS
FOSSE, BOB
   VERDON, GWEN
FOSTER, DAVID RAMSEY
   JOHNS, GLYNIS
FOSTER, NORMAN
   COLBERT, CLAUDETTE
   YOUNG, LORETTA
FOX, AARON
   FOX, WILLIAM
FOX, ADRIENNE
   BENNETT, JOAN
FOX, DIANA BENNETT
   BENNETT, JOAN
FOX, JOHN MARTIN
   BENNETT, CONSTANCE
   BENNETT, JOAN
   BENNETT, RICHARD
FOX, JR., THOMAS
   EVANS, DALE
   ROGERS, ROY
FOX, THOMAS
   EVANS, DALE
FOX, VIRGINIA
   FOX, WILLIAM
FOXX, DEBRACA
   FOXX, REDD
FOY, BRYAN
   FOY, JR., EDDIE
FOY, CATHERINE
   SENNETT, MACK
FOY, CHARLES
   FOY, JR., EDDIE
FOY, IRVING
   FOY, JR., EDDIE

FOY, MADELEINE
    FOY, JR., EDDIE
FOY, MARY
    FOY, JR., EDDIE
FOY, RICHARD
    FOY, JR., EDDIE
FOY, SR., EDWARD FITZGERALD
    FOY, JR., EDDIE
FOY, 3RD, EDDIE
    FOY, JR., EDDIE
FRABRANI, JOEL
    ROSS, KATHARINE
FRANCHETTI, ALFREDA
    FONDA, HENRY
    FONDA, JANE
    FONDA, PETER
FRANCHOT, GERTRUDE
    TONE, FRANCHOT
FRANCIOSA, ANTHONY
    WINTERS, SHELLEY
FRANCIOSA, JEAN
    FRANCIOSA, ANTHONY
FRANCIOSA, NINA
    FRANCIOSA, ANTHONY
FRANCIS, MARGARET WEST
    FRANCIS, ANNE
FRANCIS, PHILIP
    FRANCIS, ANNE
FRANCISCUS, JAMIE
    FRANCISCUS, JAMES
FRANCISCUS, JOHN ALLEN
    FRANCISCUS, JAMES
FRANCISCUS, JOLIE
    FRANCISCUS, JAMES
FRANCISCUS, KELLIE
    FRANCISCUS, JAMES
FRANCISCUS, KORIE
    FRANCISCUS, JAMES
FRANK, GERALDINE
    CLARK, DANE
FRANK, LUCILLE
    ARDEN, EVE
FRANK, MANUEL G.
    BLAINE, VIVIAN
FRANKEL, PHILIP
    ARTHUR, BEATRICE
FRANKLIN, MARY ALICE
    EDEN, BARBARA
FRANKLIN, MIRIAM
    NELSON, GENE
FRANKOVICH, JR., MICHAEL
    BARNES, BINNIE
FRANKOVICH, MICHAEL J.
    BARNES, BINNIE
    BROWN, JOE E.
FRANKOVICH, MICHELLE
    BARNES, BINNIE

FRANKOVICH, PETER
    BARNES, BINNIE
FRASER, MARJORY READ
    COLMAN, RONALD
FRASER, SARAH ELIZABETH
    LLOYD, HAROLD
FRAWLEY, JAY
    FRAWLEY, WILLIAM
FRAWLEY, MARY
    FRAWLEY, WILLIAM
FRAWLEY, PAUL
    FRAWLEY, WILLIAM
FRAZIN, GLADYS
    BANKS, MONTAGUE 'MONTY'
FREDERICK, LYNNE
    SELLERS, PETER
FREDERICK, PAULINE
    GABLE, CLARK
FREDERICKS, PAULINE
    MACK, WILLARD
FREDERIQUE, BERTHE
    JOURDAN, LOUIS
FREELEY, PAMELA
    MARVIN, LEE
FREEMAN, JOHN (BUD)
    NORTH, SHEREE
FREMANTLE, ADMIRAL SIR SIDNEY
    MASSEY, RAYMOND
FREMANTLE, MARGERY HILDA
    MASSEY, RAYMOND
FRENCH, MARY
    STEWART, JAMES
FREUND, SAMUEL JEREMIAH
    FORSYTHE, JOHN
FRIED, MARTIN
    VACCARO, BRENDA
FRIEDKIN, WILLIAM
    MOREAU, JEANNE
FRIEDLOB, BERT
    PARKER, ELEANOR
FRIEDLOB, RICHARD
    PARKER, ELEANOR
FRIEDLOB, SHARON
    PARKER, ELEANOR
FRIEDLOB, SUSAN
    PARKER, ELEANOR
FRIEND, ARTHUR
    DE MILLE, C. B.
FRIESE, HUBERTINA
    CALHERN, LOUIS
FRIESEN, BENJAMIN W.
    CANNON, DYAN
FRIESEN, DAVID
    CANNON, DYAN
FRINGS, KURT
    SOMMER, ELKE
FRIZZEL, IRENE
    BARRYMORE, ETHEL

FRIZZEL, IRENE
    BARRYMORE, JOHN
    BARRYMORE, LIONEL
FROST, BARRY
    WELCH, RAQUEL
FROST, DAVID
    CARROLL, DIAHANN
FROUD, EVELYN
    LAYE, EVELYN
FRYE, EVERETT
    MCDONALD, MARIE
FULKS, R. D.
    WYMAN, JANE
FURNESS, GEORGE CHOATE
    FURNESS, BETTY
FURRY, CAMMON
    HOPPER, HEDDA
FURRY, DAVID
    HOPPER, HEDDA
FURRY, DORA
    HOPPER, HEDDA
FURRY, EDGAR
    HOPPER, HEDDA
FURRY, FRANK
    HOPPER, HEDDA
FURRY, MARGARET
    HOPPER, HEDDA
FURRY, SHERMAN
    HOPPER, HEDDA
FUTTERMAN, MYRON
    WYMAN, JANE
FYFE, MARGARET
    YOUNG, ROBERT
GABLE, CLARK
    CRAWFORD, JOAN
    LOMBARD, CAROLE
    RUSSELL, JANE
    YOUNG, LORETTA
GABLE, JOHN CLARK
    GABLE, CLARK
GABLE, WILLIAM H.
    GABLE, CLARK
GABOR, EVA
    GABOR, ZSA ZSA
    SANDERS, GEORGE
GABOR, MAGDA
    GABOR, EVA
    GABOR, ZSA ZSA
    SANDERS, GEORGE
GABOR, VILMOS
    GABOR, EVA
    GABOR, ZSA ZSA
GABOR, ZSA ZSA
    GABOR, EVA
    SANDERS, GEORGE
GAGE, BEN
    WILLIAMS, ESTHER

GAGE, BENJAMIN
    LAMAS, FERNANDO
    WILLIAMS, ESTHER
GAGE, KIMBALL
    LAMAS, FERNANDO
    WILLIAMS, ESTHER
GAGE, SUSAN
    LAMAS, FERNANDO
    WILLIAMS, ESTHER
GAHAGAN, HELEN
    DOUGLAS, MELVYN
GAINOR, FRANK
    GAYNOR, JANET
GAINOR, HILARY
    GAYNOR, JANET
GAIZAR, MARIA
    CANTINFLAS
GALANTE, GISELE
    DE HAVILLAND, OLIVIA
GALANTE, PIERRE PAUL
    DE HAVILLAND, OLIVIA
GALBRAITH, ERLE CHENAULT
    JOLSON, AL
GALE, JANE
    LEVANT, OSCAR
GALE, JOAN
    LEVANT, OSCAR
GALLAGHER, III, THOMAS JOSEPH
    PLESHETTE, SUZANNE
GALLERY, ANN
    PITTS, ZASU
GALLERY, THOMAS
    PITTS, ZASU
GALLO, FRANK
    PERREAU, GIGI
GALLO, GINA
    PERREAU, GIGI
GALLO, TONY
    PERREAU, GIGI
GALLUCI, ARTHUR
    GABOR, EVA
    GABOR, ZSA ZSA
GALT, MAGINEL
    BAXTER, ANNE
GALT, MELISSA
    BAXTER, ANNE
GALT, RANDOLPH
    BAXTER, ANNE
GANNON, MARY
    GORCEY, LEO
GANNOWAY, AL
    CALVET, CORINNE
GANNOWAY, GARY
    CALVET, CORINNE
GANO, ALENE
    HUGHES, HOWARD
GARAVANTI, NATALIE 'DOLLY'
    SINATRA, FRANK

GARBO, GRETA
    GILBERT, JOHN
    OAKIE, JACK
GARCIA, MARIA VIDAL SILAS Y
    AUMONT, JEAN-PIERRE
GARDINER, REGINALD
    LAMARR, HEDY
GARDNER, AVA
    HUGHES, HOWARD
    ROONEY, MICKEY
    SHAW, ARTIE
    SINATRA, FRANK
GARDNER, BEATRICE
    GARDNER, AVA
GARDNER, CATHERINE
    VAN FLEET, JO
GARDNER, EDWARD F.
    BOOTH, SHIRLEY
GARDNER, INEZ
    GARDNER, AVA
GARDNER, JACK
    DRESSER, LOUISE
GARDNER, JONAS B.
    GARDNER, AVA
GARDNER, JR., WINTHROP
    HENIE, SONJA
GARDNER, MARILYNN
    SAVALAS, TELLY
GARDNER, MARY
    PREMINGER, OTTO
    RENNIE, MICHAEL
    WOOD, PEGGY
GARDNER, PAULINE
    PRENTISS, PAULA
GARFEIN, BLANCHE
    BAKER, CARROLL
GARFEIN, HERSHEL
    BAKER, CARROLL
GARFEIN, JACK
    BAKER, CARROLL
GARFIELD, JR., JOHN
    GARFIELD, JOHN
GARFIELD, JULIE
    GARFIELD, JOHN
GARFINKLE, DAVID
    GARFIELD, JOHN
GARFINKLE, MAX
    GARFIELD, JOHN
GARLAND, JUDY
    MINNELLI, LIZA
    ROONEY, MICKEY
    SHAW, ARTIE
GARNER, GRETA
    GARNER, JAMES
GARNER, KIMBERLY CLARKE
    GARNER, JAMES
GARR, TERRI
    WILDER, GENE

GARRETT, BETTY
    PARKS, LARRY
GARRETT, DIANE
    VAN, BOBBY
GARSON, GEORGE
    GARSON, GREER
GARVER, VERNA LUCILLE
    WALKER, CLINT
GARVEY, DORA
    LOVEJOY, FRANK
GARY, ROMAIN
    SEBERG, JEAN
GASSMAN, VITTORIA
    WINTERS, SHELLEY
GASSMAN, VITTORIO
    WINTERS, SHELLEY
GATES, ALLENE
    WEISSMULLER, JOHNNY
GATES, PHYLLIS
    HUDSON, ROCK
GATLEY, EDITH
    HARDING, ANN
GATLEY, GEORGE G.
    HARDING, ANN
GAUDEL, MARCELLA FRANCES
    VAUGHN, ROBERT
GAUNT, MABEL HATTERSLEY
    MASON, JAMES
GAUTHIER, JEANETTE
    GOULET, ROBERT
    LAWRENCE, CAROL
GAVILAN, ELENOR
    NOVARRO, RAMON
GAY, VIVIENNE
    SCOTT, RANDOLPH
GAYNOR, JANET
    FARRELL, CHARLES
    POWER, TYRONE
GEDDES, JOAN
    BEL GEDDES, BARBARA
GEDDES, NORMAN
    BEL GEDDES, BARBARA
GEFFEN, DAVID
    THOMAS, DANNY
GEHMAN, ABBIE
    PARSONS, ESTELLE
GEHMAN, MARTHA
    PARSONS, ESTELLE
GEHMAN, RICHARD
    PARSONS, ESTELLE
GEIGER, CONSTANCE
    SAINT JAMES, SUSAN
GEILUS, ANN
    ASTAIRE, FRED
GEISMAN, HENRY
    ALLYSON, JUNE
GEISMAN, ROBERT
    ALLYSON, JUNE

GELIEN, WALTER
    HUNTER, TAB
GELIN, DANIEL
    ANDRESS, URSULA
GEMELLI, DALE
    BACALL, LAUREN
GENARO, ROMANO
    DURANTE, JIMMY
GENDRE, HENRI
    JOURDAN, LOUIS
GENNELL, MINA
    GARLAND, JUDY
    MINNELLI, LIZA
GEORGE, BARBARA ANN
    RATHBONE, BASIL
GEORGE, FLORENCE
    CROSBY, BING
GEORGE, PHYLLIS
    EVANS, ROBERT
GERARD, JAMES
    PACINO, AL
GERARD, ROSE
    PACINO, AL
GERBER, HENRY
    GAYNOR, MITZI
GERMONPREZ, VALERIE MARGUERITE
    VON STROHEIM, ERICH
GERSHWIN, GEORGE
    LEVANT, OSCAR
GERSHWIN, IRA
    DICKINSON, ANGIE
    LEVANT, OSCAR
GESTON, SUSAN
    BRIDGES, JEFF
GHEDINI, MARIA
    BRAZZI, ROSSANO
GIBBONS, AUSTIN PATRICK
    DEL RIO, DOLORES
GIBBONS, CEDRIC
    DEL RIO, DOLORES
GIBBS, DONALD
    HAVOC, JUNE
GIBLIN, WALTER M.
    TALMADGE, CONSTANCE
    TALMADGE, NORMA
GIBSON, LOIS
    GIBSON, HOOT
GIBSON, MARGARET
    PAGET, DEBRA
GIELGUD, FRANK
    GIELGUD, JOHN
GIELGUD, LEWIS
    GIELGUD, JOHN
GIELGUD, VAL
    GIELGUD, JOHN
GIGANTI, DENISE
    MINNELLI, LIZA

GILBERT, JANE
    HOPPER, HEDDA
GILBERT, JOANNE
    PAIGE, JANIS
GILBERT, JOHN
    BRUCE, VIRGINIA
    CLAIRE, INA
    DIETRICH, MARLENE
    GARBO, GRETA
GILBERT, LEATRICE JOY
    GILBERT, JOHN
GILBERT, LINDA
    CARRADINE, JOHN
GILBERT, MACK
    MARX, GROUCHO
GILBERT, RAY
    PAIGE, JANIS
GILBERT, SUSAN ANN
    BRUCE, VIRGINIA
    GILBERT, JOHN
GILBERT, WALTER B.
    GILBERT, JOHN
GILLOOLY, JACK
    BURSTYN, ELLEN
GILMAN, RITA
    BEERY, WALLACE
GILMARTIN, JUNE
    LEVANT, OSCAR
GILMORE, VIRGINIA
    BRYNNER, YUL
GINER, MARIA
    ITURBI, JOSE
GINGOLD, BARONESS HELENE
    GINGOLD, HERMIONE
GINGOLD, JAMES
    GINGOLD, HERMIONE
GINGOLD, MARGARET
    GINGOLD, HERMIONE
GIOLUND, NELLINA
    LAINE, FRANKIE
GIRARDOT, ANNIE
    BELMONDO, JEAN-PAUL
GISH, DOROTHY
    GISH, LILLIAN
GISH, JAMES LEIGH
    GISH, DOROTHY
    GISH, LILLIAN
GISH, LILLIAN
    GISH, DOROTHY
GIST, ROBERT
    MOOREHEAD, AGNES
GLANTZ, SARAH
    BERLE, MILTON
GLANVILLE, HOPE
    ROBARDS, JR., JASON
GLASER, GLORIA
    CLARK, FRED

GLEASON, GERALDINE
  GLEASON, JACKIE
GLEASON, HERBERT
  GLEASON, JACKIE
GLEASON, LINDA
  GLEASON, JACKIE
GLEASON, RUSSELL
  GLEASON, JAMES 'JIMMY'
GLEASON, WILLIAM
  GLEASON, JAMES 'JIMMY'
GLOCKNER, EVA
  RAFT, GEORGE
GLUCK, ALMA
  ZIMBALIST, JR., EFREM
GLUSMAN, FREDERICK
  CARROLL, DIAHANN
GODDARD, ALTA
  GODDARD, PAULETTE
GODDARD, PAULETTE
  CHAPLIN, CHARLES
  MEREDITH, BURGESS
GODOWSKY, DAGMAR
  NAZIMOVA
  WINDSOR, CLAIRE
GOETZ, WILLIAM
  MAYER, LOUIS B.
GOLD, LAUREN
  CRAWFORD, BRODERICK
GOLDEN, OLIVE
  CAREY, HARRY
GOLDENBERG, JACK
  ROBINSON, EDWARD G.
GOLDENBERG, MAX
  ROBINSON, EDWARD G.
GOLDENBERG, MORRIS
  ROBINSON, EDWARD G.
GOLDENBERG, OSCAR
  ROBINSON, EDWARD G.
GOLDENBERG, WILLIE
  ROBINSON, EDWARD G.
GOLDENBERG, ZACKERY
  ROBINSON, EDWARD G.
GOLDFISH, ABRAHAM
  GOLDWYN, SAMUEL
GOLDMAN, EDWARD
  ROTH, LILLIAN
GOLDSTEIN, BERNARD
  GOULD, ELLIOT
GOLDWYN, JR., SAMUEL
  GOLDWYN, SAMUEL
GOLDWYN, SAMUEL
  BANKY, VILMA
  COLMAN, RONALD
  DE MILLE, C. B.
GOLLUMB, HELEN
  HOLLIDAY, JUDY
GOOCH, AGNES
  BUZZI, RUTH

GOODE, ESLANDA CARDOZO
  ROBESON, PAUL
GOODMAN, BERNARD
  BARA, THEDA
GOODMAN, DOROTHY
  ALLEN, STEVE
GOODMAN, LORI
  BARA, THEDA
GOODMAN, MARQUE
  BARA, THEDA
GOODRICH, BENJAMIN BRIGGS
  DE HAVILLAND, OLIVIA
GOODRICH, FRANCES
  HACKETT, RAYMOND
GOODRICH, MARCUS AURELIUS
  DE HAVILLAND, OLIVIA
GOODWIN, EDITH
  LAKE, ARTHUR
GOODWIN, GEORGE
  WINWOOD, ESTELLE
GOOGE, NOVADEEN
  WILLS, CHILL
GORCEY, AUDREY
  GORCEY, LEO
GORCEY, BERNARD
  GORCEY, LEO
GORCEY, BRANDY JOSEPHINE
  GORCEY, LEO
GORCEY, DAVID
  GORCEY, LEO
GORCEY, FRED
  GORCEY, LEO
GORCEY, JAN
  GORCEY, LEO
GORCEY, JR., LEO
  GORCEY, LEO
GORDEAN, JACK
  MONROE, MARILYN
GORDON-HOWLEY, FRANCIS
  LAWRENCE, GERTRUDE
GORDON, FERNANDA LU
  MORENO, RITA
GORDON, LARRY
  THOMAS, DANNY
GORDON, LEONARD
  MORENO, RITA
GORDON, MARY
  ARBUCKLE, FATTY
GORDON, SARAH
  BOW, CLARA
GORDY, BERRY
  ROSS, DIANA
GORE, ALTOVISE
  DAVIS, JR., SAMMY
GORE, RHEA
  HUSTON, JOHN
  HUSTON, WALTER

GORE, RHEA
  KEYES, EVELYN
GORME, CORENE
  LAWRENCE, STEVE
GORME, EYDIE
  LAWRENCE, STEVE
GORME, NESSIM
  LAWRENCE, STEVE
GORME, ROBERT
  LAWRENCE, STEVE
GOSDEN, JR., FREEMAN
  GOSDEN, FREEMAN
GOSDEN, LINDA
  GOSDEN, FREEMAN
GOSDEN, VIRGINIA MARIA
  GOSDEN, FREEMAN
GOSDEN, WALTER WAY
  GOSDEN, FREEMAN
GOSSETT, CHRISTINE
  AMES, LEON
GOULD, DEBORAH
  LAWFORD, PETER
GOULD, ELLIOT
  O'NEILL, JENNIFER
  STREISAND, BARBRA
GOULD, GLORIA
  FARNUM, DUSTIN
GOULD, JOSHUA
  GOULD, ELLIOT
  STREISAND, BARBRA
GOULD, SAMUEL
  GOULD, ELLIOT
GOULET, CHRISTOPHER
  GOULET, ROBERT
  LAWRENCE, CAROL
GOULET, JOSEPH
  GOULET, ROBERT
  LAWRENCE, CAROL
GOULET, MICHAEL
  GOULET, ROBERT
  LAWRENCE, CAROL
GOULET, NICOLETTE
  GOULET, ROBERT
  LAWRENCE, CAROL
GOULET, ROBERT
  FORD, GLENN
  LAWRENCE, CAROL
GOURLEY, LORRAINE
  JESSEL, GEORGE
GOWENS, WILLIAM R.
  REMICK, LEE
GRABLE, BETTY
  COOGAN, JACKIE
  RAFT, GEORGE
GRABLE, CONN
  GRABLE, BETTY
GRABLE, MARJORIE
  GRABLE, BETTY

GRACIE, SALLY
  STEIGER, ROD
GRAF, BERNICE
  JANSSEN, DAVID
GRAHAM, BILLY
  WATERS, ETHEL
GRAHAM, EFFIE
  FLEMING, RHONDA
GRAHAM, ELLIE
  JANSSEN, DAVID
GRAHAM, MONA
  MALDEN, KARL
GRAHAM, SHEILA
  HEFLIN, VAN
GRAHAME, JEAN
  GRAHAME, GLORIA
GRAMIAK, ANN
  PALANCE, JACK
GRANGER, FARLEY
  WINTERS, SHELLEY
GRANGER, JAIME
  GRANGER, STEWART
  SIMMONS, JEAN
GRANGER, LINDSAY
  GRANGER, STEWART
  SIMMONS, JEAN
GRANGER, SAMANTHA
  GRANGER, STEWART
GRANGER, STEWART
  SIMMONS, JEAN
GRANGER, TRACY
  GRANGER, STEWART
  SIMMONS, JEAN
GRANT, CARY
  CANNON, DYAN
GRANT, JENNIFER
  CANNON, DYAN
  GRANT, CARY
GRANT, KATHRYN
  CROSBY, BING
GRANT, MARY
  PRICE, VINCENT
GRANT, SANDRA
  BENNETT, TONY
GRANT, SHELBY
  EVERETT, CHAD
GRANVILLE, BERNARD
  GRANVILLE, BONITA
GRAVES, ELSIE
  STARR, RINGO
GRAY, LILLIAN
  GRAYSON, KATHRYN
GRAYSON, KATHRYN
  LANZA, MARIO
  MONTGOMERY, GEORGE
  POWELL, JANE
GREDE, JENNY MATILDA
  ANDERSSON, BIBI

GREDE, KJELL
    ANDERSSON, BIBI
GREELEY, GEORGE
    CLAYTON, JAN
GREEN, ADDIE
    EDWARDS, CLIFF
GREEN, ADOLPH
    HOLLIDAY, JUDY
GREEN, BARBARA BABETTE
    FURNESS, BETTY
GREEN, JOHN
    FURNESS, BETTY
GREEN, MARIE 'RITA'
    WINCHELL, WALTER
GREEN, RICHARD
    FURNESS, BETTY
GREEN, ROSE ALICE
    DONAT, ROBERT
GREENBLATT, NATHANIEL
    HOPE, BOB
GREENE, BELINDA SUSAN
    GREENE, LORNE
GREENE, CHARLES
    GREENE, LORNE
GREENE, DANIEL
    GREENE, LORNE
GREENE, GILLIAN DONNA
    GREENE, LORNE
GREENE, HERBERT SIDNEY
    ARTHUR, JEAN
GREENE, RICHARD
    HENIE, SONJA
GREENSTEIN, FRANCINE
    BARRY, GENE
GREENSTREET, JOHN
    GREENSTREET, SYDNEY
GREENSTREET, JOHN OGDEN
    GREENSTREET, SYDNEY
GREENWOOD, CHARLOTTE
    HOPPER, HEDDA
GREER, BETTEJANE
    VALLEE, RUDY
GREER, NINA
    GARSON, GREER
GREEY, MONICA
    GIELGUD, JOHN
GREGORY, PAUL
    GAYNOR, JANET
GREGSON, NATASHA
    WAGNER, ROBERT
    WOOD, NATALIE
GREGSON, RICHARD
    WOOD, NATALIE
GREVNER, COUNTESS ANTONIA VON
    EVANS, ROBERT
GREW, ELIZABETH
    BLOOM, CLAIRE

GREY, JAMES
    GREY, JOEL
GREY, JENNIFER
    GREY, JOEL
GREY, NAN
    LAINE, FRANKIE
GREY, VIRGINIA
    GABLE, CLARK
GRIER, PAM
    PRYOR, RICHARD
GRIFFIN, FRANCIS
    DUNNE, IRENE
GRIFFIN, FRANK
    PAGET, DEBRA
GRIFFIN, LISA GAYE
    PAGET, DEBRA
GRIFFIN, MARGARET
    PAGET, DEBRA
GRIFFIN, MARY FRANCES
    DUNNE, IRENE
GRIFFIN, PHYLLIS
    DANIELS, BEBE
GRIFFIN, RUELL SHAYNE
    PAGET, DEBRA
GRIFFIN, TEALA LORING
    PAGET, DEBRA
GRIFFITH, CYNTHIA
    BERNARDI, HERSHEL
GRIFFITH, D.W.
    GISH, LILLIAN
    PICKFORD, MARY
GRIFFITH, KAY
    CRAWFORD, BRODERICK
GRILKHAS, DANA
    DAY, LARAINE
GRILKHAS, GIGI
    DAY, LARAINE
GRILKHAS, MICHAEL
    DAY, LARAINE
GRIMES, TAMMY
    PLUMMER, CHRISTOPHER
GRINDE, NICK
    WILSON, MARIE
GROVER, LORAINE
    FRANCISCUS, JAMES
GRUZALSKI, JAMES
    RUSH, BARBARA
GUARDINO, JOSEPH
    GUARDINO, HARRY
GUARDINO, LOUIS
    GUARDINO, HARRY
GUARDINO, MICHAEL
    GUARDINO, HARRY
GUARDINO, MICHELLE
    GUARDINO, HARRY
GUBITOSI, JAMES
    BLAKE, ROBERT

GUBITOSI, JR., JAMES
    BLAKE, ROBERT
GUBITOSI, LOVANNY
    BLAKE, ROBERT
GUEFFEN, MENACHEM
    RIGG, DIANA
GUERIN, TERENCE
    MARTIN, DEAN
GUGLIELMI, ALBERTO
    VALENTINO, RUDOLPH
GUGLIELMI, BEATRICE
    VALENTINO, RUDOLPH
GUGLIELMI, GIOVANNI
    VALENTINO, RUDOLPH
GUGLIELMI, MARIA
    VALENTINO, RUDOLPH
GUILFOYLE, FRANCES
    CLOONEY, ROSEMARY
GUINNESS, MATTHEW
    GUINNESS, ALEC
GUION, LEROY D.
    MACDONALD, JEANETTE
    RAYMOND, GENE
GUMM, DOROTHY VIRGINA
    MINNELLI, LIZA
GUMM, DOROTHY VIRGINIA
    GARLAND, JUDY
GUMM, FRANK AVENT
    GARLAND, JUDY
    MINNELLI, LIZA
GUMM, MARY JANE SUZANNE
    GARLAND, JUDY
    MINNELLI, LIZA
GURDIN, NICHOLAS
    WOOD, NATALIE
GURIAN, MANNING
    HARRIS, JULIE
GURIAN, PETER
    HARRIS, JULIE
GUSTAFSSON, ALVA
    GARBO, GRETA
GUSTAFSSON, KARL ALFRED
    GARBO, GRETA
GUSTAFSSON, SVEN
    GARBO, GRETA
GUTTMAN, SARAH
    ROBINSON, EDWARD G.
GUZMAN, ALEXANDER
    ALBERGHETTI, ANNA MARIA
GUZMAN, CLAUDIO
    ALBERGHETTI, ANNA MARIA
GUZMAN, PILAR
    ALBERGHETTI, ANNA MARIA
GWENN, EDMUND
    WINWOOD, ESTELLE
HAAVIG, MAGNHILD SENOVIA
    MEEKER, RALPH

HACHLER, HORST
    SCHELL, MARIA
HACHLER, OLIVER CHRISTIAN
    SCHELL, MARIA
HACKER, MARIA
    MELCHIOR, LAURITZ
HACKER, MILDRED
    HACKETT, BUDDY
HACKER, PHILIP
    HACKETT, BUDDY
HACKETT, ALBERT
    HACKETT, RAYMOND
HACKETT, IVY JULIE
    HACKETT, BUDDY
HACKETT, LISA JEAN
    HACKETT, BUDDY
HACKETT, MARJORIE
    MOORE, MARY TYLER
HACKETT, SANY ZADE
    HACKETT, BUDDY
HACKMAN, CHRISTOPHER
    HACKMAN, GENE
HACKMAN, ELIZABETH
    HACKMAN, GENE
HACKMAN, EUGENE EZRA
    HACKMAN, GENE
HACKMAN, LESLIE
    HACKMAN, GENE
HAESELBARTH, EDITH SHAKESPEARE
    CARRILLO, LEO
HAGEN, UTA
    FERRER, JOSE
HAGMAN, BENJAMIN
    MARTIN, MARY
HAGMAN, LARRY
    MARTIN, MARY
HAHN, SUZANNE
    ASTIN, JOHN
HAIMER, JACK
    BLANC, MEL
HAINES, PATRICIA
    CAINE, MICHAEL
HAINES, WILLIAN
    CRAWFORD, JOAN
HAISMAN, IRENE
    DENNY, REGINALD
HAJMASSY, FRANCIS
    MASSEY, ILONA
HALE-MUNRO, BEATRICE 'BINNIE'
    LAYE, EVELYN
HALE-MUNRO, JOHN R. 'SONNIE'
    LAYE, EVELYN
HALE, JEANNE
    HALE, ALAN
HALE, JR., ALAN
    HALE, ALAN
HALE, KAREN
    HALE, ALAN

HALE, LUCY
    RITTER, THELMA
HALEY, GLORIA
    HALEY, JACK
HALEY, JOHN
    HALEY, JACK
HALEY, JR., JOHN JOSEPH
    HALEY, JACK
    MINNELLI, LIZA
HALFORD, GENEVIEVE
    GLEASON, JACKIE
HALL, CHRISTOPHER JOHN
    CARON, LESLIE
HALL, CONRAD
    ROSS, KATHARINE
HALL, DIANA
    AYRES, LEW
HALL, DORRIE
    KEATON, DIANE
HALL, FERRIS
    ASTOR, MARY
HALL, JACK
    KEATON, DIANE
HALL, JAMES NORMAN
    HALL, JON
HALL, JENNIFER CARON
    CARON, LESLIE
HALL, JON
    LANGFORD, FRANCES
HALL, JOSEPHINE
    WELCH, RAQUEL
HALL, MORTIMER
    ROMAN, RUTH
HALL, PETER
    CARON, LESLIE
HALL, RANDY
    KEATON, DIANE
HALL, RICHARD
    ROMAN, RUTH
HALL, ROBIN
    KEATON, DIANE
HALLIDAY, HELLER
    MARTIN, MARY
HALLIDAY, RICHARD
    MARTIN, MARY
HALLWARD, MICHAEL
    GRAHAME, GLORIA
HALPIN, DARLENE
    HOPPER, DENNIS
HAMAMA, FATEN
    SHARIF, OMAR
HAMEL, ALAN
    SOMERS, SUZANNE
HAMILTON, ASHLEY STEVEN
    HAMILTON, GEORGE
HAMILTON, CARRIE LOUISE
    BURNETT, CAROL

HAMILTON, DAVID HUBBARD
    HAMILTON, GEORGE
HAMILTON, ERIN KATE
    BURNETT, CAROL
HAMILTON, GEORGE WILLIAM
    HAMILTON, GEORGE
HAMILTON, JODY ANN
    BURNETT, CAROL
HAMILTON, JOE
    BURNETT, CAROL
HAMILTON, WILLIAM
    HAMILTON, GEORGE
HANDS, RITA
    GREENE, LORNE
HANDSCHUMAKER, MEGAN
    MACRAE, GORDON
HANKS, CAMILLE
    COSBY, BILL
HANKS, JR., ROBERT LOWERY
    PARKER, JEAN
HANKS, ROBERT LOWERY
    PARKER, JEAN
HANNAGAN, STEVE
    SHERIDAN, ANN
HANSON, DOROTHEA ODETTA
    COOGAN, JACKIE
HANTON, ELLEN
    O'HERLIHY, DAN
HARDIN, LILLIAN
    ARMSTRONG, LOUIS
HARDING, FRIEDA
    DILLMAN, BRADFORD
HARDING, LAURA
    HEPBURN, KATHARINE
HARDING, LULA MAE
    ROBERTSON, DALE
HARDWICKE, EDWARD
    HARDWICKE, CEDRIC
HARDWICKE, EDWIN WEBSTER
    HARDWICKE, CEDRIC
HARDY, JUANITA
    POITIER, SIDNEY
HARDY, OLIVER
    LAUREL, STAN
HARDY, ROBERT
    COOPER, GLADYS
HARGITAY, MARIA
    MANSFIELD, JAYNE
HARGITAY, MICHAEL
    MANSFIELD, JAYNE
HARGITAY, MIKLOS
    MANSFIELD, JAYNE
HARGITAY, ZOLTAN
    MANSFIELD, JAYNE
HARGRAVE, HOMER P.
    MOORE, COLLEEN
HARGRAVE, JR., HOMER
    MOORE, COLLEEN

HARRIS, KATHERINE CORRI
    BARRYMORE, ETHEL
    BARRYMORE, JOHN
    BARRYMORE, LIONEL
HARRIS, LAWSON
    DEREK, JOHN
HARRIS, MARK
    ROTH, LILLIAN
HARRIS, MILDRED
    CHAPLIN, CHARLES
HARRIS, PHIL
    FAYE, ALICE
HARRIS, PHYLLIS
    FAYE, ALICE
    HARRIS, PHIL
HARRIS, WILLIAM PICKETT
    HARRIS, JULIE
HARRISON, CAREY
    HARRISON, REX
    KENDALL, KAY
    PALMER, LILLI
    ROBERTS, RACHEL
HARRISON, GEORGE
    LENNON, JOHN
    MCCARTNEY, PAUL
    STARR, RINGO
HARRISON, HAROLD
    HARRISON, GEORGE
HARRISON, HARRY
    HARRISON, GEORGE
HARRISON, LOUISE
    HARRISON, GEORGE
HARRISON, NOEL
    HARRISON, REX
    KENDALL, KAY
    PALMER, LILLI
    ROBERTS, RACHEL
HARRISON, PETER
    HARRISON, GEORGE
HARRISON, REX
    KENDALL, KAY
    PALMER, LILLI
    ROBERTS, RACIEL
HARRISON, ROLAND
    LYON, SUE
HARRISON, SUSAN
    LYON, SUE
HARRISON, WILLIAM REGINALD
    HARRISON, REX
HARROLD, MARJORIE JANE
    LADD, ALAN
HARSHMAN, JONATHAN
    WINTERS, JONATHAN
HART, CATHERINE
    CARLISLE, KITTY
HART, CHRISTOPHER
    CARLISLE, KITTY

HARGRAVE, JUDY
    MOORE, COLLEEN
HARKIN, KATHRYN
    MOSTEL, ZERO
HARKNESS, ELIZABETH GRANT
    MONTGOMERY, ElIZABETH
    MONTGOMERY, ROBERT
HARLOW, JEAN
    EDWARDS, CLIFF
    GABLE, CLARK
    HARLOW, JEAN
    HUGHES, HOWARD
    POWELL, WILLIAM
HARMON, KRISTIN
    HILLIARD, HARRIET
    NELSON, OZZIE
    NELSON, RICK
HARMON, TOM
    NELSON, RICK
HARNICK, SHELDON
    MAY, ELAINE
HAROKOPOS, PANAYIOTIS
    MERCOURI, MELINA
HARPER, DON
    HARPER, VALERIE
HARPER, EDITH
    HAYMES, DICK
HARPER, HOWARD
    HARPER, VALERIE
HARPER, LEAH
    HARPER, VALERIE
HARRIGAN, CATHERINE H.
    CROSBY, BING
HARRIGAN, DENNIS
    CROSBY, BING
HARRIGAN, KATE
    HAYWARD, SUSAN
HARRIS, ALICE
    FAYE, ALICE
    HARRIS, PHIL
HARRIS, BETTY JEAN
    FOXX, REDD
HARRIS, CAROLINA
    BARTHELMESS, RICHARD
HARRIS, DAMIAN
    HARRIS, RICHARD
HARRIS, DERMOT
    HARRIS, RICHARD
HARRIS, IVAN
    HARRIS, RICHARD
HARRIS, JAMIE
    HARRIS, RICHARD
HARRIS, JARED
    HARRIS, RICHARD
HARRIS, JR., PHIL
    FAYE, ALICE
    HARRIS, PHIL

HART, MARTHA
    REDFORD, ROBERT
HART, MARY
    HART, WILLIAM S.
HART, MOSS
    CARLISLE, KITTY
HART, WALTER S.
    STERLING, ROBERT
HARTFORD, EDEN
    MARX, CHICO
    MARX, GROUCHO
    MARX, GUMMO
    MARX, HARPO
    MARX, ZEPPO
HARTLEY, ERNEST RICHARD
    LEIGH, VIVIEN
HARTMAN, GRETCHEN
    HALE, ALAN
HARTSHORN, GRACE DUNAWAY
    DUNAWAY, FAYE
HARVEY, DOMINO
    HARVEY, LAURENCE
HARZ, CLAUDE
    WELD, TUESDAY
HARZ, NATASHA
    WELD, TUESDAY
HASTINGS, AIMEE RAISCH
    BENNETT, CONSTANCE
    BENNETT, JOAN
    BENNETT, RICHARD
HASTINGS, DELLA
    ARMENDARIZ, PEDRO
HAUBENSTOCK, HARRY MAYER
    SCHNEIDER, ROMY
HAUSER, GAYLORD
    GARBO, GRETA
HAUSER, MADELINE
    FALK, PETER
HAUSMAN, MICHAEL
    VARSI, DIANE
HAUSMAN, WILLOW
    VARSI, DIANE
HAVEMAN, BARBARA
    OWEN, REGINALD
HAVER, BERT
    HAVER, JUNE
HAVER, JUNE
    MACMURRAY, FRED
    NELSON, GENE
HAVOC, JUNE
    LEE, GYPSY ROSE
HAWKINS, JACK
    TANDY, JESSICA
HAWKINS, SUSAN
    CRONYN, HUME
    TANDY, JESSICA
HAWKS, HOWARD
    ASTOR, MARY

HAWKS, HOWARD
    SHEARER, NORMA
HAWKS, KENNETH
    ASTOR, MARY
HAWN, EDWARD RUTLEDGE
    HAWN, GOLDIE
HAWN, KATHY
    MARTIN, DEAN
HAWN, PATRICIA
    HAWN, GOLDIE
HAWORTH, LELA
    HAYWORTH, RITA
    ROGERS, GINGER
HAWORTH, VOLGA
    HAYMES, DICK
    HAYWORTH, RITA
    WELLES, ORSON
HAYAKAWA, FUJIKO
    HAYAKAWA, SESSUE
HAYAKAWA, YOICHORO
    HAYAKAWA, SESSUE
HAYAKAWA, YOSHIKO
    HAYAKAWA, SESSUE
HAYAKAWA, YUKIO
    HAYAKAWA, SESSUE
HAYDEN, CHRISTIAN
    HAYDEN, STERLING
HAYDEN, DANA
    HAYDEN, STERLING
HAYDEN, DARRELL
    SAINT, EVA MARIE
HAYDEN, GRETCHEN
    HAYDEN, STERLING
HAYDEN, JEFFREY
    SAINT, EVA MARIE
HAYDEN, LAURETTE
    SAINT, EVA MARIE
HAYDEN, MATTHEW
    HAYDEN, STERLING
HAYDEN, RUSSELL
    CLAYTON, JAN
HAYDEN, SANDRA JANE
    CLAYTON, JAN
    HAYDEN, RUSSELL
HAYDEN, THOMAS
    FONDA, HENRY
    FONDA, JANE
    FONDA, PETER
HAYDEN, TROY
    FONDA, HENRY
    FONDA, JANE
    FONDA, PETER
HAYES, CATHERINE ESTELL
    HAYES, HELEN
HAYES, CATHY LIND
    HAYES, PETER LIND
HAYES, CLARK B.
    HAYES, GABBY

HAYES, GABBY
    BOYD, WILLIAM
HAYES, GRACE DOLORES
    HAYES, PETER LIND
HAYES, HAL B.
    GABOR, EVA
    GABOR, ZSA ZSA
HAYES, HATTIE
    HAYES, GABBY
HAYES, HELEN
    LUNT, ALFRED
HAYES, PETER MICHAEL
    HAYES, PETER LIND
HAYMES, BARBARA
    DRU, JOANNE
    HAYMES, DICK
    HAYWORTH, RITA
    IRELAND, JOHN
HAYMES, DICK
    DRU, JOANNE
    HAYWORTH, RITA
HAYMES, HELEN
    DRU, JOANNE
    HAYMES, DICK
    HAYWORTH, RITA
    IRELAND, JOHN
HAYMES, RICHARD
    DRU, JOANNE
    HAYMES, DICK
    HAYWORTH, RITA
    IRELAND, JOHN
HAYS, KATHRYN
    FORD, GLENN
HAYTON, LENNIE
    HORNE, LENA
HAYTON, LEONARD
    HORNE, LENA
HAYWARD, BRIDGET
    SULLAVAN, MARGARET
HAYWARD, BROOKE
    FONDA, JANE
    HOPPER, DENNIS
    SULLAVAN, MARGARET
HAYWARD, CYNTHIA
    FORD, GLENN
HAYWARD, LELAND
    FONDA, HENRY
    HEPBURN, KATHARINE
    HOPPER, DENNIS
    SULLAVAN, MARGARET
HAYWARD, LOUIS
    LUPINO, IDA
HAYWARD, WILLIAM 'BILL'
    FONDA, PETER
    HOPPER, DENNIS
    SULLAVAN, MARGARET
HAYWORTH, RITA
    HAYMES, DICK

HAYWORTH, RITA
    ROGERS, GINGER
    WELLES, ORSON
HAZELWOOD, JEAN
    WIDMARK, RICHARD
HEALY, MARY
    HAYES, PETER LIND
HEARNEY, GLADYS
    NAISH, J. CARROLL
HEARST, WM. R.
    PARSONS, LOUELLA O.
HEARST, WM. RANDOLPH
    DAVIES, MARION
HEATHERTON, RAY
    HEATHERTON, JOEY
HEATHERTON, RICHARD
    HEATHERTON, JOEY
HECHT, HAROLD
    LANCASTER, BURT
HECKSHER, BETTY
    CAREY, MACDONALD
HEDRICK, BUDDY
    GRAYSON, KATHRYN
HEDRICK, CHARLES E.
    GRAYSON, KATHRYN
HEDRICK, FRANCES RAEBURN
    GRAYSON, KATHRYN
HEDRICK, HAL
    GRAYSON, KATHRYN
HEEMSTRA, BARON ARNOUD VAN
    HEPBURN, AUDREY
HEEMSTRA, BARONESS ELLA VAN
    HEPBURN, AUDREY
HEES, ADA
    RAYMOND, GENE
HEFLIN, CATHLEEN
    HEFLIN, VAN
    TALBOT, LYLE
HEFLIN, EMMETT
    HEFLIN, VAN
HEFLIN, FRANCES
    HEFLIN, VAN
HEFLIN, MARTIN
    HEFLIN, VAN
HEFLIN, TRACY NEAL
    HEFLIN, VAN
    TALBOT, LYLE
HEFLIN, VANA
    HEFLIN, VAN
    TALBOT, LYLE
HEIMBERGER, FRANK
    ALBERT, EDDIE
HEINZ, NANCY
    TUFTS, SONNY
HELD, ADAH
    CRABBE, BUSTER
HELLIWELL, BERYL
    RIGG, DIANA

HELLMAN, LILLIAN
    COLBERT, CLAUDETTE
    NEAL, PATRICIA
HELM, FRANCES
    KEITH, BRIAN
HELMORE, EVELYN
    KARLOFF, BORIS
HELMS, RUTH
    NAGEL, CONRAD
HEMINGWAY, ERNEST
    COOPER, GARY
HEMINGWAY, MARIE
    RAINS, CLAUDE
HENAGHAN, JAMES
    VERDON, GWEN
HENDERSON, ANNE
    DRESSLER, MARIE
HENDERSON, CECIL
    JOHNS, GLYNIS
HENDERSON, EDWARD
    TALBOT, LYLE
HENDERSON, ELIZABETH LOUISE
    YOUNG, ROBERT
HENDERSON, ROBERT BARTON
    WINWOOD, ESTELLE
HENDERSON, SKITCH
    EMERSON, FAYE
HENDLER, HANK
    GRAYSON, KATHRYN
HENDRICKS, ANGELA
    DAY, LARAINE
HENDRICKS, CHRISTOPHER
    DAY, LARAINE
HENDRICKS, JAMES RAY
    DAY, LARAINE
HENDRICKS, MICHELE
    DAY, LARAINE
HENDRIX, DIXIE WANDA
    MURPHY, AUDIE
HENIE, LEIF
    HENIE, SONJA
HENIE, SONIA
    POWER, TYRONE
HENIE, WILHELM
    HENIE, SONJA
HENKEL, JULIETTE
    MURPHY, GEORGE
HENNESSEY, CHARLOTTE
    PICKFORD, MARY
HENRY, ADELAIDE ANTOINETTE
    DUNNE, IRENE
HEPBURN-RUSTON, JOSEPH ANTHONY
    HEPBURN, AUDREY
HEPBURN, AUDREY
    FERRER, MEL
HEPBURN, DR. THOMAS NORVAL
    HEPBURN, KATHARINE

HEPBURN, JR., THOMAS
    HEPBURN, KATHARINE
HEPBURN, KATHARINE
    HUGHES, HOWARD
    TRACY, SPENCER
HEPBURN, MARGARET
    HEPBURN, KATHARINE
HEPBURN, MARION
    HEPBURN, KATHARINE
HEPBURN, RICHARD
    HEPBURN, KATHARINE
HEPBURN, ROBERT
    HEPBURN, KATHARINE
HERINGLAKE, DORIS P.
    TUCKER, FORREST
HERLIHY, ELIZABETH
    ALLEN, FRED
HERMAN, SARAH
    BERMAN, SHELLEY
HERRIN, MARK
    GARLAND, JUDY
    MINNELLI, LIZA
HERSHELMAN, ADELINE
    GABLE, CLARK
HERSHKOWITZ, FRANCES
    ALLEN, FRED
HERSHOLT, ALLEN
    HERSHOLT, JEAN
HERSHOLT, HENRY
    HERSHOLT, JEAN
HERTLE, BARBARA
    AMECHE, DON
HERTZ, JR., JOHN
    LOY, MYRNA
HERVEY, IRENE
    JONES, ALLAN
    SAINT JOHN, JILL
    TAYLOR, ROBERT
HESSELBERG, EDOUARD G.
    DOUGLAS, MELVYN
HESSELBERG, GEORGE
    DOUGLAS, MELVYN
HESSELBERG, LAMAR
    DOUGLAS, MELVYN
HESTON, CHESTER
    HESTON, CHARLTON
HESTON, FRASER CLARKE
    HESTON, CHARLTON
HESTON, HOLLY ANN
    HESTON, CHARLTON
HEWITT, MURIEL
    RICHARDSON, RALPH
HEYMAN, HENRIETTA
    SHEARER, NORMA
HICKS, BETTY
    LANZA, MARIO
HIGGINS, GERALDINE
    DOUGLAS, PAUL

HIGGINS, LIZ
    ROMERO, CESAR
HIGHTOWER, ROBERT
    VERA-ELLEN
HILEM, JO ANNE
    TAYLOR, ROD
HILEM, MARY
    TAYLOR, ROD
HILL, GLADYS
    HUSTON, JOHN
HILL, HANNAH
    CHAPLIN, CHARLES
    GODDARD, PAULETTE
HILL, JAMES
    HAYWORTH, RITA
    LANCASTER, BURT
HILL, JOANNA
    BAER, JR., MAX
HILL, PHYLLIS
    FERRER, JOSE
HILLIARD, HARRIET
    NELSON, OZZIE
    NELSON, RICK
HILLIARD, HAZEL
    HILLIARD, HARRIET
HILTON, FRANCESCA
    GABOR, EVA
    GABOR, ZSA ZSA
    SANDERS, GEORGE
HILTON, JR., CONRAD NICHOLSON
    TAYLOR, ELIZABETH
    VON FURSTENBURG, BETSY
HILTON, SR., CONRAD NICHOLSON
    GABOR, EVA
    GABOR, ZSA ZSA
    MILLER, ANN
    TAYLOR, ELIZABETH
HIME, ADAM
    MONTGOMERY, GEORGE
    SHORE, DINAH
HIME, JENNIFER TRINITY
    MONTGOMERY, GEORGE
    SHORE, DINAH
HIME, MARK
    MONTGOMERY, GEORGE
    SHORE, DINAH
HIRD, THORA
    TORME, MEL
HIRSCH, MARY
    COBB, LEE J.
HIRSCH, RAYMOND
    PARKER, ELEANOR
HITCHCOCK, PATRICIA
    HITCHCOCK, ALFRED
HITCHCOCK, WILLIAM
    HITCHCOCK, ALFRED
HOAR, ELLEN ELIZABETH
    TERRY-THOMAS

HOBSON, ALICE
    FINNEY, ALBERT
HOCKETT, CAROLYN
    ROONEY, MICKEY
HODGES, DANIEL
    JACKSON, GLENDA
HODGES, ROY
    JACKSON, GLENDA
HODIAK, JOHN
    BAXTER, ANNE
HODIAK, KATRINA BAXTER
    BAXTER, ANNE
    HODIAK, JOHN
HOEN, ROBIN
    MACGRAW, ALI
HOFERT, ELIZABETH
    DAILEY, DAN
HOFFA, PORTLAND
    ALLEN, FRED
    MASON, JAMES
HOFFMAN, ELIZA L.
    BENNETT, RICHARD
HOFFMAN, HARRY
    HOFFMAN, DUSTIN
HOFFMAN, JENNIFER CELIA
    HOFFMAN, DUSTIN
HOFFMAN, LILLIAN
    GRABLE, BETTY
HOFFMAN, MABEL
    DURYEA, DAN
HOFFMAN, RONALD
    HOFFMAN, DUSTIN
HOHENZOLLERN, PRINCE LOUIS VON
    DAMITA, LILI
HOLBERT, SUSAN
    MCDANIEL, HATTIE
HOLBROOK, DAVID
    HOLBROOK, HAL
HOLBROOK, EVE
    HOLBROOK, HAL
HOLBROOK, HAROLD ROWE
    HOLBROOK, HAL
HOLBROOK, VICTORIA
    HOLBROOK, HAL
HOLDEN, PETER WESTFIELD
    HOLDEN, WILLIAM
HOLDEN, RICHARD
    HOLDEN, WILLIAM
HOLDEN, ROBERT
    HOLDEN, WILLIAM
HOLDEN, SCOTT PORTER
    HOLDEN, WILLIAM
HOLDEN, VIRGINIA
    HOLDEN, WILLIAM
HOLLENBECK, MABELLE
    WEBB, CLIFTON
HOLLOWAY, JULIAN
    HOLLOWAY, STANLEY

HOLM, THEODORE
    HOLM, CELESTE
HOLMAN, HERBERT LEIGH
    LEIGH, VIVIEN
HOLMAN, LIBBY
    CLIFT, MONTGOMERY
HOLMAN, SUZANNE
    LEIGH, VIVIEN
    OLIVIER, LAURENCE
HOLMES, CAROL
    DAHL, ARLENE
HOLMES, III, CHRISTIAN
    DAHL, ARLENE
HOLMSDALE, JEFFREY
    COWARD, NOEL
HOLT, TIM
    GRANVILLE, BONITA
HOOPER, MABEL
    RAYE, MARTHA
HOOVER, HERBERT
    MAYER, LOUIS B.
HOPE, ANTHONY READE
    HOPE, BOB
HOPE, FREDERICK
    HOPE, BOB
HOPE, GEORGE
    HOPE, BOB
HOPE, HONORA AVIS MARY
    HOPE, BOB
HOPE, IVOR
    HOPE, BOB
HOPE, JACK
    HOPE, BOB
HOPE, JAMES
    HOPE, BOB
HOPE, LINDA ROBERTA THERESA
    HOPE, BOB
HOPE, SIDNEY
    HOPE, BOB
HOPE, WILLIAM KELLY FRANCIS
    HOPE, BOB
HOPPER, DENNIS
    FONDA, PETER
    PHILLIPS, MICHELLE
HOPPER, HEDDA
    PARSONS, LOUELLA O.
HOPPER, II, JOHN
    HOPPER, HEDDA
HOPPER, JANE
    BOONE, RICHARD
HOPPER, JOAN
    HOPPER, HEDDA
HOPPER, JR., WILLIAM DEWOLF
    HOPPER, HEDDA
HOPPER, MARIN
    HOPPER, DENNIS
HOPPER, VIRDEEN RUTH
    EVERETT, CHAD

HOPPER, WILLIAM DEWOLF
    HOPPER, HEDDA
HOPPERT, GEORGE
    DRESSLER, MARIE
HORMEL, GEORGE
    CARON, LESLIE
    MORENO, RITA
HORNBLOW, JR., ARTHUR
    LOY, MYRNA
HORNBY, SHIRLEY
    TWIGGY
HORNBY, VIVIAN
    TWIGGY
HORNBY, WILLIAM NORMAN
    TWIGGY
HORNE, EDWIN F.
    HORNE, LENA
HORNE, JUNE
    COOPER, JACKIE
HORNE, VICTORIA
    OAKIE, JACK
HORSPOOL, JESSIE HELEN
    TANDY, JESSICA
HOSHELLE, MARJORIE
    CHANDLER, JEFF
HOUGH, STANLEY
    PETERS, JEAN
HOUGHSTON, ROBERT
    HUSTON, WALTER
HOUGHTON, KATHERINE MARTHA
    HEPBURN, KATHARINE
HOUSE, DOROTHY IRENE
    DEVINE, ANDY
HOUSE, ELIZABETH
    WHITE, PEARL
HOUSE, RON
    LAKE, VERONICA
HOVEY, WALTER
    MOORE, COLLEEN
HOVICK, JOHN OLAV
    HAVOC, JUNE
    LEE, GYPSY ROSE
HOWARD, ARTHUR JOHN
    HOWARD, TREVOR
HOWARD, CLINT
    HOWARD, RON
HOWARD, CY
    GRAHAME, GLORIA
HOWARD, FRANCES
    GOLDWYN, SAMUEL
HOWARD, JEAN
    MAYER, LOUIS B.
HOWARD, JOHN RIDGELY
    LAMOUR, DOROTHY
HOWARD, JOHN ROBERT
    BARRYMORE, JOHN
HOWARD, LESLIE
    BOGART, HUMPHREY

HOWARD, LESLIE RUTH
    HOWARD, LESLIE
HOWARD, LILIAN
    HOWARD, LESLIE
HOWARD, MARIANNE PAULETTE
    GRAHAME, GLORIA
HOWARD, RANCE
    HOWARD, RON
HOWARD, RICHARD
    LAMOUR, DOROTHY
HOWARD, RONALD
    HOWARD, LESLIE
HOWARD, WILLIAM ROSS
    LAMOUR, DOROTHY
HOWE, ANNE
    SELLERS, PETER
HOWLEY, PAMELA
    LAWRENCE, GERTRUDE
HOYT, JULIA
    CALHERN, LOUIS
HRUBA, JR., RUDOLF
    RALSTON, VERA HRUBA
HRUBA, RUDOLF
    RALSTON, VERA HRUBA
HRUNEK, RUDOLPH V.
    PALMER, BETSY
HUBER, GERDA
    DIETRICH, MARLENE
HUBERT, RICHARD
    SAINT CYR, LILI
HUDNUT, RICHARD
    VALENTINO, RUDOLPH
HUDSON, BILL
    HAWN, GOLDIE
HUDSON, OLIVER
    HAWN, GOLDIE
HUDSON, ROCK
    MAXWELL, MARILYN
    SAINT JAMES, SUSAN
HUDSON, SHARLEY JEAN
    WYNN, KEENAN
HUFF, AMANDA
    BEGLEY, ED
HUFFAKER, CLAIR
    ROSS, KATHARINE
HUFFMAN, HARRISON C.
    EDEN, BARBARA
HUGHES, CAROLYN
    SCOTT, GEORGE C.
HUGHES, DAVID
    ZETTERLING, MAI
HUGHES, HARRIET V.
    FIELDS, W.C.
HUGHES, HOWARD
    DOVE, BILLIE
    GARDNER, AVA
    GAYNOR, MITZI

HUGHES, HOWARD
    HARLOW, JEAN
    HEPBURN, KATHARINE
    MOORE, TERRY
    PETERS, JEAN
    RUSSELL, JANE
HUGHES, HOWARD ROBARD
    HUGHES, HOWARD
HUGUENY, SHARON
    EVANS, ROBERT
HUME, BENITA
    COLMAN, RONALD
    SANDERS, GEORGE
HUMPHREY, MAUDE
    BOGART, HUMPHREY
HUNT, DESIREE
    BALL, LUCILLE
HUNT, SUZY
    BURTON, RICHARD
HUNTER, CHRISTOPHER
    HUNTER, JEFFREY
    RUSH, BARBARA
HUNTER, JEFFERY
    RUSH, BARBARA
HUNTER, JOYCE
    AUER, MISCHA
HUNTER, TODD
    HUNTER, JEFFREY
HUPP, JACK
    WINDSOR, MARIE
HUPP, RICHARD
    WINDSOR, MARIE
HUSSEY, GEORGE
    HUSSEY, RUTH
HUSSEY, OLIVIA
    MARTIN, DEAN
HUSTON, ANGELICA
    HUSTON, JOHN
    NICHOLSON, JACK
    O'NEAL, RYAN
HUSTON, JOHN
    BOGART, HUMPHREY
    DE LAURENTIIS, DINO
    HUSTON, WALTER
    KEYES, EVELYN
HUSTON, PAUL ALBERRAN
    HUSTON, JOHN
    KEYES, EVELYN
    SHAW, ARTIE
HUSTON, WALTER
    HUSTON, JOHN
    KEYES, EVELYN
HUSTON, WALTER ANTHONY
    HUSTON, JOHN
HUTNER, HERBERT L.
    GABOR, EVA
    GABOR, ZSA ZSA

HUTTON, BARBARA
    GRANT, CARY
    MERRILL, DINA
HUTTON, E. F.
    MERRILL, DINA
HUTTON, MARGARET LITTLE
    SMITH, MAGGIE
HYAMS, BONNIE
    SOMMER, ELKE
HYAMS, CHRISTOPHER
    SOMMER, ELKE
HYAMS, JAY
    SOMMER, ELKE
HYAMS, JOE
    SOMMER, ELKE
HYDE WHITE, ALEXANDER 'PUNCH'
    HYDE WHITE, WILFRED
HYDE WHITE, JULIET
    HYDE WHITE, WILFRED
HYDE WHITE, MICHAEL
    HYDE WHITE, WILFRED
HYER, AGNES ANN
    HYER, MARTHA
HYER, JEANNE
    HYER, MARTHA
HYER, JULIEN C.
    HYER, MARTHA
HYLAND, DIANA
    TRAVOLTA, JOHN
ICHILOV, OFRA
    BIKEL, THEODORE
ILLIANA, VERA
    LAUREL, STAN
INCE, RALPH
    STEWART, ANITA
INCE, THOMAS
    STEWART, ANITA
INCE, THOMAS H.
    HART, WILLIAM S.
INGELS, MARTY
    JONES, SHIRLEY
INGLE-FINCH, GEORGE
    FINCH, PETER
INGOLIE, CONCERTA ANN
    FISHER, EDDIE
INGRIM, NAOMI
    HALE, ALAN
IPAR, ALI
    BRUCE, VIRGINIA
IRELAND, JILL
    BRONSON, CHARLES
    MCCALLUM, DAVID
IRELAND, JOHN
    DRU, JOANNE
IRELAND, JOHN ALFRED
    IRELAND, JILL
    MCCALLUM, DAVID

IRELAND, JOHN ANTHONY
    DRU, JOANNE
    IRELAND, JOHN
IRELAND, PETER
    DRU, JOANNE
    IRELAND, JOHN
IRELAND, SR., JOHN
    IRELAND, JOHN
IROLLE, IDA
    MASTROIANNI, MARCELLO
IRVINE, MARION
    LEDERER, FRANCIS
ISAACS, BARBARA
    CARNEY, ART
ISAACS, CHARLES
    GABOR, EVA
    GABOR, ZSA ZSA
ISLEY, PHILIP R.
    JONES, JENNIFER
ITALIANO, JOANNE
    BANCROFT, ANNE
    BROOKS, MEL
ITALIANO, MICHAEL
    BANCROFT, ANNE
    BROOKS, MEL
ITALIANO, PHYLLIS
    BANCROFT, ANNE
    BROOKS, MEL
ITURBI, AMPARA
    ITURBI, JOSE
ITURBI, MARIA
    ITURBI, JOSE
ITURBI, RICARDO
    ITURBI, JOSE
ITZKOWITZ, MICHAEL
    CANTOR, EDDIE
IVANHOE, SAMUEL ICLE
    IVES, BURL
IVES, ALEXANDER
    IVES, BURL
IVES, BEATRICE
    HAYWORTH, RITA
    WELLES, ORSON
IVES, FRANK
    IVES, BURL
IWERKS, UB
    DISNEY, WALT
JACKSON, ANNE
    WALLACH, ELI
JACKSON, EDDIE
    DURANTE, JIMMY
JACKSON, FELIX
    DURBIN, DEANNA
JACKSON, HARRY
    JACKSON, GLENDA
JACKSON, JESSICA
    DURBIN, DEANNA

JACKSON, KATE
    BEATTY, WARREN
JACKSON, MARTA
    GRANGER, STEWART
JACKSON, RICHARD EMERY
    GOSDEN, FREEMAN
JACOBI, GERALDINE
    RUSSELL, JANE
JACOBS, ALFRED
    LAURIE, PIPER
JACOBS, CHARLES
    THOMAS, DANNY
JACOBS, ELAINE
    BARRYMORE, ETHEL
    BARRYMORE, JOHN
    BARRYMORE, LIONEL
JACOBS, SHERRE
    LAURIE, PIPER
JACOBS, THOMAS
    THOMAS, DANNY
JAFFEE, BERNARD
    JAFFE, SAM
JAGGER, ALBERT
    JAGGER, DEAN
JAGGER, DIANE MARION
    JAGGER, DEAN
JAMBOR, AGI
    RAINS, CLAUDE
JAMES, CLAIR
    BERKELEY, BUSBY
JAMES, DR. CARVEL
    TALMADGE, CONSTANCE
    TALMADGE, NORMA
JAMES, EDDIE
    PROWSE, JULIET
JAMES, EDWARD
    GODDARD, PAULETTE
JAMES, ELIZABETH
    GRABLE, BETTY
JAMES, HARRY
    GRABLE, BETTY
JAMES, JESSICA
    GRABLE, BETTY
JAMES, VICTORIA
    GRABLE, BETTY
JAMESON, FRANK G.
    GABOR, EVA
    GABOR, ZSA ZSA
JAMESON, JOYCE
    VAUGHN, ROBERT
JANIS, ELSIE
    NOVARRO, RAMON
JANIS, VIVIENNE AUDREY
    CUMMINGS, ROBERT
JANSEN, VIRGINIA DEWITT
    SHAW, ROBERT
JANSSEN, EUGENE
    JANSSEN, DAVID

JANSSEN, JILL
    JANSSEN, DAVID
JANSSEN, TERI
    JANSSEN, DAVID
JANSSEN, WERNER
    HARDING, ANN
JARRETT, ARTHUR
    HOLM, ELEANOR
JAYNES, HERBERTA
    FONDA, HENRY
JEANS, ISABEL
    RAINS, CLAUDE
JEFFRIES, ANNE
    STERLING, ROBERT
JEFFRIES, FRAN
    HAYMES, DICK
JEFFRIES, LANG
    FLEMING, RHONDA
JENKINS, BARBARA PATRICIA
    BARRIE, WENDY
JENKINS, FRANK C.
    BARRIE, WENDY
JENKINS, THOMAS
    BURTON, RICHARD
JENS, SALOME
    MEEKER, RALPH
JENSEN, JONNA
    COCHRAN, STEVE
JESSEL, GEORGE
    TALMADGE, CONSTANCE
    TALMADGE, NORMA
    WINCHELL, WALTER
JESSEL, JERILYN
    JESSEL, GEORGE
JESSEL, JOSEPH AARON
    JESSEL, GEORGE
    TALMADGE, NORMA
JOHNS, MERVYN
    JOHNS, GLYNIS
JOHNSON, ANNA
    CRAWFORD, JOAN
JOHNSON, ARTHUR
    LAWRENCE, FLORENCE
JOHNSON, CHARLES
    JOHNSON, VAN
JOHNSON, CLARENCE IRWIN
    DAY, LARAINE
JOHNSON, DE ARMAN
    DAY, LARAINE
JOHNSON, DELLA
    LOY, MYRNA
JOHNSON, DELORES
    DEREK, JOHN
JOHNSON, ELIZABETH
    VON FURSTENBURG, BETSY
JOHNSON, ETHRIDGE
    DAY, LARAINE

JOHNSON,   GERALDINE
    MATTHAU, WALTER
JOHNSON, HELEN
    GIBSON, HOOT
JOHNSON, JOHN
    CARROLL, DIAHANN
JOHNSON, JOSEPH GWYNNE
    YORK, MICHAEL
JOHNSON, LAMAR
    DAY, LARAINE
JOHNSON, LYNDA B.
    HAMILTON, GEORGE
JOHNSON, MAGGIE
    EASTWOOD, CLINT
JOHNSON, MARILYN
    TUCKER, FORREST
JOHNSON, MERLE
    DONAHUE, TROY
JOHNSON, NARVILLE
    DAY, LARAINE
JOHNSON, NILA
    DAY, LARAINE
JOHNSON, RICHARD
    NOVAK, KIM
JOHNSON, RUTH
    MARX, CHICO
    MARX, GROUCHO
    MARX, GUMMO
    MARX, HARPO
    MARX, ZEPPO
JOHNSON, SCHUYLER
    JOHNSON, VAN
JOHNSON, THERMA
    DAY, LARAINE
JOHNSON, VAN
    WYNN, KEENAN
JOHNSTON, AGNES MUIR
    FARNUM, WILLIAM
JOHNSTON, CLARA
    STONE, FRED
JOHNSTON, JOHN
    GRAYSON, KATHRYN
JOHNSTON, PATRICIA KATHRYN
    GRAYSON, KATHRYN
JOHNSTON, RUBY ELAINE
    HOLBROOK, HAL
JOHNSTONE, AGNES MUIR
    FARNUM, DUSTIN
JOLLEY, SANDRA
    TUCKER, FORREST
JOLSON, AL
    KEELER, RUBY
JOLSON, ASA
    JOLSON, AL
JOLSON, JR., AL 'PETER'
    JOLSON, AL
    KEELER, RUBY

JONES, ALLAN
    SAINT JOHN, JILL
JONES, BECKY ANN
    DAMONE, VIC
JONES, BOB
    MILES, VERA
JONES, CLINTON
    GORDON, RUTH
JONES, CYRIL
    LYNLEY, CAROL
JONES, DANIEL
    JONES, ALLAN
JONES, GAIL
    HORNE, LENA
JONES, IKE
    STEVENS, INGER
JONES, JACK
    JONES, ALLAN
    SAINT JOHN, JILL
JONES, JENNIFER
    WALKER, ROBERT
JONES, JULIA
    ALBERT, EDDIE
JONES, LEWIS
    HORNE, LENA
JONES, LUCILLE
    HARDY, OLIVER
JONES, MAXINE
    JONES, BUCK
JONES, MAY
    VON STROHEIM, ERICH
JONES, PAUL
    JONES, SHIRLEY
JONES, ROBERT A.
    VANCE, VIVIAN
JONES, ROBERT EARL
    JONES, JAMES EARL
JONES, SHIRLEY
    CASSIDY, JACK
JONES, TERRY
    HORNE, LENA
JOPLIN, JANIS
    KRISTOFFERSON, KRIS
JORDAN, AL
    DAY, DORIS
JORDAN, HELEN
    BEGLEY, ED
JORDAN, JIM
    CORRELL, CHARLES
JORDAN, TED
    SAINT CYR, LILI
JORDAN, TERRY
    DAY, DORIS
JORGENSON, SUSAN
    DOUGLAS, KIRK
JOSEF, LESLIE
    GINGOLD, HERMIONE

JOSEF, MICHAEL
    GINGOLD, HERMIONE
JOSEF, STEPHEN
    GINGOLD, HERMIONE
JOSEPH, SAMUEL
    BARNES, BINNIE
JOSIE, VIRGINIA DI
    DARREN, JAMES
JOURDAN, LOUIS HENRY
    JOURDAN, LOUIS
JOURDAN, YVONNE
    JOURDAN, LOUIS
JOY, LEATRICE
    GILBERT, JOHN
JOYCE, ELAINE
    VAN, BOBBY
JOYCE, JAMES
    MENJOU, ADOLPHE
JOYCE, NORA
    MENJOU, ADOLPHE
JUDSON, EDWARD C.
    HAYWORTH, RITA
JULIEN, JAY I.
    HARRIS, JULIE
JUNOT, PHILIPPE
    KELLY, GRACE
JURADO, KATY
    BORGNINE, ERNEST
    CHRISTIAN, LINDA
    DEAN, JAMES
JURADO, LUIS
    JURADO, KATY
KAAREN, SUSANNE
    BLACKMER, SIDNEY
KAHMANN, DEE
    MARSHALL, HERBERT
KAHN, IRENE
    MARX, GROUCHO
KALB, BETTY CLAIRE
    BARRY, GENE
KALISH, CHARLES
    TUCKER, SOPHIE
KALISH, SUSANNE
    AUER, MISCHA
KALLINA, ELISABETH
    WERNER, OSKAR
KAMINKER, ANDRE
    SIGNORET, SIMONE
KANE, CAROL
    PACINO, AL
KANIN, GARSON
    GORDON, RUTH
KANTOR, AMY
    FRANCIOSA, ANTHONY
KANTOR, JUDY BALABAN
    FRANCIOSA, ANTHONY
KANTOR, VICTORIA
    FRANCIOSA, ANTHONY

KAPPELHOFF, FREDERICK WILHELM
    DAY, DORIS
KAPPELHOFF, PAUL
    DAY, DORIS
KAPSALLIS, CHRISTINA
    SAVALAS, TELLY
KARGER, FRED
    WYMAN, JANE
KARL, DENISE
    MCDONALD, MARIE
    REYNOLDS, DEBBIE
KARL, HARRISON
    MCDONALD, MARIE
    REYNOLDS, DEBBIE
KARL, HARRY
    MCDONALD, MARIE
    REYNOLDS, DEBBIE
KARL, TINA MARIE
    MCDONALD, MARIE
    REYNOLDS, DEBBIE
KARLOFF, BORIS
    SMITH, C. AUBREY
KARLOFF, SARA JANE
    KARLOFF, BORIS
KARLSSON, ANNA LOVISA
    GARBO, GRETA
KARP, BETTY
    MARX, CHICO
    MARX, GROUCHO
    MARX, GUMMO
    MARX, HARPO
    MARX, ZEPPO
KASHFI, ANNA
    BRANDO, MARLON
KASS, KATHARINE
    COLLINS, JOAN
KASS, RON
    COLLINS, JOAN
KATALIN, ULBERT
    BANKY, VILMA
KATZ, EVA
    BLANC, MEL
KATZ, MICKIE
    GREY, JOEL
KATZ, RONALD
    GREY, JOEL
KAUFMAN, GEORGE
    LOLLOBRIGIDA, GINA
KAUFMAN, GEORGE S.
    ASTOR, MARY
KAUFMANN, CHRISTINE
    CURTIS, TONY
KAY, HERBERT
    LAMOUR, DOROTHY
KAY, MONTE
    CARROLL, DIAHANN
KAY, SUZANNE
    CARROLL, DIAHANN

KAYE, CLARISSA
    MASON, JAMES
KAYE, DENA
    KAYE, DANNY
KAYE, HENRIETTE
    BACKUS, JIM
KEANE, ANTHONY
    LAKE, VERONICA
KEATON, BUSTER
    KERRY, NORMAN
    TALMADGE, CONSTANCE
    TALMADGE, NORMA
KEATON, DIANE
    ALLEN, WOODY
    BEATTY, WARREN
KEATON, DOROTHY
    KEATON, DIANE
KEATON, HARRY
    KEATON, BUSTER
KEATON, JAMES
    KEATON, BUSTER
    TALMADGE, CONSTANCE
    TALMADGE, NORMA
KEATON, JOE
    KEATON, BUSTER
KEATON, LOUISE
    KEATON, BUSTER
KEATON, MYRA
    KEATON, BUSTER
KEATON, ROBERT
    KEATON, BUSTER
    TALMADGE, CONSTANCE
    TALMADGE, NORMA
KEEL, GUNNAR
    KEEL, HOWARD
KEEL, KAIJA LIANE
    KEEL, HOWARD
KEEL, KRISTINE
    KEEL, HOWARD
KEEL, LESLIE GRACE
    KEEL, HOWARD
KEELER, GERTRUDE
    KEELER, RUBY
KEELER, MARJORIE
    KEELER, RUBY
KEELER, RALPH
    KEELER, RUBY
KEELER, RUBY
    BERKELEY, BUSBY
    JOLSON, AL
KEENAN, HILDA
    WYNN, ED
    WYNN, KEENAN
KEITH, BARBARA
    KEITH, BRIAN
KEITH, DAISY
    KEITH, BRIAN

KEITH, ELIZABETH
    KEITH, BRIAN
KEITH, MICHAEL
    KEITH, BRIAN
KEITH, MIMI
    KEITH, BRIAN
KEITH, ROBERT
    KEITH, BRIAN
KEITH, RORY
    KEITH, BRIAN
KEITH, SLIM
    COLBERT, CLAUDETTE
KEKO, BILL
    BUZZI, RUTH
KELLAWAY, EDMUND
    GWENN, EDMUND
KELLAWAY, ELSIE
    GWENN, EDMUND
KELLER, HENRIETTA
    JOLSON, AL
KELLER, MARTHE
    PACINO, AL
KELLERMAN, JOHN HELM
    KELLERMAN, SALLY
KELLERMAN, SALLY
    BLAKE, ROBERT
KELLINO, ROY
    MASON, PAMELA
KELLY, AGNES
    MOORE, COLLEEN
KELLY, BEVERLY
    COBURN, JAMES
KELLY, BRIDGET
    KELLY, GENE
KELLY, ELIZABETH ANN 'LIZANNE'
    KELLY, GRACE
KELLY, FRED
    KELLY, GENE
KELLY, GEORGE
    KELLY, GRACE
KELLY, GREGORY
    GORDON, RUTH
KELLY, HARRIET 'JAY'
    KELLY, GENE
KELLY, JAMES PATRICK JOSEPH
    KELLY, GENE
KELLY, JOHN B. 'KELL'
    KELLY, GRACE
KELLY, JOHN BRENDAN
    KELLY, GRACE
KELLY, JONES HARRIS
    GORDON, RUTH
KELLY, JR., JAMES
    KELLY, GENE
KELLY, KENNETH
    VENUTA, BENAY
KELLY, KERRY
    KELLY, GENE

KELLY, LOUISE
    KELLY, GENE
KELLY, LUCILLE
    EDWARDS, CLIFF
KELLY, MAE
    GLEASON, JACKIE
KELLY, MARGARET 'PEGGY'
    KELLY, GRACE
KELLY, MILDRED FRANCES
    MORAN, POLLY
KELLY, MIMI
    BOONE, RICHARD
KELLY, NANCY
    O'BRIEN, EDMOND
KELLY, SARAH ROSE 'PATSY'
    KEELER, RUBY
KELLY, TIMOTHY
    KELLY, GENE
KELLY, WALTER C.
    KELLY, GRACE
KEMINS, RHODA
    BORGNINE, ERNEST
KEMP, MARTHA STEPHENSON
    MATURE, VICTOR
KEMPSON, ERIC WILLIAM EDWARD
    REDGRAVE, MICHAEL
KEMPSON, RACHEL
    REDGRAVE, LYNN
    REDGRAVE, MICHAEL
    REDGRAVE, VANESSA
KEMPTON, ELIZABETH
    TAMBLYN, RUSS
KENASTON, GAIL
    DOVE, BILLIE
KENASTON, ROBERT
    DOVE, BILLIE
KENASTON, ROBERT ALAN
    DOVE, BILLIE
KENDALL, KAY
    HARRISON, REX
KENDALL, KIM
    HARRISON, REX
    KENDALL, KAY
KENDALL, MARIE
    KENDALL, KAY
KENDALL, TERRY
    HARRISON, REX
    KENDALL, KAY
KENDRICK, CAROLINE
    EDDY, NELSON
KENDRICK, ISABEL
    EDDY, NELSON
KENNEDY, CHERYL
    COURTENAY, TOM
KENNEDY, CHRISTOPHER GEORGE
    KENNEDY, GEORGE
KENNEDY, EDWARD
    LAWFORD, PETER

KENNEDY, JOHN F.
    DAVIES, MARION
    LAWFORD, PETER
KENNEDY, JOSEPH P.
    LAWFORD, PETER
KENNEDY, KARIANNE
    KENNEDY, GEORGE
KENNEDY, MERNA
    BERKELEY, BUSBY
KENNEDY, PATRICIA
    LAWFORD, PETER
KENNEDY, ROBERT F.
    LAWFORD, PETER
KENNEDY, SHARON ADELAIDE
    WAGGONER, LYLE
KENNEDY, SR., GEORGE
    KENNEDY, GEORGE
KENNEY, ANNA MARIE
    FOY, JR., EDDIE
KENT, LEO R.
    SHERIDAN, ANN
KER, AILEEN
    WELD, TUESDAY
KERLIN, WILLIAM
    DRESSER, LOUISE
KERN, ELIZABETH
    SHAW, ARTIE
KERN, JEROME
    SHAW, ARTIE
KERR-TRIMMER, ARTHUR
    KERR, DEBORAH
KERR-TRIMMER, EDMUND
    KERR, DEBORAH
KERR, DEBORAH
    COLBERT, CLAUDETTE
KERRY, NORMAN
    KEATON, BUSTER
KERRY, SONDRA
    BLAKE, ROBERT
KEYES, EVELYN
    DOUGLAS, KIRK
    HUSTON, JOHN
    HUSTON, WALTER
    SHAW, ARTIE
KEYES, SAMUEL
    KEYES, EVELYN
KHAN, JASMIN
    HAYMES, DICK
    HAYWORTH, RITA
KHAN, PRINCE ALY
    HAYWORTH, RITA
    TIERNEY, GENE
KIELESEWSKA, ELEANORA VON
    NEGRI, POLA
KIEMAST, TERESA
    MILLER, MARVIN
KIESLER, EMIL
    LAMARR, HEDY

KILBE, MARGARET
　　SANDERS, GEORGE
KILBRIDE, PERCY
　　MAIN, MARJORIE
KILEY, DAVID
　　KILEY, RICHARD
KILEY, DIERDRE
　　KILEY, RICHARD
KILEY, DOROTHEA
　　KILEY, RICHARD
KILEY, ERIN
　　KILEY, RICHARD
KILEY, KATHLEEN
　　KILEY, RICHARD
KILEY, LEO JOSEPH
　　KILEY, RICHARD
KILEY, MICHAEL
　　KILEY, RICHARD
KILLIAN, JOSIE BELL
　　MURPHY, AUDIE
KILLIBREW, EVELYN
　　FOXX, REDD
KIMMEL, MARTIN
　　DE HAVEN, GLORIA
KIND, LOUIS
　　STREISAND, BARBRA
KIND, ROSALIND
　　STREISAND, BARBRA
KING, HARRY
　　VAN, BOBBY
KINGDOM, ELSIE
　　GRANT, CARY
KINGSTON, WINIFRED
　　FARNUM, DUSTIN
　　FARNUM, WILLIAM
KIP, LENORE
　　COTTEN, JOSEPH
KIRBY, MICHAEL
　　HENIE, SONJA
KIRKLAND, ALEXANDER
　　HAVOC, JUNE
　　LEE, GYPSY ROSE
KISS, LIDIA
　　MASSEY, ILONA
KISSINGER, HENRY
　　SAINT JOHN, JILL
KITAEVA, IDA
　　LAUREL, STAN
KITT, ALMITA
　　KITT, EARTHA
KITT, ANNA PEARL
　　KITT, EARTHA
KITT, WILLIAM
　　KITT, EARTHA
KLANOWSKI, ADELAIDE
　　SWANSON, GLORIA
KLASEN, ARTHUR LAWRENCE
　　LAWRENCE, GERTRUDE

KLASS, MARTIN
　　BARRY, GENE
KLEIN, STEPHANIE
　　BASEHART, RICHARD
KLEINER, DORIS
　　BRYNNER, YUL
KLUGMAN, ADAM
　　KLUGMAN, JACK
KLUGMAN, DAVID
　　KLUGMAN, JACK
KNIGHT, ELIZABETH
　　LOMBARD, CAROLE
KNIGHT, ERIC
　　LASSIE
KNIGHT, PATRICIA
　　WILDE, CORNEL
KNIGHT, SANDRA
　　NICHOLSON, JACK
KNIPPER, OLGA
　　CHEKHOV, MICHAEL
KNITTEL, PATRICIA
　　RAINER, LUISE
KNITTEL, ROBERT
　　RAINER, LUISE
KNOX, MARGUERITE
　　VON STROHEIM, ERICH
KOERBER, ALEXANDER RUDOLPH VON
　　DRESSLER, MARIE
KOERBER, BONITA VON
　　DRESSLER, MARIE
KOHN, JOSE
　　PAPAS, IRENE
KOHNER, PAUL
　　HUSTON, JOHN
KOMINSKY, JACOB
　　KAYE, DANNY
KOMINSKY, LAWRENCE
　　KAYE, DANNY
KOMINSKY, MAC
　　KAYE, DANNY
KONEN, GRETA RICE
　　PECK, GREGORY
KONIGSBERG, LETTI
　　ALLEN, WOODY
KONIGSBERG, MARTIN
　　ALLEN, WOODY
KORDA, ALEXANDER
　　OBERON, MERLE
KORENMANN, ETHEL
　　HYDE WHITE, WILFRED
KOSOW, VICTOR
　　SIDNEY, SYLVIA
KOSTER, DOROTHY
　　IVES, BURL
KOSTER, JOSEPH
　　O'NEILL, JENNIFER
KOSTES, MARIA
　　RATOFF, GREGORY

KOUFAX, SANDY
　　WIDMARK, RICHARD
KOVACS, ANDREW J.
　　KOVACS, ERNIE
KOVACS, BETTY
　　ADAMS, EDIE
　　KOVACS, ERNIE
KOVACS, ERNIE
　　ADAMS, EDIE
KOVACS, KIP
　　ADAMS, EDIE
　　KOVACS, ERNIE
KOVACS, MIA
　　ADAMS, EDIE
　　KOVACS, ERNIE
KOVACS, THOMAS
　　KOVACS, ERNIE
KOVNER, LEONARD
　　WILLIAMS, ESTHER
KRAFT, RUTH A.
　　CUMMINGS, ROBERT
KRAL, BLANCHE
　　NOVAK, KIM
KRANZ, HELEN
　　CORTEZ, RICARDO
KRANZ, STANLEY
　　CORTEZ, RICARDO
KRASNE, FLORENCE
　　EVANS, ROBERT
KRAUSE, BARBARA
　　COOPER, JACKIE
KREBS, ANNABELLE
　　MAIN, MARJORIE
KREBS, DR. STANLEY LEFEVRE
　　MAIN, MARJORIE
KREIGER, SHIRLEY COLLEEN
　　CONTE, RICHARD
KRESKI, CONNIE
　　CAAN, JAMES
KRIMS, MILTON
　　MEADOWS, AUDREY
　　MEADOWS, JAYNE
KRISTOFFERSON, CASEY
　　KRISTOFFERSON, KRIS
KRISTOFFERSON, JR., KRIS
　　KRISTOFFERSON, KRIS
KRISTOFFERSON, TRACY
　　KRISTOFFERSON, KRIS
KRUGER, OTTO
　　YOUNG, ROBERT
KUBELSKY, MEYER
　　BENNY, JACK
KULEFF, MARCI
　　WOOD, NATALIE
KUNG, LOUIS C.
　　PAGET, DEBRA
KWAN, NANCY
　　SCHELL, MAXIMILIAN

LA BARBA, MARION SHIELDS
　　RUGGLES, CHARLES
LA GROS, STOVER
　　FARNUM, DUSTIN
LA MARR, BARBARA
　　PITTS, ZASU
LA MARR, MARVIN CARVILLE
　　LA MARR, BARBARA
　　PITTS, ZASU
LA PIERE, GEORGANNE
　　CHER
LA PIERE, GILBERT
　　CHER
LA PLANTE, LYDIA
　　LA PLANTE, LAURA
LA ROCQUE, ROD
　　BANKY, VILMA
　　DANIELS, BEBE
　　NEGRI, POLA
LA ROCQUE, WILLIAM
　　LA ROCQUE, ROD
LA SALLE, GEORGINA BELLE
　　DILLMAN, BRADFORD
LA TOUR, MONIQUE LA ROCQUE DE
　　LA ROCQUE, ROD
LABATT, FRANCES AMELIA
　　CRONYN, HUME
LABHART, IRENE
　　BARKER, LEX
LABLANCHE, FREDERICA
　　GRANGER, STEWART
LABROT, ELEANOR DE LIAGRE
　　AHERNE, BRIAN
LACHMANN, HEDWIG
　　NICHOLS, MIKE
LACKERMAN, ALBERT
　　TUCKER, SOPHIE
LADD, ALANA
　　LADD, ALAN
LADD, DAVID
　　LADD, ALAN
LADD, JR., ALAN
　　LADD, ALAN
LADD, SR., ALAN
　　LADD, ALAN
LADIN, SUSAN
　　MINEO, SAL
LAEMMLE, CARL
　　LAWRENCE, FLORENCE
LAFFERTY, FRED
　　BLAIR, JANET
LAFFERTY, JR., FRED
　　BLAIR, JANET
LAFFERTY, LOUISE
　　BLAIR, JANET
LAHR, HERBERT
　　LAHR, BERT

LAHR, JANE
    LAHR, BERT
LAHR, JOHN
    LAHR, BERT
LAKE, ALAN
    DORS, DIANA
LAKE, ARTHUR
    DAVIES, MARION
LAKE, ARTHUR PATRICK
    LAKE, ARTHUR
LAKE, BONNIE
    SOTHERN, ANN
LAKE, FLORENCE
    LAKE, ARTHUR
LAKE, JASON
    DORS, DIANA
LAKE, MARION
    SOTHERN, ANN
LAKE, SIMON
    SOTHERN, ANN
LAKE, WALTER J.
    SOTHERN, ANN
LALONDE, PATRICIA
    WHITMAN, STUART
LAMARR, HEDY
    MONTGOMERY, GEORGE
LAMAS, ALEJANDRE
    LAMAS, FERNANDO
    WILLIAMS, ESTHER
LAMAS, FERNANDO
    DAHL, ARLENE
    TURNER, LANA
    WILLIAMS, ESTHER
LAMAS, LORENZO FERNANDO
    DAHL, ARLENE
    LAMAS, FERNANDO
    WILLIAMS, ESTHER
LAMOND, STELLA
    REDDY, HELEN
LAMONT, CHARLES
    MCLAGLEN, VICTOR
LAMONT, ENID
    MCLAGLEN, VICTOR
LAMONT, LILLIAN
    MACMURRAY, FRED
LAMPHERE, DODIE
    COOGAN, JACKIE
LANCASTER, BURT
    THATCHER, TORIN
LANCASTER, JAMES
    LANCASTER, BURT
LANCASTER, JAMES STEVEN
    LANCASTER, BURT
LANCASTER, JANE
    LANCASTER, BURT
LANCASTER, JOANNA MARI
    LANCASTER, BURT

LANCASTER, JR., JAMES
    LANCASTER, BURT
LANCASTER, SIGHLE
    LANCASTER, BURT
LANCASTER, SUSAN ELIZABETH
    LANCASTER, BURT
LANCASTER, WILLIAM
    LANCASTER, BURT
LANCASTER, WILLIAM HENRY
    LANCASTER, BURT
LANCHESTER, EDITH
    LANCHESTER, ELSA
LANCHESTER, ELSA
    LAUGHTON, CHARLES
LANDAU, ARTHUR
    HARLOW, JEAN
LANDAUER, GUSTAV
    NICHOLS, MIKE
LANE, ABBE
    CUGAT, XAVIER
LANE, ALLAN
    FRANCIS THE MULE
LANE, KENT
    FLEMING, RHONDA
LANE, LOLA
    AYRES, LEW
LANE, LOUISA
    BARRYMORE, ETHEL
    BARRYMORE, JOHN
    BARRYMORE, LIONEL
LANE, LUPINO
    LUPINO, IDA
LANE, MARJORIE
    DONLEVY, BRIAN
LANE, TOM
    FLEMING, RHONDA
LANE, VIOLET MARION
    HOLLOWAY, STANLEY
LANG, JENNINGS
    BENNETT, JOAN
LANG, JESSICA
    KING KONG
LANG, JUNE
    HUGHES, HOWARD
LANG, MARGARET
    ROONEY, MICKEY
LANG, NEAL
    RAYE, MARTHA
LANGE, JOHN
    LANGE, HOPE
LANGFORD, FRANCES
    HALL, JON
LANGFORD, VASCO
    LANGFORD, FRANCES
LANGHAM, MARGARET
    STONE, LEWIS
LANGHAM, RHEA LUCAS
    GABLE, CLARK

LANGHANKE, OTTO L. W.
    ASTOR, MARY
LANGLEY, SUSAN
    CALHOUN, RORY
LANSBURY, BRUCE
    LANSBURY, ANGELA
LANSBURY, EDGAR
    LANSBURY, ANGELA
LANSBURY, ISOLDE
    LANSBURY, ANGELA
LANSBURY, JR., EDGAR
    LANSBURY, ANGELA
LANTZ, WALTER
    WOODPECKER, WOODY
LANZA, COLLEEN
    LANZA, MARIO
LANZA, DAMON
    LANZA, MARIO
LANZA, ELISA
    LANZA, MARIO
LANZA, MARIA
    LANZA, MARIO
LANZA, MARK
    LANZA, MARIO
LARAIA, JOSEPH
    CASTELLANO, RICHARD
    GOULET, ROBERT
    LAWRENCE, CAROL
LARAIA, MICHAEL
    CASTELLANO, RICHARD
    GOULET, ROBERT
    LAWRENCE, CAROL
LARSEN, ERIK
    MILES, VERA
LARSEN, EVY NORLUND
    DARREN, JAMES
LARSEN, KEITH
    MILES, VERA
LASALLE, GEORGIA
    PARKER, SUZY
LASALLE, PIERRE
    PARKER, SUZY
LASKY, BLANCHE
    GOLDWYN, SAMUEL
LASKY, JESSE
    DE MILLE, C. B.
    GOLDWYN, SAMUEL
LASKY, JR., JESSE
    HARLOW, JEAN
LASSER, LOUISE
    ALLEN, WOODY
LATELL, LYLE
    FOY, JR., EDDIE
LAUGHTON, CHARLES
    LANCHESTER, ELSA
LAUGHTON, FRANK
    LAUGHTON, CHARLES

LAUGHTON, MICHAEL
    CARON, LESLIE
LAUGHTON, ROBERT
    LAUGHTON, CHARLES
LAUGHTON, TOM
    LAUGHTON, CHARLES
LAUNER, BEATRICE
    DASSIN, JULES
LAUREL, LOIS
    LAUREL, STAN
LAUREL, STAN
    HARDY, OLIVER
LAURENCE, LOTTA
    LAWRENCE, FLORENCE
LAURENTIIS, FEDERICO DE
    DE LAURENTIIS, DINO
LAURENTIIS, FRANCESCA DE
    DE LAURENTIIS, DINO
LAURENTIIS, RAFAELLA DE
    DE LAURENTIIS, DINO
LAURENTIIS, ROSARIO AURELIO DE
    DE LAURENTIIS, DINO
LAURENTIIS, VERONICA DE
    DE LAURENTIIS, DINO
LAURIE, PIPER
    NELSON, GENE
LAWFORD, BETTY
    LAWFORD, PETER
LAWFORD, CHRISTOPHER
    LAWFORD, PETER
LAWFORD, PETER SYDNEY ERNEST
    LAWFORD, PETER
LAWFORD, ROBIN
    LAWFORD, PETER
LAWFORD, SYDNEY
    LAWFORD, PETER
LAWFORD, VICTORIA FRANCES
    LAWFORD, PETER
LAWHORN, LUCY
    BERGEN, POLLY
LAWLESS, WILLIAM F.
    WINCHELL, WALTER
LAWRENCE, CAROL
    GOULET, ROBERT
LAWRENCE, DAVID
    LAWRENCE, STEVE
LAWRENCE, GERTRUDE
    FAIRBANKS, JR., DOUGLAS
LAWRENCE, MICHAEL
    LAWRENCE, STEVE
LAWSON, LEIGH
    MILLS, HAYLEY
LAWTON, FRANK
    LAYE, EVELYN
LAYE, GILBERT
    LAYE, EVELYN
LEA, GILBERT
    THAXTER, PHYLLIS

LEACH, ELIAS
    GRANT, CARY
LEAHY, ELNORA
    KEELER, RUBY
LEAK, DORIS
    PINZA, EZIO
LEBOST, ESTELLE
    REINER, CARL
LECERF, CAROLINE
    GRANGER, STEWART
LEDERER, CHARLES
    DAVIES, MARION
    SHIRLEY, ANNE
    WELLES, ORSON
LEDERER, DANIEL DAVIES
    SHIRLEY, ANNE
LEDERER, EVELYN
    LADD, ALAN
LEDERER, JOSEPH
    LEDERER, FRANCIS
LEE, BRANDON BRUCE
    LEE, BRUCE
LEE, CHRISTINE CONNIFF
    CORTEZ, RICARDO
LEE, EVE
    FOX, WILLIAM
LEE, GYPSY ROSE
    HAVOC, JUNE
    PREMINGER, OTTO
LEE, JOHN GRIFFITN
    MOOREHEAD, AGNES
LEE, MINNIE
    WILLIAMS, GUINN 'BIG BOY'
LEE, SEAN
    MOOREHEAD, AGNES
LEE, SHANNON
    LEE, BRUCE
LEE, W. HOWARD
    LAMARR, HEDY
    TIERNEY, GENE
LEEDS, BARBARA
    MERRILL, GARY
LEIGH, JANET
    CURTIS, TONY
LEIGH, VIVIEN
    O'SULLIVAN, MAUREEN
    OLIVIER, LAURENCE
LEIGHTON, MARGARET
    HARVEY, LAURENCE
    WILDING, MICHAEL
LELEKOS, STAVROS
    PAPAS, IRENE
LEMKOW, TUTTE
    ZETTERLING, MAI
LEMMON, CHRISTOPHER
    LEMMON, JACK
LEMMON, COURTNEY
    LEMMON, JACK

LEMMON, JACK
    PARSONS, ESTELLE
LEMMON, JR., JOHN UHLER
    LEMMON, JACK
LENNON, ALFRED
    LENNON, JOHN
LENNON, JOHN
    HARRISON, GEORGE
    MCCARTNEY, PAUL
    STARR, RINGO
LENNON, JOHN CHARLES JULIAN
    LENNON, JOHN
LENNON, SEAN ONO
    LENNON, JOHN
LENZ, KAY
    CASSIDY, JACK
    JONES, SHIRLEY
LEON, ROBERT DE
    CARROLL, DIAHANN
LEONARD, AUDREY MADALENE
    RENALDO, DUNCAN
LEONARD, MABEL
    COOPER, JACKIE
LEONARD, ROBERT Z.
    MURRAY, MAE
LEONTOVICH, EUGENIE
    RATOFF, GREGORY
LEOPOLD, JOSEPH
    WYNN, ED
LEPPERT, WILLIAM
    FAYE, ALICE
    HARRIS, PHIL
    MARTIN, TONY
LERNER, ALAN JAY
    CLAYTON, JAN
LERNER, JOSEPH
    CLAYTON, JAN
LERNER, KAREN 'KIMMY'
    CLAYTON, JAN
LERNER, ROBERT WARREN
    CLAYTON, JAN
LERNER, ROBIN
    CLAYTON, JAN
LEROY, MERVYN
    ROGERS, GINGER
LESLEY, E.
    HUSTON, JOHN
    HUSTON, WALTER
LESTER, ELIZABETH
    TRYON, TOM
LESUEUR, HAL
    CRAWFORD, JOAN
LESUEUR, THOMAS
    CRAWFORD, JOAN
LETZ, EDA
    MONTGOMERY, GEORGE
LETZ, GEORGE G.
    MONTGOMERY, GEORGE

LETZ, JAMES
    MONTGOMERY, GEORGE
LETZ, LYDA
    MONTGOMERY, GEORGE
LETZ, MARY
    MONTGOMERY, GEORGE
LETZ, MATTHEW
    MONTGOMERY, GEORGE
LETZ, MAURICE
    MONTGOMERY, GEORGE
LETZ, MICHAEL
    MONTGOMERY, GEORGE
LETZ, NICHOLAS
    MONTGOMERY, GEORGE
LETZ, OLGA
    MONTGOMERY, GEORGE
LETZ, ROSE
    MONTGOMERY, GEORGE
LETZ, SAMUEL
    MONTGOMERY, GEORGE
LETZ, WILLIAM
    MONTGOMERY, GEORGE
LEVANT, AMANDA
    LEVANT, OSCAR
LEVANT, BENJAMIN
    LEVANT, OSCAR
LEVANT, HARRY
    LEVANT, OSCAR
LEVANT, HOWARD
    LEVANT, OSCAR
LEVANT, LORNA
    LEVANT, OSCAR
LEVANT, MARCIA ANN
    LEVANT, OSCAR
LEVANT, MAX
    LEVANT, OSCAR
LEVEE, JOSEPH RUSSELL
    GODDARD, PAULETTE
LEVEY, ALEDA
    ANDREWS, LAVERNE
    ANDREWS, MAXENE
    ANDREWS, PATRICIA
LEVEY, LOU
    ANDREWS, LAVERNE
    ANDREWS, MAXENE
    ANDREWS, PATRICIA
LEVEY, PETER
    ANDREWS, LAVERNE
    ANDREWS, MAXENE
    ANDREWS, PATRICIA
LEVITCH, DANIEL
    LEWIS, JERRY
LEVITT, ETHEL
    BORGNINE, ERNEST
    MERMAN, ETHEL
LEVITT, JR., ROBERT
    BORGNINE, ERNEST

LEVITT, JR., ROBERT
    MERMAN, ETHEL
LEVITT, ROBERT D.
    MERMAN, ETHEL
LEVY, FLORENCE
    CAESAR, SID
LEWIS, ANTHONY
    LEWIS, JERRY
LEWIS, CHRISTOPHER
    YOUNG, LORETTA
LEWIS, CHRISTOPHER
    LEWIS, JERRY
LEWIS, DIANA
    POWELL, WILLIAM
LEWIS, GARY
    LEWIS, JERRY
LEWIS, JANE
    YOUNG, LORETTA
LEWIS, JERRY
    MARTIN, DEAN
LEWIS, JOSEPH
    LEWIS, JERRY
LEWIS, JUDY
    YOUNG, LORETTA
LEWIS, PATRICIA
    PLUMMER, CHRISTOPHER
LEWIS, PETER
    YOUNG, LORETTA
LEWIS, RAE
    LEWIS, JERRY
LEWIS, RONALD
    LEWIS, JERRY
LEWIS, SCOTT
    LEWIS, JERRY
LEWIS, TED
    TUCKER, SOPHIE
LEWIS, THOMAS H. A.
    YOUNG, LORETTA
LEWIS, WINDSOR
    BEL GEDDES, BARBARA
LEWTON, NINA
    NAZIMOVA
LEWTON, VAL
    NAZIMOVA
LI, AGNES
    LEE, BRUCE
LI, GRACE
    LEE, BRUCE
LI, PETER
    LEE, BRUCE
LI, PHOEBE
    LEE, BRUCE
LI, ROBERT
    LEE, BRUCE
LIBERACE, ANN
    LIBERACE
LIBERACE, FRANCES
    LIBERACE

LIBERACE, GEORGE
  LIBERACE
LIBERACE, RUDY
  LIBERACE
LIBERACE, SALVATORE
  LIBERACE
LICHINE, ALEXIS
  DAHL, ARLENE
LIEBMAN, PHILIP
  DARNELL, LINDA
LIEBOWITZ, BERNARD
  LAWRENCE, STEVE
LIEBOWITZ, MAX
  LAWRENCE, STEVE
LILLBURN, MARGUERITE
  O'HARA, MAUREEN
LILLIE, BEATRICE
  KEATON, BUSTER
LIND, ISABELLE
  FARNUM, WILLIAM
LIND, JOSEPH CONRAD
  HAYES, PETER LIND
LINDFORS, TORSTEN
  LINDFORS, VIVECA
LINDLEY, AUDRA
  WHITMORE, JAMES
LINDSAY-HOGG, EDWARD
  FITZGERALD, GERALDINE
LINDSAY-HOGG, MICHAEL
  FITZGERALD, GERALDINE
LINDSAY, CYNTHIA
  GLEASON, JAMES 'JIMMY'
LINDSAY, JOHN
  LOCKHART, JUNE
LINDSAY, MICHAEL GLEASON
  GLEASON, JAMES 'JIMMY'
LINDSTROM, DR. PETER
  BERGMAN, INGRID
LINDSTROM, PIA
  BERGMAN, INGRID
LING, GLORIA JOAN
  JAGGER, DEAN
LININGER, HOPE
  LUGOSI, BELA
LIPTON, JAMES
  FOCH, NINA
LISI, GAETANO
  ROSS, KATHARINE
LISSMANN, ROSE
  PALMER, LILLI
LISTER, GLORIA
  ROMANOFF, 'PRINCE' MICHAEL
LITTLE, MARY ALICE
  DURANTE, JIMMY
LIVI, LUIGI
  SIGNORET, SIMONE
LIVINGSTON, ALAN
  HUTTON, BETTY

LLEWELLYN, LILLIE MAE
  BARTHOLOMEW, FREDDIE
LLOYD, GAYLORD
  LLOYD, HAROLD
LLOYD, GLADYS
  ROBINSON, EDWARD G.
LLOYD, GLORIA
  LLOYD, HAROLD
LLOYD, HAROLD
  DANIELS, BEBE
LLOYD, J. DARSIE
  LLOYD, HAROLD
LLOYD, JR., HAROLD
  LLOYD, HAROLD
LLOYD, PEGGY
  LLOYD, HAROLD
LOCHMAN-NIELSEN, SELMA
  HENIE, SONJA
LOCKHART, GENE
  LOCKHART, JUNE
LOCKHART, JOHN COATES
  LOCKHART, GENE
LOCKHART, JUNE
  LOCKHART, GENE
LOCKWOOD, FLORENCE
  COCHRAN, STEVE
LODER, ANTHONY
  LAMARR, HEDY
LODER, DENISE
  LAMARR, HEDY
LODER, JOHN J.
  LAMARR, HEDY
LOEW, JEANNE
  COLBERT, CLAUDETTE
LOEW, MARCUS
  MAYER, LOUIS B.
LOGAN, JOSHUA
  STEWART, JAMES
LOLLOBRIGIDA, GIOVANNI
  LOLLOBRIGIDA, GINA
LOMBARD, CAROLE
  GABLE, CLARK
  POWELL, WILLIAM
  RAFT, GEORGE
LONCIT, VILMOS
  BANKY, VILMA
LONDON, JUDITH
  KEITH, BRIAN
LONDON, JULIE
  WEBB, JACK
LONG, BARBARA
  LONG, RICHARD
LONG, CAREY
  LONG, RICHARD
LONG, GREGORY
  LONG, RICHARD
LONG, JANET
  LONG, RICHARD

LONG, JOHN
  LONG, RICHARD
LONG, NORA
  MURPHY, GEORGE
LONG, PHILLIP
  LONG, RICHARD
LONG, ROBERT
  LONG, RICHARD
LONG, SHERMAN D.
  LONG, RICHARD
LONG, VALERIE
  LONG, RICHARD
LONGENECKER, C. ROBERT
  HUSSEY, RUTH
LONGENECKER, GEORGE R.
  HUSSEY, RUTH
LONGENECKER, JOHN W.
  HUSSEY, RUTH
LONGENECKER, MARY E.
  HUSSEY, RUTH
LONGET, CLAUDINE
  WILLIAMS, ANDY
LONGET, DANIELLE
  LONGET, CLAUDINE
LONGET, ROBERT
  LONGET, CLAUDINE
LONGMORE, LOUISE
  GOULET, ROBERT
LOOMIS, ALLEN
  DAMITA, LILI
LOPEZ, JUAN
  BERNHARDT, SARAH
LORD, MARIAN
  MCLAGLEN, VICTOR
LOREN, SOPHIA
  GRANT, CARY
LORING, BEATRICE
  BICKFORD, CHARLES
LORRE, ALOIS
  LORRE, PETER
LORRE, KATHRYN
  LORRE, PETER
LOSEE, FRED
  PARKER, ELEANOR
LOTERY, DIANA
  BASEHART, RICHARD
LOUGHERY, JACKIE
  WEBB, JACK
LOUIER, CAMILLA
  WEISSMULLER, JOHNNY
LOUIS, HAROLD
  FLEMING, RHONDA
LOUISE, TINA
  MINEO, SAL
LOVE, GLADYS
  PRESLEY, ELVIS
LOVE, MELVINE
  BELAFONTE, HARRY

LOVECCHIO, JOHN
  LAINE, FRANKIE
LOVECCHIO, JOSEPH
  LAINE, FRANKIE
LOVEJOY, JUDITH
  LOVEJOY, FRANK
LOVEJOY, SR., FRANK
  LOVEJOY, FRANK
LOVEJOY, STEPHEN
  LOVEJOY, FRANK
LOVELAND, WINIFRED ADA
  SIMMONS, JEAN
LOWE, CHRISTINE
  KEELER, RUBY
LOWE, III, JOHN
  KEELER, RUBY
LOWE, JR., JOHN
  KEELER, RUBY
LOWE, KATHLEEN
  KEELER, RUBY
LOWE, THERESA
  KEELER, RUBY
LOWRENCE, ANTOINETTE
  JAGGER, DEAN
LOY, MYRNA
  NOVARRO, RAMON
  POWELL, WILLIAM
LUBITSCH, ERNST
  NEGRI, POLA
LUCAS, HARMONY
  SAINT JAMES, SUSAN
LUCAS, SUNSHINE
  SAINT JAMES, SUSAN
LUCAS, TOM
  SAINT JAMES, SUSAN
LUCCHESI, VINCENT
  MARTIN, DEAN
LUCE, CLAIRE
  ASTAIRE, FRED
LUDINGTON, DOROTHY
  MASSEY, RAYMOND
LUFT, JOEY
  GARLAND, JUDY
  MINNELLI, LIZA
LUFT, LORNA
  GARLAND, JUDY
  MINNELLI, LIZA
LUFT, SID
  GARLAND, JUDY
  MINNELLI, LIZA
LUGOSI, JR., BELA
  LUGOSI, BELA
LUKACS, JANOS
  LUKAS, PAUL
LUKE, KEYE
  OLAND, WARNER
LUKER, DIANDRA MURRELL
  DOUGLAS, MICHAEL

LUM, MABEL
  HUTTON, BETTY
LUMET, SIDNEY
  HORNE, LENA
LUND, JANA
  ULLMANN, LIV
LUNT, SR., ALFRED
  LUNT, ALFRED
LUPINO, BARRY
  LUPINO, IDA
LUPINO, GEORGE
  LUPINO, IDA
LUPINO, IDA
  DUFF, HOWARD
LUPINO, MARK
  LUPINO, IDA
LUPINO, RITA
  DUFF, HOWARD
  LUPINO, IDA
LUPINO, STANLEY
  DUFF, HOWARD
  LUPINO, IDA
LUPINO, WALLACE
  LUPINO, IDA
LVOVSKY, CECILIE
  LORRE, PETER
LYKKE-DAHN, JOHANNA
  TAYLOR, ELIZABETH
  WILDING, MICHAEL
LYNCH, KATHERINE
  VALLEE, RUDY
LYNDE, CORD
  LYNDE, PAUL
LYNDE, HOY
  LYNDE, PAUL
LYNDE, JOHN
  LYNDE, PAUL
LYNDE, RICHARD
  LYNDE, PAUL
LYNN, BETTY
  CARSON, JACK
LYON, BARBARA
  DANIELS, BEBE
LYON, BEN
  DANIELS, BEBE
LYONS, DAVID
  ROTH, LILLIAN
LYTELL, BERT
  WINDSOR, CLAIRE
LYTELL, JACK
  LA MARR, BARBARA
LYTELL, WILFRED
  WINDSOR, CLAIRE
M'DIVANI, KORAN DAVID
  MURRAY, MAE
M'DIVANI, PRINCE DAVID
  MURRAY, MAE

M'DIVANI, PRINCE DAVID
  NEGRI, POLA
M'DIVANI, PRINCE SERGE
  MURRAY, MAE
  NEGRI, POLA
MAC RAE, 'WEE WILLIE'
  MACRAE, GORDON
MACARTHUR, CHARLES
  HAYES, HELEN
MACARTHUR, JAMES
  HAYES, HELEN
MACARTHUR, JOHN
  HAYES, HELEN
MACARTHUR, MARY
  HAYES, HELEN
MACDONAGH, NELL
  BARRIE, WENDY
MACDONALD, BLOSSOM
  MACDONALD, JEANETTE
  RAYMOND, GENE
MACDONALD, DANIEL
  MACDONALD, JEANETTE
  RAYMOND, GENE
MACDONALD, ELSIE
  MACDONALD, JEANETTE
  RAYMOND, GENE
MACDONALD, GEORGE
  PARKER, JEAN
MACDONALD, JEANETTE
  HARLOW, JEAN
  RAYMOND, GENE
MACDONALD, SIR JOHN
  FORD, GLENN
MACDONNELL, DALLAS
  BURNETTE, SMILEY
MACDOUGALL, JAMIE
  FABRAY, NANETTE
MACDOUGALL, RANALD
  FABRAY, NANETTE
MACGILL, MOYNA
  LANSBURY, ANGELA
MACGRAW, ALI
  EVANS, ROBERT
  MCQUEEN, STEVE
MACGRAW, RICHARD
  MACGRAW, ALI
MACKAILL, DOROTHY
  MCCREA, JOEL
MACKENNEY, JULIA REID
  COREY, WENDELL
MACKENZIE, EDITH A.
  ASTIN, JOHN
MACKENZIE, FRANCES ELLEN
  TIBBETT, LAWRENCE
MACKENZIE, HARRY MALCOLM
  GRANGER, STEWART
MACKENZIE, MARGARET LINNIE
  ASTIN, JOHN

MACLAINE, SHIRLEY
  BEATTY, WARREN
MACLEAN, KATHLYN
  BEATTY, WARREN
  MACLAINE, SHIRLEY
MACMURRAY, FRED
  HAVER, JUNE
MACMURRAY, FREDERICK
  HAVER, JUNE
  MACMURRAY, FRED
MACMURRAY, KATHARINE
  HAVER, JUNE
  MACMURRAY, FRED
MACMURRAY, LAURIE
  HAVER, JUNE
  MACMURRAY, FRED
MACMURRAY, ROBERT
  HAVER, JUNE
  MACMURRAY, FRED
MACMURRAY, SUSAN
  HAVER, JUNE
  MACMURRAY, FRED
MACPHERSON, AMY SEMPLE
  FAIRBANKS, DOUGLAS
MACRAE, BRUCE
  MACRAE, GORDON
MACRAE, HEATHER
  MACRAE, GORDON
MACRAE, JR., GORDON
  MACRAE, GORDON
MACRAE, MEREDITH
  MACRAE, GORDON
MACRAE, SHEILA
  MACRAE, GORDON
MACVICAR, MARTHA
  ROONEY, MICKEY
MADISON, 'DOLLY'
  MADISON, GUY
MADISON, BRIDGET CATHERINE
  MADISON, GUY
MADISON, ERIN PATRICIA
  MADISON, GUY
MAGAMOLL, JUDY
  KEEL, HOWARD
MAGEE, JUNE
  WINCHELL, WALTER
MAGNANI, FRANCESCO
  MAGNANI, ANNA
MAGNANI, GEORGETTE
  MINNELLI, LIZA
MAHAFFRY, MARIE
  MCCAMBRIDGE, MERCEDES
MAHNKEN, ELAINE
  ROONEY, MICKEY
MAHONEY, 'DUCKY'
  SOMERS, SUZANNE
MAHONEY, JOCK
  FIELD, SALLY

MAITLAND, MOLLY
  MARSHALL, HERBERT
MAIXONEUVE, CAROLINE DE LA
  VON FURSTENBURG, BETSY
MAIXONEUVE, GUY VINCENT DE LA
  VON FURSTENBURG, BETSY
MAIZE, EDNA PEARL
  PAGE, GERALDINE
MAJER, MARGARET
  KELLY, GRACE
MAJOR, ELIZABETH
  FARNUM, WILLIAM
MAJOR, ISABELLE
  FARNUM, WILLIAM
MAJORS, LEE
  FAWCETT-MAJORS, FARRAH
MAKRIS, FRAN
  HAYMES, DICK
MALDEN, CARLA
  MALDEN, KARL
MALDEN, MILA
  MALDEN, KARL
MALLERY, BARBARA
  CLARK, DICK
MALLORY, EDDIE
  WATERS, ETHEL
MALLORY, PATRICIA 'BOOTS'
  MARSHALL, HERBERT
MALLORY, ROBERT
  NOVAK, KIM
MALONE, JOHN M.
  MORAN, POLLY
MALONE, MARTIN
  MORAN, POLLY
MALONEY, DR. JOHN FRANCIS
  LOCKHART, GENE
  LOCKHART, JUNE
MALONEY, PATRICIA ANN
  MURRAY, MAE
MALTESE, KAY
  HACKMAN, GENE
MANDELL, MARIA BROCK
  WEISSMULLER, JOHNNY
MANDL, FRITZ
  LAMARR, HEDY
MANGANO, SYLVANA
  DE LAURENTIIS, DINO
MANKIEWICZ, JOSEPH
  YOUNG, LORETTA
MANN, ROBERTA
  GARFIELD, JOHN
MANSFIELD, JAYNE MARIE
  MANSFIELD, JAYNE
MANSFIELD, LUCILLE
  RUTHERFORD, ANN
MANSFIELD, PAUL
  MANSFIELD, JAYNE

MANSON, CHARLES
    TATE, SHARON
MANVILLE, JR., THOMAS F.
    WINDSOR, CLAIRE
MARCH, ANTHONY
    MARCH, FREDRIC
MARCH, ELSPETH
    GRANGER, STEWART
MARCH, LINDA
    CABOT, BRUCE
MARCH, PENELOPE
    MARCH, FREDRIC
MARCHER, CORA
    MARCH, FREDRIC
MARCIANO, LAWRENCE
    LOVELACE, LINDA
MARI, PAOLA
    WELLES, ORSON
MARIE, ELLEN FRANCES
    CAINE, MICHAEL
MARIE, JULIENNE
    JONES, JAMES EARL
MARINO, FLORA
    ALDA, ALAN
    ALDA, ROBERT
MARION, CHARLES
    VERDUGO, ELENA
MARION, FRANCES
    DRESSLER, MARIE
    HOPPER, HEDDA
MARION, RICHARD ANTHONY
    VERDUGO, ELENA
MARKEY, GENE
    BENNETT, CONSTANCE
    BENNETT, JOAN
    BENNETT, RICHARD
    CLAIRE, INA
    LAMARR, HEDY
    LOY, MYRNA
MARKEY, JAMES
    LAMARR, HEDY
    LOY, MYRNA
MARKEY, MELINDA
    BENNETT, JOAN
    LAMARR, HEDY
    LOY, MYRNA
MARKHAM, MARY
    MELCHIOR, LAURITZ
MARKLE, FLETCHER
    MCCAMBRIDGE, MERCEDES
MARKS, AGNES
    EKLAND, BRITT
    SELLERS, PETER
MARKS, IRENE
    BERMAN, SHELLEY
MARKS, SADYE
    BENNY, JACK

MARLEY, CHARLOTTE MILDRED
    DARNELL, LINDA
MARLEY, J. PEVERELL
    DARNELL, LINDA
MARQUAND, CHRISTIAN
    AUMONT, JEAN-PIERRE
MARRENER, FLORENCE
    HAYWARD, SUSAN
MARRENER, JR., WALTER
    HAYWARD, SUSAN
MARRENER, WALTER
    HAYWARD, SUSAN
MARSH, CHARLES
    MARSH, MAE
MARSH, LOVEY
    MARSH, MAE
MARSH, MARGARET
    MARSH, MAE
MARSHALL, ANN
    MARSHALL, HERBERT
MARSHALL, BRENDA
    HOLDEN, WILLIAM
MARSHALL, CHARLES G.
    MARSHALL, E.G.
MARSHALL, DEGEN
    MARSHALL, E.G.
MARSHALL, GEORGE P.
    GRIFFITH, CORINNE
MARSHALL, HARRIET
    ARNOLD, EDWARD
MARSHALL, JILL
    MARSHALL, E.G.
MARSHALL, MARION
    WAGNER, ROBERT
MARSHALL, MICHAEL
    MORGAN, MICHELE
    PRESLE, MICHELINE
    ROGERS, GINGER
MARSHALL, PENNY
    REINER, CARL
MARSHALL, SARAH BEST
    MARSHALL, HERBERT
MARSHALL, TULLY
    BENNETT, CONSTANCE
    BENNETT, JOAN
MARSHALL, WILLIAM
    MORGAN, MICHELE
    PRESLE, MICHELINE
    ROGERS, GINGER
MARTI, JOSE JULIAN
    ROMERO, CESAR
MARTI, MARIA MANTILLA
    ROMERO, CESAR
MARTIN, CLAUDIA
    MARTIN, DEAN
MARTIN, CRAIG
    MARTIN, DEAN

MARTIN, DEAN
    LAWFORD, PETER
    LEWIS, JERRY
MARTIN, DEANA
    MARTIN, DEAN
MARTIN, DEWEY
    LEE, PEGGY
MARTIN, DR. HARRY W.
    PARSONS, LOUELLA O.
MARTIN, EDWARD MORRIS
    MARTIN, TONY
MARTIN, GAIL
    MARTIN, DEAN
MARTIN, GINA
    MARTIN, DEAN
MARTIN, JR., DEAN 'DINO'
    MARTIN, DEAN
MARTIN, JR., TONY
    CHARISSE, CYD
    MARTIN, TONY
MARTIN, LORETTA
    CLARK, DICK
MARTIN, MALETA
    HAVER, JUNE
    MACMURRAY, FRED
MARTIN, PRESTON
    MARTIN, MARY
MARTIN, RICCI
    MARTIN, DEAN
MARTIN, RUTH EVELYN
    HOWARD, LESLIE
MARTIN, TONY
    CHARISSE, CYD
    FAYE, ALICE
    TURNER, LANA
MARTINELLI, FRANK
    PAIGE, JANIS
MARVIN, CHRISTOPHER
    MARVIN, LEE
MARVIN, CLAUDIA
    MARVIN, LEE
MARVIN, COURTENAY
    MARVIN, LEE
MARVIN, CYNTHIA
    MARVIN, LEE
MARVIN, LAMONT W.
    MARVIN, LEE
MARVIN, LEE
    LEE, BRUCE
MARVIN, MICHELLE TRIOLA
    MARVIN, LEE
MARVIN, ROBERT
    MARVIN, LEE
MARVIS, KATHERINE
    GORCEY, LEO
    MARX, CHICO
    MARX, GROUCHO

MARVIS, KATHERINE
    MARX, GUMMO
    MARX, HARPO
    MARX, ZEPPO
MARX, ALEXANDER
    MARX, CHICO
    MARX, GROUCHO
    MARX, GUMMO
    MARX, HARPO
    MARX, ZEPPO
MARX, ANDREW
    MARX, GROUCHO
MARX, ARTHUR
    MARX, CHICO
    MARX, GROUCHO
    MARX, GUMMO
    MARX, HARPO
    MARX, ZEPPO
MARX, BERT
    WINTERS, SHELLEY
MARX, CHICO
    MARX, GROUCHO
    MARX, GUMMO
    MARX, HARPO
    MARX, ZEPPO
MARX, GROUCHO
    MARX, CHICO
    MARX, GUMMO
    MARX, HARPO
    MARX, ZEPPO
MARX, GUMMO
    MARX, CHICO
    MARX, GROUCHO
    MARX, HARPO
    MARX, ZEPPO
MARX, HARPO
    MARX, CHICO
    MARX, GROUCHO
    MARX, GUMMO
    MARX, ZEPPO
MARX, JAMES
    MARX, CHICO
    MARX, GROUCHO
    MARX, GUMMO
    MARX, HARPO
    MARX, ZEPPO
MARX, KAY
    MARX, CHICO
    MARX, GROUCHO
    MARX, GUMMO
    MARX, HARPO
    MARX, ZEPPO
MARX, MAXINE
    MARX, CHICO
    MARX, GROUCHO
    MARX, GUMMO
    MARX, HARPO

MARX, MAXINE
    MARX, ZEPPO
MARX, MELINDA
    MARX, CHICO
    MARX, GROUCHO
    MARX, GUMMO
    MARX, HARPO
    MARX, ZEPPO
MARX, MINNIE
    MARX, CHICO
    MARX, GROUCHO
    MARX, GUMMO
    MARX, HARPO
    MARX, ZEPPO
MARX, MIRIAM
    MARX, CHICO
    MARX, GROUCHO
    MARX, GUMMO
    MARX, HARPO
    MARX, ZEPPO
MARX, ROBERT
    MARX, CHICO
    MARX, GROUCHO
    MARX, GUMMO
    MARX, HARPO
    MARX, ZEPPO
MARX, SAMUEL
    MARX, CHICO
    MARX, GROUCHO
    MARX, GUMMO
    MARX, HARPO
    MARX, ZEPPO
MARX, TIMOTHY
    MARX, CHICO
    MARX, GROUCHO
    MARX, GUMMO
    MARX, ZEPPO
MARX, WILLIAM
    MARX, CHICO
    MARX, GROUCHO
    MARX, GUMMO
    MARX, HARPO
    MARX, ZEPPO
MARX, ZEPPO
    BARRIE, WENDY
    MARX, CHICO
    MARX, GROUCHO
    MARX, GUMMO
    MARX, HARPO
MASCHIO, JOHN
    MOORE, CONSTANCE
MASCHIO, MARY CONSTANCE 'GINA'
    MOORE, CONSTANCE
MASCHIO, MICHAEL
    MOORE, CONSTANCE
MASCHWITZ, ERIC
    GINGOLD, HERMIONE

MASON, ALEXANDER MORGAN
    MASON, JAMES
    MASON, PAMELA
MASON, HELEN
    WAYNE, DAVID
MASON, JAMES
    MASON, PAMELA
MASON, JAMES 'JIM'
    MASON, MARSHA
MASON, JOHN
    MASON, JAMES
MASON, PORTLAND
    MASON, JAMES
    MASON, PAMELA
MASSE, CORA ALICE DE
    AMES, LEON
MASSEY, ANNA
    MASSEY, RAYMOND
MASSEY, CHESTER D.
    MASSEY, RAYMOND
MASSEY, DANIEL
    MASSEY, RAYMOND
MASSEY, GEOFFREY
    MASSEY, RAYMOND
MASSEY, VINCENT
    MASSEY, RAYMOND
MASTERSON, JESSIE
    HARDWICKE, CEDRIC
MASTIN, WILL
    DAVIS, JR., SAMMY
MASTROIANNI, BARBARA
    MASTROIANNI, MARCELLO
MASTROIANNI, MARCELLO
    DENEUVE, CATHERINE
MASTROIANNI, OTTONE
    MASTROIANNI, MARCELLO
MATHEWS, JOYCE
    BERLE, MILTON
MATHEWS, RICHARD
    ASHLEY, ELIZABETH
MATHIAS, BESSIE
    REINER, CARL
MATHIS, JUNE
    VALENTINO, RUDOLPH
MATTHAU, CHARLES
    MATTHAU, WALTER
MATTHAU, DAVID
    MATTHAU, WALTER
MATTHAU, JENNIFER
    MATTHAU, WALTER
MATTHOW, HENRY
    MATTHAU, WALTER
MATTIOLI, LUISA
    MOORE, ROGER
MATTIS, DEE JAY
    CAAN, JAMES
MATTSON, ELINOR
    PARSONS, ESTELLE

MATURE, M. G.
    MATURE, VICTOR
MATURE, VICTORIA
    MATURE, VICTOR
MATUSCHANSKAYASKY, MILTON
    MATTHAU, WALTER
MAUND, MILDRED
    POWELL, DICK
MAXWELL, ALFRED GLENN
    ALLYSON, JUNE
MAXWELL, MARILYN
    SINATRA, FRANK
MAY, DAVID
    RUTHERFORD, ANN
MAY, ELAINE
    NICHOLS, MIKE
MAY, ETHEL
    NICHOLSON, JACK
MAY, FRED
    TURNER, LANA
MAY, GLORIA
    RUTHERFORD, ANN
MAY, JEAN BESLIN
    MAY, ELAINE
MAY, MARTY
    BANCROFT, ANNE
MAY, MARVIN
    MAY, ELAINE
MAY, MARY LOUISE
    BOND, WARD
MAYBERRY, LILY
    JAGGER, DEAN
MAYER, EDITH
    MAYER, LOUIS B.
MAYER, EDWIN JUSTIN
    TALMADGE, NORMA
MAYER, IDA
    MAYER, LOUIS B.
MAYER, IRENE
    MAYER, LOUIS B.
MAYER, JACOB
    MAYER, LOUIS B.
MAYER, JERRY G.
    MAYER, LOUIS B.
MAYER, LOUIS B.
    BANKY, VILMA
    DRESSLER, MARIE
    DURANTE, JIMMY
    GARSON, GREER
    GOLDWYN, SAMUEL
    MURPHY, GEORGE
    TAYLOR, ROBERT
MAYER, RUDOLPH 'RUDY'
    MAYER, LOUIS B.
MAYER, VALENTINE
    ROBERTS, RACHEL
MAYER, YETTA
    MAYER, LOUIS B.

MAYO, ALYCE
    FALK, PETER
MAYO, AMANDA
    BLAIR, JANET
MAYO, ANDREW
    BLAIR, JANET
MAYO, NICK
    BLAIR, JANET
MCALOON, CLAIR
    BOONE, RICHARD
MCCAFFREY, CAPT. JACK
    PARSONS, LOUELLA O.
MCCAHON, ROBERT W.
    STONE, FRED
MCCALLUM, DAVID
    IRELAND, JILL
MCCALLUM, JASON
    BRONSON, CHARLES
    IRELAND, JILL
    MCCALLUM, DAVID
MCCALLUM, PATRICIA
    YORK, MICHAEL
MCCALLUM, PAUL
    BRONSON, CHARLES
    IRELAND, JILL
    MCCALLUM, DAVID
MCCALLUM, VALENTINE
    BRONSON, CHARLES
    IRELAND, JILL
    MCCALLUM, DAVID
MCCAMBRIDGE, JOHN PATRICK
    MCCAMBRIDGE, MERCEDES
MCCAMERY, BERTHA
    WARFIELD, WILLIAM
MCCARTHY, CHARLIE
    BERGEN, EDGAR
MCCARTHY, JAMES
    ASHLEY, ELIZABETH
MCCARTHY, JOSEPH ALLAN
    LAKE, VERONICA
MCCARTNEY, JAMES
    MCCARTNEY, PAUL
MCCARTNEY, JAMES LOUIS
    MCCARTNEY, PAUL
MCCARTNEY, MARY
    MCCARTNEY, PAUL
MCCARTNEY, MICHAEL
    MCCARTNEY, PAUL
MCCARTNEY, PAUL
    HARRISON, GEORGE
    LENNON, JOHN
    STARR, RINGO
MCCARTNEY, RUTH
    MCCARTNEY, PAUL
MCCARTNEY, STELLA
    MCCARTNEY, PAUL
MCCAULEY, MARY MILDRED
    MOOREHEAD, AGNES

MCCLAIN, CLEO
   ARNOLD, EDWARD
MCCLINTIC, GUTHRIE
   WINWOOD, ESTELLE
MCCLINTOCH, ROSS
   VAN DOREN, MAMIE
MCCLURE, KEVIN
   TALBOT, LYLE
MCCONELL, MARY ROBINSON
   GISH, DOROTHY
MCCONNELL, CATHERINE
   HAYDEN, STERLING
MCCONNELL, MARY ROBINSON
   GISH, LILLIAN
MCCOOK, JOHN
   PROWSE, JULIET
MCCOOK, SETH
   PROWSE, JULIET
MCCORD, DALE
   LONG, RICHARD
MCCORMACK, ANN
   COOGAN, JACKIE
MCCORMACK, JOHN
   MOORE, COLLEEN
MCCORMICK, PARKER
   FORSYTHE, JOHN
MCCOY, RONALD
   MCCOY, 'COLONEL' TIM
MCCOY, TERENCE MICHAEL
   MCCOY, 'COLONEL' TIM
MCCOY, TIMOTHY
   MCCOY, 'COLONEL' TIM
MCCREA, DAVID
   MCCREA, JOEL
MCCREA, JODY
   MCCREA, JOEL
MCCREA, JOEL
   BENNETT, CONSTANCE
MCCREA, PETER
   MCCREA, JOEL
MCCULLAGH, JR., SAMUEL
   HOPE, BOB
MCCUTCHEON, WALLACE
   WHITE, PEARL
MCDANIEL, REV. HENRY
   MCDANIEL, HATTIE
MCDONALD, BETTY
   MARTIN, DEAN
MCDONALD, KITT
   KITT, EARTHA
MCDONALD, SR., MARIE
   MCDONALD, MARIE
MCDONALD, WILLIAM O.
   KITT, EARTHA
MCDOWALL, THOMAS
   MCDOWALL, RODDY
MCDOWALL, VIRGINIA
   MCDOWALL, RODDY

MCFADDEN, FLORENCE
   HALEY, JACK
MCGAUGHEY, MARY
   MAIN, MARJORIE
MCGEE, CATHERINE
   STANWYCK, BARBARA
MCGIBBON, ELIZABETH
   HUSTON, WALTER
MCGOVERN, LILLIAN
   FABRAY, NANETTE
MCGOVERN, MARGARET
   O'BRIEN, PAT
MCGRATH, EUGENE C.
   MOORE, TERRY
MCGRATH, MARGARET
   RENNIE, MICHAEL
MCGRAW, KATHRYN
   BROWN, JOE E.
MCGREW, CHARLES F.
   HARLOW, JEAN
MCGUANE, THOMAS
   ASHLEY, ELIZABETH
MCGUIRE, DEBORAGH
   PRYOR, RICHARD
MCGUIRE, THOMAS B.
   ROTH, LILLIAN
MCGUIRE, THOMAS JOHNSON
   MCGUIRE, DOROTHY
MCHUGH, JIMMY
   PARSONS, LOUELLA O.
MCINTOSH, ALISTAIR
   TALMADGE, CONSTANCE
   TALMADGE, NORMA
MCINTYRE, ANDERS
   MAXWELL, MARILYN
MCKAY, MARIE
   SCHILDKRAUT, JOSEPH
MCKAY, SCOTT
   SHERIDAN, ANN
MCKAY, WANDA
   CARMICHAEL, HOAGY
MCKENNA, LEONORE
   KILEY, RICHARD
MCKENZIE, FAYE
   COCHRAN, STEVE
MCKINNIES, HENRY
   HUNTER, JEFFREY
MCKITTRICK, BEVERLY
   GLEASON, JACKIE
MCKNIGHT, CLARA
   RUSSELL, ROSALIND
MCKNIGHT, ROBERT
   HEPBURN, KATHARINE
MCLAGLEN, ANDREW
   MCLAGLEN, VICTOR
MCLAGLEN, ARTHUR
   MCLAGLEN, VICTOR

MCLAGLEN, CLIFFORD
   MCLAGLEN, VICTOR
MCLAGLEN, CYRIL
   MCLAGLEN, VICTOR
MCLAGLEN, FRED
   MCLAGLEN, VICTOR
MCLAGLEN, KENNETH
   MCLAGLEN, VICTOR
MCLAGLEN, LEOPOLD
   MCLAGLEN, VICTOR
MCLAGLEN, LEWIS
   MCLAGLEN, VICTOR
MCLAGLEN, LILLIAN MARION
   MCLAGLEN, VICTOR
MCLAGLEN, RT. REV. ANDREW
   MCLAGLEN, VICTOR
MCLAGLEN, SHEILA
   MCLAGLEN, VICTOR
MCLAGLEN, SYDNEY
   MCLAGLEN, VICTOR
MCLAUGHLIN, ALYCE
   CORRELL, CHARLES
MCLEAN, GLORIA HATRICK
   STEWART, JAMES
MCMAHON, FRANCES
   DUKE, PATTY
MCMANUS, BOBBIE
   FARRELL, CHARLES
MCMATH, WILLIAM EDDINS
   ROGERS, GINGER
MCMEEKAN, DAVID JAMES
   WAYNE, DAVID
MCMURRAY, LILLITA LOUISE
   CHAPLIN, CHARLES
MCNAIR, EMILY
   ZIMBALIST, JR., EFREM
MCNORTON, HELAYNE
   BUTTONS, RED
MCNULTY, DANIEL GERARD
   DAY, DENNIS
MCNULTY, DR. JAMES
   BLYTH, ANN
   DAY, DENNIS
MCNULTY, EILEEN ALANA
   BLYTH, ANN
MCNULTY, EILEEN MARIA
   DAY, DENNIS
MCNULTY, EUGENE DENNIS
   DAY, DENNIS
MCNULTY, KATHLEEN MARY
   BLYTH, ANN
MCNULTY, MARGARET MARY
   DAY, DENNIS
MCNULTY, MARY KATE
   DAY, DENNIS
MCNULTY, MAUREEN ANN
   BLYTH, ANN

MCNULTY, MICHAEL JOSEPH
   DAY, DENNIS
MCNULTY, PATRICK
   DAY, DENNIS
MCNULTY, PATRICK JAMES
   DAY, DENNIS
MCNULTY, PAUL THOMAS
   DAY, DENNIS
MCNULTY, TERENCE GRADY
   BLYTH, ANN
MCNULTY, THERESE MARIE
   DAY, DENNIS
MCNULTY, THOMAS FRANCIS
   DAY, DENNIS
MCNULTY, TIMOTHY PATRICK
   BLYTH, ANN
MCPHAIL, ADDIE
   ARBUCKLE, FATTY
MCPHERSON, AIMEE SEMPLE
   QUINN, ANTHONY
MCQUARRIE, ZELLA
   WALKER, ROBERT
MCQUEEN, CHADWICK
   MACGRAW, ALI
   MCQUEEN, STEVE
MCQUEEN, STEVE
   LEE, BRUCE
   MACGRAW, ALI
   NEWMAN, PAUL
MCQUEEN, TERRY
   MACGRAW, ALI
   MCQUEEN, STEVE
MCQUEEN, WILLIAM
   MCQUEEN, STEVE
MEADE, HELEN
   KENNEDY, GEORGE
MEADOWS, AUDREY
   ALLEN, STEVE
   MEADOWS, JAYNE
MEADOWS, JAYNE
   ALLEN, STEVE
   MEADOWS, AUDREY
MEDICI, JANET
   DILLMAN, BRADFORD
MEDINA, PATRICIA
   COTTEN, JOSEPH
MEEKER, JR., RICHARD
   MOORE, MARY TYLER
MEEKER, RICHARD
   MOORE, MARY TYLER
MEINARDI, RUTH
   CARMICHAEL, HOAGY
MEJO, CARLO DE
   VALLI, ALIDA
MEJO, LORENZO DE
   VALLI, ALIDA
MEJO, OSCAR DE
   VALLI, ALIDA

MELCHER, MARTIN
    ANDREWS, LAVERNE
    ANDREWS, MAXENE
    ANDREWS, PATRICIA
    DAY, DORIS
MELCHER, TERRY
    BERGEN, CANDICE
MELCHIOR, AGGE
    MELCHIOR, LAURITZ
MELCHIOR, BIRTE INGER
    MELCHIOR, LAURITZ
MELCHIOR, BODIL
    MELCHIOR, LAURITZ
MELCHIOR, HELLE BIRTE
    HAMILTON, GEORGE
    MELCHIOR, LAURITZ
MELCHIOR, IB JORGEN
    MELCHIOR, LAURITZ
MELCHIOR, LAURITZ
    SLEZAK, WALTER
MELCHIOR, LEIF LAURITZ
    MELCHIOR, LAURITZ
MENJOU, ALBERT
    MENJOU, ADOLPHE
MENJOU, HENRY
    MENJOU, ADOLPHE
MENJOU, PETER ADOLPHE
    MENJOU, ADOLPHE
MENKEN, GRACE
    BOGART, HUMPHREY
MENKEN, HELEN
    BOGART, HUMPHREY
MERCER, MARY 'MIMI'
    SHIRLEY, ANNE
MERCOURI, MELINA
    DASSIN, JULES
MERCOURI, STAMATIS
    MERCOURI, MELINA
MEREDITH, BURGESS
    GODDARD, PAULETTE
MEREDITH, JONATHAN
    MEREDITH, BURGESS
MEREDITH, TALA BETH
    MEREDITH, BURGESS
MEREDITH, WILLIAM GEORGE
    MEREDITH, BURGESS
MERENDINO, DR. VINCENT
    PALMER, BETSY
MERENDINO, MISSIE
    PALMER, BETSY
MERIVALE, JOHN
    COOPER, GLADYS
    LEIGH, VIVIEN
    STERLING, JAN
MERIVALE, PHILIP
    COOPER, GLADYS
MERMAN, ETHEL
    BORGNINE, ERNEST

MERRICK, LYNN
    NAGEL, CONRAD
MERRILL, DINA
    ROBERTSON, CLIFF
MERRILL, GARY
    DAVIS, BETTE
MERRILL, MARGOT
    DAVIS, BETTE
    MERRILL, GARY
MERRILL, MICHAEL
    DAVIS, BETTE
    MERRILL, GARY
MESERVEY, FRANK
    PRESTON, ROBERT
MESERVEY, FRANK W.
    PRESTON, ROBERT
METHOT, MAYO
    BOGART, HUMPHREY
MEYER, MACK
    WINTERS, SHELLEY
MEYERS, DAVID L.
    BARRIE, WENDY
MEYERS, LEE
    VAN DOREN, MAMIE
MICKELWHITE, STANLEY
    CAINE, MICHAEL
MICKLEWHITE, MAURICE
    CAINE, MICHAEL
MIDGLEY, ANDRE
    FURNESS, BETTY
MIDGLEY, LESLIE GRANT
    FURNESS, BETTY
MIDGLEY, PETER JEDEDIAH
    FURNESS, BETTY
MIERS, FRIEDA
    WYNN, ED
    WYNN, KEENAN
MIGLIETTA, JOHN
    BARRYMORE, ETHEL
    BARRYMORE, JR., JOHN
MIGLIETTA, JOHN ROMEO
    BARRYMORE, ETHEL
MIKLENDA, MICHAEL
    MILLS, JOHN
MILBURNE, PAMELA
    HUME, BENITA
MILES, ARLENE
    TORME, MEL
MILES, CHRISTOPHER
    MILES, SARAH
MILES, DEBORAH
    MILES, VERA
    SCOTT, GORDON
MILES, JOHN
    MILES, SARAH
MILES, KELLY
    MILES, VERA

MILES, KELLY
    SCOTT, GORDON
MILES, PETER
    PERREAU, GIGI
MILES, RICHARD
    PERREAU, GIGI
MILES, ROBERT
    MILES, VERA
MILES, TAMI
    TORME, MEL
MILES, VANESSA
    MILES, SARAH
MILES, VERA
    SCOTT, GORDON
MILL, MARION
    PREMINGER, OTTO
MILLAND, DANIEL DAVID
    MILLAND, RAY
MILLAND, VICTORIA FRANCESCA
    MILLAND, RAY
MILLAR, JAMES ALEXANDER
    BOYD, STEPHEN
MILLARD, ELIZA SARAH
    KARLOFF, BORIS
MILLER, AGNES
    MCCOY, 'COLONEL' TIM
MILLER, ALLAN 'PINKY'
    MARX, ZEPPO
MILLER, ANTHONY DAWSON
    MILLER, MARVIN
MILLER, ARTHUR
    MONROE, MARILYN
MILLER, CHARLES DANIEL
    SAINT JAMES, SUSAN
MILLER, IRENE
    BALSAM, MARTIN
MILLER, KEVIN CHRISTOPHER
    MILLER, MARVIN
MILLER, M. HUGHES
    POWERS, MALA
MILLER, MARGARETT
    HOPPER, HEDDA
MILLER, MARILYN
    PICKFORD, MARY
MILLER, MELISSA
    MILLER, MARVIN
MILLER, RUTH
    BOYD, WILLIAM
MILLINO, ROSEA
    DURANTE, JIMMY
MILLS, ANNETTE
    MILLS, JOHN
MILLS, HAYLEY
    MILLS, JOHN
MILLS, JOHN
    MILLS, HAYLEY
MILLS, JOSHUA
    ADAMS, EDIE

MILLS, JR., JOHN
    MILLS, HAYLEY
    MILLS, JOHN
MILLS, JULIA
    TRUEX, ERNEST
MILLS, JULIET
    MILLS, HAYLEY
    MILLS, JOHN
MILLS, LEWIS
    MILLS, JOHN
MILLS, MARTY
    ADAMS, EDIE
MILNE, CORDELL
    SAINT CYR, LILI
MILNE, ETHEL MARION
    GARLAND, JUDY
    MINNELLI, LIZA
MILNER, DOUGLAS
    MILLER, ANN
MILNER, REESE L.
    MILLER, ANN
MIMIEUX, RENE A.
    MIMIEUX, YVETTE
MINARDOS, DEBORAH
    POWER, TYRONE
MINEO, MICHAEL
    MINEO, SAL
MINEO, SARINA
    MINEO, SAL
MINEO, SR., SALVATORE
    MINEO, SAL
MINICKER, KATE
    FISHER, EDDIE
MINNELLI, CHRISTIANA NINA
    MINNELLI, LIZA
MINNELLI, LIZA
    GARLAND, JUDY
    HALEY, JACK
MINNELLI, VINCENTE
    GARLAND, JUDY
    MINNELLI, LIZA
MINTER, MARY MILES
    ARBUCKLE, FATTY
MIRANDA, MARIA EMILIA
    MIRANDA, CARMEN
MIRON, FERNANDO D.
    HOPE, BOB
MITCHELL, FLORENCE
    RANDALL, TONY
MITCHELL, MARY ALICE
    CRAWFORD, BRODERICK
MITCHUM, CHRIS
    MITCHUM, ROBERT
MITCHUM, JAMES
    MITCHUM, ROBERT
MITCHUM, JIM
    BROLIN, JAMES

MITCHUM, JIM
    MITCHUM, ROBERT
MITCHUM, JOHN
    MITCHUM, ROBERT
MITCHUM, JULIE
    MITCHUM, ROBERT
MITCHUM, PETRINE
    MITCHUM, ROBERT
MIX, EDWIN E.
    MIX, TOM
MIX, EMMA
    MIX, TOM
MIX, ESTHER
    MIX, TOM
MIX, HARRY
    MIX, TOM
MIX, RUTH JANE
    MIX, TOM
MIX, THOMASINA
    MIX, TOM
MIX, TOM
    ABBOTT, BUD
    WAYNE, JOHN
MIZZY, ARNOLD R.
    HAVOC, JUNE
    LEE, GYPSY ROSE
MOBLEY, MARY ANN
    HUNTER, TAB
MOELLER, JOLIE
    MELCHIOR, LAURITZ
MOFFET, SALLY
    TRUEX, ERNEST
MOLL, GEORGIA
    BARRYMORE, JR., JOHN
MONROE, GLADYS BAKER
    MONROE, MARILYN
MONROE, MARILYN
    LAWFORD, PETER
    RUSSELL, JANE
MONTALBAN, ANITA
    MONTALBAN, RICARDO
MONTALBAN, CARLOS
    MONTALBAN, RICARDO
MONTALBAN, LAURA
    MONTALBAN, RICARDO
MONTALBAN, MARK
    MONTALBAN, RICARDO
MONTALBAN, RICARDO
    YOUNG, LORETTA
MONTALBAN, VICTOR
    MONTALBAN, RICARDO
MONTAND, LOUISE
    SIGNORET, SIMONE
MONTAND, YVES
    SIGNORET, SIMONE
MONTANI, VIRGIL JAMES
    NESBIT, EVELYN

MONTELLO, MERCY
    ROONEY, MICKEY
MONTEMAYOR, CARMEN
    MIMIEUX, YVETTE
MONTEZ, MARIA
    HALL, JON
MONTEZ, MARIO
    WARHOL, ANDY
MONTGOMERY, DAVID
    STONE, FRED
MONTGOMERY, DOUGLAS
    MORAN, LOIS
MONTGOMERY, ELIZABETH
    MONTGOMERY, ROBERT
    YOUNG, GIG
MONTGOMERY, FLORENCE
    ARLISS, GEORGE
MONTGOMERY, GEORGE
    SHORE, DINAH
MONTGOMERY, HENRY
    MONTGOMERY, ROBERT
MONTGOMERY, JOHN DAVID
    MONTGOMERY, GEORGE
    SHORE, DINAH
MONTGOMERY, JR., ROBERT
    MONTGOMERY, ELIZABETH
    MONTGOMERY, ROBERT
    YOUNG, GIG
MONTGOMERY, MELISSA ANN
    MONTGOMERY, GEORGE
    SHORE, DINAH
MONTGOMERY, ROBERT
    MONTGOMERY, ELIZABETH
    YOUNG, GIG
MOORE, CHRISTIAN
    MOORE, ROGER
MOORE, DEBORAH
    MOORE, ROGER
MOORE, DUDLEY
    WELD, TUESDAY
MOORE, ELIZABETH ANN
    MOORE, MARY TYLER
MOORE, EVA
    OLIVIER, LAURENCE
MOORE, GEOFFREY
    MOORE, ROGER
MOORE, GEORGE
    MOORE, ROGER
MOORE, GEORGE TYLER
    MOORE, MARY TYLER
MOORE, HARRY R. 'TIM'
    CORRELL, CHARLES
MOORE, JOANNA
    O'NEAL, RYAN
MOORE, JOHN
    MOORE, MARY TYLER
MOORE, JOHN RICHARD
    WHITING, MARGARET

MORGAN, GEORGE
    MORGAN, FRANK
MORGAN, HELEN SPEAR
    MASON, PAMELA
MORGAN, LAURA ANDRINA
    BURR, RAYMOND
MORGAN, MICHAEL
    DE CARLO, YVONNE
MORGAN, ROBERT
    DE CARLO, YVONNE
MORGEN, MARILYN
    NELSON, GENE
MORGENSTERN, ANNA GRACE
    LAURIE, PIPER
MORGENSTERN, JOSEPH
    LAURIE, PIPER
MORLEY, ALEXIS
    MORLEY, ROBERT
MORLEY, ANNABEL
    MORLEY, ROBERT
MORLEY, ROBERT
    COOPER, GLADYS
MORLEY, ROBERT WILTON
    MORLEY, ROBERT
MORLEY, SHERIDAN
    MORLEY, ROBERT
MORONDO, MADELINE
    FOY, JR., EDDIE
MOROSCO, WALTER
    GRIFFITH, CORINNE
MORRILL, DR. LEWIS
    FLEMING, RHONDA
MORRIS, BARBARA
    ANDREWS, JULIE
MORRIS, MARGARET
    BRUCE, VIRGINIA
MORRIS, MELANIE CONSTANCE
    AMES, LEON
MORRISON, ADRIENNE
    BENNETT, CONSTANCE
    BENNETT, JOAN
    BENNETT, RICHARD
MORRISON, AISSA
    WAYNE, JOHN
MORRISON, ANTONIA
    WAYNE, JOHN
MORRISON, CHARLES
    MOORE, COLLEEN
MORRISON, CLEVE
    MOORE, COLLEEN
MORRISON, CLYDE
    WAYNE, JOHN
MORRISON, ETHAN
    WAYNE, JOHN
MORRISON, JACK
    CAGNEY, JAMES
MORRISON, MARISA
    WAYNE, JOHN

MOORE, JOSEPHINE
    DILLMAN, BRADFORD
MOORE, LEROY
    BEAVERS, LOUISE
MOORE, MATT
    PICKFORD, MARY
MOORE, NORMA
    PERKINS, TONY
MOORE, OWEN
    PICKFORD, MARY
MOORE, PATRICK
    WELD, TUESDAY
MOORE, TERRY
    HUGHES, HOWARD
MOOREHEAD, REV. JOHN HENDERSON
    MOOREHEAD, AGNES
MOOREHEAD, CHESTER HIRST
    BENNETT, CONSTANCE
    BENNETT, RICHARD
MOOREHEAD, HUBERT
    EDEN, BARBARA
MORAN, CATHERINE
    NAISH, J. CARROLL
MORAN, JOSEPH A.
    RITTER, THELMA
MORAN, JOSEPH ANTHONY
    RITTER, THELMA
MORAN, MONICA
    RITTER, THELMA
MORAN, THOMAS
    MORAN, POLLY
MOREAU, ANATOLE DESIRE
    MOREAU, JEANNE
MOREAU, MICHELE
    MOREAU, JEANNE
MORENO, DENNIS
    MORENO, RITA
MORENO, EDWARD
    MORENO, RITA
MORENO, JOSE
    CANTINFLAS
MORENO, JUAN
    MORENO, ANTONIO
MORENO, RITA
    BRANDO, MARLON
MORENO, ROSE
    CASTELLANO, RICHARD
    GOULET, ROBERT
    LAWRENCE, CAROL
MOREUIL, FRANCOIS
    SEBERG, JEAN
MORGAN, ARTHUR
    NOVELLO, IVOR
MORGAN, BRUCE
    DE CARLO, YVONNE
MORGAN, CLAUDIA
    MORGAN, FRANK

MORRISON, MELINDA
    WAYNE, JOHN
MORRISON, MICHAEL A.
    WAYNE, JOHN
MORRISON, PATRICK
    WAYNE, JOHN
MORRISON, ROBERT
    WAYNE, JOHN
MORROW, DORETTA
    DAMONE, VIC
MORROW, PATRICIA
    RUSSELL, ROSALIND
MORTENSEN, EDWARD
    MONROE, MARILYN
MORTON, GARY
    BALL, LUCILLE
MOSELY, BENJAMIN J.
    MADISON, GUY
MOSS, BUDD B.
    ROMAN, RUTH
MOSS, WILLIAM
    MILLER, ANN
MOSTEL, ISRAEL
    MOSTEL, ZERO
MOSTEL, JOSHUA
    MOSTEL, ZERO
MOSTEL, TOBIAS
    MOSTEL, ZERO
MOTON, WILLIAM
    ROSS, DIANA
MOULLNER, MARIA
    MCDONALD, MARIE
MUIR, ESTHER
    BERKELEY, BUSBY
MULLANE, ALFRED
    MILLAND, RAY
MULLAVEY, GREG
    MACRAE, GORDON
MULLEN, DOROTHY HOGAN
    DALY, JAMES
MULLENGER, WILLIAM R.
    REED, DONNA
MULLER, ALMA
    MORGAN, FRANK
MULLER, KIEL
    MARTIN, DEAN
MULLIGAN, GERRY
    DENNIS, SANDY
MULROONEY, GRAYCE
    RAFT, GEORGE
MUNIER, JULIETTE
    CALVET, CORINNE
MUNSTON, JOHN
    LILLIE, BEATRICE
MUNSTON, MURIEL
    LILLIE, BEATRICE
MURPHY, ALICE
    BELLAMY, RALPH

MURPHY, ARIEL JUNE
    MURPHY, AUDIE
MURPHY, BEATRICE 'BILLIE'
    MURPHY, AUDIE
MURPHY, CHARLES EMMETT 'BUCK'
    MURPHY, AUDIE
MURPHY, DENNIS MICHAEL
    MURPHY, GEORGE
MURPHY, ELIZABETH CORINNE
    MURPHY, AUDIE
MURPHY, EMMETT BERRY
    MURPHY, AUDIE
MURPHY, EUGENE PORTER
    MURPHY, AUDIE
MURPHY, FRANCES
    NAGEL, CONRAD
MURPHY, J. W.
    MURPHY, AUDIE
MURPHY, JAMES SHANNON
    MURPHY, AUDIE
MURPHY, JOSEPH PRESTON
    MURPHY, AUDIE
MURPHY, MARY
    ROBERTSON, DALE
MURPHY, MELISSA ELAINE
    MURPHY, GEORGE
MURPHY, MICHAEL
    MURPHY, GEORGE
MURPHY, ONETA
    MURPHY, AUDIE
MURPHY, RICHARD HOUSTON
    MURPHY, AUDIE
MURPHY, TERRY MICHAEL
    MURPHY, AUDIE
MURPHY, VEDA NADINE
    MURPHY, AUDIE
MURPHY, VERNON
    MURPHY, AUDIE
MURRAY, CHRISTOPHER
    LANGE, HOPE
MURRAY, CORT
    MURRAY, KEN
MURRAY, DON
    LANGE, HOPE
MURRAY, JANE
    MURRAY, KEN
MURRAY, JANET
    ANDREWS, DANA
MURRAY, JOSEPH E.
    STAPLETON, JEAN
MURRAY, KEN
    WILSON, MARIE
MURRAY, MAE
    BEERY, WALLACE
MURRAY, PAMELA
    MURRAY, KEN
MURRAY, PATRICIA
    LANGE, HOPE

MURRAY, WILLIAM B.
    CHASE, ILKA
MURRAY,JR., KEN
    MURRAY, KEN
MUSSOLINI, ROMANO
    LOREN, SOPHIA
MUX, PEARLA
    LAMAS, FERNANDO
MYER, HAROLD
    JANSSEN, DAVID
MYERS, DOROTHY PENNEBAKER
    BRANDO, MARLON
MYERS, EDMA EMMA
    CUMMINGS, ROBERT
MYERS, JEAN
    CARNEY, ART
MYGATT, NANCY
    WHITMORE, JAMES
MYRICK, DAPHNE
    IRELAND, JOHN
MYROW, FREDRIC E.
    MIMIEUX, YVETTE
NAGEL, CONRAD
    FONTAINE, JOAN
NAGEL, FRANK
    NAGEL, CONRAD
NAISH, CAROL ELAINE
    NAISH, J. CARROLL
NAISH, PATRICK SARSFIELD
    NAISH, J. CARROLL
NATHAN, GEORGE JEAN
    GISH, LILLIAN
NATHANSEN, INGER
    MELCHIOR, LAURITZ
NATWICK, JOSEPH
    NATWICK, MILDRED
NATZKA, WINIFRED
    COBURN, CHARLES
NEAGLE, FLORENCE
    NEAGLE, ANNA
NEAL, FRANCES
    HEFLIN, VAN
    TALBOT, LYLE
NEAL, MARGARET
    NEAL, PATRICIA
NEAL, MARY ALLEN
    ROWLANDS, GENA
NEAL, PATRICIA
    COOPER, GARY
NEAL, PETER
    NEAL, PATRICIA
NEAL, TOM
    TONE, FRANCHOT
NEAL, WILLIAM BURDETTE
    NEAL, PATRICIA
NEGRETTE, ANTONIA LOPEZ
    DEL RIO, DOLORES

NEGRI, POLA
    BARRYMORE, JOHN
    CHAPLIN, CHARLES
    LA ROCQUE, ROD
    VALENTINO, RUDOLPH
NEIDES, HAL
    HAYES, HELEN
NEIL, ELEANOUR
    SHIRE, TALIA
NEILECHT, KATE
    COBB, LEE J.
NEILSEN, TRYGVE
    NELSON, BARRY
NEJEDLY, ADA
    LEDERER, FRANCIS
NELL, SUSAN
    WILDING, MICHAEL
NELSON, ALAN CHRISTOPHER
    NELSON, GENE
NELSON, ALFRED
    NELSON, OZZIE
NELSON, CAROLYN
    CAGNEY, JAMES
NELSON, DAVID
    HILLIARD, HARRIET
    NELSON, OZZIE
    NELSON, RICK
NELSON, DEBRA
    LAMOUR, DOROTHY
NELSON, DOUGLAS
    NELSON, GENE
NELSON, GENE
    POWELL, JANE
NELSON, GEORGE WALDUMAR
    NELSON, OZZIE
NELSON, GUNNAR
    HILLIARD, HARRIET
    NELSON, OZZIE
    NELSON, RICK
NELSON, JR., ERIC
    HILLIARD, HARRIET
    NELSON, OZZIE
    NELSON, RICK
NELSON, JR., HARMON O.
    DAVIS, BETTE
NELSON, LENORE
    NELSON, GENE
NELSON, LOIS
    LAUREL, STAN
NELSON, MATTHEW
    HILLIARD, HARRIET
    NELSON, OZZIE
    NELSON, RICK
NELSON, OZZIE
    HILLIARD, HARRIET
    NELSON, RICK
NELSON, RALPH
    HOLM, CELESTE

NELSON, RICK
    HILLIARD, HARRIET
    NELSON, OZZIE
NELSON, SHERRY
    STEIGER, ROD
NELSON, THEODORE
    HOLM, CELESTE
NELSON, TRACY KRISTIN
    HILLIARD, HARRIET
    NELSON, OZZIE
    NELSON, RICK
NELSON, VICTORIA LEANDRA
    NELSON, GENE
NEMEROVSKY, CLARA
    KAYE, DANNY
NERNEY, LINDSAY AVERILL
    POWELL, JANE
NERNEY, PAT
    POWELL, JANE
NERO, CARLO
    REDGRAVE, VANESSA
NERO, FRANCO
    REDGRAVE, VANESSA
NESBIT, EVELYN
    BARRYMORE, JOHN
NESBITT, DOROTHY ELIZABETH
    WYNN, ED
    WYNN, KEENAN
NETCHER, TOWNSEND
    TALMADGE, CONSTANCE
    TALMADGE, NORMA
NEUBERT, RICHARD
    SAINT JAMES, SUSAN
NEWBERN, ANN
    LANGFORD, FRANCES
NEWELL, HOPE
    DALY, JAMES
NEWLEY, ANTHONY
    COLLINS, JOAN
NEWLEY, JR., ANTHONY
    COLLINS, JOAN
NEWLEY, TARA
    COLLINS, JOAN
NEWMAN, ARTHUR
    NEWMAN, PAUL
NEWMAN, CARA
    NEWMAN, PAUL
    WOODWARD, JOANNE
NEWMAN, ELEANOR
    NEWMAN, PAUL
    WOODWARD, JOANNE
NEWMAN, JOE
    NEWMAN, PAUL
NEWMAN, MELISSA
    NEWMAN, PAUL
    WOODWARD, JOANNE
NEWMAN, PAUL
    POITIER, SIDNEY

NEWMAN, PAUL
    WOODWARD, JOANNE
NEWMAN, SCOTT
    NEWMAN, PAUL
    WOODWARD, JOANNE
NEWMAN, STEPHANIE
    NEWMAN, PAUL
    WOODWARD, JOANNE
NEWMAN, SUSAN
    NEWMAN, PAUL
    WOODWARD, JOANNE
NEY, RICHARD
    GARSON, GREER
NICHOLS, DAISY
    NICHOLS, MIKE
NICHOLS, JENNY
    NICHOLS, MIKE
NICHOLS, MAX
    NICHOLS, MIKE
NICHOLS, MIKE
    MAY, ELAINE
NICHOLSON, FLORENCE
    RUTHERFORD, MARGARET
NICHOLSON, JACK
    PHILLIPS, MICHELLE
NICHOLSON, JENNIFER
    NICHOLSON, JACK
NICHOLSON, JOHN
    NICHOLSON, JACK
NICHOLSON, VIRGINIA
    WELLES, ORSON
NIELSEN, JOHANNA AUGUSTA
    ARTHUR, JEAN
NILSSON, ANNA Q.
    HART, WILLIAM S.
    NORMAND, MABEL
NIVEN, DAVID
    BRUCE, VIRGINIA
    COLMAN, RONALD
    FLYNN, ERROL
    GRANGER, STEWART
NIVEN, FIONA
    NIVEN, DAVID
NIVEN, JAMES
    NIVEN, DAVID
NIVEN, JR., DAVID
    NIVEN, DAVID
NIVEN, KRISTINA
    NIVEN, DAVID
NIVEN, MARGARET
    BOGARDE, DIRK
NIVEN, WILLIAM GRAHAM
    NIVEN, DAVID
NIXON, ALAN
    WILSON, MARIE
NIXON, RICHARD M.
    AUTRY, GENE

NOBLE, GLORIA
    O'CONNOR, DONALD
NOEL, MILDRED LARUE
    LEMMON, JACK
NOIA, NICHOLAS DE
    O'NEILL, JENNIFER
NOLAN, JAMES
    NOLAN, LLOYD
NOLAN, JAY
    NOLAN, LLOYD
NOLAN, LLOYD
    AMES, LEON
NOLAN, MELINDA JOYCE
    NOLAN, LLOYD
NOON, BETTY ANN DE
    HAYDEN, STERLING
NOONAN, KATHERINE
    IRELAND, JOHN
NOONAN, MICHAEL
    IRELAND, JOHN
NOONAN, TOMMY
    IRELAND, JOHN
NORDBERG, MARGARETHE NOE VON
    SCHELL, MARIA
    SCHELL, MAXIMILIAN
NORDENWALD, BRUNO VON
    VON STROHEIM, ERICH
NORDENWALD, FREDERICK 'BENNO'
    VON STROHEIM, ERICH
NORMAND, CLAUDE GEORGE
    NORMAND, MABEL
NORMAND, GLADYS
    NORMAND, MABEL
NORMAND, JR., CLAUDE
    NORMAND, MABEL
NORMAND, MABEL
    SENNETT, MACK
NORRIS, EDWARD
    SHERIDAN, ANN
NORRIS, ELEANOR KATHLEEN
    KEATON, BUSTER
    VALLEE, RUDY
NORWOOD, LELA
    CHARISSE, CYD
NORWORTH, JOHN
    DRESSER, LOUISE
NOVAK, ARLENE
    NOVAK, KIM
NOVAK, JANE
    HART, WILLIAM S.
NOVAK, JOSEPH A.
    NOVAK, KIM
NOVARRO, RAMON
    DEL RIO, DOLORES
    LOY, MYRNA
NOVELLO, CLARA
    NOVELLO, IVOR

NOYES, ANN
    TRYON, TOM
NUGENT, CAROL
    ADAMS, NICK
NUTTER, RIK VAN
    EKBERG, ANITA
NUYEN, FRANCE
    BRANDO, MARLON
    CULP, ROBERT
O'BRIAN, HUGH
    CHRISTIAN, LINDA
    ROMAN, RUTH
O'BRIEN, BRENDAN
    O'BRIEN, EDMOND
O'BRIEN, BRIDGET
    O'BRIEN, EDMOND
O'BRIEN, BRIGID
    O'BRIEN, PAT
O'BRIEN, JAMES
    O'BRIEN, EDMOND
O'BRIEN, JAMES JAY
    MURRAY, MAE
O'BRIEN, JR., PATRICK
    O'BRIEN, PAT
O'BRIEN, KATHLEEN
    O'BRIEN, PAT
O'BRIEN, LAWRENCE
    O'BRIEN, MARGARET
O'BRIEN, MARIA
    O'BRIEN, EDMOND
O'BRIEN, MAVOURNEEN
    O'BRIEN, PAT
O'BRIEN, PAT
    RENALDO, DUNCAN
    TRACY, SPENCER
O'BRIEN, SR., WILLIAM
    O'BRIEN, PAT
O'BRIEN, TERENCE
    O'BRIEN, PAT
O'CONNELL, MICHAEL
    O'CONNELL, ARTHUR
O'CONNOR, ALICIA
    O'CONNOR, DONALD
O'CONNOR, BILL
    O'CONNOR, DONALD
O'CONNOR, DONALD
    FRANCIS THE MULE
O'CONNOR, DONALD FREDERICK
    O'CONNOR, DONALD
O'CONNOR, DONNA
    DAILEY, DAN
    O'CONNOR, DONALD
O'CONNOR, EDWARD JOSEPH
    O'CONNOR, CARROLL
O'CONNOR, HUGH
    O'CONNOR, CARROLL
O'CONNOR, HUGH
    O'CONNOR, CARROLL

O'CONNOR, JACK
    O'CONNOR, DONALD
O'CONNOR, JOHN EDWARD
    O'CONNOR, DONALD
O'CONNOR, KEVIN
    O'CONNOR, DONALD
O'CONNOR, LOIS
    ROBARDS, JR., JASON
O'CURRAN, CHARLES
    HUTTON, BETTY
O'DONOHUE, IRENE
    FERRER, MEL
O'FARRELL, JAMES
    VERDON, GWEN
O'FEENEY, EDWARD
    FORD, FRANCIS
O'FEENEY, JOSEPHINE'
    FORD, FRANCIS
O'FEENEY, MAMIE
    FORD, FRANCIS
O'FEENEY, PATRICK
    FORD, FRANCIS
O'FEENEY, SEAN ALOYSIUS
    FORD, FRANCIS
    WALKER, ROBERT
O'HARA, MICHAEL
    GABOR, EVA
    GABOR, ZSA ZSA
O'HERLIHY, CORMAC
    O'HERLIHY, DAN
O'HERLIHY, GAVIN
    O'HERLIHY, DAN
O'HERLIHY, JOHN
    O'HERLIHY, DAN
O'HERLIHY, LORCAN PATRICK
    O'HERLIHY, DAN
O'HERLIHY, MARGUERITE
    O'HERLIHY, DAN
O'HERLIHY, MICHAEL
    O'HERLIHY, DAN
O'HERLIHY, OLWEN
    O'HERLIHY, DAN
O'HERLIHY, PATRICIA
    O'HERLIHY, DAN
O'KEEFE, EDWARD JAMES FLANAGAN
    O'KEEFE, DENNIS
O'NEAL, GRIFFIN PATRICK
    O'NEAL, RYAN
O'NEAL, FATRICK
    O'NEAL, RYAN
O'NEAL, RYAN
    AIMEE, ANOUK
O'NEAL, TATUM
    O'NEAL, RYAN
O'NEILL, CHARLES
    O'NEAL, RYAN
O'NEILL, EUGENE
    CHAPLIN, CHARLES

O'NEILL, EUGENE
    CHAPLIN, GERALDINE
O'NEILL, JENNIFER
    GOULD, ELLIOT
O'NEILL, JR., OSCAR
    O'NEILL, JENNIFER
O'NEILL, KEVIN
    O'NEAL, RYAN
O'NEILL, OONA
    CHAPLIN, CHARLES
    CHAPLIN, GERALDINE
O'NEILL, OSCAR
    O'NEILL, JENNIFER
O'SHAY, CONSTANCE
    DUFF, HOWARD
    LUPINO, IDA
O'SHEA, MARY
    MAYO, VIRGINIA
O'SHEA, MICHAEL
    MAYO, VIRGINIA
O'SHEA, ROBERT
    RAYE, MARTHA
O'SULLIVAN, CHARLES
    O'SULLIVAN, MAUREEN
O'SULLIVAN, MAUREEN
    FARROW, MIA
    SINATRA, FRANK
O'TOOLE, CATHERINE 'KATE'
    O'TOOLE, PETER
O'TOOLE, PATRICIA
    O'TOOLE, PETER
O'TOOLE, PATRICIA 'PAT'
    O'TOOLE, PETER
O'TOOLE, PATRICK JOSEPH
    O'TOOLE, PETER
O'TOOLE, PETER
    SCHNEIDER, ROMY
OAXACA, MANUELA 'NELLIE'
    QUINN, ANTHONY
OBER, PHILIP
    VANCE, VIVIAN
OCKELMAN, H.A.
    LAKE, VERONICA
ODETS, CLIFFORD
    RAINER, LUISE
OETTINGER, EDWIN
    PARSONS, LOUELLA O.
OETTINGER, FLORENCE
    PARSONS, LOUELLA O.
OETTINGER, FRED
    PARSONS, LOUELLA O.
OETTINGER, JOSHUA
    PARSONS, LOJELLA O.
OETTINGER, RAE
    PARSONS, LOUELLA O.
OGDEN, DOROTHY
    GREENSTREET, SYDNEY

OGMORE, LORD
    HARRIS, RICHARD
    HARRISON, REX
OKELL, MARY
    BAINTER, FAY
OLAND, CARL
    OLAND, WARNER
OLAND, JONAS
    OLAND, WARNER
OLIN, KERATIN
    VON SYDOW, MAX
OLIVER, JOE ' KING'
    ARMSTRONG, LOUIS
OLIVETTE, NINA
    STOCKWELL, DEAN
OLIVIER, LAURENCE
    COOPER, GLADYS
    LEIGH, VIVIEN
OLIVIER, REV. GERARD KERR
    OLIVIER, LAURENCE
OLIVIER, RICHARD
    OLIVIER, LAURENCE
OLIVIER, RICHARD
    OLIVIER, LAURENCE
OLIVIER, SIMON
    LEIGH, VIVIEN
    OLIVIER, LAURENCE
OLIVIER, TAMSIN
    OLIVIER, LAURENCE
OLIVIER, TARQUIN
    LEIGH, VIVIEN
    OLIVIER, LAURENCE
OLSEN, JEANNE
    DURANTE, JIMMY
OLSEN, KATHERINE M.
    HUDSON, ROCK
OLSSON, GUSTAV
    ANN-MARGRET
    SMITH, ROGER
ONASSIS, ARISTOTLE
    GARBO, GRETA
ONASSIS, CHRISTINA
    BELMONDO, JEAN-PAUL
ONO, YOKO
    LENNON, JOHN
ONSTAD, NILS
    HENIE, SONJA
OPEL, GUNTHER SACHS VON
    BARDOT, BRIGITTE
OPPENHEIM, DAVID
    HOLLIDAY, JUDY
OPPENHEIM, JONATHAN
    HOLLIDAY, JUDY
ORFEI, LIANA
    REEVES, STEVE
ORLENOFF, PAUL
    NAZIMOVA

ORMPHBY, GLADYS
    BUZZI, RUTH
ORNSTEIN, ALICE
    WEAVER, DENNIS
ORNSTEIN, ROSE
    LEDERER, FRANCIS
ORR, ETHEL IRENE
    NELSON, OZZIE
ORSATTI, ALBERT
    MCDONALD, MARIE
ORSATTI, ERNEST
    MCDONALD, MARIE
ORSATTI, FRANK
    MCDONALD, MARIE
ORSATTI, VICTOR
    CALHOUN, RORY
    MCDONALD, MARIE
ORSINI, ARMANDO
    SAINT CYR, LILI
OSBORNE, ODELLE
    JONES, BUCK
OSHINSKY, HERBERT
    ROTH, LILLIAN
OSTRER, ISADORE
    MASON, PAMELA
OSTRER, PAMELA
    MASON, JAMES
OUTTEN, EVELYN
    POITIER, SIDNEY
OWEN, J. FENWICK
    OWEN, REGINALD
OWEN, JR., TONY
    REED, DONNA
OWEN, MARY ANN
    REED, DONNA
OWEN, PENNY
    REED, DONNA
OWEN, TIMOTHY
    REED, DONNA
OWEN, TONY
    REED, DONNA
OWENS, JAMES
    SHERIDAN, ANN
OWENS, PATRICIA
    ASTIN, JOHN
OZMONT, ELNORA
    AUTRY, GENE
PACINO, SALVATORE
    PACINO, AL
PAGE, DONALD
    PAGE, GERALDINE
PAGE, GERALDINE
    TORN, RIP
PAGE, LEON ELWIN
    PAGE, GERALDINE
PAGLIAI, BRUNO
    OBERON, MERLE

PAGLIAI, FRANCESCA
    OBERON, MERLE
PAGLIAI, JR., BRUNO
    OBERON, MERLE
PAHLAVI, SORAYA ESFANDIARY
    SCHELL, MAXIMILIAN
PAKULA, ALAN J.
    LANGE, HOPE
PALAHNUIK, JOHN
    PALANCE, JACK
PALANCE, BROOK GABRIELLE
    PALANCE, JACK
PALANCE, CODY JOHN
    PALANCE, JACK
PALANCE, HOLLY
    PALANCE, JACK
PALAZZOLI, GABRIELLA 'GABY'
    BARRYMORE, JR., JOHN
PALLETT, PILAR
    WAYNE, JOHN
PALMER, LILLI
    HARRISON, REX
PALMER, PATTI
    LEWIS, JERRY
PAPALEO, ANTHONY
    FRANCIOSA, ANTHONY
PAPAS, ALKIS
    PAPAS, IRENE
PAPATAKIS, NICOS
    AIMEE, ANOUK
PARDO, CARMEN
    ARMENDARIZ, PEDRO
PARIS, HARRY
    SHIRLEY, ANNE
PARKE, JEAN
    HOLM, CELESTE
PARKER, ASHLEY ALLEN
    PARKER, FESS
PARKER, DAISY
    ARMSTRONG, LOUIS
PARKER, DORIAN LEIGH
    DILLMAN, BRADFORD
    PARKER, SUZY
PARKER, DOROTHY
    BENCHLEY, ROBERT
PARKER, FLORA
    DE HAVEN, GLORIA
    PAYNE, JOHN
PARKER, GEORGE LOFTON
    PARKER, SUZY
PARKER, III, FESS
    PARKER, FESS
PARKER, JOY
    SCOFIELD, PAUL
PARKER, LESTER K.
    PARKER, ELEANOR
PARKER, RUSSELL
    VARSI, DIANE

PARKER, SR., FESS
    PARKER, FESS
PARKER, STEPHANIE SACHIKO
    BEATTY, WARREN
    MACLAINE, SHIRLEY
PARKER, STEVE
    BEATTY, WARREN
    MACLAINE, SHIRLEY
PARKER, SUZY
    DILLMAN, BRADFORD
PARKER, THOMAS A.
    PRESLEY, ELVIS
PARKS, ANDREW
    PARKS, LARRY
PARKS, GARRETT
    PARKS, LARRY
PARKS, HILDY
    COOPER, JACKIE
PARNASSUS, DR. WILLIAM
    HALEY, JACK
PARRY, FLOWER
    COOGAN, JACKIE
PARSONS, EBEN
    PARSONS, ESTELLE
PARSONS, HARRIET
    PARSONS, LOUELLA O.
PARSONS, JOHN
    PARSONS, LOUELLA O.
PASSANI, VERONIQUE
    PECK, GREGORY
PATERSON, PAT
    BOYER, CHARLES
PATLAWSKY, IDA
    TERRY-THOMAS
PATRICK, CATHERINE AMAYIA
    AMSTERDAM, MOREY
PATRICK, EVELYN
    SILVERS, PHIL
PATTEN, DICK VAN
    BALSAM, MARTIN
PATTEN, JOYCE VAN
    BALSAM, MARTIN
PATTEN, VINCE VAN
    FAWCETT-MAJORS, FARRAH
PAUL, AILEEN
    BARTHOLOMEW, FREDDIE
PAUL, BYRON
    VAN DYKE, DICK
PAUL, VAUGHN
    DURBIN, DEANNA
PAVAN, MARISA
    ANGELI, PIER
    AUMONT, JEAN-PIERRE
    DAMONE, VIC
PAVIA, CHRISTINE
    VACCARO, BRENDA
PAYNE, JOHN
    DE HAVEN, GLORIA

PAYNE, JOHN
    SHIRLEY, ANNE
PAYNE, JULIE ANNE
    DE HAVEN, GLORIA
    PAYNE, JOHN
    SHIRLEY, ANNE
PAYNE, KATHLEEN
    DE HAVEN, GLORIA
    PAYNE, JOHN
PAYNE, PETER
    PAYNE, JOHN
PAYNE, THOMAS
    DE HAVEN, GLORIA
    PAYNE, JOHN
PAYNE, WILLIAM
    PAYNE, JOHN
PAYTON, BARBARA
    TONE, FRANCHOT
PEABODY, EMILY ELIZABETH
    STEWART, JAMES
PEARSON, ELLEN
    HAYWARD, SUSAN
PEARSON, RUTH
    ALEXANDER, JANE
PEARSON, SALLY
    COOPER, GLADYS
PEARSON, SIR NEVILLE
    COOPER, GLADYS
PECK, ANTHONY
    PECK, GREGORY
PECK, CAREY
    PECK, GREGORY
PECK, CECELIA
    PECK, GREGORY
PECK, JACK
    LONDON, JULIE
PECK, JONATHAN
    PECK, GREGORY
PECK, LYDELL
    GAYNOR, JANET
PECK, SR., GREGORY
    PECK, GREGORY
PECK, STEPHEN
    PECK, GREGORY
PEEL, ROBERT
    LILLIE, BEATRICE
PEEL, SIR ROBERT
    LILLIE, BEATRICE
PEISER, ALFRED
    PALMER, LILLI
PEISER, IRENE
    PALMER, LILLI
PELTCH, FRANCES
    LYNLEY, CAROL
PEMBERTON, MARTE
    BERKELEY, BUSBY
PENDERGAST, LESTER
    CRAWFORD, BRODERICK

PENNINO, FRANCESCO
    SHIRE, TALIA
PENNINO, ITALIA
    SHIRE, TALIA
PEOPLES, JOHN
    RUSSELL, JANE
PEPPARD, BRADFORD DAVIES
    ASHLEY, ELIZABETH
    PEPPARD, GEORGE
PEPPARD, CHRISTOPHER
    ASHLEY, ELIZABETH
    PEPPARD, GEORGE
PEPPARD, GEORGE
    ASHLEY, ELIZABETH
PEPPARD, JULIE LOUISE
    ASHLEY, ELIZABETH
    PEPPARD, GEORGE
PEPPARD, SR., GEORGE
    PEPPARD, GEORGE
PEREZ, JOSE LUIS
    CLAYTON, JAN
PEREZ, LUIS ROBERTO
    CLAYTON, JAN
PERKINS, ELVIS BROOKE
    PERKINS, TONY
PERKINS, MILLIE
    STOCKWELL, DEAN
PERKINS, OSGOOD
    PERKINS, TONY
PERKINS, OSGOOD ROBERT
    PERKINS, TONY
PERREAU, JANINE
    PERREAU, GIGI
PERREAU, ROBERT
    PERREAU, GIGI
PERRIN, NAT
    MARX, GROUCHO
PERRINE, KITTY JEWEL
    MIX, TOM
PERRINE, VALERIE
    BRIDGES, JEFF
PERRY, HENRIETTA
    CANOVA, JUDY
PERRY, JOAN
    HARVEY, LAURENCE
    HUNTER, TAB
PERRY, MARGARET
    MEREDITH, BURGESS
PERSKE, WILLIAM
    BACALL, LAUREN
PESCHKOWSKY, PAUL
    NICHOLS, MIKE
PETERS, FREDERICK
    LOMBARD, CAROLE
PETERS, FREDERICK C.
    LOMBARD, CAROLE
PETERS, JEAN
    HUGHES, HOWARD

PETERS, JON
    KRISTOFFERSON, KRIS
    STREISAND, BARBRA
PETERS, LAURI
    VOIGHT, JON
PETERS, STUART
    LOMBARD, CAROLE
PETERSEN, CARL BRISSON
    RUSSELL, ROSALIND
PETERSON, JOHN
    CAULFIELD, JOAN
PETERSON, ROBERT
    CAULFIELD, JOAN
PETIT, MARGARET
    CARON, LESLIE
PETREY, EURA MILDRED
    NEAL, PATRICIA
PETTET, JOANNA
    CORD, ALEX
PHILBIN, MARY
    WILLIAMS, GUINN 'BIG BOY'
PHILENA, LUCILLE
    STONE, LEWIS
PHILLIPE, ANDRE
    GARLAND, JUDY
PHILLIPS, CHYNA
    PHILLIPS, MICHELLE
PHILLIPS, JOHN
    PHILLIPS, MICHELLE
PHILLIPS, MACKENZIE
    PHILLIPS, MICHELLE
PHILLIPS, MARY
    BOGART, HUMPHREY
PHILLIPS, MICHELLE
    BEATTY, WARREN
    HOPPER, DENNIS
    NICHOLSON, JACK
PHILLIPS, SIAN
    O'TOOLE, PETER
PHILLIPS, TITA
    PURDOM, EDMUND
PIAF, EDITH
    AZNAVOUR, CHARLES
PIALOGLOU, JOHN
    TALMADGE, CONSTANCE
    TALMADGE, NORMA
PICCIONI, PIERO
    VALLI, ALIDA
PICKARD, HELENA
    HARDWICKE, CEDRIC
PICKENS, DARYLE ANN
    PICKENS, SLIM
PICKENS, MARGARET LOUISE
    PICKENS, SLIM
PICKENS, THOMAS MICHAEL
    PICKENS, SLIM
PICKFORD, JACK
    DANIELS, BEBE

PICKFORD, MARY
    CRAWFORD, JOAN
    FAIRBANKS, DOUGLAS
    FAIRBANKS, JR., DOUGLAS
    GOLDWYN, SAMUEL
PICKLES, EDNA
    PIDGEON, WALTER
PICONE, JOSEPH
    EVANS, ROBERT
PIDGEON, CALEB BURPEE
    PIDGEON, WALTER
PIDGEON, CHARLES
    PIDGEON, WALTER
PIDGEON, DAVID
    PIDGEON, WALTER
PIDGEON, EDNA VERNE
    PIDGEON, WALTER
PIERANGELI, LUIGI
    ANGELI, PIER
PIERANGELI, PATRICIA
    ANGELI, PIER
    AUMONT, JEAN-PIERRE
    PAVAN, MARISA
PIEROSE, GEORGE
    DRU, JOANNE
PIGNATARI, FRANCISCO 'BABY'
    CHRISTIAN, LINDA
PIKE, GEORGINA
    DENNY, REGINALD
PILCHARD, FRANCES
    FERRER, MEL
PINE, VIRGINIA
    RAFT, GEORGE
PINKETT, JOHN RANDOLPH
    BAILEY, PEARL
PINZA, CELIA
    PINZA, EZIO
PINZA, CESARE
    PINZA, EZIO
PINZA, CLAUDIA
    PINZA, EZIO
PINZA, EZIO PIETRO
    PINZA, EZIO
PINZA, GLORIA
    PINZA, EZIO
PITMAN, ELEANOR
    ROBARDS, JR., JASON
PITTS, ZASU
    FRANCIS THE MULE
    LA MARR, BARBARA
PLANT, PETER BENNETT
    BENNETT, CONSTANCE
    ROLAND, GILBERT
PLANT, PHILIP MORGAN HAYWARD
    BENNETT, CONSTANCE
    BENNETT, JOAN
    BENNETT, RICHARD

PLANT, PHILIP MORGAN HAYWARD
    WINDSOR, CLAIRE
PLEMIANIKOFF, ROGER VADIM
    BARDOT, BRIGITTE
PLESHETTE, EUGENE
    DONAHUE, TROY
    PLESHETTE, SUZANNE
PLESHETTE, SUZANNE
    DONAHUE, TROY
PLOWRIGHT, JOAN
    OLIVIER, LAURENCE
PLUMMER, AMANDA
    PLUMMER, CHRISTOPHER
PLUMMER, JOHN
    PLUMMER, CHRISTOPHER
POITIER, BEVERLY
    POITIER, SIDNEY
POITIER, PAMELA
    POITIER, SIDNEY
POITIER, REGINALD
    POITIER, SIDNEY
POITIER, SHERRY
    POITIER, SIDNEY
POITIER, SIDNEY
    NEWMAN, PAUL
POLANSKI, ROMAN
    DUNAWAY, FAYE
    TATE, SHARON
POLENA, PAUL
    MARTIN, DEAN
POLETTE, EDITH
    CRENNA, RICHARD
POLTE, GEORGE
    PROWSE, JULIET
PONTI, CARLO
    DE LAURENTIIS, DINO
    LOREN, SOPHIA
PONTI, EDOUARDO
    LOREN, SOPHIA
PONTI, JR., CARLO
    LOREN, SOPHIA
POOLE, ELSIE M.
    SANDERS, GEORGE
POPE, IRENE
    O'NEILL, JENNIFER
POPE, LILLIAN
    MOORE, ROGER
PORCHIA, LOUIS A.
    HALEY, JACK
PORTAGO, MARQUIS ALFONSO DE
    CHRISTIAN, LINDA
PORTER, COLE
    WOOLLEY, MONTY
PORTER, LILLIAN
    HAYDEN, RUSSELL
PORTES GIL, EMILIO
    JURADO, KATY

POSILLICO, ANGELA
    HARPER, VALERIE
POST, MARJORIE
    MERRILL, DINA
POST, WILEY
    ROGERS, WILL
POTTER, PETER
    ASTAIRE, FRED
POTTER, PHYLLIS BAKER
    ASTAIRE, FRED
POWELL, CLARENCE
    POWELL, ELEANOR
POWELL, CYNTHIA
    LENNON, JOHN
POWELL, DICK
    ALLYSON, JUNE
    BLONDELL, JOAN
    TAYLOR, ROBERT
POWELL, ELEANOR
    FORD, GLENN
POWELL, ELLEN
    ALLYSON, JUNE
    BLONDELL, JOAN
    POWELL, DICK
POWELL, EWING
    POWELL, DICK
POWELL, HORATIO WARREN
    POWELL, WILLIAM
POWELL, HOWARD
    POWELL, DICK
POWELL, JANE
    NELSON, GENE
POWELL, JR., RICHARD KEITH
    ALLYSON, JUNE
    POWELL, DICK
POWELL, PAMELA
    ALLYSON, JUNE
    POWELL, DICK
POWELL, WILLIAM
    COLMAN, RONALD
    HARLOW, JEAN
    LOMBARD, CAROLE
    LOY, MYRNA
    RAINER, LUISE
POWELL, WILLIAM DAVID
    POWELL, WILLIAM
POWER, ANNE
    POWER, TYRONE
    WERNER, OSKAR
POWER, FREDERICK TYRONE EDMOND
    POWER, TYRONE
POWER, ROMINA
    CHRISTIAN, LINDA
    POWER, TYRONE
    PURDOM, EDMUND
POWER, TARYN
    CHRISTIAN, LINDA

POWER, TARYN
    POWER, TYRONE
    PURDOM, EDMUND
POWER, TYRONE
    CHRISTIAN, LINDA
    GAYNOR, JANET
    HENIE, SONJA
    ROMERO, CESAR
    WERNER, OSKAR
POWER, 3RD, TYRONE
    POWER, TYRONE
POWERS, GEORGE
    POWERS, MALA
POWERS, STEPHANIE
    HOLDEN, WILLIAM
PRATT, ALICIA
    BUTTONS, RED
PRATT, CHARLES RARY
    KARLOFF, BORIS
PRATT, DAVID CAMERON
    KARLOFF, BORIS
PRATT, EDWARD
    KARLOFF, BORIS
PRATT, EDWARD MILLARD
    KARLOFF, BORIS
PRATT, ELIZA JULIA
    KARLOFF, BORIS
PRATT, EMMA CAROLINE
    KARLOFF, BORIS
PRATT, FREDERICK GRENVILLE
    KARLOFF, BORIS
PRATT, GEORGE MARLOW
    KARLOFF, BORIS
PRATT, JENNIE MAE 'BETTY'
    ABBOTT, BUD
PRATT, JOHN THOMAS
    KARLOFF, BORIS
PRATT, JR., EDWARD
    KARLOFF, BORIS
PRATT, JULIA HONORIA
    KARLOFF, BORIS
PRATT, RICHARD SEPTIMUS
    KARLOFF, BORIS
PREMINGER, ERIK KIRKLAND
    HAVOC, JUNE
    LEE, GYPSY ROSE
    PREMINGER, OTTO
PREMINGER, MARK
    PREMINGER, OTTO
PREMINGER, OTTO
    LEE, GYPSY ROSE
PREMINGER, VICTORIA
    PREMINGER, OTTO
PRENDERGAST, HONORE
    AMECHE, DON
PRENTISS, PAULA
    BENJAMIN, RICHARD

PRESLEY, JESS GARON
    PRESLEY, ELVIS
PRESLEY, LISA MARIE
    PRESLEY, ELVIS
PRESLEY, VERNON ELVIS
    PRESLEY, ELVIS
PRESSLEY, JUNITA
    MARTIN, MARY
PRESSMAN, DR. JOEL
    COLBERT, CLAUDETTE
PREVIN, ANDRE
    FARROW, MIA
    O'SULLIVAN, MAUREEN
PREVIN, GIGI
    FARROW, MIA
    O'SULLIVAN, MAUREEN
PREVIN, KYM LARK
    FARROW, MIA
    O'SULLIVAN, MAUREEN
PREVIN, MATTHEW PHINEAS
    FARROW, MIA
    O'SULLIVAN, MAUREEN
PREVIN, SASCHA VILLIERS
    FARROW, MIA
    O'SULLIVAN, MAUREEN
PRICE, BRONWYN FITZSIMMONS
    O'HARA, MAUREEN
PRICE, HARRIET
    PRICE, VINCENT
PRICE, JAMES
    PRICE, VINCENT
PRICE, JR., BAMLET L.
    FRANCIS, ANNE
PRICE, LAURA LOUISE
    PRICE, VINCENT
PRICE, LEONTYNE
    WARFIELD, WILLIAM
PRICE, MARY VICTORIA
    PRICE, VINCENT
PRICE, VINCENT B.
    PRICE, VINCENT
PRICE, VINCENT LEONARD
    PRICE, VINCENT
PRICE, WILL
    O'HARA, MAUREEN
PRICHARD, MARGARET
    BOONE, PAT
PRINGLE, AILEEN
    TALMADGE, CONSTANCE
PRINGLE, JOHN
    CLAIRE, INA
    GILBERT, JOHN
PROPPER, FRANCES
    RAINS, CLAUDE
PROUSE, JULIET
    SINATRA, FRANK
PROVINE, DOROTHY
    SINATRA, FRANK

PROWSE, CLIVE
    PROWSE, JULIET
PROWSE, REGINALD
    PROWSE, JULIET
PRYOR, ARTHUR
    SOTHERN, ANN
PRYOR, ELIZABETH A'NNE
    PRYOR, RICHARD
PRYOR, FLORENCE
    STONE, LEWIS
PRYOR, JR., RICHARD
    PRYOR, RICHARD
PRYOR, RAIN
    PRYOR, RICHARD
PRYOR, ROGER
    SOTHERN, ANN
PUMPHREY, JR., MARSHALL
    MCLAGLEN, VICTOR
PUMPHREY, MARGARET
    MCLAGLEN, VICTOR
PURDOM, C. B.
    PURDOM, EDMUND
PURDOM, EDMUND
    CHRISTIAN, LINDA
PURDOM, LILIAN
    PURDOM, EDMUND
PURDOM, MARINA
    PURDOM, EDMUND
PURVIANCE, EDNA
    CHAPLIN, CHARLES
PUTCH, JOHN
    STAPLETON, JEAN
PUTCH, PAMELA
    STAPLETON, JEAN
PUTCH, WILLIAM
    STAPLETON, JEAN
QUARRY, MIRANDA
    SELLERS, PETER
QUEDENS, CHARLES PETER
    ARDEN, EVE
QUEST, ANNIE ELIZA
    COURTENAY, TOM
QUIGLEY, JR., THOMAS
    ALEXANDER, JANE
QUIGLEY, PAMELA
    ALEXANDER, JANE
QUIGLEY, THOMAS BARTLETT
    ALEXANDER, JANE
QUINE, RICHARD
    HAYMES, DICK
QUINN, ANTHONY
    DE MILLE, C. B.
    KEYES, EVELYN
QUINN, CHRISTINA
    DE MILLE, C. B.
    QUINN, ANTHONY
QUINN, CHRISTOPHER
    DE MILLE, C. B.

QUINN, CHRISTOPHER
    QUINN, ANTHONY
QUINN, DANIELE
    QUINN, ANTHONY
QUINN, DUNCAN
    DE MILLE, C. B.
    QUINN, ANTHONY
QUINN, FRANCESCO
    QUINN, ANTHONY
QUINN, FRANK
    QUINN, ANTHONY
QUINN, KATHLEEN
    DE MILLE, C. B.
    QUINN, ANTHONY
QUINN, LORENZO
    QUINN, ANTHONY
QUINN, STELLA
    QUINN, ANTHONY
QUINN, VALENTINA
    DE MILLE, C. B.
    QUINN, ANTHONY
RACETTE, FRANCINE
    SUTHERLAND, DONALD
RACKMIL, MILTON R.
    BLAINE, VIVIAN
RADIN, ANNE
    LEVANT, OSCAR
RADOVICH, ADRIENNE
    HALEY, JACK
RADOVICH, MILAN
    HALEY, JACK
RAFFERTY, FRANCES
    BYINGTON, SPRING
RAFFERTY, JR., MAXWELL
    RAFFERTY, FRANCES
RAFFERTY, MAXWELL A.
    RAFFERTY, FRANCES
RAFT, GEORGE
    GRABLE, BETTY
    LOMBARD, CAROLE
    SHEARER, NORMA
RAGEN, MAE
    VANCE, VIVIAN
RAGUSA, ANN GARDNER
    PRENTISS, PAULA
RAGUSA, THOMAS J.
    PRENTISS, PAULA
RAINER, III, PRINCE
    KELLY, GRACE
RAINS, FREDERICK WILLIAM
    RAINS, CLAUDE
RAINS, JENNIFER
    RAINS, CLAUDE
RALSTON, MARCIA
    HARRIS, PHIL
RAMBEAU, MARJORIE
    MACK, WILLARD

RAMIREZ, DARREN
    ROBERTS, RACHEL
RAMZI, SOHAIR
    SHARIF, OMAR
RANCOURT, DONNA GRANOUCCI
    BORGNINE, ERNEST
RANDALL, ADDISON 'JACK'
    BENNETT, CONSTANCE
    BENNETT, JOAN
    ROSENBLOOM, 'SLAPSIE' MAXIE
RANDALL, JAMES
    PERKINS, TONY
RANDALL, STARLITE
    PERKINS, TONY
RANDALL, TONY
    MATTHAU, WALTER
RANDOM, IDA
    BRIDGES, JEFF
RANE, JANET
    PERKINS, TONY
RANFT, ANTHONY
    RAFT, GEORGE
RANFT, CATHERINE
    RAFT, GEORGE
RANFT, CONRAD
    RAFT, GEORGE
RANFT, JOSEPH
    RAFT, GEORGE
RANFT, MICHAEL
    RAFT, GEORGE
RANFT, WILLIAM
    RAFT, GEORGE
RANKIN, ARTHUR
    HART, WILLIAM S.
    REID, WALLACE
RANKIN, DORIS
    BARRYMORE, ETHEL
    BARRYMORE, JOHN
    BARRYMORE, LIONEL
RANKIN, PHYLLIS
    HART, WILLIAM S.
    REID, WALLACE
RAPHAEL, IDA
    CAESAR, SID
RAPP, PAUL
    ADAMS, NICK
RAPPE, GRETA
    VON SYDOW, MAX
RAPPE, VIRGINIA
    ARBUCKLE, FATTY
RASE, BETTY JANE
    ROONEY, MICKEY
RATHBONE, CYNTHIA BARBARA
    RATHBONE, BASIL
RATHBONE, EDGAR PHILIP
    RATHBONE, BASIL
RATHBONE, RODION
    RATHBONE, BASIL

RATHGEBER, RALPH
    MEEKER, RALPH
RAUSE, RANDOLPH
    MEADOWS, AUDREY
    MEADOWS, JAYNE
RAVER, LUCILLE
    GOULD, ELLIOT
RAWLEY, INA
    LADD, ALAN
RAWLINGS, JUDITH
    DAMONE, VIC
RAY, ANTHONY
    GRAHAME, GLORIA
RAY, NICHOLAS
    GRAHAME, GLORIA
RAY, TIMOTHY NICHOLAS
    GRAHAME, GLORIA
RAYE, THELMA
    COLMAN, RONALD
RAYMOND, AILEEN
    MILLS, JOHN
RAYMOND, GENE
    MACDONALD, JEANETTE
REA, RUTH
    PRESTON, ROBERT
READ, ADA
    DURBIN, DEANNA
READ, JR., ALFRED C.
    WINDSOR, CLAIRE
READ, MARIAN YOUNG
    WINDSOR, CLAIRE
READE, DOLORES
    HOPE, BOB
REAGAN, J. NEIL
    REAGAN, RONALD
REAGAN, JOHN EDWARD
    REAGAN, RONALD
REAGAN, JR., RONALD
    REAGAN, RONALD
REAGAN, MAUREEN
    REAGAN, RONALD
    WYMAN, JANE
REAGAN, MICHAEL
    REAGAN, RONALD
    WYMAN, JANE
REAGAN, PATRICIA
    REAGAN, RONALD
REAGAN, RONALD
    MOORE, COLLEEN
    WYMAN, JANE
REAMES, STANLEY
    LEIGH, JANET
REAUME, HELEN EMMA
    POWER, TYRONE
REDDY, ANTONIA LAMOND
    REDDY, HELEN
REDDY, MAX
    REDDY, HELEN

REDFORD, AMY
    REDFORD, ROBERT
REDFORD, CHARLES
    REDFORD, ROBERT
REDFORD, JAIMIE
    REDFORD, ROBERT
REDFORD, SCOTT
    REDFORD, ROBERT
REDFORD, SHAUNA
    REDFORD, ROBERT
REDFORD, WILLIAM
    REDFORD, ROBERT
REDGRAVE, COLIN
    REDGRAVE, LYNN
    REDGRAVE, MICHAEL
    REDGRAVE, VANESSA
REDGRAVE, LYNN
    REDGRAVE, MICHAEL
    REDGRAVE, VANESSA
REDGRAVE, MICHAEL
    REDGRAVE, LYNN
    REDGRAVE, VANESSA
REDGRAVE, ROY
    REDGRAVE, MICHAEL
REDGRAVE, VANESSA
    REDGRAVE, LYNN
    REDGRAVE, MICHAEL
REED, DAVID
    REED, OLIVER
REED, LILIAN
    CHATTERTON, RUTH
REED, MARK
    REED, OLIVER
REED, MAXWELL
    COLLINS, JOAN
REED, OLIVER
    HARRIS, RICHARD
REED, PATRICIA
    SCOTT, GEORGE C.
REED, PETER
    RAYE, MARTHA
    REED, OLIVER
REED, SARAH
    REED, OLIVER
REED, SIMON
    REED, OLIVER
REED, SIR CAROL
    REED, OLIVER
REED, TRACY
    REED, OLIVER
REEMAN, HELEN
    TWIGGY
REESE-WILLIAMS, JOAN ELIZABETH
    HARRIS, RICHARD
    HARRISON, REX
REEVES, MYRTLE
    HARDY, OLIVER

REEVES, RUTH
    BARRYMORE, JOHN
    COSTELLO, DOLORES
REGE, HELEN
    COSTELLO, LOU
REID, JAMES HALLECK
    REID, WALLACE
REID, JR., WILLIAM WALLACE
    HART, WILLIAM S.
    REID, WALLACE
REIF, ELSIE
    BLACK, KAREN
REILLY, ROSE
    DAVIES, MARION
REINER, CHARLES
    REINER, CARL
REINER, IRVING
    REINER, CARL
REINER, LUCAS
    REINER, CARL
REINER, ROB
    REINER, CARL
REINER, SYLVIA A.
    REINER, CARL
REISE, EMMA
    WYMAN, JANE
RELINS, VEIT
    SCHELL, MARIA
REMARQUE, ERICH MARIA
    DIETRICH, MARLENE
    GODDARD, PAULETTE
REMICK, BRUCE
    REMICK, LEE
REMICK, FRANK E.
    REMICK, LEE
RENALDO, EDWIN
    RENALDO, DUNCAN
RENALDO, JEREMY
    RENALDO, DUNCAN
RENALDO, RICHARD
    RENALDO, DUNCAN
RENALDO, STEPHANIE
    RENALDO, DUNCAN
RENNIE, DAVID
    RENNIE, MICHAEL
RENNIE, JAMES
    GISH, DOROTHY
    GISH, LILLIAN
    RENNIE, MICHAEL
RENNIE, MICHAEL
    PREMINGER, OTTO
RENTZELL, LANCE
    HEATHERTON, JOEY
REUBENFINE, DR.
    MAY, ELAINE
REVENTLOW, LANCE
    SAINT JOHN, JILL

REVILLE, ALMA
    HITCHCOCK, ALFRED
REVSON, JENNIFER
    GUARDINO, HARRY
REVSON, JULIE
    GUARDINO, HARRY
REVSON, MARTIN
    GUARDINO, HARRY
REVSON, PETER
    GUARDINO, HARRY
REYNOLDS, BURT
    FAWCETT-MAJORS, FARRAH
    SHORE, DINAH
    STEVENS, INGER
REYNOLDS, BURTON 'BURT'
    REYNOLDS, BURT
REYNOLDS, DEBBIE
    ANGELI, PIER
    FISHER, EDDIE
    WAGNER, ROBERT
REYNOLDS, JOYCE
    PITTS, ZASU
REYNOLDS, RAYMOND F.
    REYNOLDS, DEBBIE
REYNOLDS, WILLIAM
    REYNOLDS, DEBBIE
RICE, EVA MARIE
    SAINT, EVA MARIE
RICH, DORIS
    CARRADINE, JOHN
RICHARD, JEAN-LOUIS
    MOREAU, JEANNE
RICHARD, JEROME
    MOREAU, JEANNE
RICHARD, TERRY
    FISHER, EDDIE
RICHARDS, WILLIAM
    ROTH, LILLIAN
RICHARDSON, AMBROSE
    RICHARDSON, RALPH
RICHARDSON, ARTHUR
    RICHARDSON, RALPH
RICHARDSON, CHARLES DAVID
    RICHARDSON, RALPH
RICHARDSON, CHRISTOPHER
    RICHARDSON, RALPH
RICHARDSON, JOELY KIM
    REDGRAVE, MICHAEL
    REDGRAVE, VANESSA
RICHARDSON, NATASHA
    REDGRAVE, MICHAEL
    REDGRAVE, VANESSA
RICHARDSON, TONY
    REDGRAVE, LYNN
    REDGRAVE, MICHAEL
    REDGRAVE, VANESSA
RICHMOND, GENEVIEVE WINIFRED
    CARRADINE, JOHN

RICKARD, GWENDOLYN
    BOLGER, RAY
RID, JOANNE
    LIBERACE
RIDDLE, BETTY JANE
    CONNORS, CHUCK
RIEGLER, MIRIAM
    BIKEL, THEODORE
RIGG, LOUIS
    RIGG, DIANA
RIJN, JOHANNA VAN
    SLEZAK, WALTER
RILEY, ANNA MAE
    KITT, EARTHA
RILEY, LEWIS
    DEL RIO, DOLORES
RINEHART, MARCELLA
    PARKER, FESS
RIPLEY, JAMES
    CANOVA, JUDY
RISKIN, JR., ROBERT
    WRAY, FAY
RISKIN, ROBERT
    LOMBARD, CAROLE
    ROGERS, GINGER
    WRAY, FAY
RISKIN, VICKI
    WRAY, FAY
RITCHIE, ROBERT
    MACDONALD, JEANETTE
RITTER, CHARLES
    RITTER, THELMA
RITTER, JONATHAN
    RITTER, TEX
RITTER, THOMAS
    RITTER, TEX
RIVERA, DIEGO
    FLYNN, ERROL
RIVERO, DIANA CANOVA
    CANOVA, JUDY
RIVERO, FHILIP
    CANOVA, JUDY
RIZZO, FRANCES MARIE
    RANDALL, TONY
ROACH, HAL
    LLOYD, HAROLD
ROBARDS, DAVID
    BACALL, LAUREN
    ROBARDS, JR., JASON
ROBARDS, III, JASON
    BACALL, LAUREN
    ROBARDS, JR., JASON
ROBARDS, JAKE
    ROBARDS, JR., JASON
ROBARDS, JR., JASON
    BACALL, LAUREN
ROBARDS, SAM
    BACALL, LAUREN

ROBARDS, SAM
    ROBARDS, JR., JASON
ROBARDS, SARA LOUISE
    BACALL, LAUREN
    ROBARDS, JR., JASON
ROBARDS, SHANNON
    ROBARDS, JR., JASON
ROBARDS, SR., JASON
    ROBARDS, JR., JASON
ROBER, RICHARD
    BARTHELMESS, RICHARD
ROBERTS, PAUL
    BURSTYN, ELLEN
ROBERTS, RACHEL
    HARRISON, REX
ROBERTS, RICHARD RHYS
    ROBERTS, RACHEL
ROBERTSON, ALAN
    NEAGLE, ANNA
ROBERTSON, CHESTER
    ROBERTSON, DALE
ROBERTSON, CLIFF
    MERRILL, DINA
ROBERTSON, CLIFFORD
    ROBERTSON, CLIFF
ROBERTSON, HEATHER
    MERRILL, DINA
    ROBERTSON, CLIFF
ROBERTSON, HERBERT WILLIAM
    NEAGLE, ANNA
ROBERTSON, MELVIN
    ROBERTSON, DALE
ROBERTSON, MERLE
    DARNELL, LINDA
ROBERTSON, REBEL LEE
    ROBERTSON, DALE
ROBERTSON, ROCHELLE
    ROBERTSON, DALE
ROBERTSON, ROXY
    ROBERTSON, DALE
ROBERTSON, STEPHANIE
    MERRILL, DINA
    ROBERTSON, CLIFF
ROBERTSON, STUART
    NEAGLE, ANNA
ROBESON, BENJAMIN
    ROBESON, PAUL
ROBESON, JR., PAUL 'PAULI'
    ROBESON, PAUL
ROBESON, JR., WILLIAM DREW
    ROBESON, PAUL
ROBESON, MARION
    ROBESON, PAUL
ROBESON, REEVE 'REED'
    ROBESON, PAUL
ROBESON, WILLIAM DREW
    ROBESON, PAUL

ROBINSON, FRANCESCA
    ROBINSON, EDWARD G.
ROBINSON, GERTRUDE
    LEIGH, VIVIEN
ROBINSON, HUBBELL
    WHITING, MARGARET
ROBINSON, JR, EDWARD G. 'MANNY
    ROBINSON, EDWARD G.
ROBINSON, JULIE
    BELAFONTE, HARRY
ROBINSON, NADINE
    COLE, NAT 'KING'
ROBISON, LIDA MARY
    CARMICHAEL, HOAGY
RODER, ERVIN
    ADAMS, NICK
RODIER, ESTHER
    DAILEY, DAN
ROGARD, FOLKE
    LINDFORS, VIVECA
ROGARD, JAN
    LINDFORS, VIVECA
ROGARD, LENA
    LINDFORS, VIVECA
ROGERS, CHARLES 'BUDDY'
    PICKFORD, MARY
    WINDSOR, CLAIRE
ROGERS, CHERYL DARLENE
    EVANS, DALE
    ROGERS, ROY
ROGERS, CLEM VANN
    ROGERS, WILL
ROGERS, DEBORAH
    EVANS, DALE
    ROGERS, ROY
ROGERS, GINGER
    ASTAIRE, FRED
    AYRES, LEW
    HAYWORTH, RITA
    HUGHES, HOWARD
    MONTGOMERY, GEORGE
ROGERS, JAMES
    ROGERS, WILL
ROGERS, JOHN
    EVANS, DALE
    ROGERS, ROY
ROGERS, JOHN LOGAN
    ROGERS, GINGER
ROGERS, JR., ROY
    EVANS, DALE
    ROGERS, ROY
ROGERS, JR., WILL
    ROGERS, WILL
ROGERS, LENORA
    SCHILDKRAUT, JOSEPH
ROGERS, LINDA LOU
    EVANS, DALE

ROGERS, LINDA LOU
   ROGERS, ROY
ROGERS, MARGARET
   FURNESS, BETTY
ROGERS, MARION
   EVANS, DALE
   ROGERS, ROY
ROGERS, MARY
   ROGERS, WILL
ROGERS, MARY LITTLE DOE
   EVANS, DALE
   ROGERS, ROY
ROGERS, MILLICENT
   GABLE, CLARK
ROGERS, ROBIN
   EVANS, DALE
   ROGERS, ROY
ROGERS, RONALD PICKFORD
   PICKFORD, MARY
ROGERS, ROXANNE PICKFORD
   PICKFORD, MARY
ROGERS, ROY
   AUTRY, GENE
   EVANS, DALE
ROGERS, SCOTT WARD
   EVANS, DALE
   ROGERS, ROY
ROGERS, VIRGINIA RUTH
   LAUREL, STAN
ROGERS, WILL
   AUTRY, GENE
   FETCHIT, STEPIN
   MCCREA, JOEL
ROHE, MARTIN F.
   VERA-ELLEN
ROHRER, VERNELLE
   PEPPARD, GEORGE
ROLAND, GILBERT
   BENNETT, CONSTANCE
   BENNETT, JOAN
   BENNETT, RICHARD
   BOW, CLARA
   NIVEN, DAVID
   TALMADGE, NORMA
ROLAND, GYL CHRISTINA
   BENNETT, CONSTANCE
   ROLAND, GILBERT
ROLAND, LORINDA ALONZO
   BENNETT, CONSTANCE
   ROLAND, GILBERT
ROLDAN, FRANCISCA
   CARRILLO, LEO
ROLLO, PRIMULA
   NIVEN, DAVID
ROMAN, ANNA
   ROMAN, RUTH
ROMAN, ANTHONY
   ROMAN, RUTH

ROMAN, EVE
   ROMAN, RUTH
ROMERO, BOLIVAR SIMON
   ROMERO, CESAR
ROMERO, CAESAR JULIUS
   ROMERO, CESAR
ROMERO, EDUARDO S.
   ROMERO, CESAR
ROMERO, FRANKLIN BENJAMIN
   ROMERO, CESAR
ROMERO, GRACIELA
   ROMERO, CESAR
ROMERO, MARIA TERESA
   ROMERO, CESAR
ROMERO, NELSON HORATIO
   ROMERO, CESAR
ROMSHE, FRANCES ADA
   DILLER, PHYLLIS
ROONEY, JR., MICKEY
   ROONEY, MICKEY
ROONEY, KELLY ANN
   ROONEY, MICKEY
ROONEY, KERRY
   ROONEY, MICKEY
ROONEY, KIMMY SUE
   ROONEY, MICKEY
ROONEY, KYLE
   ROONEY, MICKEY
ROONEY, MICKEY
   FRANCIS THE MULE
   GARDNER, AVA
ROONEY, THEODORE
   ROONEY, MICKEY
ROONEY, TIMOTHY
   ROONEY, MICKEY
ROOSEVELT, ELLIOTT
   EMERSON, FAYE
ROQUEBRUNE, MICHELINE
   CONNERY, SEAN
ROSE, BILLY
   BRICE, FANNY
   HOLM, ELEANOR
ROSE, DAVID
   GARLAND, JUDY
   HAVER, JUNE
   RAYE, MARTHA
ROSE, STUART
   BOGART, HUMPHREY
ROSEN, DIANE
   STREISAND, BARBRA
ROSEN, HARLENE
   ALLEN, WOODY
ROSENBAUM, ESTELLE
   BLANC, MEL
ROSENBERG, DAVID
   BRICE, FANNY
   HOLM, ELEANOR

ROSENBLATT, LEA
   RENALDO, DUNCAN
ROSENSTEIN, SOPHIE
   YOUNG, GIG
ROSEWELL, DR. CHARLES
   VERDUGO, ELENA
ROSS, ARTHUR
   ROSS, DIANA
ROSS, CAULFIELD
   CAULFIELD, JOAN
ROSS, CHICO
   ROSS, DIANA
ROSS, DUDLEY
   ROSS, KATHARINE
ROSS, FRANK
   CAULFIELD, JOAN
ROSS, FRANK J.
   ARTHUR, JEAN
ROSS, FRED
   ROSS, DIANA
ROSS, FRED EARLL
   ROSS, DIANA
ROSS, RITA
   ROSS, DIANA
ROSSELLINI, INGRID ISOTTA
   BERGMAN, INGRID
ROSSELLINI, ISABELLA
   BERGMAN, INGRID
ROSSELLINI, JR., ROBERTO
   BERGMAN, INGRID
ROSSELLINI, ROBERTO
   BERGMAN, INGRID
   MAGNANI, ANNA
ROSSEN, CAROL
   HOLBROOK, HAL
ROSSEN, ROBERT
   HOLBROOK, HAL
ROSSITER, AIMEE
   O'NEILL, JENNIFER
ROSSITER, DEED
   O'NEILL, JENNIFER
ROSSON, HAL
   HARLOW, JEAN
ROSTOVA, MIRA
   CLIFT, MONTGOMERY
ROTH, HERMAN
   LA MARR, BARBARA
ROTHENBERG, STANFORD
   WRAY, FAY
ROTHSCHILD, CECILE DE
   GARBO, GRETA
ROTHSCHILD, VICTOR
   VERA-ELLEN
ROWAN, DAN
   LAWFORD, PETER
ROWAN, MARY
   LAWFORD, PETER

ROWE, GEORGE H.
   HOLBROOK, HAL
ROWLAND, ADELE
   RUGGLES, CHARLES
ROWLANDS, EDWIN MERWIN
   ROWLANDS, GENA
ROWTON, C. H.
   SHERIDAN, ANN
ROYAL, GLADYS
   YOUNG, LORETTA
RUBANIS, TEODORO
   MOREAU, JEANNE
RUBENS, ALMA
   CORTEZ, RICARDO
RUBENSTEIN, BLANCHE
   WHITE, PEARL
RUBIN, CHRISTOPHER
   BRUCE, VIRGINIA
RUBIN, J. WALTER
   BRUCE, VIRGINIA
RUBIROSA, PORFIRIO
   GABOR, ZSA ZSA
RUDAS, CHRIS
   HARRIS, RICHARD
RUELLE, DANIELLE DE
   PERREAU, GIGI
RUELLE, GENE DE
   PERREAU, GIGI
RUELLE, KEITH DE
   PERREAU, GIGI
RUGGIERO, LOUIS A.
   ANDREWS, LAVERNE
   ANDREWS, MAXENE
   ANDREWS, PATRICIA
RUGGLES, CHARLES
   STONE, LEWIS
RUGGLES, WESLEY
   RUGGLES, CHARLES
RUMBOUGH, JR., STANLEY M.
   MERRILL, DINA
RUMBOUGH, NINA
   MERRILL, DINA
RUMBOUGH, STANLEY D.
   MERRILL, DINA
RUSCHA, EDWARD
   EGGAR, SAMANTHA
RUSE, LILLIAN AUGUSTA
   AHERNE, BRIAN
   DE HAVILLAND, OLIVIA
   FONTAINE, JOAN
RUSH, BARBARA
   HUNTER, JEFFREY
RUSH, ROY L.
   RUSH, BARBARA
RUSSELL, CLARA
   RUSSELL, ROSALIND
RUSSELL, GAIL
   MADISON, GUY

RUSSELL, JAMES
    RUSSELL, JANE
RUSSELL, JOHN
    RUSSELL, ROSALIND
RUSSELL, JR., JAMES
    RUSSELL, ROSALIND
RUSSELL, KENNETH
    RUSSELL, JANE
RUSSELL, LEE
    MARSHALL, HERBERT
RUSSELL, LILLIAN
    DRESSLER, MARIE
RUSSELL, LYDIA
    RICHARDSON, RALPH
RUSSELL, MARY JANE
    RUSSELL, ROSALIND
RUSSELL, PAT
    DONAHUE, TROY
RUSSELL, REV. ROY WILLIAM
    RUSSELL, JANE
RUSSELL, SR., JAMES
    RUSSELL, ROSALIND
RUSSELL, THOMAS
    RUSSELL, JANE
RUSSELL, WALLACE
    RUSSELL, JANE
RUTHERFORD, JOHN D.
    RUTHERFORD, ANN
RUTSTEIN, ANN
    ROTH, LILLIAN
RUTSTEIN, ARTHUR
    ROTH, LILLIAN
RYAN, CHENEY
    RYAN, ROBERT
RYAN, JACK
    GABOR, EVA
    GABOR, ZSA ZSA
RYAN, JONATHAN
    RYAN, ROBERT
RYAN, LISA
    RYAN, ROBERT
RYAN, NITA
    CHEVALIER, MAURICE
RYAN, ROBERT
    O'SULLIVAN, MAUREEN
RYAN, SHEILA
    CAAN, JAMES
RYAN, TIMOTHY
    RYAN, ROBERT
RYAN, TIMOTHY A.
    RYAN, ROBERT
RYRHOLM, GERTRUDE
    EDWARDS, CLIFF
SAADA, CLAIRE
    SHARIF, OMAR
SACHS, EMMA
    BENNY, JACK

SACHS, ROLF
    BARDOT, BRIGITTE
SAENZ, JOSEPHINE
    WAYNE, JOHN
SAINT JOHN, JILL
    JONES, ALLAN
SAINT, ADELAIDE
    SAINT, EVA MARIE
SAINT, JOHN MERLE
    SAINT, EVA MARIE
SAKS, DANIEL
    ARTHUR, BEATRICE
SAKS, GENE
    ARTHUR, BEATRICE
SAKS, MATTHEW
    ARTHUR, BEATRICE
SALACETOS, JOSE
    MURRAY, MAE
SALAMAN, NERULA
    GUINNESS, ALEC
SALKIND, ILYA
    THAXTER, PHYLLIS
SALTER, HARRY
    LAWRENCE, FLORENCE
SALVATORE, GIUSEPPINA
    DE LAURENTIIS, DINO
SAMANIEGOS, ANTONIO
    NOVARRO, RAMON
SAMANIEGOS, CARMEN
    NOVARRO, RAMON
SAMANIEGOS, EDUARDO
    NOVARRO, RAMON
SAMANIEGOS, JOSE
    NOVARRO, RAMON
SAMANIEGOS, LENORE
    NOVARRO, RAMON
SAMANIEGOS, LUZ
    NOVARRO, RAMON
SAMANIEGOS, M. N.
    NOVARRO, RAMON
SAMANIEGOS, MARIANO
    NOVARRO, RAMON
SAMMARCELLI, JULIO
    VALENTINO, RUDOLPH
SAMUEL, MATILDA BEATRICE
    DE MILLE, C. B.
SAN GREGORIO, BARON NICOLA DI
    GINGOLD, HERMIONE
SAN JUAN, OLGA
    O'BRIEN, EDMOND
SANBORN, MARJORIE GWYNNE
    EWELL, TOM
SANCHEZ, ELVIRA
    DAVIS, JR., SAMMY
SANDERS, GEORGE
    GABOR, EVA
    GABOR, ZSA ZSA

SANDERS, GEORGE
    GABOR, ZSA ZSA
    HUME, BENITA
SANDERS, HENRY
    SANDERS, GEORGE
SANDERS, THOMAS CHARLES
    SANDERS, GEORGE
SANDS, BENNY
    SANDS, TOMMY
SANDS, TOMMY
    SINATRA, FRANK
SANFORD, FRED
    FOXX, REDD
SANFORD, JR., FRED
    FOXX, REDD
SANGLEL, BRYNA
    DOUGLAS, KIRK
SAPERSTEIN, REBECCA
    SIDNEY, SYLVIA
SARGEANT, JESSICA
    BARTHELMESS, RICHARD
SARGENT, HOWLAND
    LOY, MYRNA
SAROYAN, ARAN
    MATTHAU, WALTER
SAROYAN, CAROL GRACE MARCUS
    MATTHAU, WALTER
SARRAZIN, BERNARD
    SARRAZIN, MICHAEL
SARRAZIN, MICHAEL
    BISSET, JACQUELINE
SARZANA, MARIELLA DI
    BOYD, STEPHEN
SAUNDERS, JOHN MONK
    WRAY, FAY
SAUNDERS, SUSAN
    WRAY, FAY
SAURA, CARLOS
    CHAPLIN, GERALDINE
SAVALAS, CANDACE
    SAVALAS, TELLY
SAVALAS, CHRISTINA
    SAVALAS, TELLY
SAVALAS, CONSTANTINE 'GUS'
    SAVALAS, TELLY
SAVALAS, DEMOSTHENES 'GEORGE'
    SAVALAS, TELLY
SAVALAS, KATHERINE
    SAVALAS, TELLY
SAVALAS, NICHOLAS
    SAVALAS, TELLY
SAVALAS, NICHOLAS CONSTANTINE
    SAVALAS, TELLY
SAVALAS, PENELOPE
    SAVALAS, TELLY
SAVALAS, PRAXITELES 'TED'
    SAVALAS, TELLY

SAVALAS, TELLY
    FALK, PETER
SAVILLE, PHILIP
    RIGG, DIANA
SAVITCH, VLADIMIR 'SPIDER'
    LONGET, CLAUDINE
SCHAAK, EDWARD VAN
    SAINT CYR, LILI
SCHAAL, DICK
    HARPER, VALERIE
SCHAEFER, IDA
    PAYNE, JOHN
SCHAFER, NATALIE
    CALHERN, LOUIS
SCHAUDER, EILEEN ANN
    WINTERS, JONATHAN
SCHAUM, ROUSEVELLE
    DAHL, ARLENE
SCHAUM, ROUSEVELLE W.
    DAHL, ARLENE
SCHEIDER, MAXIMILIA
    SCHEIDER, ROY
SCHELL, HERMANN FERDINAND
    SCHELL, MARIA
    SCHELL, MAXIMILIAN
SCHELL, IMMY
    SCHELL, MARIA
    SCHELL, MAXIMILIAN
SCHELL, KARL
    SCHELL, MARIA
    SCHELL, MAXIMILIAN
SCHELL, MARIA
    SCHELL, MAXIMILIAN
SCHELL, MAXIMILIAN
    SCHELL, MARIA
SCHENCK, JOSEPH M.
    ARBUCKLE, FATTY
    MONROE, MARILYN
    TALMADGE, CONSTANCE
    TALMADGE, NORMA
SCHENCK, NICHOLAS M.
    TALMADGE, NORMA
SCHIFF, DOROTHY
    ROMAN, RUTH
SCHILDKRAUT, RUDOLPH
    SCHILDKRAUT, JOSEPH
SCHLEE, GEORGE
    GARBO, GRETA
SCHMIDT, LARS
    BERGMAN, INGRID
SCHNEIDER, ALEXANDER
    PAGE, GERALDINE
SCHNEIDER, BERT
    BERGEN, CANDICE
SCHNEIDER, CHARLES
    ARNOLD, EDWARD
SCHNEIDER, MAGDA
    SCHNEIDER, ROMY

SCHOENBERG, MINNIE
 MARX, CHICO
 MARX, GROUCHO
 MARX, GUMMO
 MARX, HARPO
 MARX, ZEPPO
SCHOLL, DANNY
 GRIFFITH, CORINNE
SCHORR, BERTHA
 WALLACH, ELI
SCHRAFFT, ELIZABETH
 MACRAE, GORDON
SCHREIBER, LETA MARIE
 GOSDEN, FREEMAN
SCHREUER, BETSY LEWIS
 BEL GEDDES, BARBARA
SCHREUER, CARL L.
 BEL GEDDES, BARBARA
SCHREUER, SUSAN
 BEL GEDDES, BARBARA
SCHRIFT, BLANCHE
 WINTERS, SHELLEY
SCHRIFT, JOHAN
 WINTERS, SHELLEY
SCHRIMPSHER, MARY
 ROGERS, WILL
SCHROEDER, MILDRED
 LAHR, BERT
SCHULTZ, MARY JOAN
 WILDER, GENE
SCHWARTZ, CHARLOTTE
 JESSEL, GEORGE
 TALMADGE, NORMA
SCHWARTZ, MONO
 CURTIS, TONY
SCHWARTZ, ROBERT
 CURTIS, TONY
SCHWARTZ, STEPHEN
 BURSTYN, ELLEN
SCHWENKER, JR., WILLIAM MORRIS
 MURRAY, MAE
SCICOLONE, ANNA MARIA
 LOREN, SOPHIA
SCICOLONE, RICARDO
 LOREN, SOPHIA
SCOT, PAT
 NICHOLS, MIKE
SCOTT, ADRIAN
 SHIRLEY, ANNE
SCOTT, ALBERT P.
 MOORE, COLLEEN
SCOTT, ALEXANDER
 DEWHURST, COLLEEN
 SCOTT, GEORGE C.
SCOTT, BERYL
 WEISSMULLER, JOHNNY
SCOTT, CAMPBELL
 DEWHURST, COLLEEN

SCOTT, CAMPBELL
 SCOTT, GEORGE C.
SCOTT, CHRISTOPHER
 SCOTT, RANDOLPH
SCOTT, DONALD P.
 CALVET, CORINNE
SCOTT, ENID
 SARRAZIN, MICHAEL
SCOTT, GEORGE
 SCOTT, RANDOLPH
SCOTT, GEORGE C.
 DEWHURST, COLLEEN
SCOTT, GEORGE D.
 SCOTT, GEORGE C.
SCOTT, GORDON
 MILES, VERA
SCOTT, JANETTE
 TORME, MEL
SCOTT, KATHRYN
 TOOMEY, REGIS
SCOTT, MARY
 HARDWICKE, CEDRIC
SCOTT, MICHAEL
 MILES, VERA
 SCOTT, GORDON
SCOTT, PATRICIA
 SEGAL, GEORGE
SCOTT, RANDOLPH
 LAMOUR, DOROTHY
SCOTT, SANDRA
 SCOTT, RANDOLPH
SCOTT, SHELLEY
 SCOTT, ZACHARY
SCOTT, WAVERLY
 SCOTT, ZACHARY
SCOTT, WILLIAM C.
 ROTH, LILLIAN
SCRIVEN, MAE
 KEATON, BUSTER
SCUDAMORE, MARGARET
 REDGRAVE, MICHAEL
SEBASTIAN, DAVID
 MIRANDA, CARMEN
SEBASTIAN, DOROTHY
 BOYD, WILLIAM
SEBERA, MINNIE
 MALDEN, KARL
SEBRING, JAY
 TATE, SHARON
SEGAL, ELIZABETH
 SEGAL, GEORGE
SEGAL, PATRICIA
 SEGAL, GEORGE
SEGAL, SR., GEORGE
 SEGAL, GEORGE
SEITER, CHRIS
 LA PLANTE, LAURA

SEITER, WILLIAM
 LA PLANTE, LAURA
SEKULOVICH, DANIEL
 MALDEN, KARL
SEKULOVICH, MILO
 MALDEN, KARL
SEKULOVICH, PETER
 MALDEN, KARL
SELBIE, EVELYN
 ANDERSON, 'BRONCO
SELBY, ANGELICA MARY
 BRUCE, NIGEL
SELIGER, LIZZIE
 ASNER, EDWARD
SELLERS, MICHAEL PETER
 EKLAND, BRITT
 SELLERS, PETER
SELLERS, PETER
 EKLAND, BRITT
SELLERS, SARAH JANE PETERS
 EKLAND, BRITT
 SELLERS, PETER
SELLERS, VICTORIA
 EKLAND, BRITT
 SELLERS, PETER
SELLERS, WILLIAM
 EKLAND, BRITT
 SELLERS, PETER
SELSMAN, JILL VICTORIA
 LYNLEY, CAROL
SELSMAN, MICHAEL
 LYNLEY, CAROL
SELWART, TONIO
 BANKHEAD, TALLULAH
SELWYN, EDGAR
 GOLDWYN, SAMUEL
SELZNICK, DAVID O.
 JONES, JENNIFER
 MAYER, LOUIS B.
SELZNICK, MARY JENNIFER
 JONES, JENNIFER
SELZNICK, MYRON
 POWELL, WILLIAM
SENNETT, MACK
 BERKELEY, BUSBY
 NORMAND, MABEL
SEYMOUR, FRANCES
 FONDA, HENRY
 FONDA, JANE
 FONDA, PETER
SHACKLEFORD, LENA
 DOUGLAS, MELVYN
SHAHOUB, JOSEPH
 SHARIF, OMAR
SHALLECK, BENJAMIN
 ROTH, LILLIAN
SHANE, CE CE
 HUSTON, JOHN

SHARIF, TAREK
 SHARIF, OMAR
SHARPE, ALMA
 DONAHUE, TROY
SHAUNESSEY, WINIFRED
 VALENTINO, RUDOLPH
SHAW, ALEXANDER
 SHAW, ROBERT
SHAW, ANTHONY
 LANSBURY, ANGELA
SHAW, ARTIE
 GARDNER, AVA
 GARLAND, JUDY
 GRABLE, BETTY
 KEYES, EVELYN
 TURNER, LANA
SHAW, CHARLES JANSEN
 SHAW, ROBERT
SHAW, DIEDRE
 LANSBURY, ANGELA
SHAW, ELIZABETH
 SHAW, ROBERT
SHAW, GEORGE BERNARD
 DAVIES, MARION
SHAW, HANNAH
 SHAW, ROBERT
SHAW, JOANNA
 SHAW, ROBERT
SHAW, JONATHAN DOWLING
 SHAW, ARTIE
SHAW, LUCIE
 LILLIE, BEATRICE
SHAW, PENNY
 SHAW, ROBERT
SHAW, PETER
 LANSBURY, ANGELA
SHAW, STEVEN KERN
 GARDNER, AVA
 SHAW, ARTIE
SHAW, THOMAS
 SHAW, ROBERT
SHAW, VICTORIA
 SMITH, ROGER
SHAW, WENDY
 SHAW, ROBERT
SHEA, MARGARET
 NOLAN, LLOYD
SHEAN, AL
 MARX, CHICO
 MARX, GROUCHO
 MARX, GUMMO
 MARX, HARPO
 MARX, ZEPPO
SHEARER, ANDREW
 SHEARER, NORMA
SHEARER, ATHOLE
 SHEARER, NORMA

SHEARER, DOUGLAS
    SHEARER, NORMA
SHEARER, NORMA
    GILBERT, JOHN
    NIVEN, DAVID
SHEARN, EDITH
    OLAND, WARNER
SHEFTEL, STUART
    FITZGERALD, GERALDINE
SHEFTEL, SUSAN
    FITZGERALD, GERALDINE
SHELDON, ELAINE
    IRELAND, JOHN
SHELTON, JOHN
    GRAYSON, KATHRYN
SHELTON, VIOLET
    BRUCE, NIGEL
SHENBERG, MARGARET
    MAYER, LOUIS B.
SHEPHERD, CYBILL
    BRIDGES, JEFF
SHEPHERD, WILLIAM JENNINGS
    SHEPHERD, CYBILL
SHERER, ROY
    HUDSON, ROCK
SHERIDAN, GEORGE W.
    SHERIDAN, ANN
SHERIDAN, JR., GEORGE
    SHERIDAN, ANN
SHERIDAN, KITTY
    SHERIDAN, ANN
SHERIDAN, MABEL
    SHERIDAN, ANN
SHERIDAN, PAULINE
    SHERIDAN, ANN
SHERIN, EDWIN
    ALEXANDER, JANE
SHERMAN, LOVELL
    COSTELLO, DOLORES
SHERRY, BARBARA DAVIS
    DAVIS, BETTE
SHERRY, WILLIAM GRANT
    DAVIS, BETTE
SHIDLER, JOHN
    DE CAMP, ROSEMARY
SHIDLER, MARGARET
    DE CAMP, ROSEMARY
SHIDLER, MARTHA
    DE CAMP, ROSEMARY
SHIDLER, NITA
    DE CAMP, ROSEMARY
SHIDLER, VALERIE
    DE CAMP, ROSEMARY
SHIELDS, ADOLPHUS
    FITZGERALD, BARRY
SHIELDS, ARTHUR
    FITZGERALD, BARRY

SHIELDS, UNA
    FITZGERALD, BARRY
SHIMKUS, JOANNA
    POITIER, SIDNEY
SHIPMAN, HELENA
    KEITH, BRIAN
SHIPPEY, FANNY
    HEFLIN, VAN
SHIRE, DAVID
    SHIRE, TALIA
SHIRE, MATTHEW ORLANDO
    SHIRE, TALIA
SHIRLEY, ANNE
    FURNESS, BETTY
    PAYNE, JOHN
SHOEMAKER, DOROTHY
    BAXTER, WARNER
SHORE, BESS
    SHORE, DINAH
SHORE, DINAH
    MONTGOMERY, GEORGE
    REYNOLDS, BURT
SHORE, S. A.
    SHORE, DINAH
SHOTWELL, ELIZABETH
    KOVACS, ERNIE
SIDNEY, SIGMUND
    SIDNEY, SYLVIA
SIEBER, MARIA
    DIETRICH, MARLENE
SIEBER, RUDOLPH
    DIETRICH, MARLENE
SIEGEL, CHARLES 'BUGSY'
    BARRIE, WENDY
SIEGEL, CHRISTOPHER
    LINDFORS, VIVECA
SIEGEL, DONALD
    LINDFORS, VIVECA
SIEGEL, HANNAH
    BURNS, GEORGE
SIEPMAN, ERIC
    HUME, BENITA
SIGNORET, GEORGETTE
    SIGNORET, SIMONE
SILBERMAN, WILLIAM J.
    WILDER, GENE
SILBERSTEIN, CHUDNEY LANE
    ROSS, DIANA
SILBERSTEIN, RHONDA SUZANNE
    ROSS, DIANA
SILBERSTEIN, ROBERT
    ROSS, DIANA
SILBERSTEIN, TRACEE JOY
    ROSS, DIANA
SILVERLAKE, SR., ARTHUR
    LAKE, ARTHUR
SILVERMAN, KATHERINE
    ROTH, LILLIAN

SILVERS, CANDICE
    SILVERS, PHIL
SILVERS, CATHERINE
    SILVERS, PHIL
SILVERS, LOREY LOCKE
    SILVERS, PHIL
SILVERS, NANCY ELIZABETH
    SILVERS, PHIL
SILVERS, TRACEY EDITH
    SILVERS, PHIL
SILVERSMITH, SAUL
    SILVERS, PHIL
SIMMONS, CHARLES
    SIMMONS, JEAN
SIMMONS, JEAN
    BOGARDE, DIRK
    GRANGER, STEWART
SIMON, CARLY
    KRISTOFFERSON, KRIS
SIMON, MARGARET CHRISTEN
    THOMAS, DANNY
SIMON, NEIL
    MASON, MARSHA
SIMON, NORTON
    JONES, JENNIFER
SIMON, SIMONE
    NIVEN, DAVID
SIMPSON, DOROTHY
    BRIDGES, JEFF
    BRIDGES, LLOYD
SINATRA, CHRISTINE
    FARROW, MIA
    GARDNER, AVA
    SINATRA, FRANK
SINATRA, FRANK
    COLBERT, CLAUDETTE
    FARROW, MIA
    FORD, GLENN
    GARDNER, AVA
    LAWFORD, PETER
    O'SULLIVAN, MAUREEN
    PROWSE, JULIET
    SANDS, TOMMY
SINATRA, JR., FRANK
    FARROW, MIA
    GARDNER, AVA
    SINATRA, FRANK
SINATRA, MARTIN ANTHONY
    SINATRA, FRANK
SINATRA, NANCY
    FARROW, MIA
    GARDNER, AVA
    SANDS, TOMMY
    SINATRA, FRANK
SINNOTT, GEORGE
    SENNETT, MACK
SINNOTT, JOHN
    SENNETT, MACK

SINNOTT, JOHN FRANCIS
    SENNETT, MACK
SINNOTT, MARY
    SENNETT, MACK
SISTOUARIS, NIKOLAS
    CHAPLIN, CHARLES
SIX, ROBERT F.
    MEADOWS, AUDREY
    MERMAN, ETHEL
SKELTON, JOSEPH
    SKELTON, RED
SKELTON, RICHARD
    SKELTON, RED
SKELTON, VALENTINA
    SKELTON, RED
SKOFIC, JR., MIRKO
    LOLLOBRIGIDA, GINA
SKOFIC, MIRKO
    LOLLOBRIGIDA, GINA
SKYLAR, JOANNE-ALEX
    PACINO, AL
SLEDGE, ADELINE EUGENIA
    BANKHEAD, TALLULAH
SLEZAK, ERICA
    SLEZAK, WALTER
SLEZAK, INGRID
    SLEZAK, WALTER
SLEZAK, LEO
    SLEZAK, WALTER
SLEZAK, LEO LAURITZ WALTER
    SLEZAK, WALTER
SLEZAK, MARGARETE
    SLEZAK, WALTER
SLIMS, BERNICE
    FETCHIT, STEPIN
SLOAN, MICHAEL
    STONE, FRED
SLYE, ANDREW E.
    ROGERS, ROY
SLYE, MARY
    ROGERS, ROY
SMALE, KATHLEEN ROSE
    KERR, DEBORAH
SMALE, PHYLLIS
    KERR, DEBORAH
SMALL, EDWARD
    CRABBE, BUSTER
SMITH, ALEXIS
    RAFFERTY, FRANCES
SMITH, BARBARA
    LEVANT, OSCAR
SMITH, BILL
    BURSTYN, ELLEN
SMITH, CHARLES JOHN
    SMITH, C. AUBREY
SMITH, DALLAS
    ANN-MARGRET

SMITH, DALLAS
    SMITH, ROGER
SMITH, DALLAS THOMAS
    ANN-MARGRET
    SMITH, ROGER
SMITH, ELIZABETH
    MIX, TOM
SMITH, ELSIE
    HARRIS, JULIE
SMITH, ETHEL
    BELLAMY, RALPH
SMITH, GRACE M.
    TIBBETT, LAWRENCE
SMITH, GRACE MARY MATHER
    CABOT, BRUCE
SMITH, GWYNNE
    PICKFORD, MARY
SMITH, HATTIE
    MARTIN, TONY
SMITH, HONOR BERYL CLODE
    SMITH, C. AUBREY
SMITH, J. G.
    MOORE, CONSTANCE
SMITH, JACK
    PICKFORD, MARY
SMITH, JOHN CHARLES
    PICKFORD, MARY
SMITH, JORDAN
    ANN-MARGRET
    SMITH, ROGER
SMITH, JR., WALTER HILLMAN
    EVANS, DALE
SMITH, LILLA LOUISE
    BELLAMY, RALPH
SMITH, LOTTIE
    PICKFORD, MARY
SMITH, LUDLOW OGDEN
    HEPBURN, KATHARINE
SMITH, MARGARET
    WEBB, JACK
SMITH, MARY
    MACDONALD, JEANETTE
    RAYMOND, GENE
SMITH, MARY 'MIMI'
    LENNON, JOHN
SMITH, MAURICE
    SHORE, DINAH
SMITH, MINERVA
    BURR, RAYMOND
SMITH, NATHANIEL
    SMITH, MAGGIE
SMITH, NOEL M.
    FAZENDA, LOUISE
SMITH, PENNI
    CRENNA, RICHARD
SMITH, ROGER
    ANN-MARGRET

SMITH, SHARON
    KEELER, RUBY
SMITH, SIDNEY A.
    DAMITA, LILI
SMITH, TRACEY
    ANN-MARGRET
    SMITH, ROGER
SMITH, WALTER HILLMAN
    EVANS, DALE
SMITH, WENDY
    HAYMES, DICK
SMITH, WILLIAM B.
    MERMAN, ETHEL
SNEIDER, HELEN BELLE
    BEL GEDDES, BARBARA
SNELSON, EDWIN A.
    GARSON, GREER
SNERD, MORTIMER
    BERGEN, EDGAR
SNODGRESS, III, HARRY A.
    SNODGRESS, CARRIE
SNODGRESS, JOHN
    SNODGRESS, CARRIE
SNODGRESS, JR., HARRY A.
    SNODGRESS, CARRIE
SNODGRESS, MELVIN
    SNODGRESS, CARRIE
SNODGRESS, ZEKE
    SNODGRESS, CARRIE
SNYDER, CHRISTOPHER JOHN
    FURNESS, BETTY
SNYDER, DENTON MCCOY
    FURNESS, BETTY
SNYDER, ELIZABETH ANNE
    FURNESS, BETTY
SNYDER, ROY
    HILLIARD, HARRIET
    NELSON, OZZIE
SOBOL, MARION
    SEGAL, GEORGE
SOGLIO, ANTHONY
    STEVENS, INGER
SOMA, ENRICA
    HUSTON, JOHN
    HUSTON, WALTER
SOMBORN, GLORIA
    SWANSON, GLORIA
SOMBORN, HERBERT K.
    SWANSON, GLORIA
SOMBORN, JOSEPH P.
    SWANSON, GLORIA
SOMERS, BRETT
    KLUGMAN, JACK
SOMERS, LESLIE
    KLUGMAN, JACK
SOMERVILLE, MARION DUPONT
    SCOTT, RANDOLPH

SOMMER, DR. GREGORY
    NORTH, SHEREE
SOMMER, ERICA
    NORTH, SHEREE
SOMMERS, BRUCE
    SOMERS, SUZANNE
SOMMERS, JR., BRUCE
    SOMERS, SUZANNE
SOMNER, PEARL L.
    BALSAM, MARTIN
SOPHIA, ALMA
    DAY, DORIS
SOPKIN, BETTY
    TORME, MEL
SOREL, SONIA
    CARRADINE, JOHN
SOTHERN, ANN
    STERLING, ROBERT
SOUKOTINE, ELIZABETH
    FERRER, MEL
SOULE, HELEN
    KARLOFF, BORIS
SOULS, ELISE
    AUER, MISCHA
SOUTHWORTH, DOROTHY FAY
    RITTER, TEX
SPACEK, ED
    SPACEK, SISSY
SPACEK, JR., ED
    SPACEK, SISSY
SPACEK, ROBERT
    SPACEK, SISSY
SPACEK, SISSY
    TORN, RIP
SPACEK, THELMA
    TORN, RIP
SPALDING, ANNE STEVENS
    HAMILTON, GEORGE
SPARV, CAMILLA
    EVANS, ROBERT
SPAULDING, LORANDA STEPHANIE
    ZIMBALIST, JR., EFREM
SPEED, ANNIS
    ANDREWS, DANA
SPENCER-MARCUS, FREDRIQUE
    WYNTER, DANA
SPENCER, DOROTHY
    MITCHUM, ROBERT
SPIER, WILLIAM
    HAVOC, JUNE
    LEE, GYPSY ROSE
SPIVEY, INA MAE
    AUTRY, GENE
SPRECKELS, JOAN
    GABLE, CLARK
SPRECKELS, KAY WILLIAMS
    COOPER, GARY

SPRECKELS, KAY WILLIAMS
    GABLE, CLARK
SPRIGMAN, EMMA LOUISE
    COBURN, CHARLES
SQUIRES, DOROTHY
    MOORE, ROGER
ST. GERMAINE, KAY
    CARSON, JACK
ST. JOHN, AL 'FUZZY'
    ARBUCKLE, FATTY
ST. JOHNS, ADELA ROGERS
    LA MARR, BARBARA
STAAB, LINDA
    VAUGHN, ROBERT
STACK, CHARLES ROBERT
    STACK, ROBERT
STACK, ELIZABETH LANGFORD
    STACK, ROBERT
STACK, JAMES LANGFORD
    STACK, ROBERT
STACY, HEATHER
    DARBY, KIM
STACY, JAMES
    DARBY, KIM
STACY, PATRICIA
    WAYNE, JOHN
STAFFORD, JIM
    SHORE, DINAH
STAHL, C. RAY
    HYER, MARTHA
STAINER, ARTHUR
    HOWARD, LESLIE
STAINER, DORICE
    HOWARD, LESLIE
STAINER, FRANK
    HOWARD, LESLIE
STAINER, IRENE
    HOWARD, LESLIE
STAINER, JAMES
    HOWARD, LESLIE
STALLONE, FRANK
    STALLONE, SYLVESTER
STALLONE, JR., FRANK
    STALLONE, SYLVESTER
STALLONE, SAGE MOON BLOOD
    STALLONE, SYLVESTER
STANDER, ARTHUR
    PAIGE, JANIS
STANDRING, GERTRUDE
    VERDON, GWEN
STANG, JAPPE
    ULLMANN, LIV
STANHOPE, RUTH ADELIA
    TAYLOR, ROBERT
STANTON, ROBERT
    DRU, JOANNE
    HAYMES, DICK

STANWYCK, BARBARA
    TAYLOR, ROBERT
STAPLER, SHEILA
    YOUNG, GIG
STAPLETON, JOHN
    STAPLETON, JEAN
STAPLETON, JOHN P.
    STAPLETON, MAUREEN
STAPLETON, LIONEL P.
    BLAINE, VIVIAN
STAPLETON, MARIE
    STAPLETON, JEAN
STARKEY, HARRY
    STARR, RINGO
STARR, RINGO
    HARRISON, GEORGE
    LENNON, JOHN
    MCCARTNEY, PAUL
STARR, ZAK
    STARR, RINGO
STAUFFER, ERNEST 'TEDDY'
    LAMARR, HEDY
STEEL-PAYNE, ALYS MAUDE
    JOHNS, GLYNIS
STEELE, ALFRED N.
    CRAWFORD, JOAN
STEELE, ANTHONY
    EKBERG, ANITA
STEELE, TED
    WINDSOR, MARIE
STEFANOTTI, TERESA
    BENDIX, WILLIAM
STEFFEN, II, GEARY A.
    POWELL, JANE
STEFFEN, III, GEARY A.
    POWELL, JANE
STEFFEN, SUZANNE ILEEN
    POWELL, JANE
STEFFIN, MYRA
    BERKELEY, BUSBY
STEIGER, ANNA JUSTINE
    BLOOM, CLAIRE
    STEIGER, ROD
STEIGER, FREDERICK
    STEIGER, ROD
STEIGER, ROD
    BLOOM, CLAIRE
STEIN, ANNA
    SHORE, DINAH
STEINBERG, ADA
    JAFFE, SAM
STEINEM, GLORIA
    NICHOLS, MIKE
STEINHOFF, LAURA
    HAWN, GOLDIE
STENSLAND, CARL
    STEVENS, INGER

STEPHANIE, PRINCESS
    KELLY, GRACE
STEPHANS, CHRISTOPHER
    SMITH, MAGGIE
STEPHANS, ROBERT
    SMITH, MAGGIE
STEPHANS, TOBY
    SMITH, MAGGIE
STERLING, JAN
    DOUGLAS, PAUL
STERLING, JEFFREYS
    STERLING, ROBERT
STERLING, JR., ROBERT
    STERLING, ROBERT
STERLING, PATRICIA 'TISHA'
    SOTHERN, ANN
    STERLING, ROBERT
STERLING, ROBERT
    SOTHERN, ANN
    TIERNEY, GENE
STERLING, TYLER
    STERLING, ROBERT
STERN, JENNA LOUISE
    EGGAR, SAMANTHA
STERN, NICOLAS
    EGGAR, SAMANTHA
STERN, ROSE
    BRICE, FANNY
STERN, TOM
    EGGAR, SAMANTHA
STERNBERG, JOSEF VON
    DIETRICH, MARLENE
STEVENS, ANDREW
    DARBY, KIM
STEVENS, BYRON
    STANWYCK, BARBARA
STEVENS, BYRON E.
    STANWYCK, BARBARA
STEVENS, ERNEST FREDERICK
    TERRY-THOMAS
STEVENS, INGER
    REYNOLDS, BURT
STEVENS, JOHN
    TERRY-THOMAS
STEVENS, MARY
    TERRY-THOMAS
STEVENS, MILDRED
    STANWYCK, BARBARA
STEVENS, RICHARD
    TERRY-THOMAS
STEVENS, TIMOTHY 'TIGER'
    TERRY-THOMAS
STEVENS, WILLIAM
    TERRY-THOMAS
STEVENSON, BILL
    ROSS, KATHARINE
STEVENSON, VENETIA
    TAMBLYN, RUSS

STEWART, ALEXANDER MAITLAND
    STEWART, JAMES
STEWART, GEORGE
    STEWART, ANITA
STEWART, JAMES
    COOPER, GARY
    FONDA, HENRY
    RUSSELL, ROSALIND
    SULLAVAN, MARGARET
STEWART, JUDY
    STEWART, JAMES
STEWART, KELLY
    STEWART, JAMES
STEWART, LUCILLE LEE
    STEWART, ANITA
STEWART, MAJOR JAMES
    GRANGER, STEWART
STEWART, MARIANNE
    CALHERN, LOUIS
STEWART, MICHAEL
    STEWART, JAMES
STEWART, MONA
    TAYLOR, ROD
STEWART, RONALD
    STEWART, JAMES
STEWART, WILLIAM
    STEWART, ANITA
STEYN, DOORN VAN
    MOORE, ROGER
STIEFEL, ISOBEL
    DENNY, REGINALD
STILLER, MAURITZ
    GARBO, GRETA
STILLMAN, PATRICIA
    SCOTT, RANDOLPH
STILLWELL, EDNA
    SKELTON, RED
STINE, DOROTHY
    KARLOFF, BORIS
STINE, HELEN
    PARSONS, LOUELLA O.
STOCKING, LAILA
    CABOT, BRUCE
STOCKMAN, MIRIAM
    BOARDMAN, ELEANOR
STOCKWELL, GUY
    STOCKWELL, DEAN
STOCKWELL, HARRY
    STOCKWELL, DEAN
STOKES, OLIVE
    MIX, TOM
STOKOWSKI, LEOPOLD
    GARBO, GRETA
STOMPANATO, JOHNNY
    GARDNER, AVA
    TURNER, LANA
STONE, BARBARA
    STONE, LEWIS

STONE, BERTRAND MCDONALD
    STONE, LEWIS
STONE, CAROL
    STONE, FRED
STONE, CYNTHIA
    LEMMON, JACK
    ROBERTSON, CLIFF
STONE, DOROTHY
    STONE, FRED
STONE, LEWIS PRESTON
    STONE, FRED
STONE, PAULA
    STONE, FRED
STONE, PAULINE
    HARVEY, LAURENCE
STONE, ROBIN JOHN
    CALVET, CORINNE
STONE, VIRGINIA
    STONE, LEWIS
STONEHAM, CHARLES
    GOSDEN, FREEMAN
STONEHAM, JANE
    GOSDEN, FREEMAN
STONEHOUSE, RUTH
    ANDERSON, 'BRONCO BILLY'
STOREY, EDITH
    MORENO, ANTONIO
STORME, RORY
    STARR, RINGO
STOVELL, GERALDINE
    WEAVER, DENNIS
STRASBERG, LEE
    PACINO, AL
    WALLACH, ELI
STRAUSS, SARAH
    SHAW, ARTIE
STREET, DAVID
    PAGET, DEBRA
STREISAND, BARBRA
    GOULD, ELLIOT
    KRISTOFFERSON, KRIS
    NEWMAN, PAUL
    POITIER, SIDNEY
STREISAND, EMANUEL
    STREISAND, BARBRA
STREISAND, SHELDON
    STREISAND, BARBRA
STROHEIM, JOSEF ERICH VON
    VON STROHEIM, ERICH
STROHEIM, JR., ERICH VON
    VON STROHEIM, ERICH
STUART, ROD
    EKLAND, BRITT
STURTEVANT, FLORENCE
    FURNESS, BETTY
SUBER, FLORA MAE
    JONES, JENNIFER

SUE, HELEN
   BROLIN, JAMES
SULLAVAN, 'SONNY'
   SULLAVAN, MARGARET
SULLAVAN, CORNELIUS HANCOCK
   SULLAVAN, MARGARET
SULLAVAN, MARGARET
   FONDA, HENRY
   STEWART, JAMES
SULLIVAN, JAMES
   LANCHESTER, ELSA
SULLIVAN, SHEILA
   CULP, ROBERT
SULLY, DANIEL J.
   FAIRBANKS, DOUGLAS
   FAIRBANKS, JR., DOUGLAS
SULLY, ELIZABETH
   CRAWFORD, JOAN
   FAIRBANKS, DOUGLAS
   FAIRBANKS, JR., DOUGLAS
SUNDERLAND, NAN
   HUSTON, JOHN
   HUSTON, WALTER
SUNDSTEN, KAJA
   MEREDITH, BURGESS
SUPERSTAR, INGRID
   WARHOL, ANDY
SUPRENANT, LAURENT
   BENNETT, JOAN
SURACI, ANNA
   BENNETT, TONY
SUTHERLAND, ANNETTE
   BURR, RAYMOND
SUTHERLAND, KIEFER
   SUTHERLAND, DONALD
SUTHERLAND, RACHEL
   SUTHERLAND, DONALD
SUTHERLAND, ROEG RACETTE
   SUTHERLAND, DONALD
SUTHERLAND, VICTOR
   WHITE, PEARL
SUZARA, SARA JANE
   LEWIS, JERRY
SWAN, IDELLE
   DAHL, ARLENE
SWANSON, GLORIA
   BEERY, WALLACE
   MCCREA, JOEL
SWANSON, JOSEPH P.
   SWANSON, GLORIA
SWANSON, JOSEPH THEODORE
   SWANSON, GLORIA
SWANSON, NELL
   BERGEN, EDGAR
SWEET, BLANCHE
   HACKETT, RAYMOND
SWOPE, JOHN
   MCGUIRE, DOROTHY

SWOPE, MARK
   MCGUIRE, DOROTHY
SWOPE, MARY 'TOPO'
   MCGUIRE, DOROTHY
SYDOW, CARL WILHELM VON
   VON SYDOW, MAX
SYDOW, CLAS WILHELM VON
   VON SYDOW, MAX
SYDOW, PER HENRIK VON
   VON SYDOW, MAX
SYKES, NANCY LOU
   ASNER, EDWARD
SYLVIO, DON
   O'BRIEN, MARGARET
SZAVOZD, NICHOLAS
   MASSEY, ILONA
TABOR, JOAN
   CRAWFORD, BRODERICK
TABORI, GEORGE
   LINDFORS, VIVECA
TAIZ, LILLIAN
   JAFFE, SAM
TALBOT, CYNTHIA
   TALBOT, LYLE
TALBOT, DAVID
   TALBOT, LYLE
TALBOT, FLORENCE
   TALBOT, LYLE
TALBOT, MARGARET
   TALBOT, LYLE
TALBOT, STEPHEN
   TALBOT, LYLE
TALLOWN, GUS
   FITZGERALD, BARRY
TALMADGE, CONSTANCE
   BARTHELMESS, RICHARD
   DAVIES, MARION
   JESSEL, GEORGE
   KEATON, BUSTER
   TALMADGE, NORMA
TALMADGE, FREDERICK
   TALMADGE, CONSTANCE
   TALMADGE, NORMA
TALMADGE, NATALIE
   JESSEL, GEORGE
   KEATON, BUSTER
   TALMADGE, CONSTANCE
   TALMADGE, NORMA
TALMADGE, NORMA
   JESSEL, GEORGE
   KEATON, BUSTER
   ROLAND, GILBERT
   TALMADGE, CONSTANCE
TALMER, JEROME
   LEVANT, OSCAR
TAMBLYN, EDWARD
   TAMBLYN, RUSS

TAMBLYN, LAWRENCE
   TAMBLYN, RUSS
TAMBLYN, WARREN
   TAMBLYN, RUSS
TANDY, EDWARD
   TANDY, JESSICA
TANDY, HARRY
   TANDY, JESSICA
TANDY, JESSICA
   CRONYN, HUME
TANDY, MICHAEL
   TANDY, JESSICA
TATE, DEBORAH ANN
   TATE, SHARON
TATE, PATRICIA GAYE
   TATE, SHARON
TATE, PAUL J.
   TATE, SHARON
TAUROG, NORMAN
   COOPER, JACKIE
TAYLOR-YOUNG, LEIGH
   O'NEAL, RYAN
TAYLOR, BELLE
   TIERNEY, GENE
TAYLOR, DAISY GILMORE
   BACKUS, JIM
TAYLOR, DONALD
   MCDONALD, MARIE
TAYLOR, ELAINE
   PLUMMER, CHRISTOPHER
TAYLOR, ELIZABETH
   BURTON, RICHARD
   CLIFT, MONTGOMERY
   FISHER, EDDIE
   REYNOLDS, DEBBIE
   WILDING, MICHAEL
TAYLOR, ELOISE
   O'BRIEN, PAT
TAYLOR, FELICIA RODERICA
   TAYLOR, ROD
TAYLOR, FRANCIS
   TAYLOR, ELIZABETH
TAYLOR, HOWARD
   TAYLOR, ELIZABETH
TAYLOR, IDA MILLER
   MEADOWS, AUDREY
   MEADOWS, JAYNE
TAYLOR, JOSEPHINE
   LONDON, JULIE
TAYLOR, MARILYN
   GLEASON, JACKIE
TAYLOR, RACHEL
   ROBARDS, JR., JASON
TAYLOR, ROBERT
   MONTGOMERY, GEORGE
   STANWYCK, BARBARA
TAYLOR, ROD
   EKBERG, ANITA

TAYLOR, TERENCE
   TAYLOR, ROBERT
TAYLOR, TESSA
   TAYLOR, ROBERT
TAYLOR, WILLIAM DESMOND
   MORENO, ANTONIO
   NORMAND, MABEL
TAYLOR, WILLIAM STUART
   TAYLOR, ROD
TCHINAROVA, TAMARA
   FINCH, PETER
TEASDALE, VERREE
   MENJOU, ADOLPHE
TEBET, DAVID
   FABRAY, NANETTE
TEER, BARBARA ANN
   CAMBRIDGE, GODFREY
TEJADA, ARMAND
   WELCH, RAQUEL
TELL, MICHAEL
   DUKE, PATTY
TEMPLE, GEORGE
   TEMPLE, SHIRLEY
TEMPLE, GEORGE FRANCIS
   TEMPLE, SHIRLEY
TEMPLE, JOHN
   TEMPLE, SHIRLEY
TEMPLE, SHIRLEY
   AGAR, JOHN
TENDLER, HARRIET
   BRONSON, CHARLES
TERLITZKY, GLORIA
   DARREN, JAMES
TERRY-LEWIS, KATE
   GIELGUD, JOHN
TERRY, ALICE
   NOVARRO, RAMON
TERRY, CHRISTOPHER
   CRAWFORD, JOAN
TERRY, MINNIE
   GWENN, EDMUND
TERRY, PHILLIP
   CRAWFORD, JOAN
TERSMEDEN, HJORDIS
   NIVEN, DAVID
THALBERG, IRVING
   DAVIES, MARION
   GILBERT, JOHN
   HAYES, HELEN
   MAYER, LOUIS B.
   SHEARER, NORMA
THALBERG, JR., IRVING
   SHEARER, NORMA
THALBERG, KATHARINE
   SHEARER, NORMA
THALBERG, SYLVIA
   SHEARER, NORMA

THALBERG, WILLIAM
    SHEARER, NORMA
THATCHER, PHILLIP TORIN
    THATCHER, TORIN
THATCHER, TORIN JAMES BLAIR
    THATCHER, TORIN
THAW, HARRY K.
    NESBIT, EVELYN
THAW, RUSSELL
    NESBIT, EVELYN
THAXTER, SIDNEY
    THAXTER, PHYLLIS
THIERREE, JEAN-PIERRE
    CHAPLIN, CHARLES
THIESS, MANUELA
    TAYLOR, ROBERT
THIESS, MICHAEL
    TAYLOR, ROBERT
THIESS, URSULA
    TAYLOR, ROBERT
THOMAS, BLANCHE OELRICHS
    BARRYMORE, ETHEL
    BARRYMORE, JOHN
    BARRYMORE, LIONEL
THOMAS, CHARLES ANTHONY
    THOMAS, DANNY
THOMAS, JEFF
    O'CONNOR, DONALD
    SULLAVAN, MARGARET
THOMAS, LOUISE 'LULU'
    AHERNE, BRIAN
    FONTAINE, JOAN
THOMAS, MARGARET JULIA 'MARLO'
    THOMAS, DANNY
THOMAS, MARJORIE
    HARRISON, REX
THOMAS, MICHAEL
    SULLAVAN, MARGARET
THOMAS, OLIVE
    PICKFORD, MARY
THOMAS, THERESA CECILIA 'TERRE
    THOMAS, DANNY
THOMAS, WILLIAM
    SULLAVAN, MARGARET
THOMASEN, BARBARA ANN
    ROONEY, MICKEY
THOMPSON, BEATRIX
    RAINS, CLAUDE
THOMPSON, BRENDA LEE
    EVERETT, CHAD
THOMPSON, CARLOS
    PALMER, LILLI
THOMPSON, ETHEL
    WILDING, MICHAEL
THOMPSON, JOHN
    OBERON, MERLE
THOMPSON, ROBERT
    CANOVA, JUDY

THOMPSON, SALLIE
    POWELL, DICK
THOMSON, BARRY
    CHATTERTON, RUTH
THORNBURG, MARION
    HUTTON, BETTY
THORNBURG, PERCY
    HUTTON, BETTY
THORPE, DR. FRANKLIN
    ASTOR, MARY
THORPE, MARYLYN HAUOLI
    ASTOR, MARY
THORSEN, MARA TOLENE
    O'BRIEN, MARGARET
THORSEN, ROY
    O'BRIEN, MARGARET
THORSSELL, ULLA
    AZNAVOUR, CHARLES
THURLOW, CONSTANCE
    BARKER, LEX
TIBBET, WILLIAM EDWARD
    TIBBETT, LAWRENCE
TIBBETT, LAWRENCE
    TIBBETT, LAWRENCE
TIBBETT, MICHAEL
    TIBBETT, LAWRENCE
TIBBETT, RICHARD
    TIBBETT, LAWRENCE
TIBBS, CASEY
    ROSS, KATHARINE
TIBOR, HELTAI
    GABOR, EVA
    GABOR, ZSA ZSA
TIERNAN, MARGARET
    CASTELLANO, RICHARD
TIERNEY, EDWARD
    TIERNEY, LAWRENCE
TIERNEY, GENE
    STERLING, ROBERT
TIERNEY, GERALD
    TIERNEY, LAWRENCE
TIERNEY, HOWARD SHERWOOD
    TIERNEY, GENE
TIERNEY, JR., HOWARD
    TIERNEY, GENE
TIERNEY, LAWRENCE A.
    TIERNEY, LAWRENCE
TIERNEY, PATRICIA
    TIERNEY, GENE
TIFFIN, GRACE IRENE
    TIFFIN, PAMELA
TIJER, JULIO
    O'BRIEN, MARGARET
TILDEN, BILL
    DANIELS, BEBE
TILLMAN, NORMA
    AUER, MISCHA

TIMPONI, ROSINA
    GRANVILLE, BONITA
TINKER, GRANT
    MOORE, MARY TYLER
TINSLEY, KATHERINE
    MENJOU, ADOLPHE
TOBIAS, IDA
    CANTOR, EDDIE
TODD, ELIZABETH FRANCES
    BURTON, RICHARD
    TAYLOR, ELIZABETH
TODD, JR., MICHAEL
    BLONDELL, JOAN
    TAYLOR, ELIZABETH
TODD, MARY
    ANDREWS, DANA
TODD, MICHAEL
    BLONDELL, JOAN
    KEYES, EVELYN
    REYNOLDS, DEBBIE
    TAYLOR, ELIZABETH
TODD, THELMA
    PITTS, ZASU
TOLAND, LOTHIAN
    SKELTON, RED
TOMARKIN, ROBERT
    MALONE, DOROTHY
TOMLINSON, SAMUEL JOSEPH
    MAIN, MARJORIE
TOMPKINS, SAMUEL WILLIAM
    EWELL, TOM
TONE, FRANCHOT
    CRAWFORD, JOAN
TONE, FRANK JEROME
    TONE, FRANCHOT
TONE, JEROME
    TONE, FRANCHOT
TONE, PASCAL F.
    TONE, FRANCHOT
    WILDE, CORNEL
TONE, THOMAS JEFFERSON
    TONE, FRANCHOT
    WILDE, CORNEL
TOOMEY, FRANCIS X.
    TOOMEY, REGIS
TOOMEY, ORD
    TOOMEY, REGIS
TOOMEY, OTHELIA
    TOOMEY, REGIS
TOOMEY, SARAH
    TOOMEY, REGIS
TOPPING, DAN
    HENIE, SONJA
TOPPING, HENRY J. (BOB)
    TURNER, LANA
TORME, DAISY ANN
    TORME, MEL

TORME, JAMES SCOTT
    TORME, MEL
TORME, MISSY
    TORME, MEL
TORME, STEVEN
    TORME, MEL
TORME, TRACY
    TORME, MEL
TORME, WILLIAM
    TORME, MEL
TORN, ANGELICA
    PAGE, GERALDINE
    TORN, RIP
TORN, ANTHONY
    PAGE, GERALDINE
    TORN, RIP
TORN, DANAE
    PAGE, GERALDINE
    TORN, RIP
TORN, ELMORE
    TORN, RIP
TORN, JONATHAN
    PAGE, GERALDINE
    TORN, RIP
TORN, RIP
    PAGE, GERALDINE
    SPACEK, SISSY
TORNBLOM, LINNEA MARIA
    ZETTERLING, MAI
TOTH, ANDRE DE
    LAKE, VERONICA
TOTH, DIANE DE
    LAKE, VERONICA
TOTH, MICHAEL DE
    LAKE, VERONICA
TOWNE, DOROTHY
    WEBB, JACK
TOWNES, AGNES
    HOPE, BOB
TOXTON, CANDY
    TORME, MEL
TRACY, CARROLL
    TRACY, SPENCER
TRACY, JOHN
    TRACY, SPENCER
TRACY, JOHN EDWARD
    TRACY, SPENCER
TRACY, LOUISE
    TRACY, SPENCER
TRACY, SPENCER
    HEPBURN, KATHARINE
    JOHNSON, VAN
    O'BRIEN, PAT
TRAESNER, TOVE
    BORGNINE, ERNEST
TRAVAGLINI, LUCILLE
    COMO, PERRY

TRAVAJOLI, ARMANDO
    ANGELI, PIER
    PAVAN, MARISA
TRAVAJOLI, HOWARD ANDREA
    ANGELI, PIER
    PAVAN, MARISA
TRAVOLTA, ANN
    TRAVOLTA, JOHN
TRAVOLTA, ELLEN
    TRAVOLTA, JOHN
TRAVOLTA, JOE
    TRAVOLTA, JOHN
TRAVOLTA, MARGARET
    TRAVOLTA, JOHN
TRAVOLTA, SALVATORE
    TRAVOLTA, JOHN
TRAVOLTA, SAM
    TRAVOLTA, JOHN
TRAYNOR, CHARLES
    LOVELACE, LINDA
TREADWELL, LOUISE
    TRACY, SPENCER
TREMAN, ROBERT E.
    CASTLE, IRENE
TRIKONIS, GUS
    HAWN, GOLDIE
TRIMBLE, CONSTANCE CHARLOTTA
    LAKE, VERONICA
TRIMMIER, ELINOR
    WOODWARD, JOANNE
TRIPP, ROSINNE
    KERRY, NORMAN
TRIPPLET, SALLY
    TAMBLYN, RUSS
TRIPPS, BARBARA C.
    FERRER, MEL
TRIX, JANE GORDON
    WAYNE, DAVID
TROUPE, BOBBY
    LONDON, JULIE
TROUPE, CYNTHIA
    LONDON, JULIE
TROUPE, JODY
    LONDON, JULIE
TROUPE, KELLY
    LONDON, JULIE
TROUPE, REESE
    LONDON, JULIE
TROUPE, RONNE
    LONDON, JULIE
TRUEX, BARRETT
    TRUEX, ERNEST
TRUEX, JAMES
    TRUEX, ERNEST
TRUEX, PHILIP
    TRUEX, ERNEST
TRUSCOTT-JONES, ELIZABETH
    MILLAND, RAY

TRYON, ARTHUR LANE
    TRYON, TOM
TSAKLAKIS, ANTHONY J.
    WINDSOR, CLAIRE
TUBONI, ELEANOR
    MCDONALD, MARIE
TUBONI, ROSE
    MCDONALD, MARIE
TUCK, BERT
    TUCKER, SOPHIE
TUCK, LOUIS
    TUCKER, SOPHIE
TUCKER, CYNTHIA
    TUCKER, FORREST
TUCKER, FORREST A.
    TUCKER, FORREST
TUCKER, PAMELA BROOKE JOLLEY
    TUCKER, FORREST
TUCKER, SANDRA
    CARSON, JACK
TUFTS, DAVID ALBERT
    TUFTS, SONNY
TUFTS, II, BOWEN CHARLESTON
    TUFTS, SONNY
TURKEL, ANN
    HARRIS, RICHARD
TURNER, LANA
    BARKER, LEX
    LAMAS, FERNANDO
    SHAW, ARTIE
    SINATRA, FRANK
TURNER, VIRGIL
    TURNER, LANA
TURNER, YOLANDE
    FINCH, PETER
TUSHINGHAM, COLIN
    TUSHINGHAM, RITA
TUSHINGHAM, JOHN
    TUSHINGHAM, RITA
TUSHINGHAM, PETER
    TUSHINGHAM, RITA
TUTTLE, WILLIAM
    REED, DONNA
TUVIM, ABRAHAM
    HOLLIDAY, JUDY
TYLER, JEAN
    CHAMPION, GOWER
TYRELL, SUSAN
    PACINO, AL
TYSON, EMILY
    TYSON, CICELY
TYSON, WILLIAM
    TYSON, CICELY
ULLMAN, LINN
    ULLMANN, LIV
ULLMANN, VIGGO
    ULLMANN, LIV

ULMAN, HEZEKIAH CHARLES-DOUGLAS
    FAIRBANKS, DOUGLAS
ULMAN, ROBERT
    FAIRBANKS, DOUGLAS
ULRIC, LENORE
    BLACKMER, SIDNEY
URE, MARY
    SHAW, ROBERT
URMY, KEITH
    DUNNOCK, MILDRED
URMY, LINDA
    DUNNOCK, MILDRED
URMY, MARY
    DUNNOCK, MILDRED
URWICK, ADRIANNE JOY
    MATURE, VICTOR
USTINOV, IGOR
    USTINOV, PETER
USTINOV, IONA
    USTINOV, PETER
USTINOV, PAVIA
    USTINOV, PETER
USTINOV, TAMARA
    USTINOV, PETER
VACCARO, BRENDA
    DOUGLAS, MICHAEL
    MEREDITH, BURGESS
VACCARO, MARIO
    VACCARO, BRENDA
VADIM, NATALIE STROYBERG
    FONDA, JANE
VADIM, ROGER
    DENEUVE, CATHERINE
    FONDA, HENRY
    FONDA, JANE
    FONDA, PETER
VADIM, VANESSA
    FONDA, HENRY
    FONDA, JANE
    FONDA, PETER
VALENTINE, PAUL
    SAINT CYR, LILI
VALENTINO, RUDOLPH
    NEGRI, POLA
    RAFT, GEORGE
VALLEE, CHARLES ALPHONSE
    VALLEE, RUDY
VALLEE, KATHLEEN
    VALLEE, RUDY
VALLEE, WILLIAM
    VALLEE, RUDY
VALLEE, YVONNE
    CHEVALIER, MAURICE
VALLI, VIRGINIA
    FARRELL, CHARLES
VAN CLEEF, ALAN
    VAN CLEEF, LEE

VAN CLEEF, C. LEROY
    VAN CLEEF, LEE
VAN CLEEF, DEBORAH
    VAN CLEEF, LEE
VAN DEVERE, TRISH
    SCOTT, GEORGE C.
VAN DYKE, BARRY
    VAN DYKE, DICK
VAN DYKE, CARRIE BETH
    VAN DYKE, DICK
VAN DYKE, CHRISTIAN
    VAN DYKE, DICK
VAN DYKE, JERRY
    VAN DYKE, DICK
VAN DYKE, JESSICA LEE
    VAN DYKE, DICK
VAN DYKE, L. W.
    VAN DYKE, DICK
VAN DYKE, STACEY
    VAN DYKE, DICK
VAN FLEET, HUGH
    VAN FLEET, JO
VANDEN-BOOSCHE, JOSEPHINE
    CHEVALIER, MAURICE
VANDERBILT, ERSKINE GWYNNE
    WINDSOR, CLAIRE
VANDERBILT, GLORIA
    MONTGOMERY, GEORGE
VANDERBILT, WENDY
    HAMILTON, GEORGE
VANTON, MONTE
    POWERS, MALA
VANTON, VERNON
    POWERS, MALA
VARDEN, VENITA
    OAKIE, JACK
VARSI, GAIL
    VARSI, DIANE
VARSI, RUSSELL
    VARSI, DIANE
VARSI, SHAWN MICHAEL
    VARSI, DIANE
VASCONCELLOS, HELEN
    ASTOR, MARY
VASSAR, QUEENIE
    CAWTHORN, JOSEPH
VAUGHN, EDITH BAINE
    KELLERMAN, SALLY
VAUGHN, GERALD WALTER
    VAUGHN, ROBERT
VEITCH, VIOLET
    COWARD, NOEL
VELAZQUEZ, SANDRAMARIA CRISTINA
    BORGNINE, ERNEST
    JURADO, KATY
VELAZQUEZ, VICTOR
    JURADO, KATY

VELAZQUEZ, VICTOR HUGO
    BORGNINE, ERNEST
    JURADO, KATY
VELEZ, EMIGDIO VILLALOBOS
    VELEZ, LUPE
VELEZ, JOSEFINA VILLALOBOS
    VELEZ, LUPE
VELEZ, JUANA
    VELEZ, LUPE
VELEZ, LUPE
    COOPER, GARY
    TIBBETT, LAWRENCE
    WEISSMULLER, JOHNNY
VELEZ, MERCEDES VILLALOBOS
    VELEZ, LUPE
VELEZ, REMEDIOS
    VELEZ, LUPE
VENABLE, JR., REGINALD S. H.
    BAINTER, FAY
VENABLE, REGINALD S. H.
    BAINTER, FAY
VENUTA, BENAY
    CLARK, FRED
VERDON, JOSEPH
    VERDON, GWEN
VERDUGO, BEATRICE
    VELEZ, LUPE
    VERDUGO, ELENA
VERHOEVEN, DR. MICHAEL
    BERGER, SENTA
VERNAC, DENISE
    VON STROHEIM, ERICH
VERNE, KAAREN
    LORRE, PETER
VERNON, FRANCIS WILLARD
    CAGNEY, JAMES
VICKERY, JAMES
    DEWHURST, COLLEEN
VID, RENEE
    WILDE, CORNEL
VIDAL, HENRI
    MORGAN, MICHELE
VIDOR, ANTONIA
    BOARDMAN, ELEANOR
VIDOR, BELINDA
    BOARDMAN, ELEANOR
VIDOR, CHARLES
    KEYES, EVELYN
VIDOR, KING LOUIS WALLIS
    BOARDMAN, ELEANOR
    MOORE, COLLEEN
VIERTEL, PETER
    KERR, DEBORAH
VIERTEL, SALKA
    GARBO, GRETA
VILLALOBOS, JACOB
    VELEZ, LUPE

VILLANI, ROMILDA
    LOREN, SOPHIA
VILLENEUVE, JUSTIN DE
    TWIGGY
VINCENT, ANNA
    MASSEY, RAYMOND
VOGEL, BERTHE
    DASSIN, JULES
VOGT, EMMY
    CALHERN, LOUIS
VOGT, EUGENE ADOLPH
    CALHERN, LOUIS
VOIGHT, BARRY
    VOIGHT, JON
VOIGHT, ELMER
    VOIGHT, JON
VOIGHT, JAMES HAVEN
    VOIGHT, JON
VOIGHT, JAMES WESLEY
    VOIGHT, JON
VON DEHN, HYATT
    WINCHELL, WALTER
VON DEHN, MARY ELIZABETH
    WINCHELL, WALTER
VON FURSTENBURG, COUNT FRANZ
    VON FURSTENBURG, BETSY
VON, JULIA
    WARHOL, ANDY
VON, MARJORIE
    TUFTS, SONNY
VOYSEY, ELLA ANNESLERY
    DONAT, ROBERT
VRUWINK, DR. JOHN
    COSTELLO, DOLORES
WADDINGTON, EUPHEMIA
    WYATT, JANE
WAGG, KENNETH
    SULLAVAN, MARGARET
WAGGONER, BEAU JUSTIN
    WAGGONER, LYLE
WAGGONER, JASON KENNEDY
    WAGGONER, LYLE
WAGGONER, MYRON
    WAGGONER, LYLE
WAGNER, COURTNEY BROOKE
    WAGNER, ROBERT
    WOOD, NATALIE
WAGNER, KATHERINE
    WAGNER, ROBERT
    WOOD, NATALIE
WAGNER, ROBERT
    REYNOLDS, DEBBIE
    WOOD, NATALIE
WAGNER, SIEGFRIED
    MELCHIOR, LAURITZ
WAGNER, SR., ROBERT
    WAGNER, ROBERT

WALBERN, RAEMOND
    LAUREL, STAN
WALD, JEFF
    REDDY, HELEN
WALD, JORDAN
    REDDY, HELEN
WALD, TRACY
    REDDY, HELEN
WALDEN, VIVIAN FERNE
    DARIN, BOBBY
WALDO, MARGARET
    REMICK, LEE
WALKER, CHARLES
    MASSEY, ILONA
WALKER, HORACE
    WALKER, ROBERT
WALKER, JR., ROBERT
    JONES, JENNIFER
    WALKER, ROBERT
WALKER, LUCILLE NEOMA
    WALKER, CLINT
WALKER, MICHAEL
    JONES, JENNIFER
    WALKER, ROBERT
WALKER, PAUL ARNOLD
    WALKER, CLINT
WALKER, RICHARD
    WALKER, ROBERT
WALKER, ROBERT
    JONES, JENNIFER
    TAYLOR, ROD
WALKER, RUTH
    PIDGEON, WALTER
WALKER, VALERIE JEAN
    WALKER, CLINT
WALKER, WALTER
    WALKER, ROBERT
WALKER, WAYNE
    WALKER, ROBERT
WALLACE, ANN
    BOLGER, RAY
WALLACE, BERYL
    BERLE, MILTON
WALLACE, FRANK
    WEST, MAE
WALLACE, JEAN
    TONE, FRANCHOT
    WILDE, CORNEL
WALLACE, MABEL GREY
    HOWARD, TREVOR
WALLACE, SHEILA
    SANDS, TOMMY
WALLACE, WILLIAM R.
    CLAIRE, INA
WALLACH, ABRAHAM
    WALLACH, ELI
WALLACH, KATHERINE BEATRICE
    WALLACH, ELI

WALLACH, PETER DOUGLAS
    WALLACH, ELI
WALLACH, ROBERTA LEE
    WALLACH, ELI
WALLING, WILLIAM HENRY
    WOOD, PEGGY
WALLIS, HAL B.
    FAZENDA, LOUISE
    HYER, MARTHA
    RIN TIN TIN
WALLIS, HAL BRENT
    FAZENDA, LOUISE
WALLIS, JR., HAL BRENT
    HYER, MARTHA
WALLIS, MINNA
    FAZENDA, LOUISE
    GABLE, CLARK
WALSH, BILL
    ROMAN, RUTH
WALSH, IRENE
    STAPLETON, MAUREEN
WALTER, DAVID
    WALTER, JESSICA
WALTER, KATE
    GINGOLD, HERMIONE
WALTERS, BETTE LOU
    MURRAY, KEN
WALTON, EMMA KATE
    ANDREWS, JULIE
WALTON, TONY
    ANDREWS, JULIE
WANAMAKER, SAM
    STERLING, JAN
WANGEMEN, LOLA VAN
    REDFORD, ROBERT
WANGER, JUSTIN
    BENNETT, JOAN
WANGER, SHELLEY
    BENNETT, JOAN
WANGER, STEPHANIE
    BENNETT, JOAN
WANGER, WALTER
    BENNETT, CONSTANCE
    BENNETT, JOAN
    BENNETT, RICHARD
WARD, AMELITA
    GORCEY, LEO
WARD, CHRISTOPHER
    WYATT, JANE
WARD, EDGAR B.
    WYATT, JANE
WARD, EVELYN
    CASSIDY, JACK
WARD, ISABELLA
    BURR, RAYMOND
WARD, JAMES
    DEVINE, ANDY

WARD, MABEL HUBBELL
   MIX, TOM
WARD, MICHAEL
   WYATT, JANE
WARD, VALERIE
   BATES, ALAN
WARDEN, CHRISTOPHER
   WARDEN, JACK
WARDEN, JOHN F.
   WARDEN, JACK
WARFIELD, ROBERT ELZA
   WARFIELD, WILLIAM
WARHOL, JAMES
   WARHOL, ANDY
WARHOL, JOHN
   WARHOL, ANDY
WARHOL, PAUL
   WARHOL, ANDY
WARMBRODT, SARA
   TAYLOR, ELIZABETH
WARNE, MARY
   MARSH, MAE
WARNER, JACK
   DAVIS, BETTE
WARNER, JR., JOHN WILLIAM
   TAYLOR, ELIZABETH
WARNER, NORA
   DAILEY, DAN
WARREN, GEN. SIR CHARLES
   BARRIE, WENDY
WARREN, JULIE
   FORSYTHE, JOHN
WARREN, LULA STEWART
   SHERIDAN, ANN
WASSGREN, KRISTIN
   WYNN, KEENAN
WATERFIELD, BOB
   RUSSELL, JANE
WATERFIELD, JR., ROBERT
   RUSSELL, JANE
WATERFIELD, MICHAEL 'DANDY KIM'
   EGGAR, SAMANTHA
WATERFIELD, THOMAS
   RUSSELL, JANE
WATERFIELD, TRACY
   RUSSELL, JANE
WATERS, JOHN WESLEY
   WATERS, ETHEL
WAYNE, JOHN
   BOND, WARD
   CABOT, BRUCE
   FORD, GLENN
   O'HARA, MAUREEN
WAYNE, MELINDA
   WAYNE, DAVID
WAYNE, SUSAN
   WAYNE, DAVID

WAYNE, TIMOTHY
   WAYNE, DAVID
WEATHERWAX, RUDD
   LASSIE
WEAVER, DAVID
   WOOD, PEGGY
WEAVER, JOHN VAN ALSTYN
   WOOD, PEGGY
WEAVER, RICHARD
   WEAVER, DENNIS
WEAVER, ROBERT
   WEAVER, DENNIS
WEAVER, RUSTIN
   WEAVER, DENNIS
WEBB, FAY
   VALLEE, RUDY
WEBB, JACK
   LONDON, JULIE
WEBB, LISA
   LONDON, JULIE
   WEBB, JACK
WEBB, SAMUEL CHESTER
   WEBB, JACK
WEBB, STACEY
   LONDON, JULIE
   WEBB, JACK
WEBSTER, BEN
   WHITTY, DAME MAY
WEBSTER, LUCILLE
   GLEASON, JAMES 'JIMMY'
WEBSTER, MARGARET
   WHITTY, DAME MAY
WEBSTER, MURIEL
   MILLAND, RAY
WECHSLER, WALTER
   ANDREWS, LAVERNE
   ANDREWS, MAXENE
   ANDREWS, PATRICIA
WEDGEWORTH, ANN
   TORN, RIP
WEEKS, BEATRICE
   LUGOSI, BELA
WEIDLER, GEORGE
   DAY, DORIS
WEILL, RITA VALE
   GIELGUD, JOHN
WEINBERG, RITA
   BIKEL, THEODORE
WEINBLATT, SYLVIA
   MAZURKI, MIKE
WEINER, EUGENE
   ROTH, LILLIAN
WEINSTEIN, ERNA
   SCHILDKRAUT, JOSEPH
WEINSTEIN, LILLIAN
   BALSAM, MARTIN
WEISBERG, SALLY
   MUNI, PAUL

WEISENFREUND, PHILIP
   MUNI, PAUL
WEISS, ARLENE
   ALDA, ALAN
   ALDA, ROBERT
WEISSMULLER, HEIDI
   WEISSMULLER, JOHNNY
WEISSMULLER, JOHNNY
   VELEZ, LUPE
WEISSMULLER, JR., JOHN
   WEISSMULLER, JOHNNY
WEISSMULLER, WENDY
   WEISSMULLER, JOHNNY
WEITZMAN, STACEY
   WINKLER, HENRY
WELCH, DAMON
   WELCH, RAQUEL
WELCH, JAMES WESTLEY
   WELCH, RAQUEL
WELCH, TAHNEE
   WELCH, RAQUEL
WELD, DAVID
   WELD, TUESDAY
WELD, LATHROP MOTLEY
   WELD, TUESDAY
WELD, SALLY
   WELD, TUESDAY
WELD, TUESDAY
   PACINO, AL
WELLES, BEATRICE
   WELLES, ORSON
WELLES, CHRISTOPHER
   WELLES, ORSON
WELLES, ORSON
   DEL RIO, DOLORES
   HAYWORTH, RITA
WELLES, REBECCA
   HAYMES, DICK
   HAYWORTH, RITA
   WELLES, ORSON
WELLES, RICHARD
   WELLES, ORSON
WELLES, RICHARD HEAD
   HAYWORTH, RITA
   WELLES, ORSON
WELLES, SUSSIE
   DOUGLAS, PAUL
WELLMAN, KATHLEEN KENT
   FRANCISCUS, JAMES
WELLMAN, WILLIAM
   FRANCISCUS, JAMES
WELLS, EDWARD C.
   ANDREWS, JULIE
WELLS, HELEN MARY
   KERRY, NORMAN
WELLS, JOHN
   ANDREWS, JULIE

WELLS, MICHAEL
   YORK, SUSANNAH
WELLS, ORLANDO
   YORK, SUSANNAH
WELLS, RUTH
   BRENNAN, WALTER
WELLS, SASHA
   YORK, SUSANNAH
WELTER, GERALD
   CHRISTIAN, LINDA
WEMLINGER, MABEL
   TREVOR, CLAIRE
WEMLINGER, MALCOLM 'BYRON'
   TREVOR, CLAIRE
WEMLINGER, MAUDE
   TREVOR, CLAIRE
WEMLINGER, MILDRED
   TREVOR, CLAIRE
WEMLINGER, NOEL B.
   TREVOR, CLAIRE
WENHAM, JANE
   FINNEY, ALBERT
WERNER, ELEANORE
   WERNER, OSKAR
WERNER, OSKAR
   POWER, TYRONE
WERNICK, FANNY
   BRICE, FANNY
   HOLM, ELEANOR
WERTHEIM, ELSE
   SLEZAK, WALTER
WEST, BEVERLY
   WEST, MAE
WEST, BROOKS
   ARDEN, EVE
WEST, DOUGLAS BROOKS
   ARDEN, EVE
WEST, DUNCAN PARIS
   ARDEN, EVE
WEST, JOHN EDWIN
   WEST, MAE
WEST, JOHN PATRICK
   WEST, MAE
WESTBROOKE, BERTHA BELLE
   REID, WALLACE
WESTERMANN, FRANCES
   BERGEN, CANDICE
   BERGEN, EDGAR
WESTMEYER, ALMA
   VERA-ELLEN
WESTMORE, HAMILTON 'BUD'
   RAYE, MARTHA
WESTMORELAND, JAMES
   DARBY, KIM
WESTOVER, WINIFRED
   HART, WILLIAM S.
WESTPHAL, FRANK
   TUCKER, SOPHIE

WETHERALD, MAE
    BASEHART, RICHARD
WEXLER, GREGORY SIMON
    CRISTAL, LINDA
WEXLER, YALE
    CRISTAL, LINDA
WHALEN, MICHAEL
    MASSEY, ILONA
WHALEN, TOMMY
    HOLM, ELEANOR
WHEATCROFT, FLORENCE MARY
    BATES, ALAN
WHEELOCK, THOMAS
    ASTOR, MARY
WHELAN, EMMA
    HITCHCOCK, ALFRED
WHIPPLE, BAYONNE
    HUSTON, JOHN
    HUSTON, WALTER
WHITE, CORDELLA
    IVES, BURL
WHITE, EDWARD G.
    WHITE, PEARL
WHITE, FRED
    WHITE, PEARL
WHITE, GEORGE
    WHITE, PEARL
WHITE, GRACE
    WHITE, PEARL
WHITE, LORAY
    DAVIS, JR., SAMMY
WHITE, OLIVE ANN
    FARNUM, DUSTIN
    FARNUM, WILLIAM
WHITE, OPAL
    WHITE, PEARL
WHITE, SLAPPY
    FOXX, REDD
WHITE, STANFORD
    NESBIT, EVELYN
WHITE, WILLIAM EDWARD
    HYDE WHITE, WILFRED
WHITING, BARBARA
    WHITING, MARGARET
WHITING, JACK
    FAIRBANKS, JR., DOUGLAS
WHITING, RICHARD
    WHITING, MARGARET
WHITMAN, ANTHONY
    WHITMAN, STUART
WHITMAN, ELAINE
    YOUNG, GIG
WHITMAN, LINDA
    WHITMAN, STUART
WHITMAN, MICHAEL
    WHITMAN, STUART
WHITMAN, SCOTT
    WHITMAN, STUART

WHITMORE, DANIEL
    WHITMORE, JAMES
WHITMORE, III, JAMES
    WHITMORE, JAMES
WHITMORE, JAMES A.
    WHITMORE, JAMES
WHITMORE, STEPHEN
    WHITMORE, JAMES
WHITNEY, GLORIA
    BEERY, WALLACE
WHITTAKER, JAMES
    CLAIRE, INA
WHITTAKER, JULIETTE
    PRYOR, RICHARD
WHITTY, ALFRED
    WHITTY, DAME MAY
WHITTY, MICHAEL JAMES
    WHITTY, DAME MAY
WIDMARK, ANNE
    WIDMARK, RICHARD
WIDMARK, CARL H.
    WIDMARK, RICHARD
WIDMARK, DONALD
    WIDMARK, RICHARD
WIGTON, KARI
    CLARK, DICK
WILCOX, HERBERT
    NEAGLE, ANNA
WILCOX, MARGUERITE COBB
    PRICE, VINCENT
WILCOX, ROBERT
    BARRYMORE, JOHN
WILDE, LOUIS BELA
    WILDE, CORNEL
WILDE, WENDY
    WILDE, CORNEL
WILDER, JO
    GREY, JOEL
WILDER, KATHARINE ANASTASIA
    WILDER, GENE
WILDING, CHRISTOPHER EDWARD
    BURTON, RICHARD
    FISHER, EDDIE
    TAYLOR, ELIZABETH
    WILDING, MICHAEL
WILDING, HENRY
    WILDING, MICHAEL
WILDING, JR., MICHAEL HOWARD
    BURTON, RICHARD
    FISHER, EDDIE
    TAYLOR, ELIZABETH
    WILDING, MICHAEL
WILDING, LEYLA
    TAYLOR, ELIZABETH
    WILDING, MICHAEL
WILDING, MICHAEL
    GRANGER, STEWART

WILDING, MICHAEL
    TAYLOR, ELIZABETH
WILDING, NAOMI
    TAYLOR, ELIZABETH
    WILDING, MICHAEL
WILEY, ALICE NEVIN
    COREY, WENDELL
WILEY, IRENE
    EDWARDS, CLIFF
WILKERSON, BILLY
    O'CONNOR, DONALD
WILKINS, ARLENE
    ROGERS, ROY
WILKINS, LIDA ALBERTA
    BOYD, WILLIAM
WILLARD, CATHERINE
    BELLAMY, RALPH
WILLAT, IRVING
    DOVE, BILLIE
WILLETT, MARJORIE
    VAN DYKE, DICK
WILLETT, SARAH E.
    CAWTHORN, JOSEPH
WILLIAMS, ANDY
    LONGET, CLAUDINE
WILLIAMS, CARA
    BARRYMORE, JR., JOHN
WILLIAMS, CHARLES
    HUNTER, TAB
WILLIAMS, CHRISTIAN
    LONGET, CLAUDINE
    WILLIAMS, ANDY
WILLIAMS, DAVID
    LOY, MYRNA
WILLIAMS, DONALD
    WILLIAMS, ANDY
WILLIAMS, DR. JOHN
    GABOR, EVA
    GABOR, ZSA ZSA
WILLIAMS, ESTHER
    LAMAS, FERNANDO
WILLIAMS, FRANCES
    LOVEJOY, FRANK
WILLIAMS, GERTRUDE
    WOOLLEY, MONTY
WILLIAMS, JANE
    WILLIAMS, ANDY
WILLIAMS, JAY EMERSON
    WILLIAMS, ANDY
WILLIAMS, JR., DAVID
    LOY, MYRNA
WILLIAMS, KAY
    MONTGOMERY, GEORGE
WILLIAMS, LARRY C.
    MCDANIEL, HATTIE
WILLIAMS, LOU
    WILLIAMS, ESTHER

WILLIAMS, LUCILLE
    WILLIAMS, GUINN 'BIG BOY'
WILLIAMS, MALCOLM
    WILLIAMS, GUINN 'BIG BOY'
WILLIAMS, MARJORIE
    JONES, SHIRLEY
WILLIAMS, MAUREEN
    WILLIAMS, ESTHER
WILLIAMS, MINNIE LEE
    WILLIAMS, GUINN 'BIG BOY'
WILLIAMS, NOELLE
    LONGET, CLAUDINE
    WILLIAMS, ANDY
WILLIAMS, PEGGY
    TAYLOR, ROD
WILLIAMS, RICHARD
    WILLIAMS, ANDY
WILLIAMS, ROBERT
    LONGET, CLAUDINE
    WILLIAMS, ANDY
WILLIAMS, RUTH
    JONES, JAMES EARL
WILLIAMS, SR., GUINN
    WILLIAMS, GUINN 'BIG BOY'
WILLIAMS, SYBIL
    BURTON, RICHARD
WILLS, IVAH
    COBURN, CHARLES
WILLS, JILL
    WILLS, CHILL
WILLS, WILL
    WILLS, CHILL
WILLSON, SALLY
    COTTEN, JOSEPH
WILLY, CHILLY
    WOODPECKER, WOODY
WILNER, NANCY
    CULP, ROBERT
WILSON, EILEEN
    POWELL, WILLIAM
WILSON, HENRY
    HUDSON, ROCK
WILSON, JACQUELINE
    ROBERTSON, DALE
WILSON, KATHERINE YOUNG
    BARTHELMESS, RICHARD
WILSON, LUCILLE
    ARMSTRONG, LOUIS
WILSON, MARY
    ROSS, DIANA
WILSON, MILDRED
    DEAN, JAMES
WILSON, NELLIE
    REAGAN, RONALD
WILSON, WOODROW
    GREENSTREET, SYDNEY
WILTON, OLIVE DE
    KARLOFF, BORIS

WINCHEL
    WINCHEL
INCHELL, EIL
    WINCHELL, WAL
WINCHELL, GLORIA
    WINCHELL, WALTER
WINCHELL, JR., WALTER
    WINCHELL, WALTER
WINCHELL, KENYA ALISE
    WINCHELL, WALTER
WINCHELL, OWEN REED
    WINCHELL, WALTER
WINECHEL, JACOB
    WINCHELL, WALTER
WINFIELD, PAUL
    TYSON, CICELY
WINKLER, BEATRICE
    WINKLER, HENRY
WINKLER, HARRY
    WINKLER, HENRY
WINSOR, KATHLEEN
    SHAW, ARTIE
WINSTON, LEWISE
    SULLAVAN, MARGARET
WINTER, DAVID
    LOVELACE, LINDA
WINTER, PETER
    WYNTER, DANA
WINTER, ROSE
    WINTERS, SHELLEY
WINTERS, ALICE KILGORE RODGERS
    WINTERS, JONATHAN
WINTER, JONATHAN 'JAY'
    WINTERS, JONATHAN
WINTERS, LUCINDA KELLEY
    WINTERS, JONATHAN
WINTERS, SHELLEY
    FRANCIOSA, ANTHONY
WINWOOD, ESTELLE
    BANKHEAD, TALLULAH
WIRT, ROBERT
    CALVET, CORINNE
WITHERS, GRANT
    YOUNG, LORETTA
WITNEY, MICHAEL
    TWIGGY
WITTE, JACQUELINE
    NEWMAN, PAUL
WOLCOTT, NANCY
    EBSEN, BUDDY
WOLDERS, ROBERT
    OBERON, MERLE
WOLF, HAZEL ELIZABETH
    STONE, LEWIS
WOLF, HELEN
    MARSHALL, E.G.
WOLFE, ANNE MARIE
    THATCHER, TORIN

WOLFE, PETER
    DUNAWAY, FAYE
LFF, BARBARA MICHELE
    CLARK, PETULA
FF, CATHERINE NATALIE
    CLARK, PETULA
LFF, CLAUDE
    CLARK, PETULA
WOLFF, PATRICK PHILIPPE
    CLARK, PETULA
WOMACH, MATTIE MARTHA
    ROGERS, ROY
WONSO, STANLEY
    TIFFIN, PAMELA
WOOD, BETTIE SUE
    EVANS, DALE
WOOD, ELIZABETH
    STACK, ROBERT
WOOD, EUGENE
    WOOD, PEGGY
WOOD, ISABEL MARY SCOTT
    SMITH, C. AUBREY
WOOD, LANA
    WOOD, NATALIE
WOOD, MARY BELL
    KILEY, RICHARD
WOOD, NATALIE
    PRESLEY, ELVIS
    WAGNER, ROBERT
WOODALL, EDWARD
    PITTS, ZASU
WOODRUFF, CHARLES E.
    SWANSON, GLORIA
WOODS, MARY ELLEN
    BICKFORD, CHARLES
WOODS, THOMAS
    BICKFORD, CHARLES
WOODWARD, JOANNE
    NEWMAN, PAUL
WOODWARD, JR., WADE
    WOODWARD, JOANNE
WOODWARD, WADE
    WOODWARD, JOANNE
WOOLEY, WILLIAM EDGAR
    WOOLLEY, MONTY
WOOLLEY, JAMES
    WOOLLEY, MONTY
WORTIS, BEATRICE
    ARKIN, ALAN
WRATHER, CHRISTOPHER
    GRANVILLE, BONITA
WRATHER, JACK
    GRANVILLE, BONITA
WRATHER, JR., JACK
    GRANVILLE, BONITA
ATHER, LINDA
    GRANVILLE, BONITA

WRATHER, MOLLY
    GRANVILLE, BONITA
WRAY, FAY
    KING KONG
WRAY, WILLOW
    WRAY, FAY
WRIGHT, ANNA MAY
    MACDONALD, JEANETTE
    RAYMOND, GENE
WRIGHT, CATHERINE
    BAXTER, ANNE
    HODIAK, JOHN
WRIGHT, FRANK LLOYD
    BAXTER, ANNE
WRIGHT, JR., ALFRED
    DE HAVILLAND, OLIVIA
    FONTAINE, JOAN
WRIGHT, LAURIE
    WILLIAMS, ANDY
WRIGHT, SR., COBINA
    BEERY, WALLACE
WRIGHT, VIRGINIA
    BOOTH, SHIRLEY
WU, SYLVIA
    LEE, BRUCE
WUPPERMANN, GEORGE
    MORGAN, FRANK
WUPPERMANN, RALPH KUHNER
    MORGAN, FRANK
WURMAN, NORMA JEAN 'REVEL'
    KENNEDY, GEORGE
WYATT, CHRISTOPHER BILLOP
    WYATT, JANE
WYATT, WILMA W.
    CROSBY, BING
WYCOFF, CHARLES ELMER
    AMES, LEON
WYLER, WILLIAM
    SULLAVAN, MARGARET
WYMAN, JANE
    RAYMOND, GENE
    REAGAN, RONALD
WYMORE, PATRICE
    FLYNN, ERROL
WYNN, ED
    WYNN, KEENAN
WYNN, EDMUND
    JOHNSON, VAN
    WYNN, KEENAN
WYNN, EDWYNNA
    WYNN, KEENAN
WYNN, HILDA
    WYNN, KEENAN
WYNN, KEENAN
    JOHNSON, VAN
    WYNN, ED
WYNN, TRACY
    JOHNSON, VAN

WYNN, TRACY
    WYNN, KEENAN
YATES, HERBERT J.
    RALSTON, VERA HRUBA
YDE-LAKE, ANNETTE
    SOTHERN, ANN
YEAGER, AUDREY
    DARIN, BOBBY
YEWELL, MARTINE
    EWELL, TOM
YODER, MARGO
    CLARK, DANE
YOUNG, BARBARA QUEEN
    YOUNG, ROBERT
YOUNG, CAROL
    YOUNG, ROBERT
YOUNG, CLARENCE M.
    MORAN, LOIS
YOUNG, COLLIER
    DE HAVILLAND OLIVIA
    FONTAINE, JOAN
    LUPINO, IDA
YOUNG, ELIZABETH JANE
    MONTALBAN, RICARDO
    YOUNG, LORETTA
YOUNG, ELIZABETH LOUISE
    YOUNG, ROBERT
YOUNG, GEORGIANNA
    MONTALBAN, RICARDO
    YOUNG, LORETTA
YOUNG, GIG
    MONTGOMERY, ELIZABETH
    MONTGOMERY, ROBERT
YOUNG, JACK
    MONTALBAN, RICARDO
    YOUNG, LORETTA
YOUNG, JAMES D.
    COTTEN, JOSEPH
YOUNG, JENNIFER
    YOUNG, GIG
YOUNG, JOHN EARL
    YOUNG, LORETTA
YOUNG, JOSEPH
    YOUNG, ROBERT
YOUNG, KATHLEEN JOY
    YOUNG, ROBERT
YOUNG, KAY
    WILDING, MICHAEL
YOUNG, LORETTA
    GABLE, CLARK
    MONTALBAN, RICARDO
    TRACY, SPENCER
YOUNG, MARELLE
    DAMITA, LILI
    FLYNN, ERROL
YOUNG, NEIL
    SNODGRESS, CARRIE

YOUNG, POLLY ANN
    MONTALBAN, RICARDO
    YOUNG, LORETTA
YOUNG, REGINA
    CUMMINGS, ROBERT
YOUNG, THOMAS
    YOUNG, ROBERT
YOUNG, TIMOTHY
    MORAN, LOIS
YOUNG, VICTORIA
    KEITH, BRIAN
YULE, JOE
    GARDNER, AVA
    ROONEY, MICKEY
ZAGURI, BOB
    BARDOT, BRIGITTE
ZAHARIADES, BRUCE
    DUNCAN, SANDY
ZANUCK, DARRYL F.
    FOX, WILLIAM
    RIN TIN TIN
ZANUCK, RICHARD DARRYL
    FOX, WILLIAM
ZELTA, STEFANIE KAROLINE
    WERNER, OSKAR
ZERBY, CLYDE
    DARBY, KIM
ZETTERLING, JOEL
    ZETTERLING, MAI
ZIEGFELD, FLORENZ
    BURKE, BILLIE
    OWEN, REGINALD
ZIEGFELD, PATRICIA
    BURKE, BILLIE
ZIEGLER, ANNIE TAPLEY
    GORDON, RUTH
ZIEGLER, GAIL
    BLACK, KAREN
ZIEGLER, NORMAN A.
    BLACK, KAREN
ZIEGLER, PETER
    BLACK, KAREN
ZILAHY, MARIA
    LUKAS, PAUL
ZIMBALIST, EFREM
    ZIMBALIST, JR., EFREM
ZIMBALIST, III, EFREM
    ZIMBALIST, JR., EFREM
ZIMBALIST, JR., STEPHANIE
    ZIMBALIST, JR., EFREM
ZIMBALIST, NANCY
    ZIMBALIST, JR., EFREM
ZIMMERMAN, EDWARD
    MERMAN, ETHEL
ZIMROTH, PETER
    PARSONS, ESTELLE
ZITO, JIMMY
    HAVER, JUNE

ZOMAR, JOSEPH A.
    SAINT CYR, LILI
ZOTNICKAITA, BER SKIKNE
    HARVEY, LAURENCE
ZUBAREFF, VALENTINA
    CANTINFLAS

APPENDICES

A SHORT HISTORY OF THE FILM BUSINESS

The film business didn't begin in Hollywood, which was just a station on the cattle trail from central California to the railroad terminal in Los Angeles. The station had been named by the mid 1880s by the pioneering Mrs. H. Wilcox, who had wishful memories of a village in new England.

Hollywood was incorporated in 1903 but soon had to face the problems of a shortage of water and an abundance of sewerage. With no evident solutions, the residents voted in 1910, to merge with the bigger city towards the east and south, to permit Los Angeles to solve the problems.

If the beginning of the motion picture business wasn't to be found in Hollywood, one early and important step was taken not too far distant. The question had been asked as to the exact method by which a horse managed to run. The human eye had been unable to determine the absolute answer and a sportsman and business tycoon of northern California heritage, Leland Stanford, financed an inquiry into the matter.

Edweard Muybridge, photographer, was assisted by John Isaacs, engineer, in coordinating exposures of film in a series of still cameras. The photographs that resulted, when viewed in sequence, proved indisputably that all four hooves of that running horse were off the ground at the same instant. The graphic results were sent east.

In Philadelphia the films were demonstrated by Henry Renno Heyl on his zoetropic projection system. Then the same films were forwarded to Jean Louis Meisonier in Paris for a demonstration to the Academie Francaise on the subject of animal postures.

The Reverend Hannibal Goodwin attempted to obtain a United States patent in 1887 for a process that resulted in dry, flexible photographic images on a film base. But it wasn't until 1898 that he received his patent and in the mysteriously long intervention of eleven years, The Eastman Dry Plate Film Company successfully patented a similar process and began to merchandise a product.

A quarter of a century later the Reverend Hannibal Goodwin's widow would receive from the Eastman Company a compensation payment of six million dollars.

George Eastman's one-inch wide light-sensitive film on a nitrocellulose base, in strip form, was defined for a U.S. patent in 1889, and when Thomas Alva Edison needed fifty feet of the film, he was charged $2.50.

William Kennedy Dickson was working with Edison at the laboratory in Goerck Street in New York City to merge photography with their phonographic device. With the Eastman film passing the viewing point at the rate of forty frames per second, they defined a process, Kinetoscope, received a patent, made a film they called "Monkeyshines" and presented it to the public in 1894.

William Edward Greene went to the British patents office about the same time with his process of photography on celluloid. Hyphenating his wife's name to his own, Friese-Greene protected the rights to Kinematography.

Woodville Latham, experimenting with the process of projection of film devised the "Latham Loop," which permitted longer shows. His technical achievement permitted the handling of the eleven thousand foot "wide" film which was shot in 1897, in Carson City, Nevada, recording the Corbett-Fitzsimmon's boxing match.

The first major use of artificial lighting occurred in 1899. Four hundred arc lamps were positioned around the ring at Coney Island, New York, when Sharkey and Jeffries fought it out.

The enlightened Lumiere brothers, Louis and August, of

Lyon, France, took advantage of the Kinetoscope system, which Edison had not patented overseas because the foreign copyrights would have cost him $150. The Lumieres modified both the system and the name. They set the projection speed to sixteen exposures per second and called it Cinematographe. The reduced speed became the standard of the industry until sound track synchronization required an advanced rate of projection. They also employed the technique of perforated sprocket holes in the making of their fifty foot documentary, "Lunch Hour at the Lumiere Factory."

That film was first shown to a society dedicated to the encouragement of an industrial France. Parisiennes saw it in the basement of the Grand Café on the Boulevard des Capucines.

The next Lumiere film was the terrifying "Arrival of a Train at a Station." Then they made "Bathing Beach," showing to inland residents the immensity and the restlessness of the sea.

"Baby's Breakfast" was another film and featured Madame Lumiere in the titular role, while her husband could be seen in the distance drinking a bottle of beer.

The film business in France almost ended in 1897 when a fire killed 180 viewers at a charity exhibition. The blame was placed on the film, known to be combustible, until an investigation proved there was another cause for the holocaust.

The exonerated Cinematographe remained the standard projection system for almost a quarter of a century. And by the beginning of the twentieth century, film had been shown in New York City at Hammerstein's Music Hall Theatre and companies such as Vitagraph and American Biograph had been incorporated to make more films.

"The Great Train Robbery" was a sensation in 1903. Harry, Albert, Sam and Jack Warner, brothers, went into business with a travelling operation that included a print of the picture, a projector and a barrel for the film to fall into after it had passed by the lens.

In 1906 Carl Laemmle opened his first theatre in Chicago, marking the beginning of the Universal Film Co. and William Fox bought his first amusement center.

D. W. Griffith abandoned the live stage in 1907 and adopted the Biograph Studio's technique of filmmaking, which he took with him when he moved to Hollywood.

The first motion picture made in a color process was introduced in London. Kinemacolor was the descriptive word for the 1909 study of Queen Elizabeth, starring Sarah Bernhardt. The film was brought to the Unitd States by Adolphe Zukor, who had founded the Famous Players Film Co.

In 1913, "Quo Vadis" arrived from Italy. The admission price was set at one dollar at New York's Astor Theatre. It was the first use of the dollar sign at the ticket window.

"Traffic in Souls" was the first attempt to depict human sexual urges in a film for public viewing. Made by Universal at a cost of $5,700, it returned a reported $450,000.

Dustin Farnum became a celebrity when he made "The Squaw Man." The producers of that picture, Jesse Lasky and his partners, Samuel Goldwyn and Cecil B. De Mille, would all have long and independent careers making films. Even the barn where the film was shot would become a landmark, symbol of Hollywood's invention of heroic and glorified cowboys.

The value of the personality of the film actors had been observed and contracts with celebrated players were becoming expensive. Mary Pickford was getting two thousand dollars a week in 1914 from the Famous Players Co. That year, Paramount Pictures was formed to produce and release the films of Famous Players.

Two dollars was the ticket price when "Birth of a Nation" was shown in New York City. It was the year Metro Pictures was established with Richard Rowland as president of the company, Joseph Engel, treasurer and Louis B. Mayer, secretary.

When Mary Pickford found out that Charles Chaplin was collecting a salary of ten thousand dollars a week at Mutual Pictures, she soon had a new contract, guaranteeing one million forty thousand dollars in two years with bonuses based on the profits of her films.

In 1919, William Randolph Hearst incorporated Cosmopolitan Pictures, diversifying his publishing and land empire. And that same year Louis B. Mayer raised five million dollars and formed his own company.

Pickford, Chaplin, Griffith and Douglas Fairbanks formed the United Artists Corporation with Oscar Price as president. And in 1920, brothers, Harry and Jack Cohn, with a partner, Joe Brandt, established the C.B.C. Film Sales Company, with initial pride. Later they sought property for a studio and became the Columbia Pictures Corporation.

In Pittsburgh, Pennsylvania, The Duquesne Amusement Supply Company was established to sell equipment to theatre owners. They mailed out a brochure that was prophetically titled: *The Film Noise.* This newsletter would soon enough display sound equipment but in the early 1920's the newest invention that would benefit audiences and exhibitors was the ice cream machine, which had just been perfected in Youngstown, Ohio.

In 1926, "Don Juan" was shown with a fully synchronized musical score, recorded by the New York Philharmonic Orchestra. But it was in August, that year, that the "Jazz Singer" revolutionized the film business. The Warner brothers had bought the Vitagraph Company and the Stanley Theatres, whose properties would become known as Stanley Warner Theatres, as if to honor another but non-existent brother. They also acquired an interest in First National Productions.

Mergers and acquisitions were occurring in the rapidly developing film business. Almost daily new partnerships were announced.

Marcus Loew and his son, Arthur, had progressed from penny arcades to nickelodeon operations by 1924. Then they acquired the Goldwyn Pictures Company which had been formed by Edgar Selwyn and Samuel Goldfish. Goldfish had

even changed his name to conform to the company's.

To run the company, Loew acquired the services of Louis B. Mayer, who brought along his partners, Irving Thalberg and J. Robert Rubin. Loew was also involved with the operators of the Palisades Amusement Park, Nicholas Schenck, who remained through the metamorphosis of M-G-M while Joseph Schenck went with Darryl F. Zanuck and William Goetz and formed Twentieth Century Pictures.

William Fox had started a film exhibition business in a Brooklyn store in 1903 and progressed from there. He had a national company in operation by 1935, with Winfield Sheehan, general manager and Sidney Kent, president. That year he merged it with Twentieth Century Pictures and Darryl Zanuck took charge of film production. Sheehan left the new studio while Joseph Schenck stayed, a rival to his brother, a few dusty miles away, at M-G-M.

Beside these major studios there were many other companies formed to produce films. Often led by a single charismatic figure, these companies only performed as well as their leader could sustain his own performance. In 1930, a listing of film-producing companies would include names like American General, Artclass, Associated Artists, Audible Pictures, Chesterfield Motion Pictures, Empire Productions, Excellent Pictures, Inspiration Pictures, Mascot Pictures, Parthenon Pictures, Rayart Pictures, Tiffany Productions, UFA Films and WAFilms.

Eleven thousand three hundred fifty titles were indexed in a compilation of the feature films made between the beginnings of 1915 and 1930. By the end of that period more than 20,000 people worked in Hollywood film production capacities. Films had become a major source of information and education, as well as entertainment, for the country and for the world. Hollywood's films were exhibited everywhere and the players were known throughout the world. And so it came to be said, with voice over a fanfare of music: *the film business is everybody's business.*

STUDIO HIERARCHIES

COLUMBIA PICTURES CORP.
(Incorporated 1924)
COLUMBIA PICTURES INDUSTRIES, INC.

Chairman of the Board

A. Schneider	(1969–1973)
Leo Jaffe	(1973–

President

Harry Cohn	(1924–1928)
Joe Brandt	(1928–1933)
Harry Cohn	(1933–1959)
A. Schneider	(1959–1968)
Leo Jaffe	(1968–1969)
A. Schneider	(1969–1970)
Leo Jaffe	(1970–1971)
Stanley Schneider	(1971–1972)
Leo Jaffe	(1972–1973)
Alan J. Hirschfield	(1973–1978)
Frank T. Vincent	(1978–

Production Executive

Samuel Briskin	(1928–1930)
Harry Cohn	(1930–1936)
Jack Cohn	(1936–1943)
Harry Cohn	(1943–1950)
Jack Cohn	(1950–1953)
Harry Cohn	(1953–1959)
A. Schneider	(1959–1964)
M. J. Frankovich	(1964–1968)
Robert Weitman	(1968–1970)
Leo Jaffe	(1970–1971)
Stanley Schneider	(1971–1973)
David Begelman	(1973–1978)

Board of Directors

Harry Cohn	(1933–1959)
Jack Cohn	(1933–1957)
Sol Bornstein	(1933–1940)
Max Winslow	(1933–1935)
Jack Kerner	(1933–1940)
Leo M. Blancke	(1933–1966)
Nathan Burkan	(1934–1935)
A. Schneider	(1936–1976)
Charles Schwartz	(1938–1942)
N. P. Spingold	(1941–1959)
Dr. A. H. Giannini	(1941–1943)
L. J. Barbano	(1943–1944)
A. Montague	(1943–1962)
Donald S. Stralem	(1945–1976)
Arnold Grant	(1949–1953)
Henry Crown	(1949–1953)
L. Rosensteil	(1951–1952)
Alfred Hart	(1953–1975)
A. M. Sonnabend	(1953–1964)
Ralph Cohn	(1958–1960)
Mendel B. Silverberg	(1959–1965)
Leo Jaffe	(1960–
Samuel J. Briskin	(1961–1969)
Jerome Hyams	(1963–1973)
Herbert L. Barnet	(1966–1971)
Chester I. Lappen	(1966–1975)
Ben Regan	(1969–1970)
Matthew Rosenhaus	(1969–1970)
Serge Semenenko	(1969–1976)
Irving Mitchell Felt	(1970–1973)
P. H. Horowitz	(1970–1972)
R. Karp	(1970–1972)
M. F. Jordan	(1970–1972)
S. Malamed	(1970–1972)
Bernard E. Zeeman	(1970–1972)
Stanley Schneider	(1970–1973)
Howard Buhse	(1970–1976)
Paul Hallingby, Jr.	(1970–1976)
Matthew Rosenhaus	(1973–
Alan J. Hirschfield	(1973–
Herbert A. Allen, Jr.	(1974–
David Begelman	(1974–1978)
Samuel L. Tedlow	(1976–
John H. Mitchell	(1976–1977)
Robert Strauss	(1976–1977)
Irwin Kramer	(1977–
George C. Scott	(1977–
Dan W. Lufkin	(1977–
James P. Wilmot	(1978–
Jack H. Vaughn	(1978–
Sy Weintraub	(1978–

WALT DISNEY PRODUCTIONS, LTD.
(Incorporated 1929)

Chairman of the Board

Walter E. Disney	(1947–1969)
Roy O. Disney	(1969–1972)
Donn B. Tatum	(1972–

President

Walter E. Disney	(1929–1947)
Roy O. Disney	(1947–1969)
Donn B. Tatum	(1969–1972)
E. Cardon Walker	(1972–

Production Executive

Roy O. Disney	(1936–1941)
Walter E. Disney	(1941–1947)
William H. Anderson	(1960–1973)
Michael L. Bagnall	(1973–1974)
William H. Anderson	(1974–1977)
Robert W. Gibeaut	(1977–

Board of Directors

Walter E. Disney	(1953–1969)
Roy O. Disney	(1953–1973)
George E. Jones	(1953–1954)
Gunther R. Lessing	(1953–1965)
Paul L. Pease	(1953–1960)
Gordon E. Youngman	(1953–1974)
Floyd B. Odlum	(1955–1961)
Edward H. Wadewitz	(1955–1956)
John E. Barber	(1957–1971)
E. Cardon Walker	(1961–
George L. Bagnall	(1962–1974)
William H. Anderson	(1962–
Donn B. Tatum	(1966–
S. Clark Biese	(1966–1975)
Ronald W. Miller	(1970–
Raymond L. Watson	(1974–
Richard T. Morrow	(1974–
Philip Hawley	(1975–
Shirley Temple Black	(1975–1977)
Caroline Leonetti Ahmanson	(1978–
Roy O. Disney	(1978–

METRO-GOLDWYN-MAYER CORP.
(Incorporated 1919)

Chairman of the Board

George L. Killion	(1959–1969)
Robert H. O'Brien	(1969–1970)
George L. Killion	(1970–1972)
Fred Benninger	(1972–

President

Nicholas M. Schenck	(1928–1958)
Joseph R. Vogel	(1958–1964)
Robert H. O'Brien	(1964–1969)
Louis F. Polk, Jr.	(1969–1970)
James T. Aubrey, Jr.	(1970–1973)
Frank E. Rosenfelt	(1973–

Production Executive

Louis B. Mayer	(1925–1951)
Dore Schary	(1951–1957)
Robert M. Weitman	(1964–1967)
Clark Ramsay	(1967–1969)
Herbert F. Solow	(1969–1972)
Daniel Melnick	(1971–1977)
Richard A. Shepherd	(1978–

Board of Directors

Nicholas M. Schenck	(1928–1958)
J. Robert Rubin	(1928–1957)
Louis B. Mayer	(1928-1931, 35–37)
Irving Thalberg	(1928–1937)
Harry Rapf	(1928–1937)
David Bernstein	(1928–1946)
Arthur M. Loew	(1928–1935, '57)
David L. Loew	(1928–1935)
David Warfield	(1928–1946)
Edward J. Bowes	(1928–1934)
Messmore Kendall	(1928–1934)
F. J. Godsol	(1928–1931)
Edward Schaller	(1928–1934)
Felix F. Feist	(1928–1934)
E. M. Saunders	(1928–1934)
William Braden	(1928–1934)
Leopold Friedman	(1930–1955)
J. T. Mills	(1932–1934)
Charles C. Moskowitz	(1932–1946, 51–57)
Isidor Frey	(1936–1938)
William A. Philips	(1938–1939)
John R. Hazel	(1938–1943)
George N. Armsby	(1938–1943)
William A. Parker	(1938–1970)
A. Lichtman	(1938–1943)
Henry Rogers Winthrop	(1941–1955)
J. R. Vogel	(1941–1964)
Eugene W. Leake	(1943–1957)
George A. Brownell	(1952–1958)
G. Rowland Collins	(1955–1957)
Howard Dick	(1955–1957)
Benjamin Melniker	(1956–1970)
Charles M. Reagan	(1956–1957)
John Lawrence Sullivan	(1957–1970)
Fred F. Florence	(1958–1959)
Louis A. Johnson	(1958–1959)
George L. Killion	(1958–1972)
Frank Page, Jr.	(1958–1959)
K. T. Keller	(1958–1959)
Ray Lawson	(1958–1959)
Stanley Meyer	(1958–1959)
Ogden R. Reid	(1958–1959)
Joseph Tomlinson	(1958–1959)
Ellsworth C. Alvord	(1959–1964)
Omar N. Bradley	(1959–1969)
Charles Braunstein	(1959–1960)
Samuel Briskin	(1959–1960)
Bennett Cerf	(1959–1966)
Louis A. Green	(1959–1960)

Ira Guilden	(1959–1970)
Francis W. Hatch	(1959–1960)
J. Howard McGrath	(1959–1968)
Jerome Newman	(1959–1960)
Robert H. O'Brien	(1959–1970)
Philip A. Roth	(1959–1970)
Charles H. Silver	(1959–1970)
Nathan Cummings	(1960–1964)
Joseph I. Snyders, Jr.	(1960–1965)
Robert Weitman	(1965–1968)
Frank E. Conant	(1966–1972)
Philip J. Levin	(1966–1968)
James A. Rowe, Jr.	(1968–1970)
John Wanamaker	(1969–1970)
Richard L. Shall	(1969–1970)
Louis F. Polk, Jr.	(1969–1970)
John L. Loeb	(1969–1970)
Edgar M. Bronfman	(1969–1970)
Edgar R. Baker	(1969–1970)
Bernhard M. Auer	(1969–1970)
Arnold McGraw	(1970–1971)
George T. Scharffenberger	(1970–1971)
William Singleton	(1970–1971)
E. Leo Kolber	(1970–1977)
Barron Hilton	(1971–1972)
James T. Aubrey, Jr.	(1971–1973)
Arnold Daum	(1971–1975)
Kirk Kerkorian	(1971–
James D. Aljian	(1971–
Fred Benninger	(1971–
William R. Boyd	(1972–1973)
Walter M. Sharp	(1972–
Douglas Netter	(1973–1974)
Alvin Benedict	(1973–
Frank E. Rosenfelt	(1974–
Barrie K. Brunet	(1976–
Arthur G. Linkletter	(1976–
Cary Grant	(1976–
Robert W. Prescott	(1978–

PARAMOUNT PICTURES, CORP.
(Incorporated 1917)

Chairman of the Board

William H. English	(1933–1934)
Adolph Zukor	(1936–1965)
Barney Balaban	(1965–1967)
Charles G. Bluhdorn	(1967–1974)
Barry Diller	(1974–

President

Adolph Zukor	(1928–1936)
John E. Otterson	(1936–1938)
Barney Balaban	(1938–1965)
George Weltner	(1965–1967)
Charles G. Bluhdorn	(1967–1970)
Stanley R. Jaffe	(1970–1971)
Frank Yablans	(1971–1975)
Barry Diller	(1975–1976)
David V. Picker	(1976–1977)
Michael D. Eisner	(1977–

Production Executive

Jesse L. Lasky (1st V.P.)	(1928–1932)
Y. Frank Freeman	(1945–1948)
Henry Ginsberg	(1948–1950)
Y. Frank Freeman	(1950–1960)
Jacob H. Karp	(1960–1966)
Howard Koch	(1966–1968)
Robert Evans	(1968–1976)
Robin French	(1976–1977)
Arthur N. Ryan	(1977–1978)
Bob Boyett	(1978–

Board of Directors

Adolph Zukor	(1928–1965)
Gilbert W. Kahn	(1928–1934)
Jesse Laskey	(1928–1930)
William H. English	(1928–1934)
Casimir J. Stralem	(1928–1930)
Felix E. Kahn	(1928–1934)
Frank Bailey	(1928–1934)
Elek John Ludvigh	(1928–1930)
Emil E. Shauer	(1928–1930)
Sir William Wiseman	(1928–1935)
Jules E. Bruhtor	(1928–1934)
John Cecil Graham	(1928–1934)
Albert A. Kaufman	(1928–1930)
Daniel Frohman	(1928–1930)
Sidney R. Kent	(1928–1930)
Eugene Zukor	(1928–1934)
Ralph Kohn	(1928–1935)
Sam Katz	(1928–1930)
Herman Wobber	(1928–1930)
Emmanuel Cohen	(1933–1935)
Austin C. Keough	(1933–1955)
Albert D. Lasker	(1933–1934)
Maurice Newton	(1933–1966)
Walter B. Cokell	(1934–1935)
Sam Denbow, Jr.	(1934–1935)
George J. Schaeffer	(1934–1935)
Neil F. Agnew	(1935–1946)
Henry Anderson	(1935–1936)
John W. Hicks, Jr.	(1935–1944)
Russell Holman	(1935–1937)
E. Paul Phillips	(1935–1936)
R. Earl Anderson	(1936–1937)
H. K. Fortington	(1936–1937)
Y. Frank Freeman	(1936–1966)
John D. Hertz	(1936–1962)
John E. Otterson	(1936–1937)
Barney Balaban	(1938–1970)
Stephen Callaghan	(1938–1952)
Harvey D. Gibson	(1938–1951)
A. Conger Goodyear	(1938–1962)
Stanton Griffis	(1938–1966)
Duncan G. Harris	(1938–1966)
Earl I. McClintock	(1938–1964)

E. V. Richards	(1938–1949)
Edwin L. Weisl	(1939–1970)
Charles M. Reagan	(1945–1948)
Leonard H. Goldenson	(1945–1949)
Fred Mohrhardt	(1950–1954)
Paul Raibourn	(1950–1967)
George Weltner	(1950–1967)
Paul E. Manheim	(1963–1969)
James H. Richardson	(1965–1967)
Gerald H. Ruttenberg	(1967–1968)
Edwin S. Steinmetz	(1967–1968)
T. H. Neyland	(1967–1968)
John H. Duncan	(1967–1968)
Milton A. Gordon	(1967–1969)
Fred M. Kauffmann	(1967–1969)
David N. Judelson	(1967–
Charles G. Bluhdorn	(1967–
John Reynolds	(1968–1969)
Don Gaston	(1968–1970)
Joel Dolkart	(1968–1970)
Thomas M. Lewyn	(1968–
Martin S. Davis	(1968–
Stanley R. Jaffe	(1970–1971)
Frank Yablans	(1971–1976)

TWENTIETH CENTURY FOX FILM CORP.

Chairman of the Board

William Fox	(1928–1932)
H. L. Clark	(1932–1933)
E. R. Tinker	(1933–1935)
Joseph M. Schenck	(1935–1942)
Wendell L. Wilkie	(1942–1945)
Spyros Skouras	(1962–1969)
Darryl F. Zanuck	(1969–1971)
Dennis C. Stanfill	(1971–

President

William Fox (Fox)	(1915–1931)
H. L. Clark (Fox)	(1931–1932)
E. R. Tinker (Fox)	(1932–1933)
Sidney R. Kent	(1933–1942)
Spyros Skouras	(1942–1962)
Darryl F. Zanuck	(1962–1971)
Gordon Stulberg	(1971–1975)
Dennis C. Stanfill	(1975–

Production Executive

Ben Jackson (Fox)	(1925–1928)
Winfield Sheehan (Fox)	(1928–1935)
Darryl F. Zanuck	(1935–1956)
Sid Rogell	(1956–1958)
Buddy Adler	(1958–1961)
Lew Schreiber	(1961–1962)
Peter G. Levathes	(1962–1963)
Richard D. Zanuck	(1963–1972)
Dennis C. Stanfill	(1972–

Board of Directors

William Fox	(1928–1932)
Jack Leo	(1928–1930)
Douglas Tauszig	(1928–1930)
Saul Rogers	(1928–1930)
Nathaniel King	(1928–1930)
Winfield Sheehan	(1928–1933)
Charles Levin	(1928–1930)
Jacob W. Loeb	(1928–1930)
Aaron Fox	(1928–1930)
Harley L. Clarke	(1931–1934)
Matthew C. Brush	(1931–1933)
Charles W. Higley	(1931–1933)
Oscar L. Gubelman	(1931–1932)
Joseph E. Higgins	(1931–1932)
S. C. Munoz	(1931–1932)
Albert H. Wiggin	(1932–1933)
Cornelius Vanderbilt	(1932–1933)
Philip R. Clarke	(1932–1933)
Frank O. Watts	(1932–1933)
George M. Moffett	(1932–1933)
David K. E. Bruce	(1932–1933)
E. R. Tinker	(1932–1935)
Samuel W. Fordyce	(1932–1933)
Winthrop A. Aldrich	(1933–1934)
Sidney R. Kent	(1933–1942)
W. C. Michel	(1934–1969)
John D. Clark	(1934–1938)
Donald Campbell	(1934–1944)
Richard F. Hoyt	(1934–1935)
Daniel O. Hastings	(1934–1963)
Arthur W. Loasby	(1934–1935)
Ernest W. Niver	(1934–1935)
Hermann G. Place	(1934–1944)
Seton Porter	(1934–1953)
Sydney Towell	(1934–1944)
Joseph M. Schenck	(1935–1942)
John R. Dillon	(1938–1948)
Felix A. Jenkins	(1938–1947)
William P. Philips	(1938–1951)
Wilfred J. Eadie	(1941–1953)
Edwin P. Kilroe	(1941–1942)

William Goetz	(1942–1944)	H. Blackmer Johnson	(1974–1975)
Spyros Skouras	(1942–1969)	Gerald Trautman	(1974–
Wendell Wilkie	(1942–1945)	John Vogelstein	(1975–
Darryl F. Zanuck	(1942–1971)	William P. Rogers	(1976–
Thomas J. Connors	(1943–1948)	Ralph Lewis	(1975–
Donald A. Henderson	(1945–1953, 65–73)	F. Warren Hellman	(1975–
L. Sherman Adams	(1945–1959)	Donald N. Frey	(1975–
Robert L. Clarkson	(1945–1969)	William G. Karnes	(1978–
Robert Lehman	(1945–1969)	H. S. H. Princess Grace of Monaco	(1978–
Murray Silverstone	(1945–1953)		
Colby M. Chester	(1953–1962)		
Kevin C. McCann	(1953–1973)		
B. Earl Puckett	(1953–1962)		
James A. Van Fleet	(1953–1969)		
Thomas Pappas	(1960–1964)		
John L. Loeb	(1962–1963)		
Milton S. Gould	(1962–1963)		
William Wyler	(1963–1964)		
Arnold Grant	(1963–1964)		
Francis S. Levien	(1963–1968)		
Adam Gimbel	(1963–1969)		
Jerome A. Straka	(1963–1974)		
Fred L. Metzler	(1964–1966)		
Seymour Poe	(1965–1967)		
Richard D. Zanuck	(1967–1968, 70–71)		
William R. Hearst, Jr.	(1969–1976)		
William H. Mulligan	(1970–1971)		
Paul Miller	(1970–1971)		
David Brown	(1970–1971)		
John P. Edmondson	(1970–1974)		
William T. Gossett	(1970–1975)		
Harry J. MacIntyre	(1970–1976)		
William C. Keefe	(1970–1977)		
Frederick L. Ehrman	(1971–1974)		
Dennis C. Stanfill	(1971–		
John H. Johnson	(1971–		
John T. Pollock	(1971–		
Gordon Stulberg	(1971–1975)		
Malcolm A. MacIntyre	(1973–		

UNIVERSAL PICTURES, CO., INC.
(Incorporated 1925)

Chairman of the Board

J. Cheever Cowdin	(1936–1950)
Nate J. Blumberg	(1950–1960)

MCA, Inc.

Jules C. Stein	(1965–1974)
Lew R. Wasserman	(1974–

President

Carl Laemmle	(1920–1936)
R. H. Cochrane	(1936–1938)
Nate J. Blumberg	(1938–1952)
Milton R. Rackmil	(1952–1973)
H. H. Martin	(1973–

Production Executive

Martin Murphy	(1926–1932)
Carl Laemmle, Jr.	(1932–1933)
Leo Spitz	(1946–1955)
Edward Muhl	(1955–1974)
Clark Ramsay	(1974–

Board of Directors

Carl Laemmle	(1925–1936)
R. H. Cochrane	(1925–1938)
P. D. Cochrane	(1925–1938)
C. B. Paine	(1932–1935)
Phil Reisman	(1932–1933)
Helen E. Hughes	(1932–1935)
O. C. Binder	(1932–1933)
L. J. Schlaifer	(1933–1934)
Frank R. Mastroly	(1933–1935)
W. S. McKay	(1934–1937)
J. R. Granger	(1934–1935)
E. F. Walsh	(1934–1935)
J. Myer Schine	(1936–1938)
J. Cheever Cowdin	(1936–1950)
Charles Rogers	(1936–1938)
Paul G. Brown	(1936–1951)
William Freiday	(1936–1940)
Budd Rogers	(1936–1966)
Nate J. Blumberg	(1938–1961)
Daniel Schaeffer	(1938–1960)
Willis H. Taylor, Jr.	(1938–1947)
D. C. Collins	(1938–1947)
Ottavio Prochet	(1938–1949)
Charles D. Prutzman	(1939–1949)

Samuel I. Posen	(1939–1944)
J. Dabney Penick	(1939–1942)
Preston Davie	(1939–1966)
Peyton Gibson	(1941–1942)
John J. O'Connor	(1942–1962)
Allan L. Carter, Jr.	(1942–1944)
J. Arthur Rank	(1945–1953)
William German	(1945–1952)
Clifford Work	(1945–1947)
Robert S. Benjamin	(1948–1953)
G. Woodham Smith	(1948–1953)
Matthew Fox	(1948–1951)
John G. Eidell	(1950–1952)
Albert A. Garthwaite	(1950–1967)
Leon Goldberg	(1950–1954)
R. W. Lea	(1950–1957)
Franklin Nevius	(1950–1951)
Alfred E. Daff	(1952–1960)
Milton R. Rackmil	(1953–1973)
Harold I. Thorp	(1953–1966)
Samuel H. Vallance	(1953–1966)
Walter M. Heymann	(1967–1971)
Lew R. Wasserman	(1967–
Charles Miller	(1967–1977)
Mary Gardiner Jones	(1967–
Jules C. Stein	(1967–
Howard F. Ahmanson	(1968–1969)
Charles B. Thornton	(1968–
Daniel L. Ritchie	(1969–1970)
Taft B. Schreiber	(1969–1977)
Albert A. Dorskind	(1970–1971)
Berle Adams	(1970–1971)
Louis B. Lundborg	(1972–
John E. Drick	(1972–
Sidney Jay Sheinberg	(1975–
Frank Price	(1978–
Ned Tanen	(1978–
Thomas Wertheimer	(1978–

WARNER BROTHERS PICTURES, INC.
(Incorporated 1923)

President

Harry M. Warner	(1928–1957)
Jack L. Warner	(1957–1967)
Benjamin Kalmenson	(1967–1970)
Ted Ashley	(1970–1972)
Frank G. Wells	(1972–1974)
John Calley	(1974–1976)
Frank G. Wells	(1976–

Production Executives

Jack L. Warner	(1923–1945)
Harry M. Warner	(1945–1950)
Jack L. Warner	(1950–1951)
Harry M. Warner	(1951–1957)
Jack L. Warner	(1957–1970)
M. Kenneth Hyman	(1970–1971)
John Calley	(1971–1972)
Richard D. Zanuck	(1972–1973)
Frank Wells	(1973–1976)
John Calley	(1976–1978)
Guy McElwaine	(1977–1978)
Martin Elfand	(1978–
Robert Shapiro	(1978–

Chairman of the Board

Eliot Hyman	(1968–1970)
Ted Ashley	(1970–1974)
*Frank G. Wells	(1974–1976)
*Ted Ashley	(1974–1976)
Ted Ashley	(1976–

*Co-Chairmen

Board of Directors

Harry M. Warner	(1929–1959)
Albert Warner	(1929–1967)
Jack L. Warner	(1929–1968)
Waddill Catchings	(1929–1968)
Henry A. Rudkin	(1929–1937)
Sam Morris	(1929–1939)
G. E. Quigley	(1929–1930)
Herman Starr	(1929–1930)
Abel Gary Thomas	(1929–1937)
J. D. Rossheim	(1929–1930)
Moe Mark	(1930–1932)
Morris Wolf	(1930–1953)
A. Sablosky	(1930–1931)
Simon H. Fabian	(1930–1931)
H. S. Bareford	(1932–1933)
Stanleigh P. Freidman	(1932–1960)
C. S. Guggenheimer	(1933–1954)
J. P. Laffey	(1933–1935)
Samuel Carlisle	(1936–1957)
Joseph Bernhard	(1938–1946)
Robert W. Perkins	(1938–1968)
Joseph H. Hazen	(1941–1944)
Samuel Schneider	(1945–1956)
John E. Bierwirth	(1946–1953)
Serge Semenenko	(1957–1967)
Charles Allen, Jr.	(1957–1968)
Benjamin Kalmenson	(1957–1970)
Thomas J. Martin	(1957–1968)
M. Kenneth Hyman	(1967–1968)
Jerome A. Newman	(1967–1968)
Alfred Bloomingdale	(1968–1969)
Armand Deutsch	(1968–1969)
Alan J. Hirshfield	(1968–1969)
Denniston L. Slater	(1968–1969)
Samuel H. Haims	(1968–1970)
Maxwell Rabb	(1968–1970)
Eliot Hyman	(1968–1970)
Fred Weintraub	(1970–1971)
Daniel Stern	(1970–1971)
Richard D. Zanuck	(1970–1972)
Norman B. Katz	(1970–1972)
David Brown	(1970–1972)

Ted Ashley	(1970–
William Sarnoff	(1970–1973)
W. Spencer Harrison	(1970–1973)
Mo Ostin	(1971–1974)
Leo Greenfield	(1971–1975)
Ahmet Ertegun	(1971–1974)
Jacob S. Leibowitz	(1971–1975)
Gerald J. Leider	(1971–1975)
Frank G. Wells	(1971–
Steven J. Ross	(1971–
Ralph Peterson	(1971–
Charles McGregor	(1971–
Charles Greenlaw	(1971–
Jay Emmett	(1971–
John Calley	(1971–
Carroll Rosenbloom	(1973–1974)
Rich Sheperd	(1974–1975)
Myron Karlin	(1974–
Richard Lederer	(1975–1976)
M. MacSchwebel	(1976–
Guy McElwaine	(1976–1977)
Terry Semel	(1977–
David Geffen	(1977–1978)

ASTROLOGICALLY—A STATISTICAL ANALYSIS

Tabulation of the signs of the zodiac, compiled from the birthdates in the biographic section, indicates these statistical probabilities. The success factor was calculated by the standard deviation method.

SIGN	SUCCESS FACTOR
Aquarius	+17
Gemini	+14
Aries	+13
Capricorn	+ 5
Pisces	+ 1
Scorpio	− 2
Leo	− 5
Sagittarius	− 6
Taurus	− 7
Cancer	−10
Virgo	−10
Libra	−12

JANUARY

1 CUGAT, XAVIER
ANDREWS, DANA
KING KONG
WOODPECKER, WOODY
MITZI THE DOLPHIN
FRANCIS THE MULE
FOX, WILLIAM
BICKFORD, CHARLES

3 MILLAND, RAY
FURNESS, BETTY
ANDREWS, MAXENE
MOREAU, JEANNE
DAVIES, MARION
PITTS, ZASU

4 WYMAN, JANE
BENNETT, TONY
RUSH, BARBARA
CANNON, DYAN

5 AUMONT, JEAN-PIERRE
KEATON, DIANE

6 YOUNG, LORETTA
THOMAS, DANNY
MIX, TOM

7 MOORE, TERRY

8 FERRER, JOSE
PRESLEY, ELVIS
MIMIEUX, YVETTE

9 BANKY, VILMA
LEE, GYPSY ROSE
LAMAS, FERNANDO
VAN CLEEF, LEE
YORK, SUSANNAH

10 BOLGER, RAY
MINEO, SAL
BUSHMAN, FRANCIS X.
HAYAKAWA, SESSUE

11 TAYLOR, ROD
RITTER, TEX

12 RAINER, LUISE

13 STACK, ROBERT
VERDON, GWEN
TUCKER, SOPHIE

14 DANIELS, BEBE
BENDIX, WILLIAM
TRYON, TOM
DUNAWAY, FAYE

15 THATCHER, TORIN
BRIDGES, LLOYD
SCHELL, MARIA
O'BRIEN, MARGARET
NOVELLO, IVOR

16 MERMAN, ETHEL
JURADO, KATY
CAREY, HARRY

17 NORTH, SHEREE
JONES, JAMES EARL
SENNETT, MACK

18 GRANT, CARY
KAYE, DANNY
MOORE, CONSTANCE
HARDY, OLIVER

19 MADISON, GUY
STAPLETON, JEAN
FABARES, SHELLEY

20 AMES, LEON
WARFIELD, WILLIAM
NEAL, PATRICIA
BURNS, GEORGE

21 NAISH, J. CARROLL
SCOFIELD, PAUL
SAVALAS, TELLY
REEVES, STEVE

22 SOTHERN, ANN
LAURIE, PIPER
BIXBY, BILL
GRIFFITH, D. W.

23 SCOTT, RANDOLPH
DURYEA, DAN
KOVACS, ERNIE
BOGART, HUMPHREY

24 BORGNINE, ERNEST
WINWOOD, ESTELLE

25 DUNNOCK, MILDRED

26 NEWMAN, PAUL
KITT, EARTHA

27 VENUTA, BENAY
REED, DONNA
DONAHUE, TROY

28 ALDA, ALAN

29 MATURE, VICTOR
FORSYTHE, JOHN
LONGET, CLAUDINE
ROSS, KATHARINE

30 IRELAND, JOHN
WAYNE, DAVID
MALONE, DOROTHY
HACKMAN, GENE
REDGRAVE, VANESSA

31 BANKHEAD, TALLULAH
AGAR, JOHN
LANZA, MARIO
DRU, JOANNE
SIMMONS, JEAN
FRANCISCUS, JAMES
PLESHETTE, SUZANNE
WALTER, JESSICA
CANTOR, EDDIE

FEBRUARY

1 GABLE, CLARK
WHITMAN, STUART

2 GRANVILLE, BONITA
FAWCETT-MAJORS, FARRAH

3 BERMAN, SHELLEY
CORRELL, CHARLES

4 FOY, JR., EDDIE
LUPINO, IDA
BRUCE, NIGEL

5 CARRADINE, JOHN
BUTTONS, RED

6 REAGAN, RONALD
GABOR, ZSA ZSA
TORN, RIP
VAN DOREN, MAMIE
PERREAU, GIGI
NOVARRO, RAMON

7 CRABBE, BUSTER
STEWART, ANITA

8 TALBOT, LYLE
TURNER, LANA
LEMMON, JACK
DEAN, JAMES
RUGGLES, CHARLES

10 CHANEY, JR., LON
WAGNER, ROBERT
FIELDS, W.C.
HALE, ALAN
DURANTE, JIMMY

11 GABOR, EVA
REYNOLDS, BURT

12 GREENE, LORNE
TUCKER, FORREST

13 NOVAK, KIM
SEGAL, GEORGE
REED, OLIVER
LYNLEY, CAROL

14 RITTER, THELMA

15 ROMERO, CESAR
BLOOM, CLAIRE
BARRYMORE, JOHN

16 ANDREWS, PATRICIA
VERA-ELLEN
BONO, SONNY

17 HOLBROOK, HAL

18 PALANCE, JACK
KENNEDY, GEORGE
SHEPHERD, CYBILL
TRAVOLTA, JOHN
ARNOLD, EDWARD
MENJOU, ADOLPHE

19 OBERON, MERLE
MARVIN, LEE
HARDWICKE, CEDRIC
CALHERN, LOUIS

20 POITIER, SIDNEY
DUNCAN, SANDY
O'NEILL, JENNIFER

21 SHERIDAN, ANN
ROMANOFF, 'PRINCE' MICHAEL

22 YOUNG, ROBERT
MILLS, JOHN

23 HALL, JON
VARSI, DIANE
FONDA, PETER

24 SCOTT, ZACHARY
CRISTAL, LINDA
FARENTINO, JAMES
MAIN, MARJORIE

25 MARX, ZEPPO
BACKUS, JIM
HARRISON, GEORGE
CARUSO, ENRICO

26 ALDA, ROBERT
GLEASON, JACKIE
RANDALL, TONY
HUTTON, BETTY
CAMBRIDGE, GODFREY
FRAWLEY, WILLIAM

27 TONE, FRANCHOT
BENNETT, JOAN
WOODWARD, JOANNE
TAYLOR, ELIZABETH

28 MOSTEL, ZERO

29 MORGAN, MICHELE

MARCH

1 MORAN, LOIS
NIVEN, DAVID
SHORE, DINAH
BELAFONTE, HARRY
HOWARD, RON

2 ARNAZ, DESI
JONES, JENNIFER

3 HARLOW, JEAN

4 GARFIELD, JOHN
PRENTISS, PAULA
WHITE, PEARL

5 HARRISON, REX
CASSIDY, JACK
STOCKWELL, DEAN
EGGAR, SAMANTHA

6 COSTELLO, LOU

7 MAGNANI, ANNA

8 CHARISSE, CYD
REDGRAVE, LYNN
JAFFE, SAM
BEAVERS, LOUISE

9 CLARK, FRED
PAPAS, IRENE

10 MASON, PAMELA
FITZGERALD, BARRY

11 GISH, DOROTHY

12 MACRAE, GORDON

14 CAINE, MICHAEL
TUSHINGHAM, RITA
BENNY, JACK

15 CAREY, MACDONALD
TIERNEY, LAWRENCE
SABU

16 BERGEN, EDGAR
LEWIS, JERRY
NAGEL, CONRAD

17 MCCAMBRIDGE, MERCEDES
COLE, NAT 'KING'
BATES, ALAN

18 DONAT, ROBERT
TREVOR, CLAIRE
BURNETTE, SMILEY
CLARK, DANE

19 ANDRESS, URSULA

20 NELSON, OZZIE
REDGRAVE, MICHAEL
COREY, WENDELL
REINER, CARL
MELCHIOR, LAURITZ

21 BEGLEY, ED
ANDERSON, 'BRONCO BILLY'

22 MALDEN, KARL
MARX, CHICO
SCHILDKRAUT, JOSEPH

23 CRAWFORD, JOAN

25 BARNES, BINNIE
   SIGNORET, SIMONE
   COURTENAY, TOM

26 HAYDEN, STERLING
   ARKIN, ALAN
   CAAN, JAMES
   ROSS, DIANA
   JOLSON, AL

27 JANSSEN, DAVID
   YORK, MICHAEL
   SWANSON, GLORIA

28 LOVEJOY, FRANK
   BOGARDE, DIRK
   BARTHOLOMEW, FREDDIE

29 O'CONNELL, ARTHUR
   O'KEEFE, DENNIS
   BAILEY, PEARL
   CAWTHORN, JOSEPH
   BAXTER, WARNER

30 LAINE, FRANKIE
   ASTIN, JOHN
   BEATTY, WARREN

31 KILEY, RICHARD
   JONES, SHIRLEY
   CHAMBERLAIN, RICHARD

APRIL

1 POWELL, JANE
   MACGRAW, ALI
   CHANEY, LON
   BEERY, WALLACE

2 EBSEN, BUDDY
   GUINNESS, ALEC
   WEBB, JACK

3 STERLING, JAN
   DAY, DORIS
   MASON, MARSHA
   HOWARD, LESLIE

4 LANGFORD, FRANCES
   PERKINS, TONY
   NALDI, NITA

5 TRACY, SPENCER
   DOUGLAS, MELVYN
   DAVIS, BETTE
   PECK, GREGORY
   STORM, GALE

6 HUSTON, WALTER

7 GARNER, JAMES
   BARA, THEDA
   WINCHELL, WALTER

8 CHASE, ILKA
   HENIE, SONJA
   PICKFORD, MARY

9 BOND, WARD
   BELMONDO, JEAN-PAUL
   ROBESON, PAUL

10 CONNORS, CHUCK
   VON SYDOW, MAX
   SHARIF, OMAR
   ARLISS, GEORGE
   MURRAY, MAE
   MCCOY, 'COLONEL' TIM

11 GREY, JOEL
   REYNOLDS, DEBBIE

12 MILLER, ANN
   THUNDERCLOUD, CHIEF

13 KEEL, HOWARD
   WAGGONER, LYLE

14 GIELGUD, JOHN
   STEIGER, ROD
   DILLMAN, BRADFORD
   CHRISTIE, JULIE
   WINDSOR, CLAIRE

15 USTINOV, PETER
   MONTGOMERY, ELIZABETH
   CARDINALE, CLAUDIA
   REID, WALLACE
   JESSEL, GEORGE

16 HODIAK, JOHN
   NELSON, BARRY
   ADAMS, EDIE
   CHAPLIN, CHARLES

17 LAKE, ARTHUR
   HOLDEN, WILLIAM
   SHIRLEY, ANNE

18 BARRIE, WENDY
   MILLS, HAYLEY

19 MANSFIELD, JAYNE
   TALMADGE, CONSTANCE

20 FOCH, NINA
   VERDUGO, ELENA
   O'NEAL, RYAN
   LLOYD, HAROLD
   RATOFF, GREGORY

21 QUINN, ANTHONY
   MAY, ELAINE

22 ALBERT, EDDIE
   NICHOLSON, JACK

23 RENALDO, DUNCAN
   BLAIR, JANET
   TEMPLE, SHIRLEY
   DEE, SANDRA

24 MACLAINE, SHIRLEY
   IRELAND, JILL
   STREISAND, BARBRA

25 PACINO, AL

26 BURNETT, CAROL
   WILLIAMS, GUINN 'BIG BOY'

27 KLUGMAN, JACK
   AIMEE, ANOUK
   DENNIS, SANDY

28 ANN-MARGRET
   BARRYMORE, LIONEL

29 EWELL, TOM
   HOLM, CELESTE

30 ARDEN, EVE
   BRANDO, MARLON
   CALVET, CORINNE
   LEACHMAN, CLORIS

MAY

1 FORD, GLENN
   O'HERLIHY, DAN

2 AHERNE, BRIAN
   CROSBY, BING
   BIKEL, THEODORE
   HOPPER, HEDDA

3
   SLEZAK, WALTER
   ASTOR, MARY

4 HEPBURN, AUDREY

5 FAYE, ALICE
   POWER, TYRONE
   GOSDEN, FREEMAN

6
   GRANGER, STEWART
   WELLES, ORSON
   VALENTINO, RUDOLPH

7 COOPER, GARY
   BAXTER, ANNE
   HAYES, GABBY

8
   BARKER, LEX
   NELSON, RICK

9 ARMENDARIZ, PEDRO
  FINNEY, ALBERT
  JACKSON, GLENDA
  BERGEN, CANDICE
  BARTHELMESS, RICHARD

10 ASTAIRE, FRED

11 SILVERS, PHIL
  RUTHERFORD, MARGARET

12 HYDE WHITE, WILFRED
  MINNELLI, LIZA

13 COTTEN, JOSEPH
  ARTHUR, BEATRICE
  BERGER, SENTA

14 DOVE, BILLIE
  DARIN, BOBBY

15 MASON, JAMES
  ALBERGHETTI, ANNA MARIA

16 FONDA, HENRY
  SULLAVAN, MARGARET
  LIBERACE
  ARNESS, JAMES

17 O'SULLIVAN, MAUREEN
  HOPPER, DENNIS

18 COMO, PERRY
  PINZA, EZIO

20 STEWART, JAMES
  CHER

21 MONTGOMERY, ROBERT
  BURR, RAYMOND
  DAY, DENNIS
  KENDALL, KAY
  BENNETT, RICHARD

22 OLIVIER, LAURENCE
  AZNAVOUR, CHARLES
  BENJAMIN, RICHARD
  SARRAZIN, MICHAEL

23 SHAW, ARTIE
  PAYNE, JOHN
  CLOONEY, ROSEMARY
  COLLINS, JOAN
  FAIRBANKS, DOUGLAS
  GLEASON, JAMES 'JIMMY'
  MARSHALL, HERBERT

24 PALMER, LILLI
  ARBUCKLE, FATTY

25 COCHRAN, STEVE
  CRAIN, JEANNE

26 WAYNE, JOHN
  LEE, PEGGY
  LUKAS, PAUL
  TALMADGE, NORMA

27 PRICE, VINCENT
  ZETTERLING, MAI
  FARNUM, DUSTIN

28 BAKER, CARROLL

29 HOPE, BOB
  MORLEY, ROBERT
  LILLIE, BEATRICE

30 FETCHIT, STEPIN
  BLANC, MEL
  WALKER, CLINT

JUNE

1 CAULFIELD, JOAN
  CURTIS, TONY
  MONROE, MARILYN
  BOONE, PAT
  MORGAN, FRANK

2 WEISSMULLER, JOHNNY
  KELLERMAN, SALLY

3 GODDARD, PAULETTE
  GORCEY, LEO
  SAINT CYR, LILI
  DEWHURST, COLLEEN

4 RUSSELL, ROSALIND
  WEAVER, DENNIS
  BARRYMORE, JR., JOHN
  NAZIMOVA

5 BOYD, WILLIAM

7 TANDY, JESSICA

8 PRESTON, ROBERT
  WYNTER, DANA
  DARREN, JAMES
  LASSIE

9 CUMMINGS, ROBERT

10 HAYDEN, RUSSELL
  GARLAND, JUDY
  HAVER, JUNE
  MCDANIEL, HATTIE

11 WILDER, GENE
  EVERETT, CHAD

12 RALSTON, VERA HRUBA
  DAMONE, VIC

13 LYNDE, PAUL
  RATHBONE, BASIL

14 IVES, BURL
  MCGUIRE, DOROTHY
  BARRY, GENE
  EDWARDS, CLIFF

15 LOCKHART, JUNE

16 KERRY, NORMAN
  LAUREL, STAN

17 BELLAMY, RALPH
  MARTIN, DEAN
  FAZENDA, LOUISE

18 MACDONALD, JEANETTE
  MARSHALL, E.G.
  BOONE, RICHARD
  BROLIN, JAMES
  MCCARTNEY, PAUL

19 NATWICK, MILDRED
  JOURDAN, LOUIS
  ANGELI, PIER
  PAVAN, MARISA
  ROWLANDS, GENA
  WHITTY, DAME MAY
  COBURN, CHARLES

20 FLYNN, ERROL
  MURPHY, AUDIE

21 RUSSELL, JANE
  HOLLIDAY, JUDY
  STAPLETON, MAUREEN

22 CHAMPION, GOWER
  KRISTOFFERSON, KRIS

24 HARRIS, PHIL

25 HAYES, PETER LIND

26 LORRE, PETER
  PARKER, ELEANOR
  RAFFERTY, FRANCES

28 BROOKS, MEL
  MORAN, POLLY

29 EDDY, NELSON
   PICKENS, SLIM
   EVANS, ROBERT

30 HORNE, LENA
   HAYWARD, SUSAN

JULY

1 DE HAVILLAND, OLIVIA
  CARON, LESLIE
  BUJOLD, GENEVIEVE
  BLACK, KAREN
  LAUGHTON, CHARLES

3 SANDERS, GEORGE

4 ARMSTRONG, LOUIS
  MURPHY, GEORGE
  SAINT, EVA MARIE
  BOYD, STEPHEN
  LOLLOBRIGIDA, GINA
  FARNUM, WILLIAM
  MAYER, LOUIS B.
  LAWRENCE, GERTRUDE

5 MASSEY, ILONA

6 ANDREWS, LAVERNE
  STALLONE, SYLVESTER

7 STARR, RINGO

8 EMERSON, FAYE
  LAWRENCE, STEVE
  DARBY, KIM

10 LAYE, EVELYN
   ADAMS, NICK
   LYON, SUE
   GILBERT, JOHN

11 BRYNNER, YUL
   HUNTER, TAB

12 BERLE, MILTON
   COSBY, BILL
   HERSHOLT, JEAN

13 BLACKMER, SIDNEY

14 MURRAY, KEN
   TERRY-THOMAS
   ROBERTSON, DALE
   BERGEN, POLLY

15 HACKETT, RAYMOND

16 STANWYCK, BARBARA
   ROGERS, GINGER
   TUFTS, SONNY

17 DILLER, PHYLLIS
   SUTHERLAND, DONALD
   CARROLL, DIAHANN
   BANKS, MONTAGUE 'MONTY'
   CAGNEY, JAMES

18 WILLS, CHILL
   VELEZ, LUPE
   SKELTON, RED
   CRONYN, HUME
   MILLER, MARVIN
   HILLIARD, HARRIET
   LOCKHART, GENE

20 DAMITA, LILI
   ALBRIGHT, LOLA
   RIGG, DIANA
   WOOD, NATALIE

21 SMITH, C. AUBREY

22 WHITING, MARGARET

23 WILDING, MICHAEL
   DE HAVEN, GLORIA

24 BUZZI, RUTH

25 BRENNAN, WALTER

26 ALLEN, GRACIE
   VANCE, VIVIAN
   ROBARDS, JR., JASON
   LEIGH, JANET

27 WYNN, KEENAN

28 VALLEE, RUDY
   BROWN, JOE E.
   LA MARR, BARBARA

29 POWELL, WILLIAM

31 CHAPLIN, GERALDINE

AUGUST

2 LOY, MYRNA
  MERRILL, GARY
  O'CONNOR, CARROLL
  O'TOOLE, PETER

3 DEL RIO, DOLORES
  MAXWELL, MARILYN
  SCOTT, GORDON
  CORD, ALEX

5 HUSTON, JOHN
  TAYLOR, ROBERT
  OWEN, REGINALD

6 BALL, LUCILLE
  MITCHUM, ROBERT
  WARHOL, ANDY
  CARRILLO, LEO
  PARSONS, LOUELLA O.
  GIBSON, HOOT

7 BURKE, BILLIE

8 BOW, CLARA
  SIDNEY, SYLVIA
  DE LAURENTIIS, DINO
  CALHOUN, RORY
  WILLIAMS, ESTHER
  HOFFMAN, DUSTIN

9 FARRELL, CHARLES
  SHAW, ROBERT

10 HALEY, JACK
   SHEARER, NORMA
   WYATT, JANE
   FLEMING, RHONDA
   HYER, MARTHA
   FISHER, EDDIE

11 NOLAN, LLOYD
   PARKER, JEAN
   DAHL, ARLENE

12 CANTINFLAS
   DEREK, JOHN
   HAMILTON, GEORGE
   DE MILLE, C. B.

13 TOOMEY, REGIS
   RAYMOND, GENE
   LAHR, BERT
   HITCHCOCK, ALFRED

14 SAINT JAMES, SUSAN

15 BARRYMORE, ETHEL
   FORD, FRANCIS

16 PARKER, FESS
   BLYTH, ANN
   CULP, ROBERT
   VON FURSTENBURG, BETSY

17 HARDING, ANN
   O'HARA, MAUREEN
   DE NIRO, ROBERT
   WOOLLEY, MONTY
   WEST, MAE

18 WINTERS, SHELLEY
   REDFORD, ROBERT

19 MOORE, COLLEEN
   PAGET, DEBRA
   SAINT JOHN, JILL
   STONE, FRED
   LUNT, ALFRED
   BOARDMAN, ELEANOR

22 PRESLE, MICHELINE
   HARPER, VALERIE

23 KELLY, GENE
   MILES, VERA
   EDEN, BARBARA

25 KEELER, RUBY
   JOHNSON, VAN
   FERRER, MEL
   CONNERY, SEAN

26 CLAYTON, JAN

27 RAYE, MARTHA
   SANDS, TOMMY
   WELD, TUESDAY
   GOLDWYN, SAMUEL

28 O'CONNOR, DONALD
   BOYER, CHARLES

29 RENNIE, MICHAEL
   BERGMAN, INGRID
   MONTGOMERY, GEORGE
   GOULD, ELLIOT
   CHEKHOV, MICHAEL

30 BOOTH, SHIRLEY
   MACMURRAY, FRED
   BLONDELL, JOAN
   ASHLEY, ELIZABETH
   BOTTOMS, TIMOTHY
   MASSEY, RAYMOND

31 BASEHART, RICHARD
   COBURN, JAMES
   MARCH, FREDRIC

SEPTEMBER

1 DE CARLO, YVONNE

2 CHAMPION, MARGE

3 LADD, ALAN
  CARLISLE, KITTY

4 GAYNOR, MITZI
  CASTELLANO, RICHARD

5 LAWRENCE, CAROL
  WELCH, RAQUEL

7 LAWFORD, PETER

8 CAESAR, SID
  SELLERS, PETER

9 ROBERTSON, CLIFF

10 WRAY, FAY
   O'BRIEN, EDMOND

12 CHEVALIER, MAURICE

13 COLBERT, CLAUDETTE
   HAYMES, DICK
   TORME, MEL
   BISSET, JACQUELINE

14 HEATHERTON, JOEY

15 RIN TIN TIN
   COOPER, JACKIE
   BENCHLEY, ROBERT

16 PAIGE, JANIS
   BACALL, LAUREN
   FALK, PETER
   FRANCIS, ANNE

17 COSTELLO, DOLORES
   MCDOWALL, RODDY
   BANCROFT, ANNE

18 ANDERSON, EDDIE 'ROCHESTER'
   GARBO, GRETA
   BRAZZI, ROSSANO
   WARDEN, JACK
   BLAKE, ROBERT
   AVALON, FRANKIE

19 MCCALLUM, DAVID
   TWIGGY
   TRUEX, ERNEST
   CORTEZ, RICARDO

20 ROBERTS, RACHEL
   LOREN, SOPHIA

22 VON STROHEIM, ERICH
   MUNI, PAUL

23 ROONEY, MICKEY
   SCHNEIDER, ROMY
   PIDGEON, WALTER

25 RAY, ALDO
   PROWSE, JULIET
   DOUGLAS, MICHAEL

26 LONDON, JULIE
   GWENN, EDMUND
   MORENO, ANTONIO

27 MEADOWS, JAYNE
   RAFT, GEORGE

28 FINCH, PETER
   MASTROIANNI, MARCELLO
   BARDOT, BRIGITTE

29 AUTRY, GENE
   GARSON, GREER
   BRUCE, VIRGINIA
   HOWARD, TREVOR
   EKBERG, ANITA

30 KERR, DEBORAH
   DICKINSON, ANGIE

OCTOBER

1 ROSENBLOOM,'SLAPSIE'MAXIE
  MATTHAU, WALTER
  WHITMORE, JAMES
  HARVEY, LAURENCE
  HARRIS, RICHARD
  PEPPARD, GEORGE
  ANDREWS, JULIE
  HOLLOWAY, STANLEY

2 MARX, GROUCHO
  ABBOTT, BUD

3 OLAND, WARNER

4 HESTON, CHARLTON
  KEATON, BUSTER

5 JOHNS, GLYNIS
  DRESSER, LOUISE

6 LOMBARD, CAROLE
  EKLAND, BRITT

7 DEVINE, ANDY
  ALLYSON, JUNE

9 LENNON, JOHN

10 HAYES, HELEN

13 WALKER, ROBERT
   WILDE, CORNEL
   DAY, LARAINE
   TIFFIN, PAMELA

   HUME, BENITA
   JONES, ALLAN
   MOORE, ROGER
   GISH, LILLIAN

15 PETERS, JEAN
   CLAIRE, INA

16 DARNELL, LINDA
   LANSBURY, ANGELA

17 ARTHUR, JEAN
   HAYWORTH, RITA
   CLIFT, MONTGOMERY
   BYINGTON, SPRING

18 MERCOURI, MELINA
   SCOTT, GEORGE C.
   STEVENS, INGER

20 NEAGLE, ANNA
   BERNARDI, HERSHEL
   LUGOSI, BELA

22 BENNETT, CONSTANCE
   FONTAINE, JOAN
   DENEUVE, CATHERINE
   BERNHARDT, SARAH

23 DALY, JAMES
   DORS, DIANA

25 FRANCIOSA, ANTHONY
   REDDY, HELEN

26 COOGAN, JACKIE

27 CARSON, JACK
   FABRAY, NANETTE
   SNODGRESS, CARRIE

28 LANCHESTER, ELSA
   PARKER, SUZY
   ALEXANDER, JANE

29 DREYFUSS, RICHARD
   BRICE, FANNY

30 HUSSEY, RUTH
   WINKLER, HENRY
   GORDON, RUTH

31 WATERS, ETHEL
   EVANS, DALE
   BEL GEDDES, BARBARA

NOVEMBER

1 LA PLANTE, LAURA
  PALMER, BETSY

2 LANCASTER, BURT
  RUTHERFORD, ANN

3 BRONSON, CHARLES

4 DOUGLAS, PAUL
  YOUNG, GIG
  CARNEY, ART
  BALSAM, MARTIN
  ROGERS, WILL

5 MCCREA, JOEL
  ROGERS, ROY
  LEIGH, VIVIEN
  SOMMER, ELKE

6 LEDERER, FRANCIS
  GAYNOR, JANET
  NICHOLS, MIKE
  FIELD, SALLY

7 JAGGER, DEAN

8 HEPBURN, KATHARINE
  HAVOC, JUNE

9 LAMARR, HEDY
  DRESSLER, MARIE
  WYNN, ED
  WEBB, CLIFTON
  MARSH, MAE

10 BURTON, RICHARD
   SCHEIDER, ROY
   RAINS, CLAUDE
   NORMAND, MABEL

11 RYAN, ROBERT
   WINTERS, JONATHAN
   ANDERSSON, BIBI
   O'BRIEN, PAT

12 OAKIE, JACK
   KELLY, GRACE

13 STERLING, ROBERT
   WERNER, OSKAR
   CHRISTIAN, LINDA
   SEBERG, JEAN

14 POWELL, DICK
   DE CAMP, ROSEMARY
   DUFF, HOWARD
   LAKE, VERONICA
   KEITH, BRIAN

15 ASNER, EDWARD
   CLARK, PETULA
   STONE, LEWIS

16 MEREDITH, BURGESS
   TIBBETT, LAWRENCE

17 AUER, MISCHA
   HUDSON, ROCK

18 COCA, IMOGENE
   VACCARO, BRENDA

20 CANOVA, JUDY
   KEYES, EVELYN
   TIERNEY, GENE
   THAXTER, PHYLLIS
   PARSONS, ESTELLE
   DENNY, REGINALD

21 POWELL, ELEANOR
   MEEKER, RALPH
   BLAINE, VIVIAN
   HAWN, GOLDIE

22 PAGE, GERALDINE
   VAUGHN, ROBERT
   CARMICHAEL, HOAGY

23 KARLOFF, BORIS
   MARX, HARPO

24 FITZGERALD, GERALDINE
   GRIFFITH, CORINNE

25 MONTALBAN, RICARDO
   HUNTER, JEFFREY

26 GOULET, ROBERT

27 LEE, BRUCE

28 GRAHAME, GLORIA
   LANGE, HOPE
   ITURBI, JOSE

29 BERKELEY, BUSBY
   LA ROCQUE, ROD

30 MAYO, VIRGINIA
   ZIMBALIST, JR., EFREM
   CRENNA, RICHARD
   CLARK, DICK

DECEMBER

1 MARTIN, MARY
  ALLEN, WOODY
  PRYOR, RICHARD

2 HARRIS, JULIE

3 WILLIAMS, ANDY

4 DURBIN, DEANNA
  BUCHHOLZ, HORST
  BRIDGES, JEFF
  JONES, BUCK

5 DISNEY, WALT
  PREMINGER, OTTO

6 MOOREHEAD, AGNES
  HOLM, ELEANOR
  VAN, BOBBY
  HART, WILLIAM S.

7 WALLACH, ELI
  BURSTYN, ELLEN
  BAINTER, FAY

8 COBB, LEE J.
  DAVIS, JR., SAMMY
  SCHELL, MAXIMILIAN

9 FAIRBANKS, JR., DOUGLAS
  CRAWFORD, BRODERICK
  DOUGLAS, KIRK
  FOXX, REDD
  MERRILL, DINA
  GINGOLD, HERMIONE

10 LAMOUR, DOROTHY

11 ROLAND, GILBERT
   WINDSOR, MARIE
   MORENO, RITA
   MCLAGLEN, VICTOR

12 SINATRA, FRANK
   ROBINSON, EDWARD G.

13 HEFLIN, VAN
   ROTH, LILLIAN
   PARKS, LARRY
   PLUMMER, CHRISTOPHER

14 AMSTERDAM, MOREY
   DAILEY, DAN
   REMICK, LEE
   DUKE, PATTY

15 CHANDLER, JEFF

16 ULLMANN, LIV
   COWARD, NOEL

18 DASSIN, JULES
   GRABLE, BETTY
   VAN DYKE, DICK
   SMITH, ROGER
   COOPER, GLADYS

19 RICHARDSON, RALPH
   PURDOM, EDMUND
   TYSON, CICELY

20 DUNNE, IRENE

21 FONDA, JANE

23 ROMAN, RUTH
   GUARDINO, HARRY

24 HUGHES, HOWARD
   GARDNER, AVA
   CHATTERTON, RUTH

25 MAZURKI, MIKE
   MARTIN, TONY
   SPACEK, SISSY

26 WIDMARK, RICHARD
   ALLEN, STEVE

27 DIETRICH, MARLENE
   LEVANT, OSCAR
   LONG, RICHARD
   GREENSTREET, SYDNEY

28 AYRES, LEW
   NEFF, HILDEGARDE
   SMITH, MAGGIE

29 LINDFORS, VIVECA
   POWERS, MALA
   MOORE, MARY TYLER
   VOIGHT, JON

30 WILSON, MARIE
   VAN FLEET, JO
   TAMBLYN, RUSS
   NEGRI, POLA